CHRISTIAN-MUSLIM ENCOUNTERS

CHRISTIAN-MUSLIM ENCOUNTERS

Edited by

Yvonne Yazbeck Haddad

and

Wadi Zaidan Haddad

UNIVERSITY PRESS OF FLORIDA
Gainesville / Tallahassee / Tampa / Boca Raton
Pensacola / Orlando / Miami / Jacksonville

Publication of this book was sponsored in part by the Hartford Seminary, Hartford, Connecticut.

00 99 98 97 96 95 6 5 4 3 2 1

Library of Congress Cataloging-in-Publication Data

Christian-Muslim encounters / edited by Yvonne Yazbeck Haddad and Wadi Zaidan Haddad.
p. cm.
The result of a conference held on June 7–9, 1990 and sponsored in part by the Hartford Seminary, Connecticut.
Includes bibliographical references.
ISBN 0-8130-1356-9 (alk. paper). — ISBN 0-8130-1359-3 (pbk.: alk. paper)
1. Islam—Relations—Christianity—Congresses. 2. Christianity and other religions—Islam—Congresses. I. Haddad, Yvonne Yazbeck, 1935– . II. Ḥaddād, Wadīʿ Zaydān. III. Hartford Theological Seminary.
BP172.C434 1995 95-5178
261.2′7—dc20 CIP

The University Press of Florida is the scholarly publishing agency for the State University System of Florida, comprised of Florida A & M University, Florida Atlantic University, Florida International University, Florida State University, University of Central Florida, University of Florida, University of North Florida, University of South Florida, and University of West Florida.

University Press of Florida
15 Northwest 15th Street
Gainesville, FL 32611

DEDICATION

+☽

Willem A. Bijlefeld, Professor Emeritus of Islamic Studies at Hartford Seminary, enjoys an international reputation as outstanding scholar, teacher, and pioneer in the field of Christian-Muslim relations. The author of numerous works on various aspects of Islamic theology and interfaith dialogue, he has traveled widely throughout the Muslim world and is well acquainted with a great range of Muslim activities from Indonesia to Africa, to Europe and the United States.

In 1966, Professor Bijlefeld came to join Hartford Seminary, where he has served as professor, academic dean, editor of *The Muslim World*, and director of the Duncan Black Macdonald Center for Christian-Muslim Relations. Throughout his distinguished career he has been a leader in fostering better understanding of the religion of Islam, furthering dialogue among persons of faith, and promoting academic exchange among scholars of Christian-Muslim relations.

It is with extreme gratitude for the care, devotion, and skill with which Professor Bijlefeld has undertaken his lifelong task of scholarship that the present volume of essays on historical and contemporary relationships among Muslims and Christians is dedicated. His many students and colleagues, represented by the authors of the essays contained here, remain in his deep debt for the quality, depth, and range of his contributions.

CONTENTS

+☽

PART TWO   The Contemporary Situation

Regional Studies

PREFACE

+ ☽

The campus of Hartford Seminary, June 7-9, 1990, was the scene of a three-day meeting of academics engaged in dialogue on the issue of "Christian-Muslim Encounter: The Heritage of the Past and Present Intellectual Trends." Thirty scholars who have been engaged in research in the area of Christian-Muslim studies, representing both faith traditions, lectured and discussed the relationship of the two communities historically and in the contemporary worldwide context. The chapters of this volume are the result of the research done for, and the conversations held in the context of, that extended meeting.

The conference was sponsored by Hartford Seminary and cosponsored by Saint Joseph College, Trinity College, and University of Hartford. It was supported by grants from the National Endowment for the Humanities, the Connecticut Humanities Council, and Mobil Oil Corporation. Other funds were received from the Presbyterian Church USA, the United Church of Christ Board of Global Ministries, the Dutch Reformed Church in the Netherlands, the Lutheran Church of America, and the United Methodist Church. The viewpoints and beliefs expressed in these papers are those of the individual authors and do not necessarily reflect the opinions of the sponsoring organizations.

Our gratitude is expressed to the chairs and participants of the many panels conducted in the course of the conference, including former presidents of Hartford Seminary—James Gettemy, Harvey MacArthur, John Dillenberger, Michael Rion, and Interim President Jackson Carroll—and to M. Paton Ryan, president of Saint Joseph College; Walter G. Markham, dean, College of Arts and Sciences, University of Hartford; Leslie DesMangles, Trinity College; John Stack, Saint Joseph College; W. Cantwell Smith, professor emeritus, Harvard University; and Peter Bright, University of Hartford.

Particular thanks are due to Elizabeth D'Amico and Karen Gidman for their tireless efforts in the organization and administration of the conference, to Elizabeth Speight for the art work for the brochure, and to Alice Izer, Mary Jane Ross, and David Sawan who typed several versions of a number of manuscripts. Our gratitude is extended for all of these contributions without which neither the project nor this volume would have been possible.

Introduction

The fourteen-century history of the encounter between Christianity and Islam has taken many forms of conflict and cooperation, diatribe and dialogue, hatred and tolerance, community hostility and personal friendships. There has been an enormous range in terms of the kinds of contacts and responses that members of the respective communities have made with and to each other and in the various methods used to report findings to their own constituencies. At this moment, nearing the end of the twentieth century, we find ourselves in a distinctively different situation. The reality of mass communication alone has changed circumstances radically. Rather than reading in books and journals about what Muslims in various contexts are doing, we can have information at the touch of a television button. Muslims are able not only to learn immediately about events in the various Christian communities of the Western world but to know without delay the Western response to happenings in the Muslim world. We are, in effect, instantly accountable to each other.

The portrait of Islam that the Western press has put forth during the past decade suggests to Muslims that the West has not in fact always been responsible in its reporting. Muslims feel that the tendency toward sensationalism and communicating only the extremist activities of Muslim individuals and groups has reinforced a negative image of Islam in the West. Headlines talk about the menace of Islam, and some American political figures have been quoted as proposing that Islam has now replaced communism as the international enemy of Western democracy. Within the more militant wing of the Muslim community, some are suggesting that since the time of the Crusades, and continuing through the stages of Inquisition, imperialism, missionary activity, and the support of Zionism, the West has been devoted to the systematic elimination of Islam.

One issue for consideration at this meeting, therefore, was an examination of the ways in which Muslims and Christians have actually encountered one another both across the range of that historical span and in the new and often continuingly painful engagement in today's world. The other major issue addressed by participants was the nature of the scholarship that Westerners have used in their investigations of the different phenomena of Islam.

The need to hold a research conference on the topic of Christian-Muslim relations seemed to the planners to have taken on a special urgency. Scholars during the last decade increasingly have become sensitized to the fact that research on Islam has been colored by religious as well as political and cultural motivations and presuppositions that have brought into question the very corpus of literature produced on the subject of Islam and interfaith relations. Many of the ideas and attitudes that have crept into the scholarship in this field have been shaped by historical events that tend to distort rather than to enlighten. Muslims, now well aware of what has happened, are making increasing reference to Western scholarship which they see as "orientalist" in perspective, characterized by the desire to learn about Islam so as to be able to control it. They view the whole academic venture of Euro-Americans in many cases as being driven by motives that are in fact not scholarly but political and even racial.

Questions have been raised about the validity of any research on Islam and Muslims not conducted by members of that faith community. The motives of some researchers have been questioned, as well as the ability of any scholar outside the faith to understand the elements of that faith well enough to present them accurately. This in itself is not a new issue. Many scholars since Joachim Wach have addressed the question of whether a scholar must be "religious" in order to engage in research on religion and, more specifically, whether confessional commitment is a prerequisite for understanding a particular religion.[1] Such a condition, which would make it impossible to justify the incorporation of this field of study in the curriculum of a public university, is critically examined, directly and indirectly, in several of the papers presented here.

Another factor in the new situation of encounter is the current demand of Muslims for parity in Europe and in America. After more than four centuries of relative absence of Muslims in the West, following their explusion from Spain in the fifteenth and sixteenth centuries, the Islamic presence is making itself strongly felt both in Europe and in North America. Muslims are asking for equal opportunity and equal treatment under Western laws. They have become aware of the redefinition of Christianity that is going on in Europe and the United States vis-à-vis its relationship to Judaism. They see it as a kind of revisionist history that interprets Christianity as part of the continuous flow of the Judeo-Christian tradition. Muslims are asking for the same kind of acceptance, pressing Christians to acknowledge Islam as a legitimate religion in the same way that Muslims have always accepted the validity of the faith of Christianity.

The Hartford conference, therefore, was designed as a way in which to initiate a fresh look at some of the issues that have shaped Christian-Muslim encounters over the centuries and in their contemporary manifestations, and to determine if we can begin to explore new modes of scholarship and forms of communication between the two faith communities. Volumes have been written over the centuries by members of succeeding generations as the two traditions reassessed their relationship. The purpose of the conference out of which this volume grew was neither to be comprehensive in covering the whole historical scope of the encounter nor to provide a rehash of the material developed over the many centuries of interaction. It was rather to allow prominent scholars in the field an opportunity to present and discuss materials covering a wide geographical, historical, and methodological range.

In the first essay Willem Bijlefeld considers whether there is such a field of scholarship as Muslim-Christian (or Christian-Muslim) studies, pointing to the need for a critical bibliography in this area. He outlines the various disciplines that he understands legitimately to be included, noting leading works in these areas and suggesting how some of the essays included here contribute to those disciplines. The categories he proposes, in brief, are Qurʾanic and biblical studies, *ḥadīth*, "religious" legal provisions, Islam and the West, Muslim and Christian minorities, regional studies, the history of theological interaction and apologetic exchange, comparative theological studies, comparative studies in spirituality and mysticism, *daʿwa*, and mission. Bijlefeld concludes that only to the extent that collaborative and cross-disciplinary efforts characterize Muslim-Christian studies could it be designated a field of scholarship. He then goes on to consider the degree to which the scope and subject matter of the areas of Christian-Muslim studies and Islamic studies overlap but do not coincide and ends with some observations concerning the future of Christian-Muslim encounter itself and the potential impact of Muslim-Christian studies on the two communities of faith.

The rest of the essays are grouped into four general categories. First are those that deal with the heritage of Christian-Muslim relations, focusing on analysis of sacred scripture as the point of departure. Five presentations look for affirmation of the fact that openness to the validity of other religious traditions is indeed justified on the basis of some of the texts. Issa Boullata examines the Qurʾan for what he calls a principle of religious pluralism or interfaith relations. He finds such a principle in suras 2:148 and 5:48, which contain the command to vie with one another in doing good works (*fa-stabiqū ʾl-khayrāt*). Boullata analyzes the commentaries of a number of classical and modern exegetes of the Qurʾan on these verses, as well as on S. 2:256, which states clearly that there should be no compulsion in religion. The exegetes, with little exception, support his contention that these passages provide the foundation for human accountability to persons of other faiths, for interfaith dialogue and understanding, and for cooperation between Islam and Christianity.

In a similar endeavor Antonie Wessels looks at the texts of the Old and New Testaments for guidance in understanding the relationship of Christianity to other faiths. He considers three biblical texts that deal with interaction of people from different religions and cultures. In Genesis 14:18–20 the legitimacy of the priesthood of a non-Jew, Melchizedek, is recognized. Matthew 15:21–28 talks of Jesus interacting with and perhaps being influenced by a Canaanite woman. And in Acts 10:9–29 and 34–36, the encounter between Peter and Cornelius suggests that Peter's acknowledgment that "there is no partiality with God" came after he had recognized and been recognized by Cornelius's heathen messengers. Wessels argues that the controversial passage in John 14:6, "No one comes to the Father but by me," is not a judgment on other ways of salvation but a confessional statement internal to faith in Jesus the Christ. The Bible, he concludes, does offer clear examples of the importance of openness to persons of other religious traditions.

Mahmud Ayoub offers a study of the concept of sonship in the Qur'an and in the history of Qur'an commentary. He asserts that Jesus, understood as a man of faith and piety, has served as a bridge between Christianity and Islam, bringing them together in their common quest for faith and understanding. Jesus as seen by Christians, however, the divine son of God and member of the Trinity, has served only as a barrier between them. Ayoub sees his essay as an attempt to begin to break down this wall by means of an examination of the Qur'anic terms *ibn* and *walad*, both of which refer to a filial relationship. He concludes that the Christian Gospel and the Qur'an are talking about the same Jesus and are relaying essentially the same understanding of the virgin birth, working from the presupposition that we must not use the scriptures of either tradition to assess the authenticity of the doctrines of the other.

The polemical discussions that took place in the early centuries of Christian-Muslim encounter, according to Wadi Z. Haddad, had several phases, including the reliance of each on their own respective scriptures for authority, Christians learning Arabic and working with Muslim texts, and the provision of a common ground of discussion through the translation of Greek and Syriac texts into Arabic. Haddad shows in detail how the polemics of the encounter were exemplified in the *Kitāb al-Tamhīd* of al-Bāqillānī, a tenth-century Mālikī judge in Baghdad. Both prolific and contentious, al-Bāqillānī in this work, considered one of the most important Sunni texts of *kalām*, refutes not only Christians and their doctrines but others whose ideas seemed to him to impugn monotheism—particularly his sharp theological and philosophical challenge to the Christian doctrine of the incarnation and thus of the trinity. Al-Bāqillānī concludes, after lengthy argumentation, that it is clear from the text of the Christian Gospel itself that Jesus was fully and completely human and not divine.

Another such example is from the ninth century, that of the Melkite Bishop Peter of Bayt Rās, who tried to elucidate a number of aspects of the Christian doctrine of the incarnation of Jesus as Word of God in a work entitled *Kitāb al-Burhān*. Mark Swanson summarizes this text, then considers the ways in which Ibn Taymiyya, whom he calls a "Muslim controversialist," later reflected on the bishop's exposition of this complex Christian doctrine. Swanson concludes that while Ibn Taymiyya's critique is in many ways valid, challenging the viability of the wedding of biblical and Hellenistic religions, he did not really understand what Peter was trying to say. How helpful it would have been, Swanson reflects, if the two had actually been able to talk together about these issues. He notes that rarely in interfaith conversation has there been a real effort to view another's faith from within rather than from the outside or to allow that glimpse to challenge and refine one's own beliefs.

The second section offers studies on various kinds of interfaith and intercultural encounter and an examination of some of the mystical literature of each tradition. The history of encounter between Islam and Christianity is replete with attempts on the part of practitioners of each tradition to explain the tenets of their faith to members of the other. Such attempts often have been less than successful.

An example of a misinterpretation of the doctrine of another tradition is offered by Daniel Sahas in his treatment of a Byzantine perception of the Muslim understanding of God. Sahas examines a text of ritual abjuration, actually an anathema, in which a Muslim renounces the God of Muhammad and formally accepts Christianity. In the text it is said that Muhammad's god is *holosphyros*, literally made of metal beaten into a sphere. Sahas understands this as an attempt to translate the Arabic word *ṣamad* in its most literal rather than figurative sense, an attempt that he thinks might be seen as a kind of Byzantine Christian revenge for Muslim distortion of the doctrine of the Trinity. In a complex set of maneuvers reflecting what Sahas considers to have been both creative and politically expedient, anathema of the God of Muhammad was later deleted and replaced by the anathema of Muhammad himself.

Among the great Christian reformers of the sixteenth century, much has been written about Martin Luther in relation to Islam. Very little work, however, has been done on the views of John Calvin toward Muslims and their religion, and this lacuna is addressed by Jan Slomp. On the basis of Calvin's formal writings, letters, and sermons, Slomp summarizes his views on "the Turks," on their concept of God, on Muhammad, on the Qur'an, and on Muslim ceremonies and institutions. Slomp argues that Calvin had little contact with Muslims and did not know much about Islam. His real concern was to identify enemies of the evangelical movement of which he was a leader; thus he generally classified Turks with Roman Catholics (papists), from whom he was under greatest attack, as well as with Jews and pagans. His most serious critique of Muslims is that they deny the divinity of Jesus Christ. As Christian observers have done through the ages, Calvin put the blame for the erroneous ideas that the Turks have about God directly on Muhammad, citing him as responsible for deceiving former Christians into converting to a false religion. Slomp concludes that it is doubtful that Calvin had any real knowledge of the Qur'an, and that the threat posed by the Turks to the church at that time precluded his taking Islam as a religion with real seriousness.

The theme of mystical piety and devotion and its implications for interfaith understanding is dealt with in two essays in this collection. Annemarie Schimmel looks to the poetry of Jalāl al-Dīn Rūmī for images of the figures of Jesus and Mary. She notes that while the portraits of Jesus are somewhat different from those used by Christians, Rūmī's work is replete with references to Jesus as a person full of love and finding beauty in all of God's creation, as well as an ideal ascetic. Jesus' miracles—speaking in the cradle, breathing life into clay birds, quickening the dead—reveal him as one through whom life is bestowed, the great physician who heals all ailments. Mary, mother of Jesus, is portrayed as the symbol of the pure soul. Rūmī paints poetic pictures of Mary in the garden, the "bud" in whom the rose of Jesus is found.

James Royster, in an attempt to discover what he calls the transcultural, the transpersonal, and the essential, calls for dialogue that seeks for transcendence. Toward this end he provides a study of the theme of personal transformation as it is developed in the works of two great medieval mystics, teachers and metaphysicians, Muḥyī al-Dīn ibn al-ʿArabī and Meister Eckhart. While representing different religious traditions, they shared a common Judeo-Christian heritage, a Platonic and Neoplatonic background, and a grounding in Greek metaphysics. Most important, both based their speculative systems on their own personal experience of transformation, moving dialectically from duality to identity in the ultimate, the godhead, *al-ḥaqq*. Royster sees that the differences between ibn al-ʿArabī and Meister Eckhart are of less significance than the differences of each from the other members of his tradition, and that in the analysis of their writings lies the potential for dialogue in depth.

As part of an ongoing project of examining Arabic sources for references to the attitudes of Muslims of the Maghrib toward Christians, R. Marston Speight presents the results of his research on relations during the Fāṭimid period. He reports clear evidence of appreciation for the figure of Jesus, even devotion, although this was not necessarily carried over in Maghribī Muslim attitudes toward Christians. While the way of life of the Christians was given a certain degree of respect, their *dhimmī* status meant that they were clearly subordinate to Muslim authority. In some cases there seems to have been real antipathy on the part of the Maghribī Muslims toward their Christian neighbors, although Speight feels that on the whole such hostility as existed was political and not religious. Nonetheless, he sees that by the tenth century the divisions between the Christian and Muslim communities were becoming even firmer.

Several essays treat the general subject of relations between members of the two respective communities in the Middle Ages. Hadia Dajani-Shakeel provides a glimpse of interaction between Muslims and Frankish Christians in twelfth-century Syria, Lebanon, and Palestine (the Shām region) in the time of Frankish occupation. Playing the old game of divide and rule, she notes, the Franks developed alliances and counteralliances in their attempts to keep the Muslim population under control. There were two primary Frankish populations, the early settlers and their descendants and those who came later to the territory. It was the later arrivals, Dajani-Shakeel says, who intensified the military confrontations with the Muslims and finally led to Frankish defeat at the hands of Ṣalāḥ al-Dīn. On the whole, the period of coexistence of the two communities was fairly peaceful, with the civilian populations existing independent of each other and generally uninvolved in military encounters.

Also dealing with the Levant area, but at a somewhat later date, is Donald Little in his essay on the life of Christians in Mamlūk Jerusalem. This time the Christians are ruled rather than rulers, and Little discusses their life after the end of the Crusades through examination of Muslim histories, travel reports of Christian pilgrims, and Mamlūk documents. He paints a picture in which Muslims generally took seriously their responsibilities in regard to Christians, Christians as well as Jews sharing in the communal life of the city. The Mamlūks seem to have been far more tolerant of the presence of Christians in Jerusalem than the Christian pilgrims were of Muslims in what they felt to be their holy city. Pilgrim literature reflects contempt both for the Muslims whose customs they observed there and for the Orthodox Christians whom they considered to be members of "heretical" sects.

The theme of Christian pilgrim responses to the Muslims whom they encounter on their journeys to the Holy Land is continued in Jane Smith's essay on the accounts of French travelers to Islamic lands in the sixteenth to the eighteenth centuries. Citing the reports of missionaries, scientists, emissaries of the French crown, historians, and adventurers, as well as pilgrims, Smith focuses especially on these travelers' perceptions of Muslim beliefs and practices concerning death and the afterlife. On the whole they seem to have been reasonably well informed about such matters, although apparently not much familiar with the Qur'an. Smith observes that while they reject in their accounts what they view as the excessively carnal nature of Islam, exemplified specifically in the life and teachings of Muhammad, and make no attempt to apply allegorical interpretation to Muslim beliefs about the afterlife, they are actually quite restrained in their critique of everything but the Prophet himself.

A third group of essays in this collection examines some regional contexts in which one finds examples of contemporary Christian-Muslim encounters. Two of these deal with the nation of India. Christian Troll posits the thesis that the participation of Muslims in the modern republic raises new issues for Islamic political thought. He presents the perspectives of a number of contemporary Indian Muslims on the role that Muslims as a religious minority should play in cooperation with Hindus in the modern pluralistic nation state, arranging the responses he received to this question into five categories: the situation is really not new and therefore there is no problem; the situation is definitely new but the concern is political and not religious; Muslims need a radical reinterpretation of Islam, one in which the *ʿulama* (scholars of Islam) play a less significant role; politics are essential to Islam, which calls for a rule by God's law; Muslims do not need rule by the *sharīʿa* (the law), but must apply *ijtihād* (individual interpretation) to the law. Troll acknowledges the flexibility and independence of mind of these Islamic scholars in a very challenging situation, while stressing the need for yet more creative thought.

Focusing on one particular area of India, Roland Miller looks to the state of Kerala as a place that might serve as an example for interfaith relations in the country as a whole. He traces the tumultuous history of the interaction of Muslims, Christians, and Hindus in that area, which he calls the only place in the world where these three communities live together in such "numerical equilibrium." Stressing the acuteness of the danger of internal antagonism and strife in India today, he says that contemporary leaders have called for tolerance less on the basis of religious imperatives than out of the expedience of secular rationalism. He argues for a combination of mutual respect, mutual knowledge, motivation, and cooperative action, to which also must be added the spiritual ideologies that flow from the three religious traditions. Miller believes that Kerala has come a long way toward the achievement of such a combination.

One interesting contemporary model for interfaith tolerance is that provided by the Pancasila (the five foundational principles) of modern Indonesia. Olaf Schumann examines the principles of this doctrine in which religious toleration is espoused although only those religions that acknowledge one supreme being are recognized—Islam, Protestantism, Roman Catholicism, Hinduism, and Buddhism. Schumann traces the intercommunal and interreligious history that led to the establishment of the Pancasila, noting that often Muslims and Christians found themselves allied against the defenders of local custom. Since the time of President Sukarno, however, there has been a growing competition between Christians and Muslims, each accusing the other of attempting to proselytize. Encouraged by recent efforts on the part of some Muslims to find a solid theological rationale for the principles of interfaith cooperation underscored by the Pancasila, he urges Christians to engage in that same task.

J. Haafkens examines the historical development of Christian-Muslim relations in sub-Saharan Africa before 1800, during the time of European dominance from 1800 to 1960, and in the most recent period of postindependence movements. He points to positive changes in the 1960s in both the Protestant and Roman Catholic communities in the reorientation of their approaches to

Islam and describes some of the initiatives taken to foster dialogue, as well as similar efforts on the part of Muslims. This hope for genuine improvement in Christian-Muslim relations he sees as not really having been fulfilled. The phenomenon of Islamic revival has carried with it an apologetic attack on Western culture and values. Christians reject the growing hope on the part of some Muslims for implementation of the sharī'a. Despite these factors, Haafkens ends on a note of hope in that some voices within both communities are continuing to call for tolerance and dialogue.

One dramatic change in the demography of Muslim populations in the second half of the twentieth century has been the increase of their numbers in the countries of Europe. Jorgen Nielsen considers this phenomenon, providing a brief history of their arrival, some reflections on Islamic institutions in Europe, on the relationship of Muslim communities to their home countries and the influence of those countries on European Islam, and on the question of official "recognition" of Muslims. He observes that among the problems faced by Muslims in Europe are employment, tensions between European social welfare policies and traditional Muslim culture, parochial vs. secular education, and the ongoing reality of prejudice and discrimination on the part of Europeans basically unaccepting of minorities. Critical to the future of Islam in Europe are such issues as whether individual Muslims will want to participate in European society or remain separate and the extent to which Europe itself is ready and willing to adapt to the growing presence of Muslims.

Sulayman Nyang sets the context for the dialogue between Muslims and Christians in the United States by providing a concise history of the arrival and presence of immigrant Muslims and the movements of conversion to Islam of African Americans. He then identifies some of the issues that he sees as central to the dialogue. Suggesting first the importance of human rights as an arena for common action, he goes on to acknowledge three areas that he feels have been and continue to be divisive: distortions of each other's faith due to error or conviction, the "missionary" character of each of the religions, and the feelings of marginalization that Muslims experience in the United States. He concludes by drawing a distinction between secularization and secularism, identifying the former as a legitimate contributor to the impetus of dialogue.

Frederick M. Denny offers an overview of the situation of the U.S. Muslim community, immigrant and African American, in the nineties. He looks both at the various groupings within immigrant Islam and the tensions that they are experiencing as they attempt to live out their Islam in the American context, and at how the picture is complicated by the particular circumstances, including the economic kind, of indigenous Muslims. Denny offers the possibility that African Americans may be a bridge between immigrant Muslims and non-Muslim America in the United States. He posits the Islamic ideal of the *umma* or community as a key concept in fostering Muslim unity in America, suggesting that the metaphors both of melting pot and of mosaic may be useful in helping Muslims balance the tensions between racial/ethnic divisions on the one hand and the fear of total assimilation and consequent loss of values and identity on the other.

In the fourth section of this collection, scholars critique the reflections and contributions of some contemporary Muslim and Christian thinkers who have given special consideration to the matter of Christian-Muslim encounter and to understanding their own tradition in relation to the other. The first essay, by Jacques Waardenburg, provides an analysis of the ways in which some North African intellectuals have articulated their understanding of Islam as a response to engagement with the West, in particular with France. Waardenburg has selected writers who are educated and erudite, who are both aware and appreciative of French culture and thought, and who do not preach Islamic revival. Among them are the Algerian Malek Bennabi, the only writer who focuses on Islam as a religion; the Tunisian Hichem Djait, calling for a liberal, universalist spirit; the Algerian Ali Merad, who advocates a dialogue on practical issues; the Tunisian Mohamed Talbi, long-time participant in Christian-Muslim dialogue; the Moroccan Abdallah Laroui, who sees Islam not as a religion but as history and culture; and the Algerian Mohammed Arkoun, philosopher and man of letters who has provided deep intellectual challenges to interfaith dialogue.

Discussion about the nature of relationships between majority and minority communities, both descriptive and prescriptive, has been rich in the history of Muslim-Christian interaction. Analyzing some of the most recent turns in that ongoing discussion, Yvonne Y. Haddad considers literature currently being produced in Egypt relating to the role of Christians (Copts) in a Muslim state. The writers are revivalist Muslims, and the context is one in which many are calling for the institution of the sharīʿa as the constitution of the Egyptian state. As Copts reflect on their potential role in such a state, should it evolve, Muslims are providing a range of responses to questions of minority rights and responsibilities, national unity, classical doctrines concerning *dhimmī* (minority) status in Muslim lands, and contemporary nation-state models. The alternatives suggested range from specifically stated second class status for non-Muslims to creative ways in which all persons can share equally in a state which is, nonetheless, clearly Islamic in orientation.

In a tribute to the late Ismāʿīl al-Fārūqī's contributions to several decades of Muslim-Christian dialogue, Kenneth Cragg presents a frank appraisal of al-Fārūqī's attempts to understand and interpret Christianity. Both appreciative and critical in his review, Cragg claims that his Muslim colleague consistently repudiated the dimension of tragedy and the notion of paradox, each essential to a real understanding of the Christian faith. He challenges al-Fārūqī's advocacy of Abraham as the starting point for interfaith conversation, suggesting rather that we should begin and end with God. While giving great credit to al-Fārūqī for his agility and intelligence and for having acquired the technical skills to discuss Christianity at a deep level, Cragg nonetheless argues that in fact he was never really able to engage in that kind of discussion because he could not leave behind his own preconceptions.

Among Muslim writers who have reflected on the question of religious pluralism, one of the best known in the West has been Muḥammad Kāmil Ḥussein. Stressing Ḥussein's personal, nontraditional interpretation of Islam, Harold Vogelaar presents a picture of a man, a physician by profession, who had been influenced more by Western science than by philosophy or metaphysics, and who strongly believed that religion and science can form a rational whole. Stressing that people should be free to choose the religion best suited for them, Ḥussein placed his loyalty not to any religious tradition as such but to a vision of humanity. In his well-known novel *City of Wrong* he contributed to Christian-Muslim dialogue by trying to show how members of the two traditions could be allies and not rivals. Vogelaar argues that Ḥussein's work provides an excellent example of a layperson's attempt to move theology from the transcendent to the immanent and to change the focus from revelation to scientific method but that it does not go beyond what is truly Islamic.

Turning to contemporary Christian attempts to understand Islam, David Kerr considers seven writers and thinkers—Louis Massignon, Charles Ledit, Michel Hayek, George Khodr, Kenneth Cragg, Hans Küng, and W. Montgomery Watt—who since the middle of the twentieth century have tried to understand Muhammad in one way or another as a "post-Christian" prophet. They represent the Catholic, Orthodox, and Anglican traditions, and all write from Christian theological positions that range between inclusivism and pluralism. Kerr's work is based on the recognition that while Christians over the years often have shown respect for Islam and Muslims, they have had great difficulty acknowledging the legitimacy of Muhammad as a prophet. He concludes that the presentations of these scholars remain essentially intra-Christian, their treatment of prophecy and prophethood determined by Christian rather than Islamic presuppositions, and that in fact they almost all beg the more important question of whether Christian and Muslim theologies of prophethood are in fact compatible at all.

John Carman takes us back to the early work of another theologian who has devoted his life to a Christian understanding of Islam, Willem Bijlefeld. He shares his own changing responses to matters raised in Bijlefeld's doctoral dissertation, *De Islam als Na-Christelijke Religie*. The main issue for Carman here is that of *epochē*, or the phenomenological suspension of evaluation. Bijlefeld's assertion is that *epochē* is appropriate to the study of religion and evaluation to the task of theology but that, in the case of Islam, *epochē* should be invoked even in regard to theological appraisal. Earlier rejecting Bijlefeld's exception, Carman now expresses greater appreciation for it on the grounds that Christians have been unable to address adequately the matter of the prophethood of Muhammad. Calling himself a Christian inclusivist, Carman affirms that Bijlefeld's *epochē* does not preclude proclaiming the Gospel, which he asserts is essential to dialogue.

Seyyed Hossein Nasr points to seven theological and metaphysical issues, the study and elaboration of which he identifies as crucial to a real understanding between Christians and Muslims: the ways in which God manifests Himself; the meaning of finality in the two traditions; the meaning and status of sacred scripture; the differences between sacred, liturgical, and vernacular languages; sacred law in general and sexuality in particular as it is governed by sacred law; the life of Christ as seen in the two religions; and finally what he considers to be the most subtle and elusive issue, the influence of modernism and postmodernism in the conversations between the two partners. Acknowledging that many important matters have been left off this list, he defends it on the grounds that other matters have either been well discussed already or are easily resolved. The above points he sees as potentially the most divisive and therefore deserving of the theological attention of the participants in this present moment in the history of Christian-Islamic dialogue.

The research presented in the following articles is intended to open additional areas of investigation and to answer some questions. How have Muslims and Christians understood and used their scripture in defining relations with peoples of other faiths? How have some of the specific historical encounters between the two faith communities impacted the formulation of ideas about minority/majority religious communities and what kinds of literature have been written for the community of believers? What is the traditional understanding of the role of a minority religious community in a pluralistic society? Why has the study of Islam traditionally been a neglected area in the field of history of religions, and has the situation changed significantly since it was brought to the attention of the scholarly community several decades ago? From the particular vantage point of Christian-Muslim studies, the kinds of issues raised here contribute to clarification of the broader concern of the role and function of religious studies in relation to other disciplines in the humanities, in a global, an intercultural, and an interreligious context.

NOTE

1. See Wach's *Religionswissenschaft* of 1924, now available for the first time in English in his *Introduction to the History of Religions*, ed. Joseph M. Kitagawa and Gregory D. Allen (1988), esp. chaps. 2 and 4.

1

Christian-Muslim Studies, Islamic Studies, and the Future of Christian-Muslim Encounter

Willem A. Bijlefeld

Christian-Muslim Studies

During the past three decades and from within several academic disciplines, so many studies dealing in some way with both Islamic and Christian data have been published that it now makes sense to raise the question whether it would be useful to recognize the existence of a distinct field of scholarship, here tentatively designated "Muslim-Christian (or Christian-Muslim) Studies."[1]

The OCLC Bibliographical Records, consulted through EPIC in April 1991, listed a total of 1,101 entries under the subject heading "Islam—Relations—Christianity" (practically coinciding with "Christianity and other religions: Islam"). Limiting the same search for the period up to 1960 yielded 229 entries. The increase in the quantity of publications in this field during the past thirty years seems even more pronounced than the 20:80 ratio these figures suggest. Under the same subject heading, "Islam—Relations—Christianity," an RLIN search of May 1990 gave for the research libraries catalogue a total of 675 records, of which 355, more than 52 percent, had been published in the last ten years. Admittedly, not all of the older publications in the research libraries are included in this database, but even so the proportion of recent titles is startling. A highly selective bibliographical search I carried out independently to 1980—limited to publications in English, French, and German and (methodologically a far more questionable restriction) to Christian perspectives on the various aspects of this interfaith relationship—resulted in 200 titles, including books and journal articles, for the period 1900–1960 and over 1,000 for the next two decades. On the basis of the data collected, my estimate is that the number of journal articles, chapters from multiauthored volumes, and the like is at least twelve times larger than the number retrieved last year with a Dialog search from the Religion Index Data Base under the subject heading "Muslims—Relations—Christians."[2]

All of this information points to the need for a critical bibliography in this area of study. Existing bibliographical resources such as the three mentioned above are valuable ancillary aids, but they cannot serve as bibliographies and are not intended to do so. The *Index Islamicus*, an indispensable source for almost every dimension of the study of Islam, hardly touches upon this subject matter, which lies largely outside the confines of Islamic Studies as usually conceived (see "Christian-Muslim Studies and Islamic Studies" below).[3] By far the most comprehensive bibliographical project undertaken on the subject of Muslim-Christian dialogue and closely related issues is *Islamochristiana*'s "Bibliographie du dialogue islamo-chrétien," of which to date eight parts (in ten installments) have been published,[4] listing Arabic, Syriac, Armenian, Georgian, Coptic, Greek, and Latin material from the seventh to the fourteenth century. The compilers' intention is to cover the entire history of this dialogue up to the present, although they realize that "the literature on this subject grows more abundant as history progresses, to the point of becoming almost inexhaustible in our time."[5] In the first fifteen years of the journal's existence this survey has not moved beyond data from the fourteenth century, and many wonder when it will reach the latter part of the twentieth century and which criteria will be used to determine the selection of titles for that later period (the issue of languages to be included, for example). No matter when and in which precise format *Islamochristiana's* bibliography will be completed, its superb quality and its unparalleled merits as a source of documentation do not detract from the need for a complementary bibliography for the post-1950 period which would facilitate an informed assessment of what has been accomplished in this field of study since the middle of the century, would reflect the most important changes in methodology and the major shifts in areas of research, and would diminish the danger of mere repetitions in the future by suggesting priorities for new research. In order to accomplish this, the bibliography would include statements of present positions as well as literature dealing, in retrospect but not therefore necessarily less objectively, with past authors and periods and would cover a field wider and more varied than the nomenclature "Muslim-Christian Dialogue" or the term "Muslim-Christian Encounter" suggest.[6] The term Muslim-Christian Studies purports to denote a field that includes contributions from a large group of scholars (such as in history, anthropology, sociology, language and literature, history of religions, theology) working in one or more of the following ten subject areas.

Qur'anic and Biblical Studies

The following chapters by Issa Boullata and Antonie Wessels[7] illustrate the widely acknowledged fact that, while a study of biblical data relevant to the issues of religious plurality and interfaith relations can only set the framework in which also the question of Muslim-Christian relations needs to be viewed, in Qur'anic Studies one can focus directly on data about the relationship with and the attitude to (Jews and) Christians. In recent discussions of this latter material one of the noteworthy developments is the frequent emphasis on S. 5:48[8] rather than on the two verses which in the past repeatedly functioned as foci of attention—namely S. 2:62 and S. 3:85, the latter one considered of decisive importance by, for example, Boubakeur Hamza in his 1972 publication.[9]

Among the wide range of "comparative" Qur'anic and biblical studies—several of which are dangerously premature attempts at comparison[10]—the apparently never ending flow of publications on the Yūsuf/Joseph narratives is of special interest. The expositions of this passage clearly demonstrate the variety of approaches and methodologies used in scripture studies and unmistakably reveal the very diverse intentions of the authors.[11]

Ḥadīth

Although on many other points a significant amount of work has been done in the comparison of Qur'anic and *ḥadīth* data, the relation between these two sets of data on the subject of "Islam and the people of the Book" has received scant attention. Articles by R. Marston Speight[12] and Alex Wijoyo,[13] among others, show the significance of this line of inquiry. The latter's conclusion that "inasmuch as the Christians are concerned, the Ḥadīth tends to speak unfavorably of them"[14] deserves critical attention and, if found valid, a more detailed explanation of this development.

"Religious" Legal Provisions

Studies about Islamic legal provisions for Christian minorities[15] and about the civil law codes of these communities[16] fall in this third category, as does the literature dealing with Western (medieval) Christian canon law stipulations about the "infidels."[17] Moreover, several publications discuss the more strictly legal data in other contexts, for example, the history of a religious minority in a Muslim or Christian environment (the fifth subject area considered here) or the study of ḥadīth data (the second subject area, above).

Islam and the West

"Islam and the West" obviously denotes a much wider field of inquiry than can be subsumed meaningfully under Christian-Muslim Studies. Topics such as the artistic interaction between and cross-fertilization of the Muslim world and the West or the reception and assimilation of Arabic scientific literature in Europe, while not unrelated, are often covered in a way that touches only indirectly on specifically Muslim and/or Christian data. On the other hand, wide-ranging studies such as Norman Daniel's *Islam and the West*, *The Arabs and Mediaeval Europe*, and *Islam, Europe and Empire*[18] should find a place here, besides numerous other publications about this long and complex history of "the making of an image" and about the historical and theological reasons for the Western fear of Islam.[19] For the latter topic the dividing line is somewhat ambiguous: the more strictly theological Muslim assessments of Christianity and Christian evaluations of Islam fall under "The History of Theological Interaction" and "Theological Perspectives" below, while the emphasis in this fourth section as a whole, for both the Christian and the Muslim sides, is on what Daniel once described as a third level of intellectual activity, midway between "theological intellectualism on the one hand and simple folklore on the other"—that is, the opinion of "intelligent people who are not intellectuals, of common people who are not specialists."[20]

Muslim and Christian Minorities

Since its establishment in 1977, the *Journal of the Institute of Muslim Minority Affairs*[21] is making an extremely valuable contribution to the study of past and present conditions of Muslim minorities, many of whom are situated in traditionally predominantly Christian environments. Its broad range of articles about regional/national situations and the fundamental issues that arise in this context deserve careful attention, as do numerous articles published elsewhere and several monographs, some of which provide important factual data and break new ground in the reflection on this subject.

Within the section on the history and the present predicament of Christian communities under Muslim rule or in a Muslim society, a very large number of titles discuss Christian minorities in the Arab world and in the Maghrib, a field of inquiry represented in this volume by the contributions of Yvonne Haddad, Donald Little, and Marston Speight.[22] The multiauthored, recently published volume *Conversion and Continuity*[23] is an example of studies concerned with a wide geographical area but limited to the premodern period. In other publications the focus of attention is on the twentieth century, particularly on very recent developments in one specific country such as Indonesia, an area still too often considered "marginal" to the Islamic world and therefore also insufficiently recognized for its importance in any study of the relations between Muslim majorities and Christian minorities in the contemporary world.[24]

Regional Studies

Any publication assignable to the previous rubric is obviously a "regional study." It seems to make sense, however, to set apart those studies that deal explicitly with majority-minority issues, using that focus as a criterion for the division rather than the particular geographical area under consideration. With regard to the latter, the question could be raised, for example, whether the Muslim presence in some parts of western Europe should be considered a case of a Muslim minority in a predominantly Christian environment or whether it should be recognized that in those regions—not less than in the entirely different Indian context—both Muslims and Christians are (or soon may be) religious minorities. For some other nations—Nigeria is a frequently discussed instance—the national situation is that of a numerically relatively balanced coexistence, while in particular regions of the country majority-minority issues and feelings seem to determine much of everyday life.

Whatever the primary foci of these articles are, the fact that no less than six chapters in this volume analyze the "regional context" of Christian-Muslim relations[25] reflects the crucial importance of this line of research. Discussions of the Muslim-Christian encounter tend to become distressingly repetitious and dangerously unrelated to human realities unless one realizes that every encounter worth that designation is contextualized in multiple ways. The historical, cultural, regional, and personal variants of each situation need to be studied and interpreted with utmost care,[26] because they are the context in which must be studied those theological issues that seem to recur in Muslim-Christian conversations throughout history and throughout the world. "We must concern ourselves with the people and the situations, rather than the internal issues of dogma, or perhaps we had better say, with the latter only and always in the context of the former," Kenneth Cragg wrote in the early 1950s; in the same article he warned, with some words of caution, that in our contacts we should think of each other as "people involved in decisions rather than as adherents involved in dogmas."[27]

The study of the regional context is therefore not, as it were, an appendix to a previously established theological construct of what Christian-Muslim encounter entails, but an analysis of the empirical reality in which Muslims and Christians coexist and meet each other (or fail to do so), and, as such, the only basis for a responsible and meaningful agenda for Muslim-Christian dialogue.

The History of Theological Interaction and Apologetic Exchange

The issue of theological interaction between the two traditions and, more specifically, the question of the role Christian thought may have played in the historical development of Islamic theology continue to attract attention.[28] A book that sets out to study the origins of Muslim theology *with regard to the Church fathers*[29] reveals in its title the author's orientation in this matter as clearly as does an article that deals with one particular example of "The Formation of Later Islamic Doctrines as a Response to Byzantine Polemics."[30] The suggestion of any such formative Christian influence has not remained unchallenged;[31] Robert Haddad's cautious observation that "the very effort to demonstrate a one-way flow of inspiration or formative influence may be ill-advised"[32] is undoubtedly valid far beyond the particular context in which the remark was made.

Regrettably, no monograph about the classical period of Muslim polemics with Christians is as yet available to update or even replace Fritsch's German text of 1930.[33] In the first part of Anawati's excellent selective survey of the whole history of Muslim-Christian polemics, apologetics, and dialogue[34] (with special reference to Muslim authors but including a few Christian writers as well), the author deals with basically the same group of persons as does Fritsch, but (unavoidably so within the space available) the article does not contain a systematic overview of the main points in this controversy, as is provided in the 1930 publication.[35] The historical survey literature in English includes one of Windrow Sweetman's volumes on *Islam and Christian Theology*, almost entirely devoted to Christian authors (Ibn Ḥazm and al-Ghazālī are the only exceptions),[36] Dorman's 1948 study of contemporary apologetic of Islam,[37] and Gaudeul's notes and comments on the authors and the contents of a sizable number of Muslim and Christian polemical texts which he published (several of them in Arabic, with English translations) in a kind of workbook that is very useful but can hardly be considered an analytical survey of this material.[38] A large number of articles[39] and some significant monographs on individual Muslim contributors to the Muslim-Christian dialogue have been published in the past four decades (including studies on al-Ghazālī and Ibn Taymiyya[40]), which provided additional background data necessary for the compilation of a long overdue critical and comprehensive history of this polemical exchange.

Although reference has already been made to the Christian side of this polemical encounter, a few supplementary comments are in order. The most gratifying development since the early 1950s has been increased attention to other than Western (especially Latin) material. A few names of persons and fields must stand for many—Samir Khalil and Sidney Griffith for research in Arab

Christian material;[41] Harald Suermann for work on early oriental Christian, especially Syrian, writings on Islam;[42] and A. T. Khoury and Daniel Sahas for the field of Byzantine-Muslim studies.[43] An actual listing of relevant titles would also have to include, in addition to several other well-known names, a number of insufficiently noticed studies, including some unpublished doctoral dissertations such as that of Landron on Nestorian polemical writings in the period up to the beginning of the fourteenth century.[44]

Important scholarship and research in the area of Latin and later Western material also continued in the post-1950 period. Significant studies on Riccoldo da Monte di Crocci[45] and Nicholas of Cusa[46] must suffice here as illustrations of the progress made in this field of inquiry.

Theological Perspectives on Muslim-Christian Relations: Comparative Theological Studies

While much of the history of Christian and Muslim reflections on each other's faith and tradition is touched upon in the context of a discussion of the development of the apologetic-polemical exchange, a substantial amount of material, especially but not exclusively of the twentieth century, needs to be dealt with in a separate subsection. For Christian data research continues on, for instance, the sixteenth-century Reformation and Islam[47] and on Protestant theology of the next one hundred years,[48] but the focus of interest of most publications is undoubtedly the modern period. Moubarac's extremely valuable study on this subject[49] and numerous other (often far less comprehensive) surveys—seldom failing to discuss Louis Massignon, W. Cantwell Smith, and Kenneth Cragg as the key figures[50]—provide ample information on Islam as reflected in the mirror of contemporary Christian theology.

Rather than offering yet another variant of the list of Christian authors who have or have had the greatest impact on the rethinking of Christian-Muslim relationship, I would like to indicate briefly three areas in which important shifts in Christian thinking took place. The first issue seems to have gained widespread concurrence, but the second and especially the third remain intensely controversial. In the latter two cases the change is not that a broad-based agreement markedly different from the main line of Christian thought in the past has been reached, but that issues which then seemed unambiguously clear to many Christians have now become challenging questions to an ever-increasing number of them.

The same God.—In the 1950s several authors realized that they were raising a highly controversial point when they argued that we, as Muslims and Christians, notwithstanding the differences in our knowledge of God, worship the same God;[51] this conviction, however, is recently often expressed in ways that reflect the fact that there is at present almost a consensus[52] on this point among Christians of very different theological persuasions.[53] In a number of cases the worship of the One God is described explicitly as the common ground between Jews, Muslims, and Christians,[54] setting them in this respect apart from people of all other faiths. Although some sharply dissenting voices continue to be heard,[55] the acknowledgment of "the same God" has been expressed so frequently in recent times by individual authors as well as by denominational bodies that it is justifiable to maintain that what was in the past, at least as far as Protestants are concerned, the conviction of relatively few[56] has become for most of those who write about this subject an indisputable assumption in their thinking about Islam.

God's speaking through the Qur'an.—The question of the prophethood of Muhammad has been raised relatively widely and at times very explicitly by Christians in these past decades[57] and is often directly linked with the question of the Qur'an as Word of God.[58] The answers remain almost as diverse as they were, but there are significant changes in the relative frequency with which certain positions are defended. One of these responses is that of Christians who, rather than using the terminology of the Qur'an as the (or as *a*) Word of God, affirm that God has spoken and continues to speak to countless people through the Qur'an[59] and, in that sense, these Christians recognize the ministry of the Prophet Muhammad as the conveyor of this message. This, as well as any of the other answers, may have precedents in history but the new development, as stated earlier, is that in some circles in which only a few decades ago the possibility of any "theological" recognition of Muhammad did not even come up as an issue for deliberation, more and more Christians are now seeing this as a question deserving explicit discussion.

Taking Islam seriously on its own terms.—Ever since the early centuries of Christian-Muslim relations, but particularly from the 1930s onward, a current in Christian thought has assigned to Islam a "Mosaic," a "pre-Mosaic," or a "patriarchal" place in God's history of salvation,[60] often interpreting its divine mission as limited to the polytheists in Arabia or, by extension, to "pagan" populations elsewhere (especially in Africa) in later centuries. This line of thought still has its proponents, as does the characterization of Islam as ultimately a phenomenon within church history[61] and, more specifically, as a movement closely akin to Jewish-Christianity.[62] But many Christians have turned away from any such trend and have embarked upon thoughtful attempts to take Islam seriously on its own terms instead of "recognizing" it in ways—by a Christian "acceptance" of it as an early (or proto-) stage of the biblical revelation or as an offshoot of Christianity—that are in direct conflict with its own sense of identity. There are important nuances in various interpretations of Islam's "own terms" in regard to the Christians, but there can be no doubt that, in addition to other groups, the Qur'an also addresses Jews and Christians with an affirmative-corrective message, often interpreted with a one-sided emphasis on either the corrective or the affirmative side, but sometimes understood as another eye on the same reality. Many Christians are exploring what this might mean, not so much in retrospect with regard to seventh-century Christianity in the Arab environment but primarily with regard to traditional and contemporary formulations of the Christian faith worldwide.

With respect to the Muslim side of the discussion, many Christians seem to share the disappointment which Montgomery Watt expressed recently in these words: "while there are many Western Islamologists from whom Muslims have something to learn, there are no corresponding Muslim students of Christianity . . . there have been no works on Christianity by Muslims apart from works of polemics; at most, within the last decade or two Comparative Religion has been introduced as a subject at some Islamic universities."[63] It is, indeed, not in the form of more or less systematic expositions of Christianity that Muslim reflections on their relations with Christians are expressed, but rather in a variety of studies on Qur'anic passages about Christ[64] and in several pleas for Muslim-Christian dialogue. The latter group of writings shows that, notwithstanding the continuing distrust of many in the ultimate objectives of dialogue, the disillusionment of some in what it has accomplished thus far, and the ongoing discussion on the scope and prospects of Muslim-Christian dialogue,[65] this subject has occasioned important appeals to rethink what being Muslim and being Christian—and what living together—mean at this juncture in history.

While the classic works of Louis Gardet and M.M. Anawati[66] and J. Windrow Sweetman[67] are, in a sense, exercises in "comparative theology," the reference in the title of this section is rather to a large number of journal articles and a modest number of books dealing, in a more or less explicitly comparative way, with particular notions: prophethood, sin, redemption, salvation, Word of God, etc.[68] Several of these studies are devoted largely to a discussion of Qur'anic and biblical data, but, as they also take into consideration later theological developments and/or contain elements of a theological assessment of Christian-Muslim relations, they would seem to fall under this category and not under "Qur'anic and Biblical Studies" above.

Comparative Studies in Spirituality, Prayer and Devotion, Mysticism, and Ethics

Although for a long period many Muslims and Christians have been interested in each other's language of devotion, forms of worship, and spirituality, comparative studies in these areas are still relatively rare and only a few years ago it could be reported that we had just set "a first step in a dialogue on spirituality."[69] But at least many Muslim and Christian prayers have already found a well-deserved "common roof for their habitation"[70] not only in printed compilations but also in the lives of several small communities and individuals.

The topic of "the early Christian mystics and the rise of the Sufis"[71] continues to be of interest to some, but many recent publications in comparative Christian-Muslim mysticism are endeavors in the comparison of two or more individual mystics, as in James Royster's article in this volume, or studies in common language and common symbols, a highly important field of inquiry represented here by Annemarie Schimmel's contribution.[72]

With regard to ethics, issues of social and public ethics draw special attention. Questions of human rights[73] and social justice, of ethical norms binding for all people in a pluralist society, of democracy, war and peace, of religious freedom, and of equal access to educational and professional opportunities belong with numerous other issues to the concerns that are increasingly considered challenges that Muslims, Christians, and other citizens living in one society have to face together. Sustained reflection both on common grounds and on distinctive perspectives is beginning to take shape.

Daʿwa and Mission

Although significant differences between the notions of mission and *daʿwa* have been pointed out repeatedly, in some situations the words seem to refer to very similar realities and, at least after the much-discussed Chambésy Conference of 1976,[74] the two terms are often linked in the discussion. The notion of an intrinsic interrelatedness of crusades, colonial expansion, economic exploitation, and Christian mission is a recurrent theme in Muslim literature. On the Christian side, twentieth-century literature on "missions and the world of Islam" shows a number of remarkable and radical changes. While historical surveys of this particular mission history or any part thereof[75] contain much material that falls under "Theological Perspectives" above (and some that belongs under "The History of Theological Interaction"), other dimensions of it need to be brought to the fore separately: issues of ultimate objectives of missionary planning and implementation are or ought to be matters of public record, on both sides, no matter how sensitive the subject matter is.

Concluding Observations

The answer to the question raised earlier of whether it makes sense to think of the immense diversity of subject areas here denoted as one field of scholarship depends on the interpretation of this suggestion. If it is understood as a proposal to bring all the material referred to above and the various approaches together into one independent and separate branch of study, the answer is definitely negative. In this connection von Harnack's warning, voiced early in this century, comes to mind: he warned against establishing academic chairs for the at that time emerging "general history of religions" because, he emphasized, this field exists only as an endless task of many disciplines and trying to give it shape as a more or less autonomous branch of study would lead unavoidably to dilettantism.[76] The same warning is perhaps even more urgent in this case. Only to the extent that collaborative arrangements can stimulate the work done in a large number of disciplines, in various faculties, and at several academic institutions spread over all continents is it justifiable to think of Muslim-Christian Studies as one multidisciplinary field of research and scholarship. Such cross-disciplinary contacts could help a larger number of Islamic scholars and persons involved in the study of Christian relations with the Muslim world to break out of the academic isolation in which they still find themselves,[77] to become acquainted with the relevant dimensions, insights, and methodologies of several other disciplines in the humanities and the social sciences, and in turn to stimulate related research in other faculties and disciplines by the specific contribution they can make to this diversified and yet in so many ways interrelated field of study.

Christian-Muslim Studies and Islamic Studies

That the scope and subject matter of Christian-Muslim and of Islamic Studies overlap but do not coincide is evident. Islamic Studies is concerned with large areas of inquiry in Qur'anic studies, ḥadith, history, theology, law, Sufism, for instance, that are outside the perimeters of Christian-Muslim Studies; the latter is concerned not only with Islamic but also with Christian data, much of which would normally not be considered part of the field of Islamic Studies.[78]

The point is that subject matter and not methodology constitutes the essential criterion for distinguishing between Muslim-Christian and Islamic Studies. Both fields are multidisciplinary and therefore not bound to or characterized by any one method or approach,[79] and both fields invite scholars from any religious or ideological persuasion to participate.[80] A second distinction lies in the candid inclusion of the normative-theological dimension in the wide spectrum of approaches in Christian-Muslim Studies. This may well be a less fundamental difference than it appears to be. While the incorporation of the normative-theological perspective may bear upon the work done in several subject areas of this field of study, it certainly cannot function in a prescriptive manner—if for no other reason than the great diversity of theological positions represented. Moreover, the idea that "normative"[81] considerations are in fact absent and should as a matter of principle be excluded from an academic program in Islamic Studies is widely questioned. Some of these issues have been raised specifically with regard to Islamic Studies;[82] others are most frequently discussed in the context of reflections on the scope and nature of religious studies in general and history of religions in particular. While this ongoing debate obviously cannot be summarized within the confines of this chapter,[83] one conclusion can be drawn without any hesitation: the time has passed to assume uncritically that the last word about these problems was spoken with the introduction of the distinction between "descriptive" and "normative" approaches, assuming thereby that academic scholarship in the field of religion and religions should limit itself to the former—namely, the desciptive dimension. From the side of Islamic Studies an early contribution to these deliberations was Ismāʿīl al-Fārūqī's provocative 1965 article on the nature and significance of the history of religions, in which he pleaded for the necessity to incorporate the dimensions of judgment and evaluation in the history of religions.[84] The much heralded and widely accepted idea of *epochē*—a suspending, bracketing of one's own presuppositions and convictions—"is necessary but insufficient," he argued,[85] and judgment is not only desirable but possible. Historians of religion need to "agree on the priority of truth to Christian, Muslim, Jewish, Hindu and Buddhist claims to the truth,"[86] and "the search for a meta religion with which the particular may be properly understood as well as evaluated, is possible."[87] Al-Faruqi's suggestion of a determinable universal religious norm with which all particulars should be evaluated may be as unacceptable to many as Heiler's attempt to define a common substratum underlying all religious differences was to al-Faruqi,[88] but the fact that he raised so directly the issue of *religion and truth*[89] should be acknowledged as a major contribution.

More than once, regret has been expressed that the "history of religions proper has rather neglected Islam . . . and the categories of *Religionswissenschaft*, like Phenomenology of Religion, have practically never been applied to this religion."[90] A similar assessment was given by Charles Adams, who stressed the "fundamental importance" of the *epochē* aspect of the phenomenological approach,[91] particularly as far as the study of the deepest commitments of Muslims is concerned. (That this latter dimension cannot be omitted from the academic study of Islam is clear, no matter how understandable, in a sense, are the reactions of a person such as Tibawi, who judged that it is "more conducive to human understanding, and more scholarly to leave matters of faith alone."[92]) Now that more and more voices, including those of Muslims, challenge the sufficiency and the adequacy of the history-of-religions approach,[93] one wonders whether there are alternatives and whether, considering the discussion referred to above, it is desirable to move also in Islamic Studies beyond the limitations of a "descriptivist approach"[94] and beyond a religio-phenomenological *epochē* ideal, and to confront consciously and explicitly issues of truth and validity. A *conditio sine qua non* for any development in this direction is, in my opinion, a fully balanced participation of Muslims in such a program of Islamic Studies, a firm commitment of all concerned not to evade controversial issues, and an academic and social atmosphere conducive to unqualified freedom of expression for all. Much more is therefore at stake than equal numerical representation in the faculty (and student body) of Muslims and people of other faiths (and ideologies), and one is hard pressed to see this as a realizable prospect for most Western institutions of higher learning; it is probably hardly more likely as an imminent possibility elsewhere. Therefore, a combination of philological, historical, and social scientific approaches and an honest acceptance of the self-limitations implied in the principle of *epochē* remain the most responsible guidelines for programs in the field for the foreseeable future. This is one of the reasons for the importance of Christian-Muslim Studies as an interinstitutional endeavor, since this kind of collaboration would provide a framework that can stimulate contacts and exchange among persons of very different perspectives on normative issues and thus can begin to build a new network of communication and facilitate a *common* quest for "truth, goodness and beauty."[95]

Muslim-Christian Studies and the Future of Christian-Muslim Encounter

"Since we cannot avoid affecting our Muslim contemporaries in quite vital ways through our work, is it not better that we should become self-conscious about what we are doing? And is it not also an aspect of our very scholarship that we should seek this self-consciousness?"[96]

This issue, raised in 1967 by Charles Adams with regard to Islamic Studies, is no less relevant with regard to present reflections on Muslim-Christian Studies, and the implications of his statement for decisions on courses to be offered, topics to be covered, and themes to be pursued deserve careful attention in both instances. Although it would be sheer foolishness to suggest that the future of the Muslim-Christian encounter depends on what is happening or will happen in Christian-Muslim Studies, it would be shortsighted to ignore the potential impact of the various dimensions of this field of scholarship on both communities of faith and on their relations with each other. Very few, if any, of those following closely what has been accomplished in Muslim-Christian dialogue thus far are anticipating major breakthroughs in the immediate future.

Georg Evers's remarks about "disillusionment in the dialogue between Christians and Muslims"[97] after the initial enthusiasm and even euphoria among Christians about interreligious dialogue in general abated have innumerable parallels in recent Christian literature. So has his expression of awareness that not without reason the Muslim world reacted with much greater reserve on this point than many Christians did, and his appeal for patience on both sides.

But is it a matter of time and patience? In a provocative discussion of "Islam and Christianity: The Opposition of Similarities,"[98] Charles Adams warned that doctrines or positions that seem similar may "prevent us from seeing more far-reaching differences inherent in the way in which doctrines and concepts combine into an integrated whole," and concluded in relation to the distinctive characters of the two traditions: "Here the difference is so great that one may well ask whether in truth there is any hope of Christian-Muslim dialogue ever progressing beyond the stage of registering the differences with one another."[99] While acknowledging the significance of these observations as a highly needed corrective to numerous attempts to show the commonality of these two traditions on the basis of decontextualized similarities, many persons are undoubtedly unwilling to accept Adams's conclusions and continue to hope "for what they do not yet see." Such a sober patience is reflected, for example, in the writings of Georges Anawati, who in the sixties had already concluded that, except on some rare occasions in conversations between a few specialists, one should avoid a still premature dialogue on points of dogmatic divergencies and deal exclusively with what Muslims and Christians have in common in the religious, social, and cultural realms and, above all, focus on the significance of directly interpersonal contacts.[100]

In my own assessment, there are good reasons to continue to believe in the meaningfulness of Muslim-Christian dialogue even on the traditionally controversial issues, with the condition, however, that one radically parts with the pointless exchange of fully predictable questions and answers (making dialogue into a "double monologue"[101]) and finds ways to deal with these same issues under new perspectives. Needless to say, the potential for such an innovatively searching interchange is greatly enhanced when one moves beyond attempts to answer new questions on the basis of a theological position rigidly fixed in every detail and is willing to take seriously the fact, in all its implications, that theology is always "in the making."[102] Here, as in all reflections on dialogue, the problem arises of how to avoid denying the otherness and the unrestricted right to theological self-determination of the partners in the dialogue by posing as binding for them also conditions which one considers absolutely essential for oneself. In the context of an expression of firm disagreement with a remark I had made, Montgomery Watt once wrote: "Dialogue, as I see it, involves a readiness to respond positively (that is, with some degree of acceptance) to the assertions of the other religion yet without transferring one's allegiance to it. Without some readiness to learn on both sides dialogue is a kind of concealed proselytizing."[103] The clarification here intended is that the issue for me is not what my own reaction is to the suggestion that we need to be ready "to respond positively . . . to the assertions of the other religion," but the question of how far we can go excluding a large number of people, in our own and in other traditions, from wholeheartedly participating in dialogue by setting prerequisites and formulating assumptions that are very questionable or even totally unacceptable to them. One would hope that the moment is approaching when we do not need to reiterate that a mere rehearsal of centuries-old arguments is meaningless. What needs to be emphasized at present is that one makes mockery of the adventure that dialogue is and should remain if one sets as conditions certain insights, perspectives, and convictions that may (not necessarily will or must) *result* from this interplay.

Against this background, and with due recognition of the significance of the experiences and conclusions of a scholar-participant such as Anawati, it seems to me that a widespread collaboration of Muslims, Christians, and others in the academic study of the whole range of subject areas referred to in the first section of this chapter is a far more promising way toward mutual understanding and recognition than an *exclusive* focus on Christian-Muslim dialogue on theological issues. That the latter is in no way to be excluded should be clear from the preceding paragraphs. One of the very fruitful areas for common search and reflection is, in my experience, the field of theologies and philosophies of history and particularly a discussion of the manifold aspects of the question of "revelation and history"[104] (revelation as ahistorical or as intrinsically historical; history as revelation; the theological meaning of the time between the revelatory events decisively important for either tradition and the eschaton). The importance of a theologically oriented dialogue for the future of both communities of faith should not be underestimated. But the challenge for countless Muslims and Christians, in endlessly varied situations, to be "living together in dialogue,"[105] as well as the task of patient and sustained shared research and scholarship in the subject matters referred to earlier—in both cases, contacts which should never be degraded by the suggestion that they are mere preliminary steps, slowly preparing the ground for the introduction of the "real" dialogue—will undoubtedly continue to involve and affect many more Muslims and Christians than will participate in organized and structured conversations on the "internal issues of dogma." The meaningfulness of the dialogue at the doctrinal level will be determined, in final analysis, by the extent to which it can show that these *internal* issues are really our various attempts to deal, under God's guidance, with our *common* concern for the ultimate questions of human existence.

NOTES

1. The two terms are used interchangeably throughout this chapter. The term here proposed seems preferable to the more common designations such as (the study of) Muslim-Christian relations, encounter, or dialogue. One of the relatively rare occurrences in English of the expression "Islamo-Christian Studies" is in a 1980 article by Augustin Dupré La Tour ("A New Departure in Islamo-Christian Studies," *Theol. Rev.*, 3, no. 2 [1980], 5–9; repr. from *Lumen Vitae*, 35 [1980]). In this case it is clearly an adaptation of the usage in French (the article deals with the Institute of Islamo-Christian Studies of Beirut's Saint Joseph University), a language in which it is as common as *christlich-islamisch* is in German, used frequently in a very similar way as here intended, e.g., in the name of the publisher of an interesting series of studies in this field, *Christlich-Islamisches Schrifttum Verlag* in Altenberge.

2. A word of special thanks is due to Carolyn Sperl and Marie Rivero of the Library of Hartford Seminary, Hartford, Conn., for their patient and excellent help in obtaining the EPIC data as well as numerous other bibliographical particulars. Linda McKinney, Research Librarian at Trinity College, Hartford, Conn., was instrumental in securing the RLIN as well as the Dialog data mentioned above; her gracious assistance is deeply appreciated.

3. *Index Islamicus, 1906–1955*, comp. J.D. Pearson, with the assistance of Julia F. Ashton (Cambridge, England: W. Heffer & Sons, 1958) is followed by quinquennial *Supplements* (1956–60, etc., since the third supplement published by Mansell), bringing together and amplifying data appearing regularly (since 1976) in *The Quarterly Index Islamicus*.

What is stated about the *Index Islamicus* equally applies to other bibliographies such as the Middle East Libraries Committee's *Middle East and Islam*, rev. and enlarged edition, ed. D. Grimwood-Jones (Zug, Switzerland: International Documentation Center, 1979 [first ed. 1972]), followed by a *Supplement 1977–1983*, ed. Paul Auchterlonie (Zug: IDC, 1986).

4. *Islamochristiana* (Rome: Pontificio Istituto di Studi Arabi & Islamici, 1975–) published installments of this bibliography in vols. 1–7, 10, 13, and 15. The coordinator of the project is Robert Caspar.

5. Ibid., 1 (1975), 129.

6. The introduction to *Islamochristiana*'s bibliography states that texts published in the period under consideration constitute the base of their project and that studies *about* that period published in later centuries are excluded. The reason for this is the compilers' concern for objectivity, and "later studies, works by Christians, Muslims or agnostics, cannot escape the climate of their times and the ideology of their authors" (ibid., 1: 128). Equally relevant to the issue of the scope of the bibliography is the compilers' focus on dialogue at the doctrinal level, excluding studies on social, political, and economic contacts (ibid., 1: 127–28). Within the limits set for it, the "Bibliographie du dialogue islamo-chrétien" seems to fulfill its goal to become a "provisionally definitive" bibliography (ibid., 1: 131).

7. See below, chaps. 2 and 3.

8. The text was brought to the attention of many by Fazlur Rahman, "Christian Particularity and the Faith of Islam: A Muslim Response," in Donald G. Dawe and John B. Carman, eds., *Christian Faith in a Religiously Plural World* (Maryknoll, N.Y.: Orbis, 1978), pp. 69–79 (the reference to S. 5:48 is on p. 74). In a slightly revised form and under a different title the article was reprinted as appendix 2 in his *Major Themes of the Qur'an* (Minneapolis-Chicago: Bibliotheca Islamica, 1980), pp. 162–70 (p. 167); in this form it was once again reprinted in Paul J. Griffith's, *Christianity through Non-Christian Eyes* (Maryknoll, N.Y.: Orbis, 1990), pp. 102–10 (pp. 106–7). Michel Lelong derived from this text the title of his 1986 publication *Si Dieu l'avait voulu* (Paris: Ed. Tougui, 1986).

9. Si Boubakeur Hamza, *Le Coran. Traduction nouvelle et commentaires*, 2 vols. (Paris: Fayard/Denoël, 1972). In his commentary on S. al-Ma'ida (5):69 (which parallels S. 2:62), the author states that the text was abrogated by S. 3:85 (ibid., 1: 242), a somewhat surprising reasoning in light of the widely accepted chronological order of Suras 3 and 5.

10. Comparative studies should not be a beginner's exercise, as is too often the case. The "translation" of the terms and notions of one religious tradition into those of another is a demanding exercise, as Oosten pointed out with reference to the anthropological study of religion: "Translations easily imply distortions" (Jarich Oosten, "Cultural Anthropological Approaches," in Frank Whaling, ed., *Contemporary Approaches to the Study of Religion* [Berlin–New York–Amsterdam: Mouton, 1985], 2: 234–35).

11. Two of the many interestingly contrasting examples are Marilyn Robinson Waldman, "New Approaches to 'Biblical' Material in the Qur'an," *The Muslim World* 75 (1985): 1–16, and the Dutch publication by D.J. Kohlbrugge and J. van der Werf, *De Ware Jozef* (The True Joseph) (Nijkerk: G.F. Callenbach, 1973). Both studies emphasize the important point of the "decontextualized" nature of the Joseph story in the Qur'an (in contrast with its function in Genesis, where it is an integral part of one coherent history), but, while Waldman's main concern is to do justice to the "plural contexts" of the story and to show that the message of S. 12, read in its Qur'anic context, clearly is "that God's will be fulfilled no matter what" (pp. 3–5), the Dutch authors search for the one *true* Joseph and use the perceived differences between the biblical and Qur'anic narratives to substantiate their conclusion that "the true Muslim as depicted in the Qur'an is diametrically opposite to the true Joseph of the Bible" (p. 107).

12. R. Marston Speight, "Attitudes toward Christians as Revealed in the *Musnad* of al-Ṭayālisī," *The Muslim World* 63 (1973): 249–68; the article is based on a section of the author's Ph.D. dissertation, "The *Musnad* of al-Ṭayālisī: A Study of Islamic Ḥadīth as Oral Literature" (Hartford, 1970).

13. Alex Soesito Wijoyo, "The Christians as Religious Community According to the Hadith," *Islamochristiana* 8 (1982): 83–105.

14. Ibid., 102.

15. Of the literature written by persons outside the Muslim community, the classical study by Antoine Fattal, *Le statut légal des non-Musulmans en pays d'Islam* (Beyrouth: Imprim. Catholique, 1958), is perhaps hardly less controversial, in the opinion of some, than the more recent study of Bat Ye'or, *The Dhimmi, Jews and Christians under Islam*, trans. from the French by David Maisel, Paul Fenton, and David Littman (Rutherford-Madison-Teaneck: Fairleigh Dickinson University Press, 1985).

16. A good example of this category is Richard B. Rose, "Islam and the Development of Personal Status Laws among Christian Dhimmis: Motives, Sources, Consequences," *The Muslim World* 72 (1982): 159–79. Significant work in this field has been done by Herbert Kaufhold, who, after his major study *Syrische Texte zum Islamischen Recht* (Munich: Verlag der Bayerischen Akademie der Wissenschaften, 1971), published the legal collection of Gabriel of Baṣra (a significant part of which is based on a Syriac fragment in the archives of Hartford Seminary) in *Die Rechtssamlung des Gabriel von Baṣra und ihr Verhältnis zu den anderen juristischen Sammelwerken der Nestorianer* (Berlin: J. Schweitzer, 1976); the text and German translation of the Hartford fragment are on pp. 134–59, 168–99.

17. See, e.g., James Muldoon, *Popes, Lawyers and Infidels* (Philadelphia: University of Pennsylvania Press, 1979).

18. Norman Daniel, *Islam and the West. The Making of an Image* (Edinburgh: University Press, 1960; several reprints); *The Arabs and Mediaeval Europe* (London and New York: Longman, 1975; 2d ed. 1979); *Islam, Europe and Empire* (Edinburgh: University Press, 1966). There is also, however, a continuing need for detailed, sharply focused studies on various topics in the field of contacts between the Muslim world and "the West," and the importance and the diversity of this type of contribution is clearly exemplified in the current volume in chapters by Hadia Dajani-Shakeel, Jane I. Smith, and Jacques Waardenburg (12, 14, and 22, respectively).

19. See, e.g., Carsten Colpe, "Historische und theologische Gründe fur die abendländische Angst vor dem Islam," in his *Problem Islam*, (Frankfurt/M.: Athenäum, 1989), pp. 11–38. Edward W. Said stressed the ongoing impact of this fear on modern orientalism: "Modern Orientalism already carried within itself the imprint of the great European fear of Islam" (*Orientalism* [New York: Pantheon Books, 1978], pp. 253–54).

20. Norman Daniel, "Sarrasins, Chevaliers et Moines dans les Chansons de Geste," *MIDEO* 17 (1986): 115. His *Heroes and Saracens. An Interpretation of the Chansons de Geste* (Edinburgh: University Press, 1984) is of special interest in the context of Christian-Muslim Studies primarily because of its thesis that the totally distorted picture of the Saracens and their gods which the Chansons provide was not "a matter of simple ignorance. . . . We must consider the possibility that the multiplicity of Saracen gods is a deliberate fiction and intended, not to deceive, but to amuse" (ibid., p. 121; see also chaps. 6 and 12, esp. pp. 275–79).

21. Published by King Abdulaziz University, Jeddah, Saudi Arabia.

22. See below, chaps. 23, 13, and 11, respectively.

23. Michael Gervers and Ramzi Jibran Bikhazi, eds., *Conversion and Continuity*, Papers in Mediaeval Studies 9 (Toronto: Pontifical Institute of Mediaeval Studies, 1990).

24. See, e.g., in addition to his contribution to this volume (chap. 17), Olaf Schumann's "Herausgefordert durch die Pancasila: Die Religionen in Indonesien," in *Gottes ist der Orient, Gottes ist der Okzident*, Festschrift für Abdoljavad Falaturi zum 65. Geburtstag, ed. Udo Tworuschka (Cologne-Vienna: Böhlau, 1991), pp. 322–43, and François Raillon, "Chrétiens et Musulmans en Indonésie: Les voies de la tolérance," *Islamochristiana* 15 (1989): 135–67.

25. In addition to Schumann's article referred to in note 24, contributions by Christian Troll (chap. 15), Roland Miller (chap. 16), J. Haafkens (chap. 18), Jorgen Nielsen (chap. 19), Sulayman Nyang (chap. 20), and Frederick Denny (chap. 21).

26. See, e.g., the concluding section of Mohammed Arkoun, "Émergences et problèmes dans le monde musulman contemporain (1960–1985)," *Islamochristiana* 12 (1986): 135–61 (on the Muslim-Christian dialogue aspect, esp. pp. 157–61). Especially in light of the major contributions Wilfred Cantwell Smith has made to this field, it would be disgraceful if historians of religion would relegate it exclusively to the anthropological study of religion to deal with the human realities of "the Muslim in Indonesia in the twentieth century and the Muslim in Medieval Persia" and would see that discipline as the only branch of study concerned in this connection with both "the explanation of differences and the explanation of similarities"; cf. Oosten's article in Whaling, ed., *Contemporary Approaches*, 2: 252. Whereas Cantwell Smith's corrective has had a tremendous impact on work in the history of religions, it continues to be ignored by many of those who construct "theologies of religions" of a type that reduces once again the faith of other people to religious "systems" to be judged and evaluated in more or less unequivocal ways, without due reference to the rich diversity in the life of faith of those communities.

27. Kenneth Cragg, "Persons, Situations, Books," *The Muslim World* 43 (1953): 199–200.

28. The classical and often quoted study along these lines is Carl H. Becker, "Christliche Polemik und Islamische Dogmenbildung," *Zeitschrift fur Assyriologie*, 26 (1912): 175–95.

29. Morris S. Seale, *Muslim Theology: A Study of Origins with Reference to the Church Fathers* (London: Luzac & Co., 1964).

30. Daniel J. Sahas, "The Formation of Later Islamic Doctrines as a Response to Byzantine Polemics: The Miracles of Muhammad," *The Greek Orthodox Theological Review* 27 (1982): 307–24. The notion of a "borrowing" of Christian doctrines is obviously a different matter than the idea of a development in theological articulation occasioned by a *response* to Christians.

31. See, e.g., the critical remarks on the Becker-Seale line of thought by W. Montgomery Watt, *The Formative Period of Islamic Thought* (Edinburgh: University Press, 1973), pp. 98–99.

32. Robert M. Haddad, "Iconoclasts and *Muʿtazila*: The Politics of Anthropomorphism," *Greek Orthodox Theological Review* 27 (1982): 301.

33. Erdmann Fritsch, *Islam und Christentum im Mittelalter* (Breslau: Müller & Seiffert, 1930).

34. Georges C. Anawati, O.P., "Polémique, Apologie et Dialogue Islamo-Chrétiens. Positions classiques médiévales et positions contemporaines," *Euntes Docete* 22 (1969): 375–451. The first section, on the classical polemical writings (pp. 379–415), discusses fourteen Muslim authors, from al-Hāshimī to al-Suʿūdī.

35. Fritsch, *Islam und Christentum*, pp. 39–150.

36. J. Windrow Sweetman, *Islam and Christian Theology*, pt. 2, vol. 1 (London: Lut-

terworth Press, 1955). Chapter 5, "Polemical Climax," discusses Riccoldo of Monte di Crocci and Nicholas of Cusa on the Christian side (pp. 116–78) and Ibn Ḥazm and al-Ghazālī on the Muslim side (pp. 178–308).

37. Harry Gaylord Dorman, Jr., *Toward Understanding Islam. Contemporary Apologetic of Islam and Missionary Policy* (New York: Teachers College, Columbia University, 1948).

38. Jean-Marie Gaudeul, *Encounters and Clashes. Islam and Christianity in History*, 2 vols. (Rome: Pontificio Istituto di Studi Arabi & Islamici, 1984).

39. Including the articles in this volume on Ibn Taymiyya (by Mark Swanson, chap. 6) and on al-Bāqillānī (by Wadi Z. Haddad, chap. 5). In any study of Ibn Taymiyya, the letter of Paul of Antioch is bound to be discussed as well (cf. Muzammil H. Siddiqi, "Muslim and Byzantine Christian Relations: Letter of Paul of Antioch and Ibn Taymiyah's Response," *Greek Orth. Theol. Rev.* 31 [1986]: 33–45; rep. in N.M. Vaporis, ed., *Orthodox Christians and Muslims* [Brookline, Mass.: Holy Cross Orthodox Press, 1986], pp. 33–45); in this and similar instances a study may be equally relevant to the rubric of Muslim polemics as to that of Christian apologetics and controversy.

40. See, especially, Franz-Elmar Wilms, *Al-Ghazālī's Schrift wider die Gottheit Jesu* (Leiden: E.J. Brill, 1966) and Thomas F. Michel, *A Muslim Theologian's Response to Christianity: Ibn Taymiyya's al-Jawāb al-Ṣaḥīḥ* (Delmar, N.Y.: Caravan Books, 1984).

41. Since any summary bibliography would fail to do justice to their work, only one, arbitrarily chosen title is given here for each author, simply as an illustration of the contribution made: Samir Khalil, "Une théologie arabe pour l'Islam," *Tantur Yearbook 1979–80*, pp. 57–84, and Sidney H. Griffith, "The Monks of Palestine and the Growth of Christian Literature in Arabic," *The Muslim World* 78 (1988): 1–28; both articles contain a number of references to other publications by the same authors.

42. Harald Suermann, *Die geschichtstheologische Reaktion auf die einfallenden Muslime in der Edessenischen Apokalyptik des 7. Jahrhunderts* (Frankfurt/M.: P. Lang, 1985); "Orientalische Christen und der Islam," *Zeitschrift für Missionswissenschaft und Religionswissenschaft* 67 (1983): 120–36; "Ein Disput des Jôhannàn von Litharb," *CIBEDO. Beiträge zum Gespräch zwischen Christen und Muslimen* 3, no. 5–6 (1989): 182–90; a bibliographical note on the same Syriac Christian author in *Islamochristiana* 15 (1989): 169–74.

43. Of A. Th. Khoury's numerous publications on Byzantine theology (polemics) and Islam, only a few can be mentioned here: *Les théologiens byzantines et l'Islam*: vol. 1, *Textes et auteurs (VIIIe–XIIIe s.)*, 2d ed. (Louvain: Nauwelaerts, 1969); vol. II, *Polémique byzantine contre l'Islam (VIIIe–XIIIe s.)*, 2d ed. (Leiden: E.J. Brill, 1972); "Apologétique byzantine contre l'Islam (VIIIe-XIIIe s.)," *Proche Orient Chrétien* 29 (1979): 242–300; 30 (1980): 132–74; 32 (1982): 14–49.

Since his doctoral dissertation *John of Damascus on Islam* (Leiden: E.J. Brill, 1972), Daniel J. Sahas has published several articles and chapters on various aspects of Byzantine-Muslim relations, including his contribution in this volume (chap. 7).

44. Bénédicte Landron, "Apologétique, polémique et attitudes nestoriennes vis-à-vis de l'Islam entre le VIIIE et le début du XIVe siècle" (thèse de doctorat, Université au Paris, Sorbonne, 1978).

45. Of the newer literature, special mention should be made of the work of Jean-Marie Mérigoux, including "Un précurseur du dialogue islamo-chrétien, frère Ricolodo,"

Revue Thomiste 73 (1973): 609–21; "L'ouvrage d'un frère Prêcheur florentin en Orient à la fin du XIIIE siècle, le 'Contra legem Sarracenorum' de Riccoldo da Monte di Croce," *Memorie Domenicane* n.s. 17 (1986): 1–144; "Lettres du Fr. Riccoldo adressées à l'Eglise du Ciel," *Sources* (Fribourg, Switzerland) 12 (Sept.-Oct. 1986): 204–12.

46. See Ludwig Hagemann, *Der Kur'ān in Verständnis und Kritik bei Nikolaus von Kues: Ein Beitrag zur Erhellung islāmisch-christlicher Geschichte* (Frankfurt/M.: Josef Knecht, 1976).

47. E.g., Victor Segesvary, *L'Islam et la Reforme: étude sur l'attitude des reformateurs zurichois envers l'Islam (1510–1550)* (Lausanne: Ed. L'Age d'Homme, 1978); and, for Calvin, the remarks by Jan Slomp (chap. 8 below).

48. H. Brenner, "Protestantische Orthodoxie und Islam. Die Herausforderung der türkischen Religion in Spiegel evangelischer Theologen des augehenden 16. und des 17. Jahrhunderts." Theol. diss., Heidelberg, 1986.

49. Youakim Moubarac, *Récherches sur la Pensée Chrétienne et l'Islam dans les temps modernes et à l'époque contemporaine* (Beirut: Publ. de l'Université Libanaise, 1977). The introduction and the first two chapters set the stage for the discussion of explicitly Christian material, pp. 133–555.

50. A few illustrations of such summary overviews must suffice: Youakim Moubarac and Guy Harpigny, "L'Islam dans la réflexion théologique du christianisme contemporain," in *Concilium* 116 (1976) [Project 10: Chrétiens et Musulmans]: 28–38 (with a section "En Orient Chrétien," referring to, among others, Joseph Dourra Haddad, Michel Hayek, Paul Khoury, and Georges Khodr); Jean-Paul Gabus, "Approches Protestantes de l'Islam" in Jean-Paul Gabus, Ali Merad, and Youakim Moubarac, *Islam et Christianisme en dialogue* (Paris: Ed. du Cerf, 1982), pp. 13–32, 51–62; and, finally, the far more elaborate analysis of some German, Dutch, and American Protestant authors as well as of Cragg and Cantwell Smith in Klaus Hock, *Der Islam in Spiegel westlicher Theologie* (Cologne-Vienna: Böhlau, 1986).

51. An interesting example of a strongly qualified recognition of our worshiping the same god (as Jews, Muslims, and Christians) is Eric Bishop's 1948 article, in which he writes: "It seems sometimes as if we scarcely worship the same God—anyhow our ideas of Him are quite obviously not the same. If it were absolutely and not relatively true that we 'worship the same God,' would there be either a Jewish or an Islamic problem?" (E. F. F. Bishop, "The Jerusalem that Now Is," *Int. Review of Missions* 37 [1948]: 432–34).

52. Youakim Moubarac, "Approches chrétiennes de l'Islam vu d'Orient," in *Islam et Christianisme en dialogue* (see note 50), p. 92, used the consensus language already in 1982. For a reference to an earlier discussion of the issue of "the same God," see John Carman's observations in chap. 27, this volume.

53. An example on the evangelical Christian side is James P. Dretke, *A Christian Approach to Muslims: Reflections from West Africa* (Pasadena, Calif.: William Carey Library, 1979), appendix A, "The Same God," pp. 203–6.

54. Two illustrations of this suggested parallelism of Christian-Jewish and Christian-Muslim relations on this point suffice. First, Samuel Zwemer's statement made in the 1940s: "No Jew since Paul's day, any more than Paul himself, was ever conscious of a change of 'gods' when he accepted Christ as Saviour and Lord. The same is true of every

Moslem convert today" ("The Allah of Islam and the God revealed in Jesus Christ," *Theology Today*, April 1946, reprinted in *The Muslim World* 36 [1946]: 309). And, second, Robert W. Jenson's remark: "It is surely the gospel mandate to baptize Jews who are brought to ask for it, but we do not regard them, as we do pagans, as thereby first beginning to worship the true God. In our judgment the church's relation to Islam must in this respect be like its relation to Judaism" ("God and Jesus: Theological Reflections for Christian-Muslim Dialog" [Minneapolis, Minn.: American Lutheran Church, Division for World Mission and Inter-Church Cooperation, 1986], p. 66).

55. For publications until the mid-1950s, see, e.g., my *De Islam als Na-Christelijke Religie* (The Hague: van Keulen, 1959), pp. 59–62, 100–109. For later literature the section in Paul Schwarzenau, "'Kommt herbei zu einem gleichen Wort zwischen uns' (Koran, Sure 3:64)—Biblische und koranische Grundlagen für den christlich-islamischen Dialog," in *Gottes ist der Orient*, p. 499, where he mentions as recent examples of a denial of "the same God" notion M. Basilea Schlink, *Wo liegt die Wahrheit? Ist Mohammeds Allah der Gott der Bibel*? (Darmstadt-Eberstadt: Verl. Evang. Marienschwesternschaft, 1982), and Marius Baar, *Das Abendland am Scheideweg* (Asslar: Schulte and Gerth, 1979; English translation, *The Unholy War*, trans. Victor Carpenter [Nashville: T. Nelson, 1980].)

56. Within the Roman Catholic tradition the affirmation of the worship of the same God has been the dominant pattern for centuries. A few examples of this affirmation in other Christian circles in past centuries and in the first half of the twentieth century are given in my *De Islam*, pp. 80–91.

57. See in this volume chap. 26 by David Kerr. Besides the carefully selected major contributions that he reviews, numerous other recent references to this issue deserve attention: Robert Caspar, "Pour une vision chrétienne du Coran," *Islamochristiana* 8 (1982): 25–55; Claude Geffré, "Le Coran, une Parole de Dieu différente?" *Lumière et Vie* 163 (July–August 1983): 21–32; Michel Lelong, *Deux Fidélités une espérance* (Paris: Ed. du Cerf, 1979), esp. pp. 85–87; Michel Lelong, "Mohammed, prophète de l'Islam," *Studia Missionalia* 33 (1984): 251–75, esp. pp. 266–75; Jan Slomp, "Can Christians Recognize Muhammad as a Prophet?" in Jan Slomp, ed., *Witness to God in a Secular Europe* (Geneva: Conference of European Churches, 1985), p. 28 ["Mohammed erkennen als Profeet?" *Wereld en Zending* 13 (1984): 231–37]; Theo Sundermeier, "Die religiöse und politische Herausforderung des Islam," *Evangelische Mission. Jahrbuch* 15 (1983): 37–49.

58. Wilfred Cantwell Smith initiated the discussion in many Protestant circles by his Yale lecture "Is the Qur'an the Word of God?" *Questions of Religious Truth* (New York: Charles Scribner's Sons 1967), pp. 37–62), repr. *Religious Diversity*, ed. Willard G. Oxtoby (New York–London: Harper & Row, 1976), pp. 22–40. From the Roman Catholic side, one of the major contributions in recent years is Robert Caspar's article in *Islamochristiana* mentioned in note 57; his extended study formed the background for the discussion on this topic in the Muslim-Christian Research Group (Groupe de Récherche Islamo-Chrétien, GRIC) that led to the document *The Challenge of the Scriptures: The Bible and the Qur'an*, trans. Stuart E. Brown (Maryknoll, N.Y.: Orbis, 1989), esp. pp. 47–76 (the French original was published Paris: Ed. du Centurion, 1987). As far as a Christian perspective on the Qur'an is concerned, the joint study group suggested seeing

"the Qurʾan as an authentic Word of God, but one in part essentially different from the Word in Jesus Christ" (*Challenge*, p. 73).

In his important comments on this publication, Jacques Jomier described the outcome of this project as a helpful beginning of the discussion but considered its conclusions unconvincing and judged the theological exploration of the scriptures in Muslim-Christian dialogue still premature ("Eine neue Form des christlich-islamischen Dialogs," *CIBEDO Beiträge* 2, no. 2 [1988]: 38–44, an abridged German translation of his review in *Revue Thomiste* 87 [1987]: 690–97).

59. The emphasis is on the words "through the Qurʾan," used to distinguish this statement from some Christians' affirmation that God does speak "directly" to human hearts everywhere, usually without the medium of "the sacred page" or, as a participant in the International Missionary Conference at Edinburgh, 1910, expressed it, God is speaking to Muslims "not through any word of the Koran, or through doctrines of Islam, but through His Spirit" (*The Report of Commission IV* [Edinburgh-London: Oliphant, Anderson & Ferries], p. 127).

60. See Georges C. Anawati's critical remarks about this distinction between chronological and "paracletical" time (i.e., time of the Holy Spirit, the order of God's plan of revelation/salvation) in "An Assessment of the Christian-Islamic Dialogue," in Kail C. Ellis, ed., *The Vatican, Islam, and the Middle East* (Syracuse, N.Y.: Syracuse University Press, 1987), pp. 57 ff.

61. In Friedrich Schwally's second edition and complete revision of Theodor Nöldeke's famous *Geschichte des Qorans*, Schwally deplores the fact that Christian "theologians still insufficiently realize that Islam belongs to Church History" (ibid., vol. II [Leipzig: Dieterich'sche Verlagsbuchhandlung, 1919], 209). Frequently this idea was expressed in the form of a characterization of Islam as "a Christian sect"; some well-known examples of this designation are listed in my *De Islam*, pp. 98–99 (see p. 89), including those of Adolf von Harnack (1874), Frank H.F. Foster (1932), and Duncan Black Macdonald (1933). Recent, often extremely sharp criticisms of this usage are in a sense justifiable, as indicated above, but one should not overlook the fact that many (certainly not all) late nineteenth- and early twentieth-century authors who used this language did so in an attempt to express their conviction of a fundamental affinity between the Muslim and Christian traditions, seeking to counteract radically negative attitudes to Islam at the time still dominant in many circles. One illustration of the criticism here referred to is Gordon E. Pruett, "Duncan Black Macdonald: Christian Islamicist," in Asaf Hussain, Robert Olson, and Jamil Qureshi, eds., *Orientalism, Islam, and Islamists* (Brattleboro, Vt.: Amana Books 1984), pp. 125–76, esp. pp. 150 ff.

62. The notion of Islam as an (Arabic) form of Jewish Christianity was propounded in the last quarter of the nineteenth and the first quarter of the twentieth century by several scholars, among them von Harnack (1877), F.M. Zahn (1888), and Adolf Schlatter (1918) (for bibliographical references see my *De Islam*, pp. 99, 275–76, where H.J. Schoeps [1949] is mentioned as one of the relatively rare reccurrences of this idea in the following decades). In recent years this suggestion was reintroduced in the theological discussion especially by Hans Küng, not in terms of a direct borrowing but rather as a

remarkably analogous development; see Hans Küng, Josef van Ess, Heinrich von Stietencron, and Heinz Bechert, *Christianity and the World Religions*, trans. Peter Heinegg (Garden City, N.Y.: Doubleday, 1986), pp. 123–24; "Christianity and World Religions: The Dialogue with Islam as One Model," *The Muslim World* 77 (1987): 92 ff.

63. W. Montgomery Watt, "The Study of Islam by Orientalists," *Islamochristiana* 14 (1988): 209–10.

64. While several of these publications follow the traditional controversial pattern, others are breaking new ground in various ways. Of particular importance is Mahmoud Ayoub's insistence that the Qur'anic references to Jesus must be understood as cohesive within the total message of the Qur'an: what is presented is "a fully Islamic Christology based . . . on the Islamic view of man and God" ("The Death of Jesus, Reality or Delusion? A Study of the Death of Jesus in Tafsīr Literature," *The Muslim World* 70 [1980]: 94). See also his study in this volume, chap. 4.

65. See section below p. 21. One important instance of contemporary Muslim reflections on the issue of interfaith relations is found in the work of Muḥammad Kāmil Ḥussein; see in this volume Harold Vogelaar's analysis, chap. 25.

66. Louis Gardet and M. M. Anawati, *Introduction à la théologie musulmane. Essai de théologie comparée* (Paris: J. Vrin, 1948).

67. J. Windrow Sweetman, *Islam and Christian Theology. A Study of the Interpretation of Theological Ideas in the Two Religions*, pts. 1 and 2, vol. 1; pt. 1, vol. 2 (London: Lutterworth Press, 1945–55).

68. A few randomly selected titles on this equally arbitrary list of topics: Jacques Jomier, "Prophétisme biblique et Prophétisme Coranique," *Revue Thomiste* 77 (1977): 600–609; Thomas J. O'Shaughnessy, "Sin as Alienation in Christianity and Islam," *Boletín de la Asociación Española de Orientalistas* 14 (1978): 127–35; Muzammil Husain Siddiqi, "The Doctrine of Redemption: A Critical Study," in Khurshid Ahmad and Zafar Ishaq Ansari, eds., *Islamic Perspectives* (Leicester, U.K.: The Islamic Foundation, 1979), pp. 91–102; three articles in *Studia Missionalia* 29 (1980): Ary A. Roest Crollius, "Salvation in the Qur'an," 125–40; Kenneth Cragg, "God and Salvation (An Islamic Study)," 155–66; and Jacques Jomier, "Le salut selon l'Islam," 141–54; Siegfried Riedel, *Sünde und Versöhnung in Koran und Bibel* (Erlangen: Verlag der Ev. Luth. Mission, 1987); two articles in *Orthodox Christians and Muslims* (see note 39): Mahmoud Mustafa Ayoub, "The Word of God in Islam," pp. 69–78, and Maximos Aghiorgoussis, "The Word of God in Orthodox Christianity," pp. 79–103; Thomas J. O'Shaughnessy, *Word of God in the Qur'an*, 2d rev. ed. (Rome: Biblical Institute Press, 1984).

69. Stuart E. Brown, "A First Step in a Dialogue on Spirituality: Impressions of a Conference," *Islamochristiana* 12 (1987): 169–76; "La IVe Recontre islamo-chrétienne de Tunis (21–26 avril 1986): 'La spiritualité, exigence de notre temps,'" ibid., pp. 163–67.

70. Kenneth Cragg, comp., *Alive to God: Muslim and Christian Prayer* (London: Oxford University Press, 1970), p. vii.

71. Margaret Smith, *The Way of the Mystics. The Early Christian Mystics and the Rise of the Sufis* (New York: Oxford University Press, 1978; first publ. in 1931 as *Studies in Early Mysticism in the Near and Middle East*).

72. Chaps. 10 and 9 below.

73. See the important collection of articles on this subject in *Islamochristiana* 9 (1983), a volume devoted almost entirely to the theme of "Les droits de l'homme en Islam et en Christianisme" (pp. 1–248).

74. "Christian Mission and Islamic Daʿwah," *Int. Review of Missions* 65, no. 260 (1976): 365–460; the text was reissued, with a new preface, under the same title, *Christian Mission and Islamic Daʿwah: Proceedings of the Chambésy Dialogue Consultation* (Leicester: The Islamic Foundation, 1982). See also Klaus Hock, "Christliche Mission und islamische Daʿwa: 'Sendung' und 'Ruf' in geschichtlichen Wandel," *CIBEDO Beiträge* 3, no. 1 (1989): 11–26.

75. See, e.g., Andreas Waldburger, *Missionare und Moslems: Die Basler Mission in Persien 1833–1837* (Basel: Basileia Verlag, 1985), and Lyle L. Vander Werff, *Christian Mission to Muslims, the Record: Anglican and Reformed Approaches in India and the Near East, 1800–1938* (South Pasadena, Calif.: William Carey Library, 1977). One of the most interesting sections in Waldburger's study deals with C. G. Pfander's naive Europe-centered thinking and its consequences for his assessment of then existing conditions in, and the future of, "the Orient": *Missionare*, pp. 100–115.

76. Adolf von Harnack in his famous lecture, *Die Aufgabe der theologischen Fakultäten und die allgemeine Religionsgeschichte* (Giessen: J. Ricker, 1901), pp. 10, 20–21.

77. Claude Welch's observation that "Islam would seem to be a field particularly in need of . . . the creation of structures for interrelating religious with literary and cultural studies" is still relevant to the present situation (*Graduate Education in Religion: A Critical Appraisal* [Missoula: University of Montana Press, 1971], p. 63). What Leonard Binder reported a few years later about Middle East specialists seems to apply equally to more than a few of those involved in Islamic Studies at the present: "It was widely agreed that Middle East specialists are often isolated within their departments and at the same time intellectually estranged from other Middle East specialists of different disciplinary persuasions" ("Area Studies: A Critical Reassessment," in Leonard Binder, ed., *The Study of the Middle East* [New York–London: John Wiley & Sons, 1976], p. 22). In his *Europe and the Mystique of Islam* (Seattle-London: University of Washington Press, 1991), Maxime Rodinson comments on "the Orientalists' self-satisfied acceptance of their academic ghetto" (p. 117) and stresses the urgent necessity of contact with other disciplines, in this post-philological-dominance phase of Islamic studies (pp. 79–82 and elsewhere). While there are a growing number of individual scholars who have broken out of this "isolationist" position and who bring a variety of perspectives from other disciplines to bear upon their study of Islam, this development seems to have had only a modest impact on the structure of many Islamic Studies *programs*.

78. To the exceptions belong, e.g., Christian data considered in the context of a study of Qurʾanic references to (the scriptures, beliefs and practices of) Christians and in connection with an examination of Muslim responses to Christian polemical or apologetic writings.

79. A concise overview of the variety of approaches applied to the study of Islam is offered, e.g., by Charles J. Adams, "Islamic Religious Tradition," *The Study of the Middle East*, pp. 34–54. While programs in Islamic Studies frequently find their academic place in departments/faculties of religious studies, one can hardly overestimate the signifi-

cance of work done in this field as well as in Christian-Muslim Studies by persons primarily involved in other departments and other branches of the humanities and social sciences. Two arbitrarily chosen titles must suffice to illustrate the availability of publications in the field of literature that are immediately relevant to the subject matter of Western images of, and Christian responses to, Islam: Ahmad Haydar, "Mittelalterliche Vorstellungen von dem Propheten der Sarazenen, mit besonderen Berücksichtigung der Reisebeschreibung des Bernhard von Breidenback (1483)," Diss. Phil., Freie Universität, Berlin, 1971, and Roswitha Wisniewski," Christliche Antworten auf den Islam in frühmittelalterlicher deutscher Dichtung," in Albert Zimmermann and Ingrid Craemer-Ruegenberg, eds., *Orientalische Kultur und Europäisches Mittelalter* (Berlin–New York: Walter de Gruyter, 1985), pp. 103–11.

80. The words "Muslim-Christian" in the designation of this field of research and scholarship are definitely not intended as a reference to the religious background of the participants-contributors, as seems to be the case, e.g., with the use of the same word combination in the name "Muslim-Christian Research Group" (GRIC), mentioned in note 58 above.

81. Limiting the notion of "normative" to "religious" (as, among many others, Adams seems to be doing in the section "Normative or Religious Approaches," *The Study of the Middle East*, pp. 35–41) obscures the fact that many other "normative" perspectives have influenced and at times determined the work in Islamic Studies.

82. Many of the recent critiques of orientalism are entirely or mostly discussions of Western scholars involved in the study of Islam, and the accusations of imperialistic motivations and racist distortions are frequently aimed most directly at this particular field. See also above, note 19, and below, note 92.

83. An excellent selective bibliography, "Allgemeine Literatur zur Methode und Theorie der Religionsforschung," is given by Jacques Waardenburg, *Religionen und Religion. Systematische Einführung in die Religionswissenschaft* (Berlin–New York: Walter de Gruyter, 1986), pp. 257–64; of the approximately 130 entries almost 90 percent date from the last two decades.

84. Ismāʿīl Ragi al-Fārūqī, "History of Religions: Its Nature and Significance for Christian Education and the Muslim-Christian Dialogue," *Numen* 12 (1965): 35–65, 81–86. Al-Fārūqī maintains that without this aspect of evaluation as an integral part of the discipline, a history of religions remains "a mere boodle bag in which religio-cultural wholes have just been put one beside the other in eternal and cold juxtaposition"; ibid., p. 48. For an assessment of Ismāʿīl al-Fārūqī see Kenneth Cragg, chap. 24 this volume.

85. Al-Fārūqī, "History of Religions," p. 51.

86. Ibid., p. 61.

87. Ibid., p. 56.

88. Ibid., p. 53.

89. Mentioning a single title from among the many important contributions to this discussion in later years may seem unfair, but Donald Wiebe's *Religion and Truth: Towards an Alternative Paradigm for the Study of Religion* (The Hague: Mouton, 1981) does deserve special attention as a provocative and stimulating introduction to the issues involved.

90. Annemarie Schimmel, "Islam" in *Historia Religionum, Handbook for the History of Religions* (Leiden: E.J. Brill, 1971), 2: 208.

91. Adams, in *Study of the Middle East*, pp. 50, 52–53. The author returned to this same point ten years later but then with the observation that "the strong, indeed almost exclusive, textural and philological orientation of traditional Islamic Studies" was giving way to a more varied approach and "to a more mutually fructifying relation between those occupied with learning about Islam and those who are principally interested in the phenomenon of religion" (Charles J. Adams, foreword in Richard C. Martin, ed., *Approaches to Islam in Religious Studies* [Tucson: University of Arizona Press, 1985], pp. viii–ix).

92. For a brief study of Tibawi and two other Arab critics of orientalism see Donald P. Little, "Three Arab Critiques of Orientalism," *The Muslim World* 69 (1979): 110–31; Tibawi's remark here referred to is quoted on p. 113. (The other critiques discussed are those of Anouar Abdel-Malek and Edward Said.)

93. Cf. Ismāʿīl al-Fārūqī's comment quoted above, note 85.

94. See the first of Wiebe's final conclusions, *Religion and Truth*, p. 228.

95. Ismāʿīl al-Fārūqī used this word combination in his articulation of the final purpose of history of religions: "the putting under the light of consciousness the progress or movement of the ship of humanity towards truth, goodness and beauty" (*Numen* 12 [1965]: 60). In many Christian reflections on a basis for the recognition of God's presence in the lives of people of faith, of whatever tradition they are, reference is made to Gal. 5:22, the list of "the fruit of the Spirit," beginning with Love. The emphasis on "ethical" criteria has led to the warning of some that this is an evasion of the question of truth and a "dereligionizing" or at least "detheologizing" of the interreligious dialogue. But in a proposal such as that of Peggy Starkey, "love" is presented exactly as criterion for *truth*; "Agape: A Christian Criterion for Truth in the Other World Religions," *Int. Rev. of Missions* 74, no. 296 (1985): 425–63.

96. Charles J. Adams, "The History of Religions and the Study of Islam," in Joseph M. Kitagawa, ed., *The History of Religions: Essays on the Problem of Understanding* (Chicago-London: University of Chicago Press, 1967), p. 193.

97. Georg Evers, "Christen und Muslime im Gespräch," *Evangelische Mission. Jahrbuch 18* (1986): 86–87. The article was published originally in *Missio-Pastoral*, 4 (1983).

98. Chapter 18 in Roger M. Savory and Dionisius A. Agius, eds., *Logos Islamikos. Studia Islamica in honorem G.M. Wickens*, (Toronto, Ontario: Pontifical Institute of Mediaeval Studies, 1984), pp. 287–306.

99. Ibid., p. 306.

100. Anawati, in *Euntes Docete* 22 (1969): 450, where he refers to an earlier statement of this conclusion, in his article "L'Islam à l'heure du Concile, Prolegomènes à un dialogue islamo-chrétien," *Angelicum* 41 (1964): 145–68.

101. Peter Antes, "Dialog oder doppelter Monolog? Bemerkungen zum Gespräch zwischen Christen und Muslim," in *Gottes ist der Orient*, pp. 425–37.

102. In the sense in which Wensinck distinguished, also for Islam, "creeds" from "confessions of faith" (A.J. Wensinck, *The Muslim Creed: Its Genesis and Historical Development* [Cambridge: University Press, 1932], pp. 1, 202, and elsewhere).

The fact that some trends in contemporary (Western) Christian theology are far from conducive to Christian-Muslim dialogue has been stressed by, among others, Smail Balic ("The Western theologians who distance themselves from the God of revelation open up a gulf which could make Muslim-Christian dialogue impossible") ("The Image of Jesus in Contemporary Islamic Theology," in Annemarie Schimmel and Abdaljavad Falaturi, eds., *We Believe in One God* [New York: Seabury Press, 1979], pp. 1–2, 7); and by Peter Antes (dealing especially with the tendency toward a radical transformation of theology into anthropology), "Theologie als Dialoghindernis?," in Ludwig Hagemann and Ernst Pulsfort, eds., *Festschrift für A. Th. Khoury zum 60. Geburtstag* (Altenberge: Telos, 1990), pp. 29–39.

103. William Montgomery Watt, *Islamic Revelation in the Modern World* (Edinburgh: University Press, 1969), pp. vi–vii.

104. In brief references (1971, 1982, 1986, and 1990) to this issue as, in my opinion, one of the most fruitful items for the theological agenda of Muslim-Christian conversations, I have made reference to remarks extremely significant in this connection by, among others, Seyyed Hossein Nasr—"To the claim of Küng that both Christians and Moslems believe in God as the historical God, I would respond in the negative" (*The Muslim World* 77 [1987]: 102); Smail Balic—"Islam did not arise out of the history of a covenant with God, as in the case of Judaism. An intimate connexion between God and man based on interaction in history is unknown to Islam" (*We Believe in One God*, pp. 2–3); and Abdaljavad Falaturi—"There is no reason to conceive of revelation as something temporal or historical" ("The Experience of Time and History in Islam," *We Believe in One God*, pp. 65–66). In his contribution to this volume, chap. 28, Nasr draws attention to the (related) issue of historical finality in the religious sense as one of the questions of great theological significance in Christian-Muslim dialogue. An illustration of Christian reflections on this issue occurs in Hans Zirker, *Christentum and Islam: Theologische Verwandschaft und Konkurrenz* (Düsseldorf: Patmos, 1989), pp. 55–71, 148–61 passim. Revelation and history in modern Muslim theology, and contemporary (Arab) Muslim philosophies (or theologies) of history are perhaps, as far as Western literature is concerned, most helpfully analyzed in Rotraud Wielandt, *Offenbarung und Geschichte im Denken moderner Muslime* (Wiesbaden: Franz Steiner, 1971) and Yvonne Y. Haddad, *Contemporary Islam and the Challenge of History* (Albany: State University of New York Press, 1981), esp. pp. 75–144.

105. Already in the closing statement of the first Protestant-Orthodox-Catholic "Consultation on Dialogue," held in Kandy, Sri Lanka, February–March 1967, a great deal of attention was given to this challenge of "Living in Dialogue" (*Study Encounter* 3, no. 2 [1967]: 54–55).

PART ONE

The Historical Heritage

Sacred Scriptures as the Point of Departure

2

Fa-stabiqū ʾl-khayrāt: A Qurʾanic Principle of Interfaith Relations

Issa J. Boullata

The Qurʾan, the foundation on which the religion of Islam is based, expresses in a number of ways a fundamental tolerance of earlier religions whose faith, like that of Islam, centers on the one and only God. It can be said, in this regard, that one of the doctrinal principles enunciated in the Qurʾan is that of religious pluralism. In this essay I explore the elements constituting this Qurʾanic principle, with particular reference to the ethics of interfaith relations commended in the Qurʾan as a requirement.

To begin with, the Qurʾan teaches that it is God who permits that there be more than one religious community in the world. If He willed otherwise, He would have made humankind one single community (*umma*). This idea is repeated several times in the Qurʾan:[1] "And if God had so willed, He could surely have made you all one single community" (S. 5:48); "And had thy Sustainer so willed, He could surely have made all mankind one single community" (S. 11:118); "For, had God so willed, He could surely have made you all one single community" (S. 16:93); "Now had God so willed, He could surely have made them all one single community" (S. 42:8).

In all these Qurʾanic expressions, there is a purpose adduced to religious pluralism in the divine scheme of things. Thus each of the above-quoted four verses continues with a clear indication of this purpose: "but [He willed it otherwise] in order to test you by means of what He has vouchsafed unto you" (S. 5:48); human beings "continue to hold divergent views" (S. 11:118); God "lets go astray him that wills [to go astray], and guides aright him that wills [to be guided]" (S. 16:93); and "He admits unto His grace him that wills [to be admitted]" (S. 42:8). However, the Qurʾan also points out in the same verses that there is human accountability with regard to religious pluralism, as when it says: "and you will surely be called to account for all that you ever did" (S. 16: 93), or: "the evildoers shall have none to protect them and none to succour them [on Judgment Day]" (S. 42:8).

It is true that the Qur'an also says that humankind once were all members of a single community (S. 2:213; S. 10:19). It does not specify the time of such primal religious unity among humans except to say that it existed in the past. Yet the Qur'an recognizes the divergent human views that have appeared in history by God's will and that have eventually led to religious pluralism. God's decree in this regard was to permit such differences, for the Qur'an says: "And had it not been for a decree that had already gone forth from thy Sustainer, all their differences would indeed have been settled [from the outset]" (S. 10:19). God's design was rather to guide humankind in their religious pluralism by sending them prophets with divine revelation. The Qur'an says: "whereupon God raised up the prophets as heralds of glad tidings and as warners, and through them bestowed revelation from on high, setting forth the truth, so that it might decide between people with regard to all on which they had come to hold divergent views" (S. 2:213).

Thus, although human beings have been divided into diverse religious communities, they have not been left without divine guidance. Addressing the various communities, the Qur'an says: "Unto every one of you We appointed a [different] law and way of life" (S. 5:48); and similarly: "for, every community faces a direction of its own, of which He is the focal point" (S. 2:148). And immediately following these statements in these two verses there is a command addressed to all the communities, which says: "*fa-stabiqū 'l-khayrāt*"—that is, "Vie, therefore, with one another in doing good works" (S. 2:148) and "Vie, then, with one another in doing good works" (S. 5:48). This command has been variously rendered in English. One rendering says: "Then strive together (as in a race)/ Towards all that is good" (S. 2:148) and "so strive/ As in a race in all virtues" (S. 5:51).[2] Another version says: "so be you forward in good works" (S. 2:143) and "So be you forward in good works" (S. 5:52)[3] and a third says: "so compete in [doing] good deeds" (S. 2:148) and "but compete rather in doing good deeds" (S. 5:48).[4]

In spite of the various shades of meaning that these renderings offer, they all capture important aspects of the essence of the command in Arabic, given to all religious communities: there should be vying with one another among them, there should be striving together as in a race; there should be competition, not against one another, but rather in a concerted effort to do good works, to do good deeds; there should be emulation leading toward all that is good and in all virtues. Each community is thus commanded to go forward in its good efforts, undertaken in conjunction with the others and in harmony with them. It seems abundantly clear that there is here a manifest Qur'anic principle of interfaith relations, based on a harmonious religious pluralism, and urging believers of all faiths to do good. This principle is in tune with other verses in the Qur'an which state that God's purpose in creating the diversity of humankind is that people might come to know one another despite their different languages and colors, as in S. 49:13: "O men! Behold, We have created you all out of a male and a female, and have made you into nations and tribes, so that you might come to know one another. Verily, the noblest of you in the sight of God is the one who is most deeply conscious of Him. Behold, God is all-knowing, all-aware" and in S. 30:22: "And among his wonders is the creation of the heavens and the earth, and the diversity of your tongues and colours: for in this, behold, there are messages indeed for all who are possessed of [innate] knowledge!"

In the above quotations from the Qur'an there is no mention of any specific religious community. However, when the Qur'an elsewhere does mention specific religious communities whose faith centers on the one and only God, it recognizes the existence of good people within each community and announces that they deserve divine reward. This theme strengthens the principle of religious pluralism, as it implicitly rejects all notions of exclusivism and election in Islam. In other words, the Qur'an does not favor one religious community over another. In S. 2:62, the Qur'an says: "Verily, those who have attained to faith [in this divine writ], as well as those who follow the Jewish faith, and the Christians, and the Sabians—all who believe in God and the Last Day and do righteous deeds—shall have their reward with their Sustainer; and no fear need they have, and neither shall they grieve." This theme is repeated in S. 5:69. Thus the Muslims, Jews, Christians, and Sabians are all considered to be religious communities through which human beings can attain salvation by belief in God and the Last Day, and by doing righteous deeds.

In order to ascertain how Muslims have themselves understood the Qur'anic command *fa-stabiqū 'l-khayrāt*, which I consider to be an important prooftext in this discussion, recourse will be made to a number of Muslim commentators on the Qur'an.

Let me start with al-Ṭabarī (d. A.D. 923) who, in his multivolume *Tafsīr*, brought together vast materials of traditional Qur'anic exegesis that had been gathering (mostly by oral transmission) in the first three centuries of Islam, to which he often added his own opinion or judgment on the validity of earlier interpretations. His commentary retains much of the debates of his time and those of his predecessors' times with regard to many issues. I will focus on the issue of religious pluralism reflected in the commentary on the above-quoted verses.

A look at the two Qur'anic instances (S. 2:148 and S. 5:48) where the command *fa-stabiqū 'l-khayrāt* occurs shows that it is given in the context of assuring Prophet Muhammad of the truth in God's Qur'anic revelation, even though Jews and Christians do not accept it as such and therefore do not accept Qur'anic prescriptions as binding on them. In the former instance (S. 2:148), the contention is about accepting the *qibla*, the direction of prayer toward which believers are enjoined in the Qur'an to turn their faces. In the second instance (S. 5:48), the issue is acceptance of Prophet Muhammad's judgment according to Qur'anic criteria. In both cases, the Qur'an emphasizes the separate character of each religious community as a specific entity. As mentioned above, the Qur'an says in this context (S. 2:148): "for, every community faces a direction of its own, of which He is the focal point." And it says (S. 5:48): "Unto every one of you have We appointed a [different] law and way of life."

Every translation, as we have said, is an interpretation, and this English rendering is a particular case in point. Though in my opinion it conveys the correct Qur'anic meaning, it does so more by seeking support from past Muslim exegetes with a specific frame of mind than by closely following the letter of the Arabic text in these verses. The pivotal Arabic word in the text of both verses is *kull*, which is rendered in S. 2:148 as "every community" and in S. 5:48 as "every one." In both verses, the Arabic is *li-kull-in* (unto each), a usage of the *iḍāfa* in which the second member of the construct is not mentioned but is replaced by the nunation *(-in)* which Arab grammarians call *tanwīn al-ʿiwaḍ* or *tanwīn al-taʿwīḍ* (nunation of compensation), thus leaving the genitive following *kull* unspecified and tantalizingly inviting Qur'anic exegetes to interpret it according to the context and the way they understand it.

In both instances, al-Ṭabarī interprets *li-kull-in* by providing a specified genitive after *kull*, saying that *li-kull-in* means *li-kulli ahli millatin* ("unto the people of every [religious] community").[5] He supports this interpretation by quoting orally transmitted materials going back through a chain of authorities to the earliest Muslim generation. With regard to S. 2:148, he quotes authorities offering variations on this theme, some of whom specifically refer to Jews, Christians, and Muslims as the religious communities intended, as each faces a prayer direction of its own; he also quotes Ibn ʿAbbās (d. A.D. 688), who generalizes the reference to people of all religions.[6]

With regard to S. 5:48, al-Ṭabarī explains that there has been difference of opinion in the interpretation of *li-kull-in*. One opinion holds that it refers to the people of the different religious communities and that the text means God has appointed a different law and way of life unto every religious community. Al-Ṭabarī mentions the authorities holding this opinion, and among them Qatādā (d. A.D. 735) says specifically that the Torah has a law, the Gospel has another, and the Qur'an has yet another, adding that religions are one but the laws of each are different. Al-Ṭabarī, however, states that according to another opinion the text refers only to the community of Muhammad and that the Muslims are addressed in it, *li-kull-in . . . min-kum* meaning *li-kulli-kum* ("unto every one of you"); the explanation is: for every one who enters Islam and recognizes Muhammad as his own prophet, God has appointed the Book revealed to

Prophet Muhammad as a law (*shirʿatan*) and as a way of life (*minhājan*).[7] To document this opinion, al-Ṭabarī gives a single quotation with a chain of authorities going back to Mujāhid (d. A.D. 722), who interprets *li-kull-in . . . minkum* as *li-kulli-kum*, and explains that the text means: whoever enters the religion of Muhammad has the Qurʾan as a law and way of life.[8]

Of the two opinions, al-Ṭabarī considers the first one as more likely to be correct, that is, the opinion holding that the text refers to the people of every religious community, to each of whom God has appointed a law and a way of life. And he justifies his preference by saying that if the text meant the community of Muhammad only, which is one community, the sentence following it ("And if God had so willed, He could surely have made you all one single community") would have no comprehensible meaning. Furthermore, al-Ṭabarī puts his preferred interpretation in the context of the immediately preceding verses, of which vv. 44–45 refer to the prescriptions of the Israelites in the Torah that the Jews have to obey, and vv. 46–47 refer to the prescriptions of the Christians in the Gospel that the followers of Jesus have to obey. He then shows that the text of S. 5:48 falls in place, as it refers to the Book revealed to Muhammad by whose prescriptions he has to act, because he and his community have been given a law which is different from the laws of previous prophets and communities.[9]

It is evident from this interpretation that al-Ṭabarī is in support of the Qurʾanic principle of religious pluralism. He accepts the Qurʾan's recognition of the existence of other religious communities and he documents his view by quoting a number of authorities from the first generation of Muslims. Like them, he acknowledges that God has revealed a different law and way of life to each religious community and that each of them is legitimate as a religious entity fostering the salvation of its votaries, in spite of the fact that the nature of religion is ultimately one.

The major Muslim exegetes after al-Ṭabarī agree basically with his interpretation. Both al-Zamakhsharī (d. A.D. 1144) and al-Bayḍāwī (d. A.D. 1286), for example, reflect the debate in al-Ṭabarī's *Tafsīr*. They do not mention his chain of authorities but accept the gist of their understanding. With regard to the Qurʾanic command *fa-stabiqū ʾl-khayrāt*, the two instances of it in the Qurʾan are differently interpreted. That in S. 2:148 is said to be about the geographical direction of prayer during Muslim worship, namely, the *qibla*, as well as about related matters.[10] Al-Bayḍāwī specifies those matters as the ones through which happiness in this world and the next (*saʿādat al-dārayn*) may be achieved.[11] These are the things over which Muslims should compete, according to al-Zamakhsharī and al-Bayḍāwī, with regard to the first instance of *fa-stabiqū ʾl-khayrāt* (S. 2:148). As for the second instance of this command, which appears in S. 5:48, al-Zamakhsharī simply says it means: hasten to them [i.e., to the good deeds] and try to get ahead of one another [in achieving] them.[12] The context of his interpretation of the previous sections of this verse, particularly regarding *li-kull-in*, gives one to understand that the command is addressed to all people, irrespective of the religious community to which they belong. Al-Bayḍāwī amplifies the meaning of this command by saying it means: hasten to them [i.e., to the good deeds] in order to seize the opportunity and achieve the merit of precedence and priority.[13] Like al-Zamakhsharī, he gives one to understand that the command is addressed to all people, whatever their religious community. But neither of them is as specific as al-Ṭabarī with regard to this matter. It would seem that, with Islam being firmly established in their time, it was not necessary for them to be specific and to interpret this command as addressed to people of all religious faiths.

Before turning to some modern exegetes, let me first mention one of the later commentaries, a rather short but very popular one, the *Tafsīr al-Jalālayn* of Jalāl al-Dīn al-Maḥallī (d. 1459) and Jalāl al-Dīn al-Suyūṭī (d. 1505). This commentary interprets both instances of *li-kull-in* (S. 2:148 and S. 5:48) to mean each of the *umam* (plural of *umma*), and it considers the text to be implicitly addressed to all religious communities.[14] Hence, *fa-stabiqū ʾl-khayrāt* is presumed to be addressed to people of all religions. According to this commentary, the command in S. 2:148 means "hasten to deeds of obedience and accept them;"[15] and in S. 5:48 it means "hasten to them,"[16] that is, to these deeds, in obedience to God's prescriptions. The authors of this commentary do not seem to have any problem with this Qurʾanic principle of interfaith relations in a society of religious pluralism.

Now to a couple of modern commentaries: *Tafsīr al-Qurʾān al-Ḥakīm*, known as *Tafsīr al-Manār*, written by Muḥammad Rashīd Riḍā (d. 1935), who followed the method and sometimes the wording of Muḥammad ʿAbduh's (d. 1905) lectures at al-Azhar;[17] and *Fī Ẓilāl al-Qurʾān*, written by Sayyid Quṭb (d. 1966) and partially revised before his death.[18]

With regard to the command *fa-stabiqū ʾl-khayrāt* in S. 2:148, *Tafsīr al-Manār* says that it means: "hasten to every kind of good deed by acting, and let every one of you strive to precede others to it by following the guiding leader, and not by following passion. This command is general and directed to the religious community of the call; it is not specific to the believers who have responded to God and the Messenger."[19] This interpretation is in line with that of *li-kull-in*, earlier in the same verse, which is said to mean: "to every one of the religious communities."[20]

With regard to the command in S. 5:48, *Tafsīr al-Manār* is more elaborate. After explaining that *li-kull-in . . . min-kum* means: "to every messenger or to every religious community of you, O Muslims and Scripturalists (*kitābiyyūn*), or O people,"[21] it says the following, further on, with regard to the command *fa-*

stabiqū ᾿l-khayrāt: "it is incumbent on all of you to hasten to good deeds and to hurry to them because they are specifically the intended purpose of all laws and ways of religion. Why then, O people, do you look at the difference and the dissimilarity [among religious communities] without seeing the wisdom of difference and the intention of religion and law? Is this not abandoning guidance and following the ways of passion? Hastening to do good works is indeed what avails in this world and the next. . . . And so, you should consider [different] laws to be a cause for competition in good deeds, and not a cause for enmity by rivalry in deeds of bigotry."[22]

In his interpretation of this Qur᾿anic command, Rashīd Riḍā exhibits an open-mindedness reminiscent of that of his mentor, Muḥammad ʿAbduh. He is also in harmony with the major exegetes of the Islamic tradition. For him, difference among religious communities should be an occasion to compete in good deeds, and not an occasion for fanatic deeds breeding hostility and ill will among people of different faiths. There is divine wisdom in religious dissimilarities which should be recognized; there is a divine intention behind religious pluralism which should not be overlooked. God's guidance, therefore, should be adhered to as expounded in holy books; and human passions and whims should not be allowed to dominate interfaith relations. Furthermore, Rashīd Riḍā sees this command as a general one addressed to any religious community heeding the divine call; it is not specific to Muslims who have responded to God's call and that of Muhammad, His Messenger.

In contrast, Sayyid Quṭb sees this command as one addressed specifically to Muslims. Commenting on the text of S. 2:148 he says: "[God] turns away the Muslims from listening to People of the Book and occupying themselves with their teachings. He suggests to them to be upright in their own way and in accordance with their own direction. For unto every group there is a direction, so let Muslims hasten to good, let them not be distracted from it by anything; they will all end up with God, who is capable of gathering them and rewarding them ultimately." Quṭb then quotes the Qur᾿anic verse and adds: "By this, God turns away the Muslims from being preoccupied with the plots, intrigues, interpretations, and statements of the People of the Book; He turns them away to action, and [bids them] to hasten toward good works while remembering that their return is unto God, that God is all-powerful, and that nothing is beyond Him and nothing eludes Him."[23]

When Quṭb comes to S. 5:48, he understands it in an even more specific way as addressed to Muslims in confirmation of the Sharīʿa, which they should not tamper with in an attempt to reconcile themselves with people of other faiths. After citing the Qur᾿anic verse he adds: "By that, God—may He be praised—has closed all Satan's doors, especially those that appear to be good and to reconcile hearts and unify ranks by being lax with regard to anything of

God's Sharīʿa, in return for satisfying everybody or in return for what they call unity of ranks! God's Sharīʿa is more permanent and more precious than [attempts] to sacrifice a part of it in return for anything that God has decreed not to be! People have been created, each with a predisposition, each with a predilection, each with a way, each with a road. They have been created thus for a wisdom of God's. God has then offered them guidance and left them to compete, and He has made this a test by which they would be rewarded upon their return to Him, and unto Him they shall return!"[24]

The specificity and the distinctiveness of the Muslim community are very important matters in the thought system of Sayyid Quṭb.[25] To him, the teachings of the Qurʾan divide humanity into Islam and Jāhiliyya (pre-Islamic era), and there is nothing in between. According to him, since the Qurʾan is God's last true message to humanity, other scriptural religious communities are subsumed under Islam. Their beliefs and practices are only validated by what the Qurʾan teaches, not by what they claim their scriptures teach. Sayyid Quṭb understands the implementation of the Sharīʿa of the Qurʾan to be the hallmark of Muslim specificity and distinctiveness, and a dutiful acceptance of God's governance (*Ḥākimiyya*) over humanity, which he sees as the only governance that ensures justice, peace, and salvation.[26] Thus, any religious pluralism that equates other religions with Islam tampers, in his view, with its specificity and distinctiveness and is unacceptable because it allows laxity in the full implementation of the Sharīʿa. To him, interfaith relations are possible only if the supremacy of Islam and that of its Sharīʿa are recognized; it would be best if all humankind would recognize Islam as their religion and its Sharīʿa as their law and way of life.

In his earlier, unrevised version of *Fī Ẓilāl al-Qurʾān*, Sayyid Quṭb was not as radical as he sounds in his later, revised version. Not that he compromises any of his principles in his earlier work, for he accepts in it the Qurʾan's teaching that People of the Book have knowingly suppressed the truth found in their scripture or corrupted their sacred texts. But when he comes to S. 2:148, he says: "However, every group and every individual has a direction to move in, a path to follow. And so, let the concern of every group and every person be to move toward good and hasten to it."[27] After quoting the verse he says, "Then in the end, all paths will meet with God and you will be gathered in front of Him, for He is the one capable of gathering you all from the various paths and diverse places."[28]

Similarly, Sayyid Quṭb's interpretation of S. 5:48 in the earlier version is less radical than in his revised one. He explains that the verse seeks to comfort the Messenger by lightening the impact of Jewish rejection on him and by assuring him that he is not required to make all people into one religious community, for God has appointed a way of life unto each community. "And if God had so willed, He could surely have made you all one single community" (S. 5:48). But, Quṭb adds, God tests every group according to its own way.[29]

Sayyid Quṭb's earlier exegesis is certainly more in line with that of the major exegetes of the Islamic tradition. Like them, it accepts the existence of other religious communities legitimized by God's wisdom and it believes the Qur'an is exhorting them all to compete in good works on an equal footing with Muslims. In the end, God will judge all believers, each in accordance with the law and way of life of his or her own religious community. To my mind, this interpretation is genuinely Qur'anic and historically Islamic, and anything else is a temporary aberration conditioned by temporal needs of a sociopolitical or a sociopsychological nature.

Those who argue for the claim of Islam to exclusion quote such verses as S. 3:19 and S. 3:85, in which self-surrender unto God (*al-islām*) is understood to refer to the religion of the Muslim community alone (al-Islām). S. 3:19 says: "Behold, the only [true] religion in the sight of God is [man's] self-surrender unto Him"; and S. 3:85 says: "For, if one goes in search of a religion other than self-surrender unto God, it will never be accepted from him, and in the life to come he shall be among the lost." While there is a definite possibility that self-surrender unto God can mean Islam as historically realized through the message of Prophet Muhammad, the Qur'an often uses the words *islām* and *muslim* in a general way to express one's commitment to God or self-surrender unto Him. In this sense, the Qur'an speaks of Abraham as a *muslim* in S. 3:67: "Abraham was neither a 'Jew' nor a 'Christian' but was one who turned away from all that is false, having surrendered himself unto God: and he was not of those who ascribe divinity to aught beside Him." But this is another issue which I do not want to discuss in this paper exploring the pluralistic dimension of the Qur'anic message.

It is true that the Qur'an declares the Muslim community to be the best that has been raised up for humankind, as they enjoin the doing of what is right and forbid the doing of what is wrong in the context of faith in God (S. 3:110). It is also true that the Qur'an declares God has willed Muslims to be a community of the middle way so that they might bear witness before humankind (S. 2:143). Therefore, other religious communities are implicitly meant, to whom Muslims should bear witness as a community of the middle way. Furthermore, the Qur'an has specifically prescribed kindness and tact and gracious manners for Muslims when dealing with people of other faiths, and in it the Prophet himself is commanded in the following words: "Call thou [all mankind] unto thy Sustainer's path with wisdom and goodly exhortation, and argue with them in the most kindly manner: for, behold, thy Sustainer knows best as to who strays from His path, and best knows He as to who are the right-guided" (S. 16:125).

And yet, one of the highest Qur'anic principles of interfaith relations remains that which says there ought to be no coercion or compulsion in matters of religion: "*lā ikrāha fī 'd-dīn*" (S. 2:256). Coupled with that are the two references to *fa-stabiqū 'l-khayrāt*, which as we have seen require human beings of all faiths to vie with one another in doing good works. I believe that we have in these passages the basis for interfaith dialogue and cooperation which has the potential for leading us to a better world, if only people would heed and have goodwill toward one another.

NOTES

1. Qur'anic texts quoted here in English are from *The Message of the Qur'an*, translated and explained by Muhammad Asad (Gibraltar: Dar al-Andalus, 1980), unless otherwise indicated.

2. Abdullah Yusuf Ali, *The Holy Qur'an, Text, Translation and Commentary* (n.p.: Khalīl Al-Rawāf Publication, 1946).

3. Arthur J. Arberry, *The Koran Interpreted* (London: Oxford University Press, 1964).

4. T.B. Irving, *The Qur'an, The First American Version, Translation and Commentary* (Al-Hajj Taʿlim ʿAli) (Brattleboro, Vt.: Amana Books, 1985).

5. Maḥmūd Muḥammad Shākir, ed., *Tafsīr al-Ṭabarī* (Cairo: Dār al-Maʿārif bi-Miṣr, n.d.), 3: 192, 10: 386.

6. Ibid., 3: 192–93.

7. Ibid., 10: 385–86.

8. Ibid., 10: 386.

9. Ibid.

10. Abū al-Qāsim Jār Allāh Maḥmūd Ibn ʿUmar al-Zamakhsharī, *Al-Kashshāf ʿan Haqā'iq al-Tanzīl wa-ʿUyūn al-Aqāwīl fī Wujūh al-Ta'wīl*, 4 vols. (Beirut: Dār al-Kitāb al-ʿArabī, n.d.), 1: 205; Abū Saʿīd ʿAbd Allāh Nāṣir al-Dīn al-Bayḍāwī, *Anwār al-Tanzīl*, 4 vols. (Cairo: Dār al-Kutub al-ʿArabiyya al-Kubrā, n.d.), 1: 199.

11. Al-Bayḍāwī, *Anwār al-Tanzīl*, 1: 199.

12. Al-Zamakhsharī, *al-Kashshāf*, 1: 640.

13. Al-Bayḍāwī, *Anwār al-Tanzīl*, 2: 153.

14. Jalāl al-Dīn al-Suyūṭī wa Jalāl al-Dīn al-Maḥallī, *Tafsīr al-Jalālayn* (Beirut: Dār al-Kitāb al-Lubnānī/al-Sharika al-Ifrīqiyya li-l-Ṭibāʿa wa-l-Nashr, n.d.), 24, 114.

15. Ibid., 24.

16. Ibid., 114.

17. Muḥammad Rashīd Riḍā, *Tafsīr al-Qur'ān al-Ḥakīm* (known as *Tafsīr al-Manār*), 4th printing (Cairo: Dār al-Manār, 1954).

18. Sayyid Quṭb, *Fī Ẓilāl al-Qur'ān*, 4th printing (Beirut: Dār al-ʿArabiyya li-l-Ṭibāʿa wa-l-Nashr wa-l-Tawzīʿ, n.d.).

19. Riḍā, *Tafsīr al-Manār*, 2: 22.

20. Ibid., 21.

21. Ibid., 6: 412–13.

22. Ibid., 420.

23. Sayyid Quṭb, *Fī Ẓilāl al-Qur'ān*, 2: 22–23.

24. Ibid., 6: 165.

25. Ibid., 2: 9.

26. Ibid., 6: 143–69.

27. Sayyid Quṭb, *Fī Ẓilāl al-Qur'ān*, first printing (Cairo: Dār Iḥyā' al-Kutub al-ʿArabiyya, 1953), 2: 12.

28. Ibid.

29. Ibid., 6: 67. For more on Quṭb's exegesis, see Olivier Carré, *Mystique et Politique: Lecture révolutionnaire du Coran par Sayyid Qutb, Frère musulman radical* (Paris: Les Éditions du Cerf/Presses de la Fondation Nationale des Sciences Politiques, 1984).

3

Some Biblical Considerations Relevant to the Encounter Between Traditions

Antonie Wessels

"God calls each culture to cross its own frontiers."[1]

"In his speaking and acting Jesus crosses all separative borders between human beings: religious (in contact with Romans and Samaritans), moral (prostitutes and publicans), institutional (regarding the sabbath or the prescriptions for purity), national and sexual (the Canaanite or Samaritan woman)."[2]

This essay is designed to try to answer a question: Can we learn anything from the Old and New Testaments, directly or indirectly, that could guide us in our present attempts to understand the relationship between Christianity and people of other faiths? How can the Bible help us to address the question of interreligious dialogue?

Clearly the Bible does not deal directly with some of the questions raised by modern theologians in the contemporary world. Nonetheless, biblical texts have certainly been used in discussions about the approach that Christians take toward people of other faiths. Sometimes texts are cited as proof that the Christian faith (or for that matter the Israelite or Jewish faith) is opposed and even superior to other religions. The Bible is here exploited to underline the antithesis between Christians and people of other faiths, and to emphasize Christianity as the exclusive way to salvation. Passages often cited in this context are: "And there is salvation in no one else, for there is no other name under heaven given among men by which we must be saved" (Acts 4:12), and "No one comes to the Father but by me" (John 14:6).

Others offer "prooftexts" in support of the universalistic outlook of both the Old and the New Testaments, and openness toward those "who are outside" (see, e.g., Colossians 4:5; 1 Thessalonians 4:12). "For from the rising of the sun to its setting my name is great among the nations, and in every place incense is offered to my name, and pure offering, for my name is great among the nations, says the Lord of hosts" (Malachi 1:11). "In past generations he allowed all the nations to walk in their own ways; yet he did not leave himself without witness, for he did good and gave you from heaven rains and fruitful seasons, satisfying your hearts with food and gladness" (Acts 14:16–17).

The significance of these "universalistic" texts, as they are interpreted, and the variations in the way they are understood in the context of interreligious dialogue, can be illustrated by the titles of books such as W.A. Visser t'Hooft's *No Other Name: the Choice Between Syncretism and Christian Universalism*[3] and Paul Knitter's *No Other Name? A Critical Survey of Christian Attitudes Toward the World Religions.*[4] Both use the same text from the book of Acts in the title, but one adds a question mark. It is in the area between the absence and the presence of this question mark that the discussion regarding the significance of the Bible for interreligious dialogue ranges. On the one side are those who fear syncretism and betrayal of the uniqueness of the name of Jesus Christ, and on the other those who assume a more inclusive stance which does not preclude adherence to the uniqueness of the name, but is characterized by less apprehension regarding syncretism.

In reality, Acts 4:12 ("no other name") does not deal with the relationship of Christians toward other religions, but with the healing ministry of Peter and John. In answer to the question of the rulers, elders, and scribes asking by what power they did this healing (Acts 4:7), they replied, "[b]y the name of Jesus Christ of Nazareth . . . And there is salvation in no other name" (Acts 4:10,12). This response is not a sermon dealing with penance or a missionary tract, but a witness in a courtroom. It is also not correct to read this text as meaning that the name of Jesus is in competition with the name of God. Jesus' name means that God saves. And "no other name" does not represent a statement regarding other religions and other names—the Buddha, Muhammad, or even Moses—but is a witness, a declaration, respecting the name of the one (not Jesus himself, but God) through whom salvation is achieved. It is also stretching the meaning of John 14:6 to read into it a judgment concerning other ways to salvation such as the Buddhist eightfold path, the Islamic *sharīʿa*, or the Jewish Torah. This text is intended not as a judgment of other religions, but as a confessional statement about the character of the path Jesus Christ followed: *the via crucis.*[5]

Kenneth Cragg has offered some helpful interpretation of these two texts: "We may cite Peter, addressing the rulers of the people in Acts 4:12, and saying, 'neither is there salvation in any other,' and assume that this is a verdict which answers all questions. Such an assumption would miss the point that he is addressing hearers who all, being Jews, share, in some sense, however disparate, the Messianic hope. He is affirming that this hope, which is their unanimous way of being saved is, in fact, realized in the crucified-reject, Jesus the Lord. Peter is disconcertingly identifying a shared hope, not prejudging an unknown Asian scene. Or there is the word of Jesus that 'no man comes to the Father but by me' (John 14:6). Truly we come to the Father, in experience and in language, through the Son. But is this to say that no man, otherwise, comes to the Creator, to the Lord, as indeed did Abraham and the psalmist?"[6]

Among the biblical texts that deal with the meeting of people of other cultures and religions I would like to look specifically at three: Genesis 14:18–20 about Abram and the king of Jerusalem, Matthew 15:21–28 on Jesus and the Canaanite woman, and Acts 10:9–29 and 34–36 describing the encounter between Peter and Cornelius. Christian mission is often described as "the crossing of frontiers."[7] How does this apply to Abraham (who, of course, figures strongly in the Jewish, Christian, and Muslim traditions) in this Old Testament story, to Jesus as he crossed the border between Israel and Palestine, and to Peter as the foundation on whom the church is said to be built? I will attempt to exegete these passages, and then to ask what might be their significance for contemporary encounters of people of different faiths as well as for the transmission or "translation" of the Gospel to other religious or nonreligious contexts.

A Canaanite Blesses Abram (Genesis 14:18–20)

In Genesis 12:2 we read that Abram was blessed by God and called from Ur to become himself a blessing in Canaan. This blessing also plays an important role in the story about the meeting between Abram and the king of Salem (Jerusalem), Melchizedek. Genesis 14:1–11 describes the war being waged among certain kings, and the taking of Abram's nephew Lot as prisoner by the kings of Sodom and Gomorrah. Abram pursued them, defeated the kings and liberated Lot. On his way back he was received by Melchizedek in a place not far from Jerusalem, and offered the bread and wine of hospitality through which peace was established. Abram recognized Melchizedek not only as king but as priest, thereby implying that he, or at least the narrator of the story, acknowledged El as worshiped by Melchizedek to be identical with Jahweh,[8] the same God who led him from Ur of the Chaldees (Genesis 12:1).

Genesis 14:20 says that Abram after the blessing gave a tenth of everything to Melchizedek. This story, which of course was written at a much later time, may be significant for the following reason: after his conquest of Jerusalem King David wanted to make the city, not claimed by other Israelite tribes, his capital and a cultic and political center. But Jerusalem, former stronghold of the Jebusites, had long been viewed by Israelites as a foreign city.[9] The people of Israel therefore were accustomed to seeing Jerusalem, where altar and throne were or became closely connected, as alien and heathen. As a result most Israelites preferred to give tithes to local sanctuaries rather than to the central sanctuary in Jerusalem.

The intention behind the story of Abram giving tithes to Melchizedek could, then, have been to legitimize the call to Israel to tithe to the priest of the central sanctuary in Jerusalem. Thus when Israelites in the time of David and Solomon gave tithes to a former Canaanite sanctuary in Jerusalem, they were following the example of Abram.[10] The only other place in the Old Testament where Melchizedek is mentioned is in Psalm 110:4: "The Lord has sworn and will not change his mind: You are priest for ever after the order of Melchizedek." Thus the dignity of the priest Melchizedek was transmitted to the Davidic kings.

In the New Testament the letter to the Hebrews takes up this theme. Melchizedek's name is explained as meaning "king of righteousness" and "king of peace" (Hebrews 7:2). The writer of the letter to the Hebrews sees the messianic expectations fulfilled in him (Jesus) who is also high priest after the order of Melchizedek (Hebrews 7:17). In other words, in the New Testament the priesthood of the Canaanite king Melchizedek becomes symbol and prototype of a more important priesthood, and Jesus becomes the fulfillment of a prophecy given to an originally Canaanite cult.

Jesus Crosses Frontiers: The Encounter of Jesus with the Canaanite Woman (Matthew 15:21–28)

This story tells of one of the rare occasions that Jesus operated outside his own country, Palestine. He himself came from Galilea, from the city of Nazareth from where no good was expected to come (John 1:47). As is so often true, persons considered to be "other" or different in Jesus' time were looked down upon. But was even Jesus himself an exception? According to our pericope, at a certain point in his ministry Jesus visited Tyre and Sidon in what is today Lebanon. Here we are told that he met with a woman who was not a Jew but a Canaanite (or a Syrophoenician, as in Mark 7:26).

Gospel accounts relate that Jesus had contacts inside his own country with non-Jews, particularly Samaritans. We also hear of a meeting between Jesus and a Roman centurion (Matthew 8:5–13). In the narrative under consideration Jesus, however, goes a step farther and meets a non-Jew outside Israel. This Canaanite woman asked Jesus, of whose healing powers she presumably had heard, for help on behalf of her daughter who was possessed. Readers of the New Testament with certain expectations of Jesus have been surprised to find that initially Jesus did not give even the slightest response to her cry, nor did his disciples react very kindly. Irritated that she kept shouting at him, they urged Jesus to send her off. Then Jesus uttered words that have been considered by some to be even shocking: "I am only sent to the lost sheep of the house of Israel" (15:24). But even that did not discourage the woman, who threw herself in front of Jesus pleading for help. Jesus' response to her may be seen to be as harsh as anything he said during the course of his ministry: "It is not fair to take the children's bread and throw it to the dogs" (15:25). It might be argued that here we have a prime example of the kind of prejudice of people of one nation and culture toward outsiders. Yet undeterred, the woman even seemed to agree with the designation of dog when she answered, "Yes, Lord, even the dogs eat the crumbs that fall from their master's table" (15:27). Then Jesus answered, "O woman, great is your faith! Be it done for you as you desire" (15:28).

Some have viewed this story as proving that one can always appeal to God through Jesus and that the appeal will be heard.[11] The question remains, however, whether this story may not communicate something more than that. Might it be that part of its purpose is to show not only how Jesus influenced the life of the Canaanite woman, but that he in turn was affected, influenced, even changed? Jesus and his disciples had scriptural grounds for aversion toward her (see Genesis 9:25, "Cursed be Canaan; a slave of slaves shall he be to his brother"), which may explain something of the hesitation he seemed to exhibit in responding to her plea. Is it possible that through this encounter Jesus came to the realization that, despite the fact that he was a Jew and she a Canaanite, he could and should help her? Even more directly, might one argue that through his encounter with this woman Jesus came to understand that faith was not something one found only within Israel?

Something similar seems to have happened on an earlier occasion after Jesus' encounter with the Roman centurion, to which he gave expression with the rather remarkable words, "I tell you solemnly, nowhere in Israel have I found faith like this" (Matthew 8:10). Taking into consideration such scriptural assurances as "[Jesus] learned obedience through what he suffered" (Hebrews 5:8) and "Jesus increased in wisdom and in stature, and in favor with God and man" (Luke 2:52), it seems quite possible to argue that he increased in wisdom precisely because of what he experienced, through the people he encountered, including this woman of another culture and another faith in another land.

Hospitality: The Encounter Between Peter and Cornelius (Acts 10:9–29, 34–36)

"Truly I perceive that God shows no partiality" (10:34). This statement is no doubt rightly viewed as one of the key passages in this long chapter dealing with "the conversion of Cornelius." I would like to argue that it should perhaps be applied not only to Cornelius, however, but also to "the conversion of Peter." Initially Peter seems to have thought that despite the assertion of Romans 2:11 that "God shows no partiality," there was in fact partiality in the election of Israel above the nations.[12] But "Truly I perceive" seems clearly to indicate that Peter had a new insight and a new understanding.

Peter was living at the time of this encounter in Joppa, the guest of a tanner named Simon (10:6, 9:43). Perhaps his choice to live with someone whose profession was despised as unclean was already preparing him for what was to come.[13] During the time of prayer, we are told, he became hungry (often prayer and fasting are conducive to receiving new insights) and had a vision of a table bearing clean and unclean animals descending out of heaven before him; he heard a voice saying, "Rise, Peter; kill and eat" (10:12). The thought of eating an unclean animal was so abhorrent to Peter that his immediate response was, "No, Lord; for I have never eaten anything that is uncommon or unclean" (10:14). Three times he heard the voice repeating the same message: "What God has cleansed, you must not call common" (10:15). But how could this message be legitimate?

After the vision Peter did in fact discover through a series of steps that what he had seen and heard came from God. The most immediate, and perhaps most important, of these steps was the extension of hospitality to the "heathen" messengers sent by Cornelius. Peter gave them shelter for the night, thus calling them to be his guests (10:23). In the Middle East hospitality is a sacred matter. "Do not neglect to show hospitality to strangers, for thereby some have entertained angels unawares" (Hebrews 13:2). In the guest God himself is present. The Gospel is replete with references to ways in which Jesus gave hospitality the highest of priorities, including his own role as guest among publicans and sinners (Luke 5:27–32), his attention to the caring hospitality of the good Samaritan (Luke 10:25–37), and the parable of the royal banquet (Matthew 22:1–14). It seems clear that Peter, in order to follow in Jesus' footsteps, needed also to exhibit this kind of hospitality.

So as Peter gave his guests shelter he discovered that it was actually Cornelius, the "heathen," who served as the vehicle for God's initiative toward him. His next step was then to accompany them to Cornelius, by whom he in turn was received as guest. To enter the home of a non-Jew was no doubt difficult for Peter, as illustrated in Galatians 2:11–21. But God made clear to Peter in his vision that he was "Not to call any man common or unclean" (Acts 10:28). Thus Peter was able to say to Cornelius that after he was sent for he came "without objection" (10:29).

It was only after he had received the messengers as guests and he himself had been received as a guest by Cornelius that Peter came to the understanding that "there is no partiality with God" and that "in every nation anyone who fears him and does what is right is acceptable to him" (10:34–35). The content of Peter's sermon was shaped by the experience he had as host and then as guest of the "heathen" messengers. While Peter was still preaching, the Holy

Spirit came upon all who heard the word. And it was then, on the basis of this divinely inspired hospitality experience, message, and outpouring of the Holy Spirit, that Peter was led to take the final step of baptism in the name of Jesus Christ (10:47–48).

Conclusion

In a recent volume Sri Lankan theologian Aloysius Pieris convincingly describes what he sees as the interplay of three elements in Western theological discussions on non-Christian religions: (1) the academic and philosophical approach to religious dialogue; (2) the instrumentalization or apologetic use of non-Christian thought, in favor of Christianity; and (3) the power-consciousness of the church.[14] In the early church, dialogue was conducted mainly in terms of Greek thought rather than of Greek religious practice, more with "pagan" philosophy than with "pagan" religion. Then a tradition arose whereby Christianity learned to instrumentalize philosophy. And finally dialogical contact with Greek culture coincided with the emergence of Christianity as a political power. That meant that the spread of Christianity in Europe coincided with the spread of its authority and that thereby the church lost its original zeal for "incarnational praxis." "The permanent need for dialogue and for continuous incarnation ceased to be felt."[15] Later on, the open conflict and even war with Islam reinforced the church's renunciation of dialogue. Thus with the advent of the great missionary era in the sixteenth century, the church took the same attitude toward Asian religions that it had adopted vis-à-vis Islam and European paganism.[16] One of the causes for the early church's negative stance respecting the religious aspects of Greco-Roman culture was the putative Old Testament rejection of other religions.

This is why careful examination of the Old Testament text is so crucial to contemporary theology of religion. In the use of the Bible in the context of interreligious dialogue arguments are often taken from the Old Testament to emphasize that other gods and other religions are the antithesis of the prophetic message. Reliance on Baal, for example, is harshly attacked by the prophet Hosea, and the confrontation between Elijah and the priests of Baal at Mount Carmel (1 Kings 18:20–46) is well-known. But it is important to realize that in reality there existed an interaction between the faith of Israel and the non-Israelite religious environment that is not always assessed negatively in the Old Testament. Kenneth Cracknell rightly points out that the "distinctive ideas" of the Old Testament stand out only when seen against the background of its environment. "So we are all profoundly aware of the pluralistic matrix in which the Old Testament came to birth. Yet too little attention has so far been paid to the theological implications of the world of many faiths and religious traditions even for the shapers of the Old Testament themselves. How did they perceive the relationship between God's action in Israel and the 'creative redemptive activity towards humankind' by the 'judge of all the earth'?"[17]

In fact, the Old Testament often manifests a greater openness and a less "nervous" attitude toward possible syncretism than is generally assumed. "And in every place incense is offered to my name," we read in Malachi 1:11. The story of Naaman (2 Kings 5:17–19) describes Elisha telling Naaman to go in peace after he confessed that he would enter the temple of Rimmon. The name Rimmon goes back to the Akkadian Ramanu, the name of the Babylonian god of thunder, Hadad Rimmon, associated with the Syrian god Hadad (also called Baal-Shamem or Baal). Could Elisha's response to Naaman be interpreted as a kind of concession to idolatry and therefore, if not approval, at least a form of toleration of syncretism?

According to Karl Barth some of the Old Testament figures like Melchizedek are not only an "object of mission" and message but foreigners who have something urgently important to say. They were involved, according to Barth, in a kind of ministry and mission on behalf of God.[18] Besides the Canaanite Melchizedek one could cite in this connection Balaam (Numbers 22–24); the prostitute Rahab (Joshua 2:12), who was counted among the believers by the writer of the letter to the Hebrews (11:31) and called an example by James (2:25); the Moabite Ruth who was cited as a mother in the genealogy of David and Jesus; and the Persian king Cyrus who in Isaiah is called shepherd (44:28) and anointed one (45:1) of the Lord.

The story of the Canaanite who blessed Abram is an illustration that the relationship of Israel toward the Canaanites and the Canaanite religious context is not a negataive one, that it can show the positive contribution of the secular environment and preexisting "pagan" religions. A message is being flashed to us that religion is never a new and pure creation by God "but a synthesis of the best under a new inspiration from God."[19] It is true that the relationship toward Baal is generally antithetical, but that is never the case for the belief in El.[20] The Canaanite environment had a great impact on the way of expression and presentation of Israelite faith.[21]

The Old Testament certainly does contain consistent prophetic criticism of confrontation with and resistance against "other gods," particularly where worship of these involves injustice. But that does not mean that all Canaanite culture and religion was rejected, or that nothing good could come from Canaan. There is both discontinuity and continuity between the faith of Israel and Canaanite culture. Canaan was an inspiration for Israel not only at the cultural and literary level,[22] but also in the area of religions, as the story of Abram's meeting with Melchizedek could demonstrate.

Karl Barth says about the notable "heathen" personages in the Bible, such as Melchizedek, that it is not by virtue of natural theology or any kind of natural human relationship to God that these foreigners occupy a prominent position. Rather they owe their place in the Old Testament to Jesus Christ who announces himself as the great Samaritan in them in a kind of second, outer circle of self-revelation. These vehicles of revelation thus have, in Barth's opinion, no significance in themselves: "There is no Melchizedek without Abraham, there is no Abraham without Christ."[23]

In my opinion Barth's position entails a far too narrow method of biblical interpretation, one which ignores the independent meaning of each book of the Bible and does not do justice to the sense of the Old Testament in its own right.[24] In Barth's kind of interpretation one cannot do justice to the fact that according to the Genesis story Abram was actually blessed by a Canaanite priestly king.

As for the story of Cornelius, one can deduce from it that the notion of hospitality must be seen as one of the most important keys for understanding the proper relationship between Christians and people of other cultures and religions. The encounter between Peter and Cornelius shows that "conversion" is not predictable but may take a shape and course different from what is expected. Interreligious contact involves interaction between addressees and addressers, a communication dialectic whereby the partners involved both give and receive.

Lesslie Newbigin in his latest book[25] tries to insist that one should not assume the message of the Cornelius story to be that the missionary outreach is unnecessary. It was the telling of the story that provided the occasion for the radical new experience which made Cornelius a Christian, and which dramatically changed the church's own understanding of its Gospel. This may be true, but the point is that Cornelius's messengers took the initiative by going to Peter, and that Peter got around to telling the story of Jesus only after several events had influenced them: the thrice repeated vision, his reception of and by "foreign" and "heathen" guests and hosts. The radical new experience that made Cornelius a Christian was an equally radical new experience for Peter and has been for the church, built on this Peter, ever since. "Peter had his first 'gentile' baptism (if we may so speak)," says Kenneth Cragg.[26]

Finally one may ask, can anything good come from a Canaanite man (Melchizedek) or a Canaanite woman? Abraham was blessed through a Canaanite priest, Jesus learned from a Canaanite woman and Peter was led by a gentile, albeit a God-fearing one, to the perception that God does not show partiality. It would seem that "conversion" is a mutual process whereby all involved learn that God's mercy extends to all humankind. The Canaanite, the Syrophonecian woman, and Cornelius were active agents in changing, moving, converting, blessing the "missionary." God's original blessing of Abram did not preclude his receiving an additional blessing from another. If this is already true for Abram, the father of all believers, is it not the more so for those who want to follow his footsteps in their encounters with people of other faiths?

NOTES

1. Alyward Shorter, *Toward a Theology of Inculturation* (Maryknoll, New York: Orbis, 1988), p. 107.

2. F.O. van Gennep, *De terugkeer van de verloren vader* (Baarn: Ten Have, 1989), p. 468.

3. London, 1963.

4. London, 1985.

5. See Pinchas Lapide's *Everyone Comes to the Father*, the very title of which mitigates against an exclusivist or judgmental interpretation.

6. Kenneth Cragg, *The Christian and Other Religions* (Oxford: Mowbrays, 1977), p. 79.

7. See, e.g. Horst Burkle, *Missionstheologie* (Stuttgart: W. Kahlhammer, 1979).

8. A further indication that Abram (or the narrator) recognized El as Jahweh is found in the narrative of Abram's contact with the king of Sodom, where we are told that Abram swears by this God (El): "I have sworn to the Lord God Most High, maker of heavens and earth" (Genesis 14:22).

9. See Ezekiel 16:3: "Your origin and your birth are of the land of the Canaanites; your father was an Amorite, and your mother a Hittite."

10. In the time of King Solomon a certain priest, Zakok, was nominated high priest in Jerusalem. The similiarity to Melchizedek is not coincidental. In a sense Zakok, who was a priest in Jerusalem before the conquest by David, continued the priesthood of Melchizedek after the conquest.

11. See, e.g., Karl Barth, *Kirchliche Dogmatik* (Munich: Kaiser Verlag, 1935), p. 7, where he cites with approval Martin Luther's interpretation to this effect.

12. See Gerhard F. Kittle, *Theologisches Worterbuch zum Neuen Testament* (Stuttgart: W. Kahlhammer, 1959), 6: 780–81.

13. See G. Staehlin, *Die Apostelgeschichte* (Göttingen, 1968); D.E. Haenchen, *Die Apostelgeschichte* (Göttingen: Vandenhoeck & Ruprecht, 1968), p. 287.

14. Aloysius Pieris, *Love Meets Wisdom: A Christian Experience of Buddhism* (Maryknoll, N.Y.: Orbis, 1988), p. 23.

15. Ibid., p. 22.

16. Ibid.

17. Kenneth Cracknell, *Towards a New Relationship: Christians and People of Other Faith* (London: Epworth, 1986), p. 44.

18. Karl Barth, *Kirchliche Dogmatik*, vol. 2 (Zurich, 1948), pp. 469–70.

19. Caroll Stuhlmueller, cited in Cracknell, *Towards a New Relationship*, p. 36.

20. Cf. Antonie Wessels, "Biblical Presuppositions for or against Syncretism" in J.D. Gort, H.M. Vroom, R. Fernhout, and A. Wessels, eds., *Dialogue and Syncretism: An Inter-*

disciplinary Approach (Grand Rapids, Mich.: Eerdmans; Amsterdam: Ed. Rodope, 1989), pp. 52–65.

21. J.C. de Moor, *Uw God is mijn God; over de oorsprong van het geloof in de ene God* (Kampen: Kok, 1988), p. 80. Speaking of biblical attitudes toward non-Jewish religions, P. Rossano writes, "When it [the Bible] meets with forms of pure religion or with forms that are reconcilable with faith in the God of the Covenant, it welcomes them and takes them up: it is enough to refer to the cases of Melchisedek, of Jethro, of Job, non-Jewish religious personalities, who were nevertheless recognized and praised for their faith" ("Lordship of Christ and Religious Pluralism," *Bulletin of the Secretariat for Non-Christians* 15, no. 1 (1980): 25–26.

22. See T. Worden, "The Literary Influence of the Ugarit Fertility Myth on the Old Testament," *Vetus testamentum* 3 (1953): 173–97.

23. Barth, *Kirchliche Dogmatik*, 2: 470.

24. Cf. what K.H. Miskotte in *Als de goden zwiggen: over de zin van het oude testament* (Amsterdam, 1956) calls "het tegoed van het Oude Testament" (p. 189).

25. *The Gospel in a Pluralistic Society* (Grand Rapids: Eerdmans; Geneva: World Council of Churches Publishers, 1989), p. 168.

26. *Paul and Peter: Meeting in Jerusalem* (Bible Reading Fellowship, No. 7, 1980), p. 69.

4

Jesus the Son of God: A Study of the Terms *Ibn* and *Walad* in the Qur'an and *Tafsīr* Tradition

Mahmud Mustafa Ayoub

Jesus Christ, Son of Mary, the Spirit of God, and His Word, has provided both a bridge between Christian and Muslim faith and piety and a great theological barrier between the Christian church and the Muslim *umma*. For Islamic faith, Jesus, like Adam, is a special creation of God, but unlike Adam, he is free from sin. He is a "blessed" and righteous servant of God, "high-honored in this and the next world, and one of those who are nearest to God" (S. 3:45).

For Muslim piety, Jesus is a model of true Islam, or total submission to God. He lived in God's presence, free from all attachments to this world and its vain pleasures. He is a source of hope and solace for the poor and oppressed, and a stern reproach for the rich and greedy oppressors. He is an example of true piety and trust in God for the Sufis, the "friends of God," and through his gracious miracles he embodies for all faithful Muslims God's gift of life and healing.

This Jesus of faith and piety, the man who "went about doing good,"[1] feeding the hungry, healing the sick in heart and body, and restoring dead brothers and sons to their bereft mothers and sisters,[2] is the bridge linking the two communities in their quest for faith and holiness. Jesus the "Christ," the "eternal logos," the "Word made flesh," the "Only Begotten Son of God" and second person of the trinity has been the barrier separating the two communities and long obscuring the meaning and significance of Jesus, the "Word of God," to Muslim faith and theology. Doctrines such as the divinity of Jesus and the Trinity have been the subject of sharp debate between Muslims and Christians, a debate that transcends the plane of human history and that will finally be decided between God and Jesus on the day of resurrection.[3]

I am convinced that this theological barrier is not an impenetrable wall dividing our two communities. Rather, in the spirit of the divine challenge for Muslims to seek harmony and concord with the People of the Book through dialogue and "fair exhortation,"[4] this wall could be transformed into a beacon of light guiding us all to God and the good. This essay is a humble attempt to make a small breach in this wall.

The present essay will examine the theological significance of two important Qur'anic terms: *ibn* and *walad*, both signifying a filial relationship. *Ibn* ("son"), which is used only once in the Qur'an in relation to Jesus, may be understood metaphorically to mean son through a relationship of love or adoption. The term *walad*, on the other hand, means "offspring," and thus primarily signifies physical generation and sonship. It is this latter term that is often used by Qur'an commentators to argue against the Christian concept of Christ's divine sonship. The Qur'an, however, as we shall see when we study these two terms closely, does not use the term *walad* specifically to refer to Jesus. That is to say, the Qur'an nowhere accuses Christians of calling Jesus the *walad* offspring of God.

The purpose of this endeavor is twofold. It is first to stress the need to take our scriptures seriously in what they say and not to use one as a criterion to judge the truth and authenticity of the other. This does not mean that we should treat our scriptures as isolated sacred texts completely divorced from their own time and history. God speaks to us in our historical and existential human condition, and to attempt to hear His voice in isolation from human history is to miss the essential message of His Word.

The second purpose is to reflect on the situation to which the Qur'an seems to have addressed its critique of the Christian doctrine of the divine sonship of Christ. If, as we may well discover, the historical situation which the Qur'an presupposed in its primary address no longer obtains, then the challenge for us all is to go beyond that situation and seek other and deeper meanings of God's word to our own existential situation.

To do full justice to this subject is far beyond the scope of this study. I shall therefore limit myself to the Qur'an and some of its representative commentators. Before turning to these, however, a few remarks on God's role in the conception of Christ as presented in the Gospel and the Qur'an are necessary. We shall as well take a brief look at a classical Arab Christian theologian for a concrete example of the language Arab Christians used to translate the Gospel account, before examining more closely the language that grew out of the Qur'anic account for Muslims. It is hardly necessary to argue that neither the Qur'an nor early Muslim traditionists were aware of the theological doctrines of the church fathers and church councils in their debate with Christians, but they were aware of Christian piety, liturgy, and worship.

The language of the two scriptures is highly symbolic and allegorical. The Gospel of Luke, which is our primary source on the nativity of Christ, analogous to the Qur'an, describes the conception of Jesus thus: "'The spirit of the

Lord shall come upon you,' the angel said to Mary, 'and the power of the Highest shall overshadow you: therefore also that holy thing (***hagion***)[5] which shall be born of you shall be called the Son of God.'"[6]

The language of this verse is clearly circumspect. It implies no sexual union or divine generation of any kind. Furthermore, while Luke's description agrees both in form and spirit with the Qur'anic idea of the conception of Christ, the language of the Qur'an is far more graphic and open to interpretation.

The Qur'an makes two references to God's direct intervention in the conception of Jesus. The first is put in the context of the miraculous birth of John (Yaḥyā) to Zechariah and his wife who was long past the age of child bearing. God says: "We answered his prayers and granted him Yaḥyā and restored for him his spouse. They were surely diligent in the performance of good deeds and called upon Us in fervent hope and fear. They truly lived in awe of Us." Then of Mary He continues: "And she who guarded well [lit. fortified] her chastity [lit. generative organ], and thus We breathed into her of our spirit, and We made her and her son a sign [or miracle, *'Āya*] for all beings" (S. 21:90–91). Here God includes Mary among the prophets and the righteous, those who call upon Him in fervent devotion and righteous fear.

In the second instance the Qur'an speaks of Mary as a righteous woman who lived in strict chastity and obedience to God: "And Mary daughter of ʿimrān who guarded well her generative organ *farjahā*, and thus We breathed into it of our spirit" (S. 62:12). This bold and graphic statement appears to have shocked traditionists and commentators, so that most of them either tried to cover it up with different and farfetched significations or glossed over it without comment.

Al-Ṭabarī, and following him a number of other commentators, interprets the verse as follows: "God means to say that she guarded her bosom with her garment from Gabriel, peace be upon him." Al-Ṭabarī then explains: "Any opening or hole in a chemise is called *farj*. Likewise, any crack or opening in a wall is a *farj*." Thus al-Ṭabarī interprets the verse to read: "'and thus We breathed' into the opening of her chemise which is her *farj* 'of our spirit' of Gabriel who is the 'spirit'."[7]

Ibn Kathīr interprets the phrase "guarded well her generative organ" to mean: "safeguarded and protected it. Guarding well *iḥsān* signifies chastity and high birth." He comments on the phrase, "and thus We breathed into it of our spirit" thus: "that is, through the angel Gabriel. This is because God sent him to her, and he took for her the form of a man of good stature (S. 19:17). God commanded him to breathe into the breast of her chemise. His breath went down and penetrated her generative organ, and thus caused her to conceive Jesus."[8] Ibn Kathīr, like al-Ṭabarī and all other commentators and traditionists, insists on God's transcendence; hence it is inconceivable that He would directly intervene in such intimate human affairs. Ibn Kathīr also tries to harmonize later Muslim tradition with the Qur'an without resorting to a radical interpretation of the sacred text.

The Mālikite jurist al-Qurṭubī observes that early *tafsīr* authorities held that by *farj* God here meant bosom, *jayb*. This, he argues, is because "God said, 'and thus We breathed,' for Gabriel breathed into her bosom not into her generative organ." Al-Qurṭubī further reports that the reading (*qirā'ah*) of Ubayy is, "and thus We breathed into her bosom of our spirit." Al-Qurṭubī concludes: "It is possible that the verse means that Mary safeguarded her generative organ, and that God breathed the spirit into her bosom." He interprets the phrase, "and We breathed" to mean: "We sent Gabriel and he breathed into her bosom of our spirit, that is one of our spirit, which is the spirit of Jesus."[9]

Abū Ja'far al-Ṭūsī, the jurist doctor of the Shī'ī community, as well as his well-known disciple al-Ṭabarsī, read the words, "We breathed into it" literally. Al-Ṭūsī says: "It has also been held that Gabriel breathed into Mary's generative organ, then God created Christ in it." Al-Ṭabarsī reports yet another interpretation which he obviously does not accept: "It is said that the verse means, 'We created Jesus in her womb and breathed into him the spirit, and thus he became a living person.'" This reading rests on the fact that both *farj* and *masīḥ* (Christ) are masculine. Hence, the word *fīhi* into him/it could refer to either. This interpretation is perhaps meant to dissociate both God and Gabriel from the impurities of human generation.[10]

It is noteworthy that contemporary commentators have nothing significant to say about this verse. The late Iranian religious scholar Muḥammad Ḥusayn Ṭabāṭabā'ī simply observes that Mary is the only woman mentioned by name in the Qur'an, and that she is mentioned in over thirty *sūras*. The assertion, moreover, that Mary "guarded well her chastity" is meant to exalt her above the calumnies of the Jews. This is also the view of Sayyid Quṭb.[11]

The language of both the Gospel and the Qur'an is poetic and celebrative, not scholastic, or even strictly speaking theological. In both, this marvelous event is announced as glad tidings to Mary and linked to prophetic history as a miracle of special significance. In both scriptures, it is God and not an angel who manifests His power directly in the conception and birth of Christ.[12] God breathed His spirit into Adam directly,[13] and this gave him priority over the rest of His creation. God also declares, using the "We" of majesty, that He directly breathed of His spirit into Mary, thus making her and her child a divine sign for humankind, and making the miraculous child a manifestation of divine mercy.

From the foregoing it must be concluded that the Gospel and the Qur'an are speaking about the same Christ, the "son of Mary," child of God, His Word and spirit. Furthermore, neither the Qur'an nor the Gospel nativity story implies that God had a female consort in Mary, or a physically engendered son in Christ. But have the two theological and scholastic traditions been speaking about the same Jesus?

The question here posed has concerned Muslim and Christian thinkers from the beginning, and has thus produced a vast and fascinating body of literature on both sides. We shall choose one Christian savant, theologian, and cleric as representative of the classical Syro-Arabic Christian tradition. In his interesting work *Maymar fī Wujūd al-Khāliq wa'l-Dīn al-Qawīm*,[14] Theodore Abū Qurra attempts, in the spirit of reasonable and "fair dialogue," to prove God's attributes of engendering—*wilādah*—and procession or emanation, *inbithāq*. His argument rests on an analogy not between Adam and Christ, but rather between Adam and God. It is an unusual argument.

Abū Qurra begins by asserting that God's existence can be known, or inferred, from Adam's existence. He then contrasts the nature of the two: Adam is finite but God is infinite in life, power, knowledge, and all the other attributes which He shares with Adam. Adam, moreover, was a creature of God, hence all his attributes or excellences over other earthly creatures were bestowed upon him by the Creator.

The most excellent attributes which Adam possessed are *wilāda*, engendering; *inbithāq*, emanation or procession; and *riʿāsa*, headship. He thus argues: "We saw that Adam did engender [another being] who was like him in nature, and proceeded, or issued forth, *inbathaqa* from him [another being]. We also saw that he was head over the one [Eve] who was like him. Since, therefore, Adam was a progenitor, and was head of her who issued forth from him, it follows that He who made him progenitor and head must necessarily Himself be father and head over him who is like Him." Abū Qurra again contrasts the essential differences between Adam and God. Adam engendered his son through a female by means of sexual union and brought him up. Eve came out of Adam's body, and thus diminished him. Moreover, Adam preceded both his spouse and sons, and his headship over them is not one of like nature and desires between him and them.

"On the other hand," Abū Qurra continues, "God's engendering of His son was from Him, and in like manner was the procession of His Holy Spirit. There was no female, sexual union, conception, or rearing; nor was any priority in time among them. Rather, from eternity they all were together. God's headship, moreover, over those who are of Him presupposes no difference among them. Rather they are like Him in nature, will, eternity and desire [*hawā*]. There is no difference whatsoever among them except one is father and the other begotten, and the third issued forth. The father among them is also the Godhead."

Abū Qurra further argues that it is by means of the attributes of engendering and headship that Adam was distinguished from the dumb beasts and other lowly creatures. If therefore God does not possess these two excellences, then Adam is more excellent than God. Nor is it rational to suppose that Adam was head over those who were like him, but God is head of all creatures. If neither Adam nor any other human being would accept to be head of swine, beasts, and bedbugs, then how can we describe God as head of such creatures? Nor can it be said that God is only head of angels and humankind because His nature is more different from human nature than is that of the lowliest creatures.

Abū Qurra concludes: "God, blessed and exalted be He, is without doubt head or chief. He is not, moreover, the head of all creatures, but the head of those who are like Him. He thus begot a son, and a spirit proceeded out of Him. He is therefore like Adam and Adam is like Him in engendering and headship." This mystery, Abū Qurra asserts, fulfills God's word: "So God created man in His own image, in the image of God he created him" (Gen. 1:27 RSV).[15]

It can be clearly seen from the foregoing that Christian theology, and this may be asserted of creed and liturgy as well, has used human language to describe divine activity. It went far beyond the third Evangelist in speaking of Jesus as the actual son of God. Abū Qurra's language in particular would leave no doubt in the mind of a Muslim reader that Jesus is the son of God, engendered by Him from eternity. For, while Abū Qurra uses *ibn* for son, he always uses the verb *walada*, to engender, or give birth to, when speaking of God the father and Jesus His son. In fact this direct language remains the language of Syro-Arabic liturgy and worship to this day.

As we shall see presently, on the basis of the Gospel and the Qur'an the disagreement between Christians and Muslims is not over the Divine sonship of Christ, figuratively speaking, but over his divinity. This is understandable, for Christology remains the foundation stone of the Church and the greatest challenge to her unity and faith.

As has already been observed, the term *ibn* with reference to Jesus as son of God occurs only once in the Qur'an. We have also noted that this term has both an actual and metaphorical or figurative connotation. This fact has been recognized by most commentators. Two issues will concern us in this discussion. The first is the source or origin of this concept, in the view of Qur'an commentators, and the second its significance to Christian faith and history.

The term in question occurs in verse 30 of sūra 9, which is one of the latest sūras of the Qur'an. The verse, furthermore, is part of a crucial passage that regulates the sociopolitical and religious relations of an already well established Muslim state with the communities of the Book, particularly Jews and Christians. The tone of the entire passage is highly polemical; this is especially reflected in later commentaries which in turn reflect the political and military tensions between Christendom and the world of Islam. There is as well a broader religious and moral dimension to this debate which is clearly discernible in the verse under discussion as well as the one following it. The two verses read: "The Jews say ʿUzayr [Ezra?] is the son of God, and the Christians say Christ is the son of God. That is their saying with their own mouths; they resemble the saying of those who rejected faith before them. God curse them, how they perpetrate falsehood! They took their rabbis and monks as lords instead of God, as well as Christ the son of Mary. Yet they were commanded to worship the One God, there is no god but Him; glorified is He over all that they associate with Him."

With regard to this alleged error, commentators relate the following tale:

When Jesus was taken up to heaven[16] his "true followers" lived by the true religion. They fasted during the month of Ramaḍān and prayed facing the Kaʿba. In other words, they were Muslims. Then arose many wars between them and the Jews.

Among the Jews lived a brave man called Būlus (Paul) who persecuted the Christians and killed many of them. Paul one day said to his fellow Jews: "If Jesus had the truth, then we have been rejecters of faith, and our abode shall be the Fire. We shall surely be losers if they enter Paradise and we be consigned to Hell. I will therefore deceive them and lead them astray."

To this end he hamstrung his horse and threw dust on his head, pretending remorse. He claimed that a voice addressed him from heaven saying: "No repentance will be accepted from you unless you become a Christian."

Christians believed him and took him to their church where he remained for a whole year, never leaving the sanctuary. There he learned the Gospel, and all Christians believed him. He then went to Jerusalem and left a man called Nasṭūr (Nestorius) as his representative over his followers.

Paul then began to teach his followers that Jesus, God, and Mary were three gods. He sent emissaries to Byzantine territories to teach the people that Jesus had a divine and human nature.[17] He also taught that Jesus was not a man or a body; rather he was God. He propagated this doctrine through another of his emissaries, called Jacob. He chose a third representative, a man called Malka, and taught him that Jesus was, is, and will forever be God.

Paul told each of the three men: "You are my representative; go forth, therefore, and call others to your belief." Having thus completed his scheme, Paul then told his followers: "I saw Jesus in a dream, and he was pleased with me. I shall therefore sacrifice myself for his pleasure." He thus went to the altar and slew himself.[18]

The purpose of this tale is to explain the origin of the three major Eastern Christian sects: the Jacobites, Nestorians, and Melkites, as the names of the three men indicate. The assertion that early Christians were actually *muslims* reflects, first, the high place that Christ occupies in Muslim faith and piety and, second, the persistent belief that Christianity is essentially a true religion. For this reason many commentators, even recent ones, insist that not all Christians say that "Jesus is the son of God."[19] It must also be remarked that a number of commentators seriously doubted the truth of this tale. Thus al-Alūsī, for instance, remarks that this is "a strange [tale] which can hardly be true."[20]

It was earlier observed that this debate has a political dimension which is clearly reflected, according to changing circumstances, in different commentaries. Ibn Kathīr, who lived in Syria in the aftermath of the Crusades, puts the verse squarely in its polemical framework. He says: "This is an incitement by God of the people of faith to fight with the rejecters of faith of the Jews and Christians for uttering such evil words and for their calumny against God."[21]

Fakhr al-Dīn al-Rāzī, a noted theologian/philosopher and Qurʾan commentator who lived closer in time if not in place to the Crusades, goes even further in his invective against this concept and those who subscribe to it: "There is no meaning to association [*shirk*] except if a person takes another object of worship beside God. If we were to ponder well this point, we would surely see that the rejection of faith of idol-worshippers is less serious than that of the Christians. This is because an idol-worshipper does not say that his idol is the creator or god of the universe. Rather he regards it as an object which would bring him nearer to God. Christians, on the other hand, profess divine incarnation [*ḥulūl*] and union [*ittiḥād*], and this is the worst kind of rejection of faith." Thus, Rāzī continues, "God favored the Christians with the acceptance of the *jizya* or poll tax from them because they allied themselves outwardly to Moses and Jesus and claimed to live by the Torah and the Gospel. Hence, because of these two great apostles and their two great scriptures, and because the forefathers of these Jews and Christians followed the true religion, God decreed acceptance of the jizya from them. Otherwise, there is in reality no difference between them and the associators."[22]

In spite of his harsh denunciations, Rāzī was a rationalist theologian who did not accept easy answers and thus generally gave his opponents a fair hearing. He asks rhetorically how all Christians could come to believe in this concept when neither Jesus nor his disciples could have uttered such a falsehood? Rāzī was not convinced by the Paul story. He rather says: "I believe it to be nearer to the truth to say that perhaps the word son [*ibn*] occurs in the Gospel to denote high honor, as the word *khalīl* (intimate friend of God) denotes high honor.[23] Then because of the enmity between Jews and Christians, the latter wishing to exalt Jesus by claiming a similar falsehood to that of the Jews, they exaggerated their claim and interpreted the word son literally to signify actual sonship. This idea was accepted by the foolish among them, and thus did this false belief spread among the followers of Jesus; but God knows best the truth of the matter."[24]

The view that the word *ibn* is used metaphorically in the Gospel to express a relationship of love and intimacy is shared by most commentators. Some have even concluded that Christians misunderstood their own scriptures. Al-Alūsī, who was a well-known Sufi and thus more prone to look for mystical inner meanings in all scriptures, says: "It seems to me that Christians found the term *ibn* used for Jesus and the word father for God in their Gospel, and erred in their understanding of what is actually intended by these terms, hence they said what they said."[25]

Muḥammad Maḥmūd Ḥijāzī, a more recent commentator, blames this grave misunderstanding on foreign ideas and philosophies. "Ancient Christians used this term to express love and high honor. But when pagan philosophy spread among them, they began to apply it literally claiming that Christ was the son of God, or that he was God. They are, moreover, all agreed that a unitarian *muwaḥḥid* is not a Christian."[26]

The well-known reformer Muḥammad Rashīd Riḍā in his *Tafsīr al-Manār* devotes much space to this verse. He uses as one of his primary sources the Arabic Encyclopedia of the famous Christian thinker Buṭrus al-Bustānī. Riḍā agrees that ancient Christians used the word *ibn* to denote one who is beloved or especially favored by God. They were, however, influenced in their error by Indian beliefs concerning Krishna, and other such heathen ideas. Under the influence of Greek philosophy, church councils three hundred years after Christ and his disciples formulated the doctrine of the Trinity. Riḍā insists, however, that there are many Christian thinkers who have rationally rejected the Trinity, and thus are true unitarians. He may have heard of the Unitarians or perhaps other nineteenth century Western critics of the Trinity.[27] Sayyid Quṭb, who was one of the sharpest critics of the West and of Western civilization, also argued that the idea of Divine sonship has no basis in either original Judaism or Christianity.[28]

Whereas the term *ibn* occurs only once in the Qur'an and clearly refers to Jesus, the term *walad* occurs fifteen times, although only two refer to Jesus directly. Moreover, the majority of these verses are referred by most commentators to the Makkan Arabs who claimed that their goddesses Allāt, al-ʿUzza, and Manāt were daughters of God and that angels were also His daughters.[29] Thus Jews and Christians are often added by implication.

It must be further observed that in most cases the Qur'an uses the verb *ittakhadha* (took unto Himself) rather than begot, or any other verb suggesting actual generation. The verb *ittakhadha*, if anything, implies a relationship of adoption. Yet most commentators argue strenuously against attributing an offspring to God, this being allegedly an erroneous Jewish and Christian belief.

As we review some of these verses it will become clear that both the Qur'an and its exegetes are actually arguing for God's absolute Oneness and transcendence. Moreover, since the three most immediately known communities—

the Jews, Christians, and non-Muslim Arabs—were accused of this form of associationism, then by analogy the concepts of God's transcendence, *tanzīh*, and oneness, *tawḥīd*, came to distinguish Muslims from all other communities. While this conclusion is nowhere stated, it seems to be behind the arguments of both the Qur'an and its interpreters.

Finally, before we turn to the verses themselves, it must be observed that the language in most of them is the same. They contrast God's transcendence, omnipotence, origination of all things, and sovereignty over all His creation with human nonself-sufficiency, and hence the need for offspring.[30]

The Qur'an declares: "They say that God took unto Himself an offspring; glorified be He! Rather to Him belongs whatever is in the heavens and the earth; all are subservient to Him. The originator of the heavens and the earth, when He decrees a thing He says to it 'be,' and it is" (S. 2:116–17). These two verses are typical of the Qur'anic arguments against the error of ascribing offspring to God. It may be that the emphasis on God's power to create *ex nihilo* through His word of command, *kun*, led commentators to include the Christians in their critique. Otherwise, the two verses just cited constitute an independent statement following a reference to the direction of prayer. Some commentators relate the two verses to verse 114, which reproaches those who bar people from entering God's places of worship and seek to destroy such places. This surely cannot at that time have referred to the Christians.

Al-Ṭabarī nevertheless simply states: "These are the Christians who claim that Jesus is the son of God." He then advances the following argument against this claim: "How could Jesus be an offspring (*walad*) of God when he must be in one of these places, either in the heavens or in the earth. Yet to God belongs all that is in them." Then addressing the Christians directly, al-Ṭabarī continues: "If Christ was a son as you claim, he would not have been like all the other subservient creatures of God which are in the heavens and the earth in manifesting God's handiwork in him."[31]

Ibn Kathīr regards the two verses under discussion as a refutation of the claims of Christians, Jews, and the Associators among the Arabs. Ibn Kathīr generally repeats al-Ṭabarī's argument, but in somewhat stronger language. He argues: "An offspring is engendered by two compatible beings. But God, exalted and blessed be He, has no equal or partner in His greatness and majesty. Since, moreover, He has no consort, how could He have an offspring?"

Ibn Kathīr concludes his critique with two *ḥadīth* traditions stressing the gravity of such an error. The first is a *ḥadīth qudsī* (prophetic reports of Divine utterances) in which God says: "The children of Adam have uttered lies about me, yet they had no reason. They have insulted me and they had no right to do so. As for their lies, it is their saying that I cannot bring them back to life as they were before. Their insult is their saying that I have an offspring. Far glorified am I above having a consort or offspring." The second is a Prophetic ḥadīth in which the Prophet is reported to have said: "No one is more patient with the hurt He hears from human beings than God. They ascribe to Him offspring, and yet He provides for them and grants them sound health."[32]

A good example of the argument from transcendence is stated by the Andalusian jurist and Qurʾan commentator al-Qurṭubī. He first argues that the verse applies to all—Jews, Christians, and Makkans. He continues: "Far exalted is God above their claim that He took unto Himself an offspring. He is God the exalted, one in His essence and attributes. He did not engender, so that He would need a female consort, and how could He have an offspring when He has no consort? He created all things, nor was He begotten so that other things preceded Him, high exalted is His majesty above what the wrongdoers and deniers say."

Al-Qurṭubī then advances the usual argument, namely that "God is the creator of all that exists in His creation, and if all is His creation, then none of His creatures can be His offspring: *waladiya*, engendering, implies sameness of species and temporality; while *qidam*, eternality, implies unicity (*wiḥdāniya*) and permanence. God, glorified be He, is eternal, *azalī*, the One and 'Unique, *aḥad*, eternal refuge, *ṣamad* who does not beget, nor was he begotten. Nor is there anyone equal unto Him' (S. 112). Furthermore, sonship clearly contradicts slavehood (*riqq*) and subservience. How can an offspring be a slave? This is impossible and anything which implies an impossibility is itself impossible."[33]

Few among the commentators here studied see a difference between *ittikhādh*, "taking something unto oneself," and actual engendering. The Turko-Persian Sufi Ismāʿīl Ḥaqqī discusses this important difference thus: "Taking something unto oneself can mean either making or creating such a thing, in which case [the maker is one and unique], or it means making, that is to say God made one of His creatures a child and claimed that he is His child, not that He engendered him in reality. As it is impossible for God to engender in reality, it is likewise impossible for Him to adopt or take unto Himself a child. Thus God elevated Himself above what they say about Him in His saying, 'glorified is He.'"[34]

Abū Jaʿfar al-Ṭūsī argues in a scholastic fashion that this verse indicates the impossibility of God having a child in any way. This he argues, is because, "if all that is in the heavens and the earth is His possession, then both Jesus and the angels who are brought near to Him are slaves under His dominion. A child must by necessity be of the same genus as his father, but the object of an act is never of the same genus as the subject. Every corporeal being is an object of God's act. There is therefore no one like Him in any way. Exalted be He above the attributes of His creatures."[35]

The great theologian-philosopher Fakhr al-Dīn al-Rāzī advances several scholastic arguments against the possibility of God engendering or in any way having offspring. The first is the argument from necessity and contingency. God alone necessarily exists in Himself and the existence of all else is contingent on Him. Moreover, God alone is eternal and all else is created in time. "It therefore follows that everything other than God is created in time, and hence preceded by nonbeing. This also means that all things came into being through God's creative act and His power of bringing things from nonbeing into being. From this it follows that everything other than God is His slave and possession. It is therefore impossible that anything other than He be His offspring."

Al-Rāzī's second argument is that of eternity and temporality: "This being which is ascribed to God as His offspring must be eternal. If he is eternal, then it matters not which of the two we regard as father and which as son. If, on the other hand, the child is temporal, then he was created by him who is eternal, and is therefore his slave, and thus cannot be his child."[36]

Al-Alūsī sums up most of the arguments so far discussed and others as well in the following brief commentary on the phrase "To Him belongs whatever is in the heavens and the earth": "This is a refutation of their claim and an explanation of the things which follow from that erroneous claim, namely: likening [God the eternal] to temporal phenomena of human generation and begetting, and the need of the father for a child who would fulfill his need, as well as the inevitable passing away of all composite beings which are dependent on one another. For the wisdom in human generation is to preserve the human species through the continuous succession of its examples. This is because no one individual can last forever. All this is impossible for God, for He is eternal and everlasting, absolutely self-sufficient, most exalted above resembling His creatures."[37]

Sayyid Quṭb always sought to relate early Muslim history to present realities. He thus argues that this erroneous belief was held by all three communities, Jews, Christians, and Makkan Arabs, all of which are represented today by international crusadism, Zionism, and communism. The original source of such ideas was Greek philosophy, the Muslim champions of which introduced into Islam ideas alien to it. Islam draws an absolute distinction between the Creator and all created things. Yet ideas such as Ibn al-ʿArabī's *waḥdat al-wujūd*, "unity of being," can easily accommodate notions of divine sonship.[38]

We have discussed these two verses at some length because, although they do not refer to Jesus, commentators have used them to advance most of their arguments against the view that God may beget or in any way have a child. There is no need for us in the limited scope of this essay to study each of the remaining occurrences of the term *walad*. Two, however, do call for some attention as they refer directly to the Christian belief in Christ's divine sonship. In the first God reproaches the Christians for holding such an extreme position in their faith. In the second Jesus counsels his people not to hold such a view.

"O people of the Book, do not exceed the proper bounds in your faith, and speak only the truth about God. Christ Jesus, the son of Mary, was only a messenger of God and His Word which He sent forth to Mary, and a spirit from Him. Accept faith, therefore, in God and His messengers, and do not say three. Desist, and it will be better for you. God is only one God, glory be to Him that He should have an offspring. To Him belongs all that is in the heavens and the earth, and God is a sufficient guardian" (S. 4:171).

It must be noted that the Qurʾan declares the Christian belief in the Trinity to be an extremist religious position. The matter of God having a child is mentioned only in passing as part of this extremism in faith. The verse further asserts that Jesus, Mary's child, is God's Word which He "sent forth," or cast into Mary, as the word *alqāhā* seems to suggest. Here again, what is God's role in the conception and birth of Christ? Commentators unfortunately have not pondered this question.

Al-Ṭabarī comments briefly on the verse as follows: "God is not as you say, you who claim that God is the third of three. This is because he who has an offspring is not God. Likewise, it is not possible that he who has a consort can be a god worthy of worship. Rather, God to whom belongs true Divinity and worship is one God alone worthy of worship. He has no offspring, progenitor, consort, or partner."[39]

Al-Zamakhsharī presents the following brief, but interesting exegesis: "Jesus is called 'word of God' and 'word from Him' because he came into being only through God's word and His command without the intervention of a father or sperm. He is also called 'the spirit of God' and 'a spirit from Him' because he is possessed of a spirit and a body, and because he came into being not through a part of one possessed of a spirit, such as a sperm which proceeds from a living father. Rather, Jesus was a special original creation, originated [*ukhturiʿa ikhtirāʿan*] by God in His power."

Al-Zamakhsharīī interprets the word *alqāhā*, "sent it forth," to mean "He caused it to reach Mary and be in her." Following a brief analysis of the doctrine of the Trinity, al-Zamakhsharī concludes: "God called Jesus Son of Mary to affirm that he is her child, and not the son of God."[40]

After repeating the usual argument that Jesus cannot be God's offspring because he is part of His creation, al-Qurṭubī adds with rhetorical sarcasm: "If it is possible for God to have one offspring, then why not many? Thus anyone in whom is wrought a divine miracle would be a child of God."[41]

For al-Ṭabarsī God's Oneness is the word of truth which Christians are enjoined to "speak about God." He says: "Say that He, exalted be his majesty, is One without associate, consort or offspring. Say not of Jesus that he is the son of God, or that he is like Him because this is not 'speaking the truth.'"[42]

While earlier commentators saw a special creation in Jesus as "the word of God," more recent ones have consistently attempted to play down any distinction between Jesus and the rest of humankind. For example, al-Ṭabarsī reports that some say the meaning of the phrase "and His Word which He sent forth to Mary" is: "He created it in her womb."[43] The contemporary Egyptian thinker Muḥammad Maḥmūd Ḥijāzī, as a good representative of this modern trend, says: "Every birth of a child has one manifest cause which is the coming together of two people of the opposite sex, and a real cause which is the will of God expressed in His word 'be'. Since in the case of Jesus the first cause does not apply, there is no doubt that he was created through the second cause which is the word 'be' which God conveyed to Mary through the angel Gabriel."

Ḥijāzī further argues that Jesus is not the spirit of God but he was strengthened by a spirit from God. "It is a spirit which God brought into being, and not a part of Him, as Christians have understood it. Otherwise everything would be part of God." The author then blames the Church for deviating from original Christianity which was founded on faith in the One and only God.[44]

Muḥammad Rashīd Riḍā addresses more directly than any other commentator the question why the term *walad* is used in the Qur'an to critique the Christian belief in the Divine sonship of Christ rather than the term *ibn*, which is more commonly used by Christians to express their belief. "The reason for this choice," he argues, "is to show that if they intend actual son, then this son must be a child born through the insemination of his mother by his father, and this cannot be said of God. But if they mean son in the metaphorical rather than the true sense, as the term is used in the books of the Old and New Testaments to refer to Israel, David, the peace makers and others of the righteous, then it has nothing to do with divinity, nor would Jesus have any special status." Riḍā then compares Jesus with Adam, Eve, and the angels, all of whom came into being without the process of human generation, and concludes: "They are all God's servants and His creatures."[45]

The last instance I wish to consider in this study is not without difficulty. The relevant passage reads: "This is Jesus, the word of truth concerning whom they are in doubt. It is not for God to take a child unto Himself; glory be to Him, when He decrees a matter He says to it 'be,' and it is. God is surely my Lord and your Lord, so worship Him. This is a straight way" (S. 19:34–36).

These three verses raise many crucial questions. How are we to understand the phrase "This is Jesus, the word of truth"? Is Jesus himself "the word of truth," or is what the Qur'an says about him the word of truth? Does the doubt—and hence conflict and arid debate—that has characterized Muslim and Christian relationship with Christ concern him or the "word of truth"? Finally, is the Prophet Muhammad or Jesus the Christ counseling us all to worship God our Lord?

These and many other questions have not concerned Qur'an commentators. To repeat what they have said in interpretation of this passage is to repeat the same arid and by now all too familiar debate.

The Qurʾan and the Gospel are both agreed that God is God, the Lord of all His creation. They both affirm that "His will is done" in His universe. Jesus himself insisted that not his will but the will of Him who sent him must be done. What then is the message of the Qurʾan in its insistence that God alone is God?

The words with which we began this essay, and with which we will conclude it, enjoin that God alone should be worshipped: "They took their rabbis and monks as lords instead of God," and yet, "they were enjoined to serve God alone" (S. 9:31). Were the Qurʾan to speak to today's Muslims directly, it might add, "their 'ulamā'"; "their imāms"; "their politicians"; "their ideologies"; and even "their religion." The message of these verses is not meant for Christians only but for Muslims as well. For Christians, it is to remind them that God alone is God. As for Muslims, it is to remind them that the Truth is God.

NOTES

1. Acts 10:38.

2. See Luke 7:12–17 and John 11:1–44.

3. See S. 5:116–19, which is a colloquy between Christ and God, and which, according to Qurʾan commentators and traditionists, is yet to take place on the day of judgment. See Michel Ḥāik, *al-Masīḥ fī al-Islām*, 2d ed. (Beirut: Catholic Press, 1961), p. 278.

4. Striving for a unity of faith and purpose between the Muslims and the People of the Book is an oft repeated injunction in the Qurʾan. See for examples S. 3:64, 29:46, and 16:125.

5. I am grateful for the help of my friend and colleague G. Sloyan who gave me a literal translation of this verse.

6. Luke 1:35. I have followed the King James punctuation.

7. This interpretation is reported by commentators on the authority of the well-known early traditionist/jurist of Baṣra Qatāda ibn Diʿāma al-Sadūsī. Muḥammad B. Jarīr al-Ṭabarī, *Jāmiʿ al-Bayān ʿan ʾĀy al-Qurʾān*, 30 vols. (Beirut: Dār al-Fikr, 1398/1978), 28: 110.

8. ʿImād al-Dīn Abī al-Fidāʾ Ibn Kathīr, *Tafsīr al-Qurʾān al-ʿAẓīm*, 2d ed., 7 vols. (Beirut, Dār al-Fikr, 1389/1970), 7: 65.

9. Abū ʿAbd Allāh Muḥammad B. Aḥmad al-Anṣarī al-Qurṭubī, *al-Jāmiʿ li-Aḥkām al-Qurʾān*, ed. Aḥmad ʿAbd al-ʿAlīm al-Burdūnī, 2d ed., 20 vols. (Cairo: Dār al-Kātib al-ʿArabī, 1387/1967), 18: 203–4.

10. Abū Jaʿfar Muḥammad Ibn al-Ḥasan B. ʿAlī Ibn al-Ḥasan al-Ṭūsī, *al-Tibyān fī Tafsīr al-Qurʾān*, ed. Aḥmad Qāṣir al-ʿAmilī, 10 vols. (Beirut: al-Aʿlāmī, n.d.), 10: 54–55; and Abū ʿAlī al-Faḍl ibn al-Ḥasan al-Ṭabarsī, *Majmaʿ al-Bayān fī Tafsīr al-Qurʾān*, 30 vols. (Beirut: Dār Maktabat al-Ḥayāt, 1380/1961), 28: 129.

11. See Muḥammad Ḥusayn al-Ṭabaṭābāʾī, *al-Mīzān fī Tafsīr al-Qurʾān*, 2d ed., 20 vols. (Beirut: al-Aʿlāmī, 1394/1974), 19:345; and Sayyid Quṭb, *Fī ẓilāl al-Qurʾān*, 7th ed., 8 vols. (Beirut: Dār Iḥyāʾ al-Turāth al-ʿArabī, 1391/1971), 8: 174–75.

12. The phrases in *Sūrah* 19:21, "it is a thing easy for me. . . . It is a matter al-

ready decided" and in the Gospel of Luke 1:35, "The spirit of the Lord shall come upon you and the power of the Highest shall overshadow you," suggest God's direct involvement in and control of the conception, birth, and life of Jesus.

13. See S. 15:29 and 38:72 where God declares (addressing the angels concerning Adam, his earthly creature) in exactly the same words: "When I shall have shaped him and breathed into him of my spirit, then fall prostrate before him."

14. Theodore Abū Qurra, d. c. 825, was a noted Jacobite theologian and bishop of Ḥarrān. The work under consideration is vol. 3 of the series *Al-Turāth al-ʿArabī al-Masīḥī* (Christian Arab heritage). The work is a pietistic theological argument for the existence and nature of God and the truth of the Christian faith edited by Fr. Ighnatius Dīk (The Vatican: Institute of Islamic and Arabic Studies, 1982).

15. Ibid., pp. 221–22.

16. For a discussion of Muslim views of Jesus' ascension to heaven, see my article "Towards an Islamic Christology: The Death of Jesus, Reality or Delusion?" *The Muslim World* (April 1980).

17. I have thus rendered the vague phrase *Wa-Wajjaha ilā al-Rūm wa-ʿallamahum al-lāhūt waʾl-nāsūt.*

18. Niẓām al-Dīn al-Ḥasan Ibn Muḥammad Ibn al-Ḥusayn al-Qummī al-Nīsābūrī, *Gharāʾib al-Qurʾān wa-Raghāʾib al-Furqān*, ed. Ibrāhīm ʿAtwa ʿAwaḍ, 1st ed., 30 vols. (Cairo: al-Bābī al-Ḥalabi, 1384/1964), 10: 72; and ʿAlāʾ al-Dīn ʿAlī ibn Muḥammad ibn Ibrāhīm al-Baghdadī al-Khāzin, *Lubāb al-Taʾwīl fī Maʿānī al-tanzīl*, 4 vols. (Beirut: Dār al-Maʿrifa, n.d.), 2: 319.

19. See, for example, Ismāʿīl Ḥaqqī, *Rūḥ al-Bayān*, 10 vols. (Beirut: Dār al-Fikr, n.d.), 3: 415; and Muḥammad Ibn ʿAlī Ibn Muḥammad al-Shawkīnī, *Fatḥ al-Qadīr al-Jāmiʿ bayn fannay al-Riwāya waʾl-Dirāya min ʿilm al-Tafsīr*, 3d ed., 5 vols. (Beirut: Dār al-Fikr, 1393/1973), 2: 352.

20. Abū al-Faḍl Shihāb al-Dīn Maḥmūd al-Alūsī, *Rūḥ al-Maʿānī fī Tafsīr al-Qurʾān al-ʿAẓīm waʾl-Sabʿ al-Mathānī*, 30 vols. (Beirut: Dār al-Fikr, 1398/1979), 10: 82.

21. Ibn Kathīr, *Tafsīr al-Qurʾān al-ʿAẓīm*, 3: 385.

22. Fakhr al-Dīn al-Rāzī, *Al-Tafsīr al-Kabīr*, 1st ed., 30 vols. (Cairo: al-Maṭbaʿa al-Bahiyya al-Miṣriyya, 1357/1938), 16: 33–34.

23. This is applied to Abraham in the Qurʾan: "God took Abraham for an intimate friend" (S. 4:125), which has come to be used by Muslims as part of his name: Ibrāhīm al-Khalīl.

24. Al-Rāzī, *Al-Tafsīr al-Kabīr*, p. 34.

25. Al-Alūsī, *Rūḥ al-Maʿānī*, 10: 82.

26. Muḥammad Maḥmūd Ḥijāzī, *Al-Tafsīr al-Wāḍiḥ*, 6th ed., 30 vols. (Cairo: Maṭbaʿat al-Istiqlāl al-Kubrā, 1389/1969), 10: 45.

27. Muḥammad Rashīd Riḍā, *Tafsīr al-Manār*, 2d ed., 12 vols. (Beirut: Dār al-Maʿrifa, n.d.), 10: 328–29.

28. Quṭub, *Fī Ẓilāl al-Qurʾān*, 8: 171.

29. See S. 53:22 and below in this discussion.

30. See in this regard Q. 10:68 where God is called *al-ghanī* (the rich, self-sufficient, or one who has no need of any kind). This verse is referred by most commentators, however, primarily to the Makkan Arabs.

31. Al-Ṭabarī, *Jāmiʿ al-Bayān*, 1: 403.
32. Ibn Kathīr, *Tafsīr*, 1: 280–81.
33. Al-Qurṭubī, *al-Jamiʿ li-Aḥkām al-Qurʾān*, 2: 85.
34. Ḥaqqī, *Rūḥ al-Bayān*, 1: 213.
35. Al-Ṭūsī, *al-Tibyān*, 1: 426–27.
36. Al-Rāzī, *al-Tafsīr al-Kabīr*, 4: 25–27.
37. Al-Alūsī, *Rūḥ al-Maʿānī*, 1: 136.
38. Quṭb, 1: 142–44.
39. Al-Ṭabarī, 6: 26. See also pp. 24–26.
40. Abū al-Qāsim Jār Allāh Maḥmūd Ibn ʿUmar al-Zamakhsharī, *al-Kashshāf ʿan haqāʾiq al-Tanzīl wa-ʿuyūn al-aqāwīl fī Wujūh al-Taʾwīl*, 4 vols. (Beirut: Dār al-Kitāb al-ʿArabi, n.d.), 1: 584.
41. Al-Qurṭubī, 6: 25.
42. Al-Ṭabarsī, *Majmaʿ al-Bayān*, 5: 300.
43. Ibid.
44. Ḥijāzī, *al-Tafsīr al-Wāḍiḥ*, 6: 18–20.
45. Riḍā, *Tafsīr al-Manār*, 6: 87.

5

A Tenth-Century Speculative Theologian's Refutation of the Basic Doctrines of Christianity: Al-Bāqillānī (d. A.D. 1013)

Wadi Z. Haddad

Although the initial development of Islam took place in an environment characterized predominantly by polytheism, the formative period was also one in which there was contact with Jews and even some Christians. With the movement into the Medinan period the distinctiveness of Islam was set in contrast to the doctrines of Judaism and Christianity. Thus the Qur'an provides some basic teachings about both of these faiths that have served as the foundation of the relationships among them.

When Islam began to spread beyond the borders of Arabia it moved initially into territories that were predominantly Christian. As a result, parallel to developments of Islamic jurisprudence and law and the exegetical literature of the Qur'an, a corpus of polemic literature arose that specifically addressed Christian doctrines. This literature was shaped and influenced by contacts between Muslims and Christians. Each side sought to demonstrate the truth and superiority of its own doctrines. In the initial encounter each group resorted to its own scripture as the final authority. The dialogue soon proved futile since, on the one hand, the Muslim interlocutor believed that the text of the Christian scripture had been corrupted and consequently was and is invalid and, on the other, the Christian respondent did not accept the Qur'an to be divine revelation at all.

Muslims have always come to the discussion table, as it were, self-assured as to the absolute validity of the Qur'an and, with that as a point of departure, most of them also convinced that the Hebrew and Christian scriptures suffer from emendations and interpolations. For Muslims the verses of the Qur'an itself set the general principles for religious debate. These principles are, in essence and affirmed by the word of the Qur'an, that (1) "Religion with God is al-Islam";[1] (2) "Whoever accepts a religion other than Islam, it will not be accepted from him";[2] and (3) "Dispute not with the People of the Book except with that which is better. . . ."[3] This last principle serves as the basic sanction for dialogue and debate; because of their assurance that the Qur'an is superior to the scriptures that preceded it, certainly in their perverted form, Muslims know that what they have is in fact better, as the verse enjoins.

In the first phase of the polemical discussions between Muslims and Christians, then, both sides resorted primarily to quoting from their own scriptures to prooftext their arguments. In the matter of the Trinity, for example—the central issue of contention between the two faiths—Muslims turned to the Qur'an for such verses as that which exhorts the Christians not to exaggerate in what they say about the Messiah, that he was only a messenger of God, a Word conveyed to Mary and a spirit from God. "Say not 'three'—Cease! [it is] better for you! Allah is one God. Far is it removed from his transcendent majesty that He should have a son" (S. 4:171). In an even stronger tone the Qur'an proclaims that those who say that God is the Messiah, son of Mary, are disbelievers, as are those who proclaim God to be the third of three. There is only one God and whoever insists on three will come to a painful end.[4]

A second stage in the polemical debate appears to have begun after the Muslims secured their hold over the Arabian Peninsula, Syria, Mesopotamia, Persia, North Africa, and the Iberian Peninsula. The people of the Muslim empire slowly began to learn Arabic, the language of their conquerors. Quicker to acquire the new linguistic medium were non-Muslim scholars and religious leaders, living mainly in the urban centers of the new empire. Once they mastered Arabic they were able to read the Qur'an and discover firsthand what they had before learned only by way of their partners in disputation. Moreover, Christians now translated the Bible into Arabic,[5] making it accessible to Muslim scholars. Polemical discussion thus was able to take on added dimensions. In addition to quoting their own scriptures, both sides began to quote and interpret the sacred writings of the other to support their own argumentation and to refute the affirmations of their opponents. This scarcely served to move the discussions forward, however, as each side contested the understanding and interpretation of its scripture by the other.[6]

The third stage in the polemical encounter began after the establishment of *Dār al-Ḥikma* (literally the "House of Wisdom"), the institute of philosophy begun by the ʿAbbāsid caliph al-Maʾmūn in Baghdad in 830. The basic purpose of the institute was the translation into Arabic of Greek and Syriac texts on philosophy, medicine, alchemy, astronomy, astrology, and mathematics. Once these materials were available in translation, Muslims were able to study the disciplines firsthand. Arab and Muslim philosophers dealing with these Greek and Syriac materials soon began to equal and even outnumber their Christian teachers. What this development did for Christian-Muslim conversation was very significant. For the first time there was actually a common ground of discussion, with both Christian and Muslim philosophers and logicians arguing their doctrinal differences on the basis of the mutually accepted authority of Aristotelian philosophy and logic.

Not that this latest stage in the ongoing disputations served to put an end to the style and method of the earlier polemics. In accordance with their level and scope of education, scholars on both sides continued to produce works of polemical apology. Indeed the number of men of letters who were well versed in Aristotelian philosophy was actually quite meager; many Muslim theologians and jurists renounced such methodology as alien to the spirit and the terminology of the Qur'an. More important, perhaps, is the fact that the aim of the disputations relying on philosophical argumentation often was less to convince (or convert) an adversary than to silence one by presenting a seemingly plausible argument which served at the same time to reassure the presenter's fellow believers and to confirm their already-held faith. Al-Bāqillānī himself, to whose argumentation we shall turn shortly, returns to the polemic and apologetic defense of the faith characteristic of his predecessors. Far from ever resolving differences, such arguments seem somehow to have been perceived as necessary in order to address the challenge of confrontation as it was met anew by each generation of Christian and Muslim scholars and theologians. Thus the large and still-surviving body of polemical literature.

Nonetheless, and despite reliance on traditional rhetoric, argumentation did develop in defense of God's unicity using Aristotelian logic. The first to employ it to challenge the Christian concept of the Trinity was the Arab philosopher Abū Yūsuf Yaʿqūb ibn Isḥāq al-Kindī (d. ca. 866–70) in his *Refutation of the Christians.* Although al-Kindī's work is not extant, thanks to the classical method of refutation his arguments can be reconstructed from the response prepared by the Jacobite (Monophysite) Christian Yaḥyā ibn ʿAdī (893–974).[7] Yaḥyā, known as a logician, uses the same type of logic as that employed by al-Kindī to refute his arguments and to demonstrate, at least to Yaḥyā's own satisfaction, the validity of the concept of the Trinity.

The playing field for the debates between al-Kindī and Yaḥyā was understood by philosophers and logicians in both communities who themselves were addressing the same issues. Certain Muslim speculative theologians had already made use of this kind of reasoning in buttressing their doctrinal positions in discussions with representatives of other Muslim schools of theology. They now began to draw on these philosophical arguments in combatting Christian theologians and philosophers in relation to the doctrine of God and of the incarnation. Such a theologian was Abū Bakr Muḥammad ibn al-Ṭayyib ibn al-Bāqillānī (d. 1013/403). He utilized the arguments of al-Kindī, though not exclusively, in responding both to Ibn ʿAdī and to other Christian polemicists.

Al-Bāqillānī, a tenth-century Mālikīte judge in Baghdad, belonged to the Ashʿarite school of theological interpretation. A recognized theologian, philosopher, and scholar, he has been cited as the Mujaddid (reformer of the age) of the fourth century.[8] He is reputed to have been particularly articulate in his response to Christians, silencing them with the eloquence of his answers and the incisiveness of his critique. Al-Bāqillānī is said to have devoted his life to teaching and writing, often preaching to the public as well as participating in special missions on behalf of the rulers of his time. A prolific writer, he is reported to have sat down after evening prayer and written some thirty to forty pages of text. Then after morning prayer he would have his words read back to him and make whatever additions he felt appropriate.[9]

Al-Bāqillānī is revered by many subsequent Muslim scholars for his decisive and indisputable arguments made in defense of *ahl al-sunna*. He is noted for his ridicule of all those he opposed, both Muslim and non-Muslim; the sharpness of his tongue earned him the epithet "*sayf al-sunna wa-lisan al-umma*" (sword of the Sunna and tongue of the milla).[10] According to one story his reputation was so threatening to the Shīʿa community that one Twelver Shīʿī upon seeing him coming whispered, "Here comes Satan!" Al-Bāqillānī, hearing the comment, responded "If I am Satan, you are *kuffār* (unbelievers) and I was sent to you."[11] Another tale relates a visit al-Bāqillānī made to the king of Byzantium. Forced to enter through a low door so as to illustrate his humility before the king, al-Bāqillānī countered by turning around and entering with his rear first.[12] When the king requested that he take off his turban and shoes he refused, declaring, "I am of the learned men of the Muslims and what you are seeking is humiliation and diminution. God has elevated us with Islam and strengthened us with our prophet Muhammad."[13]

The voluminousness of al-Bāqillānī's writing is borne out by the record that he actually wrote some fifty-five books, of which only a few are extant. That he was contentious as well as prolific seems to be indicated by the fact that at least twelve of these volumes contain the term *radd*, or refutation, indicating that he was in the business of seriously confronting those about whose ideas he was writing. The volume in which the present challenge to the Christians concerning the Trinity is contained is, however, entitled simply *Kitāb al-Tamhīd*.[14] The material in question is presented in a chapter titled "Bāb al-kalām ʿalā al-Naṣārā," or "Chapter on the refutation of the Christians," in which in fact he does provide a refutation of the basic doctrines of Christianity.[15] It is clear from the fact that al-Bāqillānī incorporates the discussion and refutation of the Christians in a major work on Muslim theology, and specifically in the context of a discussion of the Muslim doctrine of God, that he understands it to be relevant to understanding the nature of God.[16]

The *Kitāb al-Tamhīd* is considered to be one of the most important Sunni texts of *kalām* because of the author's comprehensiveness and clarity in distinguishing between doctrines and presenting dialogical proofs and rational argumentation. It differs from other refutations in the degree to which it is dealing with Greek philosophy and logic. Because it was designed to respond to Christians who were using this terminology in Arabic, it is in the form of a philosophical-theological treatise. Thus to the modern reader it may appear rather dense and difficult to read.

As an Ashʿarite, al-Bāqillānī affirmed the importance of reasoned reflection to prove that the One, eternal and unique God has "objective," essential attributes. These attributes he defined as coeternal with God's essence, although he somewhat paradoxically described them as being "neither He (the essence of God) nor other than He." Ashʿarites generally held that the attributes of God are seven in number: life, knowledge, power, will, speech, vision, and hearing. Al-Bāqillānī himself posited an eighth attribute, that of *baqāʾ*, eternality or permanence.

Like other Ashʿarites before and after him, al-Bāqillānī categorically rejected any notion of incarnation, or indwelling of the divine, or any of the attributes of the divine in the human form or in any created physical form. He perceived that any contiguity of the divine with the temporal created world would serve to render the divine temporal, and therefore liable to change, decay, and death—an impossible ascription to the self-subsistent and eternal God. Muslims, however, believe that God has communicated with humanity at different times through messengers and prophets whom He has chosen from among humanity to receive His message. God's revelation to Muhammad, embodied in the Qurʾan, was understood by early Muslims to be the very "speech of God" and has been accepted as such by all those who affirm God's attributes as eternal. The problem arose when the question was raised whether this meant that the Qurʾan itself is eternal or noneternal. The ensuing controversy over this issue was sharp and severe.

The Ashʿarites, al-Bāqillānī among them, held to the position that the Qurʾan is God's uncreated speech. Members of the opposing Muʿtazilite school, on the other hand, believed the Qurʾan to be God's speech, but created. This they based on their conviction of the pure unicity of God and thereby the necessity of denying that there could be any essential or objective attribute different or separate from the divine essence. The Muʿtazilites, after temporary success, finally found themselves losers of the debate. The Ashʿarite and other traditionalist theologians, however, were left with the task of explaining just how the Qurʾan—the book, paper and ink, the recitation by human voice, the sequence of letters and words, all of which denote temporality and createdness—is actually related to the uncreated speech of God. The seeming paradox that this question presents has been rationally resolved neither by the Ashʿarites in general nor by al-Bāqillānī in particular.

This question of the relationship of God's speech to His attributes, and specifically to the Qur'an as His speech, therefore remains in the background of the critique that al-Bāqillānī brings to the Christian doctrines of the Trinity. In the meantime the Christian apologists, in light of the relentless Muslim criticism of Christian belief in the Trinity and in the divinity of Christ, attempted to explain and justify their views by using not only scripture but analogical reasoning, analogies drawn from human experience and observation. These analogies remained unconvincing to Muslims, however, who rejected them on the grounds that logically no analogy drawn from the visible created world could apply to the invisible and eternal God.

With the development of Muslim philosophy in the ninth century and Ash'arite theology in the tenth, then, Christian apologists began to employ philosophical argumentation and Ash'arite theological concepts in the formulation of their own defense. In some cases, as with Yaḥyā ibn 'Adī, both were used. It is with these same philosophical, rational, and analogical arguments, therefore, that al-Bāqillānī writing at the end of the tenth century challenges his Christian counterparts as we see in passages from *Kitāb al-Tamhīd*.

Three things are important to note about al-Bāqillānī's work. First, he directs his refutation not only to the Christians but to others whose ideas appear to him either to deny the existence of the God of revelation or to reject strict monotheism. Thus in the volume as a whole he addresses the "naturalists" (chapter 4), the astrologers (chapter 5), the dualists (chapter 6), the Magians [*al-majūs*] (chapter 7), the Christians (*al-Naṣārā*) (chapter 8), the Brahmans (chapter 9), and the Jews (chapters 12–15).[17] Second, with the exception of the chapters concerning the Jews, these refutations were set in the context of al-Bāqillānī's discussion of epistemology (chapter 1), the knowables and existents (chapter 2), and, most significantly, after his discussion of the existence of God and His attributes (chapter 3).[18] Third, he sets out to refute not Christianity in the abstract, nor the generality of Christians, but the specific doctrines of the Christian denominations of his day. He is well acquainted with the basic theology of the Melkites, Nestorians, and Monophysites and though he does not quote or refer to any Christian theologian or work by name, for the most part he presents their views accurately.

In the *Kitāb al-Tamhīd*, then, al-Bāqillānī specifically rebuts the Christian arguments in relation to the nature of God, the Trinity, the divinity of Christ, and the doctrine of the incarnation—that is, the divine and the human hypostases in Christ.

Al-Bāqillānī begins his refutation of the Christians by questioning the validity and appropriateness of attributing substance (*jawhar*),[19] to God. This seems to be a reference to the use of the term by Yaḥyā ibn 'Adī, among other Christian philosophers and theologians. Yaḥyā had stated that "one of the first principles of philosophy is that all existent things consist of either substances or accidents, and since God cannot be an accident He must be a substance."[20] Al-Bāqillānī rejects this line of argumentation, for while he accepts the definition as applicable to existent created objects, he suggests that it is anthropomorphism to think that God might be compared with existent, visible objects.[21]

Al-Bāqillānī's argument is based on the Aristotelian definition and classification of existent things into three categories: pure substance or atoms, composite bodies, and accidents. Substances and bodies accept one genus of accidents. Since the Creator cannot in any way resemble that which is created, it is unacceptable to subsume the creator God into any of these three categories. It is repugnant to say that God is a body, an atom, a substance, or an accident.

These arguments appear to be based on al-Kindī's *Refutation of the Trinity*, in which by using Aristotle's *Isagoge* he argues that the three persons of the Trinity must of necessity be categorized as genus, species, persons, or accidents and thereby not eternal.[22] Al-Kindī considered the hypostases as composites of a common *jawhar* and one distinctive quality; composites, as understood by all philosophers, could not be eternal because composition necessitates the existence of a cause and causality means temporality.

Al-Bāqillānī argues cogently here by suggesting that since Christians like Ibn ʿAdī have attributed "substance" to God by analogy with visible and rational existent beings, they should try to extend that analogy. Any such extension, he believes, will lead one to acknowledge the absurdity of applying the first premise to the Creator. Then pushing farther, he emphasizes the common agreement of the philosophers that substances (including rational substances) by definition are the locus for accidents. Therefore, he asks, can Christian philosophers avoid the conclusion that, given their affirmation of God's substantiality, He must then be receptive to accidents like all other substances?[23] Al-Bāqillānī, of course, is quite aware of the distinction that Christian theologians and philosophers make between noble and ignoble substances, the latter accepting accidents and assuming a locus and the former not.[24] Thus he asks rhetorically, "Why then not make the same distinction between bodies, and call [God] a body (*jism*), a Noble Body?"[25]

He then attempts to refute the concept of three hypostases (*aqānīm*) as interpreted by Eastern Christian theologians. Ibn ʿAdī, a senior contemporary of al-Bāqillānī, had affirmed that the Trinity is of one substance with three hypostases, that is, three distinctive or different characteristics, attributes or qualities. These he designated as "*jūd*, *ḥikma*, and *ḥawl*, i.e. goodness, wisdom and power."[26] In another treatise he affirms that "Christians do not say or believe that the hypostases are identical in every respect . . . rather they [Christians] view them as identical in one respect and different in another respect."[27]

In a further effort to undermine the idea of the Trinity, al-Bāqillānī tries to demonstrate the arbitrariness of limiting the hypostases/attributes to three. Why not two, he asks, or four or fourteen or fifteen? Taking the model put forth by some Christian theologians that the Trinity is based on God's three attributes of existence, knowledge, and life, he questions why one might not assume another hypostasis, for example power, thus by implication upsetting the trinitarian notion. If Christians were to argue that power is life, and therefore one and the same hypostasis, he asks, why would they not also admit that knowledge and life are the same? That, he observes, would make God two rather than three hypostases! Thus he tries to discredit the limitation of God's essential attributes to three. Christian theologians, having tried to explain the Trinity to Muslims by using the familiar Muslim concept of God's attributes, thus found the argument turned in on them by the logical scrutiny of a thinker like al-Bāqillānī.

The other major issue that al-Bāqillānī raises in his *Kitāb al-Tamhīd* is that of the meaning of the two natures of Christ, the unity of the Word with the body. He tries to demonstrate the various ways in which this unity is understood by the Jacobites, Nestorians and Melkites, raising reasonable objections to the analogies that they offer to try to explain the two natures in one body. His main argument is this: "Whether unity is perceived as an admixture of the two natures or contiguity or indwelling (*hulūl*) or separate, there is the fact that the word, eternal—according to you [Christians]—is united with the body of Christ in time. But why would the word uniting with the body in time be exempted from being originated/created, in accordance with the philosophical premises we all share?"[28]

Al-Bāqillānī quotes the Christian affirmation regarding the incarnation that "The Word (i.e., the Son) dwelt in the body of Christ."[29] Then he presents his understanding of the various Christian interpretations of this indwelling or union. Many Christians have expressed the unity of Christ as the "mixing and intermingling" of the divine and human natures, he says, "like water when mixed with wine or milk if poured into them."[30] He wrongly attributes this position, which is actually Jacobite, to the Nestorians. Then, correctly presenting a Jacobite position, he says that the Jacobites claim that "the Word of God was transformed (*inqalabat*) into flesh and blood in the uniting (*biʾl-ittiḥād*),"[31] while others understood the unity to be the adoption of the body as the only form (*haykal*) in which the Word dwells and functions. But, he says, adherents of the latter concept differed in regard to the modality of the appearance of the Word in human form. Most of these Monophysite Jacobites upheld the idea of the mixture of the human and the divine, but some rejected this concept of mixing and offered various analogies for the presence of the Word in the body such as the reflection of a person in a mirror,[32] or the stamp that an engraved ring leaves on wax or clay. Without naming his source, al-Bāqillānī quotes a Christian writer: "I say that the word has united with the body of Christ in the sense that it has entered into it (*ḥallathu*), without touch, mixture, or intermingling, in the same manner that I say that God is [dwells] in heaven but does not touch it or mix with it, and just as I say that reason (*al-ʿaql*) is a substance (*jawhar*) which exists [lit. dwells] in the soul while it is not mixed with the soul or in contact with it."[33]

Al-Bāqillānī does not quite understand the position of the Byzantines or Melkites, which he refers to as al-Rūm. While he correctly portrays their affirmation that "the unity of the Word with the body means that the two have become one," he wrongly attributes to them and to the Nestorians the Jacobite concept of admixture and intermingling.[34] He then shifts the argument against the Melkites so as to address their concept of the humanity of Christ. He notes the difference between them and the Nestorians and Jacobites. The latter believe that the Word was united with a "specific man" (i.e., Jesus of Nazareth) to the exclusion of all others. The Melkites, on the other hand, hold that the Word united with "universal man," that is, with "humanity which is the common substance of all human beings." This, al-Bāqillānī chides, results in Christ being both universal and particular: universal in relation to his humanity and particular in relation to the Trinity. He concludes that this is both illogical and impossible, later reinforcing his refutation by indicating the logical impossibility of a "universal man" born of a "particular woman."[35]

To prove that Christ could not be both divine and eternal, al-Bāqillānī introduces a new line of argument. "All Christians," he says, "agree that this unity in Christ is an act (*fiʾl*) by which unity has been achieved and the Christ has become Christ."[36] But if this be so, who is the agent (*al-fāʿil*) of the act? Or does the act have no agent? Al-Bāqillānī shows how Christians cannot deny that acts and events have agents, and goes on to argue against other possible answers that Christians might give. "If they say that unity is the act of an agent who was united in it," he asks, "then who is the agent, the substance (*al-jawhar*) alone which unites the hypostases? Or the hypostases alone? Or both? Or one of the hypostases?"[37] Logically, he concludes, none of these possibilities is viable, and he then proceeds to tackle the issues from a different angle.

Affirmed by the Qurʾan in S. 4:157,[38] Muslims believe that the crucifixion of Christ never took place. But for the sake of argument al-Bāqillānī is willing to grant the Christian claim, clearly for his own purposes. He uses belief in the crucifixion to further his own objection to the Christian perception of the unity of the divine and human natures in Christ, and implicitly his objection to the idea of redemption. Focusing on the moment of crucifixion and death, he asks whether at that point the union of the "son" with the body still continued. If on the one hand the answer is affirmative, the implication is that the eternal Son of God was indeed crucified and killed. But if that were true, he argues, it would mean that the Father and the Holy Spirit also died, which he as well as Christians would consider a patent absurdity. On the other hand, if the response to the question were negative and the two natures of Christ were not held in union at the time of crucifixion, it would mean abandonment of the doctrine of unity and admission that at least at that moment Christ was only a human.[39] This, of course, is the ultimate aim of al-Bāqillānī's argument—to establish that Jesus was only a man and that he had but one nature.

Al-Bāqillānī continues his argument by trying to show how Abraham and Moses, as well as Jesus, were also united with the word of God at some point. This simile between these prophets and Jesus is, he knows, unacceptable to Christians. Anticipating the Christian response that the deeds of Christ prove his uniqueness, he points to the confirmation in the Hebrew scriptures that Moses too produced phenomenal miracles and thus qualifies as divine in the same way as the Christians lay claim for Jesus. To the Christian claim that the deeds of Moses were given by God in answer to his supplication, al-Bāqillānī retorts that the same could be said in regard to the miracles of Jesus.[40]

It is no surprise to find that al-Bāqillānī's conclusion after this series of argumentations is that on the basis of the text of the Gospel itself, it is clear that Jesus was completely and only human. He quotes some of the words of Jesus to show that he was obviously a human being addressing his God in the same manner as did the other prophets. Here is Jesus invoking God before raising Lazarus from the dead: "I thank you, Father, that you listen to me. I know that you always listen to me, but I say this for the sake of the people here, so that they will believe that you sent me";[41] Jesus praying in the Garden of Gethsemane: "My father, if it is possible take this cup of suffering from me! Yet not what I want, but what you want";[42] and Jesus' final words while hanging on the cross: "My God, my God, why did you abandon me?"[43]

On the basis of sophisticated philosophical argumentation al-Bāqillānī succeeds, at least in his own understanding, in devastating the assertions of his Christian opponents that Jesus the Christ was possessed of a dual nature. Jesus could be of one nature only, concludes al-Bāqillānī, and that is the human and not the divine. Argumentation aside, of course, it is clear from the beginning that the conclusion was foregone, and that rhetorical artistry is probably successful in such debates only to the extent to which it supports already deeply held convictions.

NOTES

1. S. 3:19. All quotes are taken from *The Glorious Qurʾan*, translated by Muhammad Marmaduke Pickthall (Mecca al-Mukarramah: Muslim World League, 1977).

2. S. 3:85.

3. S. 29:46. The verse continues, "unless it is with the oppressors. And say: We believe in that which was revealed to us and to you, and our God and your God are one and to Him we surrender as Muslims."

4. "They surely disbelieve who say: Lo! Allah is the Messiah, son of Mary" (S. 5:72). "They surely disbelieve who say: Lo! Allah is the third of a three; when there is no God save the One God. If they desist not from their so saying a painful doom will fall on those of them who disbelieve" (S. 5:73).

5. There are some indications that this might have been done shortly after A.D. 639 at the request of a Muslim general. See, e.g., F. Nau, "Un Colloque du Patriarche Jean avec L'Emir des Agareens," *Journal Asiatique* 11, no. 5 (1915): 225–79.

6. For a brief survey of early polemics, see Harry Garland Dorman, *Toward Understanding Islam* (New York: Bureau of Publications, Teachers College, Columbia University, 1948).

7. See "Un Traite de Yaḥyā Ben ʿAdī" in *Revue de l'Orient Chrétien* 22 (Tome 2, no. 22, 1920), 4–14. For a discussion of Yaḥyā's response see Majid Fakhry, *A History of Islamic Philosophy* (New York and London: Columbia University Press, 1970), pp. 221–25, and Robert Henry DeValve, "The Apologetic Writings of Yaḥyā ibn ʿAdi" (Ph.D. thesis, Hartford Seminary, 1973), pp. 132 ff.

8. Cited in Abū Bakr Muḥammad ibn al-Ṭayyib ibn al-Bāqillānī, *Iʿjāz al-Qurʾān*, ed. Aḥmad Ṣaqr (Cairo: Dār al-Maʿārif bi-Maṣr, 1954), p. 56.

9. Ṣaqr in al-Bāqillānī, *Iʿjāz*, pp. 38–42.

10. Abū Bakr Muḥammad ibn al-Ṭayyib ibn al-Bāqillānī, *al-Inṣāf*, ed. Muḥammad Zāhid ibn al-Ḥaṣan al-Kawtharī (Cairo: Maktab Nashr al-Thaqāfa al-Islāmiyya, 1950), p. 7. It is reported that the inscription on al-Bāqillānī's tomb reads as follows: "This is the tomb of the blessed imām, the pride of the umma, the tongue of the milla, the sword of the sunna, the pillar of religion, the protector of Islam, Abū Bakr Muḥammad ibn al-Ṭayyib al-Baṣrī, may God have mercy on him" (Al-Qadī ʿIyāḍ, *Tartīb al-Madārik* [Cairo, 1966], p. 23). Numerous tales about al-Bāqillānī tell of his encounters in debate with Christians, concluding that the incisiveness of his argumentation caused them finally to be stunned into silence.

11. "Do you not see that we have sent the satans to the unbelievers to incite them with fury?" S. 19:83; al-Kawthārī, in al-Bāqillānī, *Al-Inṣaf*, p. 6.

12. Ibid., p. 8.

13. Al-Bāqillānī, *Iʿjāz al-Qurʾān*, p. 31. Invited to partake of a meal, he also refused on the grounds that it might contain pork. Assured that it would not, he pretended to eat even though he did not see anything forbidden on the banquet table. The encounter between al-Bāqillānī and the king offered the opportunity for a number of such tales of the qāḍī's nerve, wit, and courage.

14. Edited by Richard J. McCarthy, S.J. (Beirut: al-Maktaba al-Sharqiyya, 1957). Schefer's manuscript indicates clearly in the designation of the complete title of al-Bāqillānī's work that it is actually a refutation: "Al-Tamhīd fīʾl-radd ʿalā al-mulḥida al-muʿaṭṭila waʾl-rāfiḍa waʾl-khawārij waʾl-muʿtazila." C.H. Derenbourg, *Les manuscripts arabes de la collection Schefer à la Bibliotèque Nationale* (Extract du Journal des Savants, Mars–Juin 1901) (Paris, 1901), p. 10.

15. While one finds references to monographs, in earlier times, devoted to the refutation of central Christian doctrines, only a few have survived. Al-Kindī's philosophical refutation, for example, can only partially be retrieved from Yaḥyā ibn ʿAdī's response (see note 7 above); three refutations of Christians by al-Ashʿarī have not survived (see Richard J. McCarthy, *The Theology of Al-Ashʿarī* [Beirut: Imprimerie Catholique, 1953], pp. 211–12, 227 [numbers 1, 84, 86]). An exception to this is the brief refutation by Abū Manṣūr al-Māturīdī (d. 333 A.H./A.D. 944) in his theological work *Kitāb al-Tawḥīd*, ed. Fathalla Kholeif (Beirut: Dar el-Machreq Éditeurs, 1970), pp. 210–15. The section is entitled "The opinions of the Christians concerning the Christ and their refutation," and follows the presentation of "proof of the prophethood of the prophets and especially the mission of Muhammad—blessings and peace be upon him."

16. Contrast this with al-Māturīdī, *Kitāb al-Tawḥīd*, who treats "the views of the Christians concerning Christ" under the rubric of prophetology (pp. 210–15).

17. Al-Bāqillānī, *Kitāb al-Tamhīd*, ed. Richard J. McCarthy (Beirut: Libraire orientale, 1957), pp. 34–131, 160–90. Since the refutation of the Jews was not addressed to their concept of God, it came in the context of (after) al-Bāqillānī's discussion of the prophethood of Muhammad and of the Qurʾan. The scheme of al-Bāqillānī's treatment of non-Muslim religions and ideologies in *Kitāb al-Tamhīd* seems to follow the scheme of al-Ashʿarī, as Richard J. McCarthy suggests ("The works of al-Ashʿarī," translated from Ibn ʿAsākir's *Tabyīn* with comments by McCarthy, in R.J. McCarthy, *The Theology of al-Ashʿarī* [Beyrouth: Imprimerie Catholique, 1953], pp. 211–12). But since al-Ashʿarī's *Fuṣūl* has not survived, we cannot ascertain al-Bāqillānī's dependence on him in regard to either methodology or content.

18. al-Bāqillānī, *Kitāb al-Tamhīd*, pp. 6–33.

19. Īliyya of Niṣibīn (A.D. 975–1027), a contemporary of al-Bāqillānī, wrote that "when [the Christian] translators set out to translate their Syriac works into Arabic, they sought to find an expression which exactly renders the term *kiyān* . . . but they could not find any . . . they utilized the term *jawhar* because they could not find a better term" (Ludwig Horst, trans., *Das Metropoliten Elias von Nisibis Buch vom Beweis der Wahrheit des Glaubens* [Colmar: E. Barth, 1886], p. 2, as cited in Muḥyī al-Dīn al-Iṣfahānī, *Epître sur l'Unité et la Trinité, Traite sur l'Intellect, Fragment sur l'âme*, texte arabe edité et annoté par M. Allard et G. Troupeau [Beirut: Imprimerie Catholique, 1962], p. xviii).

20. Augustine Perier, *Petits Traités Apologétiques de Yahya Ben ʿAdi* (Paris: J. Gabalda and Paul Geuthner, Eds., 1920), p. 53.

21. Al-Bāqillānī, *Kitāb al-Tamhīd*, p. 77.

22. See Perier, *Yaḥyā Ben ʾAdī*, p. 186.

23. Ibid.

24. Al-Bāqillānī, *Kitāb al-Tamhīd*, p. 78.

25. Ibid.

26. Ibn ʿAdī, in Perier, *Petits Traités*, pp. 43, 66 (The creator is described as *jawād*, *ḥakīm*, and *qadīr*, that is as good, wise and having power, representing the Father, the Son/logos, and the Holy Spirit respectively). Other theologians have ascribed different sets of attributes to God, such as life, knowledge, and power, or existence, life, and knowledge. See al-Iṣfahānī, *Epître sur l'Unité*, p. 43.

27. Ibn ʿAdī, in Perier, *Petits Traites*, p. 42.
28. Al-Bāqillānī, *Kitāb al-Tamhīd*, p. 89.
29. Ibid., p. 87.
30. Ibid.
31. Ibid.
32. This is the analogy made by Yaḥyā ibn ʿAdī. See Perier, *Petits Traités*, pp. 12–18.
33. Al-Bāqillānī, *Kitāb al-Tamhīd*, p. 88.
34. Ibid., p. 91.
35. Ibid., pp. 94–95.
36. Ibid., p. 96.
37. Ibid.
38. "And because of their [the Jews] saying: We slew the Messiah Jesus son of Mary, Allah's messenger—They slew him not nor crucified, but it appeared so unto them; and lo! those who disagree concerning it are in doubt thereof. They have no knowledge thereof save pursuit of conjecture; they slew him not for certain."
39. Al-Bāqillānī, *Kitāb al-Tamhīd*, pp. 97–98.
40. Ibid., pp. 98–99.
41. John 11:41–42. All quotes are taken from *Good News Bible: Today's English Version* (New York: American Bible Society, 1976).
42. Matthew 26:39; cf. Mark 14:36 and Luke 22:42.
43. Matthew 27:46; cf. Mark 15:34.

6

Ibn Taymiyya and the *Kitāb Al-Burhān*: A Muslim Controversialist Responds to a Ninth-Century Arabic Christian Apology

Mark N. Swanson

In or shortly after the year A.D. 1317, the celebrated Ḥanbalī reformer Taqī al-Dīn Aḥmad ibn Taymiyya wrote his *al-Jawāb al-Ṣaḥīḥ li-man Baddala Dīn al-Masīḥ* (The correct reply to those who have changed the religion of Christ).[1] This massive work—it fills more than a thousand pages in the most recent printed edition[2]—is formally a response to an elaboration of the twelfth-century apology of Paul of Antioch, Melkite bishop of Sidon.[3] In the course of his response, however, Ibn Taymiyya made polemical use of another Arabic Christian text: a late recension of a tenth-century work of history, the *Annals* of Eutychius (Saʿīd ibn Baṭrīq), Melkite patriarch of Alexandria.[4]

The recension of the *Annals* known to Ibn Taymiyya—essentially the same as that available to Western scholars through the editions of Edward Pocock or Louis Cheikho[5]—was a much-interpolated reworking of Eutychius' original text.[6] In fact, the material cited by Ibn Taymiyya comes from a variety of sources: the actual text of Eutychius,[7] additional historical material,[8] a Melkite refutation of Nestorianism,[9] and finally, a lengthy passage from a work known as the *Kitāb al-Burhān*, "The book of the demonstration."[10] It is this passage from the *Kitāb al-Burhān*, and Ibn Taymiyya's response to it, that we shall examine in this chapter.

The *Kitāb al-Burhān* and the Melkite Apologetic Project

The *Kitāb al-Burhān*, well known through the edition of Pierre Cachia with English translation by Montgomery Watt,[11] has been widely assumed to be another work of the patriarch Eutychius,[12] but recent studies indicate that its author was one Peter, Melkite bishop of Bayt Rās (Capitolias) in the Transjordan, who probably wrote toward the end of the ninth century.[13] The work is of interest as one of the "trajectory" of eighth and ninth century Arabic Melkite apologetic writings[14] which begins with the ancient apologetic treatise preserved in *Sinaitica Arabica* 154,[15] continues by way of the works of Theodore Abū Qurra[16] and the encyclopaedic *Jāmiʿ Wujūh al-Īmān*,[17] and finally arrives at the *Kitāb al-Burhān*.

The *Kitāb al-Burhān*[18] provides a number of insights into the character of this trajectory of texts. A student of Greek patristic literature might notice that it begins with an Arabic paraphrase of some paragraphs from the *De Fide Orthodoxa* of John of Damascus,[19] and ends with an Arabic version of some pages of a Greek polemic attributed to Athanasius.[20] At the same time, however, an Islamicist such as Montgomery Watt is impressed by the degree of Islamic influence that he detects, which he believes is best explained by a conscious apologetic purpose.[21] It is this double-sidedness that is responsible for much of the fascination of these early Arabic Melkite texts. They seek to express the doctrinal deposit of the Greek-speaking Church in clear Arabic. But they also seek to make the Christian faith comprehensible within the Islamic milieu, both to gain Muslims' respect and tolerance and to urge wavering Christians to remain true to the faith of their fathers.[22]

It would be helpful to know how Muslims of the period responded to this Melkite project. Unfortunately, direct responses to the works of the earliest Melkite apologists in Arabic by their Muslim contemporaries have not been preserved,[23] and those texts that we do possess respond more fully to Nestorian and Jacobite teachings than to Melkite ones.[24] It is therefore a matter of some interest that Ibn Taymiyya dedicates a lengthy passage in his *Jawāb* to material from the *Kitāb al-Burhān*. Here, if more than four centuries late, is a serious response by a Muslim scholar to an early Christian attempt to express the faith of the fathers in Arabic, and in an Islamic environment.

Ibn Taymiyya's Responses to Peter's Arguments

True to form, Ibn Taymiyya spilled far more ink in responding to Peter's text than he did in copying it out.[25] Time and again we read that the incarnation or indwelling of the Creator in a creature is impossible[26] and that Christian confessional and apologetic vocabulary consists largely of irrational, scripturally unauthorized innovations.[27] These criticisms are entirely predictable given Ibn Taymiyya's well-known positions on *tawḥīd* and the sources of correct speech about God.[28] However, it is not Ibn Taymiyya's general criticisms that interest us here, but rather the way he uses his formidable analytical and dialectical powers to dissect particular arguments or linguistic usages that he finds in Bishop Peter's text.[29] In what follows we will give five brief examples, and then conclude with a few observations.

Allah and His Word and His Spirit

The section of the *Kitāb al-Burhān* cited by Ibn Taymiyya begins with a presentation of the Incarnation of the Word of God from the Virgin Mary.[30] A noteworthy feature of this presentation is its description of God the Trinity as "Allah and his Word and his Spirit."[31] While this description draws on biblical language—with "ho theos" translated as Allah—in the *Kitāb al-Burhān* it is given weight by an apologetic argument which Peter took from John of Damascus to the effect that God cannot be without a Word and a Spirit.[32] Not all the early Arabic Melkite apologists appear to have been convinced of the adequacy of this Allah/Word/Spirit triad;[33] the author of the *Jāmiʿ Wujūh al-Īmān*, in particular, insists upon the confession that Allah is the Trinity, Father, Son, and Holy Spirit.[34] But despite possible misgivings about its specifically Christian theological adequacy, the apologetic utility of the triad Allah/Word/Spirit is obvious. Does not the Qurʾan describe Jesus as the Word of Allah and a Spirit from him?[35] But if so, what objections could Muslims possibly have to the Christian trinitarian or christological confessions?[36]

Ibn Taymiyya has no difficulty in thinking of a few. In particular, he objects to the way Peter predicates the words "create" and "Creator" not only of Allah, but also of the Word and of the Spirit. Is there then one creator god, or three?[37] Is it not a clear contradiction to speak, as Peter does, simultaneously of creation by the Word (which Muslims may accept) and of the Word who himself creates a humanity for himself?[38] Is it not obviously polytheistic (*shirk*) when the Christian claims that the Word created a man for himself "with the concurrence of God the Father and the help of the Holy Spirit"?[39] Furthermore, Ibn Taymiyya asks: What is this Creator-Word? Drawing from the discussions of the various schools of Islamic *kalām*, he lists five possible definitions of "Word of God," but finds that none of them supports Christian claims.[40] Similarly, Christian claims about the Spirit are in clear contradiction to the testimonies of scripture, in particular the Qurʾan.[41]

The Veiling of God

The *Kitāb al-Burhān* proceeds to a discussion of the "veiling"—*iḥtijāb*—of God in the Incarnation.[42] Here we meet another old apologetic move, the ground for which is made explicit in the *Jāmiʿ Wujūh al-Īmān*: "the Incarnation . . . is [God's] veiling himself under the flesh, and that because human beings have no access to God's Speech except by revelation or from behind a veil,"[43] a clear citation of S. 42:51. Peter gives this move a new twist by combining it with his view of the human person as a trichotomy: material body, "bloody" or animal soul, and rational, logical spirit. The result, for Peter, is a succession of veilings which bind immaterial and material together: God takes the human spirit, made in his image, as the veil most fit for him; the spirit, in its turn, has the animal soul as a veil, which in its turn has the physical body as a veil.[44] In this way the immaterial, invisible God may be seen in what is material.

Peter's "veiling" theory does not commend itself to Ibn Taymiyya. Earlier in the *Jawāb* he points out that S. 42:51 opposes rather than supports the Christian case, since the veil is something that screens and separates divinity from humanity. To take the Qur'anic verse seriously is to deny the possibility of the Incarnation.[45] As for Peter's theory of a succession of veilings which allows the invisible God to be seen in a material body, Ibn Taymiyya has two objections. First, all the scriptures agree that no one may see God at all.[46] Second, the idea of a succession of veilings contradicts the essentials of the Christians' own confession! Christians claim that the Word was made flesh, that this Word was present from the moment of conception in the womb of Mary,[47] and that it remained united with the dead body of the crucified Jesus.[48] We might summarize Ibn Taymiyya's insight thus: Christians believe in incarnation, not inanimation.[49]

The One Divine Hypostasis of Christ

Having presented his peculiar version of the "veil-apology" for the Incarnation, Peter goes on to a straightforward assertion of the neo-Chalcedonian doctrine of the two natures of Christ within the single hypostasis of the Logos.[50] He does this with a sophistication new for the Arabic Melkite literature. Indeed, the *Kitāb al-Burhān* is our first witness for a sentence such as the following in Arabic: "The Word of God in its hypostasis became the hypostasis of that humanity whose essence was completed through its enhypostatization by the hypostasis of the Word of God."[51] This new precision is in large part enabled by a terminological innovation: *qiwām* instead of the familiar *uqnūm* for hypostasis,[52] which allows Peter to press the verb *qawwama*[53] into service as an equivalent of *enyphisteimi*.

This, we might say, is all Greek to Ibn Taymiyya. He fails to realize that *qiwām* is equivalent to the familiar *uqnūm*. Furthermore, despite frequent assertions in the section of the *Kitāb al-Burhān* copied out by Ibn Taymiyya that Christ's one *qiwām* is that of the Word of God,[54] Ibn Taymiyya understands the precise opposite: the *qiwām* of the Word of God is Christ.[55] This misunderstanding is Ibn Taymiyya's starting point for a sustained burst of indignation, and a lengthy polemic against all—not only or even particularly Christians—who would make the Creator in any way dependent upon the creature.[56]

God's Similitudes

Peter illustrates his presentation of the Incarnation with analogies: the Word of God, begotten of the Father yet incarnate in human flesh, is like the rays which, begotten of the sun, fill a house with light and heat; or like the word which, begotten of the intellect, becomes embodied in material paper.[57] Such analogies, of course, are familiar from patristic literature; they took on great importance for Arabic-speaking Christians searching for apologetic tools. Peter concedes that his analogies are inadequate to describe God, but, using language that echoes Qur'anic affirmations, claims both biblical and Qur'anic justification for their use: "God has always set forth similitudes for his worshipers in all his Books."[58]

It is well known that Ibn Taymiyya was by no means a foe of analogical argument. He taught that the Qur'an itself speaks of God using the *qiyās al-awlā*, by which attributes of perfection are predicated of God, and every defect denied him.[59] Therefore he does not simply dismiss Christian analogies, but rather examines them with all the attention of a jurist confronted with an unfamiliar legal *qiyās*. In every case, he finds the alleged points of comparison lacking. For example, the rays of the sun fill many houses with light and heat, not just one. Furthermore, they are not begotten of the sun and do not subsist in the sun, but are, rather, an effect external to the sun subsisting in the air. So then, where are the points of comparison between the rays of the sun in a house and the Word of God incarnate in Christ?[60] In fact, Ibn Taymiyya can turn the analogy to his own advantage: it may, in some ways, illustrate God's light and guidance and spirit in the hearts of the believers.[61]

A Typology of Mixtures and the Two Natures of Christ

Peter's presentation of the Melkite doctrine of the Incarnation leads into a polemic against non-Melkite Christians[62] in which he again makes use of analogies. The Jacobites see Christ's two natures as mixing like wine and water,[63] while the Nestorians think of a mixture like that of water and oil.[64] The hypostatic union in Christ, however, is not like any mixture of two material things,[65] but rather is a mixture of the immaterial with the material, such as the soul and the body in the one human being, or fire and iron in the one glowing mass,[66] or the sun with earth and water, or even filth and corruption.[67] In such a mixture, essences are neither confused or transformed nor changed from their proper "state" (*ḥāl*) or "activity" (*fiʿāl*).[68]

Ibn Taymiyya finds this last assertion, that the hypostatic union does not involve the uniting natures in any change of state (*ḥāl*) or activity (*fiʿāl*), to be improbable, and sets out to refute it on the basis of Peter's own analogies.[69] For example, it is nonsense to claim that the union of body and soul in a single living person does not result in a change of states or activities: is an animated body really in the same "state" as a dead body?[70] Furthermore, there can be no neat sorting of activities between body and soul; each is a coparticipant in all the activities of the one person.[71] Here we might note that some of Ibn Taymiyya's observations are reminiscent of those of the Christian opponents of Chalcedon,[72] and that many Chalcedonian theologians, including John of Damascus and Theodore Abū Qurra, had expressed reservations about the use of the body/soul analogy.[73] As for the example of the union of iron and fire in a single glowing mass, Ibn Taymiyya claims that rightly interpreted, it demonstrates that the result of such a union is a new thing, a new reality, a new essence.[74] Therefore Peter's own analogies refute his attempt to shield the divinity of Christ from the mutability and passions of his humanity.[75]

Concluding Remarks

One cannot read these two texts without a deep sense of regret that they were not the opening exchange in an in-depth discussion. Many of Ibn Taymiyya's criticisms of Peter's text are extremely insightful and helpful. First, he indicates a number of points where Bishop Peter's language should have been defined and sharpened. What does it mean that the Word created a man for himself "with the concurrence of God the Father and the help of the Holy Spirit"? What precisely are the "states" and "activities" of Christ's natures which are said not to have changed in the hypostatic union?

Second, Ibn Taymiyya's criticisms of Bishop Peter's apologetic devices could have helped Christians to understand the risks involved in using them. Apologetics, after all, involves a movement away from a faith's own ground, away from its reservoirs of language and narrative and practice. To cite another's scripture is to expose oneself to criticism on the basis of the other's hermeneutics; to use another's language is to risk being understood in quite unintended ways. For example, while the apologetically formulated triad Allah/Word/Spirit may have been useful as an emergency defense of Christian monotheism, and could well have served as an opening move in an ongoing discussion, we see from Ibn Taymiyya's response that it presents too little of a challenge to Islamic presuppositions to be an adequate presentation of what Christians mean by the triune God. In fact, when this formula is combined with more robust trinitarian claims (such as the confession that each of the trinitarian persons plays a role in creation) the result is language which is quite plausibly rejected as *shirk*.[76]

Third, Ibn Taymiyya penetrates to the central paradox of Christian teaching when he criticizes Bishop Peter's rather clumsy attempts to shield Christ's divinity from his humanity, whether by his theory of multiple veilings, or by his one-sided emphasis on the distinction of the two natures of Christ. Ibn Taymiyya's criticisms, in effect, pose the question: can Christianity's marriage of biblical and Hellenistic religion last? Is it really possible simultaneously to hold to a real Incarnation of the Word of God and to a belief in God's *apayeia*, his immunity to change?

While welcoming Ibn Taymiyya's insights, we should also acknowledge the shortcomings of his response. His complete failure to comprehend Peter's presentation of the neo-Chalcedonian christology is most unfortunate. He never grasped that the Melkite doctrine of the incarnation meant anything other than the piecing together of God and a man,[77] even though the neo-Chalcedonian christology aims to avoid precisely this kind of *shirk*. Furthermore, Ibn Taymiyya certainly made no attempt to understand Christian positions "from within." He is confident, for example, that the five definitions of "Word of God" that he culls from the Islamic *kalām* exhaust all the possibilities. Whether Christians might have yet another definition is simply not a question that he asks.

While we may regret the fact that these texts did not initiate an ongoing dialogue, we should not be surprised. Although Peter of Bayt Rās uses apologetic formulations developed for use in the Islamic environment, one suspects that he is in fact far more concerned about Nestorian and Jacobite Christians than he is about Muslims. Similarly, even while reading *al-Jawāb al-Ṣaḥīḥ li-man Baddala Dīn al-Masīḥ* one senses that Ibn Taymiyya is far more concerned about the dangers posed by speculative Sufism[78] than he is about those posed by Christianity. The kind of concern about another's faith which would lead one to attempt to understand it "from within" and to allow it to challenge and refine one's own faith hardly existed in the days of Peter of Bayt Rās or of Ibn Taymiyya. It is rare enough in our own day. And thus we may turn from our study of these texts all the more grateful to a scholar such as Willem Bijlefeld, who has embodied such concern and who has helped many of us to sense its rightness.

NOTES

1. Taqī al-Dīn Aḥmad Ibn Taymiyya's work has been printed twice. The more recent edition (still available in Cairo) is *al-Jawāb al-Saḥīḥ li-man Baddala Dīn al-Masīḥ*, 4 vols. in 2 (Cairo: Maṭbaʿat al-Madanī, n.d.) (hereafter cited as *JS* I–IV). The first major Western study of the work was Ignazio Di Matteo, *Ibn Taymiyya, o Riassunto del suo opera al-Jawab al-Sahih li-man baddala din al-Masih* (Palermo, 1912). The best guide to this work now is Thomas F. Michel, *A Muslim Theologian's Response to Christianity: Ibn Taymiyya's al-Jawāb al-Saḥīḥ* (Delmar, N.Y.: Caravan Books, 1984) (hereafter cited as Michel), which includes an English translation of nearly one-third of Ibn Taymiyya's text. See p. vii for the dating of the work. See also Muzammil Husain Siddiqi, "Muslim and Byzantine

Christian Relations: Letter of Paul of Antioch and Ibn Taymiya's Response," in N.M. Vaporis, ed., *Orthodox Christians and Muslims* (Brookline, Mass.: Holy Cross Orthodox Press, 1986), pp. 33–45; Siddiqi has presented a thesis on this subject to Harvard University.

2. It is to be noted that *JS* III, p. 275–IV, p. 328, is a different work by Ibn Taymiyya, the *Takhjīl ahl al-Injīl*. See Michel, pp. 370–82.

3. Introduction, editing, and French translation by Paul Khoury, *Paul d'Antioche: Évêque Melkite de Sidon (XIIe s.)*, Recherches publiées sous la direction de l'Institut de Lettres Orientales 24 (Beirut: Imprimerie Catholique, 1965), text no. III. Also see Michel, pp. 87–96, for a discussion of Paul's apology, and its expansion into the "Letter from Cyprus," which is the text to which Ibn Taymiyya responded.

4. *JS* III, pp. 5–125, deals with material from the *Annals*. This section is preceded by a lengthy citation from another work, al-Ḥasan ibn Ayyūb's apology for his conversion to Islam (*JS* II, p. 313–III, p. 4), which recently has been reedited and translated into Dutch by Floris Sepmeijer, ed. and trans., *Een Weerlegging van het Christendom uit de 10e Eeuw: De brief van al-Hasan b. Ayyub aan zijn broer ʿAli* (Kampen, The Netherlands: W. van den Berg, 1985).

5. Edward Pocock, *Contextio Gemmarum, sive, Eutychii Patriarchae Alexandrini Annales*, 2 vols. (Oxford: H. Robinson, 1658–59); Louis Cheikho, *Eutychii Patriarchae Alexandrini Annales*, *Corpus scriptorum christianorum orientalium* vols. 50–51 = ar. t. 6–7 (Beirut: E. Typografico Catholico, 1906–9) (hereafter cited as Cheikho). An annotated Italian translation of Cheikho's edition has recently appeared: Bartolomeo Pirone, *Eutichio, Patriarca di Alessandria (877–940): Gli Annali*, Studia Orientalia Monographiae, no. 1 (Cairo: Franciscan Centre of Christian Oriental Studies, 1987). Actually, the text of the *Annals* used by Ibn Taymiyya was somewhat superior to that preserved in Pocock's or Cheikho's editions, as may be seen by comparing the parallel passages in their editions and Ibn Taymiyya's *Jawāb* with the modern edition of the *Kitāb al-Burhān* (see note 11 below).

6. For the history of this text see Michel Breydy, *Études sur Saʿid ibn Batriq et ses sources*, CSCO vol. 450 = subs. t. 69 (Louvain: E. Peeters, 1983), pp. 29–87.

7. Now available in the edition and German translation of Michael Breydy, *Das Annalenwerk des Eutychios von Alexandrien: Ausgewählte Geschichten und Legenden kompiliert von Saʿid ibn Batriq um 935 A.D.*, CSCO vol. 471–72 = ar. 44–45 (Louvain: E. Peeters, 1985).

8. Notably an account of the Nestorian heresy; *JS* III, pp. 5–38 (cf. Cheikho, pp. 89–158).

9. *JS* III, pp. 38–39, 43–44, 46–48 (cf. Cheikho, pp. 159–61). Gérard Troupeau has made a French translation of these sections, with Ibn Taymiyya's refutation: "Ibn Taymiyya et sa réfutation d'Eutych," *Bulletin d'Études Orientales* 30 (1978): 209–20.

10. *JS* III, pp. 51–53, 84–85, 88, 103–7 (cf. Cheikho, pp. 161–67).

11. Pierre Cachia, ed., and W. Montgomery Watt, trans., *Eutychius of Alexandria: The Book of the Demonstration (Kitab al-Burhan)*, CSCO vols. 192, 209 = ar. t. 20, 22 (edition) and vols. 193, 210 = ar. t. 21, 23 (translation) (Louvain: Secrétariat du Corpus SCO, 1960–61) (hereafter Cachia I–II and Watt I–II, respectively).

12. It was Georg Graf's authority that held sway here. He first suggested the attribu-

tion of the work to Eutychius in "Ein bisher unbekanntes Werk des Patriarchen Eutychius von Alexandrien," *Oriens Christianus* n.s. 1 (1911): 227–44.

13. The attribution to Eutychius is decisively refuted by Breydy, *Études*, pp. 73–87. The attribution of the work to Peter of Bayt Rās is suggested by Samir Khalil, "La littérature melkite sous les premiers abbassides," *Orientalia Christiana Periodica* (Rome) 56 (1990): 483–85, and is discussed at length in my "Some Observations on the 'Pseudo-Eutychian' *Kitāb al-Burhān*," to be published.

14. On the following group of texts considered together as a set (or "trajectory") see Rachid Haddad, *Le trinité divine chez les théologiens arabes (750–1050)*, Beauchesne Religions 15 (Paris: Beauchesne, 1985), p. 65, or Sidney H. Griffith, "The Monks of Palestine and the Growth of Christian Literature in Arabic," *The Muslim World* 78 (1988): 20–28.

15. An edition and English translation were published by Margaret Dunlop Gibson, *An Arabic Version of the Acts of the Apostles and the Seven Catholic Epistles, from an Eighth or Ninth Century MS in the Convent of St. Catherine on Mount Sinai, with a Treatise 'On the Triune Nature of God,' Studia Sinaitica* no. 7 (London: C.J. Clay & Sons, 1899), pp. 2–36, 74–107. The (inaccurate) title of the apologetic treatise is supplied by Mrs. Gibson. Fr. Samir Khalil, who is preparing a new edition, has discovered a date (of sorts) on a page left unedited by Mrs. Gibson (f. 110v): 746 years since the establishment of Christianity. Assuming that the Incarnation is intended, and that the calendar being used is the Melkite Era of the Incarnation which begins on September 1, 9 B.C. (see Samir Khalil, "L'ère de l'Incarnation dans les manuscrits arabes melkites du 11e au 14e siècle," *OCP* 53 (1987): 193–201), a date of A.D. 738 results.

16. A thorough bibliography is given in Samir Khalil, "Thiyudurus Abū Qurra," *Majallat al-Majmaʿ al-ʿIlmī al-ʿArabī, al-Qism al-Suryānī* (Baghdad) 7 (1984): 138–60.

17. The most complete manuscript of this text is British Library or. 4950. Sidney Griffith's edition and English translation will soon be appearing in the CSCO.

18. A major study of content of the *Kitāb al-Burhān* is much needed. For now, see Georg Graf, *Die Philosophie und Gotteslehre des Jahjâ ibn ʿAdî und späterer Autoren: Skizzen nach meist ungedruckten Quellen* (Münster: Aschendorffschen Buchhandlung, 1910), pp. 56–62, and Avril Mary Makhlouf, "The Trinitarian Doctrine of Eutychius of Alexandria (877–940 A.D.)," *Parole de l'Orient* 5 (1974): 5–20.

19. Compare Cachia I, pars. 1–4, with *De Fide Orthodoxa* I, 3. The best edition of the Damascene's text is Bonifatius Kotter, ed., *Die Schriften des Johannes von Damaskos herausgegeben vom Byzantinischen Institut der Abtei Scheyern: II. Ekdosis akribēs tēs orthodoxou pistēo, Esposito Fidei*, Patristische Texte und Studien, vol. 12 (Berlin and New York: Walter de Gruyter, 1973) (hereafter cited as Kotter); and see the English translation by Frank H. Chase, Jr., *Saint John of Damascus: Writings*, vol. 37 of The Fathers of the Church: A New Translation (Washington, D.C.: Catholic University of America Press, 1958) (hereafter cited as Chase). Makhlouf ("Eutychius," pp. 5–9) notes that the whole of part 1 of the *Kitāb al-Burhān* shows affinities to the Damascene's great theological summary.

20. The *Quaestiones ad Antiochum ducem*, no. 137 (*Patrologia Graeca* 28:648–700). See G. Graf, "Zu dem bisher unbekannten Werk des Patriarchem Eutychios von Alexandrien," *Oriens Christianus* n.s. 2 (1912): 136–37.

21. Watt I: iii–iv.

22. Sidney Griffith has discussed this Melkite project in a number of essays. See, for example, "The Monks of Palestine," or "Greek into Arabic: Life and Letters in the Monasteries of Palestine in the Ninth Century; the Example of the *Summa Theologiae Arabica*," *Byzantion* 56 (1986): 117–38.

23. Ibn al-Nadim notes in his *Fihrist* that the Muʿtazilite ʿĪsā ibn Ṣabīḥ al-Murdār wrote a refutation of Theodore Abū Qurra (Bayard Dodge, *The Fihrist of al-Nadim, a Tenth-Century Survey of Muslim Culture*, 2 vols. [New York and London: Columbia University Press, 1970], 1: 394), but this text has not been preserved. This is by no means unusual. ʿAbd al-Majīd al-Sharfī has compiled a list of forty-three Muslim refutations of Christianity which were written before the end of the tenth century but have not come down to us. See his *al-Fikr al-Islāmī fī al-Radd ʿalā al-Naṣārā ilā Nihāyat al-Qarn al-Rābiʿ/al-ʿĀshir* (Tūnis: al-Dār al-Tūnisiiyya li-l-Nashr and Algiers: al-Muʾassasa al-Waṭaniyya li-l-Kītab, 1986), pp. 163–70.

24. Dodge, *The Fihrist of al-Nadim*, pp. 368–69.

25. Donald P. Little ("Did Ibn Taymiyya Have a Screw Loose?" *Studia Islamica* 41 [1975]: 101) cites a letter to Ibn Taymiyya from his friend al-Dhahabī: "I do not expect you to accept my words or hearken to my admonition; instead you will strive to produce volumes in refutation of this one page."

26. E.g., *JS* III, p. 82.

27. E.g., ibid., pp. 58–59.

28. In particular: God is *al-Ṣamad*, supremely independent of all things, which for their part are completely dependent upon him (ibid., p. 122/8). The Creator is entirely other than his creatures, and utterly exalted over them (ibid., p. 83/19–20). Certain knowledge of God comes from the apostles and prophets (ibid., p. 84/7–8), but sound reason will never oppose the authentic prophetic teaching (ibid., p. 69/15–19). It is strictly forbidden to say of God that of which one does not have certain knowledge (ibid., pp. 69–70).

29. A few examples might illustrate the dialectical richness of Ibn Taymiyya's text. He relentlessly exposes the infelicities of Peter's language, as, for example, when Peter denies "confusion"—*ikhtilāṭ* or *takhlīṭ* (= *sygkhysis*)—to the "mixture"—*khalṭa* or *mukhālaṭa* (= *mixis, epimixia*)—of divinity and humanity in Christ (ibid., 108). Occasionally he pauses to give a brief lesson in Arabic grammar (e.g., ibid., p. 69)! He pounces on unsupported assertions, such as Peter's assertion that the human spirit is *alṭaf min laṭīf al-khalāʾiq siwāhā* (ibid., p. 64), and contradictory statements, such as those of Peter about *iltihām*, on the one hand, and *iḥtijāb* on the other (see below). He poses dilemmas (exclusive disjunction or *taqsīm*), for example (*JS* III, pp. 65–67): "When (according to you) God united with Christ, did people see [God] or not?" He takes Peter's statements as premises for analogical deductions leading to absurd results (the *argumentum ad hominem* or *ilzām*), for example (ibid., p. 61): if the Creator was Mary's son, he was under her authority; isn't it more fitting that the Creator be Mary's husband, and have authority over her? Or he may allow Peter's premises only to draw good Islamic conclusions from them, as when he appropriates Peter's sun analogies (see below, notes 30–34).

The analysis of Ibn Taymiyya's dialectic would be greatly facilitated by an edition of his *Tanbīh al-Rajul al-Ghāfil ʿalā Tamwīh al-Jadal al-Bāṭil*; see George Makdisi, "The Tanbīh of Ibn Taimīya on Dialectic: The Pseudo-ʿAqilan Kitāb al-Farq," in Sami A. Hanna, ed., *Medieval and Middle Eastern Studies in Honor of Aziz Suryal Atiya* (Leiden: E.J. Brill, 1972), pp. 285–94. Much helpful material is to be found in Josef Van Ess, "The Logical Structure of Islamic Theology," in G.E. Von Grunebaum, ed., *Logic in Classical Islamic Culture: First Giorgio Levi Della Vida Biennial Conference* (Wiesbaden: Otto Harrassowitz, 1970), pp. 21–50; and Van Ess, *Die Erkentnisslehre des ʿAdudaddin al-Ici: Übersetzung und Kommentar des Ersten Buches seines Mawaqif*, Akademie der Wissenschaften und der Literatur: Veröffentlichungen der orientalischen Kommission, vol. 22 (Wiesbaden: Franz Steiner, 1966), pp. 381–97.

30. Cachia I, pars. 107–8.

31. This description is fundamental to the apologetic treatise in *Sinai ar.* 154 (see note 15 above).

32. Compare Cachia I, pars. 30–33, 35, with *De Fide Orthodoxa* I, 5–7, 8. This part of *De Fide Orthodoxa*, in its turn, is essentially copied from an anonymous Greek treatise of the mid-seventh century (*De Sacrosancta Trinitate, P.G.* 77:1119–74; see B. Fraigneau-Julien, "Un traité anonyme de la Sainte Trinité attribué à Saint Cyrille d' Alexandrie," *Recherches de Science Religieuse* 49 (1961): 188–211, 386–405), which in its turn is dependent at this point on Gregory of Nyssa, *Oratio Catechetica* 1–2 (P.G. 45:13–17; James Herbert Srawley, ed., *The Catechetical Oration of Gregory of Nyssa* (Cambridge: Cambridge University Press, 1956), pp. 6–15, and see p. xxxi).

33. Modern students of John of Damascus warn that his argument that God cannot be without a Word and a Spirit should not be taken as a "proof" in the strict sense of the word, but is rather a (not entirely convincing) apologetic attempt directed especially to those who do not accept the witness of scripture. See Jakob Bilz, *Die Trinitätslehre des heiligen Johannes von Damaskus*, Forschungen zur christlichen Literatur- und Dogmengeschichte, vol. 9, pt. 3 (Paderborn: Ferdinand Schöningh, 1909), pp. 31–38.

34. *Jamīʿ Wujūh al-Īmān*, chap. 14, *wajh* 1 (BL or. 4950, f. 76a). That Allah is the Trinity is also asserted later in the *Kitāb al-Burhān* itself (Cachia I, par. 170).

35. Some Qurʾanic verses cited in the eighth-century apologies preserved in *Sin. ar.* 154 (see note 15 above) and another eighth-century Melkite apology, *Sin. ar.* 434, ff. 171a–181b, are: *Al ʿUmran* (3):39, 45; S. 4:171; S. 16:102.

36. A century before the *Kitāb al-Burhān*, a monk writing to a Muslim sheikh had asked: "Why does one who has this in his Scripture ask about Christ and his [hypostatic] union?" (Sin. ar. 434, f. 176a: *Fa-man kān hādhā fī kitābihi, limā yasʾal ʿan al-Masīḥ wa ʾitiḥādihi?*) Similarly John of Damascus: "Since you say that Christ is Word and Spirit of God, how do you scold us as *Associators*?" (Daniel J. Sahas, *John of Damascus on Islam: The "Heresy of the Ishmaelites"* (Leiden: E.J. Brill, 1972), pp. 136–37).

37. *JS* III, pp. 53–54.

38. Ibid., pp. 54–55.

39. *bi-masarrat al-ʾab wa-muʾāzarat rūḥ al-qudus*: ibid., pp. 52/5–6, 53/14, 57–58.

40. Ibid., pp. 55–56.

41. Ibid., p. 57.

42. Cachia I, par. 109.

43. BL or. 4950, f. 117b/8–11.

44. This is an extreme version of a patristic idea: John of Damascus, following Gregory of Nazianzus, speaks of the nous as the intermediary between "the purity of God and the grossness of the flesh" (*De Fide Orthodoxa* III, 6 [Kotter, p. 121; Chase, p. 280]).

45. *JS* II, pp. 166–69.

46. *JS* III, pp. 65–67.

47. Which, according to the medicine of his day, meant that the Word was united with lifeless matter for four months. Ibid., p. 63/6–7.

48. This idea was new with Gregory of Nyssa, but it quickly became standard Orthodox teaching. See L.R. Wickham, "Soul and Body: Christ's Omnipresence," in Andreas Spira and Christoph Klock, eds., *The Easter Sermons of Gregory of Nyssa: Translation and Commentary*, Patristic Monograph Series, no. 9 (Philadelphia: Philadelphia Patristic Foundation, Ltd., 1981), p. 285.

49. *JS* III, pp. 64–65, 67–68.

50. Cachia I, pars. 110–11. A good introduction to this christology is found in John Meyendorff, *Christ in Eastern Christian Thought* (Crestwood, N.Y.: St. Vladimir's Seminary Press, 1975), esp. chap. 5, "God Suffered in the Flesh," pp. 69–89.

51. *sarat kalimat āllah bi-qiwāmiha qiwāman li-tilka al-nāsūt allatī kamala jawharuhā bi-taqwīm qiwām kalimat allāh iyyāhā*, Cachia I, par. 109 (p. 69/12–13).

52. The Jacobite apologist Abū Rā'iṭa had used *qiwām* in christological contexts before, but as the equivalent of *hyparxis*. See the comments of Rachid Haddad, *Trinité*, pp. 177–78, and Sidney H. Griffith, "Habib ibn Ḥidmah Abū Rā'iṭa, a Christian *mutakallim* of the First Abbasid Century," *Oriens Christianus* 64 (1980):185.

53. We also find the forms *muqawwim*, *muqawwam*, and *taqwīm*.

54. I find this asserted eleven times in the passage cited from the *Kitāb al-Burhān*; see Cachia I, pars. 110, 111, and 123, and *JS* III, pp. 52/18–53/4, 107/16–23. Unfortunately, three of these instances are garbled in the text as cited by Ibn Taymiyya. See next note.

55. The addition of a *lam* to one of Peter's sentences contributed to the misunderstanding: "[Christ], by the unity of that one hypostasis, the hypostasis of the creative Word of God," [is one with the Trinity and one with humanity] was construed as "[Christ], by the unity of that one hypostasis [becomes] a hypostasis *for* the creative Word of God": *fa-huwa bi-tawḥīd dhālika al-qiwām al-wāḥid qiwām li-kalimat allāh al-khāliqa*; ibid., pp. 52/23–53/1 = 68/22–23, 70/20–23.

56. Ibid., pp. 68–84, English translation in Michel, pp. 312–23.

57. Cachia I, par. 112.

58. *lam yazal allāh yaḍrib li-ʿibādihi al-amthal fī jamīʿ kutubihi*, Cachia I, p. 71/1. Cf. S. 2:26, S. 30:58, S. 39:27, etc.

59. See Ibn Taymiyya, "Sharḥ al-ʿaqīda al-Iṣfahāniyya," *Majmūʿat fatāwā Shaykh al-Īslam Taqī al-Dīn Ibn Taymiyya al-Ḥarrānī*, vol. 5 (Cairo: Maṭbaʿat Kurdistān al-ʿIlmiyya, 1329 A.H.), pp. 43, 74–75; and al-Suyūṭī's abridgement of Ibn Taymiyya's *al-Radd ʿalā manṭiq al-Yūnān*, in ʿAlī Sāmī al-Nashshār, ed., *Ṣawn al-Manṭiq wa l-Kalām ʿan Fann al-Manṭiq wa al-Kalām* (Cairo: Maktabat al-Khānjī, 1947), pp. 252, 255. Note that the *qiyās*

shumūlī (Aristotelian syllogism) and the *qiyās tamthīlī* (the *qiyās* of the jurists) may not be applied to God because either would equate God and some created thing.

60. *JS* III, pp. 84–87.

61. Ibid., p. 87 (where Ibn Taymiyya cites the Qur'anic *mathal* in S. 24:35); and similarly, pp. 116–17.

62. Cachia I, pars. 113–23.

63. Ibid., pars. 116, 119.

64. Ibid., pars. 117, 120.

65. Ibid., par. 121.

66. Ibid., pars. 122–23. These analogies, of course, were much used during the christological disputes of the fifth and sixth centuries.

67. Ibid., par. 115. The original use of this analogy may have been to respond to the questioner scandalized by the thought of the Word of God dwelling in a woman's womb, as in the *Jāmiʿ Wujūh al-Īmān*, chap. 18, question 6 (BL or. 4950, ff. 119v–120r).

68. Cachia I, pars. 113–16. Note especially par. 115, p. 72/2.

69. *JS* III, pp. 108–22.

70. Ibid., pp. 108–11.

71. Ibid., pp. 111–12.

72. For whom the analogy of the union of soul and body in a single human being was especially beloved, since the resulting human being has a single human nature.

73. See, for example, John of Damascus, *Contra Jacobitas*, P.G. 94, col. 1465bc; Theodore Abū Qurra, "Letter to David the Jacobite," in Qusṭanṭīn Bāshā, *Mayāmir Thawūdurus Abī Qurra Usquf Ḥarrān* (Tripoli, Lebanon: n.p., 1904), pp. 104–17

74. *JS* III, pp. 113–15.

75. *ma dhakarahu min al-amthāl wa al-shawāhid, fa-hiya ḥujja ʿalayhi*, ibid., p. 108/14.

76. Eerdmann Fritsch, speaking of Arabic Christian attempts to present the doctrine of the Trinity, once observed: "je mehr man das Dogma aus apologetischer Absichten abschwachte, umso größer wurde die Verwirrung der Begriffe und umso leichter die Widerlegung" (*Islam und Christentum im Mittelalter: Beiträge zur Geschichte der muslimischen Polemik gegen das Christentum in arabischer Sprache*, Breslauer Studien zur historischen Theologie, vol. 17 [Breslau: Verlag Müller & Seiffert, 1930], p. 109).

77. See, for example, *JS* III, pp. 110/6–8, 114/1–2.

78. See, for example, *JS* III, pp. 73–84, 118–21. For background, see Michel, pp. 5–14; or Muhammad Umar Memon, *Ibn Taimiya's Struggle Against Popular Religion*, Religion and Society 1 (The Hague and Paris: Mouton, 1976), pp. 26–46.

Contacts and Comparisons

7

"Holosphyros"? A Byzantine Perception of "The God of Muhammad"

Daniel J. Sahas

Among the works of Nicetas Choniates (ca. 1155–ca.1215/6), or "Acominatos,"[1] the twelfth-century historian, imperial secretary, and public official in the time during the Comneni and Angeli dynasties, and appended to the XXth Book of his *Thesaurus Orthodoxiae*,[2] there is a text attributed to him entitled *Nicetae. Ordo qui observatur super iis qui a Saracenis ad nostram Christianorum puram veramque fidem se convertun* (By Nicetas. Order followed on those who return from the faith of the Saracens to the pure and true faith of us Christians).[3] In fact, this is not the complete liturgical order of conversion but the text containing only the *apotaxis*, that is, the statement of renunciation of (lit. "siding aside from") Islam, as well as the *syntaxis*, the statement of affirmation of (lit. "siding with") the Christian faith recited by a Muslim in front of the baptistry when admitted to the Church as a catechumen.[4] Baptism follows at a later time.[5] That this text, therefore, has been termed by Western scholarship as "Formula of abjuration," is not entirely accurate. More accurately, it is a public statement of renunciation of one's previous faith, with an affirmation of one's new faith; and this only as part of a lengthier process of an elaborate ritual of conversion.

The last of the anathemas and the conclusion of the *apotaxis* part reads as follows:

> And on top of all these, I anathematize the god of Muhammad, about whom he [Muhammad] says that "This is one God, *holosphyros* [made of solid metal beaten to a spherical shape] who neither begat nor was begotten, and no-one has been made like him." Thus, by anathematizing everything that I have stated, even Muhammad himself and his *sphyrelaton* [beaten solid] god, and by renouncing them, I am siding with Christ, the only true God; and I believe . . .[6]

With this anathema Islam, as a faith in God, is summarily renounced.

Orders of conversion of Jews and Manicheans to the Church with formulas of abjuration such as this can be traced back to pre-Islamic times.[7] The particular *Ordo* of conversion from Islam to Christianity must be dated from before the time of Nicetas Choniates, or the year 1180 when Emperor Manuel I Comnenos (1143–1180) ordered the deletion of this anathema. Montet,[8] in summarizing other suggestions, has rightly observed that the fact that the *syntaxis* mentions veneration of icons as part of Orthodox faith and practice allows us to assume that such a declaration dates from at least the year 843, when the veneration of the icons became a fully celebrated doctrine of the Church, if not even from earlier, when the II Council of Nicea (787) condemned iconoclasm and defined the theology of the icons. Sylburg dates the text earlier than 1152 and Cumont cites reasons why its date may be even much earlier.[9]

On the basis of internal evidence, namely that the list of Muhammad's successors renounced in this *Ordo* stops at the name of the Umayyad caliph Yazīd I (680–683, a possible *terminus post quem*), as well as that parts of the text are verbatim reproductions from John of Damascus' (ca.655–ca. 749) treatise on Islam, Cumont has concluded that this particular declaration was composed as early as the second part of the seventh century, after the Arab domination of Syria.[10] However, one needs to be mindful of the fact that the expression *holosphyros* appears nowhere in the writings of John of Damascus and that a formal, uniform, and widely used text of ritual abjuration presupposes frequent and widespread conversions from Islam to the Byzantine Church; something that did not begin happening before the end of the ninth and especially during the tenth century, after the Byzantines had scored some significant military victories and had reclaimed some of the former Byzantine lands and populations from the Arabs.[11]

Somewhere else, therefore, and in a different age, the source and the origin of the *holosphyros*, especially in its polemic and derogatory meaning, must be sought. When in 1180 emperor Manuel I Comnenos ordered its deletion from the catechetical books of the Church, the anathema had already become entrenched into the *Ordo* via the Byzantine polemic literature. No wonder, therefore, that his proposal was met with vehement opposition. Two interrelated matters are raised here: (1) What was the meaning of *holosphyros*, and how did this perception develop in the mind of the Byzantine controversialists; and (2) what were the motives and the implications of the twelfth-century controversy over the deletion from or the retention of the *holosphyros* in the *Ordo*?

Holosphyros in the Byzantine Polemics

The adjective *holosphyros* appears in a number of variations and synonyms in the Byzantine anti-Islamic literature, such as *holosphairos* (all spherical); *sphyropectos*, *sphyrelactos*, or *sphyrelatos* (wrought with the hammer), and *holobolos* (beaten to a solid ball). One can also find the adjective *prosphyros* as a synonym for *holosphyros*. Clearly, the word "holosphyros" and its synonyms represent an attempt at rendering in Greek and in a monolectic way the exact meaning of the Arabic word *ṣamad* in S. 112:2. This becomes evident in the Greek apologetic writings of the Greek- and Arabic-speaking Melkite bishop of Ḥarrān, Abū Qurra (ca. 750–ca. 820). He rendered the sūrat *al-Tawḥīd* this way:

> God is single, God is *sphyropectos* [beaten solid to a ball], who has neither given birth nor was he born, and no-one has been his counterpart.[12]

In retrospect it becomes obvious that later Byzantine controversialists, utilizing Abū Qurra's translation of *al-Tawḥīd*, focused on the figurative expression of *sphyropectos* or *holosphyros*. They used it literally and in a polemical manner, giving it the meaning of a lifeless *thing* that gives no birth and is not begotten! However, this was not Abū Qurra's intention. To him it is the theology of the *al-Tawḥīd, as a whole*, that is objectionable and at variance with the Christian theology. In prefacing his translation, Abū Qurra contrasts the teaching of Muhammad and the Christian belief in a God of three hypostases (*trisypóstaton*) with the following words:

> The deranged pseudoprophet of the Hagarenes, Muhammad, under the influence of the devil, used to say that "God has sent me to shed the blood of those who say that divinity is by nature of three hypostases, and of those who do not say God is single.

It is only after this preface that he continues with the translation of *al-Tawḥīd*.[13]

Prior to Abū Qurra, John of Damascus had avoided the temptation to translate the *al-Tawḥīd*, thus bypassing the linguistic hurdle of the loaded word *ṣamad*. Instead, in chapter 100/1 of the *De Haeresibus*, he summarized faithfully the essential teaching of Islamic monotheism and of Sūra 112 with the following words: "He [Muhammad] says that there is one God, *creator of all*, who is neither begotten, nor has he given birth."[14] Not only did he not misrepresent the Muslim theology but, perhaps intentionally, he avoided tampering with the Qur'anic idiom of *ṣamad* for fear of causing confusion and misunderstanding, as the subsequent history eloquently proved.

Bartholomeos of Edessa (ninth century), who dealt primarily with matters of practice ethics and popular traditions rather than with theological matters, in his *Contra Mahomet*[15] states the *al-Tawḥīd* in a way that combines the renderings of John of Damascus and the wording of Abū Qurra:

> He [Muhammad] says about God that, this is God, who created all things, and no-one has been like him, but he is God *holosphyros* who has neither given birth nor has he been born, but he is one God; and everyone who divides him, or makes one like him, will have no salvation but an unbearable and eternal hell.[16]

In his *Elenchus et Confutatio Agareni*[17] Bartholomeos states also that God in the Qur'an is referred to as *Allāh*, *Ṣamad*,[18] *Jamet*,[19] "[corruption of the Arabic *Jāmid*] which mean, obviously, [that he is] *holosphyros* and *holobolos*, that he can be held, and that he has a shape."[20] This is the first instance in which the word *holosphyros* is explained as a material thing that has shape and can be handled. One may discern, however, Bartholomeos' reluctance to make this explanation a definitive statement, or to capitalize on such an interpretation. Perhaps he knew enough Arabic to remain polemical, without consciously distorting the meaning of *ṣamad*. By stating also the other two names of God, Allāh and Jamet (especially the latter), he seemed to recognize that such names could not possibly be synonymous with *ṣamad*, with the meaning of a material substance.

The one who made *ṣamad* an object of misinterpretation is Nicetas of Byzantium (842–912), the "Philosopher," one of the most extreme Byzantine polemicists of Islam.[21] In his Refutation of the Qur'an, chapter 18,[22] he writes this about the *al-Tawḥīd*:

> The one hundred and eleventh[23] petty myth reads as follows: "Say, He is God one, God *holosphyros*. He has neither given birth, nor has he been begotten and no one is like him." If *holosphyros* does not mean the shape of a sphere, it does mean density and compression which are characteristics of solid.[24]

Nicetas of Byzantium seems to be the first controversialist who interpreted the adjective *holosphyros* in such a way as to depict Allāh as a depersonalized, material God, and Islam as a gross idolatry. In a longer statement he explains further:

> The author of this laughable writing who was in no happy position to even make an orderly statement on either one of the two [subjects, i.e., theology and natural sciences], except only to stammer in some way, wandered about. Regarding God he uttered this godless statement, that God is something spherical or rather, as he said, "God is holosphyros," thinking of him as something solid; otherwise he could not have a spherical shape. Being then, according to him, *a material sphere*, he [God] can neither be heard nor seen, mentally; which means that he is unable to act, unless someone else moves him, and he is even carried mindlessly with the face downwards.[25]

Nicetas is convinced that Muhammad believed in and spoke of a God who is a material object with which there can be no meaningful relationship; an object which in itself is incapable of acting, unless someone else moves it! Such a pathetic perception of God would, of course, set Christianity and Islam completely apart from and in collision with each other. One has the feeling that, in the narrowness of Nicetas, Byzantine Christianity took its revenge for the Qur'ānic and populist distortion of the Christian doctrine of the Trinity.[26]

Nicetas took particular exception to this issue, so much so that, in the nineteenth chapter of his *Refutation of the Qur'ān*, devoted to it a whole chapter entitled, "Towards those who say that God is *holosphyros*; he begat not nor was he begotten."[27] In this chapter Nicetas contrasts the Muslim theology to the Christian belief in God who in every respect—essence, power, will, eternity, and activity—is infinitely superior to all things, and who for this reason can bring everything into being *ex nihilo*. Nicetas never suspected that Islamic theology was teaching precisely the same thing. He distinguishes three kinds of material substances: solid (corporeal), nonsolid (incorporeal), and that which is made of the two. The characteristics of a corporeal substance are being three-dimensional, density, and consistency.[28] The characteristics of an incorporeal substance are being found everywhere, not being above everything even though it is incorporeal, and being circumscribable and a thing nevertheless. But what one would say about the essence or the substance of the creator? Only that he is *beyond* substance or essence (*hyperousion*). Density, consistency, and the triple dimensional characteristic are not, therefore, applicable to him. Thus, according to Nicetas, Muhammad has failed in his perception of God as *holosphyros*, even if one wants to consider the emptiness (meaning the incarnation) of the Son and Word of God in the biblical sense.[29] Because, according to Nicetas, the emptiness of the Word of God and his incarnation have to do with a power, movement, and energy which is *beyond* movement, *beyond* power, and *beyond* energy.[30] He calls, then, upon Muhammad not to shy away when he hears that the consubstantial and coeternal Word of the Father is the creator and restorer of all creation; for he is *beyond* substance. The incarnate Word of the Father is of the kind that is *beyond* substance, and *in a manner* that is beyond substance—that is, "divine."[31]

> Let no-one, therefore, say that if He was not born he gave no birth, either. Because we see that as he was not born, he was not created either. These two are necessary qualities of him who is without beginning. But we see that even though he were not created, yet he created . . . It would have been, therefore, better if he [Muhammad] had said that, because He himself was not born, He gave birth, in the same way as because He himself was not created, He created.[32]

Thus, rather than as an essential attribute, Nicetas explains the Islamic notion of *ṣamad* as a derivative of God's not giving birth and of not being begotten; which implies that, according to Nicetas, God's being a creator is denied in Islam—even his Being as such!

John of Damascus never followed this line of logic to deny the Muslims a belief in God as creator. He had stated, however, that to cut off the Word and the Spirit from the essence of God is tantamount, from the point of view of Christian theology, to making God a being who is "senseless and lifeless . . . like a stone, a piece of wood or any of the inanimate objects."[33]

The example of Nicetas of Byzantium was followed by Euthymios Zegabenos (11th–12th c.), contemporary to Emperor Alexios I Comnenos (1081–1118)[34] who commissioned him to write the *Panoplia Dogmatica* against the Bogomils for the council of Constantinople in 1110–1111. For his chapter 28, Zegabenos used the writings of Bartholomeos of Edessa, *Elenchus Agareni* and *Contra Mahomet.* He wrought an almost verbatim amalgamation of the statements made by Nicetas with a further elaboration of his own to say:

> He [Muhammad] calls God *holosphryos*, that is spherical. Shape implies and it is a characteristic of something solid,[35] dense and compressed.[36] As a material sphere, according to him, God cannot be heard or seen and, as it happens, he is brought forth with the face down[37] and rolls down in a disorderly manner.[38]

Euthymios Zegabenos amplified further Nicetas' perception of the *holosphyros* as a spherical God made of matter. If Nicetas perceived and treated *ṣamad* literally and explained it as a material spherical ball, Zegabenos added some jest to the image and made it roll downhill erratically. It was at this juncture that the deletion of the anathema against "the God of Muhammad" was proposed by Emperor Manuel I Comnenos; a proposal that started a controversy in 1180 between the Byzantine Church and the state, with little influence on the subsequent Byzantine anti-Islamic literature.[39]

The *Holosphyros* Controversy

Emperor Manuel I Comnenos proposed that the "anathema to the God of Muhammad" be deleted from the master *Catechesis* of the cathedral of Saint Sophia and from all catechetical books.[40] He reasoned that it was scandalous that Muslims "be made to blaspheme God in any manner"[41] when converting to Christianity. What exactly ensued from this proposal represents two different perceptions of Islam based on different understandings, or rather lack of understanding, of *holosphyros*; a misunderstanding that developed into a major clash between the Byzantine Church and state in 1180.[42]

Nicetas narrates that the emperor presented his proposal to Patriarch Theodosios[43] and to the bishops who were members of the patriarchal synod with "massive introductory arguments."[44] In an unflattering way, Nicetas remarks that Manuel did not understand the meaning of *holosphyros* and that his *tomos* or thesis on the subject was done with the help of "flatterers and learned men"[45] (implying, of no ecclesiastical education) of the imperial court. The *tomos*, according to Nicetas, defended the "silly tale (I would not call it theology) of Muhammad," assailing openly the previous emperors and hierarchs of the Church as "ignorant and thoughtless men, for having allowed the true God to be anathematized."[46] The bishops objected to the imperial proposal vehemently, arguing that the anathema was not directed against God, the maker of heaven and earth, but against

> the *holosphyros* god who is neither begotten nor did he beget, fabricated by the jocular and demoniacal Muhammad; for God is believed by Christians to be Father, and this [faith] prohibits completely such absurd and frivolous words of Muhammad.[47]

Apparently this *tomos* had little effect on the hierarchy, because Manuel had to issue a second and more extensive one in which he used rhetoric (something which Nicetas calls "bait")[48] to make his argument sound more dogmatic. It is regrettable that we do not possess the text of these imperial statements to be able to read Manuel's rationale against the anathema and his own understanding of the *holosphyros*.[49] One can only surmise the content and style of the *tomos* from Nicetas' story, which is less than objective. However, Nicetas admits that in the second *tomos*,

> so plausible did reason make the word appear . . . that it was very convincing, by virtue of the diverse scope of the issue, the attractiveness of its elaborate argument, and in the careful examination of the meaning of its contents;[50]

so much so, that "almost the *holosphyros* God about whom Muhammad spoke so foolishly would have been glorified as the true God had not the patriarch resisted strenuously."[51] The emperor invited the bishops to consider the issue again. The patriarch and the bishops sailed to the palace of Scoutarion in Damalis, where the ailing emperor had gone to benefit from its mild climate. The church delegation was received by the influential subsecretary Theodore Mantzoukis who, announcing to the bishops that the health of the emperor would not allow him to see them personally, handed to them the imperial "documents." One of the documents dealt with the doctrinal matter, which required their signature. The other, according to Nicetas, was a belligerent letter. In this Manuel was accusing Theodosios and the bishops of being intransigent, informing them that if they did not sign the *tomos* he would call a major council to which he intended to invite the Pope. "For I would be ungrateful and irrational," the Emperor said in this document,

> if I would not return to God, my king and the king of all, a minute fraction of the good things I have received from him, by making every effort so that He, being a true God, may not be subjected to anathema.[52]

The deletion of this anathema was for Manuel an ideological matter and a matter of common sense and personal integrity.

Such a threat, coming after the 1054 schism, frightened no one. Its impact may have had the opposite effect, if any, as it hardened further the traditionalist and anti-Latin elements in the hierarchy. Eustathios of Thessalonike, "filled with indignation by what was read and not bearing to hear that the true God is believed to be *something holosphyr*, a fabrication of a demoniacal mind,"[53] stood up and made this extraordinary and passionate declaration:

> I would have my brains in my feet and (showing the [episcopal] mantle on his shoulders) I would be wholly unworthy of this office were I to regard as true God the paederast, the camel-like master and the teacher of every abominable act.[54]

It is obvious that Eustathios contradicted himself and had missed the point of the debate completely. On the one hand the God of Islam is, to him, a material object, a "something" rather than an absolute unity, simplicity, and uncompounded entity; on the other hand, Muhammad is made to be God! It seems that Eustathios' contention was with Muhammad himself rather than with Muslim theology. From then on nothing else mattered. The issue of *holosphyros* was only coincidental. His outburst made a profound impression upon the other bishops who "were struck dumb by what they had heard."[55] This is an interesting insight into the dynamics of the *holosphyros* debate. The bishops of the Church had a remote sense and an outrageous view of Islam, which rendered any substantive discussion of the *holosphyros* issue irrelevant.

The whole story is actually one of a clash between two polarities within the twelfth-century Byzantine society, represented by Eustathios on the one hand and Emperor Manuel on the other, or by Mantzoukis himself, if one wants to read literally the wording "ho tou grámmatos hypagoreutés" (he who dictated, or composed, the writing), which Nicetas uses for Theodore Mantzoukis.[56] Dumbfounded by Eustathios' reaction, Mantzoukis returned to the Emperor who

> perturbed by the report of what had been said, gave an artful defense of his position, commending forbearance as never before. He counted himself among the most orthodox of Christians and asserted that he came from most holy parents, while shunning the censorious and the scoffers. He urgently appealed that a judgement be made between him and the archbishop of Thessalonike, for he said that if he should be absolved of believing in a god who is a paederast and of distorting the faith, then a just punishment should be imposed upon him who belched out blasphemies against the annointed of the Lord. However, should he be condemned as glorifying another god than Him whom Christians worship, then he would learn the truth and be deeply grateful to the one who should convert him from error and initiate him into the truth.[57]

In actuality, the emperor was calling for a public showdown between himself and Eustathios. Only the intervention of the moderate Patriarch Theodosios, who charmed the emperor with his reasonableness, deflected a punishment for Eustathios. Manuel pardoned Eustathios and accepted "the reasons he chose to give for his defense," but not without adding to him words of reprimand: "Being a wise man you should not show yourself to be foul-mouthed or inordinately overbold of tongue."[58]

The *tomos* was read, praised by everyone as "reverently orthodox," and the assembly adjourned itself agreeing to sign it. Both parties claimed victory; the bishops for having won over the objections of the emperor, and the emperor for having achieved "with a few words" what the previous *tomos* had not succeeded in doing. One may surmise that these "few words" were not the words of the second *tomos*, which was more extensive, rhetorical, and dogmatic than the first, but rather the direct challenge the emperor had posed to the bishops; to prove, that is, that accepting the "god of Muhammad" makes one, indeed, a non-Christian.

When the synod gathered on the next day in the patriarchal house to take action on what had been agreed the day before, the bishops were not the same men. They demanded further deletions and changes in the *tomos* before signing it. The emperor accused them of "inconstancy, fickleness and lack of intelligence."[59] A tenuous agreement was finally reached, by which the anathema against "the god of Muhammad" was to be deleted and replaced instead by an anathema against "Muhammad and all his teaching."

At this point Nicetas injects the story of the bishop of his hometown of Chonae, his own godfather, also named Nicetas. The bishop had foretold that Manuel would reign and live longer than his grandfather Alexios but that toward the end of his life he would go mad.[60] In the historian's own words, while different theories had been advanced as to the possible signs of the emperor's madness,

> when the controversy over the above-mentioned doctrine was initiated and the emperor recklessly contended the first time that the god glorified by Muhammad as *holosphyros*, who is neither begotten nor begets, is the true God, everyone agreed that this was the fulfilment of the prophecy because this doctrine, being wholly the opposite of the truth, was truly and absolutely the worst kind of madness.[61]

According to Nicetas, the time when the doctrinal controversy began, the illness of the emperor prior to March, and his death in September 1180, all coincide to uphold this prophesy. Behind this narrative one has to read Nicetas' own objection to the deletion of the anathema. The *Ordo*, which is attributed to him, contains the anathema intact. Nicetas, as a frontier man, had not many reasons to be particularly understanding and fond either of the Muslims[62] or, as a staunch anti-Latin and a pious person, of the conduct of pro-Western Manuel. He had set high moral standards for himself and demanded the same from others, including emperors, especially on matters of sexual conduct. He had his own reasons, therefore, to be intransingent toward the Muslims and unsympathetic toward the emperor: Manuel's overtures toward the Muslims were as contemptible to Nicetas as the emperor's earlier love affair with his own brother's daughter, Theodora.

Of Emperor Manuel I Comnenos, the key player in the *holosphyros* controversy, we only need mention here that, unlike his father,[63] he was an admirer of the West and a great spender on entertainment. He had married twice, both times to Western princesses—Bertha of Sulzbach, renamed Irene, sister-in-law of Conrad III, king of Germany, and Mary, a French lady of rare beauty, daughter of the prince of Antioch.[64] At the same time, Manuel had been a devoted supporter of monasticism (in its right place) with a passion for theological discussions,[65] and a man with a strong hand on matters of the Church.[66] In 1170 and 1171 he had initiated dialogues of union with the Armenian patriarch Nerses IV, with whom he had exchanged letters through a personal envoy, the philosopher Theorianus. While he was attempting union with the Armenians, Manuel was making similar gestures toward the Monophysites and the Jacobites of Syria. He had even attempted to bring the Orthodox and the Latin churches together. In 1170 representatives of Pope Calixtus II (1168–1178) sat in synod with Patriarch Michael III (1170–77) and the Constantinopolitan bishops. But the two sides differed so much from each other that this synod came to an early end.[67] Although conciliatory, Manuel was stern against heresy. For example, he did not hesitate to condemn the bishop Demetrius of Lampses, Crete, his personal envoy to the West who, in his effort to challenge the Latin doctrine of the *filioque*, advocated the Origenistic doctrine of subordination of the Son to the Father, teaching that John 14:28 ("the Father is greater than I") refers to the divine nature. Manuel dealt with this doctrinal matter swiftly. He convened a synod in Constantinople (1166) and asked that all biblical references to the Father be collected and discussed in synod. This synod condemned Demetrius[68] and had its decree engraved on a plaque and placed in the church of Saint Sophia. Manuel took also severe measures against the opponents of this synod. All these may point to the political and the theological acumen of Manuel but they do not explain his motives in having the particular anathema "to the God of Muhammad" deleted from the *Ordo*.

Byzantine emperors showed particular interest in expanding Christianity, especially among non-Christian prisoners of war.[69] Manuel seems to have been one of the most prominent emperors in this respect. His enthusiastic interest in promoting Christianity has been the point that historians of his reign and orators have noticed the most. In fact, most of the surviving orations (*Engomiastikoi Logoi*) written in honor of Byzantine emperors are for this particular emperor.[70] Manuel is praised by Euthymios Malakes as "another Abraham," who multiplied his nation "by giving birth to children through wars."[71] It is not unreasonable to assume that the characteristic reference to Abraham can be taken as pointing to the conversion of Muslims, known to the Byzantines for their claim as descendants of Abraham and perpetrators of *dīn Ibrāhīm*. At this precise point Malakes justifies his praise of Manuel with Jesus' dialogue with the Jews: "They answered to him, 'Abraham is our father.' Jesus said to them, 'If you were Abraham's children, you would do what Abraham did.' "[72] This dictum must have served as Manuel's incentive for seeking to convert Muslims to Christianity. Even Eustathios Katafloros, the bishop of Thessalonike, who opposed Manuel vehemently on the "anathema to the God of Muhammad," praises the emperor for "bringing to God those who are in an alien religion," for "leading to the knowledge of God those who live apart," and for "filling [with them] God's court of sheep."[73]

The desire to expand the influence of Christian Byzantium, coupled with an intense interest in matters of the Church, personal piety, and religious conviction,[74] led Manuel I Comnenos to tackle the absurdity of the anathema against "the God of Muhammad" and the distorted meaning of the *holosphyros*, openly and courageously, in spite of the entrenchment of these notions in the Byzantine mentality and in its anti-Islamic literature, and thus to facilitate conversion for Muslims. The latest flare up of the *filioque* and the trinitarian controversy with the Latin West not only did not contribute to any better understanding of Islam, but made the hierarchy of the Byzantine East even more intransigent and introverted. However, Manuel I Comnenos' openness and his desire for dialogue, union, and conversion, even as a political expediency, allowed him to take a creative posture toward Islam and the Muslims; a very different one from that of his contemporary Byzantine hierarchy—definitely a radically different one from that of the crusading West.

NOTES

1. Born in Chonae (Konia, Konya or Khonia) near the biblical city of Collosae in Phrygia, he is surnamed "Choniates." For his other surname "Acominatos," see *O City of Byzantium, Annals of Niketas Choniates*, trans. Harry J. Magoulias (Detroit: Wayne State University Press, 1984), p. 367, n. 2. On Nicetas' life, see Magoulias' introduction, pp. ix–xxviii. At the age of nine (ca. 1164) Nicetas was sent to Constantinople where, under the guardianship of his brother Michael, later the archbishop of Athens (1182–1204), he studied under Eustathius, later the archbishop of Thessalonike. One may want to keep in mind this relationship between Nicetas and Eustathius in order to appreciate Nicetas' siding with his spiritual master rather than with his imperial one in the *holosphyros* controversy. Before 1180, the date of death of Emperor Manuel I Comnenos (1143–1180), Nicetas served as imperial secretary. Later, and during the reign of Angeli (1185–1204), he ascended to the highest ranks of political life to become in the end destitute and a refugee during the Fourth Crusade (1204). His *Historia* in twenty-one books, a monumental work covering the period 1118–1207, is the most significant source of information on the reign of Manuel I, and on the controversy over the *holosphyros*. Critical

edition of Nicetas' history, *Nicetae Choniatae. Historia.* Recensuit Ioannes Aloysius van Dieten, Corpus Fontium Historiae Byzantinae, vol. 2, pt. 1 (Berlin: Walter de Gruyter, 1975); hereafter cited as Nicetas' *Historia.* Translation by Magoulias, as stated above. The references are to von Dietem's edition and to Magoulias' translation, whenever this translation has been used.

2. PG 140:105A–121C.

3. PG 140:124A–136C. Subsequently referred to as *Ordo.* The text of the *Ordo* in the *Patrologia Graeca* is the one published by F. Sylburg in 1595, *Saracenica sive Moamethica opera Friderici Sylburgii*, vet. ope. bibliothecae palatinae (Heidelberg, 1595), pp. 74–91.

4. Montet has published a critical edition of the part of the *Ordo* which contains the twenty anathemas against Islam, i.e., the *apotaxis*, from three mss (*Palatinus* 233 (P) 14th c.; *Vindobonensis* 306 (V) 14th c.; *Bruxellensis* (B) dated March 1st 1281), collated by Franz Cumont, which also contain similar formulas of abjuration of Judaism and Manichaeanism. Ed. Montet, "Un rituel d'abjuration des musulmans dans l'église grecque," *Revue de l'Histoire des Religions* 53 (1906): 145–63, at 145; text, pp. 148–55.

5. Cf. Daniel J. Sahas "Liturgical Orders of Conversion from Islam to the Byzantine Church" (15th Annual Byzantine Studies Conference, Amherst, Mass., 1989; unpublished).

6. PG 140:134A.

7. Cf. Franz Cumont "L'origine de la formule grecque d'abjuration imposée aux musulmans," *Revue de l'Histoire des Religions*, 64 (1911): 143–50, at 143. The format of a positive statement of faith and a list of renunciations can be observed even in the original Nicene-Constantinopolitan Creed, where after the statement of faith several anathemas were appended denouncing the teachings of Arius and Nestorius against whom the creed was formulated ("and those who say that there was a time when he [Christ] was not, are anathematized by the catholic Church"). One hardly needs to be reminded of the earliest use of creeds in the context of baptism, and of the fact that the early creeds of the Church are compilations of *baptismal* statements. The Orthodox ritual of baptism contains, until today, the rite of exorcisms and the recital of the Nicene Creed which precedes the sacrament of baptism. In Islam also the various creeds consist of positive statements of faith and renunciations of heretical beliefs or statements. Cf. the Fiḳh Akbar I, and the Waṣîyat of Abû Ḥanîfa in A.J. Wensinck, *The Muslim Creed: Its Genesis and Historical Development* (London: Frank Cass & Co., 1965). The ʿAbbāsids also introduced a ritual cursing the Umayyads, with the name of Muʿāwiya first on the list!

8. Montet, "Un rituel," pp. 146–47.

9. Franz Cumont, "Une formule grecque de renonciation au Judaism," *Bormannheft der Wiener Studien* (24, no. 2), 233–34; cf. Montet "Un rituel," p. 146, n. 1. Formulas of abjuration of Judaism and Manichaeanism (and, therefore, possibly of Islam as well) seem to go back to the end of the ninth century, and during the Patriarchate of Photius (858, 867, 877–886). Cf. Brinkmann, *Die Theosophie des Aristokritos* (Rhein., Germany, Mus. LI, 1896), p. 273; and Franz Cumont, "La conversion des Juifs byzantins au IXe siècle" *Revue de l'instruction publique en Belgique*, 46 (1903): 8–15.

10. Cumont, "L' origine," pp. 144–49. The writing of John of Damascus referred to here is chapter 100/1 of his book *De Haeresibus*, ed. Bonifatius Kotter, *Die Schriften des Johannes von Damaskos*, vol. 4, *Liber de haeresibus: Opera polemica* (Berlin: Walter de

Gruyter, 1981), pp. 60–67. On John of Damascus and an analysis of this text, see Daniel J. Sahas, *John of Damascus on Islam: The "Heresy of the Ishmaelites"* (Leiden: E. J. Brill, 1972), pp. 51–95.

11. I have discussed these matters in a paper entitled "The Tenth Century in the Byzantine Muslim Relations" presented at the 23d Annual Meeting of the Middle East Studies Association. Toronto, 1989, unpublished.

12. *Opusculum*, XX, PG 97:1545C. On Abū Qurra with a survey of his references to Islam, see Sidney H. Griffith "The Controversial Theology of Theodore Abû Qurra (c.750–c.820 A.D.), a Methodological Comparative Study in Christian Arabic Literature" (Ph.D. diss., Catholic University of America, 1978); and various studies by the same author, such as "Theodore Abû Qurrah's Arabic Tract on the Christian Practice of Venerating Images," *Journal of the American Oriental Society* 105, no. 1 (1985): 53–73; "Comparative Religion in Apologetics of the First Christian Arabic Theologians," *Proceedings of the Patristic, Mediaeval and Renaissance Conference* 4 (1979): 63–87.

13. PG 97:1545C. Of interest here is the key phrase "to theion physei trisypóstaton" (divinity is by nature of three hypostases). The spelling might be in the dative case, *physei*, rather than *physin*. This is the definitive Christian terminology of the trinitarian doctrine, which the learned bishop uses properly; it is not the Qurʾanic understanding of the Trinity. Obviously, Muhammad could not have been aware of or keen to argue the difference between "physis" and "hypostasis," which had caused bitter and lengthy christological controversies among the Christians; nor could he have been aware of the distinction between the two made with reference to Christ and in the context of *christological* definitions, rather than with reference to the divine essence.

14. PG 94:765A; Kotter, *Die Schriften*, 4: 61.

15. PG 104:1448–57.

16. PG 104:1453C.

17. PG 104:1384–1448.

18. Spelled *Samêt*.

19. I do not know to which epithet of God this name corresponds. It may be a corruption of *al-majīd* (the Glorious one, in S. 11:73, 85:15), or of *al-wājid* (the Existing), which does not appear in the Qurʾan although it frequently occurs in the scholastic theology. Or, most likely, this may be the equivalent of *al-jāmiʿ* (the Assembler of all, again, on the last day, as in S. 3:9; 4:140). Cf. D. B. Macdonald, "Allāh," in *The Shorter Encyclopedia of Islam* (Ithaca, N.Y.: Cornell University Press, 1965), pp. 34–35.

20. PG 104:1385C.

21. On Nicetas, see Adel-Théodore Khoury, *Les théologiens byzantins et l'Islam. I: Textes et auteurs (VIIIe–XIIIe s.)* (Louvain: Éditions Nauwelaerts, 1969), pp. 110–62.

22. PG 105:768B–777C.

23. The numerical discrepancy is interesting for the history of the text of the Qurʾan, as Nicetas and other Byzantines knew, perhaps, the Qurʾan with one hundred and thirteen chapters, with an integrated text of sūras 8 and 9.

24. PG 105:776B.

25. A figurative expression by which Nicetas wants, perhaps, to say that God is an impersonal being altogether. PG 105:705D–708A. Emphasis is mine.

26. Cf. S.4:171; 5:73.

27. PG 105:784C–788B.

28. PG 105:785A.

29. Cf. Philippians 2:6–8.

30. PG 105:785B.

31. PG 105:785C.

32. Ibid.

33. Kotter, *Die Schriften*, 4: 63.

34. On Euthymios Zegabenos, see Khoury, *Les Théologiens*, chap. 11, pp. 235–48, and Andreas N. Papavasileiou, *Euthymios-Ioannes Zygadenos: Vios-Syngraphai*, (Nicosia, 1979).

35. Cf. Nicetas of Byzantium, PG 105:705D.

36. Cf. *ibid.*, 105:776B.

37. Cf. *ibid.*, 105:708A.

38. *Panoplia Dogmatica*, Tit. 28, PG 130:1341B.

39. Cf. for example, John VI Cantacuzenos. This Byzantine emperor (1341–55) turned monk (d. 1383), in his 4th oration or dialogue *Against Muhammad* (PG 154:676B–692C) calls Muhammad "a godless devil" who worships and preaches God as

> *holosphairos* and utterly cold, who was not born nor did he give birth, not realizing, the wretched one, that he is worshipping a solid thing and not God. Because a sphere is some kind of solid, and coldness is characteristic of solid things. (ibid., 692BC)

Emperor Manuel II Palaiologos (1391–1425), as if trying to supplement Cantacuzenos, makes a contrast between this "solid and utterly cold" god of Muhammad to God of Christianity:

> We, Oh you [Muslims], believe in one God, father almighty maker of heaven and earth and of all things visible and invisible, without beginning, without end, without a body, without passion, impalpable, untouchable, intangible, without shape, without form, not *holosphairos* as you do, invisible, unseen, incomprehensible, inconceivable, unknowable, eternal, undefined, indescribable, uncontainable, intransitive, immovable, unchangeable, incorruptible, unapproachable, uncommunicable, according to the essence by everything of the creation, and, in summary, known not by his qualities, as we said earlier, but by what can be said *about* him in an apophatic rather than in an affirmative way. (*Manuel II, Palaiologos: Dialoge mit einem "Perser,"* ed. Erich Trapp [Wien: In Kommission bei Herman Böhlaus Nachf, 1966], p. 122.3–10)

In his 11th oration Manuel makes reference to the Christian scriptures to show that the biblical typological language and the apophatic language of the Christian theology are not contradictory to, or in any tension with, each other, and in a pointed and sarcastic way he remarks that it must be strange and difficult to try to convince Muslims that "sitting on the right" or "on the left" are figurative expressions used about God, since they believe that God, who is without shape, is *holosphyros*. Cf. ibid., p. 134.24–29.

Finally, Symeon of Thessalonike (d. 1429) in his *Dialogue against the heresies* (PG 155:77–81) and in chapter 14, "Against the gentiles," writes:

> The most impious one [Muhammad] dares to call himself superior to Christ and to know God made of crystal and *holosphairos*. (PG 155:77D)

It is interesting that by the fifteenth century the Muslims had already been perceived as gentiles, and the god of Islam as a material "beaten rounded sphere" and now, for the first time by Symeon, as "made of crystal"!

40. Nicetas makes a distinction between the *catecheticon pyction* (tablet of catechesis) and *catecheteria biblia* (books used as catechetical instruments). The former implies a firm, official "mother tablet," or the cathedral text, from which all other churches derived the material for their services, the texts of baptismal confessions or declarations of converts, and the instruments of instruction for the initiates (*Historia* 213/121). Chalandon interprets *pyction* as a slab of marble housed in the cathedral of St. Sophia on which the catechetical text of the Church was inscribed. Ferdinand Chalandon, *Les Comnène. Études sur l'Empire byzantine au XIe et au XIIe siècles*, vol. II (2) *Jean II Comnène (1118–1143) et Manuel I Comnène (1143–1180)* (New York: Burt Franklin, 1912), p. 661.

41. Nicetas, *Historia* 213/Cf.121.

42. The *holosphyros* controversy was a serious enough incident during the reign of Emperor Manuel to have attracted the attention of contemporary and subsequent historians and chroniclers. Cf. the *Synopsis Chronike* by an anonymous author, ed. N.K. Sathas, *Mesaionike Bibliotheke*, 7: 303–7; Dositheos Notaras, *Paraleipomena ek tes Historias peri ton en Hierosolymois patriarcheusanton*, ed. A. Papadopoulos-Kerameus, *Analekta Hierolymitikes Stachyologias*, 1 [1891 (Bruxelles, 1963)], pp. 247–49.

43. Theodosius I Borradiotes, Patriarch of Constantinople (1178–1183).

44. Nicetas, *Historia*, 213.

45. Ibid., 214/121.

46. Ibid., The *Historia* is a document not only of Manuel's but also of Nicetas' own attitude towards Islam.

47. Ibid., 213–14/Cf. 121.

48. *Historia*, 215/122.

49. Franz Dölger, *Regesten der Kaiserurkunden des oströmischen Reiches von 566–1453*, vol. 2: *Regesten von 1025–1204* (München-Berlin: R. Oldenbourg, 1925), p. 87, #1529, 1530.

50. *Historia*, 214/121–22.

51. Ibid., 215/122. Patriarch Theodosios I Borradiotes was of Armenian origin. Whether his attitude toward Islam had anything to do with the frontier mentality, as was perhaps the case with Nicetas himself, one cannot say with certainty.

52. Nicetas, *Historia*, 216, cf. 122.

53. Nicetas, *Historia*, 216/cf. 122; the underlining is mine. Eustathios was probably born in Constantinople. For the question of his birthplace, see Phaidon I. Koukoules, *Thessalonikes Eusathiou. Ta Laographica* (Athens, 1950), 1: 3ff. A monk, deacon of St. Sophia, teacher of rhetoric, and eventually metropolitan of Thessalonike (1175), he became well known for his comments on Homer and Pindar. However, when in 1832 his theological treatises were published (*Opuscula*, ed. Tafel), Eustathios was recognized also as a theologian and a reformer of monasticism. He wanted to see the monks restored as examples of moral and spiritual life, and the monasteries as centres of cultivation of letters. He wrote orations, letters and other pieces of literature. Phaidon I. Koukoules, *Thessalonikes Eustathiou. Ta Laographica* (Athens, 1950), and *Thessalonikes Eustathiou. Ta Grammatica* (Athens, 1953).

54. Nicetas, *Historia*, 216, cf. 122. To what extent did Nicetas of Byzantium make an impact upon the philosopher and rhetorician Eustathios of Thessalonike is an interesting, but separate question.

55. Ibid.

56. A strong personality, but of mild manners, he was one of the most intimate and trusted under-secretaries and envoys of Manuel. Michael Choniates, Nicetas' brother and archbishop of Athens, addressed to him five letters, which provide some insight into Mantzoukis' personality and office. Cf. Sp. P. Lambros, *Michael Acominatou tou Choniatou. Ta Sozomena*, vol. II [repr. Groningen: Verlag Bouma's Boekhuis N.V. 1968], Letters #27, 30, 34, 54, and 59.

57. Nicetas, *Historia*, 217/122–23.

58. Ibid., 218/123.

59. See ibid.

60. Ibid., 219/123–24.

61. Ibid., 220/124.

62. One has the impression that the real players in this controversy were Theodore Mantzoukis and Eustathios of Thessalonike, and their equivalent Emperor Manuel Comnenos and Nicetas Choniates. Chonae, a frontier Byzantine town, was occupied by the Seljuks after the battle of Manzikert (1071). They were evicted in 1090, but in 1191–92 Turkish troops pillaged the town, profaned and destroyed the altar, the pulpit, and mosaic icons of the renowned church of the Archangel Michael. Also Nicetas became bitter at Emperor Theodore I Laskaris (1204–22) for ceding Chonae to Manuel Mavrozomês, the father-in-law of the sultan of Iconium. Cf. Magoulias, p. xi.

63. Emperor John II Comnenos (1118–43). Nicetas Choniates called John "the crowning glory, so to speak, of the Komnenian dynasty to sit on the Roman throne, and one might well say that he equalled some of the best emperors of the past and surpassed the others" (*Historia*, 47/27).

64. A.A. Vasiliev, *History of the Byzantine Empire 324–1453* (Madison: University of Wisconsin Press, 1961), p. 376.

65. J.M. Hussey, *The Byzantine World*, (New York: Harper Torchbooks, 1961), p. 62.

66. With the approval of Patriarch Nicholas IV (1147–51) he had his name placed in one of the *typika*. Whether also he, personally, had something to do with the shortening or the deletion of some hymns from church services, is not entirely clear. Cf. Jean Baptiste Pitra, *Hymnographie de l'Église Grecque* (Rome: Impr. de la civita cattolica, 1867), p. 62; P. Trempelas, *Ekloge Hellenikes Orthodoxou Hymnologias* (Athens, 1949), p. xxx.

67. Vasileios K. Stefanides, *Ekklesiaspīke Historia* (Athens: Asper, 1959), pp. 414, 416, 381, n. 2.

68. The synod, in which the patriarchs of Constantinople, Antioch, and Jerusalem participated, stated that John 14:28 refers to the human nature, although it can also apply to the second person of the Trinity, since the Word and Logos who proceeds from the Father has his cause in the Father. Stefanides, *Historia*, pp. 426–27; Chr. Papadopoulos, *He Ekklesia Constantinoupoleos epi Komnenon* (1948), p. 31.

69. Cf. *De Ceremoniis*, II, 49. This policy seems to present a clear contrast at least to the earliest Muslim policy. Cf. Francesco Gabrieli, *Muhammad and the Conquests of Is-*

lam, pp. 103 ff. Also the so-called "Ordinance of Umar" forbids the instruction of the Qur'an by non-Muslims and the imitation of Islamic customs by Christians.

70. K.G. Bonis, "Ho Thessalonikes Eustathios kai oi dyo 'Tomoi' tou Autocratoros Manuel I Comnenou (1143/80) hyper ton eis ten Christianiken Orthodoxian methistamenon Moamethanon," *Epeteris Byzantinon Spoudon* (Athens) 19 (1949): 162–69. Subsequently referred to as "Eustathios."

71. K.G. Bonis, *Euthymiou tou Malake, metropolitou Neon Patron (Hypate) (deuteron hemisy xii hekatont), Ta sozomena. Teuchos B'. Dyo Engomiastikoi Logoi, nyn to proton ekdidomenoi, Eis ton autocratora Manuel I ton Comnenon (1143–80)* (Athens, 1949) 1: 526; and Bonis, "Eustathios," p. 1629

72. John 8:39. Bonis, *Malakes*, 1: 526.28, and "Euthymios," p. 162, n.2

73. Cf. W. [Vasilii Eduardovich] Regel, *Fontes rerum byzantinarum* (Petropoli: S. Eggers & S. and I. Glasunof; Leipzig: Voss' Sortiment (G. Haessel, 1892–1917), 1: 49.23; Bonis, "Eustathios," p. 163, n.1.

74. Euthymios Malakes praises Manuel for the zeal burning his heart and for the care for the churches which is devouring his soul. With similar words Eustathios of Thessalonike praises Manuel. Bonis, *Euthymios*, p. 150; Bonis, "Eustathios," p. 163. The official documents related to matters of the Church issued by Manuel have been published in Dölger, *Corpus des griechischen Urkunden*, 2: 62 ff.

8

Calvin and the Turks

Jan Slomp

The recent arrival of almost seven million new Muslims in western Europe alone has, to borrow the phrase coined in Great Britain, put theology on full alert. Since its inception in 1988 the Islam in Europe Committee of the Conference of European Churches and the Council of Roman Catholic Bishops Conferences in Europe have decided to approach the theological faculties of Europe in order to generate theological reflection and to explore the question of how the challenge of this new Muslim presence can be met. Particularly important among the disciplines that have bearing on the issue are church history and the history of Christian thought. It is hoped that through an examination of dimensions of Christian historical thought that heretofore generally have been ignored, we may be able to add new and useful insights to our knowledge of the fourteen centuries of contact between Christianity and Islam.

I present this essay as a contribution to such historical investigation, surveying the most important aspects of the faith of the Muslims, or so-called Turcs, in the writings of John Calvin. Among the topics covered are Calvin's views on the "Turkish" concept of God, on Muhammad and the Qur'an, and on Muslim ceremonies and institutions. I conclude with some brief thoughts about whether, despite the rather negative view of Islam that Calvin seems to convey, his theology may in some way lend itself to the formulation of a Christian theology of Islam.

Primary sources are the 59 volumes of Calvin's *Opera* (abbreviated as CO) and the five volumes of the *Supplementa Calviniana* (abbreviated SC) thus far published.[1] Most of Calvin's political comments are found in his letters and especially in his some 2,400 sermons.[2] There are fewer references to the Turks in the *Institutes* and in Calvin's other systematic works than in his commentaries and sermons because of the somewhat casual nature of the latter, which makes them more appropriate to a sermon than to a systematic treatise.[3]

Little work has been done to date on this aspect of Calvin's writings,[4] although the views of some other reformers on the religion of Islam have received at least brief treatment.[5] The present essay starts from the actual references to

Islam and the Turks in Calvin's published works, with particular attention to his theological positions.

The Historical Context and Its Reflection in Calvin's Writings

The Turkish presence was unquestionably very real in the life of John Calvin. He was contemporary to the powerful Turkish emperor Sulayman I (known to the Turks as Qānūnī, "the lawgiver," and to the Christian world as "the magnificent"); Suleiman lived from 1494 or 1495 to 1566, Calvin from 1509 to 1564. The other two great powers in Calvin's day were the king of France and the even stronger house of Habsburg, which under Charles V ruled over the greater part of Germany including the Southern and Northern Netherlands, Austria, and Spain. Twice the king of France, Francis I (1515–47), sought and once obtained the help of the Ottoman emperor against his enemies, despite the strong disapproval of many of his subjects.[6] Calvin, who wrote an introductory letter to this same Francis I in his *Christianae Religionis Institutio* (1536), followed with grave concern whatever foreign policies "his" king was pursuing. (Particularly troubling to him were developments in Hungary, where the Calvinist form of the Reformation had gained influence and momentum, and the king's decision to repress the "heretics.")

It is clear that Calvin had only very casual knowledge about Islam and its teachings and had relatively little opportunity to come into contact with Muslims. There is some evidence that he may have seen, and perhaps even met, members of the Turkish delegation which disembarked in Marseilles in 1534 on their way to meet the king of France. In his commentary on Daniel 3:21, "Then these men were bound in their mantles, their tunics, their hats and their other garments" (RSV), at any rate, he explained the garments with a reference to the Turks of his own day, saying that although not many of them appear among us, we know what the dress of Turks looks like (*CO* 40: 360).

In a number of places, as we shall see, he classified Turks generally with others that he felt to be enemies of the evangelical movement.[7] In 1532, for example, Charles V prescribed regular prayer days against the Turks. In 1541 reformed preachers in Strasbourg and Geneva urged the city magistrates to introduce similar days of prayer and penitence. The prayer used in Geneva was included in the introduction to Calvin's sermons on Jeremiah and Lamentations. A part of that reads: "[Lord], do not allow that those should perish over whom according to thine holy will thy name was invoked, and that the Turks, pagans, papists and other unbelievers would glorify while blaspheming thee" (*SC* 6: xxviii).

In many of Calvin's writings we find that his commentary on the Turks was really an occasion to vent his obvious criticism of Roman Catholics (often referred to simply as "the Papists"). Calvin became indignant at Pope Paul III in 1541 because the latter apparently indicated that he thought the Protestants were an even greater danger to the church than the Turks. In one of the longest texts he wrote against Papists and Turks he said, "To leave nothing to imagination as far as shamelessness is concerned, the dirty mouth [of the Pope] dares to call into question which of the two might be more inimical to Christ, the Protestants or the Turks." In 1544, in a letter to his old friend Farel, he expressed his indignation about the freedom enjoyed by the visiting Turkish allies of the French king, while evangelical Christians were severely restricted.

Calvin's frustration with the pope, however, must not be seen to overshadow his genuine worry about the Turkish reality. There was no doubt that he considered the Turks to be the cruellest and most powerful enemies one could imagine. "The [European/German] princes have great difficult mustering 10,000 horses for their army," he said, "while the Turks with the greatest ease and little cost feed 100,000 horses [and men] on the battlefield" (*CO* 30: 448). He wrote to Melanchton in September of 1557 that he had heard people say that the seacoast of Apulia (in Italy) was devastated by a Turkish fleet. Such references to Turkish military successes throughout his works indicate his clear opinion that some areas of Europe were at the complete mercy of the Turks.

He did, however, see similarities between the Turks and the Romans, insofar as their many successes led them to think that they enjoyed a kind of special divine grace. The more the Turks enjoyed victory, the more they insulted the doctrine of Christ. Calvin was particularly harsh on persons he thought might be accused of doing anything to aid the Turks. He chastised those (European and other) powers who, greedy in their attempts to gain support and protection, opened their gates for the Turks both in Asia and in Europe (*CO* 36: 308). It is clear in the same commentary (chap. 13:5) that he did not necessarily think that there was an imminent danger from the Turks, although the warning came in handy in his general arguments (*CO* 36: 260). His main theme was European responsibility for Turkish successes. In a commentary on Jeremiah 13:21 he remarked, "Whose fault is it that the Turks could so easily penetrate . . .? You have prepared a way of access through the sea . . . consequently your harbors were open for them. And they have carried out their great cruelty to their full satisfaction against your subjects; all these things were accomplished by you. You are therefore the authors of all these evils."[8]

In the fourteenth sermon on Luke (1:65–68) Calvin expressed his opinion that he knew what the Turks thought about Christianity. "The papists have their imaginations about God and so have the Turks, and even more. When they realize . . . that they make the whole world tremble with the result that they grow and expand even more—when this is the case it seems to them that we [Christians] have a religion that is just a phantasy and that we are misguided." Calvin realized that if the Turks were to conquer all of Europe it would be the end of Christianity as a power to be reckoned with. "The danger exists that there will be a greater barbarity in Christianity than ever before," he observed in sermon 28 on Daniel 11:30–32, "because the Turk will be able to come to gain everything. After that he will cause Christianity to be abolished to such an extent that there will be no memory left of it."

The Turks in those days were redoubtable adversaries for Charles V. France was too weak to present by itself a counterweight to Charles's ever-expanding empire. The permanent threat of Ottoman conquest actually favored the growth of Protestantism, but Calvin was not so shortsighted as to expect anything positive from a shift in the balance of power in favor of the Turks. Much of his commentary in regard to the Turkish menace was a response to the long struggle with the Ottomans in Hungary. The times of greatest military activity in Hungary find their reflection in frequent references to the Turks in his writings and sermons. In letter 190 to his friend Farel he said that the emperor, Charles V, feared a Turkish attack, and discussed various opinions as to the probability and nature of such an attack (*CO* 11: 177). And in letter 626, written by a Hungarian theologian to Calvin on March 26, 1545, we read about the sad state of Hungary devastated by the Turks and by indigenous tyrants. Letter 1615 written to Calvin on March 24, 1552 by Ambrosius Morbanus, who had preached in Hungary and Poland, says that Hungary was on the eve of a struggle with the Turks, and a letter from Melanchton in October of that year talks about Turkish armies having occupied two important cities and having destroyed the army of Ferdinand (*CO* 14: 308).

Calvin was convinced that European countries should be defended against the Turks but, like Luther, he opposed the idea of a crusade for which church funds should be allocated[9] (Pannier, 269). He felt that the churches had their own obligations of a more spiritual nature, particularly the organizing of days of penitence and prayer, and should not be drawn directly into preparations for war.

Calvin and Turkish Theology

In Calvin's *Institutes*, his major and best known work, the doctrine of God the Creator and sovereign Lord of all, the one whom we call Father, occupies a central place. Except for the word "Father," similar terms could have been used about the message contained in the Qur'an. It might even be possible to suggest some parallels between the Meccan prophet and the Genevan reformer, such as in the way they conceived the relevance of their respective messages as formative forces for constructing a society in agreement with divine injunctions.

It is unlikely that Calvin perceived these similarities in mission and message, however, for he had very little positive to say about the way Turks (Muslims) speak about God, Muhammad, and the Qur'an. The *Institutes* contain only a few references to the Turks. Such mention as there is clearly comes in the context of Christian theological debate and often seems to set up Islam as a foil for denigrating Christian opponents and preaching his own doctrine of Christianity. Critique of the Turks also provides an opportunity for him to express the christocentrism that so characterizes his writings. It is clear that in his opinion the greatest omission of the Turks is their failure to acknowledge the centrality of Christ, outside of whom there can be no true knowledge of God. In the *Institutes* 2:6.4 we read:

> Faith in God is faith in Christ. John's saying has always been true. He that does not have the Son does not have the Father (1 John 2:23). For even if many men once boasted that they worshipped the supreme Majesty, the Maker of heaven and earth, yet because they had no mediator it was not possible for them to taste God's mercy and thus be persuaded that he was their Father. Accordingly, because they do not hold Christ as their head, they possess only a fleeting knowledge of God. From this it also came about that they lapsed into crass and foul superstitions and betrayed their ignorance. So today the Turks, although they proclaim at the top of their lungs that the Creator of heaven and earth is God, repudiate Christ and substitute an idol in place of the true God.[10]

This difference in the doctrine of God had consequences for Calvin in terms of the words that can or cannot be used in prayer. God as Father played a central role in his theology, and this he clearly found missing among the Turks. "Hence it also follows that the right way to pray is [other than] do the Turks and other profane nations. For as Paul asserts, faith is not true unless it claims and brings to mind that sweetest name of Father (*suavissimum illud patris nomen*)" (*Institutes* 3:13.5).

In a defense of his doctrine of predestination against some of his critics, Calvin also mentioned the Turks (*CO* 9: 315); he seems not to have been aware that they also have a doctrine of divine election. This reference is found in a polemical treatise written in 1558 entitled *Calumniae nebulonis cuiusdam . . . doctrinam Ioh. Calvini De occulta dei providentia ad easdem responsio*. The tone is harsh, probably reflecting that taken by those who in turn had criticized him: "What is left to be done is to defend the glory of the eternal God against your cruel, sacrilegious remarks. You contend that I surreptitiously introduce the devil in place of the true God. Certainly whatever God one may fabricate, all pious people have to worship and adore that only one who, more than 25 centuries ago, with the exception of a period of the descendants of Abraham, has suffered so that the whole human race has wandered in utter darkness." Calvin accused his opponent of preferring human reason, "which has extinguished in its blindness all the glory of God," to scripture. "It is therefore not astonishing," he says to his adversary, "that you are prepared to mix, promiscuously, whatever religions there are, to the extent that the opinion can be held that the Turk is a worshipper of God [*Dei cultor*], the Turk who taken in by Muhammad's deliria (or: hallucinations/confusions) adores who knows what unknown power [*numen*]."

Calvin seemed to know about the beautiful names of God which Muslims take from the Qurʾan and use in their worship and theology. "With whatever beautiful titles Turks and Jews adore God, one is still bound to hold the opinion that the name of God, once it is separated from Christ, becomes an empty idea" (*CO* 47: 115).[11] In a commentary on Acts 22:14, "the God of our fathers," Calvin stated in the same vein: "Whenever there is a question of religion we learn from Paul's example that no new, piously meant, God should be imagined as the Papists and the 'Mahumetistae' and all other heretics are used to do, but we should hold on to that God who has revealed himself long ago through law and many oracles." Several things are striking in this comment. One is that Calvin did not doubt that the people he disagreed with meant well. The second is that he used the word "Mahumetistae," whereas he usually followed the common terminology of "Turks." The third is that he considered law and prophets (oracles) sufficient as a decisive source of revelation refuting the three parties he disagreed with.

The idea that God is not really known unless He is seen in the perspective of Jesus Christ was a permanent feature in Calvin's thought and deeply influenced his assessment of the religion of the Turks. In a sermon on Micah 4 delivered on December 12, 1550, he said, "When we talk to the Turks they will certainly say that they believe in God the creator of heaven and earth. But we see that they deny Him openly when they are not prepared to receive him by whom he has intended to manifest Himself to us, that is to say our Lord Jesus Christ, without whom we cannot know God. And as far as the Jews are concerned, they still have a veil before their eyes" (*SC* 5: 127, 35–38). The same thought was more strongly put in the third sermon on Melchizedek (Gen. 14): "The Turks, the Jews and the Papists abuse this holy name, going so far as to sully it, as the Turks who adore what they fabricate in their brains and blaspheme (in this way) the living God. He who does not have the Son does not have the Father, according to the words of St. John that when the Son is not honored the Father takes this as an insult. . . . Consequently the Turks adore/worship a devil under the name of God" (*CO* 23: 680).

This theme continued throughout the years of Calvin's writing and preaching. In 1551, commenting on 1 Peter 1:3 to explain the words "et Pater domini" he said, "Those who form in their mind a concept of the bare (nudum) majesty of God have an idol[12] instead of God, as the Jews and the Turks" (*CO* 55: 210).[13] A similar idea was expressed in 1556 in sermon 183 on Deuteronomy 32: "As when today the Turks boast enough that they worship the God who created heaven and earth. What is their God like? It is but an idol. The Jews say, We want to serve God, but their God is only an idol. And why? Because the divinity which is in Christ is unknown to them." The same idea was contained in the commentary on Ephesians 1:15–18, in which we again find an attack on the Roman Church: "As for the Turks, they will say again and again, 'God almighty creator of heaven and earth.' The Papists protest quite often that they believe in God just as do the Turks and Jews. But the Papists fight against the truth" (*CO* 51: 316). For Calvin these three—Jews, Papists, and Turks—in changing order, were like three impostors who deviate from the truth. In 1559 on a commentary on Isaiah 25:9 he remarked: "Although the Jews, the Turks and the unbelievers contend that they worship God the creator of heaven and earth, in fact they worship an imagination [*fictitium*] as their God." And on the 19th of January in 1563, little more than a year before his death, he said in a sermon on 2 Samuel 23:3: "The Turks today derive glory for themselves from the name of God, but still they imagine and fabricate such a God as seems good to them."[14]

One might imagine that the expression "God of Abraham," as in Acts 3:13 (*CO* 48: 68), might have prompted Calvin to make more positive mention of the Turks for whom Abraham plays such a central role. But no reference to the Qur'anic Abraham is to be found. Calvin probably did not even know that he is mentioned in the Qur'an; his knowledge of its contents was slim and he seems to have made no effort to change that. Calvin actually used his commentary on this verse to criticize the Turks once again by saying, "But the Turks claim loudly that they worship God as creator of heaven and earth," rather than to relate positively to the strong affirmation of the God of Abraham as it is actually present in the Qur'an. And as he apparently did not know about the role of Abraham in the Qur'an, Calvin did not seem to have been aware that Jesus occupies a place of honor in that scripture and that he and his mother are defended against Jewish calumnies. Otherwise he would not have said in sermon 14 on Ephesians 2:16–19, in yet another attack on his three "imposters": "The Jews blaspheme on the one hand our Lord Jesus Christ, and the Turks deride him and hold him for a phantom, and the Papists rob him of most of his graces."

Among all the texts in which Calvin made mention of the beliefs of the Turks, there is only one in which his rejection of the Turkish idea of God seems to have led to a kind of self-searching. In his commentary on Isaiah 36:19–20, written in 1559, he says:

> Where are the gods of Hamath . . .? When the godless predominate we should not think that God's power is broken. When therefore nowadays the Turk becomes presumptuous because he has already subjected so many Christians for such a long period, we should not be worried as if God had become weak and defenseless; . . . but we must repent for the many ways by which both the Greeks and the Asians have provoked His anger, as long as horrible tribes, portentous in their lusts, are reigning in these regions. Terrible superstitions and godlessness have grown; therefore a severe punishment will be called for to suppress the scandalous deeds of those who profess falsely the name of God. On the one hand [there is] the prosperity of the Turks, and on the other in the orient a terrible breakup of society. We see [Turks] reckless and erecting the crests of their helmets against our religion. (*CO* 36: 613)

Calvin and Muhammad

In Calvin's view one man in particular has to be blamed for the wrong notions that Turks have of God and that is Muhammad, who is mentioned more than twenty-five times in Calvin's writings. "We observe the Turks, how they have so much put up their defenses as they have followed the deceptions [*tromperies*] of Muhammad," he said in sermon 11 on 2 Timothy 2:8–13 (*CO* 54: 138). "They are really such fables, that if [the Turks] had not become all dull they could immediately see through the stupidity contained in them. But what happened? God has let loose His vengeance in the sense that He has put them in the wrong direction [*en sens réprouvé*]; this happened because of their ingratitude, because they were Christian bastards just like the Papists." It is clear that Calvin saw the Turks (Muslims) as former Christians who were deceived by Muhammad. In sermon 48 on Daniel 12:8–13 he said that the interpretation of what is meant by the periods of time in this apocalyptic passage must be in direct reference to the time when Muhammad began to pervert and corrupt the Christian faith.[15] Over the centuries various suggestions have been made to explain who might have been meant in 2 Thessalonians 2:8 by "the lawless one." Calvin's response was that "Paul . . . does not speak of one man but about the government which will be occupied by Satan so that he might erect the seat of abomination right in the center of the temple of God. . . . Because Mahomet, apostate as he was, has alienated the Turks from Christ" (*CO* 52: 197).

Just as he dealt with Turks and Papists in the same way, so he mentioned the pope and Muhammad (as well as the Jews) in the same breath. Continuing the same text, he said, "Let us have a look at the horrible disintegration of life under the Papal system on the one hand, and after that the deceiver Muhammad[16] and how he has seduced his whole sect, and thirdly the Jews, how blind they are." The Turks probably were mentioned before the Jews because they posed a greater threat for Calvin. From deceiver to corrupter is but a step, as we see in sermon 26 on Daniel 9 published after Calvin's death (*CO* 4: 14; 5: 99).[17] This sermon states that Muhammad had corrupted the greater part of the world, setting an example for other sects which always want to say and invent something new. "All sects that exist today," he said, "have come out of this mud puddle. This happens when one is not content with the pure doctrine of the gospel."

Another parallel in Calvin's treatment of Islam and papacy is the fact that neither pope nor prophet is content with revelation as given in holy scripture. They speak as from one mouth, he said in sermon 28 on 1 Timothy 4:1–2. He called Muhammad "the companion of the Pope who has done his very best to seduce those poor people who were enraged and saturated and poisoned by his false doctrine. He (Mahomet) says that the Holy Spirit has revealed him everything." Calvin then went on to indicate that similar things apply to the pope (*CO* 53: 340). In sermon 16 on Job 4:12–19 Calvin attributed this lack of contentment with Holy Scripture to a kind of "diabolic curiosity." The religion of the Turks, he said, is based on curiosity. Muhammad has said that he was the one who had to bring full revelation besides the gospel. Because of that, the Turks have become dull and insensitive to the point where now they amuse themselves with things that are foolish and dull. That, says Calvin, is the righteous vengeance of God in turning them in the wrong direction (*CO* 33: 204).

The same idea is found in Calvin's commentary on John 15:26. "Mahomet and Pope have a principle of religion in common: perfection of doctrine is not contained in Scripture but in something higher that was revealed by the Spirit. From the same swamp anabaptists and libertines are scooping their frenzied ideas" (*CO* 47: 335). And again in a sermon on Deuteronomy 18:9–15 delivered on November 27, 1559: "Oh there are these high mysteries which the Pope has invented in addition to the Gospel, making the same claim as Mahomet does when he says that the Alchoran is sovereign wisdom itself. They are two horns of the Antichrist" (*CO* 27: 502).[18]

Calvin rejected the claim of the Papists that some of their religious practices dated back to the early church, just as he rejected the Turks' claim that they had the truth because they had already existed a thousand years, or their claim that their religion went as far back as creation. Superstitions are just as old, he noted. Muhammad's religion enjoys the same kind of spiritual food as the Papists, he observed in his 1561 *Responsio ad Versipellem mediatorem*; in other words, "they both draw water from the same dirty old well" (*CO* 9: 536). The main difference between Christianity and Islam, Calvin said a number of times, is the latter's refusal to acknowledge the relationship of God and Jesus Christ.

"When the Turks put their Muhammad in the place of God's Son, and when they do not recognize that God is manifested in the flesh, which is one of the principle articles of our faith, then they are guilty of perversities and are leading so many people astray that they deserve to be put to death" (*CO* 27: 261).[19]

Calvin and the Qur'an

References to the Qur'an in Calvin's works are few and far between. Not a single *sūra* is literally quoted. He did not show a keen interest, as did Luther and Melanchton, in the enterprise of Theodorus Bibliander and Oporinus in Basel to get the Latin translation of Robert of Ketten (1143) printed some four hundred years after it had been completed.[20] On November 10, 1542 his old friend Oporinus wrote to Calvin asking for his help.[21] But we have no reply from Calvin. Did his letter get lost? Or was he not interested in a printed Qur'an? Or did he perhaps actually agree with opponents of publication in Basel who had been instrumental in getting Oporinus into prison for a short while, and was he thus so embarrassed by the request that he did not want to show where his sympathies really lay? After reading the letters and studying Calvin's references to the Qur'an I am inclined to think that the last is highly likely, but as yet we do not have enough evidence on which to build a case.[22]

Three references should be noted in which Calvin mentioned the Qur'an, all in exegetical context. In a sermon on Job 33 he returned to his theme of the sufficiency of holy scripture (*CO* 35: 64). Both Papists and Muslims are said not to be content with revelation as it is found in the Old and New Testaments: "The Papists contend that when we have what is contained in Holy Scripture it is not enough, but that there are other mysteries which God has reserved for His church. How did they fabricate all this? Exactly in the same way Mahumet has said that his Alcoran was the great perfection. So also the Pope says that there are secrets which have been preserved in addition to Holy Scripture." In his commentary on John 16:14, we read that Muhammad preached that without his "Alcoran" people would remain children (*CO* 47: 363). The last reference is in a sermon on 2 Timothy 1:6–8 (*CO* 54: 37). Speaking about the wicked, he said that "some of them are so strong in their resistance against the word that it does not make much difference whether one preaches against them from the Bible or from the Qur'an. They are crude people who only think of filling their stomach."

Of major importance in Calvin's experience was the affair concerning Michael Servet, a Spanish medical doctor and author on religious subjects who was accused of antitrinitarianism. As a doctor and scholar of medicine, Servet more than likely was acquainted with medical works by Arabs, probably in translation.[23] One can assume, therefore, that he might well have been influenced by these contacts with Muslim scholarship. Among the questions put to Servet in 1553 was one specifically dealing with the Qur'an and asking Servet to testify whether he considered it to be a book full of blasphemies (*CO* 8: 765). Since Calvin was undoubtedly the author of the question, one can see his own opinion reflected.

Calvin and Islamic Institutions

Despite his obvious critique of Islam, Calvin (like Luther) occasionally exhorted Christian believers to greater faithfulness by describing the zeal of the followers of Muhammad. In spite of the fact that they had not accepted the Gospel, for which reason he had no tolerance of them, he saw Muslims as admirable in the ardent way in which they practiced their religion. In a sermon delivered on August 8, 1549 on Jeremiah 18:11–14 he warned his audience: "In view of the examples of the heathens, we will be less excusable if we have not served God. . . . See how obstinately [the Turks] follow the law of Mahomet" (*SC* 7: 153). He drew attention again to the great devotion of the Turks in his sermon on Micah 4 on December 12, 1550: "One should also watch the Turks; . . . they are filled with a rage and diabolic pride; how much they seek to devote themselves to their Mahommet, even to the point that they see no problem in giving their life for their law" (*SC* 5: 127).[24] Calvin applied these kinds of observations to his audience when he said, "If we look at ourselves, do we try as hard to follow the vocation to which God has called us? . . . The only thing Turks are intended to do when they practice all their stupidities is, as they say themselves, to serve God" (*CO* 49: 672).[25] In this sixth sermon on Deuteronomy 33:18–19, delivered on July 3, 1556, he stated that "Papists and Turks who talk quite a lot about God have nevertheless no assurance; there is only in their case question of giving themselves to all stupidities and behavior as apes, which they say are based on their good intention."

While he may have admired the tenacity of the Turks in practicing their faith, Calvin did not hesitate to criticize the particular elements of their religion as he understood them. He knew, for example, that the Turks practiced circumcision, but said (second sermon on Ephesians 2:11–13) that in the end they do not benefit from it since there is no promise attached to it. For that reason, and because they behave as unbelievers, he actually listed the Turks as among the uncircumcised (*SC* 1: 18).[26] He also participated in the critique of the institution of marriage and the position of women in Islam when he called Muhammad "a corruptor of conjugal faithfulness" (*CO* 41: 270). He was highly critical of the practice of taking several wives, which he saw as the result of Muhammad's giving in to all kinds of lusts; in *Praelectiones in Danielem* 11:37

he states that "Muhammad has allowed that men practise brute licentiousness when they collect wives by buying them; by doing so they corrupt faithfulness in marriage."

One might question whether Calvin ever considered mission work among the Turks. The well-known Protestant missiologist Gustav Warneck (1834–1910) was of the opinion that not only missionary activity but the very idea of mission in the modern sense is missing in the work of the reformers. This does not seem to be entirely true in the case of Calvin, however; in at least two texts he clearly gave some thought to the possibility of Turkish conversion. In a section on baptism in the *Institutes* we read: "If a Turk should offer himself for baptism we could not easily baptise him unless he gave a confession satisfactory to the church." And in his sermon on Jeremiah 18:13–16 the possibility of a "missio Dei" is suggested but with no consequences for human commitment: "What to think, if God today would call the Turks to His knowledge and if He would hold them to be His own and if after that there would be a rebellion, they would be condemnable" (*SC* 6: 156).

It does appear that Calvin did not really think any form of preaching to the Turks would make sense because they were beyond reach: "They are apostates and as apostates have to be left to God. . . . They are alienated from true religion" (*CO* 50: 307). They are obstinate (implying a warning to the believers not to be that way) and Satan has deceived them (*CO* 50: 307). Satan's deceit rules commonly over Papists, Turks, and Jews (*CO* 31: 315).[27] The result is that they are hardened in their errors. "They are obstinate in their imaginations," he said, and consequently "they reject the grace which was acquired for the whole world by Jesus Christ. The Jews do the same. And the Papists, although they do not say it openly, show it in actuality. If the Turks and the Papists seek a more perfect wisdom elsewhere, burdened by innumerable deceipts as they are, they deserve to get drowned in the labyrinth of their errors (*CO* 47: 91).[28] In fact, while like Luther he generally tried to tar the Turks, the Jews, and the Papists with the same brush, Calvin's intense personal concern for the attacks of the Papists led him to portray them as worse than the either the Jews or the Turks and Saracens.

Conclusion

It is clear that Calvin followed the stereotypes of his time in remarking on the Turks and their religion. The observation of Norman Daniel that "the Reformers do not seem to have conceived Islam any differently [than did other medieval authors]"[29] appears to be justified by what we have found in Calvin's writings. The image of Islam to which he was exposed in his upbringing seems to have been confirmed by the events of his time and age as well as by the writings of such contemporaries as Luther and Erasmus, whom he held in high esteem. And he made no attempt to modify that image in his own writings. Of the many quotations about the Turks in Calvin's works, only a few contain any sort of positive evaluation. The immediate threat of the Turks for the Christian church and Christendom in his own day clearly prevented him from taking their religion seriously. Terms such as "Calvino-Turcism,"[30] coined by some to denote a kind of alliance between Protestants and Turks, or "Calvino-Turcismus,"[31] used by some Roman Catholic polemists, hardly seem fair or appropriate in the light of Calvin's obvious critique of the religion of Islam. And yet it is not difficult to see how Calvin's joint attack on Papists and Turks could easily have prompted such an equation.

Yet if one leaves out the negative references to the particular beliefs of the Turks that we have seen in Calvin's thought, the claim can be made that he did in fact give serious thought to the phenomenon of religion in general. Two Dutch scholars, J.H. Bavinck and Hendrik Kraemer,[32] have tried to use his ideas of "sensus divinitatis" and "semen religionis" for a theology of religions. Through his humanist training in classical studies (he wrote, for example, on Seneca's *Clementia* when he was in his early twenties), he knew the religion of the ancient Greeks and Romans better than he understood the faith and practice of his contemporary, the Turkish sultan, and his coreligionists.

Nonetheless it is obvious that there are some real similarities between the thought of Calvin and the main thrust of the Qur'anic message. The sovereignty and glory of God are at the center of both. One can only wish that Calvin had been able to study the Qur'an, available to him as it was printed by his friend Oporinus, and that he had done so with an open-mindedness that could have allowed for a more constructive reflection on the basic tenets of Islamic thought.

REFERENCES

Calvin's writings

Ioannic Calvini, *Opera Quae Supersunt Omnia*, ed. Wilhelm Baum, Eduard Cunitz, and Eduard Reuss (59 vols.) (Neukirchen, Germany: Neukirchener Verlag der Buchhandlung des Erziehungsverein 1863–1900). Abbreviated in this essay as *CO*, the first number indicating the volume and the second the page.

Jean Calvin, *Supplementa Calviniana* (Sermon inédits), ed. Erwin Mulhaupt et al. (5 vols. to date; 3 and 4 are missing, vol. 7 the last) (Neukirchen: Neukirchener Verlag der Buchhandlung des Erziehungsverein 1936–81). Abbreviated as *SC*.

About Calvin and the Turks

Jacques Pannier, "Calvin et Les Turcs," *Revue Historique* 124 (1937): 168–86.

Robert White, "Castellio Against Calvin: The Turk in the Toleration Controversy of the Sixteenth Century," *Bibliothèque d'Humanisme et Renaissance* 46, no. 3 (1984): 573–86. (I owe this source to Prof. Dr. Francis Higman of the Institut d'Histoire de la Réformation of the University of Geneva, letter dated July 25, 1989.)

Other studies about Calvin

H. Bergema, "De betekenis van Calvijn voor de zending en de missiologie," in *Vox Theologica* 29 (1958–59): 44–54.

W. de Greef, *Johannes Calvijn Zijn werk en geschriften* (Kampen, The Netherlands: KOK Publishers, 1989), p. 236. (Helpful for dating references in cases where dates are not indicated in *CO*.)

H. A. Oberman, *De Erfenis van Calvin zijn Grootheid en Grenzen* (The Netherlands: Kampen, 1988), p. 57.

Jean Rilliet, *Le vrai visage de Calvin* (Toulouse: Privat, 1982), p. 179.

Richard Stauffer, "Calvin," in Menna Prestwick, ed., *International Calvinism 1541–1715*, 2d ed. (Oxford: Clarendon, 1986), pp. 15–38.

Other sources

Mohammad Arkoun, *La Pensée Arabe* (Paris: P.U.F., 1975).

J.H. Bavinck, *Religious Besef en Christelijk Geloof*, 2d ed. (Kampen, The Netherlands: KOK Publishers, 1949, 1989); Calvin, on pp. 142–48.

Willem A. Bijlefeld, *De Islam als Na-Christelijke Religie: een Onderzoek naar de Theologische Beoordeling van de Islam* (The Hague: Van Keulen N.V., 1959), p. 351.

Kenneth Cracknell and Christopher Lamb, *Theology on Full Alert* (The Hague: Van Keulen, 1986), p. 142.

Norman Daniel, *Islam and the West, the Making of an Image* (Edinburgh: Edinburgh University Press, 1960), p. 443.

Erasmus, *Opera Omnia* (Amsterdam, N.Y.: Elsevier Science Publishers, 1986).

W. Hartner, "Arrêt de la culture scientifique," in R. Brunschvig and G.E. Von Grunebaum, eds., *Classicism et Déclin Culturel dans l'Histoire de l'Islam* (Paris: Maisonneuve, 1957).

H. Kraemer, *Religion and the Christian Faith* (London: Lutterworth, 1956), passim (p. 461).

Youakim Moubarac, *Recherches sur la Pensée Chrétienne et l'Islam dans les temps modernes et a l'Époche Contemporaine* (Beirut: L'Université Libanaisé, 1977), p. 612.

V.J. Parry, "Suleiman I" in *Encyclopaedia Britannica* (Chicago, 1973), 21: 388–89.

Victor Segesvary, *L'Islam et la Réforme* (Lausanne: Éd. l'Age d'Homme, 1978), p. 301.

Manfred Ullman, *Islamic Medicine* (Edinburgh: Edinburgh University Press, 1978), p. 138.

NOTES

1. Translations are from Latin and French texts (except for the *Institutes*, for which (J. T. M. Neill's translation was used) because Dutch libraries do not contain all the English translations of Calvin's writings that are available in America and Great Britain.

2. In a recent biography of Calvin, Richard Stauffer remarks on Calvin's interests in exegesis and preaching: "It is . . . wrong to claim, as has sometimes been done, that Calvin was the man of a single book or that 'Calvinism' can be reduced to the Institutes alone. Great as that theological summa is, it does not eclipse the products of the exegete and the preacher" (Prestwick, p. 30).

3. The commentaries were written in Latin to serve an ever increasing readership abroad before they were translated into French, German, Dutch, and other languages. The sermons were all delivered in French.

4. Until 1984 there was only one study about Calvin and the Turks, published in 1938 by Jacques Pannier. Prof. Dr. Francis Higman, director of the Institut d'Histoire de la Réformation in Geneva, drew my attention to a second study about Calvin and the Turks by Robert White, entitled "Castellio against Calvin: The Turk in the Toleration Controversy of the Sixteenth Century." See Egil Grislis "Luther and the Turks," *The Muslim World* 64 (July 1974): 180–93 and (October 1974): 275–91.

5. Several new studies concerning Luther and the Turks were published in 1982 for the fifth centennial of Luther's birth, including one by the author. In 1978 Victor Segesvary published *L'Islam et la Réforme*, in which he deals with the attitude of the reformers of Zurich vis-à-vis Islam. A. G. Weiler has done some work on Erasmus (who wrote a major study *De bello Turcis inferendo*), but further study on this thinker is needed.

6. "Christendom was scandalized to see the 'most Christian king' allied with infidels and heretics'" (*Encyclopaedia Britannica*, 1973, s.v. "France").

7. Calvin had no illusions about the true intentions of the Turks, as in Letter 158 dated February 1539 to his friend Farel. "Some kings," he writes, "in astonishing craziness [*mira rabie*] are eager to bring an army against us [Protestants] and are fully equipped for it. But really they are held back by more prudent and wise people who expect that the Turk would not remain quiet if he would see Germany preoccupied by internal wars."

8. In a sermon delivered on August 5, 1549 (*SC* 6: 137, line 30) he reminded his congregation of Adam, who after the fall shouts in vain, "Helas, woe to me." "It is unavoidable therefore," Calvin said, "that we are in the same situation and that we have all the time to shout 'helas' when we are bereft of all the grace of God [by our own fault,

like Adam] and when we are under the domain of the Turks and the Antichrist. But all our shouting and crying will be to no avail at all."

9. Jacques Pannier, "Calvin et les Turks," *Revue Historique* 124 (1937): 269.

10. Cf. Pannier, p. 285 and White, p. 584, n. 35.

11. W.A. Bijlefeld (*De Islam als Na-Christelijke Religie* [The Hague: van Keulen N.V., 1959], p. 185) quotes these last lines in Latin, preceded by the comment, "This does not mean that we reject every non-trinitarian confession about God. We refuse to accept Calvin's statement *hoc tenendum est Dei nomen, quem a Christo separatum nihil quam inane esse figmentum*," the only quotation of Calvin in this work on Christian theological opinion about Islam.

12. He uses the word "idolum," which probably did not have the strong modern connotation of idol. It may, according to the commentators and editors of the *Supplementa*, convey the meaning of an *idée fixe*. Cf. Daniel J. Sahas, " 'Holosphyros?' A Byzantine Perception of 'The God of Muhammad,' " in this volume.

13. In the same year writing on the Epistle of John 2:22 he states, "Unde sequitur, the conclusion is that the Turks, Jews and similar people instead of God hold on to a mere idol." In another text (*CO* 36: 420) he refers to the fact that the Turks are said to worship a fictitious God.

14. The following ten lines elaborate this with a decisive reference to Romans 1:25, "because they exchanged the truth about God for a lie"(RSV). The complete text is printed in *Supplementa Calviniana 1: 703*. Similar references are found in a number of Calvin's other writings. See, e.g., his commentary on Psalms 135:5 (*CO* 32: 358), "whosoever moves away from God falsely pretends to use God's name, as today do the Jews and the Turks, who while professing to worship the creator of the world only make jokes (meras nugas agunt)"; commentary on John 11:3 (*CO* 47: 151): "Turks and Jews claim in vain, when they do not respect Christ, that they worship God. In this way they try to tear God apart (Deum a se ipso divellere); commentary on Deuteronomy 6:1–4 in a sermon delivered on July 15, 1555 (sermon 15, *CO* 26: 247): "The Turks today will say that they worship God the creator of heaven and earth, but it is only an idol they worship."

15. Pannier (23 ff.) says that Calvin disagrees with Luther and Melanchton on the exegesis of these texts.

16. Cf. sermon LXXVII on Deuteronomy 11:16–21: "[T]he Papists will protest a lot that they want to serve God the creator of heaven and earth, as do the Jews and the Turks who are creating for themselves a labyrinth of superstitions, as a result of the fact that this deceiver Mahomet has enchanted them."

17. I was not able to find the exact date of its delivery.

18. This reference to the two horns of the Antichrist may be a slip of the pen, because in sermon 11 on Daniel 8:6 he does not follow Luther's exegesis of the two horns (Pannier 283). "He intends to speak about either Muhammad or the Antichrist," Luther had stated (*CO* 41: 441).

19. Sermon 88 on Deuteronomy 38, delivered September 20, 1555. This very strict observation seems to contradict a more tolerant statement about how to treat Muslims in the first edition of the *Institutes* (White, passim).

20. See Bijlefeld, *De Islam*, 84 ff. for a treatment of Bibliander's and Luther's roles in this affair.

21. This letter was printed in the *Thesaurus Epistolicus Calvinianus* in vol. 11 of Calvin's *Opera*, pp. 464 ff.

22. Pannier (pp. 278–89) has dealt at length with this matter.

23. Arab medicine in those days was still dominant in Europe. See Manfred Ullman, *Islamic Medicine* (Edinburgh: Edinburgh University Press, 1978), p. 69: "The Spaniard Michael Servetus [Miguel Servede, 1509–53], in his book *Christianismi restitutio* which appeared in 1553 and which in the same year brought him to the stake in Geneva, gives a presentation of the lung circulation which resembles Ibn-an-Nafis so strongly that one can hardly reject a direct influence." (See also W. Hartner, p. 336.)

24. "By what madness (rabie) are the Turks hit when there is question of keeping the deliria of Mahomet, for which they voluntarily spend their blood and life," he wrote in his 1559 commentary on Isaiah 44:14 (*SC* 37: 115).

25. Commentary on 1 Corinthians 10:19–24; *CO* 49: 672.

26. In a sermon on June 1, 1562 on 2 Samuel 1:20 (ed. Hans Bueckert, 1961).

27. Commentary on Psalm 32, about 1561.

28. Sermon 30 on 1 Timothy 4:1–5.

29. See Daniel pp. 280, 307. Daniel's conclusion that "facts" that tended to show the falsity of Islam were preferred to all others applies not only to medieval writers but also to Calvin and several of his contemporaries.

30. For a fuller explanation see Evans, p. 197.

31. "Calvino-Turcismus, id est calvinisticae perfidiae cum mahometana collatio" (Moubarac, p. 43).

32. J.H. Bavinck, *Religieus Besef en Christelijk Geloof* (Kampen, The Netherlands: KOK Publishers, 1949; 2d ed., 1989), p. 142, quoting Calvin according to whom man has by nature "sensus divinitatis naturali instinctu"; H. Kraemer, *Religion and the Christian Faith* (London: Lutterworth Press, 1956), p. 79, about Bavinck's religious consciousness and Christian faith, and pp. 169–71, about Calvin's position quoting the same texts from the "Institution" as Bavinck.

9

Jesus and Mary as Poetical Images in Rūmī's Verse

Annemarie Schimmel

Poets in Islamic lands, and especially in the Persianate world, used to derive their imagery largely from the Qur'an, and from Qur'anic narratives about the prophets. These appear in the entire corpus of classical poetry, be it lyrical or epic, panegyric or mystical, although they are often strangely transformed.[1] One also finds allusions to Christian themes such as the scene well-known in classical Arabic poetry of drinking bouts in monasteries and the image of a seductive hair style called a "cross" which inspired love poets. But these themes do not concern us here.

Among the Qur'anic prophets, Jesus, the last messenger before Muhammad, plays a special role. Mentioned several times in the Qur'an, along with his virgin mother, he is generally referred to as ʿĪsā ibn Maryam, and also called *masīḥ*, "Messiah, Christ." Sometimes he appears as *rūḥ Allāh*, "God's spirit," and now and then as *nabī*, "prophet." Poets made reference not only to the Qur'anic narratives about this messenger, miraculously conceived as a proof of God's omnipotence and able to cure the sick and quicken the dead; they were also aware of the legends that had grown around his personality. The picture poets draw of Jesus is full of love, even though some poetical images may sound strange to a Christian reader.

From early days onward Jesus appears as the ideal ascetic.[2] Sufi lore knows many stories about him as a paragon of meekness and love of God, an idea based on the Qur'anic statement (S. 57:27) that there is kindness and mercy in the hearts of those who follow the Gospel, Jesus' special book. In this context it is important to remember that the rare references from the Gospel are usually allusions to the Sermon on the Mount. Stories from the Apocrypha were taken over very early. One story that seemed to have been very dear to Mawlānā Rūmī[3] concerns the answer Jesus gave to someone who asked him: "What is the heaviest thing in the world?" He answered: "God's wrath." Asked how to find rescue from this Divine wrath he replied: "Suppress your own wrath and oppress your own anger."

The way of Jesus, as often shown in Muslim literature, is that of abstinence and asceticism—however, as the Prophet said, "there is no monkery, *rahbāniyya*, in Islam." Thus in a famous passage of *Fīhi mā fīhi* (chap. 17) Rūmī dwells upon the necessity of marriage as a means of spiritual purification by "putting up with the absurdities of women." This, he claims, is the way of Muhammad and of the strong; those who cannot carry such a burden are advised to go to the desert and follow the way of Jesus by living far away from the world to achieve at least something of the spiritual path.

Although Jesus was the paragon of asceticism, he was seen by Rūmī as not at all sinister and dour looking but rather always smiling, contrary to his cousin John who never laughed: "The smiling was from confidence, and the frowning was from fear" (D 12885). The different behavior of the two prophets is explained in *Fīhi mā fīhi* (chap. 11):

> Jesus, upon whom be peace, laughed much; John, upon whom be peace, wept much. John said to Jesus: "You have become exceedingly secure against the subtle deceits, that you laugh so much." Jesus replied: "You have become all too unmindful of the subtle, secret and wonderful graces and kindness of God that you weep so much." One of God's friends was present when that happened. He asked God: "Which of them has the higher station?" God answered: "He who thinks better of Me"—that is to say: "I am with my servant's thought about Me. Every servant has an image and an idea of Me. Whatever picture he forms of Me, there I am."

Therefore allusions to the "sugarlike smile" of Jesus occur frequently in Rūmī's verse, and he admonishes his listeners to learn from Jesus how to laugh at the grief and worries caused by lust, male and female (D 21021)—that is, to be beyond worldly attachment.

Out of the most important quality of Jesus, the love of God, emerges his love of all creatures. Overlooking ugliness, he sees beauty in everything created by God, for as his soul was beautiful he could discover beauty everywhere. The most famous story in this respect, elaborated not by Rūmī but by both Niẓāmī and ʿAṭṭār, is that of Jesus and his disciples passing by a dead dog. While the disciples complained about the stench and the appalling view of the carcass, Jesus pointed to the shining white teeth of the dead creature. This story found its way even into German literature and is quoted by Goethe in his *West-Ostlicher Divan.*[4]

Jesus' ascetic life is highlighted in the allusions to Matthew 8:20, that the Son of Man has no place to put his head. He is the homeless wanderer, as Rūmī dramatically tells in *Fīhi mā fīhi* (chap. 11): when Jesus tried to find shelter in a jackal's den he was driven out by a revelation because his presence disturbed the jackal's whelps. This story (making use of a pun between the Arabic words *āwā*, "jackal," and *ma'wā*, "shelter") is used to instruct the reader that it is preferable to have a spiritual Beloved, a Divine Lord who drives His lover into the wilderness in constant quest for Him, than to live comfortably without knowing the yearning for God. Stories that Jesus did not build a house or own anything that would make life more comfortable were elaborated by Rūmī's predecessors Sanā'ī and especially ʿAṭṭār. Did he not use only half a brick as a pillow to rest his head? But when Satan told him, says ʿAṭṭār, that even this broken brick proved that he had not yet severed his bonds with the world, he threw it away.[5]

One understands well why the saying "The world is a bridge; pass over it but do not stay on it" was attributed to Jesus; it has been quoted frequently by the Sufis and is written in fine calligraphy over the gate of Akbar's palace city Fathpur Sikri. Rūmī therefore tells his audience, "Become a Jesus—if you have no house, let it be so!" (D 20645). Such stories and images are often connected with Jesus' dwelling place in the fourth heaven. Rūmī claims, "I am not bound to a house, for like Jesus my dwelling place is in the fourth heaven" (D 18388).

One of the miracles mentioned only in the Tradition (*ḥadīth*) is that Jesus could walk on water (as he did, according to the Gospels, on Lake Gennesaret). Early Sufi texts ascribe to the Prophet Muhammad the remark: "If my brother Jesus had had more *yaqīn*, [absolute certainty], he would have walked in the air."[6] This story, well-known among the Sufis, inspired Rūmī to some allusions where he puns on the name of Mary, Maryam, and *yam*, "ocean" (33481). Jesus is not only the perfect ascetic but also the man of prayer: "He went to the fourth heaven on the wings of prayer" (D 2559), said Rūmī, and a sincere prayer will be answered (as Sanā'ī had already stated) by Jesus' saying "Amen" from the fourth heaven.[7] In profane literature, then, the term "the prayer of Jesus" can be used as a symbol for something extremely protective and helpful.

It would be a special task to follow the way allusions to the Gospels appear in Sufi poetry; suffice it to mention that Sanā'ī has an impressive rendering of Christ's saying that one should rather pluck out one's eye than look at something prohibited,[8] advice apparently well-known even in medieval Indo-Muslim circles.

But how did the mystical poets, in the first place Rūmī, elaborate the data given in the Qur'an about Jesus? His creation through the breath of God was administered by Gabriel and has served time and again to point out God's omnipotence.

He makes appear a child without father,
He makes the child speak in the cradle,

says ʿAṭṭār in the *Pāndnāma*. This figure of speech is commonplace in hymns of praise. For while Mary had vowed a fast which included silence (S. 3:41), her son spoke in the cradle to defend her innocence (S. 19:31): "Lo, I am God's servant. God has given me the book and made me a prophet. Blessed be He who made me wherever I be, and He has enjoined me to pray, and to give alms, as long as I live, and likewise to cherish my mother." The silence of Mary and the speech of the child is a favorite topic with the poets, so much so that writers could use it in their chains of oath formulas, like Waṭwaṭ who swears, "By the faith in the questions of Jesus in the cradle."[9] Rūmī, like other poets, uses this image in spring poems when

> the once deposed narcissus becomes the overseer of the kingdom
> and the buds, like Jesus, are intelligent and can recite (D 18166).

Or, in another example:

> The wind seeking and running, the waters washing their hands—
> We [are] talking in a way like Christ while the dust is silent like Mary (D 17351)

This mysterious talk of Jesus is the soul's talk: for is not the human soul bound in the body like Jesus in the cradle? (D 16689).

Much later, after Jesus had proved his role as prophet and servant of God by talking in the cradle, he made a table prepared come down from heaven: "For them it was a feast, a meal, and a proof of his mission" (S. 5:111 f.). This table (after which S. 5 received its name) is connected with Jesus' statement that he never told his followers to take him and his mother as two deities. The mysterious table is a sign of Divine grace, comparable to the manna and quails that were given to the children of Israel in the desert:

> From the lovely desert of Moses and from the table of Jesus—
> What kind of dainties and food and sweets is this, O God! (D 1052)

But Rūmī knows well that people will not be satisfied with this divinely sent table, as they had complained when Moses miraculously produced food in the desert (M 1:83). (The miracles of Moses and Jesus often appear as parallels in poetry.)

The table of grace, the spiritual food, is generally mentioned by Rūmī in poems that praise fasting, for

> It is the rule of Your kindness to give a table from heaven
> to those who fast like Christ. (D 19904)

According to the Qurʾan (S. 3:43; 5:110) Jesus could fashion little clay birds into which he breathed to make them alive "with God's permission": Rūmī therefore sees himself as a clay bird that learns to fly when the beloved breathes into him (D 14962).

In the same verses of the Qur'an Jesus is mentioned as quickening the dead, and it is this quality of his that is very often alluded to in poetry. For it makes him the ideal symbol of the spiritual leader who quickens the dead souls, as well as of the Beloved who is able to revive those who have been slain on the path of love and longing. In this connection the name of Lazarus, ʿĀzar, is often mentioned by poets, including by Khāqānī (who had a thorough knowledge of Christian traditions). Rūmī may claim to see even the dead dancing in their shrouds at the return of the longed-for beloved: "Is this the blowing of the trumpet or a second Jesus?" (D 21736). For Jesus is not only the one who can breathe new life into an individual. He is also the one who will appear to inaugurate a happy time of forty years after killing the *dajjāl* before the resurrection and Last Judgment begin; he is "a sign of the Hour" (S. 43:61). Thus, poets fond of personifying abstractions (and this is one of Rūmī's stylistic peculiarities) can say that Jesus (= the beloved) "will kill the *dajjāl* 'Grief' when he returns" (D 4789).

The beloved is, for Rūmī, "the prophet of the sick" (D 19646); he is so powerful that he can give life to a thousand Jesuses (D 12666). Other loving exaggerations of this kind are not lacking in his verse. Sometimes, however, it is not the beloved but Love itself that is equated with Jesus, for Love revives the dead and heals the sick:

As Love is the Jesus of the age and seeks someone dead—
Die completely before its beauty, like me, and don't fear! (D 12918)

The idea that Jesus quickens the dead often takes a turn which may sound frivolous to the Christian reader but is used thousands of times in Persian and Persianate poetry from the earliest days. The life-bestowing breath of Christ is the equivalent of a kiss. This is logical, for from antiquity the exchange of kisses was considered an exchange of souls, the soul being contained in the breath. One of the best known examples of this imagery is Rūmī's oft-imitated verse:

When someone asks you: "How did Christ quicken the dead?"
Then give me a kiss in his presence: "Thus!" (D 19180)

Expanding the idea that Jesus' breath grants new life, not only a kiss but almost everything enjoyable can be compared to it. Thus in Rūmī's verse the sound of the harp or other musical instruments has "the quality of Jesus's breath" (D 26636), that is, gives new life to the soul. This, however, seems to be restricted to his imagery as his compositions were generally triggered by music.

The most common usage, on the other hand, is the combination of Jesus and spring or the spring breeze (D 22658). For spring is the time when the "martyrs," the plants which appear dead, slain by winter's cruelty, resurface from their shrouds (D 21172)—an elegant elaboration of the Qur᾿anic proof of resurrection. One of the oldest Persian lyricists, Abū ᶜAlī Marvazī, had used the combination of Christ and spring;[10] as did many other writers through the centuries, including Anvarī and Saᶜdī.

In many cases, though rarely in Rūmī's verse, Jesus and his breath are combined with Khiḍr, who grants the seeker the Water of Life: both of them could symbolize the beloved and his kiss. The same imagery has been applied in panegyric poetry as well. As early as in the days of Maḥmūd of Ghazna, Farrūkhī compared his patron to Jesus, just as later Khāqānī praises the ruler who, being the "Jesus of the age," has quickened the country's dead body—that is, has reestablished its prosperity. Later poets, especially in India, sometimes twisted this very theme ironically, asking whether in their day there was any difference between the shop of Christ and that of a vet.[11]

Besides as reviver of the dead, Jesus appears even more frequently as the great physician who heals all ailments and grants sight by means of his *fusun*, his incantation, to those born blind (cf. S. 4:100). But his healing breath is a sign of God's creative breath:

> Sometimes He breathes and makes a Jesus son of Mary
> So that the one with a breath like Jesus becomes a witness to His breath.
> (D 30659)

For it was the pre-eternal Divine grace that was active in his miracles as in those of other prophets.

In his quality as physician Jesus is usually called *ṭabīb*, and Rūmī claims, "We are skilled physicians for we are disciples of Christ" (D 15549). It is only the beloved's Christ-like breath that can heal those who have fallen ill from longing (D 1766). Since Christ can heal the blind-born, *akmah*, his name appears sometimes in connection with *surma* or *kuḥl*, the collyrium or antimony used to brighten the eye and to strengthen the eyesight.

> I was an eye full of pain, so I grasped Jesus (D 16624)

> Why should the eye weep all the time when it has found collyrium from the prophet Christ? (D 31682)

Thus asks Rūmī, who also tells a lovely story about an ascetic who was blamed by worldly people because of his uninterrupted weeping. He is admonished,

> Do not grieve about your eyes when Jesus is yours—
> Don't seek the life of the *body* from your Jesus. (M 2: 449 ff.)

For even if the bodily eyes are lost, the eyes of the spirit will be opened.

But in order to be blessed by such a transformation one must look at Jesus and not at his donkey (D 12254), that is, seek a spiritual cure and not a material one. Once such a healing process has been performed, Rūmī calls those who have experienced it to enter the cosmic dance:

> The blind and the deaf in this world who were healed by the son of Mary,
> are called by him to enter the mystical dance. (D 2100)

The same idea of transformation leads Rūmī to call Jesus the Great Alchemy that produced spiritual changes in man, "who transforms your copper into gold" (D 25598).

Jesus can heal almost every ailment, but there is one illness even he is unable to cure by means of his miracle-working breath. That is foolishness. Rūmī elaborates this idea in an entertaining story in the *Mathnavī* (M 3: 2570 ff.): Jesus was seen running as if he were fleeing from wild lions, withdrawing to a mountaintop to retreat from the world. The reason for his behavior, as he explains, it is that there are too many fools around him and these are the only people whom even he cannot cure.

The main difference between Qur'anic and biblical christology is found in the negation by the Qur'an of Jesus' crucifixion. Sūra 4:155–57 states that "they did not kill him and did not crucify him but We lifted him up and made someone to look like him." Persian writers sometimes connect the word *tarsa*, "Christian" and its other meaning "afraid"; Rūmī uses this expression to denote *guman*, "doubtful thought," because the true believer does not think that Christ has been crucified (D 7642). And the four-pointed cross becomes a symbol of the four elements of which the world is made:

> Far be the portico of joy from fire and water and dust and wind!
> The composition of the true confessors of Unity be as far away from those
> four simple elements as from the cross! (D 7215)

It is the Christians who have invented such things, and Mawlānā has told in great detail in the first book of the *Mathnavī* how a Jewish vizier helped his king to uproot the Christians by disguising himself as a zealous Christian hermit. Before committing suicide, he distributed his "will" to his twelve closest Christian friends. But as each document contradicted the other, the followers of the twelve leaders began to fight among themselves and were extinguished, with the exception of those who studied the Gospels intensely and found the name of *Aḥmad* (= the most praised one, *perikletos*)—that is, the *paraklet*—and became as it were Muslims *avant la lettre*. A similar criticism of "Jewish rancor" appears once more in the end of the *Mathnavī* (6: 3267–70): A treacherous vizier wanted to cheat Jesus and went out in the hope of becoming the leader of the people who followed Christ, but because he looked like Jesus it was he who was crucified in Jesus' place.

The place to which Jesus was uplifted is, according to tradition, the fourth heaven. Thus he becomes a symbol of the spiritual ascension of the soul:

> You draw the Jesus "Soul" from dust (*tharā*) beyond the Pleiads (*thurayyā*)—
> Without above and below you draw him every moment to the Highest Lord. (D 35788)

For this reason it is said:

> The soul that belongs to the Divine Throne goes toward Jesus;
> The soul that belongs to Pharaoh goes toward Qārūn. (D 8677)

For Jesus, symbol of the spiritual part of man, is sometimes contrasted in poetry with Qārūn, the biblical Korah, who hoarded immense treasures and was swallowed by the earth due to their weight. Sanā'ī seems to have been the first poet to allude to Jesus and Qārūn together in one verse;[12] the comparison then became commonplace.

The poets often mentioned Christ's heavenly abode: living in this lofty place, "What has he to do with grieving about heat or cold?" (D 11661). And even more: "What has Jesus, dwelling in the fourth heaven, to do with the church?" (D 1283). Astrologically speaking, the fourth heaven is the place of the sun. For this reason Rūmī could mention Jesus even more in this connection than other writers would, because it enabled him to allude to the miracles of his spiritual beloved Shamsaddīn, the "Sun" of Tabrīz: through him, the representative of Muhammad, the power and glory of earlier prophets manifests itself.

It may seem strange that Jesus, the Spirit of God, appears not in the immediate presence of the Divine Throne but only in the fourth heaven, even though this is the central sphere because of the sun. Whatever the reason for the tradition (which may have developed from an aversion to the Christian formula of Jesus "sitting at God's right hand"), the Sufis found an explanation: although Jesus was perfect in his asceticism, he still carried a comb and a cup with him. Seeing someone combing his hair with his fingers, he threw away the comb and, discovering that one could drink water from the fountain by using the palm of one's hand, he parted with the cup. And yet, it was discovered that he had a needle in his garment, and for a spiritual being like him, "a needle will become a veil like the treasure of Qārūn" (D 27085). Rūmī had taken over the story of the needle from Sanā'ī who, as it seems, had used it for the first time in mystical Persian poetry:

> Had he not carried that needle with him,
> He would have arrived just beneath the Throne of God.[13]

The source for Sanā'ī is probably al-Ghazālī's *Iḥyā' 'ulūm al-dīn*. Somewhat later, 'Aṭṭār alluded to it in his Persian epics, as did Ibn al-Jawzī in his Arabic prose work. Poets of the sixteenth and seventeenth centuries speak of the needle and the long thread, a thread which is "extended hope," *ṭūl al-amal*, a quality disliked by the Sufis. As for the meaning of the original story, Jāmī, following Rūmī, explains that such a needle "is like a thorn in the foot of the *himmat* [spiritual high ambition] of Jesus"[14]—the more spiritualized one becomes the more dangerous is even the smallest attachment to anything that is part of "the world."

Less mystical poets, however, would compare the beloved's slender waist to the needle of Jesus, or claim that their bodies were much more worn out than his needle while (and because) the beloved's lips are finer than the *rishta-i Maryam*, the extremely fine thread Mary spun. These images, used in Khāqānī's poetry, sound quite exaggerated to a modern Western reader, who might enjoy better a verse by Ghanī Kashmīrī stating that even Jesus' breath can work only if there is an innate capacity to receive it—even he will not be able to make the needle's blind eye able to see.[15]

The fourth heaven, place of high spirituality, is often contrasted in poetry with the world of matter, as symbolized by Jesus' donkey. One knows that

> Jesus used to ride on a donkey out of modesty—
> Otherwise, how would the morning breeze ride on a donkey's back? (D 35585)

In Rūmī's work the combination of Jesus and donkey occurs so frequently that one wonders what the reason might be. It seems impossible to assume that a dim remembrance of early Christian days had survived, when in the time of Emperor Severus around A.D. 200, a picture of a crucified donkey was drawn in the Palatin to ridicule and shock the Christian community in Rome. In any case, the donkey had a bad reputation as an extremely stubborn and, more than that, sensual creature (works like Apuleius's *Golden Ass* come to mind, and Rūmī's *Mathnavī* contains some coarse and even obscene donkey stories). Sanā'ī had used the Jesus-donkey contrast to point to the contrast of soul and matter:[16] the soul should not sleep in the mud like a donkey, as Rūmī says (D 31107). Again, the "donkey in the mud" image is found frequently in both Sanā'ī's and 'Aṭṭār's verse. They repeat with slight variations the idea that the loving soul goes to heaven like Jesus and one need no longer care for the dead ass (D 1090)—that is, man's material part.

> Jesus son of Mary went to heaven, and his donkey remained here—
> I remained on earth, and my heart went up. (D 19085)

In a considerable number of stories and verses Rūmī tells of the loss of a donkey and interpreting them one finds that to lose the donkey is, in the end, not really a loss (D 14608) but rather a gain because after losing the material mount the soul can fly to heaven (D 20053). Those who serve the "donkey," the world of matter, do not understand anything of mysteries; therefore one should not cast so many delicate words of the Jesus "Soul" into the ass's heart and ear (D 18523) or offer the dainties of Jesus, such as selflessness and spiritual intoxication (D 31341), to the donkey in his stable; in short, one should not cast pearls before swine. For, as Sanāʾī says:

How could the donkey know Jesus's worth?
How could the deaf know David's melodies?[17]

Rūmī, however, thinks that kindly Jesus would probably not withhold candy from the donkey, even though the stupid creature is more interested in straw (M 6: 152).

It is amazing to see what foul language Rūmī uses when emphasizing the contrast between spirit and matter. Could one speak of Christ and at the same time smell a donkey's urine or dung (D 26025)? And, "Far be the ass's arse from the cradle of Jesus!" (D 11698). For

The lip that has kissed the ass's arse—
how could it find the sweet kiss of Christ? (D 1070)

There is no end to such remarks in Rūmī's *Dīvān*—remarks which at times bring a blush to the translator who tries to render his poetry into another language.

Yet, despite all his aversion to "material donkeys," Rūmī never gives up hope—Love can transform even an ass:

When the donkey drinks the wine of Jesus,
at some point he will sprout wings. . . . (D 10730)

The Jesus-donkey combination remained alive in Persian poetry throughout the centuries until Ghanī Kashmīrī in seventeenth-century India says in an amusing turn of the image: "Anyone who talks about Jesus in front of the beloved's life-bestowing lips, is a donkey!"[18]

Jesus, spirit from the Divine Spirit, stands beyond the multiple sects and creeds. He is, as Rūmī states (M 1: 500), *yakrang*, "unicolored"; he adheres to the one truth and thus comes to represent those who have taken the *ṣibghat Allāh* (S. 2:132), the "coloring" or "baptism" of God by which all the various colors of this world are washed off so that the saint or prophet appears in the radiant white garb of Divine Light. This idea had already been expressed by Sanāʾī, who admonishes his reader:

Take away this seven-colored gown from your hand,
Take a unicolored robe like Jesus

So that you may walk on the water like Jesus
And travel with sun and moon![19]

As Jesus is frequently called "Son of Mary" it is natural that his virgin mother should play an important role in Persianate poetry. Was she not, as the *Musnad* of Ibn Ḥanbal states, one of the four best women that ever lived on earth? The poets loved Mary (a love still visible, for example, in the visits of pious Turks at Mary's alleged tomb near Ephesus), and Mawlānā Rūmī is no exception. However he seems to be the only major poet to have devoted a full chapter (of his *Mathnavī*, M 2: 3602–13) to the story how Yaḥyā, John the Baptist, bowed in worship before Christ while still in his mother's womb.

The Qurʾanic statements about Mary begin with her birth and her mother's vow. Zacharias, her relative, was made her guardian, and whenever he came to bring her food in the inner chamber where she lived she had already received food from the Unseen and had seen the fruits of Paradise. (The term *miḥrāb*, used in the Qurʾan for this chamber, inspired the pious to write this story, or at least its beginning, around *miḥrābs* in mosques all over the world.) Rūmī quotes this story and the prayer of Zacharias through which his old, barren wife became pregnant in *Fīhi mā fīhi* (chap. 44) as proof of God's omnipotence, which is displayed at such occasions. Mary had vowed her virginity to God and the Qurʾan describes how Gabriel, the Holy Spirit, presented himself to her as "a man without fault" (S. 19:17). Rūmī dwells upon the story of the annunciation in the third book of the *Mathnavī* (M 3: 1700 ff.) and tells it with such tenderness that it almost sounds as if it were taken from a medieval Christian book of devotions. It happened during her bath that the spiritual form came to her to blow into the shirt which she had taken off—hence later poetical allusions to the "breath in her sleeve."

Mary could easily become a symbol of the pure soul (D 18042) or the heart made pregnant by the Divine spirit (D 5475), and Rūmī once equates the gift that came to her from the Unseen with the *amāna*, the entrusted good mentioned in S. 33:72. But he knew that one thing is required to make the "Heart"—Mary pregnant with Jesus, and that is pain, grief, and sorrow:

The thought, touched by grief as though that were Gabriel,
becomes pregnant with two hundred Jesuses. (D 24406)

And, even more beautiful:

If the treasure "Grief for Him" is in your heart, that heart becomes "light upon light" (S. 24:35)
like the lovely Mary who has Jesus in her womb. (D 5490)

Phrases of this kind appear in Rūmī's verse rather often but images alluding to Mary's virginity and pregnancy can be found in less spiritual connections as well. This is the case especially when poets speak of their novel "virgin" thought which then results in the eloquent child Jesus and his sweet words.

Even an untutored reader may perhaps understand that, as Khāqānī says, the lips of the beloved seem to give birth to a Jesus in such a way that a Mary seems to be hidden in the friend's mouth;[20] but when an eighteenth-century poetaster in India compares the wine bottle to Mary who carries in her womb the fragrant Jesus, the life-bestowing wine, one may not exactly relish the image.

At the end of her pregnancy Mary was overcome by birth pangs and, as the Qur'an tells, went to a dried-up date palm which she grasped, and the tree showered fruits upon her. It is this kind of fruit that called out to Mary: "Eat, drink and be in good mood!" (S. 19:25), that the faithful should eat (D 1213). The giving of fruit by the barren tree parallels the miracle of Zacharias's barren wife giving birth to John (D 35797): in all these events it is the breath of God that acts (D 13058). For Rūmī it is once more the question of "pain" that is central in his allusions to the dry palm tree (M 2: 93). Had Mary not felt the pangs of labor she would never have received such a sweet gift. Just like Mary's virginity and pregnancy, the miracle of the dates was also alluded to by poets to point to their creativity: "The word is a witness to the virgin, that is, my thought as the date palm is for Mary's miracle,"[21] and it did not take long for authors to compare the reed pen that produced sweet words to the dry date palm that yielded sweet fruit.[22]

That Mary took a vow of silence led to her son's defense of her and thus, her silence and his eloquence are often juxtaposed:

> Sometimes, like Jesus, we have become all tongue;
> Sometimes, like Mary, we have a silent heart. (D 17402)

Likewise her fasting, which is "a preparation of Divine Love" (D 32065) is seen in relation to the table of Jesus (D 26303).

One of the loveliest usages of the image of Mary is her connection with the garden. Although the Qur'an states that she and her son were given a quiet place with springs (S. 23:52), it seems unlikely that this remark contributed much to the garden imagery. It was the experience of the revival, the miraculous new birth of greenery in spring that inspired the poets to use such a combination, which goes back to the earliest days of Persian poetry. Kisā'ī wrote, "It seems that the midnight breeze became Gabriel so that the roots and dry trees became Mary!"[23] Rūmī has taken over this idea with a rather daring extension:

> The wind seems to be Gabriel and the trees Mary:
> Look at the hand-play, like that of husband and wife! (D 21030)

The result of such a play between wind and trees is the birth of the Jesus "Rose"

(D 10589), again not a novel image. Long before Rūmī, Abū ʿAlī Marvazī had sung:

> The Mary "Bud," in whose womb the rose "Jesus" is found
> comes with her face opened like the paradisiacal virgins![24]

Such an image reminds the Christian reader of one of the old Christmas carols, which begins in German "Es ist ein Ros entsprungen."

Persian poets have also compared the cloud that becomes pregnant from the wind to Mary,[25] and in seventeenth-century India the monsoon cloud that brings sweet fruits[26] appears in a similar comparison. Other authors might invent more mundane images; Rūmī, however, loved to speak mainly of Mary and the garden in spring. In swinging rhythms he sings of all the branches which look

> as if they were Marys, pregnant by the angel's breath;
> They are all houris, born from amidst the dark dust. (D 30260)

Mary, the lovely branch which, touched by the sweet breeze, gave birth to the Jesus-like rose—that was a theme dear to many writers. But Rūmī emphasizes one aspect of Mary in particular: he repeats time and again that only pain and suffering made Mary, the pure soul, experience spiritual pregnancy and helped her to receive the sweet fruits when pain seemed unbearable. Alluding to the "birth of Jesus in the soul" in several verses of his *Dīvān*, he has fully elaborated the idea in *Fīhi mā fīhi* (chap. V):

> It is pain that guides a person in every enterprise . . . It was not until the pain of labor appeared in Mary that she made for the tree . . . Those pangs brought her to the tree, and the tree which was withered became fruitful. . . .
> The body is like Mary. Everyone of us has a Jesus within him, but until the pangs manifest in us our Jesus is not born. If the pangs never come, then Jesus rejoins his origin by the same secret path by which he came, leaving us bereft and without portion of him.

Thus, the birth of Christ in the soul was expressed by a Muslim mystic in Anatolia half a century before Eckhart in Germany spoke of this central experience of the mystic in Christianity.

Author's Note:

This article is the nucleus of a future book on the theme of Jesus and Mary in Persian poetry. Rūmī's works quoted: *Dīvān-i kabīr*, ed. Badīʿuzzamān Furūzanfār, 10 vols. (Tehran: Tehran University Press, 1957 ff.)—D with the line numbers; *Mathnawīyi maʿnawī*, ed. Reynold Alleyne Nicholson, 8 vols. (London: Luzac, 1925–50); M with number of the book and line.

NOTES

1. See, e.g., Asin Palacious, "Logia et agrapha Domini Jesu," in *Patrologia orientalis* 13 (1919): 335–431, 19 (1926): 532–624; Michael Hayek, *Le Christ de l'Islam* (Paris: Éd. du Seuil, 1959); Roger Arnaldez, *Jesus fils de Marie, prophète de l'Islam* (Paris: Desclée, 1980); Abdal Jalil, *Marie et l'Islam* (Paris: Beauchesne, 1950); Olaf Schumann, *Der Christus der Muslime* (Gutersloh: Gerd Mohn, 1975); James Robson, "Stories of Jesus and Mary," *The Muslim World* 40 (1960): 235–42; W.N. Wyham, "Jesus in the Poetry of Iran," *The Muslim World* 42 (1960): 104–11.

2. S. Tor Andrae, *In the Garden of Myrtles*, trans. Birgitta Sharpe (Albany: State University of New York Press, 1988).

3. M 4: 113–115; *Fīhi mā Fīhi*, ed. Badīʿuzzmān Furūzanfār (Tehran: Tehran University Press, 1328sh/1959); English trans. Arthur J. Arberry, *Discourses of Rūmī* (London: London University Press, 1961), chap. 64.

4. Johann Wolfgang von Goethe, *West-Ostlicher Divan*, hrsg. Ernst Beutler (Leipzig: Dietrich, 1943), "Noten und Abhandlungen: Allgemeines" (S. 192).

5. Sanāʿī, *Ḥadīqat al-Haqīqat wa Ṭarīqat al-Sharīʿat*, ed. Mudarris Razavī (Tehran, Tahuri, 1329sh/1959), p. 317; Farīduddīn ʿAṭṭār, *Muṣībatnāma*, ed. N. Wisal (Tehran, Zawwar, 1338sh/1959), chap. 36/10. For references to Jesus in ʿAṭṭār's epics, see Hellmut Ritter, *Das Meer ser Seele* (Leiden: E.J. Brill, 1957), index s.v. Jesus.

6. Abū Naṣr as-Sarrāj, *Kitāb al-Lumaʿ fī'l-Taṣawwuf*, ed. Reynold Alleyne Nicholson, (London: Luzac; Leiden: E.J. Brill, 1914), p. 155.

7. Sanāʾī, *Ḥadīqa*, p. 635.

8. Ibid., p. 353ff.

9. Rashīduddīn Waṭwaṭ, *Dīvān*, ed. Saʿīd Nafīsī (Tehran: Barani, 1339sh/1960), p. 26.

10. ʿAwfī, *Lubāb al-Albāb*, ed. Edward G. Browne and Mohammad Qazwini (London-Leiden: Luzac and Brill, 1903, 1906), 2: 340.

11. Ṭālib-i Āmulī, quoted in S. M. Ikram, *Armaghan-i Pak* (Karachi: Government of Pakistan Press, 1953), p. 279.

12. Sanāʾī, *Ḥadīqa*, p. 443.

13. Ibid., p. 392.

14. ʿAbdurraḥmān Jāmī, *Dīvan-i Kāmil*, ed. Hāshim Riẓā (Tehran: Payruz, 134sh/1962), p. 199, nr. 172.

15. Muḥammad Aṣlaḥ, *Tadhkirat-i Shuʿarā-i Kashmīr*, ed. Sayyid Ḥusāmuddīn Rahsdī, 5 vols. (Karachi: Iqbal Academy, 1969–70), 2: 999.

16. Sanāʾī, *Ḥadīqa*, p. 304.

17. Sanāʾī, *Mathnavīha*, ed. Mudarris Razavī (Tehran: University Press, 1343sh/1965), "Sayr al-ʿibād ilā ʾl-maʿād," line 13.

18. S.M. Ikram, *Armaghan-i Pak*, p. 241.

19. Sanāʾī, *Ḥadīqa*, p. 132.

20. Khāqānī Shirvanī, *Dīvan*, ed. Ẓiaʾuddīn Sajjāḍī (Tehran: Zawwar, 1338sh/1959), ghazal p. 564.

21. Khāqānī Shirvanī, *Dīvan*, p. 24.
22. Jāmī, *Dīvan-i Kamīl*, p. 227 nr. 247.
23. ʿAwfī, *Lubāb al-Albāb*, 2: 46.
24. Ibid., 2: 341.
25. Ibid., 2: 111.
26. Naziri, *Dīvan*, ed. Mazāhir Muṣaffā (Tehran: Amir Kabir, 133osh/1961), ghazal nr. 48.

10

Personal Transformation in Ibn al-ʿArabī and Meister Eckhart

James E. Royster

To discover and thereby uncover the deep similarities and identities in the *theoria* and *praxis* of two mystic theologians from different religious traditions is to provide a basis, perhaps the only authentic basis, for genuine appreciation of their inevitable differences. To the extent that the two thinkers reliably expound their respective traditions, one finds a unified/unifying foundation for valuing differences between the two traditions. Esoteric unicity enhances the significance of exoteric multiplicity. Conjunction envalues disjunction. Knowing one, we honor two.

Further, to discover the transcultural within the multicultural is to discover the transtemporal, the essential, and thereby to open to fresh manifestation. Opening to the timeless provides occasion for theophany. Meeting at common depth is meeting beyond difference and thereby meeting where only One is. Dialogue in depth is not only mutually informative but also potentially transformative. To the extent that the Sacred is met, transcendence occurs and thus transformation. Just as all authentic religion thrusts toward transcendence, so does dialogue in depth. Just as authentic religion is transformative, so dialogue in depth may be. The comparison of two prominent mystics of medieval times, Ibn al-ʿArabī and Meister Eckhart, offers an example of the potential for mutual exchange, discovery, transcendance, and thus transformation that lies in dialogue in depth.

Common Background and Orientation

Few have shaped the development of Islamic spirituality as profoundly as Muḥyī al-Dīn Muḥammad ibn ʿAlī ibn al-ʿArabī (560/1165–638/1240). He is the author of perhaps 700 different works, principal among which are *al-Futūḥāt al-*

Makkiyya (The Meccan Revelations), containing 560 chapters and a projected 17,000 pages in a forthcoming critical edition, and, his most influential work, *Fuṣūṣ al-Ḥikam* (Bezels of Wisdom), twenty-seven chapters setting forth the essential teachings of as many prophets, the book itself having been revealed to Ibn al-ʿArabī in a dream. "The most prolific of all Sufi writers," Ibn al-ʿArabī is commonly known as "al-Shaykh al-Akbar," the Greatest Master, not merely for the quantity of his output but most importantly for its depth and originality.[1]

Among the medieval mystics of Christianity, none stands out more than Meister Eckhart (1260–1328?). Highly popular during his own time and in the immediately following years, his reputation all but disappeared for several centuries. The last century and a half, however, has seen a gradually increasing interest in his work until, at the present time, he is almost unrivaled among the Christian mystics of medieval times.[2] Meister Eckhart was a teacher, preacher, and administrator in the Dominican order whose continuing influence is based on two groups of writings. His Latin works—unfinished, and with some lost—are made up of carefully executed theological treatises and exegetical commentaries. His German works consist mainly of sermons, many of which were preached to the Beguines, ascetic and pious laywomen who lived in loosely organized houses patterned after convents, and several treatises composed for purposes of consolation or instruction. As might be expected, Meister Eckhart's vernacular works are more creative and daring in expression than his formally written Latin works. Each set of writings affords insight into his mind and heart.[3]

Although separated by their respective religio-cultural milieus, Ibn al-ʿArabī and Meister Eckhart share a common religio-cultural substructure, the Judeo-Christian-Islamic world view. Although not overlapping in residence or travel (Germany and France for Meister Eckhart; Spain, North Africa, and the Middle East for Ibn al-ʿArabī), the two shared what might be designated the greater Euro-Mediterranean region. Although each lived in a different time, a mere twenty years separates the death of Ibn al-ʿArabī from the birth of Meister Eckhart.

Ibn al-ʿArabī and Meister Eckhart demonstrate several similarities in their respective approaches to religious truth. Both draw from a common, albeit broad, intellectual domain, the Platonic and Neoplatonic, and interpret and apply the central perspectives of Greek metaphysics to and within their respective traditions.[4] In addition, each may have read theologians and philosophers who worked from within the other's primary religio-intellectual tradition. For example, Meister Eckhart knew Ibn Sīnā (Avicenna) and Ibn Rushd (Averroes) and Ibn al-ʿArabī may well have been acquainted with the Alexandrian church fathers.[5] This common heritage and possible cross-fertilization notwithstanding, Ibn al-ʿArabī and Meister Eckhart drew most heavily from the philosophers, theologians, exegetes, and mystics of their respective, immediate traditions, Islam and Christianity.

No literary authority, however, could hold rank with the Bible for Meister Eckhart or the Qurʾan for Ibn al-ʿArabī. The central tenets in each theosophist's system were authenticated in scripture, albeit often creatively—that is, nontraditionally—interpreted. Each believed that there are deeper, hidden meanings that only become apparent to those who are ready for them.[6] For example, Ibn al-ʿArabī, writing to novices on the Sufi path, asserted: "There are infinite meanings within the verses of the Holy Qurʾan, within every word, changing with your states and levels, knowledge and understanding."[7]

The historical sources cited so far, equally available to many others in the twelfth- to fourteenth-century Christian and Muslim worlds, fail in themselves to account for the uniqueness and subsequent far-reaching influence of the Shaykh al-Akbar and the Meister. This all-too-brief excursus into "horizontal" sources is intended only to highlight the all-important "vertical" Source that fecundates the distinctive contribution of the two mystics. Without the direct contact that each had with the divine, without the theophanies directly witnessed as each opened to the One Ultimate, neither could have produced the profound, original, and authoritative works that he did.[8]

The "speculative systems" of Ibn al-ʿArabī and Meister Eckhart are far from merely speculative. Both men founded their thought on their own direct, personal experience.[9] Ibn al-ʿArabī's imaginal world, a *barzakh* (isthmus, intermediate region) between the sphere of incorporeal spirit and the material world, was a realm of immediate experience for him.[10] According to his own report the entire contents of *Fuṣūṣ al-Ḥikam* came to him from this realm. In chapter 367 of *al-Futūḥāt al-Makkiyya* and in his *Kitāb al-Isrāʾ*, Ibn al-ʿArabī recounts his own personal *miʿrāj* (ascension), observing that "my voyage [to Allah] was only in myself."[11] That this was not mere fantasy unrelated to waking life is indicated in the Shaykh's note that "from the day I attained this station [i. e., the final station, that of pure servanthood] I have not possessed any living thing, indeed not even the clothing I wear."[12] His subjective, imaginal experience had a direct influence on the way he lived his life objectively. Ibn al-ʿArabī uses the intimately experiential term *dhawq*, "tasting," to designate the authoritative knowledge that comes through personal experience, thus distinguishing this knowledge from the ordinary knowledge that is gained through the mere transmission of information. "[True] knowledge," he affirms, "comes only through tastings."[13]

Even while stressing the decisive importance of personal experience, Ibn al-ʿArabī and Meister Eckhart were both quite reticent, apparently out of a sense of humility, about conveying their own private experiences, Meister Eckhart being somewhat more reserved even than Ibn al-ʿArabī. Though it is rare in the

Meister's writings, one does occasionally find the personal pronoun. "Here God's ground is my ground and my ground is God's ground. Here I live from my own as God lives from His own." Again, "God and I are one. Through knowledge I take God into myself, through love I enter into God."[14] Some interpreters believe that the enigmatic phrase, "pregnant with Nothing," in Meister Eckhart's sermon on Paul's Damascus Road blindness is itself the record of a personal experience, written in the third person as Paul himself occasionally did (e.g., in 2 Cor. 12:2 ff.): "It appeared to a man as in a dream—it was a waking dream—that he became pregnant with Nothing like a woman with child, and in that Nothing God was born."[15] Finally, by means of an analogy, Meister Eckhart affirms direct and immediate experience as the source of knowledge: "If a person lives in a beautifully painted house, other people who have never been inside may indeed have opinions about it; but the one whose house it is *knows*. In the same way I am certain that I live and that God lives."[16]

Metaphysics

Ibn al-ʿArabī and Meister Eckhart were both metaphysicians of the highest order. And both understood metaphysics in a traditional sense, as "the science of Ultimate Reality" and "a wisdom which liberates," to use Seyyed Hossein Nasr's characterization.[17] It is, in fact, their investigation of being as well as beyond-being and their understanding of the connection between being and knowledge that mark them as traditional metaphysicians.[18] *Waḥdat al-wujūd*, commonly translated "Oneness of Being," identifies Ibn al-ʿArabī's fundamental metaphysical perspective. Derived from *wajada*, however, *wujūd* also carries the sense of finding. Chittick notes that Ibn al-ʿArabī's "main concern is not with the mental concept of being but with the experience of God's Being, the tasting (*dhawq*) of Being, that 'finding' which is at one and the same time to perceive and to be that which truly is."[19] Similarly, Austin believes that in using *wujūd* Ibn al-ʿArabī intended to "convey the meaning of the Oneness of both Being and Perception in the perfect and complete union of the one and only Reality." He points out further that *wajada* carries the idea "of being and therefore objectivity, and that of perception and therefore subjectivity, both of which [are] one in *the* Reality."[20] Since finding occurs within and by means of awareness, and perception is itself awareness, we can indeed conclude that *wujūd* conveys the oneness of being and awareness (or consciousness), in the Ultimate as Source and in the one who "ones" with the One. Ontology and epistemology, being and knowing, are a single reality, distinguishable but not divisible.[21]

The Ultimate for Ibn al-ʿArabī is the Essence, God in Himself and thus unrelated to any created thing. The Essence is unknowable and unnameable. At best only negative assertions can be postulated of Him since any positive propositions would be necessarily limiting and therefore incorrect. Izutsu indicates that Ibn al-ʿArabī distinguishes between the Essence in itself, on one hand, and in relationship, on the other, by means of *al-Aḥad* and *al-Wāḥid*: "The Aḥad is the pure and absolute One—the reality of existence in a state of absolute undetermination, the prephenomenal in its ultimate and unconditional prephenomenality—whereas the Wāḥid is the same reality of existence at a stage where it begins to turn toward phenomenality." The *Aḥad* is "the One standing beyond all determination" while the *Wāḥid* is "the One with internal articulations."[22] In some contexts Ibn al-ʿArabī employs *al-Ḥaqq* and Allah, in others He-ness and Lordship, to make this distinction between the Absolute in itself and in relationship to created entities.[23] While the terminology may change, the distinction itself—even though it lies in the dualistic nature of the human mind and not in the essential nature of the Ultimate—remains consistent.

Ibn al-ʿArabī responds to the central ontological question, why is there anything rather than nothing, by means of a *ḥadīth qudsī*: "I was a Treasure but was not known. So I loved to be known, and I created the creatures and made Myself known to them."[24] Thus, love is the initiating movement giving existence to all created things.[25] Ibn al-ʿArabī further develops his understanding of creation by using another metaphor he draws from the prophetic tradition, the Breath of the Merciful. Immediately prior to creation an intense pressure, even distress (*karb*, derived from a root meaning "to overload"), led to the merciful spewing forth of all that is. Ibn al-ʿArabī writes: "The Cosmos is manifested in the divine Breath by which God relieved the divine Names from the distress they experienced by the nonmanifestation of their effects." A few lines later, poetically, he affirms:

> All is essentially in the Breath,
> As light is, in essence, in the dark before dawn.[26]

The manifest emerges out of the nonmanifest as light emerges out of darkness at dawn. Austin notes that mercy (*raḥma*) is "the very principle of creation by which all created things exist and by which all the latent potentialities [the Divine Names] within the 'divine mind' are released into actuality."[27] Thus we see that love and mercy, two words implying a movement toward another, lie at the very heart of Ibn al-ʿArabī's ontology and cosmogony. All-that-is emerges out of the Absolute by means of love/mercy.

Meister Eckhart's metaphysics is strikingly similar in some respects to that of the Shaykh al-Akbar. In the prologue to his unfinished *Opus Tripartitum* Eckhart asserts: "Existence is God [*esse est Deus*]."[28] By this identification of existence with God he affirms the unity of being, since God is essentially Unity/One. Unity, in itself totally devoid of distinction, is for Eckhart Absolute and prior to all differentiation. Following Boethius in his *Consolation of Philosophy*, Eckhart explains the relationship of the transcendentals: "As the good and true are grounded and established through existence and in existence, so also existence is grounded and established in the one and through the one."[29]

Eckhart's assertion that existence is God does not mean that he held a pantheistic view; for him the existence that marks all created things is borrowed. Insofar as (*in quantum*) anything is, its existence is derived and therefore the existent entity is not self-sufficient. Created things are in themselves nothing: "Everything created is nothing of itself." Eckhart also declares God to be Nothing when he attributes existence to creatures. If existence or being is attributed to creatures then it must be denied of God; therefore, in relationship to the beingness of created entities, God is Nothing.[30] In maintaining that God is Nothing Eckhart is also asserting that God is purity of being, or the being of being. Eckhart's dialectic amounts to a refusal to reduce God to existence while maintaining an essential relationship between God and created things. We also see how Eckhart, like Ibn al-ʿArabī, makes statements that seem contradictory but that are in fact consistent in terms of underlying principle. The meanings of particular terms or expressions may change from one context or argument to another, while consistency in principle prevails throughout the larger metaphysical framework.

Eckhart indentifies God as *intelligere* (depending on context—intellect, intelligence, understanding, knowing) and equates being and intelligence in God. "Where isness is not understanding, there is never unity," Eckhart claims.[31] In fact, his ascription of nonbeing to God is partly by way of giving priority to God as Intellect. At the same time, in other contexts, he affirms the priority of being to intelligence.[32] What is of interest for our purposes here is that Meister Eckhart, like Ibn al-ʿArabī, finds an essential identity between being and knowing in God. While the discursive mind distinguishes between them, in the unity of the divine they are one. To be is to know and to know is to be. And, according to macrocosm/microcosm homology, or the esoteric principle of Hermes Trismegistus, "as above, so below," in man too consciousness is reality and reality is consciousness.

Though the terminology is different, Eckhart, like Ibn al-ʿArabī, distinguishes between God as He is commonly known in religion, on the one hand, and as a reality prior to this known God, on the other hand—that is, between God and Godhead. "Before there were creatures, God was not 'God': He was That which He was. But when creatures came into existence and received their *created* being, then God was not 'God' in Himself—He was 'God' in creatures." Even more boldly, the Meister exclaims: "Let us pray to God that we may be free of God that we may gain the truth and enjoy it eternally, there where the highest angel, the fly and the soul are equal," that is, where Absolute Oneness prevails.[33] Eckhart's Godhead, John Caputo summarizes, "signifies God as He is in Himself, apart from any name we give to Him and apart from His relation to creatures."[34]

Indeed, the Godhead cannot be named since all naming necessarily limits. While Eckhart prefers apophatism to kataphatism, he also recognizes that negation too limits that to which it is applied. Even unity, though appearing positive, implies the negative—that is, nonmultiple and nondivided. Therefore, Eckhart believes it necessary to negate negation when referring to the Godhead. "The negation of negation," he writes "is the purest affirmation and the fullness of the term affirmed."[35] He also points out that the "negation of a negation is transcendently acknowledged as God's affirmation of himself." This is divine knowledge, the self-knowledge of the Godhead, principally known from the standpoint of pure Intellect, which becomes available only through the most radically detached intellection.[36]

The Godhead, as we have seen, is in itself totally without distinction. Eckhart takes up the question of creation in terms of *bollitio* and *ebollitio*, boiling and boiling over. *Bollitio* marks the arising of the Persons of the Trinity and *ebollitio* accounts, in Eckhart's scheme, for the production of all created things.[37] Thus, all distinctive entities have their ultimate origin in the Godhead and take on created status by right of emanating from and flowing out of the Godhead. This flowing from does not, however, constitute essential or absolute separation. "When the Father begat all creatures," Eckhart exclaims, "He begat me also, and I flowed out with all creatures and yet remained in the Father." He illustrates his point by noting how the very words he is speaking remain in him even while flowing out to his audience.[38] Fox regards this "remaining in" as Eckhart's "expression of the authentic and altogether orthodox doctrine of panentheism . . . , that all is in God and God is in all."[39]

In his German sermons Eckhart uses *ursprunc* (literally, primitive [*ur*-] springing) to designate the movement of entities out of the Godhead. A similar term, now obsolete, *ursprinc*, denotes effervescence, efflorescence. As with Ibn al-ʿArabī, creation according to Meister Eckhart also results from an inner pressure and is seen as a kind of eruption. Reiner Schurmann introduces the term "dehiscence" to describe Eckhart's sense of creation. Dehiscence refers to the bursting forth of seeds from their mature pods or fruits, the first step in a new round of production. He writes: "God, man, and the world unveil themselves in their first 'dehiscence' (*uzbruch*, *Ausbruch*, or *uzvluz*, *Ausfluss*) from their origin, without a why."[40] Unlike the Shaykh, Eckhart does not postulate a motive for the creative process. *Sunder warumbe*, "without a why," is Eckhart's final "motive,"—motiveless motive—for creation. It is also man's only proper "motive" for worshipping the divine. The only entirely acceptable reason for loving God, Eckhart asserts, is because He is God.[41] And with this consideration we move from metaphysics to transformation, from exhalation to inhalation, to use a metaphor appropriate to Ibn al-ʿArabī, or from *exitus* (exit) to *reditus* (return), according to Eckhart.

Transformation

Ibn al-ʿArabī's concept of the Perfect Man (*al-insān al-kāmil*) dominates much of his thought.[42] He treats the concept on two levels, universal and individual. In his development of the Perfect Man on the macrocosmic level Ibn al-ʿArabī takes up such topics as *al-ḥaqīqa al-muḥammadiyya*, "man" as *imago dei*, and mankind as the apex of the creative hierarchy. Rather than investigate these dimensions of Ibn al-ʿArabī's metaphysical anthropology, we shall content ourselves to take up his understanding of the Perfect Man on the microcosmic level, particularly as his thought bears on the transformation of "ordinary" man into the Perfect Man. Even as saintship (*walāya*) is prerequisite to both prophethood and apostleship, so it is the basis or essential quality of the Perfect Man. The Perfect Man is a saint in the fullest sense. All that would separate him from God has been annihilated (*fanāʾ*) and he subsists (*baqāʾ*) in a state of constant awareness that ultimately only God is (*waḥdat al-wujūd*).[43]

No dimension of Ibn al-ʿArabī's concept of the Perfect Man is more important than that of the divine names.[44] Here we have the heart of his anthropology and his soteriology. Every man, as man, contains all of the divine names *in potentia*. This, in fact, is what places man at the top of the hierarchy of created beings, ahead even of angels. Only the Perfect Man, however, contains all of the divine names *in actu*, that is, is aware of their presence and activity within his nature, and is, therefore, one "who does what is proper for [the reason that] is proper as [it] is proper."[45] Ibn al-ʿArabī notes that "the certain, enduring, perfect sage is he who treats every condition and moment in the appropriate manner, and does not confuse them."[46]

Ibn al-ʿArabī writes: "When God willed in respect of His Beautiful Names (attributes) . . . that their essences . . . should be seen, He caused them to be seen in a microcosmic being which . . . contains the whole . . . and through which the inmost consciousness of God becomes manifested."[47] Describing his own spiritual ascension (*miʿrāj*) and arrival at the "Muhammadan station" where he realized that he was "among the heirs of Muhammad's comprehensiveness," Ibn al-ʿArabī writes that "God removed from me my contingent dimension." As a result, he continues, "I attained in this nocturnal journey the inner realities of *all* the Names, and I saw them all returning to One Subject and One Entity: that Subject was what I witnessed, and that Entity was my Being."[48] In this experience Ibn al-ʿArabī came to an immediate awareness of the Unity of Being; here he "tasted" *al-Ḥaqq*, the Real, as being/consciousness, distinguishable but not different.

The Perfect Man, aware that his essential nature is constituted by all the divine names, knows himself to be in a state of balance or equilibrium vis-à-vis the divine names in their comprehensiveness. No particular name or quality rules compulsively to the exclusion of others. Proper relationships exist between names that might otherwise appear contradictory. An overall dynamic equilibrium is maintained as precedence is given, when appropriate, to beauty over wrath, generosity over justice, humility over magnificence, etc.[49] Because of his truly comprehensive nature, the Perfect Man intuitively knows, given a particular circumstance or context, which divine qualities warrant manifestation. Of all beings only man, given the comprehensiveness of his nature, occupies the role of servant (*ʿabd*) of Allāh—the name "Allāh" itself indicating, for Ibn al-ʿArabī, comprehensiveness. It follows then that only the Perfect Man in the individual sense exhibits servanthood fully. Ibn al-ʿArabī writes: "Perfect man is separated from him who is not perfect by a single intangible reality, which is that his servanthood is uncontaminated by any lordship whatsoever."[50] Thus devoid of any separate-self-sense, or ego, the Perfect Man cannot contaminate a given situation by introjecting any factor foreign to the full and free exercise of divine will.

The comprehensive, equipollent qualities of the Perfect Man lead him to a fundamentally dialectical mode of being in the world. While all humans occupy an intermediate position between the Real (*al-Ḥaqq*) and the phenomenal (*al-khalq*), only the Perfect Man is capable of maintaining an actual and dynamic balance. Most humans "forget" their true nature and find themselves drawn to the phenomenal, thus "shirking, in their cosmic animality, their responsibility as spiritual beings."[51] In his chapter on Noah in *The Bezels of Wisdom* Ibn al-ʿArabī writes poetically:

> If you insist only on His transcendence, you restrict Him,
> And if you insist only on His immanence, you limit Him.
> If you maintain both aspects, you are right.[52]

Ibn al-ʿArabī calls the person who operates out of the dialectical mode, the both/and rather than either/or way of seeing, a "Possessor of Two Eyes" (*dhūʾ-lʿaynayn*), basing this epithet on the Qurʾan (S. 90:8): "Have We not appointed for him two eyes." The Possessor of Two Eyes maintains God's incomparability and comparability simultaneously. He understands the Absolute both to reveal and to conceal Himself at one and same time. God is the Outward (*al-ẓāhir*) and the Inward (*al-bāṭin*). The Absolute is one and undivided (in Itself) but also multiple (in manifestation, *tajallī*).[53] Among other places, the Shaykh develops his dialectical understanding in his chapter on Joseph in *The Bezels of Wisdom* where, referring to the Absolute in relation to man, he concludes: "He is at once our identity and not our identity."[54] Aware of Abū Bakr's dialectical insight, "Incapacity to attain comprehension is itself comprehension," Ibn al-ʿArabī himself introduces a concise formula to represent the dialectical relationship he sees between the Real and the world, "He/not He" (*huwa lā huwa*).[55]

The comprehensiveness, equilibrium, and dialectic of the Perfect Man leads him to see God in all forms. Ibn al-ʿArabī points out that "the gnostic sees things in principle and in forms, so being complete [in his knowing]. If, in addition to that, he sees the Breath [of the Merciful], he is perfect as well as complete [in his knowing]. He sees only God as . . . that which he sees."[56] Describing another insight gained through his *miʿrāj*, Ibn al-ʿArabī asserts that "God (*al-Ḥaqq*) can only *be* in (external) reality through the form of the creature (*al-khalq*), and that the creature can only be there (in reality) through the form of God. This circularity . . . is what actually exists and is the way things are."[57] This all-inclusive insight leads Ibn al-ʿArabī to one of his most daring claims: "It is God who is worshipped in every object of worship, behind the veil of (the particular) form." Ibn al-ʿArabī gives considerable attention to the way in which belief limits. Belief (*iʿtiqād*) denotes the tying of a knot and implies a strong attachment to a particular idea.[58] The Shaykh declares: "He who delimits God [according to his own belief] denies Him in everything other than his own delimitation, acknowledging Him only when He reveals Himself within that delimitation. But he who frees Him from all delimitation never denies Him, acknowledging Him in every form in which He appears."[59] Summarily and unambiguously, Ibn al-ʿArabī affirms: "In every object of worship it is God Who is worshiped."[60]

A great number of principles and practices of transformation from the perspective of Ibn al-ʿArabī could be taken up. Instead only one, itself fundamental and pervasive, will be introduced, namely, detachment. In his gentle, pastoral tract for beginners on the spiritual path, Ibn al-ʿArabī sets forth many different attitudes to be taken and ways to live: divest yourself of worldly goods, beware of egoistic wishes, live in the present, expect no return, do not be satisfied in your spiritual state, choose less rather than more, etc.[61] Common to all these injunctions and others in this primer is the disposition to dis-value, or at best, to attribute only minimal, relative value to created things. The novice is enjoined to stand free of all that might distract from the divine, to disengage from the mundane world in order to know God. In his manual on spiritual retreat, *Journey to the Lord of Power*, the Shaykh identifies numerous stages along the way and concludes his description of each stage with the words, "if you do not stop with this," before moving to the next stage. He notes: "If you let go . . .

then He will free you from that mode." Why is detachment essential? Because "if you become enamored of this world, it will trip you, and you will be exiled from God."[62]

Detachment is by no means a principle of transformation designed only for those just beginning the spiritual journey. In the *Futūḥāt* Ibn al-ʿArabī declares that one must develop "nonattachment to any engendered things" if one is to come to esoteric knowledge (*bāṭin*).[63] He indicates that it is by means of detachment that Muhammad journeyed ever upward on his *miʿrāj* to Allah. Muhammad said to the Throne, which would have distracted him with its "earthly" concerns: "Do not disorder for me my detachment." When Muhammad finally came into the presence of God Himself, Allah—as if reserving these insights to the very end, thereby emphasizing their ultimacy—said to him: "I am far removed from time and place and state of being . . . , from boundaries [and] that which is limited and that which is measured." And then summarily, "I in My perfection am far removed from anything . . . to which one may cling."[64] One may not cling, in fact, even to the spiritual. Concluding *Journey to the Lord of Power*, Ibn al-ʿArabī declares that "it is not possible for the door of the invisible world and its secrets to be opened while the heart craves for them."[65] Thus we see that for Ibn al-ʿArabī, the comprehensive prerequisite to spiritual realization, to gnosis—from beginning to end—is detachment.

Meister Eckhart's entire soteriology is inspired by the promise set forth in 2 Corinthians 3:18: "We shall be completely transformed and changed into God." Commenting on this verse, he confesses: "I am so changed into him that he produces his being in me as one, not just similar."[66] Elsewhere, delineating the process somewhat more fully, he notes: "When a man accommodates himself barely to God, with love, he is unformed, then informed and transformed in the divine uniformity wherein he is one with God."[67] He clarifies that the higher powers of the soul—will, reason, memory—"are not God, but were created in the soul and with the soul, [and therefore] must be stripped of themselves and transformed into God alone, and born in God and from God, so that God alone may be their father, for in this way they are also sons of God and the only-begotten son of God."[68] This passage introduces the two principal dimensions of man's return to the divine. These are the birth (*geburt*) of the Son (or Word) in the soul, and the breakthrough (*durchbruch*) to the Godhead. Eckhart also indentifies here what is required of humans if this process is to occur, namely, stripping, or detachment, as he more frequently names it.

Before taking up each of these key concepts in Eckhart's understanding of the transformational process, it may be good to discuss his notion of the Nobleman, designated also the Good Man, the Just Man, etc. This is Eckhart's parallel to Ibn al-ʿArabī's Perfect Man on the microcosmic level, as a realizable condition within the realm of our humanness. It is the Nobleman who has experienced the birth of the Son in the soul and broken through to the Godhead. He and only he can say, "God and I, we are one. I accept God into me in knowing; I go into God in loving."[69] In his sermon on the Nobleman, Eckhart underscores the oneness that marks the relationship between this kind of man and God. In his outer life, as he lives in the world and moves among his fellow humans, "the nobleman takes and draws all his being, life and blessedness from God, by God and in God." In a sermon on justice, Eckhart writes that the "just person is one who is conformed and transformed into justice. The just person lives in God and God in him," and seeks nothing for himself.[70] At the same time, in his innermost self, in the depth of his soul, one with the Godhead, where no created thing exists, the Nobleman is "one with One, one from One, one in One, and in One, one everlastingly."[71]

Indicating that the Just Man is one who acts properly, appropriately, within whatever conditions that may prevail, Meister Eckhart introduces a quote from the *Institutes* of Justinian: "That man is just who gives everyone what belongs to him." He then elaborates by noting that the Just are "those who give God what is his, and the saints and the angels what is theirs, and their fellow man what is his." This quality of appropriateness in daily living is the Just Man's way of honoring God, possible only in the total absence of ego, of any vestige of a separate-self-sense. Those honor God, Eckhart, avers, "who have wholly gone out of themselves, and who do not seek for what is theirs in anything . . . , who are not looking beneath themselves or above themselves or beside themselves or at themselves, who are not desiring possessions or honors or ease or pleasure or profit or inwardness or holiness or reward or the kingdom of heaven."[72]

While the ontological presence of God marks every human being, the birth of the Son/Word in the soul is conditional. The prerequisite condition is that of honoring God, that of absolute selflessness, absolute humility. "If God is to enter, the creature must exit."[73] Eckhart is referring not only to one's outer life, one's personality, relationships, activities, but also to "the soul's foundation . . . , its most hidden part," there where no creature, action, knowledge, or image can enter, the place of silence and unknowing.[74] With this condition of emptiness and silence prevailing, the Birth of the Son in the soul may take place. In a brief but daring disquisition on this mystical birth, Eckhart writes: "The Father gives birth to His Son in the soul in the very same way as He gives birth to him in eternity. . . . The Father begets His Son unceasingly, and furthermore, I say, He begets me as His Son and the same Son. I say even more: not only does He beget me as His Son, but He begets me as Himself and Himself as me, and me as His being and His nature. . . . All that God works is one: therefore He begets me as His Son without any difference."[75] In *The Book of Divine Consolation*, Eckhart explains something of what he means by this birth of the Son in the soul: "I am the son of everything which forms me and gives birth to me in its image and likeness."[76] The birth of the Son in the soul means that one has become so completely purified of creatureliness that God's nature and will are free to manifest in and through one without any obstruction whatsoever. One lives in perfect conformity with the dynamic movement of the divine in time and space. This birth in the soul has real implications for both the inner and outer person. The Meister notes: "A man so fashioned, God's son, [is] good as the son of goodness, just as the son of justice."[77]

The other major category according to which Meister Eckhart discusses the return of the soul to its Origin is the breakthrough (*durchbruch*) to the Godhead. In a sermon treating this theme, Eckhart identifies the intellect as the higher power of the mind/soul (*sele*) that rests at nothing short of returning to its Ground. "It aspires," he claims, "to God not as he is the Holy Spirit nor as he is the Son: it flees from the Son. Nor does it want God inasmuch as he is God. Why? Because, as such, he still carries a name. . . . It wants him as he is the marrow . . . , the nucleus . . . , the root . . . from which goodness exudes."[78] In another sermon the Meister declares that "the spark in the soul, which has never touched either time or place . . . , rejects all created things, and wants nothing but its naked God, as he is in himself." This spark or light, he further asserts, "is not content with the Father or the Son or the Holy Spirit . . . , is not content with the divine nature's generative or fruitful qualities . . . , is not content with the simple divine essence in its repose." Instead, this light wants "to know the source of this essence, it wants to go into the simple ground, into the quiet desert, into which distinction never gazed." He concludes his description of this final and total retreat to the Godhead by noting that "in the innermost part, where no one dwells, there is contentment for that light, and there it is more inward than it can be to itself, for this ground is a simple silence, in itself immovable, and by this immovability all things are moved."[79]

The relationship of the birth of the Son in the soul to the breakthrough to the Godhead, *geburt* to *durchbruch*, is not spelled out clearly by Eckhart. To the extent, however, that one can speak of order or progression in reference to Godhead and the soul, given their common Ground, we may argue that since the Son, the second person of the trinity, emerges in and from the Godhead in the *bollitio* and *ebollitio* of *exitus*, the *reditus* is properly to and by and as the Son. This, of course, is true only from the perspective of time; from the perspective of eternity we can only maintain silence. A further clarification is offered by Caputo who notes, quite properly, that the essential precondition for each transformational movement is the same, namely, detachment. He points out also that "unity with the Son and unity with the Godhead are inseparable; it is not possible to achieve one with the other. But this is not to say that they are the same." He observes further that "the breakthrough to the Godhead is *more radical* than the birth of the Son and indeed the ground and basis of it." At the same time, "the birth of the Son *crowns* and *perfects* the unity with the Godhead as fruitfulness perfects virginity." Finally, Caputo notes that "unity with the Godhead is the *basis* of the mystical union; the birth of the Son is its *completion*."[80]

Reference has been made several times to detachment, one of the most crucial and emphasized themes in all of Eckhart's preaching and teaching. In fact, in a list of four subjects he is "wont to speak about," Eckhart lists detachment (*abegesheidenheit*, Middle High German; *abgeshiedenheit*, Modern German) as the first.[81] In his treatise "On Detachment," he declares that he finds "no other virtue better than a pure detachment from all things"; he praises detachment "above all love, . . . above all humility, . . . above all mercifulness," seeing it, indeed, as the source of all virtue. The Meister says that true detachment calls "for the spirit to stand as immovable against whatever may chance to it of joy and sorrow, honor, shame and disgrace, as a mountain of lead stands before a little breath of wind." His understanding of detachment does not lead him to advocate withdrawal or renunciation. "The outer man may be active," he argues, while "the inner man remains wholly free and immovable."[82] He was not one to countenance quietism or rapturous ecstasy. In his sermon on Mary and Martha he openly favors Martha as one who has integrated a contemplative awareness with an active life.[83] Elsewhere Meister Eckhart argues that if a person is in a state of rapture and comes to know of a sick man in need of a bowl of soup, it is "far better . . . out of love to desist from this [rapture] and to serve the poor man."[84]

Detachment for Eckhart is not just from the immediate tangibles of the outer world. It is also, and even more importantly, an inner orientation of the psyche that opens up timelessly to what is, what has been, and what yet will be. "It is not enough for a man's disposition to be detached just for the present moment when he wants to be bound to God, but he must have a well-exercised detachment from what is past and from what is yet to come."[85] True detachment excludes nostalgia and regret, anticipation and longing. As a condition of inwardness, detachment requires retreat from feeling, intention, thought, imagery, memory, indeed, from the myriad of subjective "objects" that typically constitute inner awareness. "A person should be removed from all senses and turn all his powers inward, and attain forgetfulness of all things and of himself."[86] Eckhart points out that "just as no multiplicity can disturb God, nothing can disturb or fragment [the detached] man, for he is one in that One where all multiplicity is one and is one unmultiplicity."[87]

Nowhere does the Meister outline the unconditional demands of detachment more thoroughly than in his homily on the poor in spirit (Matthew 5:3).

"A poor man," he says, "wants nothing, and knows nothing, and has nothing." To want nothing means that a person must be "as free of his own created will as he was when he did not exist." Eckhart argues that as long as "you have a will to fulfill God's will, and a longing for God and for eternity, then you are not poor; for a poor man is one who has a will and longing for nothing." Second, "a man should be set as free of his own knowing as he was when he was not." This means that he is "to live as if he does not even know that he is not in any way living for himself or for the truth or for God. Rather, he should be so free of all knowing that he does not know or experience or grasp that God lives in him." Finally, "having nothing," for Eckhart, does not refer to external possessions but to the sense of a place within which God reigns and works. "Poverty of spirit is for a man to keep so free of God and of all his works that if God wishes to work in the soul, he himself is the place in which he [works]. . . . God is his own worker in himself."[88]

A second major notion that Eckhart uses to convey this absolute abandon to and reliance on God is "letting-go" or "letting-be" (*gelazenheit*, MHG, *gelassenheit*, Mod. Ger.). Analyzing Eckhart's unique use of the term, Schurmann prefers to render it in English as "releasement" and concludes that it conveys several key notions: voluntary emptying of both outer and inner life (things and images), death to individuality and birth to beingness in general, dissolution of the difference between created beingness and uncreated beingness, and, finally, being's own way of being.[89] All of this is implied when Eckhart declares: "Where the creature ends, there God begins to be. God asks only that you get out of his way, in so far as you are creature, and let him be God in you."[90]

Living according to the principles of detachment and letting-be results in living "without a why" (*sunder warumbe*). Eckhart argues that as long as "you perform your works for the sake of the kingdom of heaven, or for God's sake, or for the sake of your eternal blessedness" you have not come to the deepest and most correct understanding. He refers to one's innermost being where "God's ground is my ground, and my ground is God's ground" and says that "it is out of this inner ground that you should perform all your works without asking, 'Why?'."[91] Elsewhere he indicates that one should love God because of God, truth because of truth, justice because of justice, and goodness because of goodness.[92] The seventeenth-century mystical poet Angelus Silesius aptly conveys this essential perspective of Meister Eckhart:

> The rose is without why; it blooms because it blooms;
> It cares not for itself; asks not if it's seen.[93]

Bernard McGinn rightly observes that a person who "lives without a why is able to find God in all things."[94] Commenting on 1 John 4:9, "we live in Him," Meister Eckhart expounds: "We must understand Him equally in all things, in one not more than another, for He is equally in all things."[95] Eckhart here acknowledges experientially what he elsewhere treats ontologically as one pole of God's dialectical relationship to beings, namely, God's indistinctness from all distinct entities, given the unity of being (*esse est Deus*).[96] Writing on detachment and the possession of God, Eckhart notes that "whoever really and truly has God, he has him everywhere, in the street and in company with everyone, just as much as in church or in solitary places." Such a person has God present in his dispositions, intentions, and love; indeed, "has God essentially [and thus] grasps God divinely." This means that "God shines in all things [and] forms himself for the man out of all things." Such a person "grasps everything as divine and as greater than things in themselves are" (since things are, apart from God, nothing). For the Nobleman, the Just Man, whose entire life, inner and outer, is marked by detachment, letting-be, and without why, "all things become . . . nothing but God."[97]

In a sermon on the Nobleman (Luke 19:12), Meister Eckhart underscores the dialectical outlook that marks such a person: "to have nothing is to have everything," "the humble person and God are one and not two," "the more we seek . . . the less we find."[98] The dialectical outlook is stressed further by the Meister in a formal treatise on the same text. Here he draws attention repeatedly to "a noble man who *went out* into a far country . . . *and returned* [emphasis added]." In this treatise Eckhart affirms that "man finds God in the One, and he who will find God must be one." That a dialectical outlook is essential to a deeper unitive awareness is indicated by his discussion of distinction and indistinction. "In distinction we do not find either one, or being, or God, or rest, or blessedness. . . . Be one, so that you may find God! And truly, if you were indeed one, you would also remain one in distinction, and distinction would be one to you." Finally, he affirms, "we can see created things without distinction and transformed from every form and made unlike every likeness in the One that is God himself." Indeed, the Nobleman is "noble because he is one and because he knows God and created things in one."[99]

Summary and Import

Both Ibn al-ʿArabī and Meister Eckhart are fully aware of the fundamental and pervasive duality that marks the immediate experience of all humans. Unlike most, however, they refuse to accept this duality—pernicious in many of its forms as the precondition of all conflict and suffering—as necessary to the human condition. Instead, each constructs a metaphysical system founded on his own personal experience that moves from the obviousness of duality through the tension and ambiguity of a dialectic to the harmony of union and, finally, to identity in the All/Ultimate, *al-Ḥaqq*/the Godhead. With transformative principles and powers encoded in the cosmos, each sees human nature as entirely capable of undertaking this journey from finitude to infinity, provided, of course, that such fundamental and essential principles as detachment and love are not simply talked about but actually applied.

It goes without saying that there are differences, some significant, between Ibn al-ʿArabī and Meister Eckhart. These differences, however, are far less significant—and that because they are entirely nonvolatile—than the differences that exist between each of these savants and many, if not most, of those who make up their respective religious traditions. Each of these theosophical mystics has been regarded as heretical, Meister Eckhart even formally so.[100] The opposition directed to each is but one expression of the duality that is endemic to the human condition and that becomes aggressive when assumptions of finality or superiority are held.

We may, perhaps, safely conclude that Ibn al-ʿArabī would have agreed—and would have understood the teaching—when Meister Eckhart declared: "He who wants to understand my teaching of releasement [letting-be] must himself be perfectly released."[101] And equally that Meister Eckhart would have agreed—and understood—when Ibn al-ʿArabī declared: "Everything is He, and of Him and from Him and to Him."[102]

NOTES

1. William C. Chittick, *The Sufi Path of Knowledge: Ibn al-ʿArabī's Metaphysic of Imagination* (Albany: State University of New York Press, 1989) p. x f.; Ibn al-ʿArabī, *The Bezels of Wisdom*, trans. and intro. R.W.J. Austin, Classics of Western Spirituality series (New York: Paulist Press, 1980), p. 13; A. Ates, "Ibn al-ʿArabī," *The Encyclopedia of Islam*, new ed., ed. Bernard Lewis et al. (Leiden: E.J. Brill, 1971), 3: 708.

2. Only Meister Eckhart and one other author receive two volumes in the acclaimed series Classics of Western Spirituality.

3. Frank Tobin, *Meister Eckhart: Thought and Language* (Philadelphia: University of Pennsylvania Press, 1986), pp. 17–23; Edmund Colledge and Bernard McGinn, trans. and intro., *Meister Eckhart: The Essential Sermons, Commentaries, Treatises, and Defense*, Classics of Western Spirituality (New York: Paulist Press, 1981), pp. 62–68.

4. A.E. Affifi, *The Mystical Philosophy of Muhyid Din-Ibnul ʿArabi* (London: Cambridge University Press, 1939), pp. 112, 156 f., 174–94; Seyyed Hossein Nasr, *Three Muslim Sages: Avicenna-Suhrawardi-Ibn ʿArabi* (Cambridge, Mass.: Harvard University Press, 1964), pp. 100–2; James M. Clark, *The Great German Mystics: Eckhart, Tauler and Suso* (Oxford: Basil Blackwell, 1949), p. 118 f.; Colledge and McGinn, *Essential Sermons*, p. 64; Tobin, *Thought and Language*, p. 57.

5. Tobin, *Thought and Language*, p. 46; Colledge and McGinn, *Essential Sermons*, 83; Affifi, *Mystical Philosophy*, p. 87.

6. Ibn al-ʿArabī, *Bezels of Wisdom*, pp. 18 f., 22; Nasr, *Three Muslim Sages*; Colledge and McGinn, *Essential Sermons*, pp. 28 f.

7. Muḥyiddīn Ibn al-ʿArabī, "What the Student Needs" (*Mā la budda minhu liʾl murīd*), trans. Tosun Bayrak al-Jerrahi, *Journal of the Muhyiddin Ibn ʿArabi Society* 5 (1986): 44; for a different rendering, though substantially the same, see Arthur Jeffery, ed., *A Reader on Islam* (The Hague: Mouton, 1962), p. 651.

8. See, e.g., Nasr, *Three Muslim Sages*, pp. 100 f.

9. While the question of the determinative relationship of belief and experience (i.e., which comes first and determines the other) remains open and continues to be vigorously debated, this writer works with the position that experience is prior to and determinative of intellectual formulation in cases of profound or deep experience, though existing objective structures of belief probably do determine surface or exoteric experiences and may indeed color expressions of even deep or esoteric experience. See Steven T. Katz, ed., *Mysticism and Philosophical Analysis* (New York: Oxford University Press, 1978); Katz, *Mysticism and Religious Traditions* (New York: Oxford University Press, 1984); Robert K.C. Forman, *Meister Eckhart: The Mystic as Theologian* (Warwick, N.Y.: Amity House, forthcoming).

10. For an exhaustive discussion of the imaginal world in Ibn al-ʿArabī see Henry Corbin, *Creative Imagination in the Sufism of Ibn ʿArabī*, trans. Ralph Manheim, Bollingen Series 91 (Princeton: Princeton University Press, 1969).

11. James M. Morris, "The Spiritual Ascension: Ibn ʿArabī and the Miʿrāj," pts. 1 and 2, *Journal of the American Oriental Society* 107, no. 4 (1987): 634; 108, no. 1 (1988): 69–77, see 73.

12. Ibid., pp. 108, 1: 73, n. 198.

13. Chittick, *Sufi Path of Knowledge*, p. 220.

14. Maurice O'Connell Walshe, trans. and ed., *Meister Eckhart: Sermons and Treatises*, 3 vols. (Dorset, England: Element Books, 1978), 1: 117, 2: 136. While this use of "I" does not prove that Meister Eckhart is here describing his own personal experience, it is certainly highly suggestive in this regard.

15. Ibid., 1: 157, 161.

16. Matthew Fox, intro. and comm., *Breakthrough: Meister Eckhart's Creation Spirituality in New Translation* (Garden City, N.Y.: Image Books, 1980), p. 140.

17. Seyyed Hossein Nasr, ed., *The Essential Writings of Frithjof Schuon* (Amity, N.Y.: Amity House, 1986), p. 27.

18. Alvin Moore, Jr., review of *Survey of Metaphysics and Esoterism*, by Frithjof Schuon in *Avaloka: A Journal of Traditional Religion and Culture* 3 (Winter 1988–Summer 1989): 53.

19. Chittick, *Sufi Path to Knowledge*, p. 3.

20. R.W.J. Austin, introduction to Ibn al-ʿArabī, *Bezels of Wisdom*, 26; see also Annemarie Schimmel, *Mystical Dimensions of Islam* (Chapel Hill: University of North Carolina Press, 1975), p. 267; John T. Little, "Al-Insān al-Kāmil: The Perfect Man According to Ibn al-ʿArabī," *The Muslim World* 77 (January 1978): 46.

21. Chittick, *Sufi Path of Knowledge*, p. 91.

22. Toshihiko Izutsu, "Ibn al-ʿArabī," in *The Encyclopedia of Religion*, Mircea Eliade, ed.-in-chief (New York: Macmillan, 1987), 6: 556; see also Chittick, *Sufi Path of Knowledge*, pp. 59–76.

The *Aḥad* is the pure and absolute One—the reality of existence in a state of absolute undetermination, the prephenomenal in its ultimate and unconditional prephenomenality—whereas the *Wāḥid* is the same reality of existence at a stage where it begins to turn toward phenomenality.

23. Toshihiko Izutsu, *Sufism and Taoism: A Comparative Study of Key Philosophical Concepts* (Berkeley: University of California Press, 1983), p. 23; Chittick, *Sufi Path of Knowledge*, p. 313.

24. Chittick, *Sufi Path of Knowledge*, p. 66. Ibn al-ʿArabī was fully aware of the fact that this tradition was not found in the standard collections. He believed, however, that it was "sound on the basis of unveiling," i.e., by means of direct perception of the imaginal world, which is to say, by means of the intuition of those capable of understanding. See ibid., p. 391, n. 14.

25. See Izutsu, *Sufism and Taoism*, p. 136.

26. Ibn al-ʿArabī, *Bezels of Wisdom*, p. 181. See Izutsu, *Sufism and Taoism*, pp. 131–33; Chittick, *Sufi Path of Knowledge*, pp. 127–30.

27. Austin, introduction, Ibn al-ʿArabī, *Bezels of Wisdom*, p. 29.

28. Meister Eckhart, *Parisian Questions and Prologues*. Trans. and intro. Armand A. Maurer (Toronto: Pontifical Institute of Mediaeval Studies, 1974), p. 93; Edmund Colledge, "Meister Eckhart: His Time and His Writings," *The Thomist* 42 (April 1978): 244.

29. Eckhart, *Parisian Questions*, pp. 96, 32.

30. Bernard McGinn, ed., *Meister Eckhart: Teacher and Preacher*, Classics of Western Spirituality (New York: Paulist Press, 1986), pp. 153, 396.

31. C.F. Kelley, *Meister Eckhart on Divine Knowledge* (New Haven, Conn.: Yale University Press, 1977), p. 147.

32. Tobin, *Thought and Language*, pp. 35–38.

33. Walshe, *Sermons and Treatises*, 2: 271.

34. John D. Caputo, "Fundamental Themes in Meister Eckhart's Mysticism," *The Thomist* 42 (April 1978): 211.

35. Bernard McGinn, "The God beyond God: Theology and Mysticism in the Thought of Meister Eckhart," *Journal of Religion* 61 (January 1981): 8. See also Eckhart, *Parisian Questions*, p. 33.

36. Kelley, *Divine Knowledge*, pp. 112, 80.

37. McGinn, *Teacher and Preacher*, p. 391.

38. James M. Clark, *Meister Eckhart: An Introduction to the Study of His Works with Anthology of His Sermons* (London: Thomas Nelson and Sons, 1957), p. 212.

39. Fox, *Breakthrough*, p. 72.

40. Reiner Schurmann, *Meister Eckhart: Mystic and Philosopher* (Bloomington: Indiana University Press, 1978), p. 112; see pp. 111–21.

41. Walshe, *Sermons and Treatises*, 1: 98.

42. Little notes that this is the most controversial of all Ibn al-ʿArabī's doctrines. See Little, "*Al-Insān al-Kāmil*," p. 43.

43. Izutsu, *Sufism and Taoism*, pp. 218, 265.

44. In fact, Chittick writes, "The divine names are the single most important concept to be found in Ibn al-ʿArabī's works" (*Sufi Path of Knowledge*, p. 10).

45. Ibid., p. 174; Affifi, *Mystical Philosophy*, pp. 81 f.

46. Muḥyiddīn Ibn al-ʿArabī, *Journey to the Lord of Power*, trans. Rabia Terri Harris (London: East West Publications, 1981), p. 59.

47. Reynold A. Nicholson, *Studies in Islamic Mysticism* (Cambridge: Cambridge University Press, 1921), p. 154.

48. Morris, "Spiritual Ascension," pp. 72 f.

49. Chittick, *Sufi Path of Knowledge*, pp. 27, 370–72; Chittick, "Belief and Transformation: The Sufi Teaching of Ibn al-ʿArabī," *The American Theosophist* 74 (1986), 5: 182–84.

50. Chittick, *Sufi Path of Knowledge*, p. 372.

51. Austin, introduction, Ibn al-ʿArabī, *Bezels of Wisdom*, p. 35.

52. Ibid., p. 75.

53. Chittick, *Sufi Path of Knowledge*, pp. 361–63; Izutsu, *Sufism and Taoism*, pp. 23 f., 30, 32, 48 f.

54. Ibn al-ʿArabī, *Bezels of Wisdom*, p. 127.

55. Chittick. *Sufi Path of Knowledge*, pp. 3 f, 113–15.

56. Ibn al-ʿArabī, *Bezels of Wisdom*, p. 127.

57. Morris, "Spiritual Ascension," p. 74.

58. Chittick, "Belief and Transformation," p. 186.

59. William C. Chittick, "Eschatology," in Seyyed Hossein Nasr, ed., *Islamic Spirituality I: Foundations*, *World Spirituality: An Encyclopedic History of the Religious Quest*, no. 19 (New York: Crossroad, 1987), pp. 388 f: also Ibn al-ʿArabī, *Bezels of Wisdom*, p. 149.

60. Ibn al-ʿArabī, *Bezels of Wisdom*, p. 78.

61. Muḥyiddīn ibn al-ʿArabī, "What the Student Needs," pp. 33–35 passim; see also Jeffery, *Reader*, pp. 640–55 passim.

62. Ibn al-ʿArabī, *Journey to the Lord of Power*, pp. 39–48 passim. Ibn al-ʿArabī uses the phrase "if you do not stop with this" twenty times in this tract.

63. Chittick, *Sufi Path of Knowledge*, p. 245.

64. Arthur Jeffrey, "Ibn alʿArabī's Shajarat al-Kawm," *Studia Islamica* 11 (1959): 154, 156, 158.

65. Ibn al-ʿArabī, *Journey to the Lord of Power*, p. 63.

66. Colledge and McGinn, *Essential Sermons*, p. 188. For discussion of Eckhart's use of 2 Cor. 3:18 see Karl G. Kertz, "Meister Eckhart's Teaching on the Birth of the Divine World of the Soul," *Traditio* 15 (1959): 359 f.

67. Walshe, *Sermons and Treatises*, 2: 119.

68. James M. Clark and John V. Skinner, *Meister Eckhart: Selected Treatises and Sermons Translated from Latin and German with an Introduction and Notes* (London: Faber and Faber, 1958), p. 111. For a discussion of why this passage ought not to have been construed as heretical see Colledge, "Meister Eckhart: Times and Writings," p. 249 f.

69. Colledge and McGinn, *Essential Sermons*, p. 188.

70. Ibid., p. 246; Fox; *Breakthrough*, p. 464.

71. Colledge and McGinn, *Sermons and Treatises*, p. 247.

72. Ibid., p. 185.

73. Richard Kieckhefer, "Meister Eckhart's Conception of Union with God," *Harvard Theological Review* 71 (July–October 1978): 210 f.

74. Fox, *Breakthrough*, p. 294.

75. Walshe, *Sermons and Treatises*, 2: 135. This is one of the many teachings of Meister Eckhart formally condemned in the papal bull of 1329, *In agro dominico*. See Colledge and McGinn, *Essential Sermons*, p. 79.

76. Clark and Skinner, *Selected Treatises*, p. 111.

77. Ibid. See Forman, *Mystic as Theologian*, chap. 6; Caputo, "Fundamental Themes," pp. 217–22.

78. Schurmann, *Mystic and Philosopher*, p. 57.

79. Colledge and McGinn, *Essential Sermons*, p. 198.

80. Caputo, "Fundamental Themes," pp. 222, 224. See also McGinn, "God Beyond God," p. 10; Forman, *Mystic as Theologian*, chap. 7.

81. Walshe, *Sermons and Treatises*, 1: 177; also McGinn, "God Beyond God," p. 4.

82. Colledge and McGinn, *Essential Sermons*, pp. 258–94 passim.

83. McGinn, *Teacher and Preacher*, pp. 338–44.

84. Kieckhefer, "Meister Eckhart's Conception of Union," p. 222.

85. Colledge and McGinn, *Essential Sermons*, p. 276.

86. Kieckhefer, "Meister Eckhart's Conception of Union," p. 221.

87. Colledge and McGinn, *Essential Sermons*, p. 252.

88. Ibid., pp. 199–203 passim."

89. Schurmann, *Mystic and Philosopher*, p. 210.

90. Raymond B. Blackney, *Meister Eckhart: A Modern Translation* (New York: Harper and Row, 1941), p. 127. For a discussion of "letting be," as well as a comprehensive look at Meister Eckhart's influence on a twentieth-century philosopher, see John D. Caputo, *The Mystical Element in Heidegger's Thought* (Athens: Ohio University, 1978), pp. 118–27.

91. Colledge and McGinn, *Essential Sermons*, p. 183.

92. Reiner Schurmann, "The Loss of the Origin in Soto Zen and in Meister Eckhart," *The Thomist* 42 (April 1978): 307.

93. Caputo, *Mystical Element*, p. 61. For further indication of Meister Eckhart's influence on Angelus Silesius, the pen name of Johannes Scheffler (1624–77), see ibid., index, passim; Frederick Franck, trans., *The Book of Angelus Silesius* (Santa Fe, N.M.: Bear and Company, 1985); Maria Shrady, trans. and foreword, and Josef Schmidt, intro. and notes, *Angelus Silesius: The Cherubinic Wanderer*, Classics of Western Spirituality (New York: Paulist Press, 1986). While neither of the latter two works properly acknowledges Meister Eckhart's extensive influence on Scheffler—as he himself failed to do, though understandably at the time in light of Eckhart's heretical status in the Roman Catholic Church, to which Scheffler converted from Lutheranism—it is quite evident.

94. Bernard McGinn, "Meister Eckhart: An Introduction," in Paul E. Szarmach, ed., *An Introduction to the Medieval Mystics of Europe* (Albany: State University of New York Press, 1984), p. 253.

95. Clark, *Meister Eckhart: Introduction*, p. 235.

96. McGinn, *Teacher and Preacher*, p. 187; see also McGinn, "God Beyond God," p. 7.

97. Colledge and McGinn, *Essential Sermons*, pp. 251–54 passim.

98. Fox, *Breakthrough*, pp. 166–69 passim.

99. Colledge and McGinn, *Essential Sermons*, pp. 240–45 passim. For further obser-

vations on the dialectical in Eckhart see Fox, *Breakthrough*, pp. 196–98; Kelley, *Divine Knowledge*, pp. 106–13; Maria R. Lichtmann, "The 'Way' of Meister Eckhart," in Valerie M. Lagorio, ed., *Mysticism: Medieval and Modern*, Salzburg Studies in English Literature, dir. Erwin A. Sturzl, Elizabeth and Renaissance Studies, ed. James Hogg (Salzburg: Institut fur Anglistik und Amerikanistik, Universitat Salzburg, 1986), pp. 96–100.

100. Steps are currently under way to effect a rescinding of the indictment of Meister Eckhart in the papal bull *In argo dominico*. See Richard Woods, *Eckhart's Way* (Wilmington, Del.: Michael Glazier, 1986).

101. Schurmann, *Mystic and Philosopher*, p. xv.

102. Ibn al-ʿArabī, *Journey to the Lord of Power*, p. 25. This final paragraph is not intended to foreclose dialogue but to suggest something of the deep experiential openness that must be brought to dialogue if it is to move beyond a mere exchange of positions, however amicably pursued, and become mutually transformative within the embrace of the divine itself.

11

Muslim Attitudes toward Christians in the Maghrib during the Fāṭimid Period, 297/909–358/969

R. Marston Speight

This study is part of a long-range project to investigate Arabic sources in chronological order for the purpose of finding references to attitudes of Maghribī Muslims toward the Christians in their presence.[1] As in previous studies of this series, the references cited reflect attitudes conveyed incidentally or indirectly, since they occur in discourse or literary works that have other purposes than to describe attitudes toward believers of another religion.

The Fāṭimid rulers came into power during the tenth Christian century in Ifrīqiya, roughly the area of the Maghrib (North Africa) now known as Tunisia.[2] Christians did not constitute an important element of the North African population, although they were a living presence, a reminder both of previous centuries when the Church figured as a major religious influence in the region and of the long, gradual decline of Christianity as it was replaced by Islam.[3] No one knows how the Christian faith first came to North Africa, but historical records take up the story of a developing Church toward the end of the second Christian century. The faith continued to expand for the next three to four hundred years. In the fifth century six hundred bishops presided over widely dispersed communities of believers. Their orientation was always toward Rome, the political, economic, military, and religious power in the Western world, although the Christians encountered serious persecution from the state religion of Rome. Church history in North Africa is marked by the brilliant achievements of figures such as Tertullian (d. ca. 230), Cyprian (d. 258), and Augustine (d. 430).

As the Roman Empire declined in the fifth century the Church also faltered and a slow diminution of its influence began. The coming of Islam in the last half of the seventh century signaled the beginning of a new religious and cultural orientation for North Africa. The Fāṭimid period of the tenth century was a particularly convulsive time in the history of the Maghrib. The people of that period faced a new crisis in their experience as a Muslim community. Divisive forces tried the unity of the Islamic *umma* almost to the limit. Buffeted as they were by Shīʿite and Khārijite revolutionaries, by Mālikites concerned with preserving the status quo, not to speak of ideological controversies between Ḥanafites and Mālikites, and between Muʿtazilites and Traditionists, the people seem, according to the meager sources available, not to have been much concerned with the slowly dwindling population of Christians. So only a partial view of Muslim attitudes toward them emerges from the evidence. Indication of the Christian presence is not lacking, as attested to in the work of Tadeusz Lewicki[4] and H. R. Idris[5] who described Christian centers in various parts of Ifrīqiya and the area now known as Algeria.

Even though the Fāṭimid caliphs were in control of the military, political, and economic forces of the area, social and religious conditions remained marked by the Sunni Mālikism that had been forming the Maghribī religious mentality during the previous century. The biographical encyclopedias[6] covering the Fāṭimid period tell of many stalwart Mālikite scholars and ascetics who withstood the pressure of the Fāṭimid domination, sometimes even to the point of giving their lives for refusing to yield. One of the most outstanding of these was Ibn Abī Zayd al-Qayrawānī (d. 386/996), whose life spanned more than two-thirds of the Maghribī phase of Fāṭimid rule. Ibn Abī Zayd is well known for his treatise on Mālikite belief and practice, the *Risāla*, which has been widely used throughout the Muslim world, even to the present, and translated into several languages. His other writings have existed up to now only in manuscript form.

In 1982 two Tunisian scholars published Ibn Abī Zayd's *Kitāb al-Jāmiʿ*,[7] a brief compendium of material on Islamic law and history. It is a supplement to a larger work, the *Mukhtaṣar* or *Epitome* of the *Mudawwana* of Saḥnūn (d. 240/854),[8] the primary teacher of Mālik's way in North Africa. The *Mukhtaṣar* has survived only in fragmentary form. Ibn Abī Zayd's *Jāmiʿ* contains sayings of Mālik, along with those of some of his companions and others. Composed for the instruction and edification of the community, it gives a selection of prophetic *ḥadīth* and sayings from great scholars of the past. The book is not an original treatise, but is intended simply to transmit the learning and advice of the pious fathers to the generation of its compiler. Selective in its presentation, however, it provides a glimpse at information which Ibn Abī Zayd considered particularly important for Maghribī Muslims to know as guidance for their thought and practice in the mid-tenth century.

Respect for Jesus

As might be expected given the high place accorded by the Qurʾan to ʿĪsā, Son of Mary, the *Jāmiʿ* of Ibn Abī Zayd gives evidence of respect and even veneration for the Prophet of the Christians. In the chapter on "The Excellence of Medina" we read: "It is said that there remains in the room[9] a place for a tomb where ʿĪsā, Son of Mary (may the blessing and peace of God be upon him) [and upon our Prophet][10] will be buried.[11] God knows whether it is true or not!"[12]

In a chapter on virtues and good manners, Ibn Abī Zayd cites the following, without indicating the source: "ʿĪsā Son of Mary (may blessing and peace be upon our Prophet and upon him)[13] said, 'Do not speak much without remembering God, lest your hearts become hard. A hard hearted person is far from God Most High.' "[14] This record is found in *al-Muwaṭṭāʾ* of Mālik (56.3),[15] one of the most widely known collections of ḥadīth in North Africa. The saying as found there continues:

> Do not take notice of the sins of others, nor look at them as though you were lords. Rather, look at your own sins as though you were slaves.[16] And when people either suffer[17] or enjoy well-being, have mercy on those who suffer and praise God for the well-being of the others.

This saying attributed to Jesus reflects a piety akin to that seen in the Gospels, even though textually it is not found in those documents.[18]

In calling attention to the preceding texts that show respect for Jesus, I am not claiming that such respect necessarily reflects a similar respect for Christians. Since Jesus is a prophet of Islam it was natural for Muslims to express their veneration for him regardless of how they might feel toward their Christian neighbors. Many factors contributed to a feeling of estrangement between the two communities of faith. Elements of theological controversy marked Muslim-Christian relations from the beginning of Islam and as religious polemics intensified, the two groups tended to separate in spirit.[19] The political rivalries of the Mediterranean region also exacerbated the estrangement. Where members of the two faiths lived together in tenth-century North Africa the Muslims were in a position of power. They had isolated the Christians socially, at least to a degree, by virtue of the *dhimmī*, or protected citizen, status. So respect for Jesus and respect for Christians did not necessarily go together. But neither was there absolute discontinuity between the two. Appreciative texts about Jesus found in Ibn Abī Zayd's book show that the best Mālikite thought of the era considered it important to keep alive the Qurʾanic regard for Jesus. Supporting that regard is the Qurʾanic acknowledgment of religious ties with Christians, the followers of Jesus. The following extracts from Ibn Abī Zayd's compilation express the nuanced position of Muslims vis-à-vis their Christian neighbors.

Respect for Christians

As *dhimmī* people, that is, protected citizens belonging to a minority religion, the Christians were definitely subordinate to the Muslim authority. Elsewhere I have commented on the humanity of the *dhimmī* status as seen in its historical context.[20] The following injunction illustrates how Mālikite law endeavored to regulate the dominance of the religious majority so as not to infringe on the rights of the minority. The saying, attributed to Mālik, is given twice by Ibn Abī Zayd, in the chapters on moral behavior and good manners: "If a traveler stops at a *dhimmī's* house he should take nothing from his host family unless they give it freely."[21]

Other injunctions deal with commercial relations between Christians and Muslims and their restrictions. "Mālik said, There is no harm in renting a house from a Christian or a Jew provided that no wine or swine have been sold in it."[22] Wine drinking and eating pork were two major barriers to Christian-Muslim interaction. Muslims tried to avoid any contamination by these unlawful substances, as well as any entanglement, even indirectly, with the practice of usury.

> [Mālik] found it repugnant to receive money from a Christian that had been used in the purchase of wine or the practice of usury. But he did not find it objectionable to take money from a Christian in payment of a debt, even as God has authorized the collection of the minority tax (*jizya*) from the Christians.[23]

Once account had been taken of incidental hindrances due to scruple, there was no limitation to business dealings between the two communities. "Mālik said, There is no harm in a Christian receiving money from you in a business transaction."[24]

In a chapter of Ibn Abī Zayd's *Jāmiʿ* on medicine and magic, Ibn Wahb (d. 197/813), an early Mālikite scholar from Egypt, is quoted as saying: "I do not object to the incantations used by the People of Scripture.[25] I follow the ḥadīth of Abū Bakr who said, 'Make incantations with the Book of God.' He [Ibn Wahb] did not accept Mālik's aversion to that practice."[26] Abū Bakr's statement had reference to an incantation made by a Jewess to cure an illness of ʿĀʾisha (*al-Muwaṭṭāʾ*, 50.4). Ibn Wahb's opinion illustrates the practice of crossing over easily from one tradition to another as Muslims and Christians interacted with each other.[27] Along the same line, al-Layth (d. 175/791), an Egyptian student of Mālik, is cited as saying,

> There is no harm in hanging something from the Qurʾan above the bed of a woman in childbirth or a sick person, if it is enclosed in leather or placed in a tube (I do not like a tube of iron). I have seen in some accounts (*ḥadīth*): This saying shall be prescribed for a woman in the pains of childbirth: "Anna gave birth to Mary. Mary gave birth to Jesus. Come out, O child, the earth is calling for you! Come out, O child!"[28]

This saying for a woman in childbirth lies entirely within an Islamic setting but its use, especially at such a crucial moment in life, could not help but accentuate the commonality that exists between the Christian and Muslim traditions.

Related to the above texts showing respect for Christians and their tradition is the legend that tells of the influence of a hermit in the foundation of the Fāṭimid refuge-city, Mahdiyya. The story is told in a thirteenth-century historical work on the North African phase of the Fāṭimid period.

> When [Abū ʿUbayd Allāh] al-Mahdī[29] was looking for a place to build his capital city he found a spot that pleased him, and there was a hermit monk (*rāhib*) [presumably Christian], who lived there in a cave. Al-Mahdī asked him what the place was called. The hermit replied, "This is the island of the caliphs."[30] He was pleased with this name.[31]

This story gives an auspicious aura to the founding of a storied Islamic city. The fact that a Christian hermit is the central figure[32] testifies to the general respect that Muslims felt for people of that faith.

The legend about a hermit and the building of Mahdiyya calls to mind a story found in the book by an eleventh-century geographer, Abū ʿUbayd al-Bakrī (d. 487/1094), *Kitāb al-Masālik waʾl-Mamālik*, a work that is not far removed from the time of the Maghribī Fāṭimids.

> There is a mountain [in northeastern Ifrīqiya] called Adar from which Sicily can be seen. Around that mountain there is a community devoted to the service of God. They have given up the world and live in the area of the mountain along with the wild animals. Their dress is made from rushes (*bardiyy*) and their food is taken from the plants of the earth and the fish of the sea, only as they have need. Many of them are known for the power of their supplicatory prayers. This mountain is well known because of the people who have lived there humbly before God [*tirām*, pl. of *tarīm*?] since the conquest of Ifrīqiya.[33]

The religious faith of these people is not identified, but since they are said to have lived in the area (modern Cap Bon, Tunisia) from the time of the Muslim conquest, that is, during a period of Christian ascendancy, it is likely that they were Christians. If they were not of Christian faith they were at least probably influenced by Christian hermits. Al-Bakrī, the Muslim geographer who recorded this account, included material pertaining to the dominant socioreligious and economic climate of the times. So this text seems to reflect a feeling of respect, perhaps awe, on the part of Muslims for the worshiping community of Adar.

Degrees of Antipathy toward Christians

Turning from expressions of respect and tolerance we discover another attitude among the Mālikite leaders of the community. This is seen, for example, in a book by Abū al-Ḥasan al-Qābisī (d. 403/1012), a younger contemporary of Ibn Abī Zayd. He is mainly known for his book on pedagogy for methods of teaching.[34]

Al-Qābisī writes strongly against mixing children and teachers from the religions of Islam, Christianity, and Judaism in the same classroom. From this it may be assumed either that sometimes children from the three faiths were together in the same school or that people considered grouping them together for the same instruction. Drawing upon Mālik's authority, al-Qābisī says that Christians and Jews are forbidden either to teach their books to Muslims or to teach the Qur'an to Muslims. He commends such a prohibition because he feels that Christians and Jews are not reliable with regard to their scriptures. In support of this he tells the story of the Jew Kaʿb al-Aḥbār who came to ʿUmar and stood before him. Holding out a well-worn copy of the Jewish scriptures, he said, "O Leader of the Faithful, this book contains the Torah; shall I read from it?" ʿUmar was silent. Then he said that if he knew it was the Book that was revealed to Moses, he would read it day and night. Kaʿb was silent.[35] Al-Qābisī goes on to say, calling on Mālik as his authority, that Muslim teachers should not have Christians or Jews in their classes to learn either the Qur'an or other subjects.

Other evidence exists, however, of some mixing of the religious groups in the schoolrooms. This is seen in Al-Qābisī's condemnation elsewhere of Muslims taking part in the festivals of the "people of unbelief" (*ahl al-kufr*).[36] The details of this prohibition constitute a text that has puzzled and intrigued scholars for a long time. H.R. Idris studied it at length;[37] after citing the text I shall take issue with his interpretation. Al-Qābisī wrote:

> In like manner it is blameworthy to accept (gifts) on the holidays of the people of unbelief. These include Christmas, Easter (or Passover?) and al-Abandās (?) in our country, St. John's Nativity (al-ʿAnṣara) in Andalusia; and the Baptism of Jesus (al-Ghiṭāṣ) in Egypt. All of these are festivals of unbelievers, to which a teacher of Muslims has no claim. And if anyone brings him something he should refuse it, even if it is offered in deference to him. Muslims should not join willingly in such practices, by adorning themselves in finery and making preparations. The children should not amuse themselves by making huts (*qibāb*) for Abandas or by merry-making at Christmas. All of these practices are unbecoming to Muslims. They should be forbidden, and the teacher should refuse any favors that might be offered him so as to show the ones who are ignorant that such activities are sinful and should be stopped. They should be ashamed of having taken part. They should attach no importance to the practices and abstain from them.[38]

It is obvious that the puzzling feature of this text is the meaning of Abandās, a festival celebrated in Ifrīqiya. H.R. Idris, in the article previously cited, assumes that all of the festivals listed are Christian, and then by an ingenious argument arrives at the tentative conclusion that Abandās refers to the celebration of the Kalends of January, a vestige of ancient Roman ritual life. In the Near East Christians celebrated this festival on January 1 of the Julian calendar and it was called al-Qalandas. It was unknown in North Africa, but if this is the word intended by al-Qābīsī's "Abandās" then it could mean, Idris argues, that there was an influx of orientals into Ifrīqiya during or before al-Qābīsī's lifetime and that the festival of al-Qalandas was taken up by Christians around him, only to disappear with the passage of time. Idris has difficulty in fitting the "huts" (*qibāb*) into this interpretation. I think it possible that the list of festivals includes both Jewish and Christian ones. The Jews figure prominently in the literature of the period. The word for Easter, "al-Fiṣḥ," is also used for Passover. And the linking of "huts" (*qibāb*) with the unknown word, Abandās, makes one think of the festival of booths, Succoth, of the Jews. A *qubba* (sing. of *qibāb*) is, properly speaking, a vaulted structure. In the text in question the word could be loosely used for the booths or huts of Succoth, since one of the laws of that festival states that the structures must be roofed. An additional sign of the wide participation of the Maghribī population in Jewish practices is seen in a statement by the historian Ibn ʿIdhārī (seventh/thirteenth century) that some Berbers had the custom of fasting on Thursday and Monday, and if this fast was broken a fine of domestic animals had to be paid.[39] These were Jewish fast days.[40]

I suggest, therefore, that al-Fiṣḥ is just as likely to refer to Passover as to Easter and that Abandās, the origin of which remains a puzzle, might well refer to Succoth, or the Jewish Festival of Booths.

Attitudes in the Fāṭimid Seat of Power

Although the Fāṭimids are known to have been tolerant toward the Christians under their rule and to have employed them in many of the government offices and other posts of public service,[41] there seems to have been little connection in the caliphs' minds between indigenous Christians and those outside the realm of Fāṭimid authority. No doubt this was due to the threat that Christian power, especially in Byzantium, posed to the Fāṭimid expansion. Before describing the official attitude toward the Christian enemy, I should point out that the *dhimmī* status of indigenous Christians was not without its dark side. This has been reflected in Mālikite sources already discussed. At one point a Mālikite biographer,[42] dwelling on Shīʿite oppression of the Mālikite religious establishment, observes that under the Shīʿites, the Mālikites were treated like *dhimmīs*. This is a telling comment on the less than ideal social position of Christians and Jews.

The information on high-level attitudes toward Christians is drawn from a passage in a published work of al-Qāḍī al-Nuʿmān (d. 363/974),[43] the outstanding Ismāʿīlī jurist of the Maghrib period of the Fāṭimid dynasty, and from the poetry of Ibn Hānī al-Andalusī, the court poet of the Fāṭimids in Ifrīqiya.[44]

S.M. Stern noticed the text in question from the pen of al-Qāḍī al-Nuʿmān, before the book in which it is found became available in published form, and he presented it along with an English translation, with notes, in *Byzantion*, 20 (1950): 239–58. His study is entitled, "An Embassy of the Byzantine Emperor to the Fatimid Caliph al-Muʿizz."

The tenth century witnessed frequent periods of fighting and truce between the Fāṭimids and the Byzantine Empire. At times the Rūm, as Muslims called the Greek enemy, and the Fāṭimids were at peace with each other as they faced common enemies or planned further strategies for conquest or reconquest. At other times they were locked in fierce conflict, at sea and on land, especially in Sicily and southern Italy. The visit and agreement recounted in the text in question took place in 346/957–58 at the caliph's residence in al-Manṣūriyya in Ifrīqiya. Al-Nuʿmān recorded in eloquent detail the conversational exchanges of the visit and the attitudes of the two protagonists, the caliph and the Byzantine ambassador.

Without going over all aspects of the document, I call attention to the vivid impression the account conveys of proud, triumphant power shown by al-Muʿizz and of groveling humiliation shown by the ambassador. The Fāṭimid's disdain for the religion of his interlocutor plays a large part in the exchange. In view of the well-known tolerance of the Fāṭimids toward Christians and Jews under their rule,[45] there is no reason to believe that the haughty scorn toward the Christian and his religion was more than another example of religion being used to accentuate the ill feeling of one side against another in the epic struggle for political and economic supremacy in the Mediterranean.[46] The same kind of exchanges were going on at that time in the Middle East. There, as the exchanges recorded by Gustave Schlumberger testify,[47] the Christian ruler or spokesman showed just as arrogant a spirit toward the Muslims as the Muslim did toward the Christian. In the text here under consideration the Christian is completely subdued, reduced to obsequiousness.

Language of Contempt

The choice of words in al-Nuʿmān's text is particularly significant in that he, the narrator, was a part of the scene he describes. So there seems little likelihood that epithets and expressions used would have been interpolated from another context. Although the Christian emperor is called *malik* (king) twice, the usual title given for the Christian emperor is *ṭāghiya*, or tyrant of the Rūm (Byzantines). Once he is called *ṣāḥib al-Qusṭanṭīniyya* (ruler of Constantinople).

The ambassador, repeatedly called the *ʿilj* (coarse person, unbeliever; Stern translates it "barbarian"), is depicted in a humiliating position, always deferring to the caliph, begging, entreating, supplicating in behalf of his master. He pleads for an embassy from the Fāṭimid ruler to the court of Byzantium so that his master might rejoice and receive the emmissary worthily, given the great love that his master has for the caliph. He brought rich gifts to the Fāṭimid court, and al-Muʿizz deigned to accept them. He also brought tribute money as a condition of truce but the Muslims called the money *jizya*, that is, the tax of a subjugated, protected people.

Indirectly but pointedly, al-Muʿizz accuses the emperor of weakness, since his authority was overridden on several occasions. The ambassador showers fulsome praise upon the caliph for the wisdom of his words, but in so doing he only intensifies his humiliation, for the expressions he uses are colored with blasphemous allusions, influenced by his false Christian doctrines. By contrast, the Fāṭimid imām, al-Muʿizz, is a model of rectitude and piety. He promises not to attack the Rūm as long as they do not break their agreement. He will not, he affirms, behave deceptively or treacherously as is the custom of the Rūm to act. He would like to open correspondence with the emperor on the subject of religion but he believes that the Byzantine ruler would not be interested. At any rate, he, al-Muʿizz, is ready to do anything, as long as it is for God's sake and for the faith. Faced with the shockingly irreverent praise addressed to him by the ambassador, the imām rebukes him and takes refuge in a humble spirit before God.

Poetic Diatribe

Turning to the poetry of Muḥammad Ibn Hānī al-Andalusī (d. 362/973), it is not surprising to find elaboration of the scornful reproach against Christians seen in the account of al-Nuʿmān. Ibn Hānī consecrated his considerable poetic skill entirely to the enhancement of the Fāṭimid dynasty. He was one of the most effective exponents of Ismāʿīlī doctrine. As such, the things he says about Christians are directed to the Byzantine power that stood in the way of the Fāṭimid expansion. Professor Mohammed Yalaoui, whose analysis of the Fāṭimid poet's work forms the basis of my remarks here,[48] finds the Byzantines attacked in only seven of the less than one hundred poems in the Ibn Hānī *dīwān*.[49]

The poet adds other words to the vocabulary of contempt: The emperor is called "al-Jāthilīq," or Catholicos, a curious term, since among Christians it refers to heads of the Nestorian, Armenian, and Georgian churches. According to the *Catholic Encyclopedia* it originally signified the head of a church who was dependent on a patriarch but who also acted as the patriarch's vicar. From its use in another poem, referring to a simple innkeeper who happened to be a Christian, it appears that to Ibn Hānī the word is nothing but a sobriquet.

Ibn Hānī uses the word *dumustuq* ("domestic") to refer to the emperor. This was the name of a rank in the Byzantine army, first seen in 759.[50] While it is possible that the term evolved to be applied to the emperor himself as head of the armed forces,[51] it is also possible that it is used by the poet in a derisive way, since it referred properly to a rank under the emperor's authority.

Other terms of ridicule applied to the Greek enemy in the Ibn Hānī corpus are: *Aʿājim* (sing. *Aʿjam*), "barbarians," those who do not speak Arabic; *mushrikūn*, "polytheists"; and *Banū al-Aṣfar*, "sons of the yellow," an epithet that had been used since the earliest days of Muslim contact with the Greeks.[52] Various theories seek to explain its origin, the simplest one being that it refers to the color of the skin.

The poems of Ibn Hānī are more concerned with the military exploits of the Fāṭimid armies and fleet than with religious matters. However, in a few cases the poet pointedly addresses religious barbs at the Christian enemy:

> "The dumustuq threw away his crucifixes when he saw the victory that God granted [to al-Muʿizz]"[53] and "May they worship another God than the Christ, for the religion of the monks will provide no refuge from your arms (al-Muʿizz)";[54] similarly, "May the unbelievers (*aʿlaj*) know well that even as you (al-Muʿizz) have been exalted the cross has been brought low."[55]

In one poem he complains about some prisoners of war who were forced by the Byzantines to become Christians.

> They abandoned Islam upon the threat of his (the Byzantine's) sword, even while showing magnificent fortitude.
>
> They followed the way of the apostates, but this did not insure for them continued life.
>
> Have they been satisfied with empty promises, when behind those words were treachery and sharpened blades of iron?[56]

These few examples from a short period of Maghribī history add some details to the record of Muslim-Christian encounter through the ages. They are to be put alongside studies of Christian attitudes, the details of which will probably be found not to differ much from the Muslim ones. The tenth century marked another stage in the hardening of lines between the two communities of faith.

NOTES

1. Published articles in this series are: R. Marston Speight, "Témoignage des sources Musulmanes sur la presénce chrétienne au Maghreb de 26/647 à 184/800," *IBLA: Revue de l'Institut des Belles Lettres Arab* (Tunis) 129 (1972): 73–96; "The Place of the Christians in Ninth Century North Africa, According to Muslim Sources," *Islamochristiana* 4 (1978): 47–65.

2. See "Fāṭimids," with bibliography, in *Encyclopaedia of Islam* (new ed.).

3. For a modern survey of North African Christianity see Joseph Cuoq, *L'Église d'Afrique du Nord du IIe au XIIe Siècle* (Paris: Éditions du Centurion, 1984).

4. Lewicki, *Études maghrébines et soudanaises*, vol. 1. Varsovie: Éditions scientifiques de Pologne, 1976.

5. Idris, *La Berberie Orientale sous les Zirides Xe–XIIe siècles*. Paris: Adrien-Maisonneuve, 1962.

6. For example, see al-Qāḍī ʿIyād, *Tartīb al-Madārik wa-Taqrīb al-Masālik Li-Maʿrifat Aʿlām Madhab Mālik*, 8 vols. Rabat: Wizārat al-Awqāf wa-ʾl-Shuʾūn al-Islāmiyya, 1965–83.

7. Ibn Abī-Zayd al-Qayrawānī, *Kitāb al-Jāmiʿ fī al-sunan wa-al-adab wa-al-maghāzī* (Beirut: Muʾassasat al-Risāla; Tunis: Al-Maktaba al-ʿAtīqa, 1982).

8. See Speight, "The Place of Christians."

9. The room (*al-Ḥujra*) of ʿĀʾisha in Medina where Muhammad, Abū Bakr and ʿUmar were buried.

10. The phrase, "and upon our Prophet" is found in only one of the two manuscripts used to prepare this edition of *al-Jāmiʿ*. It may have been added by a scribe who was not quite as serene about the equality of all prophets as others may have been (S. 4:150–52).

11. A tradition in Islam says that after Jesus' return to earth he will live forty years and then die. See "ʿĪsā" in *E.I.* (new ed.).

12. Ibn Abī Zayd, *Kitāb al-Jāmiʿ*, p. 141.

13. See note 10 above.

14. Ibn Abī Zayd, *Kitāb al-Jāmiʿ*, p. 169.

15. It is also found in Al-Tirmidhī, *Sunan*, zuhd, 47, where it is attributed to Muhammad and transmitted by Ibn ʿUmar.

16. Slaves who are on guard against their sins out of fear lest their masters learn about their wrongdoing (Zarqānī).

17. Because of their sins (Zarqānī).

18. See, for example, Matthew 7:1–5, 21–23.

19. For documentation of this religious tension as reflected in the ḥadīth literature, see R. Marston Speight, "Attitudes Toward Christians as Revealed in the *Musnad* of al-Ṭayālisī," *The Muslim World* 63 (1973): 249–68.

20. Speight, "The Place of Christians," p. 65.

21. Ibn Abī Zayd, *Kitāb al-Jāmīʿ*, pp. 188, 223. The two versions are slightly different from each other.

22. Ibid., p. 191.

23. Ibid., pp. 190–91.

24. Ibid., p. 191.

25. Christians and Jews.

26. Ibn Abī Zayd, *Kitāb al-Jāmiʿ*, p. 239.

27. For another example, this time from the Christian side, see Speight, "Témoignage sur la presence chrétienne," pp. 94, 95.

28. Ibid., pp. 239–40. The formula for women in childbirth has its basis in the Qurʾanic account of the birth of Mary (S. 3:35, 36) and of Mary's giving birth to Jesus (S. 19:23).

29. The first Fāṭimid Caliph (r. 298/909–323/934).

30. Mahdiyya was situated on an island-like spur of land jutting 1,400 meters into the sea.

31. Ibn Ḥammād, *Histoire des Rois Obaïdides (Les Califes Fatimides)*. Trans. and ed. M. Vondeheyden. (Paris: Paul Geuthner; Algiers: Jules Carbonel, 1927), p. 21.

32. Similar legends exist regarding the founding of the cities of Fez and Tunis (Speight, "Témoignage sur la présence Chrétienne," p. 83).

33. See Aḥmad Fuʾād al-Ahwānī, *Al-Taʿlīm fī Raʾy al-Qābisī min al-Alūsī, Abū al-Faḍl Shihāb al-Dīn Maḥmūdī: Rūḥ al-Maʿānī fī Tafsīr al-Qurʾān al-ʿAẓīm wa-Sabʿ al-Mathāni.* 30 vols. Beirut: Dār al-Fikr, 1398/1979. See also Le Baron de Slane, ed., *Description de l'Afrique Septentrionale par Abou-Obeid-el-Bekri.* (Algiers: Imprimerie du Gouvernment, 1957), p. 84.

34. See al-Ahwānī, *Al-Taʿlīm*. This book contains the text of al-Qabisi's *Al-Risāla al-Mufaṣṣala*.

35. Ibid., p. 280.

36. Ibid., p. 301.

37. Idris, "Fêtes chrétiennes célébrées . . . en Ifriqiya à l'époque ziride," *Revue Africaine* 98 (1954): 261–76.

38. Al-Ahwānī, *Al-Taʿlīm*, p. 301.

39. See Ibn ʿIdhārī, *Histoire de l'Afrique.*

40. See "Fasting and Fast Days," in *Encyclopaedia Judaica.*

41. Cuoq, *L'Église d'Afrique du Nord*, pp. 158–60; Abdel-Wahab, "Coup d'oeil général sur les apports ethniques étrangers en Tunisie," *Cahiers de Tunisie* 18, nos. 69–70 (1970): 151–69; see p. 157.

42. Al-Qādī ʿIyāḍ, *Tartīb al-Madārik*, vol. 5, p. 303.

43. Al-Qāḍī al-Nuʿmān, *Kitāb al-Majālis waʾl-Musāyarāt*. This Arabic text is the basis of the remarks to follow.

44. Yalaoui, *Un poète chiite d'Occident . . . Ibn Hani al-Andalusi.*

45. Ibid., p. 322.

46. Ibid.

47. Exchanges between the caliph in Baghdad and Nicephorus Phocas, the Byzantine emperor (ca. 964), in Gustave Schlumberger, *Un Empereur Byzantine au Dixième Siècle: Nicéphore Phocas* (Paris: Librairie de Firmin-Didat et Cie, 1980).

48. Yalaoui, *Un poète chiite*, p. 322.

49. Ibid., p. 291.

50. See "domestique," in *Grand Larousse Encyclopédique.*

51. This is Yalaoui's interpretation, *Un poète chiite*, p. 323.

52. See "Asfar," in *E.I.* (new ed.).
53. Yalaoui, *Un poète chiite*, p. 325.
54. Ibid., pp. 325–26.
55. Ibid., p. 326.
56. Ibid., p. 333.

12

Some Aspects of Muslim-Frankish Christian Relations in the Shām Region in the Twelfth Century

Hadia Dajani-Shakeel

The First Crusade resulted in the conquest of most of the Shām region (Syria, Lebanon, and Palestine) by Christian armies. The Muslims retained a few internal cities such as Aleppo, close to the northern Frankish states; Homs and Hama, close to Tripoli; and Damascus, close to the Latin Kingdom of Jerusalem, in addition to a few fortresses in the north. Each of these cities was controlled by an independent Saljuk ruler, who was more inclined to deal with the Franks than with his coreligionists. Taking advantage of this situation, the Franks played one Muslim ruler against the other, thus weakening the Islamic front. This policy governed the politics of the area for more than two decades, until the rise to power of ʿImād al-Dīn Zangī in A.D. 1127. ʿImād al-Dīn started the *jihād* against the Franks that, after his death, was carried on by his son Nūr al-Dīn, and then by Ṣalāḥ al-Dīn.

ʿImād al-Dīn unified many of the northern petty states under his command, creating an Islamic front close to Edessa. From his capital in Aleppo, he started launching planned attacks on Edessa and other Frankish-held territories in the north, culminating in the fall of Edessa in A.D. 1144 Five years later, Nūr al-Dīn expanded the Islamic front against the Franks of Syria to include Damascus (A.D. 1154). This placed him beside the Latin Kingdom of Jerusalem and Antioch. Finally, Ṣalāḥ al-Dīn united Egypt and Syria under his command in A.D. 1174, thus endangering the Latin Kingdom on two fronts, the Egyptian as well as the Syrian.

From his base in Damascus, Ṣalāḥ al-Dīn launched a systematic campaign to reduce both the Syrian Frankish territories and the Latin Kingdom. His military efforts were crowned with his victory at Ḥiṭṭīn in A.D. 1187 and the resulting recovery of most of Palestine. This led to the Third Crusade, which succeeded in recovering some of the coastal Palestinian cities from Ṣalāḥ al-Dīn and helped to preserve a small Latin Kingdom that lasted for almost another century until A.D. 1292.

During the two centuries of Muslim-Frankish conflict in the Shām region the demography changed as European communities, especially in the coastal cities, replaced the native Muslim population. The rural areas, on the other hand, continued to be inhabited by the original population: Muslims, Eastern Christians, and Armenians, though they were administered by Frankish rulers. The Franks had to deal with the Muslims of the area at two levels: with the Muslim communities under their control and with the neighboring independent Muslim rulers.

To understand the nature of the diplomatic relations between Muslim and Frankish leaders, it is important briefly to consider the nature of the relationship between the Muslims and the Franks, within the Frankish territory.

Relations between the Muslims and the Franks

Following the initial conquest of the Shām region by the Franks, between A.D. 1095 and 1121, the Muslim population was split into three groups: the slaves, the *fallāḥīn* or peasants, and the city people. The slaves were the Muslims captured from areas that had resisted the Franks; they and their descendants gained freedom only upon conversion to Christianity. The fallāḥīn formed most of the population of the Latin Kingdom and the Syrian principalities; they were under the rule of the lord of their area of residence.[1] The displaced Muslims were those who had fled their area of residence during the Frankish conquest but later returned. These, according to Ibn Jubayr, "returned because of love for their homeland."[2] However, to live in their former territories they required a safe conduct (*amān*)[3] from the Frankish authorities of those particular areas. Amāns usually included stipulations restricting the rights and privileges of Muslims: Muslims under Frankish rule had to pay a poll tax, which amounted to one *dīnār* and five *qīrāṭs* per person, as well as farm rents, often paid in kind.[4]

The treatment of the Muslims under Frankish rule differed from one landlord to another and from one community to another. Those communities that resisted their landlords received harsh treatment; among such communities were the villages of Jammaʿil, Yasuf, Marada, and others near Nablus, known as the *maqādisa*. Inhabitants of these villages rebelled several times against the Frankish authorities (A.D. 1113, 1155, 1187),[5] to achieve semi-independence and, further, to stop paying the poll tax, which they considered illegal. The maqādisa felt oppressed especially under the rule of Balian of Ibelin; one of their descendants, Ibn Ṭūlūn al-Ṣāliḥī, described Balian as a tyrant who committed many atrocities against the peasants from the Nablus area, such as amputating their legs for disobedience. According to al-Ṣāliḥī, Balian would charge his Muslim subjects four times more in poll tax than other Frankish lords with the aim of subjugating them. Such treatment led to the departure of some of the Muslim leaders with their families to Damascus in A.D. 1150, and to their settlement with the help of Nūr al-Dīn Zangī in al-Ṣāliḥiyya.[6] In sharp contrast to the treatment of the maqādisa by Balian was their treatment by a Frankish administrator representing Baldwin, king of the Latin Kingdom of Jerusalem. This administrator was kind to the Muslims, often informing them of the intentions of Balian against them; it was his information about a plot by Balian to assassinate the leader of the maqādisa (Sheikh Aḥmad ibn Muḥammad al-Maqdisī) that precipitated their migration to Damascus.[7] Ibn Jubayr, the Andalusian pilgrim to the Muslim East, refers to many Muslims who were living so comfortably under Frankish rule that some of their neighboring Muslims, under Muslim rule, envied them. He points out however, that they paid the Franks half of the land produce as well as a poll tax of one dīnār and five qīrāṭs. In addition, they paid a light tax on fruits. But they owned their residences. Ibn Jubayr also mentions an area near Bānyās (on the Syrian coast) where Muslims and Franks shared the land and its produce equally: even their cattle grazed together undisturbed.[8]

Despite the cooperation and coexistence among some rural communities, however, Muslims and Franks formed two distinct societies. Each community was controlled by its own laws. Often Muslim leaders conducted their own affairs, though responsible to the Frankish authorities.[9]

Two distinct Frankish populations emerged in the twelfth century. They were *al-faranj al-sharqiyyīn* ("Eastern Franks"), the early settlers and their descendants, and *al-faranj al-ghurabā* ("alien Franks"), the new settlers. The Eastern Franks included some of mixed parents: Franks and Armenians, Franks and native Christians, or Franks and Muslim converts.[10] They developed a better understanding of their Muslim neighbors and even tried to maintain better diplomatic relations with them. In contrast, the new settlers were less tolerant, aggressive, and continually seeking expansion into new territory. They persistently championed the ideals of the early crusaders, who considered the Muslims a political as well as a religious enemy.[11] Usāmā Ibn Munqidh, an Arab scholar and knight, ambassador of the Damascene authorities to some Frankish rulers, described the difference in attitude and the tension between the Eastern Franks and the new settlers in the following anecdote:

> Each of the new settlers (Franks) in the Frankish territories, is more crude than those who have adapted and associated with the Muslims.

> Once, when I was in Jerusalem, I entered the Aqṣā Mosque area to pray. Near the Aqṣā Mosque, there was a small mosque which the Franks had transformed into a chapel. Whenever I entered the Aqṣā Mosque area, the Templars vacated that mosque for me to pray. I entered the Mosque once, started my prayer, exclaimed "*Allāhu-Akbar*." All of a sudden a Frank rushed toward me, grabbed me with his hands, and turned my face toward the East saying: "Pray in this direction." A group of Templars drove him away from me. I started to pray again, when, taking advantage of the Templars' lack of attention, the same man attacked me again. He turned my face toward the East, repeating: "Pray in this direction only." The Templars again drove him away from me, apologizing that the man was a *gharīb*, a new arrival. He had not seen anybody praying in any direction other than the east. I responded: "Enough of the prayer for the time being." When I left the mosque, I wondered about the devil and about the change in his color, about his shudder and agitation on seeing the prayer performed in the direction of the Qibla.[12]

The new arrivals from Europe often forced the native Franks to revoke their treaties with the Muslims, to expand into their territory. Thus, the revoking of an existing treaty upon the arrival of recruits or settlers became an accepted practice in the East.[13]

The attitudes of the new settlers intensified the military confrontation between the Muslims and the Franks throughout the twelfth century. Three major confrontations eventually led to the downfall of the Franks in the area. The first was the Second Crusade (A.D. 1148), which was instigated by the fall of Edessa to the forces of ʿImād al-Dīn Zangī in A.D. 1144. Despite a warning from the Syrian Franks, this crusade aimed at conquering Damascus. It disrupted an existing agreement between King Baldwin III and his close ally in the area, Muʿīn al-Dīn Unūr, governor of Damascus. When the crusade failed, the natives and the Franks blamed each other.[14] However, this crusade contributed to the rise of Nūr al-Dīn Zangī in Damascus. He subsequently reduced the Syrian Frankish territory and laid the basis for the recovery of Palestine and most of the Syrian coast.

The second major encounter was the attempt by King Amalric, encouraged by the Hospitallers and the Byzantine emperor, to conquer Egypt in A.D. 1169. By invading Egypt, Amalric broke a binding treaty with his allies, the Fāṭimid establishment and the *wazīr* Shāwar. The latter had no choice but to invite the forces of Nūr al-Dīn Zangī, which were led by Asad al-Dīn Shirkūh and Ṣalāḥ al-Dīn, the enemies of both the Fāṭimids and Amalric. The invasion of Egypt by Amalric resulted in the rise of Ṣalāḥ al-Dīn to power. William of Tyre, a native Frankish historian and advisor to King Amalric, lamented that Amalric undertook such a dangerous adventure, since it led to the decline of the Franks in the East. "O wicked madness of an insatiable and greedy heart! From a quiet state of peace into what a turbulent and anxious condition has an immoderate desire for possessions plunged us!" He pointed out that the wealth of Egypt was flowing into the kingdom (in the form of payments for their alliance and promised support against Asad al-Dīn). Also, the borders of the Latin Kingdom were secure, at least from the Egyptian front.[15] With the rise of the Ayyubids to power, however, the kingdom had to contend with enemies from both the north (Syria) and the south (Egypt).

The third major contribution to the downfall of the Franks was the repeated series of attacks by Reynald de Chatillon, a European adventurer, on the caravans between Egypt and Syria, despite a binding *hudna* (truce) with Ṣalāḥ al-Dīn. One such attack was on a caravan from Egypt to Damascus which included soldiers, supplies, and money. Reynald captured all the soldiers and looted the supplies and money. This outraged Ṣalāḥ al-Dīn, who asked Reynald to return all the booty. Reynald refused. Consequently, Ṣalāḥ al-Dīn vowed that if he captured Reynald, he would kill him. This incident was a major factor contributing to the Battle of Ḥiṭṭīn.[16]

Coexistence between the Muslims and the Franks in the East

Despite the wars between the Muslims and the Franks on one front or another, the routine of life continued without any interference. Ibn Jubayr, who traveled in Syria and Palestine around A.D. 1184, reflected on the war and peace situation in the area. He points out that while the armies of both the Muslims and Christians (Franks) faced each other in battle, trade caravans continued to travel between the two parties without any interference or harassment. The following example reflects the situation of coexistence between Muslims and Christians. Ṣalāḥ al-Dīn marched with all his Muslim forces to attack the fort of Karak, which blocked the route to the Ḥijāz, and hence jeopardized the pilgrimage by the land route. Throughout the duration of the attack the movement of caravans between Egypt and Syria continued unabated, as did that of merchants between Damascus and Acre, and of Christian (Frankish) merchants through Muslim territory. The Muslims paid a tax to the Christians through whose lands they passed, while the Christian merchants paid a tax on their wares to the Muslims. Coexistence and moderation thus triumphed. While the armies clashed in battle, the civilians lived on in peace.[17]

Ibn Jubayr's remarks may be referring to an ideal situation. Other medieval authors, however, refer to similar conditions. Coexistence between Muslims and Franks was a natural outcome of a neighborly relationship that lasted for almost two centuries. Muslims and Franks exchanged commodities, wares, food products, and textiles. Reflecting on the relationship between the Latin Kingdom and Egypt under the Fāṭimids, William of Tyre says: "Our people could enter the territories of Egypt without fear and carry on commerce and trade under favourable conditions. On their part, the Egyptians brought to the realm foreign riches and strange commodities hitherto unknown to us. As long as they visited us, they were an advantage and an honour to us. Moreover, the large sums spent by them every year among us enriched the fiscal treasury and increased the private wealth of individuals."[18]

Some Muslim merchants lived in Acre after getting an *amān* allowing them to stay there for a limited period. They usually rented residences close to the coast from Frankish landlords.[19] The Italian trading communities in the East as well as the Italian states contributed to the exchange of merchandise and travelers between the two areas. This occurred in challenge of the kings of the Latin Kingdom. Italian maritime states provided war supplies to Ṣalāḥ al-Dīn's government in Egypt. Also, Italian representatives frequently visited Ṣalāḥ al-Dīn's court.[20]

As the war and peace situation prevailed on land, it also prevailed at sea. Galleys carrying people and merchandise passed between the two territories peacefully, although there were some unlucky ones that were inconvenienced by adventurers looking for booty. Since the Franks controlled the coast from Antioch to Gaza, Muslims traveling by the sea route needed an amān from the Frankish authorities for safe passage. The amān and a cross were usually shown to the Frankish authorities,[21] who would then allow the Muslims safe passage. The law of the sea was often broken; although the Muslims and the Franks had an agreement stipulating that vessels protected by an amān should not be attacked, this agreement was broken in several instances by the Franks. Two of the victims of such breaches were the families of Usāmā Ibn Munqidh and the chronicler Ibn al-Athīr. Usāmā reports that his family, traveling from Egypt to Damascus, had secured an amān from King Baldwin III, through Nūr al-Dīn Zangī. When their galley entered Frankish waters at Acre, the king (according to Usāmā) sent his men to the galley, while he watched by the shore. The king's men broke the galley with axes, claiming that it had broken accidentally in their waters. This could have been regarded as a violation of the amān, which could have invited in turn the revenge of Nūr al-Dīn. By claiming that the captured vessel broke in their waters, the Franks legalized the confiscation of the vessel, for their law of the sea provided them with an excuse to confiscate it along with its contents—both human and material. Members of Usāmā's family were thoroughly searched while their goods, including clothes and jewelry, were seized. Usāmā's collection of rare books was also impounded.[22]

Ibn al-Athīr was more fortunate, for his family recovered part of their confiscated merchandise. He mentions that in A.D. 1171 some galleys were traveling from Egypt to Damascus. At Latakia the Franks confiscated two of these galleys, loaded with commodities, claiming that due to some damage in the galleys water had seeped into them. This was enough excuse for them to seize the galleys and their contents. Nūr al-Dīn protested their violation of the amān and sent raiding detachments into their territories in Antioch, Tripoli, ʿArqa, and elsewhere. His vehement response forced them to acknowledge their violation of the amān and the truce (*hudna*) between them and Nūr al-Dīn. They returned the confiscated merchandise.[23]

Among the prime targets of the Franks were the Andalusian Muslims, traveling by the sea route to Syria. They would be commandeered to the Frankish ports and sold in the markets to buyers who would then sell them again to Muslim philanthropists and rulers for high prices.[24]

Diplomacy

During a period of two centuries of war and peace between the Muslims and the Franks, the nature of diplomacy changed. Their treaties became more binding and more elaborate as they were properly recorded and registered. This was a departure from the earlier form of diplomacy, or "sword diplomacy." The attitude of the early crusaders toward their Muslim counterparts clearly shows this earlier type of diplomacy. The representatives of the Fāṭimid government, who arrived at Antioch in A.D. 1096, were to confirm a treaty of peace with and assess the power of the leaders of the First Crusade. They were received graciously by those leaders, who had not yet captured Antioch. However, when the Egyptians left Antioch along with an accompanying Frankish delegation, countless heads of Muslims were presented to them as a gift to the Fāṭimid caliph and his wazīr.[25] Two years later, when another Egyptian delegation went to meet the Crusade leaders at ʿArqa, near Tripoli, for further negotiations, the victorious Frankish leaders dismissed the members of the delegation. They were advised to inform their rulers in Egypt that the Franks not only rejected their terms, but would also march on Egypt upon having conquered Jerusalem.[26]

The negotiations between Peter the Hermit and Kerbogha of Mosil offer another example of such crude diplomacy. Peter, knowing that the Franks encamped outside Antioch needed a truce, met Kerbogha (who was then besieging them) and warned him and the other Muslims either to surrender or to convert to Christianity. On his part, Kerbogha invited Peter and the Franks to convert or perish.[27]

During the early years of the confrontations, negotiations between Muslims and Franks continued through ambassadors representing Muslim and Frankish rulers. Native Christians and Armenians often served as ambassadors to the Franks. However, in the second half of the twelfth century a new generation of bilingual Eastern Franks conducted the negotiations for their rulers. Among these were Hugh of Caesarea, who negotiated a treaty with the Fāṭimid authorities in A.D. 1171, and the son of Humphrey of Toron (Ibn al-Hunfrī), who negotiated the peace between Ṣalāḥ al-Dīn and King Richard that concluded the Third Crusade. Some of the Eastern Frankish rulers, like Raymond III of Tripoli and Reynald of Sidon, conducted their own peace negotiations with Ṣalāḥ al-Dīn.[28] Reynald also represented Conrad Marquis of Montferrat, the ruler of Tyre, in his negotiations with Ṣalāḥ al-Dīn during the Third Crusade. These negotiations concerned a pact between Ṣalāḥ al-Dīn and the marquis against King Richard. Ibn Shaddād, one of Ṣalāḥ al-Dīn's advisors, noted that on one occasion a messenger came to Ṣalāḥ al-Dīn's camp in Acre with the information that the representative of the marquis was awaiting an appointment with the sultan. Ṣalāḥ al-Dīn sent orders to receive him with full respect. Thus a tent was pitched for him, with the necessary cushions and furniture befiting his (Frankish) leaders. After he had rested, he was called to meet with Ṣalāḥ al-Dīn.[29]

Among the most outstanding Muslim ambassadors to the Franks was Usāmā Ibn Munqidh. He often traveled to the Latin Kingdom either to release some captives or to conclude treaties for Muᶜīn al-Dīn Unūr. He would represent his father and uncle, the lords of Shayzar, in negotiations with the Frankish rulers of Antioch and other Syrian principalities. He developed many friendships among these rulers.[30] Another outstanding ambassador was al-Malik al-ᶜĀdil, Ṣalāḥ al-Dīn's brother, who was also his chief negotiator with King Richard during the Third Crusade. Al-ᶜĀdil and Richard became such good friends that they addressed each other as brother, and Richard was so impressed by al-ᶜĀdil that he offered him his sister Joanna in marriage. The offer was welcomed by Ṣalāḥ al-Dīn and accepted by al-ᶜĀdil; the union might have materialized had it not been for the intervention of the clergy in the camp of Richard.[31] They, according to Ibn Shaddād, insisted that since Joanna was widowed, she needed permission from the pope to remarry. Richard then offered his niece as a substitute for his sister, saying that there should be no objection to her marriage with al-ᶜĀdil. But Ṣalāḥ al-Dīn refused it, saying that the negotiations were over the marriage between al-ᶜĀdil and Richard's sister (Joanna); having wasted much time negotiating over Joanna, Ṣalāḥ al-Dīn felt that Richard was distracting them with the issue of marriage from other more urgent matters.[32]

Treaties

To understand the process of diplomacy between the Muslims and the Franks in the East, it is necessary to understand something of the Islamic notion of peace in the twelfth century.

Muslim jurists of the time defined *jihād* as a defensive war aimed at protecting the lives of Muslims, their territory, and property. This is a departure from the notions of *dār al-Islām* and *dār al-Ḥarb* discussed by some of the earlier jurists. Especially in the second half of the twelfth century, Muslims emphasized the liberation of Islamic territory and Islamic shrines that had been transformed into palaces and churches. From the Islamic point of view, war that aimed at neither conversion nor expansion was considered just. On the other hand, the notion of peace required protecting Muslims from falling under the rule of the enemy. Thus peace was also defensive, especially during the first few years of the First Crusade when there was total absence of Islamic leadership. In their peace process Muslim rulers tried to adhere to the Islamic instructions on peace. So did the Franks in their dealings with their Muslim counterparts, though they did not abide by their commitments as the Muslims did.

Arabic sources use several terms meaning peace, like *silm* and *salām*, *ṣulḥ*, *hudna*, *muhādana*, *muwādaʿa*, *musālama*, and *amān*. *Silm* and *salām* refer to peace in general, meaning the ending of hostilities with the enemy: "It is not inconsistent with Islam's ultimate goal if a peace treaty is concluded with the enemy, whether from expediency or because of a setback. Making treaties with non-Muslims is permitted by Divine legislation."[33] This is confirmed by the Qurʾanic verse that says: "And if they incline to peace, you also incline to it, and trust in God."[34] The process of *salām* was normally concluded after long negotiations, following truces or *hudan* (sing. *hudna*).

The term *hudna* in Arabic, with synonyms *muhādana*, *muwādaʿa*, and *ṣulḥ*, "is a form of *ʿaqd* (a tie or conjunction) signifying an agreement on a certain act which has the object of creating legal consequences."[35] Al-Qalqashandī defines the hudna as an agreement to cease all kinds of hostility between two warring factions. It is subject to renewal or nonrenewal and can be a first step toward setting up a more permanent peace. Jurists stipulated certain conditions for concluding hudan, stating that they should be in the interest of the Muslims.[36] This was not the situation early in the twelfth century though the only interest was to gain time for defending a certain territory. Jurists also demanded that the hudan should be sanctioned by the highest Islamic authority. Early in the twelfth century, certain Muslim rulers signed hasty truces with their enemies. But Nūr al-Dīn, and after him Ṣalāḥ al-Dīn (A.D. 1148–93), were intent on carrying on their war and peace activity in the name of the Abbassid caliph, and were supported by an investiture from the Abbasid caliph of the time.[37] By doing this, they universalized the notions of jihād and peace.

There were certain rules for the duration of the hudna. Some jurists stated that it should not last more than a year, with four months as minimum. Others, such as al-Shāfiʿī, allowed Muslims to extend it to ten years if they were weak. This was after the model of *ṣulḥ al-Ḥudaybiyya*, concluded between the Prophet

Muhammad and the Makkans. The Mālikites, on the other hand, set no time limit to the hudna. A hudna agreed upon by warring parties was binding on both throughout the stipulated period.[38]

According to the rules of hudan, the warring parties should agree to support each other against the enemies of either party. They would also agree to release captives, escort them to their respective territories, and ensure the safety of merchants and their merchandise passing through or residing in each other's territories. The victor could ask for an annual tribute to be delivered at a specified period or ask to retain the villages and towns that had been captured.[39]

As mentioned earlier, however, the hudan were of limited duration, their renewal negotiable. If one of the feuding parties decided against renewing a hudna upon its expiry, it was expected to inform the other party of its intentions. In the meantime, both parties were expected to ensure the safety of transient residents or merchants from each other's communities in their territory. If a party broke a hudna, it incurred severe punishment from the other.[40]

Before Nūr al-Dīn and Ṣalāḥ al-Dīn (A.D. 1149–93), whose power matched that of their enemy, the Franks hardly abided by the laws of the hudan or amāns, as indicated in the introduction. When they joined the Second Crusade against Damascus they broke a binding agreement, hudna, with the governor of Damascus, Muʿin al-Dīn Unūr, a good friend of the kings of Jerusalem. The shrewd Unūr, realizing that the Franks were humiliated by the defeat at the gate of Damascus and that he needed their support against Nūr al-Dīn, renewed his truce with them upon their request.[41]

Some of the Frankish kings or princes planning to annul a hudna with their counterparts often used to make excuses such as that some new arrivals had come from Europe with the intention of expanding and that they themselves were unable to stop these newcomers.[42] As William of Tyre mentions, Amalric, who wanted to annul his treaty with Shāwar in order to invade Egypt at a time he thought was convenient, concocted and circulated many stories about Shāwar. He claimed that the Egyptian wazīr was constantly sending messengers to Nūr al-Dīn and secretly imploring his aid. Shāwar, according to Amalric's story, claimed for his part that it was entirely against his own wishes that he had joined in any treaty of peace with the enemy, and that he desired to withdraw from the agreement he had made with the king. Having prepared public opinion for his adventure, Amalric marched against Egypt. William of Tyre, who was against breaching the agreement with Egypt, mentions that certain Franks disagreed with Amalric's claims. "They assert that the war made against him (Shāwar) was unjust and contrary to divine law; that it was merely a pretext invented to defend an outrageous enterprise. Hence it was, they maintain, that the Lord, who strictly judges the secrets of the heart and conscience, wholly withdrew his favour from us and refused to grant success to our iniquitous undertaking."[43] William of Tyre's sharp criticism of Amalric's revoking of the treaty reflects a departure from the attitude of other chroniclers of the crusade.

Early in the chapter I mentioned other examples of violations of hudan or peace or amān. As indicated, synonyms for the term hudna include *muwādaʿa* and *musālama*. The first means that the two warring parties agreed on mutual peace so that their communities might live peacefully, though for a limited period. The second means that both parties wanted peace and security.[44] Many of the medieval Muslim chroniclers use the terms interchangeably. Ibn al-Qalanisi refers to several hudan, muwādaʿāt, musālamāt between two rulers of Damascus—Tughtikin and Muʿīn al-Dīn Unūr—and certain Latin kings and Frankish lords. Ibn al-Athīr, Abū Shāma, and others refer to hudan concluded between ʿImād al-Dīn Zangī and some of the Franks of Syria. One hudna was between him and Joscelin, the count of Edessa, in A.D. 1127. ʿImād al-Dīn was in the process of consolidating his power against the Urtuqid rulers of northern Syria, and needed to protect his back from the Franks. He proposed a hudna with Joscelin, who accepted it on certain conditions, which were in turn accepted by ʿImād al-Dīn. The truce, to last for two years, worked in favor of ʿImād al-Dīn, who extended his boundaries to Edessa. Soon after, in A.D. 1137, ʿImād al-Dīn attacked the Frankish fort of Barin (Montferrand) in the valley of the upper Orontes, capturing the fort with many of the Frankish knights and dignitaries including King Fulk of Anjou (of Jerusalem).[45]

The negotiations over the surrender of Montferrand in A.D. 1137 and the resulting truce deserve to be discussed here as an example of medieval diplomacy. William of Tyre's account of these negotiations is more detailed than the Islamic. He indicates that when ʿImād al-Dīn attacked the fort of Montferrand in A.D. 1137, the besieged, who included many of the Frankish lords as well as the king of Jerusalem, sent messengers to the princes of Antioch and Edessa seeking military support. They responded by sending some detachments to the fort. However ʿImād al-Dīn, informed about the approaching forces, decided to negotiate with the besieged. He sent them envoys to make overtures of peace, says William of Tyre. "They (the envoys) were instructed to say to the king and his nobles that the fortress, already half demolished, could not hold out much longer; that the Christians, exhausted by starvation, had lost courage and had no longer strength to resist. His own army, on the contrary, possessed in abundance all things necessary." ʿImād al-Dīn proposed that out of respect for the king he was ready to return all the prisoners he had captured, to allow the king and other besieged lords to depart to their territories peacefully, on condition that they surrender the fort to him. The besieged "received the proffered terms with great eagerness and were astonished that such humanity could exist in a man so cruel." They accepted the terms, and a final agreement was concluded. Consequently, the count of Tripoli was released with a large number of captives. The king along with his entourage also left the fort, "receiving kindly treatment from the enemy." Then the fort was surrendered to ʿImād al-Dīn.[46]

ʿImād al-Dīn's victories persuaded many of the minor Frankish rulers in the north of Syria to ask for ṣulḥ. Others, whose territory came under attack by ʿImād al-Dīn, sent him delegations to propose the surrender of their territory. The ruler of Ḥārim asked for hudna, offering to surrender half of his territory to ʿImād al-Dīn.[47]

The rise of ʿImād al-Dīn to power, his expansion in northern Syria and his recovery of Edessa marked the beginning of the shift in power and diplomacy that continued until the end of the twelfth century.

Other Aspects of Muslim-Frankish Diplomacy in the East

Alliances and Counteralliances

When the Franks entered the Shām in A.D. 1095, they became an important factor in the area by playing the game of divide and rule. They allied themselves with some rulers against others, and lent their support to any Muslim ruler who sought it against another. By these maneuvers they asserted their presence in the area. Early in the century there was much demand for their services, for the Muslim rulers were disunited. Once the Islamic front was united, however, Muslims' dependence on Frankish support decreased. Instead, some Frankish rulers started to seek military support of the Muslims against their own people. One such example was Alice, the daughter of King Baldwin of Jerusalem and the young widow of Bohemond, the prince of Antioch. Following her husband's death in A.D. 1130, Alice decided to maintain her sovereignty over Antioch, but was opposed by the statesmen there. Consequently, she tried to contact ʿImād al-Dīn Zangī through one of her loyal employees. Through an envoy she sent him a message requesting military aid and a valuable present: "a snow-white palfrey shot with silver. The bridle and other trappings were likewise of silver and even the silken saddle cloth was white, so that uniformity prevailed throughout."[48] The unfortunate messenger, however, was intercepted on his way to Aleppo and returned to Antioch where he was interrogated by King Baldwin, who had gone to discipline his daughter. The envoy confessed the details of the plot and was executed. This episode may have given ʿImād al-Dīn a place in medieval Western romance.

Another prominent Frankish leader to deal with Muslims against other Franks was Raymond III of Tripoli, one of the closest allies of Ṣalāḥ al-Dīn. He contributed unintentionally to the fall of the Latin Kingdom by allowing Ṣalāḥ al-Dīn access to his territory around Tiberias. This privilege enhanced Ṣalāḥ al-

Dīn's march against the Latin Kingdom and his subsequent victory at Ḥiṭṭīn in A.D. 1187,[49] the victory marking the end of the first Latin Kingdom.

The Franks also lent their support to many Muslim rulers against other Muslims, as mentioned. Among such rulers were Muʿīn al-Dīn Unūr, the governor of Damascus, and Shāwar, the wazīr of the Egyptian Fāṭimid caliph al-ʿĀḍid. Muʿīn al-Dīn was a close friend of King Fulk of Anjou, of Jerusalem. He often used to visit the court in ʿAkkā and the holy places in Jerusalem. Afraid of ʿImād al-Dīn Zangī's conquest of Damascus in 1139, Muʿīn al-Dīn sought a defense alliance with King Fulk against ʿImād al-Dīn. He offered to pay the king twenty thousand pieces of gold monthly for the necessary expenses and to help the king recover the city of Bānyās from the agent of ʿImād al-Dīn.[50] Muʿīn al-Dīn's alliance with the kings of Jerusalem was only annulled by King Baldwin III during the Second Crusade, but was renewed soon after the end of that crusade.[51]

The most serious alliance between Muslim and Frankish rulers against other Muslims was the alliance between the Egyptian wazīr Shāwar and King Amalric of the Latin Kingdom against the forces of Nūr al-Dīn Zangī in Egypt in A.D. 1171. This alliance, aimed at protecting Egypt from Asad al-Dīn Shirkūh and Ṣalāḥ al-Dīn, the officers of Nūr al-Dīn, encouraged Amalric to invade Egypt with the intent of conquering it. However his attempt was foiled, his treaty terminated, and his ally Shāwar eventually assassinated.[52] The doomed invasion resulted in the rise of Ṣalāḥ al-Dīn, who eventually reduced the Latin Kingdom.

Prisoners of War

In a discussion of diplomatic relations between Muslims and Franks one cannot overlook the exchange of prisoners, an important factor in the peace negotiations. Ibn Jubayr, who witnessed the condition of Muslim captives in the Latin Kingdom of Jerusalem, was greatly moved by their plight. "Among the disasters witnessed in their territory (Frankish), is the sight of Muslim captives in shackles performing hard labour like the slaves. Also the sight of Muslim female captives wearing iron anklets . . . Hearts would burst with pity for them, but this does not help."[53]

The prisoners included some of the dignitaries of both sides as well as Muslim pilgrims from Andalusia, in addition to prisoners captured during raids on each other's territory. Some of those were never rescued, others fled from their captivity to Islamic or Frankish territories, still others were freed as a condition for peace treaties, and some were ransomed by certain rulers and philanthropists. Some of the Frankish princes in captivity used to raise money to ransom themselves. Thus trading in prisoners was a thriving business in the twelfth century.

The prisoners, who included men, women, and children, were numerous in both Muslim and Frankish territories. The real victims of captivity, however, were women on both sides. They were used as domestics, mistresses, wives, or slaves often sold in the thriving slave markets. Some Muslim women, fearing the gloomy fate, committed suicide, while some Frankish women chose monastic life after freedom from captivity. Two examples serve as illustration.

One is reported by Usāmā Ibn Munqidh, a witness to the events about a Muslim Kurdish woman from Shayzar named Raffūl, who was captured during an attack by the Franks and the Byzantines on the town (A.D. 1137). Her father almost lost his mind, walking in the streets of the town, telling people that Raffūl had been captured. One day, while Usāmā was walking along the river in Shayzar, he noticed a distant black item. He asked one of his associates to find out about that black item. The man went and found Raffūl dead, covered with a dark blue dress. She had thrown herself from the horse of the Frank who had captured her.[54]

Another incident, reported by Usāmā about a Muslim woman captured by one of the Franks of Antioch, reflects on the Islamic view of honor and shame and the fear of Muslim women of being molested by the enemy. Usāmā points out that the captured Muslim woman had been married to his uncle ʿIzz al-Dīn for some time before she was divorced. However, when Ibn Munqidh heard that his former wife had been captured, he was outraged and said: "I will not allow a woman I had married to stay in the captivity of the Franks." Thus, he paid five hundred dīnārs for her release and sent her back to her family.[55]

There are also many reports reflecting the fears of the Franks about their women falling into the hands of their enemies, the Muslims. One example concerns a noble lady, the wife of Renier, surnamed the Brus, the lord of Bānyās. Renier's wife was taken to Damascus along with a large number of captives in A.D. 1131, when Tāj al-Mulūk Būrī of Damascus conquered Bānyās. She spent two years in captivity and was released after a truce was concluded between the Damascene authorities and the king of Jerusalem. According to the terms of the truce, all Frankish captives in Damascus were to be released. "She was returned to her distinguished husband after an absence of two years," says William of Tyre, "and he graciously restored her to her position as his wife. Later, however, he discovered that her conduct while with the enemy had not been altogether discreet. She had not preserved the sanctity of the marriage couch as a noble matron should. Accordingly, he cast her off. She did not deny her guilt, but entered a convent of holy women at Jerusalem, took the vows of perpetual chastity, and became a nun."[56]

As noted, during the initial stage of the crusade many Muslim women forced into conversion to Christianity married Franks; many Frankish women became and married Muslims. Both produced a generation that contributed to better understanding between the two communities in the East, though they could not stop the wars which were continuously inflamed by new European settlers into the Shām region.

The situation of war and peace between Muslims and Franks in the Shām region continued for two centuries, until A.D. 1292. After the termination of the remaining Frankish posts in the Shām and Palestine, some Franks returned to Europe while others remained in the area where they became part of its population. Arabic names such as the *ifranjī*, *ifranjiyya* (family descending from a Frankish woman), *ṣalībī* (crusader), and others attest to their assimilation in the culture and its population.

The relationship between the Muslims and the Franks enriched Arabic historical writings, religious and profane poetry, and Arabic fiction, as well as the art of drafting official documents to the Franks.

NOTES

1. Jean Richard, *The Latin Kingdom of Jerusalem*, trans. J. Shirly (Amsterdam: North Holland Publishing Co., 1979), 1: 131–34.

2. Muḥammad Ibn Jubayr, *Riḥlat Ibn Jubayr* (Beirut: Dār al-Hilāl, 1981), p. 252.

3. Franks adopted the Islamic rules for granting *amāns*. Hence, they granted *amāns* to individuals as well as to whole communities. For details on *amāns*, see Majid Khadduri, *War and Peace in the Law of Islam* (New York: AMS Press, 1979), pp. 170–71; Aḥmad Ibn ʿAlī al-Qalqashandī, *Ṣubḥ al-Aʿshā fī Ṣināʿat al-Inshā* (Cairo: Al-Muʾassasa al-Miṣriyya li-l Taʾlīf waʾl-Tarjama wa ʾl-Nashr, [n.d.]), 13: 322–23.

4. Ibn Jubayr, *Riḥlat*, pp. 246–48.

5. Richard, *Latin Kingdom*, 1: 133.

6. Muḥammad Ibn Ṭūlūn al-Ṣaliḥī, *Al-Qalāʾid al-Jawhariyya fī Tārīkh al-Ṣāliḥiyya* (Damascus: Maktab al-Dirāsāt al-Islāmiyya, 1949), 1: 26–28.

7. Al-Ṣāliḥī, 1: 27–28.

8. Ibn Jubayr, *Riḥlat*, pp. 246–48.

9. Richard, *Latin Kingdom*, 1: 133.

10. See the remarks of Fulcher of Chartres in James Brundage, *The Crusades: A Documentary Survey* (Milwaukee, Wis.: Marquette University Press, 1962), pp. 74–75.

11. The best representation of this attitude is by Jacque de Vitry in his *The History of Jerusalem*, trans. A. Steward (London: The Palestine Pilgrims Text Society, 1896).

12. Usāmā Ibn Munqidh, *Kitāb al-Iʿtibār* (Princeton: Princeton University Press, 1930), pp. 134–35.

13. ʿAbd al-Raḥmān al-Maqdisī abū Shāma, *Kitāb al-Rawḍatayn fī Akhbār al-Dawlatayn al-Nūriyya wa ʾl-Ṣalāḥiyya* (Cairo: Al-Muʿassasa al-Miṣriyya al-ʿĀmma li ʾl-Taʿlīf wa ʾl-Tarjama wa ʾl-Nashr, 1962), vol. 1, pt. 1, p. 259. Just before this incident in A.D. 1156 a *hudna* was concluded between Nūr al-Dīn and King Baldwin III. Nūr al-Dīn had agreed to pay the king 800 Syrian dīnārs. The agreement was recorded.

14. Hans Eberhand Mayer, *The Crusades* (Oxford: Oxford University Press, 1981), pp. 106–7.

15. William of Tyre, *A History of the Crusades* (New York: Cambridge University Press, 1988), 2: 357–58.

16. ʿIzz al-Dīn Ibn al-Athīr, *Al-Kāmil fī ʾl-Tārīkh* (Beirut: Dār al-Kutub al-ʿIlmiyya, 1987), 10: 142. Also, see Mayer, *Crusades*, pp. 130–31.

17. Ibn Jubayr, *Riḥlat*, pp. 234–35.

18. William of Tyre, *History*, 2: 358.

19. Ibn Jubayr, *Riḥlat*, p. 248.

20. See Abū Shāma, *Kitāb al-Rawḍatayn*, vol. I, pt. 2, pp. 621–22.

21. Ibn Munqidh, *Kitāb al-Iʿtibār*, p. 34.

22. Ibid., pp. 34–35.

23. ʿIzz al-Din Ibn al-Athir, *Al-Tarikh al-Bahir fi ʾl-Dawla al-Atbakiyya* (Baghdad: Al-Muthanna, 1963), pp. 154–55.

24. Ibn Munqidh, *Kitāb al-Iʿtibār*, pp. 81–82.

25. Muṣṭafā Al-Kinānī, *Al-ʿAlāqāt bayn Ganawā wa ʾl-Fāṭimiyyīn fī ʾl-Sharq al-Awsaṭ, 1095–1171 A.D.* (Alexandria: Al-Hayʾa al-Miṣriyya al-ʿĀmma li ʾl-Kitāb, 1981), p. 129.

26. William of Tyre, *History*, 2: 326.

27. For details, see ibid., 2: 282–83.

28. See ibid., 2: 321; Bahāʾ al-Dīn Ibn Shaddād, *Al-Nawādir al-Sulṭāniyya wa-Maḥāsin al-Yūsufiyya* (Cairo: Al-Dār al-Miṣriyya li ʾl-Taʾlīf wa ʾl-Tarjama, 1964), pp. 97, 202, 204, 240. Ibn Shaddād points out that Reynold of Sidon was well versed in Arabic, Islamic history, and *ḥadīth*. He had two Muslim instructors (ibid., p. 97). Raymond III was such a good friend of Ṣalāḥ al-Dīn that the Franks accused him of converting to Islam. See Ibn al-Athīr, *Al-Kāmil*, 10: 144.

29. Ibn Shaddād, *Al-Nawādir al-Sulṭāniyya*, p. 199.

30. Ibn Munqidh's autobiography *Kitāb al-Iʿtibār* makes several references to his mission to the Franks and to his friendship with them.

31. The marriage between al-ʿĀdil and Joanna was seen as a solution for the future of the Holy Land. It was a part of the peace negotiations according to which both would rule Palestine. Had the marriage taken place, Joanna would have taken a gift from Richard of the Palestinian coast from Acre to Jaffa. Al-ʿĀdil would have taken from Ṣalāḥ al-Dīn the remaining part of Palestine, in addition to his own *iqṭāʾ* (land grant). See Ibn Shaddād, p. 195.

32. Ibid., pp. 194–96, 203–4. Ibn Shaddād adds that Joanna rejected the proposal of marrying a Muslim. Thus, Richard proposed that al-ʿĀdil convert to Christianity (ibid., p. 196).

33. Khadduri, *War and Peace*, p. 202.

34. S. 8:61.

35. Khadduri, p. 203.

36. Al-Qalqashandī, *Subḥ al-Aʿshā*, 14: 7.

37. See Abū Shāma, *Kitāb al-Rawḍatayn*, vol. I, pt. 2, p. 623. Also see Ibn al-Athīr, *Al-Bāhir*, p. 157.

38. Al-Qalqashandī, *Subḥ al-Aʿsha*, 14: 8.

39. Ibid. 14: 9–10.

40. For examples, see Ḥamza Ibn al-Qalānisī, *Dhayl Tārīkh Dimashq* (Beirut; Matbaʿat al-Ābāʾal-Yasūʿiyyīn, 1908), pp. 236–37, 263–64.

41. See Ibn al-Qalānisī, *Dhayl Tārīkh Dimashq*, p. 304.

42. For examples, see Abū Shāma, *Kitāb al-Rawḍatayn*, vol. I, pt. 1, p. 259.

43. William of Tyre, *History*, 2: 350.

44. Al-Qalqashandī, *Subḥ al-Aʿshā*, 14: 3.

45. Ibn al-Athīr, *Al-Kāmil*, 9: 244; Ibn al-Athīr, *Al-Bāhir*, pp. 39–41.

46. William of Tyre, *History*, 2: 91–92. Also see Mayer, p. 91.

47. Ibn al-Athīr, *Al-Bāhir*, p. 42. For other treaties, see Abū Shāma, *Kitāb al-Rawḍatayn*, vol. 1, pt. 1, pp. 242, 258–59.

48. William of Tyre, *History*, 2: 44. Also see Steven Runciman, *A History of the Crusades* (New York: Cambridge University Press, 1988), 2: 183–84.

49. Ibn al-Athīr, *Al-Kāmil*, 10: 141–42.

50. Ibn Munqidh, *Kitāb al-Iʿtibār*, p. 139, William of Tyre, *History*, 2: 106, 148–49.

51. Ibn al-Qalānisī, *Dhayl Tārīkh Dimashq*, pp. 303–4.

52. Al-Maqrīzī, *Ittiʿāẓ al-Ḥunafāʾ bi akhbār al-Aʾimma al-Fāṭimiyyīn al-Khulafāʾ* (Cairo: Al-Maʿhad al-ʿIlmī al-Faransī, 1964), 2: 282–90; William of Tyre, *History*, 2: 318–21.

53. Ibn Jubayr, *Riḥlat*, pp. 252–53.

54. Ibn Munqidh, *Kitāb al-Iʾtibār*, pp. 149–50.

55. Ibid., p. 71.

56. William of Tyre, *History*, 2: 77.

13

Christians in Mamlūk Jerusalem

Donald P. Little

In an article published in 1985, I discussed the status of Jews in Mamlūk Jerusalem.[1] Despite the scarcity of reliable information on this Jewish community under Muslim rule, I concluded that the few Jews living in the Holy City at this time were well organized, with their own officials recognized by the Mamlūk government, and were integrated as a minority in the Muslim society of the city. Perhaps because they were so few and maintained a low profile, they lived for the most part in peace with their Muslim neighbors. In fact, on one occasion, a Muslim dignitary intervened with the state on behalf of a Jew believed to have been wronged by its officials. Jews lived and owned property in integrated neighborhoods and conducted business transactions with Muslims. Nevertheless, on another occasion they were forbidden by the government to sell meat to Muslims, on the basis of a dubious interpretation of the *sharīʿa* on this issue. In other words, the Jews constituted a protected, though vulnerable minority in late-fourteenth-century Jerusalem, whom the Mamlūks treated in accordance with the principles of *dhimma* as long as it was in Mamlūk and Muslim interests to do so.

In this paper, I shall try to determine the status of the second component of *ahl al-kitāb* (people of the book) in this Mamlūk city, the Christians. In theory, at least, we should expect to learn much more about the Christians than the Jews, given the fact that the Christian presence in the city was larger and stronger than that of the Jews. In practice, however, the sources for the status and activities of the Christians are predictably less forthcoming than historians would like. Of three types, these sources include histories written by Arab Muslims, travelogues recorded by Christian pilgrims, and Mamlūk documents. These I have supplemented with secondary studies.

As is well known, the only major Arabic history of Jerusalem under the Mamlūks is *al-Uns al-Jalīl fī Tārīkh al-Quds waʾl-Khalīl* (Splendid Familiarity with the History of Jerusalem and Hebron) by the Ḥanbalī *ʿālim*, Mujīr al-Dīn al-ʿUlaymī (d. 928/1521–22, a few years after the Ottoman conquest).[2] This work is a compendium of Mujīr al-Dīn's vast knowledge of Jerusalem, consisting of descriptions of the monuments and quarters of the Mamlūk city, a sketch of its history and legends, biographies of its scholars and religious and political officials, and a chronicle of its events during the author's own lifetime. Other than Mujīr al-Dīn, Muslim historians of the Mamlūk period took very little interest in the city since by this time, with the end of the Crusades, it played a negligible role in the political and economic affairs that attracted the interest of historians. Except for unusual or extraordinary events, Jerusalem is rarely mentioned in Mamlūk chronicles; thus the importance of Mujīr al-Dīn's work.

It is noteworthy that Mujīr al-Dīn was aware of twenty churches and monasteries in the city, but mentioned only the four that he considered most important: the Church of the Resurrection (Kanīsat al-Qiyāma), called by Muslims Kanīsat al-Qumāma—the Church of Rubbish—to which pilgrims came every year, Mujīr al-Dīn says, from Anatolia, Europe, Armenia, Egypt, Syria, and elsewhere; the Church of Zion, associated with the Franks; the Church of Mar Yaqub, also known as the Monastery of the Armenians; and the Church of the Cross (Kanīsat al-Muṣallabiyya), associated with the Georgians.[3] In addition, Mujīr al-Dīn mentions the existence of a quarter in the city called Ḥarat al-Naṣārā, without specifying the religious identification of its inhabitants.[4] Otherwise, Christians are mentioned in Mujīr al-Dīn's work only when they made themselves conspicuous by engaging in public disputes with the Muslim establishment of the city, most notably when the Franciscan fathers of Mt. Zion became embroiled in quarrels with the Muslim authorities over ownership of the grotto alleged to be the Tomb of David. According to Mujīr al-Dīn, this controversy raged in 894 and 895/1489–90 during the reign of Sulṭān Qāʾiṭ Bāy, when the Franciscans of the Mt. Zion Monastery built two churches on sites associated with Mary and David. After the issuance of decrees from Cairo and the convocation of councils in Jerusalem, the Franciscan church over the Tomb of David was torn down in 895 and constituted as a mosque, but only after the matter had been investigated on orders from Cairo. Muslim judges in Jerusalem discounted the Franciscans' claim to the Tomb of David since it had been granted to the Muslims by Sultan Jaqmaq's decree in 856/1452; thus the Franciscans' new church had been illegally built on the site of a mosque.[5] But the dispute over Mt. Zion deserves a monograph of its own. Here I should merely like to emphasize that the Christians of Jerusalem did not loom large in Mujīr al-Dīn's consciousness unless and until they threatened Muslim interests in some way. Even then, the Muslims made an effort to examine the legality of the Christians' claims and to judge them in accordance with the evidence.

Christian pilgrim literature on the Holy Land is not lacking for the fifteenth century. Despite political turmoil in Europe, the fall of Constantinople to the Ottomans in 1453, and the irreversible reemergence of Jerusalem as a Muslim city within a Muslim empire,[6] "the stream of pilgrim travel to the Holy Places of Palestine still ran full."[7] For 1458 alone, no less than six narratives of the annual pilgrimage embarking from Venice for Palestine have survived.[8] But the fullest, most personalized, and therefore most useful of these fifteenth-century journals is the *Fratis Felicis Fabri Evagatorium* by a Dominican friar of Zurich and Ulm,[9] popularized by the English novelist H. F. M. Prescott. Prescott aptly characterizes the fifteenth-century pilgrimage literature as a combination of "devotional reflections with personal experiences; [it] jumbles together pagan myths, Christian belief, and garbled history; records the measurements of the Holy Sepulchre and the chant of little Moslem boys at school; and in addition may offer to the reader such advice, information, and instruction as is now to be found in the volumes of Baedeker."[10]

As interesting as this literature may be as a record of the impressions of tourists, whose attitudes toward the holiest places of Christendom were, then as now, based on the holy geography of the Bible, and who had scant interest in Palestinian Muslims except as implacable enemies of the faith who held the Christian shrines in captivity, the literature does pose obvious problems for historians of the Muslim-Christian encounter. Nevertheless, cumulatively these memoirs yield an invaluable record of the Mamlūks' success in organizing and controlling the pilgrimage trade to their own financial and diplomatic advantage, and the pilgrims' distress and disgust at being exploited and extorted as tourists both by Muslim guides and customs officials and by Venetian Christian sea captains who transported the pilgrims to the Holy Land. It is a record also of the utter contempt, based on serene misunderstanding, with which the Western pilgrims regarded the Muslims. This contempt was surpassed only, perhaps, by scorn for the Christians of the eastern "heretical" sects, be they Syrians, Greeks, Armenians, Georgians, Nubians, Jacobites, Chaldeans, or Ethiopians. While there are exceptional examples of Christian pilgrims' charity for their strange cousins in the faith, Friar Felix was not atypical when he "declared that he preferred, and would more readily trust, a Moslem than a Greek Christian."[11] The Syrians, he said "in truth are not Christians, but children of the devil."[12] The Nestorians are "led astray by errors of the worst kind,"[13] the Armenians "are sunk in divers errors,"[14] and the Maronites "are heretics."[15]

Blatantly biased as the travel accounts may be, they do reflect the historical reality that the Mamlūks tolerated the presence of Christians in Jerusalem, both as visitors and as residents of Christian institutions. From Friar Felix we learn, for example, that in 1483 there were twenty-four Franciscans living in the monastery on Mt. Zion, plus two quartered in the Church of the Holy Sepulchre as custodians of the Latin Church's altars. In addition, five Franciscan women lived close to the monasteries and performed menial chores for the friars.[16] While it is clear that the movements of Felix and the other pilgrims in the Holy City were restricted and controlled, it is also evident that as long as they were able to abide by the Mamlūks' rules and distribute *bakshīsh* they could visit their holy places, perform the rituals and buy relics and other souvenirs. Thus Felix was able to lodge in the Franciscan monastery and visit numerous Christian shrines. To climax the visit, some 150 pilgrims spent three nights' vigil in the Church of the Holy Sepulchre, praying, attending mass, and viewing the sights of the Church, including the spectacle of other, indecorous, pilgrims.[17] While they were certainly subject to harassment and extortion from their Muslim hosts, the fact remains that Mamlūk Jerusalem remained accessible to Christian pilgrims throughout the fifteenth century.

That the Mamlūks took seriously their responsibilities and obligations toward the Christian *ahl al-kitāb* of Jerusalem is most convincingly demonstrated in the documents issued by the Mamlūk government to such groups as the Franciscans of Mt. Zion and the Georgians of the Monastery of the Cross. In the case of the Franciscans—whose custody over "the Church of Mt. Zion, the Virgin's Chapel in the Holy Sepulchre, the tomb of St. Mary in Jehoshaphat, and the cave of Nativity in Bethlehem" had been secured from the Mamlūk sultan in 1291 upon the payment of 32,000 ducats[18]—some twenty-eight Mamlūk documents, both decrees and court records, have been published.[19] All of these relate in some way or another to the Franciscans' requests for protection from harassment and for permission from the Muslim authorities to maintain, repair, or expand their holdings in Jerusalem and Bethlehem. Although the Mamlūk authorities and courts were usually inclined to grant these concessions, their decisions were made against a background of imperial considerations. More precisely, the monks' repeated petitions for concessions and favored treatment became factors in the Mamlūks' relations with foreign Christian powers, including the governments of Abyssinia, Spain, and Italy, plus the Corsairs.[20] In this respect the Franciscans probably reached the nadir of their fortunes in 1365, when Sultan Muayyad retaliated for a Latin (Cypriote) attack on Alexandria by arresting the Mt. Zion Franciscans. According to one account, the friars were taken to Damascus, imprisoned, and later executed,[21] while another reports that they were taken to Cairo where they were incarcerated for three years.[22] Although retaliatory measures were not so drastic in the fifteenth century, the Mamlūks did not hesitate to take action against the Franciscans and other Christians of Jerusalem in order to bring pressure against their European adversaries. Thus in 1422, in response to Corsair and Catalan raids against Alexandria and Beirut, Sulṭān Barsbay arrested thirteen Latin pilgrims in Palestine, the Genoese and Venetian consuls in Jerusalem, and all the monks of Zion; for good measure he ordered the Church of the Holy Sepulchre to be closed.[23] In 1440 the Franciscans were imprisoned on the charge of spying for the Hospitallers of Rhodes.[24] After a third attempt to take Rhodes failed in 1444, pilgrims and monks in Jerusalem were arrested and taken to Cairo as hostages.[25] In 1451 the Franciscans were pilloried in the streets of Jerusalem and imprisoned in Cairo, again as a result of Mamlūk-Christian conflict in the Mediterranean.[26] Corsair raids against Alexandria and the Syrian coast led Qa'iṭ Bāy in 1476 to arrest all of the Franciscans in Jerusalem and Bethlehem and hold them as hostages in Cairo.[27]

Given the Franciscans' vulnerability to Mamlūk reprisals, it is not surprising that the monks should have petitioned periodically for documents reaffirming the rights and concessions granted to them by earlier sultans but obviously breached in times of expediency. Three such royal decrees have been preserved and published by the Franciscans, one from Sulṭān Barsbay in 831/1428, another from Khushqadam in 866/1462, and another from Qa'iṭ Bāy in 876/1472.[28] Although all three of these documents date from the late Mamlūk period, they refer to and confirm similar decrees from their predecessors Baybars, Qalāwūn, al-Nāṣir Muḥammad, Ḥasan, Shᶜabān, Barqūq, Faraj, Shaykh, Muẓaffar, Tatar, al-Ṣāliḥ, Barsbay, Jaqmaq, Inal—virtually the whole gamut of important Mamlūk sultans, stretching back two centuries. These decrees are extremely valuable for the explicit declaration of rights and privileges that the Mamlūks were willing to concede to a foreign Christian community in Jerusalem. They can be summarized as follows:

1. The Franciscans are granted freedom of movement, between their churches and monasteries, and between Jerusalem and their homes, without molestation on the roads or at Muslim ports.
2. They have free access to the Church of the Holy Sepulchre, when it is open, and they cannot be forced to open their churches and monasteries in Bethlehem and ᶜAyn Kārim.
3. They are permitted to perform their rites and celebrate their festivals and, more specifically, to conduct services in the Chapel at Golgotha.
4. They may maintain and repair their dwellings.
5. They may eat and drink what they like, including grape products.
6. Their death estates are payable to the monks. They are not responsible for Latins who die in the Holy Land.
7. They are not to be molested by any Mamlūk officials or denied the alms (*ṣadaqa*) sent to them from abroad.
8. If Franks commit hostile acts against Muslims, the monks shall not be held responsible, because "they have cut themselves off from the world."

While it is true that these rights are guaranteed specifically to the Franciscans, recently discovered documents in the Monastery of the Cross indicate that the Georgians also enjoyed privileges guaranteed to them by the Mamlūks as *dhimmīs*. An *amān* granted to the Georgians by Sulṭān al-Muẓaffar Ḥājjī (1346–47) "meant that according to the *Sharīᶜa* their personal security and their property were under the sultan's protection."[29]

Finally, a decree should be mentioned regarding the status of the various Christian communities in the Church of the Holy Sepulchre. Although the original marble plaque on which it was inscribed has long since disappeared, the indefatigable van Berchem had access to a tracing of it which he transcribed and translated. Issued by the Sulṭān al-Ghūrī in 919/1513, the decree guarantees to the Eastern Christian monks and nuns entering the Holy Land—Melkites, Jacobites, Georgians, Abyssinians, Greeks, and Copts—exemption from paying certain fees, tolls, and taxes normally charged pilgrims by the Mamlūks. This exemption was granted, of course, on the grounds of the monks' and nuns' religious vocation as recognized in documents issued to them by previous Muslim rulers.[30]

Mention should also be made of the Ḥaram documents from the Shāfiʿī Court in late fourteenth-century Jerusalem, specifically for the light they shed on the Christians of the city. Unlike the previous documents, they were issued not to or for organized religious institutions but for ordinary citizens of Jerusalem. However, since almost all the documents originated in the Shāfiʿī Court, for the most part they concern Muslims. Nevertheless, a preliminary survey of the more than nine hundred documents that I have catalogued[31] turned up a handful which deal with Christians. While these few records do not reveal anything new or earthshaking, they do provide documented hints of the activities and status of Christian residents of Jerusalem and vicinity during the fourteenth century.

To be specific, I have identified thirteen documents which directly concern Christians. Of these, three record real estate transactions. No. 350, dated 795/1393, is a testimony certified by court witnesses that a house in the Christian quarter (Ḥārat al-Naṣārā) has reverted to the Public Treasury (Bayt al-Māl) because its Christian owner, Yaʿqūb al-Naṣrānī, has died without heirs. No. 15 is a bill of sale, dated 743/1443, for another house in the Christian quarter, near the Monastery of Basil, which one Rizq Allāh ibn Būluṣ, the Melkite Christian (al-Naṣrānī al-Malakī), bought from the Muslim Public Treasury in Jerusalem.[32] How the house came into the possession of Bayt al-Māl the document does not state. One might speculate that it was part of an escheat estate which, in the absence of certifiable heirs, rightly or wrongly reverted to the state as was the case with Yaʿqūb al-Naṣrānī. In any case, because ownership of the property bought by Rizq Allāh was not clear, a Shāfiʿī judge certified the treasury's claim to it so that the sale could be conducted without liability to the vendor or purchaser. To eliminate all doubt from the transaction, a document on *verso* attests to the validity of the certification on *recto*. These documents provide evidence, then, of the ability of Christians to buy and own property held by Mamlūk institutions in Jerusalem and of the accessibility of Muslim courts in cases involving Christians. Although the action may have originated with the Public Treasury, the certification of the Shāfiʿī Court obviously worked to the benefit of the buyer as well as the vendor, so that the Christian's right to his property was in effect guaranteed by the Muslim court. Document no. 98 is a lease, dated 706/ 1307, for a shop in Bayt ʿAnyā (a village northwest of Jerusalem).[33] In this case, a Christian from another village—Bayt Rīma, in the vicinity of Ludd—rented a shop from a Mamlūk officer acting on behalf of the Mamlūk supervisor of the Islamic sanctuaries of Jerusalem and Hebron (Nāẓir al-Ḥaramayn al-Sharīfayn), al-Amīr Sayf al-Dīn Bulghāq. While one might guess that the shop was somehow connected with the *waqf*s (religious endowments) which Bulghāq was charged with administering for the benefit of the Muslim sanctuaries, the document gives no corroboration of this possibility. Nevertheless, it is noteworthy that Christians could rent business property from Muslim officials. Document no. 311, dated 745/1344, does give explicit evidence of the use of taxes on Christians (from the village of Majdal Fāḍil) for the benefit of the Dome of the Rock and al-Masjid al-Aqṣā.[34]

The largest group of our documents falls in the category of estate inventories, or records authorized by the Shāfiʿī Court of the assets and liabilities of persons who had died in Jerusalem or who were on the verge of death, along with a declaration of the heirs to the estate. Estate inventories served the interests of the testator, as a kind of will, but also the interests of the state, since the Public Treasury stood to inherit the residue of estates for which heirs were lacking. Whether or not the Muslim Public Treasury was legally entitled to a share in Christian or Jewish estates was a moot point throughout the Middle Ages, but the Mamlūks did not hesitate to appropriate dhimmi estates when need and opportunity coincided.[35] In any event, the Ḥaram collection contains estate inventories for eight Christians, three women and five men, dating from the years 793–96/1390–94. Interestingly enough, six of these persons were residing in monasteries or convents—two in Dayr al-Ḥarfūsh in Ḥārat Ṣahyūn (the Zion quarter),[36] one at Dayr al-Bala/Baghla in Ḥārat al-Naṣāra,[37] one at Dayr al-Aqbāṭ (the Coptic convent),[38] one in Dayr Mār Mattī in Ḥārat al-Naṣāra,[39] and one at Dayr al-ʿĀmūd.[40] Of the two others, one, Yūsuf al-Bannā, was living in Ḥārat Ṣahyūn in a house which he had set up as an endowment for himself and his wife during their lifetime and for the benefit of a convent (Dayr al-Sīq) thereafter.[41] The second, Sutayta al-Dimashqiyya, was residing in a house endowed for the same convent.[42] This means that all eight persons were living in residences associated with Christian institutions. All, moreover, were living in quarters designated as Christian.

All eight persons were identified as Christians, either by the *nisba* (attribution of name to the faith) al-Naṣrānī or al-Naṣrāniyya in their names or by the phrase *min al-Naṣārā*. One, Afrusha, was further specified as a Jacobite (Yaʿqūbiyya) nun living in the Coptic convent. Apparently she had been married at some point, since her heirs are named as a son and daughter, absent in Cairo.[43] Besides the nun, we can determine the professions of only two others from their nisbas. ʿAlam Ibn Yūsuf was an occulist (*kaḥḥāl*).[44] Yūsuf Ibn Saʿīd was a mason or builder (*bannā*).[45] If the estate inventories are a reliable index of wealth, all eight seem to have been of modest means, possessing little more than clothes, implements, and a few furnishings. Although Yūsuf al-Bannā owned his own home, he owed debts to several Christians and Muslims. But Sulaymān al-Shawbakī was solvent and enterprising enough to entrust 700 *dirhams* to another Christian for investment in the raisin market.[46] And Rashīd al-Shawbakī had incurred a sizable debt of thirty-six gold *dīnārs* in deferred bride price to his wife, a sufficiently large sum to pay for a bride at that time to indicate that Rashīd must have been a man of means.[47]

It is interesting, but not surprising, that all the Christians had Christian spouses, often from the same town or village. Nevertheless, some degree of mobility in the family can be inferred from the fact that several had heirs not present in Jerusalem, said to be absent in such remote places as Upper Egypt, Cairo, Alexandria, Ḥiṣn ʿAkkār (near Tripoli), and Damascus.[48] Perhaps because estates with inaccessible heirs would be difficult to settle, officials of the Bayt al-Māl were present when four of the inventories were made.[49] Seven of the eight were conducted with the authorization of the Shāfiʿī Court in Jerusalem according to a standard format used to inventory the estates of Muslims. One took the form of an *iqrār*, or legal acknowledgment, again with the authorization of the Shāfiʿī Court and with Muslim witnesses.[50]

The evidence from the Ḥaram documents, slight though it may be, suggests that the Christians, like the Jews, were well integrated into the life of Jerusalem. They could work, own property and engage in commercial transactions with fellow Christians and Muslims, and establish pious endowments. They seem to have been subject to the same regulations as Muslims in settling their estates, which may or may not have worked to their advantage, depending on the Christian and Muslim laws of inheritance and the claims of the state on residual estates. They had access to Muslim courts, legal procedures, and documents. It should also be noted that Christians who misbehaved were subject to the jurisdiction of Muslim courts, as court record no. 642 shows.[51] This document describes an investigation under the auspices of the Shāfiʿī Court into the attack and mutilation of a Muslim by three alleged assailants, all identified as Christians, on a farm in the village of Ṭakūʿ in 796/1394. The report gives no indication that the attack, in which the Muslim suffered the loss of a hand and blows to his brain, involved religious differences, though this possibility need not be discounted. In any event, the document does show that Christian-Muslim encounters in and around late fourteenth-century Jerusalem were not always placid and tranquil.

Taking into account the evidence from Arabic Muslim chronicles, Christian pilgrim literature, and Mamlūk documents, what can be said of the status and activities of Christians and Christian institutions in Jerusalem under the Mamlūks? At the risk of being labeled what Jean-Pierre Peroncel-Hugoz calls a "professional Muslim"—that is, an orientalist who "take[s] advantage of the propaganda budgets of most Arab states to enjoy receptions, scholarships, conferences, junkets, symposia, and seminars" and in return has "felt obliged, in writing or speaking about Islam, the Muslim world, or the Arabs, to adopt an attitude in which an excess of reverence, deliberate omissions, or worse, distortion or servility, have damaged truth, scholarship, and most seriously mutual understanding between Muslims and non Muslims"[52]—at the risk of all this, I would nevertheless conclude that the Mamlūks treated the Christians in their holiest city in accordance with the principles of *dhimma*. In an atmosphere singularly lacking in the spirit of interfaith dialogue or even encounter, the Mamlūks and the Muslim bureaucracy gave Christian institutions, residents, and pilgrims considerable latitude to conduct their affairs as they saw fit, as long as they acted in accordance with law and custom so that religious, social, and political equilibrium could be maintained in the city. In effect this means that Christians were free to think what they liked of Muslims (as well as other Christians) and to lament Muslim domination of their holy places as long as they did so discreetly. On those rare occasions when Christians were so intrepid as to disparage Islam in public, they could expect to be silenced, with violence, by the Muslim religious establishment.[53] If Muslims infringed the rights guaranteed to Christian institutions, those organizations could count on the Muslim authorities to redress their grievances. Nevertheless, the foreign Christian residents in the city were subject to the rule of a military oligarchy (some of whom, it should not be forgotten, were of Christian origin) who did not hesitate to exploit them as hostages in times of conflict with Christian powers. Be that as it may, even when Franciscans became martyrs, others who were obviously aware of the calculated risk they would run took their place in Jerusalem, no doubt reassured by the treatment the Christians normally received from the Muslim government. Although the Christians in Jerusalem were vulnerable, certainly, and subject to the will of the Muslim majority, for the most part the majority was kept disciplined and controlled in the interest of social and political stability. As a result the life of the Christians of Mamlūk Jerusalem was not a bad one, insofar as we can judge the quality of life in medieval societies.

NOTES

1. Donald P. Little, "Ḥaram Documents Related to the Jews of Late Fourteenth Century Jerusalem," *Journal of Semitic Studies* 30 (1985): 227–64, 368–70.

2. Mujīr al-Dīn al-ʿUlaymī, *al-Uns al-Jalīl fī Tārīkh al-Quds wa ʾl-Khalīl*, 2 vols. (Amman: Maktabat al-Muḥtasib, 1973).

3. Ibid., 2: 51.

4. Ibid., 2: 54.

5. Ibid., 2: 347–52.

6. R.J. Mitchell, *The Spring Voyage: The Jerusalem Pilgrimage in 1458* (London: John Murray, 1964), pp. 18–28.

7. H.F.M. Prescott, *Jerusalem Journey: Pilgrimage to the Holy Land in the Fifteenth Century* (London: Eyre and Spottiswoode, 1954), p. 15.

8. See Mitchell, *Spring Voyage.*

9. Translated as *The Wanderings of Felix Fabri*, "Palestine Pilgrims' Text Society," reprinted in 2 vols. from the 1887–97 ed. (New York: AMS Press, 1971).

10. Prescott, *Jerusalem Journey*, pp 14–15.

11. Ibid., p. 184.

12. *Wanderings*, 2: 389.

13. Ibid., 2: 388.

14. Ibid.

15. Ibid., 2: 389.

16. Prescott, *Jerusalem Journey*, p. 119.

17. Ibid., pp. 115–42.

18. F.E. Peters, *Jerusalem: The Holy City in the Eyes of Chronicles, Visitors, Pilgrims and Prophets from the Days of Abraham to the Beginnings of Modern Times* (Princeton: Princeton University Press, 1985), p. 422, citing Friar Felix, *Wanderings*, 2: 380.

19. [Noberto Risciani] *Documenti e Firmani* (Jerusalem: Tipografia dei PP. Francescani, 1936). These documents are the subject of a monograph by Aḥmad Darrāj, *Wathā'iq Dayr Ṣahyūn bi l-Quds al-Sharīf* (Cairo: Maktabat al-Anglū al-Miṣriyya, 1968).

20. See Aḥmad Darrāj, *al-Mamālīk wa 'l-Firanj fī al-Qarn al-Tāsi' al-Hijrī—al-Khāmis 'Ashar al-Mīladī* (Cairo: Dār al-Fikr al-'Arabī, [1961]).

21. Peters, *Jerusalem*, p. 423.

22. Darrāj, *al-Mamālīk*, p. 21.

23. Ibid., p. 32

24. Ibid., p. 55

25. Ibid., p. 58.

26. Ibid., p. 74.

27. Ibid., p. 106.

28. Risciani, *Documenti*, pp. 127, 165, 290–317, 328–47.

29. Butrus Abu-Manneh, "The Georgians in Jerusalem in the Mamluk Period," in *Egypt and Palestine: A Millenium of Association (868–1948)*, ed. Amnon Cohen and Gabriel Baer (New York: St. Martin's Press, 1984), p. 105.

30. Max van Berchem, *Matériaux pour un corpus inscriptionum arabicum*, pt. 2. *Syrie du Sud*, bk. 1. Jerusalem "Ville" (Cairo: L'Institut Français d'Archéologie Orientale, 1922), pp. 378–402.

31. Donald P. Little, *A Catalogue of the Islamic Documents from al-Ḥaram al-Sharīf in Jerusalem* (Beirut: Orient Institut DMG, 1984).

32. Ibid., pp. 250, 277–78.

33. Ibid., p. 298.

34. Ibid., p. 256.

35. For discussion of this point see my "Ḥaram Documents Related to Jews," pp. 242–43, 253–55.

36. Little, *Catalogue*, nos. 511 and 758, pp. 132, 165.

37. Ibid., no. 474, p. 126.

38. No. 384, p. 103.

39. No. 846, p. 223.

40. No. 503, p. 131.

41. No. 550, p. 141.

42. No. 521, p. 135.

43. No. 384.

44. No. 758.

45. No. 550.

46. No. 846.

47. No. 503. For the size of bride prices, see my "Relations between Jerusalem and Egypt during the Mamlūk Period according to Literary and Documentary Sources," in *Egypt and Palestine*, p. 86. Reprinted in Little, *History and Historiography of the Mamlūks* (London: Variorum Reprints, 1986).

48. Nos. 511, 384, 758, 550, 521, in that order.

49. No. 511, 521, 550, 758.

50. No. 846.

51. Little, *Catalogue*, p. 272.

52. *The Raft of Mohammed: Social and Human Consequences of the Return to Traditional Religion in the Arab World*, trans George Holsch (New York: Paragon House. 1988), pp. 1–2.

53. E.g., the execution of an Ethiopian Christian who disparaged Muhammad and a similar fate for a Christian who disparaged ʿAlī and Fāṭima. Mujīr al-Dīn, *al-Uns*, 2: 265, 317.

14

Old French Travel Accounts of Muslim Beliefs Concerning the Afterlife

Jane I. Smith

From the earliest moments of awareness that the religion of Islam was not a passing phenomenon but a reality to be reckoned with, Western Christendom evinced a range of responses—fear, ridicule, righteous indignation, theological rejection, scholarly inquisitiveness, cultural fascination. Those who for a variety of reasons found themselves visitors to Islamic lands from the turn of the millenium through the renaissance and enlightenment displayed all of these responses, while generally sharing the world view that recognized little of value beyond Christian Europe. Many have argued that medieval voyagers were so certain of the absolute and exclusive truth of Christianity, and that Europe was the center of the world, that it was impossible for them to see Islam and Muslim peoples as anything other than misguided, false, or evil.[1] It also may be the case that the very encounter with the other precipitated a consciousness of cultural, social, and religious differences that engendered the feelings of superiority that are usually thinly veiled in such voyagers' reports and writings.

The lure of Islamic lands, and in particular the Holy Land, was nonetheless strong over the centuries and travelers made arduous journeys for reasons that ranged from personal piety to ecclesiastical or diplomatic mission to scientific investigation. It is clear from the written reports of those travels available to us that despite their ostensible reasons for journeying, few were able to resist at least some kind of commentary on the peoples inhabiting these Muslim countries and, in many cases, reflection on the customs and beliefs of the followers of the Prophet, whom by definition they considered to be false. Often these observations were superficial and clearly not reflective of what Muslims themselves would have acknowledged. In many cases, however, it is apparent that the reporters did take the trouble to avail themselves of Islamic informants and texts, and much of what is related provides an interesting and not always inaccurate glimpse of what life, and belief, entailed for Muslims in the lands of the Middle East in centuries past.

Before the turn of the millenium few Western Europeans traveled to Muslim countries. Those who did go were restricted both by the language barrier and by their fearful preconceptions of the "stranger" to be encountered, and brought back only very superficial impressions of the religion of Islam.[2] Gradually travel from Europe to other parts of the world became easier, particularly after the opening of the overland route to the Holy Land. Although individuals from various parts of the Western world went to Jerusalem, the majority traveled from a few provinces of France—especially Burgundy, Normandy, and Aquitaine—as well as from the area of the Rhineland.[3]

While western Europe began to acquire some knowledge of Islam through the reports of those who for one reason or another had occasion to visit Muslim lands, on the whole there was little interest in or curiosity about the religion and culture of Islam in the early centuries of travel.[4] After the thirteenth century this situation changed somewhat, and increasing numbers of travelers from the West began to acquire and disseminate more accurate knowledge about things Islamic. Scholastics became involved with the translation of Arabic texts for missionary or polemic purposes and the learned in western Europe in general were more interested in knowing something about the religion of Islam.

Pilgrims and travelers to Palestine and other parts of the Islamic world in the thirteenth, fourteenth, and fifteenth centuries often provided highly descriptive impressions and eyewitness accounts of Muslim life, practices, and beliefs.[5] As trade opportunities expanded and diplomatic missions increased, so did knowledge of Muslim peoples. By the sixteenth and seventeenth centuries, public interest in accounts of Muslim life and customs was high and a large number of travel books flooded the European market. Some of what was transmitted concerning Islamic doctrines and practices seems to have been couched in as vivid a language and interpretation as possible to add to the appeal of the report, partly to assuage the public's desire for sensationalism.[6] As contacts with the Ottoman Empire became more direct and the Western understanding of Muslims in some senses less clouded, attention often focused more on what they did, how they lived, than on what they believed. To some extent this may reflect the growing appeal of the "exotic" in the Europe of that day.

For the purposes of opening one fairly narrow window on the kinds of information provided by travelers I have selected a sampling of visitors to Muslim lands that offers a representative range in terms of purpose, area, and time of visit; and one theological theme as illustrative of the kinds of reporting on the religion of Islam that was made available to the home constituencies of these visitors. We will look at the reports of French travelers made primarily in the sixteenth through the eighteenth centuries. In brief these reports were made by pilgrims, missionaries and other clergy, scientists, emissaries of the French crown, consuls, historians, and adventurers, and told of visits made to Egypt,

North Africa, and Turkey as well as to the Holy Land and environs. (Biographical and bibliographical information is provided at the end of this chapter under "Reports Cited," in chronological order of travel; references in the text are to pages in these works.)

Of the various doctrines of the religion of Islam that may have been of interest to these travelers, one that clearly caught their imagination was the set of practices and beliefs related to death and life after death, including resurrection, judgment, and consignments to the abodes of punishment and reward. It is noteworthy that the theme of death and afterlife was discussed or at least mentioned in one way or another in almost all of the more than thirty separate reports reviewed in this study. In some cases there were genuine attempts to portray Muslim beliefs accurately; in others the subject provided a convenient focus for general polemic about Islam, Muslims, and in particular the Prophet Muhammad. So as to get an overview of the material presented in these reports, let us look at some of the topics that seem to have held for them the greatest interest.

Death, Dying, and Burial

A number of writers treat the dying process in some detail. Although they do not overtly ridicule the elements of this process, it is clear that they use them to support their conviction that Islam greatly overemphasizes the sensual nature of life after death. When a Muslim (Turk) is so sick that it appears he is about to die, says Eugène Roger, a *santon* or priest comes to console him with the assurance that after death the afflicted will be healthy and vigorous in paradise, where he will be able to dance, sing, drink, and eat as much as he wants and will have beautiful girls to caress him (265).[7]

Our observers are much taken by descriptions of the lamentations over the deceased. The demonstrative nature of these expressions of grief suggests a culture very different from that of the Westerners. Marcel Ladoire notes that some of the women are paid to shout and cry, and that nothing is as horrible to hear as that shrill screaming and howling (392–93). Women are "rented to cry," and it is a dreadful thing to hear the groaning of women screaming goodbye to the departed (Pierre Dan, 275–76).[8] The women who follow the body to the grave are said to dance not to the sound of a violin but to the cadence of castanets, striking these on cheek and chest with such fury that they appear to be on fire, their eyes burning like candles issuing forth from their heads. The clamor and shouting is interlaced with diabolical words, "so strange that it seems as if they are straight from hell" (Eugène Roger, 265–66). Several authors note that while there are no burials in public mosques, some persons erect mosque-like structures in which they can be laid to rest. Others are put in public graves in a special area located apart from the city.[9]

None of the writers appears to have had access to Muslim accounts of the process of death as experienced by the dying person him- or herself.[10] Roger alone gives some theological content to the dying process when he says, "All those who profess the law of Mahomet are obliged to believe in predestination. Thus they do not apprehend either the plague, or death, without saying, 'If God has determined that I have the plague, I cannot flee from it because it will take me wherever I am. And if he wishes to exempt me, I will have nothing to fear'" (264). He cites this as a poor excuse for the Turks not taking personal responsibility for their lives.[11]

Questioning and Punishment in the Grave

A number of the travelers seem to have some acquaintance with popular Muslim beliefs about the fate of the deceased immediately after death. Several comment that after being washed, the dead one is wrapped in a shroud with the feet and head left free and is placed in a sitting position, because of the commandment of Muhammad in relation to the coming of the two black questioning angels (Pierre Belon, 174b; Louis Deshayes, 273). (One adds that this is a custom taken from the Jews who bury their dead sitting in the same posture as a doctor in his chair to show that the deceased are wise masters to teach us to live well [Dan, 275].)

A commonly reported version of the descriptions of the terrifying creatures, which is quite true to some Islamic (though non-Qur'anic) accounts, goes as follows: Immediately when the dead one is put in the tomb two angels black as pitch[12] come to meet him, holding in their hands an iron club and a dreadful hook respectively. They command the deceased to rise to his knees and to take back his soul. Then they question him as to his obedience to the law of Muhammad and his having lived a life of virtue. If the response is adequate, the black angels leave to be replaced by two angels whiter than snow "who pour into his spirit a thousand sweet consolations, and become his inseparable companions during his sojourn, assisting him to the end of the world" (Michel Baudier, 620). Alas, if the deceased is unable to respond successfully, the black inquisitors remain to torment him, one striking him on the head with the mallet so that he sinks into the earth, while the other pulls him up with the hook so that the punishment can be administered without ceasing until the day of resurrection.[13] Baudier comments that this crazy belief terrorizes the Turks to the point where they are often heard to pray, "Deliver us Lord from the angel examiner, from the torment of the grave, and from the way that leads men to perdition" (621).[14]

For the most part commentary on death and afterlife is offered by these observers in a somewhat abstract way, not related to their own experiences as travelers in Muslim countries. In a rare exception Jacques de Villamont, writing at the turn of the seventeenth century, relates that when he and his guide ventured too close to a Muslim cemetery near Jerusalem, Turks pelted them with stones. His interpreter explained the reverence that Muslims have for their tombs and their dead, and their desire that everyone share that respect.

The Day of Resurrection

There is very little mention by these writers of the natural cataclysms signaling the end of the world that are so graphically described in the Qur᾿an. A few note that at the day of judgment, the end of the world, a trumpet will sound and all men and angels will die. When the trumpet sounds again they will all be resuscitated. Belon cites the Book of the Zuna (Sunna)[15] as saying that the sheep that are killed on the Easter day of the Turks, Bairam, will enter paradise on the day of judgment. According to Belon, the reason that Turks sacrifice many sheep on their Easter is because they believe "that they will pray on the day of judgment for those who were the cause of their being sacrificed" (175a–b).

He then tells a story about two angels who are said to be hanging in a cavern in Babylon by their eyebrows. Sent by God as judges among the people of that land, these angels descended from heaven to do their work each day and ascended each evening. One day they came upon a beautiful woman who was complaining about her husband. So lovely was she that they thought to tempt her and prayed that she would submit to them. She agreed, on condition that they teach her the prayer that gave them the virtue to ascend to heaven. But as soon as the crafty woman learned the prayer she went straight to heaven, leaving the angels both frustrated and punished by God with having to hang by their eyebrows until the day of judgment. Belon adds darkly that some say the angels daily teach the art of necromancy to the people in that area (175b).

The destruction of the earth at the day of resurrection, mentioned only by Baudier and attributed to *azoare* (ṣūra) 22:6,[16] will come without warning with the speed of a blink. This he suspects may be an allusion to the passage in the Gospel indicating that the arrival of the Son of Man will be like a quick burst of light which leaves the east and in a moment sends its light to the rest of the world all the way to the west. But, he assures the reader, this was not the way Muhammad understood it. In a passage much like several sections of the Qur᾿an, he says that suddenly a terrible trembling of the earth will transfix men with terror, and goes on to mention pregnant women aborting, men walking as if drunk, mountains reduced to powder, etc. Baudier attributes much of the information that Muhammad had about the end of the earth to conversations with his preceptor monk Sergius and with a Jewish acquaintance, Abdia ben Belon, although he is quick to assure the reader that Muhammad got things confused (625–26).[17]

Discussion of Islamic eschatology frequently serves as the occasion for a defense of Christian doctrine. Baudier, for example, reports the Muslim tradition about resurrected persons waiting miserably for the judgment, swimming in the sweat of their own apprehensions, and going from one prophet to another looking for intercession. These are listed, as in the Islamic eschatological writings, as Adam, Noah, Abraham, Moses, and finally (before Muhammad) Jesus. Each save Muhammad is disqualified because of some specific condition or misdeed. While the reason is unclear in Baudier's version, the Islamic material suggests that Jesus is inappropriate as intercessor not for any sin of his own but because some of his followers took him and his mother for divinities.[18] Baudier does seem to understand that, for he comments, "Here this impious Arab attacked again the divinity of the Son of God!" (629–30). This kind of defense of Christian doctrine is also evident in de Villamont's reflection on the Turkish belief that the day of judgment is near. Referring to a prophesy of "their Mahomet" that the law will only last one thousand years, he calls them the thousand years of the apocalypse, of Gog and Magog, that is, of the Arabs and the Tartars and Turks mixed together. "And at least the devil taught to Mahomet the ruin of his sect," de Villamont reflects, "he first having learned the writings of the holy prophets" (204b).

The judgment process itself, so graphically detailed in the Qur'an, seems to hold only moderate interest for most of these reporters. In what appears to be a kind of attempt to find commonalities between Muslim and Christian beliefs, Roger says, "They call the day of judgment Joumelhasab [*yawm al-ḥisāb*], and like us they believe that it will take place in the valley of Jehosaphat, where Mahomet (according to what they say) will be found as judge" (268). He goes on to describe Muhammad's Throne, a huge column of marble, which the Turks have expressly set on the top of the wall of Jerusalem, looking out on the valley of Jehosaphat, "where our Savior made his entrance on the day of palms." He remarks on the blowing of the trumpet, the obliteration of all living creatures save God, the resuscitating rain of mercy, and Muhammad's interrogation of all souls.[19] De Villamont also refers to Muhammad's role as judge, although without relating it to Christian doctrine. Giving instructions to pilgrims coming to the Holy Land, he says that "if you climb to the mount of Olives, I warn you that turning your gaze on the walls of Jerusalem you will see a small column of three or four feet on which the Turks believe that their false Mahomet will come on the day of judgment to sit and judge them. He will have the form of a sheep, and they of a fly" (204b–205a).[20]

The Abodes of Recompense

Several writers seem well acquainted with the *miʿrāj* or night journey of the Prophet Muhammad and use it as an introduction to their commentary on the Muslim concept of heaven. Belon, for example, mentions the "pleasant voyage that Mahomet pretended to have made to paradise at night while asleep, and the great follies that he recounted concerning the paradise of the Turks" (175b). According to the version often cited by these observers Muhammad was sleeping with his wife Axa (ʿĀʾisha) when the angel Gabriel knocked on his door to take him on the trip. What seems to intrigue the narrators more than Gabriel's remarkable appearance (with seventy pairs of wings, whiter than snow and shining more than crystal) is the encounter between Muhammad and Alborach (Burāq), the steed that was to carry him to heaven. They thoroughly enjoy the fact that Burāq would not let the Prophet mount until he promised that the horse would be the first beast to enter paradise, Roger even noting that the animal turned his hind quarters to Muhammad and gave him several blows with his foot until the promise came. (At various points in their commentaries we see that the Christian writers were disgusted at the thought of animals having access to paradise.)

The Muslim heavens are clearly of great interest to the travelers and in several cases they spend many pages recounting detail about them. "Mahomet speaking of the matter of which heaven is made said that God created it from smoke, and that he established the firmament on the point of the horn of a bullock, and that the trembling of the earth proves the emotion of the bullock because having all the earth on his head makes him tremble. The Turks believe now the thousand follies that Mahomet has made them listen to" (Belon, 178a). The sevenfold structure of paradise is described in elaborate detail, made of gold and silver and enriched with pearls and precious gems. Rooms and halls, gardens, fountains and rivers are the subject of interest, as well as the tree that contains all of paradise, its leaves of gold and silver and its branches reaching as far as the walls of heaven. Belon notes that on each leaf of this tree is written the name of Muhammad after the name of God. It is from this passage, he says, that the Turks have taken the most singular of their prayers, which he recites in phonetics (revealing it to be the *shahāda* or testimony to God and his Prophet). If a Christian imprudently were to utter these words, he says, he would either have to become a Turk or be killed.[21]

Roger reports that the levels of paradise are like great countries. They are paved respectively with silver, gold, pearls, emeralds (this fourth pleased Muhammad most, he says, in memory of which he took green for his livery, which is the reason Jews and Christians are not permitted to wear this color[22]), crystal and fire. The seventh is a delicious garden with fountains and rivers of milk, honey, and wine. Here apple trees bear fruit whose seeds change into girls not subject to purgations like those below. The entrance to this paradise is guarded by a multitude of angels of diverse and monstrous forms. Some are like men having the heads of cows with horns, each of which has forty thousand coils with forty days of travel between one coil and another. Imagine, says Roger to his reader, what manner of horns these must be, and if you are a good mathematician calculate the length they must have. Elaborating on numbers of heads, mouths, and tongues, each tongue speaking seventy thousand kinds of languages with which it praises God, he invites us to admire this ingenious multiplication. He concludes his description with a fairly atypical sarcasm, saying, "But let us leave this paradise and quit these reveries, fearing that these monsters will bite us. So many mouths and so many horns are capable of giving great terror!" (218).

Most engaging to the imagination of many of these observers, as might be expected, are the beautiful virgins of paradise. This description by Belon is the prototype of many such to follow: "And after the Turks have drunk and eaten their fill in this paradise, then the pages adorned with jewels and precious stones and with rings on their arms, hands, legs and ears will come to the Turks, each holding a lovely plate of gold in his hand and carrying a large lemon or fruit which the Turks take to smell. And suddenly each Turk will have put it next to his nose, and from it will come out a beautiful virgin well adorned with lovely things, who will embrace the Turk, and the Turk her, and they will remain fifty years thus embracing each other without separating, taking together the pleasure of all sorts that man has with a woman." At the end of the fifty years God will say to them: "Get up, my servants, and rejoice in my glory. Because you will never die again and will not have any sadness or displeasure." And raising their heads they will see God face to face. After this interlude each Turk will take his virgin again, lead her to his room in the palace where he will find things to eat and drink, and will thus remain with her without ever any fear of dying (178a–b). Reflecting on these Muslim descriptions of paradise, Belon comments that what is said about pages and virgins is clearly reflected in the Turkish Serai (palace) where women are well guarded and shut up behind walls.[23]

Writing about the same time as Belon, Guillaume Postel brings up the matter of paradise in the context of a discussion of the Muslim idea of God. "It is God who has created the paradise of Adam, there where the waters run below, where there are fruits and rivers of wine, milk and honey, all flesh and fowl to eat well, large beautiful women who are always virgins, who have big eyes like ostriches and all the pleasures that are in the world" (87). Postel understands the importance of those human virtues that in fact guarantee entrance into paradise (which he recognizes as the paradise of Adam) and a place at the right hand of God. Specifically, the saved will be those who believe that there is one God without partner, who have fed their women well and visited orphans and who have paid the tithe to the Prophet of God, helped the injured and the elderly. He says of paradise that it is "there where God has predestined, because he is the one who makes whomever he pleases believe and be damned or saved" (87–88).

One might expect that these writers would pay considerable attention to the terrors of the fire in their descriptions, but for the most part that is not the case. Postel says that it is God who has prepared the fiery fire (*l'enfer de feu*) of burning pitch, and he describes the tree which bears stinking fruit, bitter, full of poison, eaten by the damned who have not wanted to believe in the Prophet of God and who have done the opposite of those things that get the good into heaven. After concluding that they will be there forever with the Devil, eating poison, he says in what is a clear reference to the Qur'an 7:50–51: "And they will demand water from those in Paradise who will mock them at this hour and will say to them, Where are those whom you have adored and have made gods? Taste in this hour the evil that you have done and for which you are mocked" (87).[24]

And de Villamont notes that one of the differences between the saved and the damned is that the latter will be distinguishable from each other, known by their own names written on their foreheads and charged with the heavy burden of their own sins. Unlike others, he mentions the Qur'anic bridge of Sirat [Sherat Cuplissi], which cuts like a razor. The greatest sinners fall from the bridge into an ardent blaze, from which they are periodically removed and refreshed in a morass of stinking water. At the pit of the fire is the tree which he calls Saiarata, Azacon, or Roozo Saytanin,[25] with fruit resembling a devil's head from which the damned eat (207a).

But it is the heavens that are most interesting to the travelers, no doubt because of their apparent abundance of sensual joys. "This imaginary paradise that Mahomet provided to his Mussulmins and faithful sectarians of the law," says Nicolas Bénard, "is filled with nothing but delicacies, good food, and carnal and mundane pleasures" (328). After fully describing these pleasures he says that the faithful of the sect of Muhammad will dine at a table made of diamond all of one piece measured to be seven thousand days long and longer. Bénard chides Muhammad, whom he calls a false promiser, saying that this is a subject that leads to laughter and mocking of the ridiculous imaginings of the pseudoprophet. As if this were not enough, he says, Muhammad had to go on to give his followers more to hope for, specifically the beautiful and virgin nymphs who will come from the fruit carried on the golden plates by the pages of heaven. "There are many other follies and reveries that one could tell on this subject contained in the Alcoran, obviously less true than the gossip of a good woman" (329–30).

It is obviously what they perceive as the sexual promises of Muslim paradise that both intrigue and shock these reporters. The number of heavens was multiplied, says Baudier, since the pleasures and sensual delights that Muhammad promised could not be contained in just one. But the pleasure that tops all the others will be the pleasure of women. Muhammad made them the perfection of all sovereign good in their beauty, their graces, and their attractions, with clear eyes, large like eggs, which they will only open to look at their husbands. Referring to them as Hors (*ḥūr*), he says that the most powerful attraction of these lovely ones is their modesty. Noting the Islamic tradition that if one of them should spit into the ocean the sea would lose its bitterness and its waters become sweeter than honey, he says that it is perhaps the reason why men of a neighboring province of France, when they let their reason carry them to the folly of love, have learned to gather the spittle of the women that they idolize and swallow it in their presence in order to testify to the excess of their affection. These feminine beauties of the heaven of the Turks will not exactly be of the human race, he says, but created from the sky, like the souls, for the pleasure of the Muslims.[26]

Few of these writers resist the temptation to use the descriptions of the pleasures of paradise to condemn the Prophet as their author. Typical is the late-eighteenth-century remark of C.F. Volney, who places his reference to the Muslim paradise in the context of a sharp condemnation of the Prophet. Calling the Qur'an "a composition so flat and so fastidious that there is nobody capable of reading to the end," he says that in it one finds that "heaven presents itself open to whoever fights for its cause. The houris offer their arms to the martyrs. The imagination blazes up. And the proselyte says to Mahomet, Yes, you are the Messenger of God. Your word . . . is infallible. Walk, I will follow you." What can be the consequence of such a message, he asks, but to establish the most absolute despotism in the one who orders and the blindest devotion in the one who obeys? That was the goal of Muhammad, who did not want to clarify, but to reign (362).

Women in the Afterlife

A subject that always has been of great and continuing interest to those who visit Muslim lands is the situation of women. It is not surprising, then, that the question of women in relation to the reward of paradise captured the imagination of many of the travelers in our survey.

Contrary to the clear affirmations of the Qur'an, in general these writers seem persuaded that women will not be able to share in the pleasures of the celestial gardens and palaces.[27] Several equate what they observe about the nonparticipation of women in the mosque with women lacking access to heaven. "Women never go to the mosques to do their prayers," says Phillippe de Fresne-Canaye, "but remain at home, because the law does not permit them to enter into paradise, but to remain at the door" (105–6). Others note that there are special places outside the mosques where women are relegated, as when Pierre Lescalopier reports that in front of the mosques there are doors where the Turkish women do their devotions. The reason for this is that only the circumcised can enter into paradise or into "temples." Women cannot be circumcised and therefore will not enter paradise, so God will provide for them some beatitude at the door (paralleled by their location outside the entrance to the mosque) (40).

Noting the festive atmosphere of paradise where everyone is having a wonderful time, Roger comments that this is only for the Muslim men, not their wives. "Those, by what they say, will soil all the beauty of this place. That is why they will not enter there at all, but will have a part of it where all the happiness will consist of regarding the joys of the men. Oh unhappy condition of the Turkish women!" he laments, "because they are slaves in this life, and miserable in the other. See in what they place the beatitude of the true observers of their law!" (269).

Not one of the writers commenting on women in relation to the afterlife attributes to them the role which in truth the Qur'an guarantees. Dan, writing in the mid-seventeenth century, says the Muslim paradise is only for men, women being excluded according to the teaching of the Qur'an, and adds that women will have a place apart where all their joy will be in regard to that of the men. He is rather more specific than the others about the fact that the pleasure of the men will be in the maidens of paradise, suggesting his understanding that in the Islamic view earthly wives would complicate matters were they to be present.

Using the account of a specific event to reflect on women in relation to paradise, R.P. Robert de Dreux recalls the tale about a Turk who was having dinner with the French ambassador. The guest was shocked to see that Madame Ambassador was eating with them. He asked if the women of France ate with the men and was told that they do. "But," he said, "do the women of France hope to go after this life to paradise with the men?" "Yes," answered Madame, "and we even hope to be in a better place than they if we are faithful to God." "Ah! How happy the women of France are," he cried in admiration, "and how unhappy are ours, since those of France are in paradise in this life, and hoping to be again in the other world, and since on the contrary our women are as in the fire in this world, living like slaves without hope of ever entering our paradise." De Dreux adds that this is because according to the law of the Turks, women will have only a little paradise which will be like an antechamber to that of the men (101).[28]

Writing in the eighteenth century Chevalier d'Arvieux reports that women are exempt from the responsibility of fasting. "Why should they subject themselves to a painful law in which they do not hope for any reward in the other world?" he asks. "For Mahomet has excluded them from paradise" (2:175). And Volney in the latter part of the same century remarks that as passionately fond as Muhammad was of women, he did not do them the honor of treating them in the Qur'an as if they were members of the human species. Not only does he not mention them in regard to religious ceremonies or the reward of the next life, says Volney, but "it is even a problem with the Mahometans, whether women have souls."[29]

The Carnal Nature of Islam

It is clear throughout these writings that what is most disturbing—and intriguing—to the writers about Muslim understanding of the abodes of the afterlife is what they see as the obvious physical and sensual nature of rewards and punishments of heaven. A few note this in a rather neutral way, such as le-Gouz, who says the senses and the souls both will have their pleasures because "man will not be completely happy if all the parts do not have their recompense and the full joy of their objects" (32). Most, however, express themselves to be repelled by what they see as raw carnality. Muhammad had long been considered a voluptuary by Western Christian observers, and the seemingly sensual nature of the punishments and rewards served to corroborate the prejudice that most of these writers must already have had.[30] From the *Voyage de George Lengherand* in 1485–86 we read that Muhammad promised his followers that they will drink and eat in paradise, and that the beatitude will consist in all forms of sensuality that the body can experience, including sodomy. The author reflects that one should not be surprised given what he has seen about the way they live. "And I believe that their manner of living is the greatest horror of the world, enjoying luxuries of which they have no conscience and holding them in virtue, showing their nature as dogs with the men pissing squatting like women!" (181).[31]

Some credit this perceived sensual nature of paradise to an inability of Muhammad and the Turks to understand higher realms of nature. As for the recompense that he promises them after life, it is all material, they say, pertaining completely to the senses and prescribed to accommodate the grosser spirits who are not capable of comprehending an intellectual beatitude (Deshayes, 273). Pierre Bergéron observes that the reason Muhammad's sect grew was because of his emphasis on the freedom of the flesh, which he extended into paradise designed for the lecherous and intoxicated. He notes that not all Muslims were trapped in that way of thinking, recalling figures such as Avicenna and Averroes who, with Plato, Aristotle, and other good philosophers, had a better understanding of virtue which is not at all in the flesh. Alas, he says, it is this same brutality that made Muhammad want to make the beasts participants in his paradise (9–10).

Baudier, who in his lengthy excursis on Muslim views of the afterlife generally does not offer much judgmental commentary, cannot resist venting his disgust at the sensuality of Muhammad's heaven and hell: "This ignorant Arab only put the sovereign felicity of souls at the pleasure of the bodies, and in sensualities, and not in the vision of God who is the unique source of sovereign good. Also he attributes pains only to the senses and not to the privation of the ineffable vision [of God], which is the greatest of all the tragedies of the damned, and the most afflicting of their pains" (645). And somewhat later he adds, "[Mahomet's] voluptuousness and brutal mind only feeds on the dirty delicacies of sensuality, and is blind to those of the soul. . . . Not content to have had a bordello on earth . . . he lifts it up to heaven" (662).[32]

Some connect the theme of carnality with what they (are predisposed to) perceive as the brutal nature of Muslims. Among others, says Dan, the Arabs and the "Mahometan Moors" have this brutality so strongly implanted in their souls that if they come to kill a Christian, they think they are assured of going straight to heaven, where they will enjoy those filthy pleasures (*sales delices*) that Muhammad promised them. That is what gives them the audacity so willingly to take the life of a Christian. Dan here warns his Christian readers about the dangers of travel in Turkey and in Barbary (27). In a later section he says it is the promise of carnal voluptuousness that keeps the Arabs reading the Qur'an, which he calls a detestable book full of abominations, fables, and ridiculous discourses, its greatest appeal to the Arabs being the prospect of beautiful women who will recompense them in heaven (265–66).

The final denouement for the prophet Muhammad is suggested in no uncertain terms by Bénard, in his commentary on the Islamic afterlife, as a direct consequence of Muhammad's licentiousness resulting in a damnable law and doctrine. Referring his readers to Psalm 7:15 and Exodus 15:10,[33] he concludes with obvious pleasure that "God has hurled this impious and evil one to the depth of the fire where he has fallen like a mass of lead, thrown into the furious and deep waters, there to receive the eternal punishment which he has earned with his sectarians!" (331–32).

Conclusion

On the whole, it must be said that many of these observers seem to have been rather well informed about popular—though often not Qur'anic—views of the afterlife.[34] They seem to have had little understanding of Muslim texts, or of the distinction between Qur'anic doctrines and what are in fact the elaborations of often weak *ḥadīths*. But there is also not a great deal in the travelers' descriptions that does not bear some relationship to what is found in eschatological manuals and other popular Islamic writings about the afterlife. What is missing is any attempt to understand the allegorical or symbolic nature of these narratives. One can suppose that such an omission is both because it was not easily available to these persons, who for the most part were not scholars of Islam, and because it would not have served the purposes of those who saw themselves as critical reviewers of Muslim practices and beliefs and who at least in some cases hoped to titillate a waiting audience.

The question of the degree to which the treatment of this material in the respective texts really reflects the writers' preconceived notions about the religion of Islam, however, is not so easy to assess. Not only are some far more charitable than others (or less inclined to invective), but on the whole the subject of the afterlife was treated with considerably less criticism, mockery, and scorn than one might expect given the obvious cultural (and religious) predilections of the writers.[35] In relatively few cases do we find extended critique of the afterlife ideas themselves; most writers confine themselves to a fairly straightforward description with only an occasional taunt (in many cases, one suspects, to pique the interest of the potential readership).

Undeniably, however, little effort is spared in taking aim at the Prophet Muhammad. To the extent to which the doctrines were criticized it was less for their content as such than simply because they were presented as having been authored by the false prophet who copied, invented, lied, and schemed. I have included the editorial remarks of the authors whenever possible to help the reader understand the extremely low esteem in which Muhammad has been held by Western Christians. These inclusions may somewhat skew the image of the reports, which were substantially more objective than critical when taken as a whole. However they do serve to underscore the observation that while Christians through the ages have had varying responses to Muslims as a people, and even to the theological doctrines of Islam, their charity has been rarely in evidence when it comes to Muhammad. Thus while we see only a few instances in which the doctrines of afterlife themselves are given serious critique, they are damned by association as the flights of fancy and the false promises of an imposter who would be well assigned, in the opinion of most Christians of that age, to the depths of the very hells that he himself is said to have created.

Reports Cited (in chronological order of travel)

1. *Voyage de Georges Lengherand, mayeur de Mons en Haynaut, à Venise, Rome, Jerusalem, Mont Sinai et le Kayre* (Mons: Masquillier & Dequesne, 1861). Lengherand in 1485–86 undertook a voyage which was, in the words of the editor of his narrative, "in the old and pious tradition of the pilgrimage to the tomb of Jesus Christ" (p. v).

2. Jean Thénaud, *Le Voyage d'Outremer* (Paris: Ernest Léroux, 1884). In 1512, five years after the conquest of Egypt by Sultan Selim, Thénaud traveled from the monastery of Franciscan friars at Angoulême to Egypt on a political mission authorized by the count of Angoulême.

3. Guillaume Postel, *De la République des Turcs* (Poitiers: E. de Marnef, 1560). Among the more learned of the early travelers, Postel was the first professor of Hebrew and Aramaic at the Collège de France and author of an Arabic grammar. He was sent by Francis I on a diplomatic mission to Constantinople in 1535 and again in 1549, and he used the occasions to bring back classical Islamic manuscripts and to record his impressions of the country.

4. Pierre Belon, *Les observations de plusieurs singularitez et choses mémorables . . . en Grèce, Asie . . .* (Paris: Gilles Corrozet, 1555). A botanist and scientific attaché of the French government, Belon went from Turkey in 1546 to Egypt and the Holy Land. In addition to scientific studies he published this more general work on his observations in Muslim lands.

5. Jean Chesneau, *Le Voyage de Monsieur d'Aramon* (Paris: Ernest Léroux, 1887). In 1547 Chesneau traveled to Constantinople as secretary to Gabriel de Luitz, seigneur d'Aramon, who was the French ambassador to Turkey. Chesneau chronicled the voyage of d'Aramon with commentary on the life and customs of the Muslims.

6. Philippe du Fresne-Canaye, *Le Voyage du Levant* (Paris: Ernest Léroux, 1897). Raised as a Roman Catholic, Philippe became a Huguenot at a young age. He traveled extensively throughout Europe and in 1573, at the age of twenty-one, went to the Levant as a tourist where he stayed for less than a year. He was acquainted with the writings of Belon, Thevet, Postel, and de Nicolay.

7. E. Cleray, "Le Voyage de Pierre Lescalopier 'Parisien'" in *Revue d'Histoire Diplomatique* 35 (1921): 21–55. A young bourgeois Frenchman, Lescalopier visited Constantinople in 1574 on a trip which included stops in many of the

great cities of the Mediterranean. His reflections on his journey were recorded in a narrative journal.

8. Jacques de Villamont, *Les Voyages du Seigneur de Villamont* (Paris: Claude de Montroeil, 1600). This work, extremely popular at the turn of the century, describes Villamont's trip in 1589–90 to Tripoli.

9. Nicolas Bénard, *Voyage de Hierusalem* (Paris: Denis Moreau, 1621). Chevalier of the order of St. Sepulchre of Notre Seigneur Jesus Christ, Bénard went to the Holy Land in 1617 at the age of twenty in the company of a missionary in Constantinople.

10. Louis Deshayes, Baron de Courmenin, *Voiage de Levant fait par le comandement du roy en l'année 1621* (Paris: A. Taupinart, 1632). Deshayes was sent in 1621 by the French king as special ambassador to Palestine to establish a consulate for the protection of missionaries and pilgrims. His travels took him first to Constantinople, from which much of his information was taken, and then to Jerusalem.

11. Pierre Bergéron, *Relation des Voyages en Tartarie* (Paris: Jean de Heuqueville, 1634). Advocate in the parliament of Paris, Bergéron was an enthusiastic traveler who indicates in this work that he was familiar with the writings of many famous adventurers, including Marco Polo.

12. Michel Baudier, *Histoire générale de la Religion des Turcs* (Rouen: Jean Berthelin, 1641). Although there is little evidence that Baudier himself traveled in Muslim lands, he has been cited as the seventeenth-century writer who did more than any other to popularize a knowledge of Turkish history, government, customs, and religion in France. He was official historiographer for the king of France.

13. Eugène Roger, *La Terre Saincte* (Paris: A. Bertier, 1646). Roger, recollect and missionary to "barbarie," stayed in the Holy Land for five years by the order of his superiors. He described the forty nations of different religions who inhabited Jerusalem and Bethlehem, giving special notice to Christian holy places.

14. Pierre Dan, *Histoire de Barbarie et de ses Corsaires. Des Royaumes, et des Villes d'Alger, de Tunis, de Sale, et de Tripoli* (Paris: Chez Pierre Rocolet, 1649). Dan, "Ministre et Supérieur du Convent de l'ordre da la S. Trinité," wrote his history in six books with the express intent of illustrating the "barbarous" nature of the Turks and especially what he considered to be their harsh treatment of Christian captives.

15. Francois de la Boullaye-le-Gouz, *Les Voyages et Observations* (Paris: F. Clousier, 1653). Identified in the frontispiece to this work as "Cardinal et prince de la Sainte Eglise Romaine, premier Prestre, grand Bibliotéquaire du Vatican, et Protecteur de la nation Maronite," Boullaye-le-Gouz observed Islamic customs while visiting Constantinople.

16. R.P. Robert de Dreux, *Voyage en Turquie*, published and annotated by Hubert Pernot (Paris: Société d'Édition "Les Belles Lettres," 1925). A clergyman and diplomatic traveler, Père de Dreux accompanied an envoy of the French crown to Constantinople in the late 1660s. He served as chaplain and official recorder of the customs of the Turks.

17. *Nouveaux Mémoires des Missions de la Compagnie de Jésu dans le Levant*, II (Paris: Nicolas le Clerc, 1717). The anonymous author of these memoirs was a missionary in Egypt and the Levant who shared his reflections on the Muslims in a series of letters written to his superior.

18. Marcel Ladoire, *Voyage fait à la Terre Sainte en l'année 1719* (Paris: J.R. Coignard, 1720). Vicaire de la Terre Sainte, La Doire registered his impressions of a trip to Jerusalem in a journal dedicated to the count of Toulouse. Along with an account of the manners and customs of the Turks he gave great attention to the rebuilding of the Holy Sepulchre.

19. Laurent d'Arvieux, *Mémoires du chevalier d'Arvieux . . . contenant ses voyages à Constantinople, dans l'Asie, la Syrie, la Palestine, l'Egypte et la Barbarie*, I (Paris: C.J.B. Delespine, 1735). D'Arvieux was envoy of the king of France to the Porte as well as to the counsels of Aleppo, Tripoli, and the Holy Land.

20. C.F. Volney, *Voyage en Syrie et en Egypte pendant les années 1783, 1784, & 1785*, II (Paris: Volland Librarie, 1787). Traveling to Syria and Egypt for pleasure and study in 1782–84 while a young man, Volney distinguished himself by learning Arabic and living for an extensive period in a Druze convent. He wrote to persuade other travelers of the importance of such cultural immersion.

NOTES

1. Voyagers were unequipped to recognize the diversity of the Muslim communities to which in varying degrees they were exposed. The fundamental criterion they applied when describing the faith of Islam was the fact that it was not Christian. See Jean-Paul Roux, *Les Explorateurs au Moyen Age* (Paris: Fayard, 1981), p. 241.

2. For an interesting historical survey of the development of Western views of Islam, see Philippe Sénac, *L'Image de l'Autre* (Paris: Flammarion, 1983).

3. Jonathan Sumption, *Pilgrimage: An Image of Medieval Religion* (Totowa, N.J.: Rowman and Littlefield, 1975), pp. 115–17. One of the earliest extant French reports of the lives and religious beliefs of Muslims was that of Guibert, Abbot of Nogent-sous-Coucy (1053–c.1124). In his *Gesta Dei* he provides a detailed chronicle of what he saw as Muhammad's evil life and demise. See John Benton, *Self and Society in Medieval France. The Memoires of Guibert of Nogent* (New York: Harper, 1970), p. 10. Benton notes the abbot's acknowledgment that his sources were not beyond question.

4. A fragment from the journal of an anonymous French pilgrim traveling in the Holy Land in 1382 indicates that the writer was more concerned about the high tariffs he had to pay to the Muslims than he was about describing their beliefs and practices

(H. Omant, "Journal d'un Pélerin Français en Terre-Sainte [1383]," *Revue de l'Orient Latin* 3 [1895]: 457–59).

5. Among the few extant French reports from these centuries are the well-publicized accounts of Ghillebert de Lannoy in 1422 and Bertrandon de la Broquière in 1432–33. Clearly their primary concern was not religion, in that they had been sent by the duke of Bourgogne, Philippe le Bon, on military reconnaissance respectively to Syria and Egypt, and to Syria and Asia Minor. Even de la Broquière, however, occasionally added to his investigations some attention to the beliefs of the people with whom he was coming into contact. He tells the story of a conversation with a slave named Hayaldoula (Abd Allah) who described to him Muhammad's coffin in Mecca in a circular chapel. The slave said that sometimes pilgrims after seeing the coffin ask to have their eyes pierced because they will never see anything more worthy ("disans qu'ilz ne pevent ny ne veullent jamais veoir plus digne chose"). De la Broquière says he actually saw two such people with their eyes pierced. He follows this narrative about these customs with the comment that "when the day of judgment comes, Muhammad will put in paradise as many people as he wishes, and that they will have women, milk and honey as much as they will want" (pp. 57–58) (*Voyage d'Outremer de Bertrandon de la Broquière*, trans. Charles Schefer [Paris: Ernest Léroux, 1892]).

6. See Norman Daniel, *Islam, Europe and Empire* (Edinburgh: University Press, 1960), p. 15. Daniel notes earlier (p. 10) that visitors to Muslim lands seem to have preferred to pass on traditional reports of theological matters and information that was out of date to finding and disseminating more accurate information.

7. According to Jacques de Villamont, if the priest sees that the patient is not dying, he brings the Qur'an and reads seven times the relevant passages (204a–b).

8. Laurent Chevalier d'Arvieux adds that the families of the dead wail as if they wanted to sell their tears, and that they scratch their faces and arms and pull out their hair (337). He goes on, generously, to note that such practices are not all blameworthy in the case of women because once they are in the grave they will never be seen again, Muhammad having had the severity to exclude them from paradise "and to send them by grace to the suburbs of the place of bliss" where they will mix with Christians (337).

9. Personal items such as scimitar, warclub, quiver, and bow (or silver mitre in the case of a woman) may be taken with the deceased to the grave but removed before burial, says Roger (265–66). In writing about the Turks of Constantinople, Sieur de la Boulaye-le-Gouz discusses the fact that the turbans placed on the stone representing the dead vary according to the condition of the deceased. A Janissary wears one more pleated than a pasha, etc. "And as for a woman, they put on her a coiffure in accord with her quality to distinguish her from others" (40).

10. A number of Muslim texts deal with this phenomenon, as with other details of Islamic eschatology. See Abū Ḥāmid al-Ghazālī's *al-Durra al-Fākhira* (eleventh century); Ibn Qayyim al-Jawzīya's *Kitāb al-Rūh* (fourteenth century); Jalāl al-Dīn Suyūṭī's *Bushrā al-Ka'īb bi-Liqā'i al-Ḥabīb* (fifteenth century); Abū Layth al-Samarqandī's *Kitāb al-Ḥaqā'iq wa'l-Daqā'iq* (seventeenth century); and the anonymous *Kitāb Aḥwāl al-Qiyāma* (seventeenth century).

11. The same considerations, he says, mean that the Turks do not even use remedies

for their infirmities. "See how coarse they are and so little caring for their health that they do not look for better nourishment in sickness than in health" (264).

12. The names of these angels (who are also described in Islamic traditions as black) reflect the Arabic names Munkar and Naqir, and are rendered by these reporters as Mungir or Mongir and Quarequir, Granequir, or Guauegir.

13. The anonymous eighteenth-century author of *Nouveaux Mémoires* comments on tales he has heard that the suffering of the dead in their graves is so great that passersby should pour buckets of water on the dead to give them some refreshment. Tufts of hair are left on the heads of those buried, he says, so that an angel can come from time to time to change their positions and so that Muhammad can find a hold when he comes to transport them to paradise (317–18).

14. Belon says that at the command of these angels the deceased puts on his soul "just (says the Alcoran) like a man puts on his shirt" (174b). The questioning of the angels has terrified the Turks so much, he says, that part of the funeral prayer is to say, "Lord God, deliver me from the interrogation of the two angels, and from the torment of the grave and from the bad road, Amen" (175a). Roger comments that the punishing blows and retrieval with hooks are the purgatory of the Turks (270). There is some confusion among these writers as to whether or not Muslims believe in purgatory, and no attempt at a redefinition of what that might mean in Islamic terms.

15. Belon says that besides the Qur'an the Turks observe the commandments of another book, which they call Zuna de Mahomet, meaning road or law, i.e., following the counsel of Muhammad, which book (composed of six separate books) his disciples wrote after his death (174a).

16. The term *azoare* is commonly used by these writers for *sūra* or chapter of the Qur'an. Pierre Bergeron says that the Turks understand all the law in a book, called *Alcoran* or *Alfurcan*, which Muhammad composed in Mecca. They call the chapters in it *sura*, or *surata*, and vulgarly *azoara*, *Alfurcan*, i.e., verse or separate chapter (13, 15–16). Dan in a section entitled "About the Alcoran and its abominations, fables and ridiculous discourses" says that the *Alcoran* is divided into several chapters called azores, adding that "in fact this infamous and detestable book is also called by some of them *Alfurkan*" (267).

17. After a lengthy discussion of the angel of death Baudier reports that the world will be empty for the space of forty years, during which God will speak of the deplorable sin of man, and will say to himself, "Where are now these superb princes and these proud kings who insolently ruled over the earth? What has become of their empires, and where is now this swollen power, which made them the terror and the dread of other men?" (626–27). Cf. Abū Ḥāmid al-Ghazālī's *al-Durra al-Fākhira*: "Then God will manifest Himself in the clouds, seizing the seven heavens in His right hand and the seven earths in His left, saying, "O world, O worldly one! Where are your masters? Where are your chiefs? You have beguiled them with your splendors and with your beauty you have kept them from concern for things of the hereafter" (*The Precious Pearl*, trans. Jane I. Smith [Missoula, Mont.: Scholars Press, 1979], p. 44).

18. "But Jesus says, 'Truly my mother and I have been taken as gods, apart from God. How could I intercede for you when I have been worshipped along with Him and designated as His son and He called my father?'" (ibid., p. 58).

19. LaDoire is less charitable. He likens the stone where Muhammad will preside to a cannon looking out on the valley of Jehosaphat across the tomb of Absalom. The "Mahometans" say so many impertinences on the subject, he comments, that he will not repeat them for fear of annoying the reader (380).

20. Belon, in discussing souls suffering the fire, says that all good Turks who have been temporarily punished will be carried out by Muhammad and washed pure in a fountain of paradise. He refers to the belief that Muhammad will change himself into a lamb and that the Turks will become like fleas. "And coming from the fire to put them in paradise, he will succour them so that the so-called fleas will fall inside and take the form of other Turks" (179a).

21. In reference to the tree in the middle of paradise, de Villamont also refers to the fate that befalls the Christian who inadvertently pronounces the syllables "Alla, Ille, he, allah, Mahomet Rezul, allah" (206a).

22. In the fourth paradise are many angels, he says, including the angel of death Melek el mouti (*malik al-mawt*), who is extremely large and holds the records of human deeds. In the same paradise is an angel called Bka (or Bxa), who cries continually for the sins and miseries of the damned.

23. He cites a tradition noted by several others that Muhammad once said that if one of these virgins went out of the Serail of paradise at midnight she would give light to all of the world as does the sun.

24. Postel concludes his quite accurate description of Muslim notions of God and the abodes of eternity with a damning commentary on the motivations of the Prophet. "All his speech, badly constructed as it is, is written out of wiliness [*astuce*] and cunning [*cautelle*], and half in imitation of the obscure chapters of the Hebrew prophets, there where he speaks by ambiguity and doubt in the person of God, after Gabriel, or by himself without naming the person who speaks. To this end, that he is able to persuade the believing people that it is God who is speaking when it is he himself" (88–89).

25. The Qur'an calls this tree Shajarat al-Zaqqūm.

26. The longest reference to the *ḥūr* in the Qur'an is in sūra 55: "In them [the gardens] are those who are chaste, with glances restrained, whom neither man nor *jinn* has before touched . . . like rubies and coral . . . is there any reward for goodness but goodness? . . . In them are those who are good, beautiful . . . *ḥūr* well-guarded in pavilions . . . whom neither man nor *jinn* has before touched" (from vv. 56–57).

27. In one of the earliest reports of this collection, that of Frère Jean Thénaud, the reference to women in relation to matters of death and afterlife has not to do with their fate but with their role in helping guarantee the felicity of the one in the grave. Each Friday, he observes, women go to visit the tombs of their dead on which they throw great quantities of aromatic matters such as jasmine, baselic, roses, and scented oils, on the smells of which he says the Saracens believe that their deceased feed (51).

28. Gilles Veinstein in the introduction to an edited volume on eighteenth-century France explains the title of the book when he cites the remark of the Turkish ambassador to France in 1720–21 that the country makes real the *ḥadīth* "Le monde est la prison des croyants et le paradis des infidels" (*Mehmed Effendi, Le paradis de infidèles* [Paris: Librairie François Maspero, 1981], p. 7).

29. C.F. de Chasseboeu f. Comte de Volney, *Travels through Syria and Egypt in the years 1783, 1784, and 1785*, trans. from the French (London: G. Robinson, 1805), vol. 2. His is the only mention found in these reports of the (incorrect) opinion that women are soulless in the Islamic understanding.

30. This predisposition is evidenced early. In Michelant and Raynaud's *Itinéraires à Jérusalem*, a kind of compendium of descriptions of the Holy Land gathered from the eleventh to the thirteenth centuries, reference is made to these carnal pleasures: "par l'entuschement Mahumeth ki nule honestete ne enseignera ne reddur de vertu, mais delices charneles e ke plest au cors, est ia tute corrumpeue e pasture au diable" (ed. Henri Michelant and Gaston Raynaud [Osnabruck: Otto Zeller, 1966], 130).

31. Nicolas de Nicolay, dauphin of Arfeuile, writing in the middle of the sixteenth century, assures his readers that the faith of the Mahometistes, both Turks and Moors, evidences the most blatant hypocrisy and damnable superstition precisely because their manner of living with its feigned holiness and vain devotion is so beastly and so far from true religion (*Les Navigations, Peregrinations et Voyages faicts en la Turquie* [Antwerp: G. Silvius, 1576], pp. 99–100).

32. For Roger the paradise of Muhammad is one continual "caresme-prenant" (equated with the reveling of Shrovetide) where there are only festivities, dances, and farces (169). De Dreux comments that in order better to seduce the Jews and the Christians, Muhammad put in "his Alcoran" some maxims of their religion, "which he accommodated to the sensuality of the corrupt nature that was found in many of his sectarians" (121).

33. He cites the Latin "Et ecce incidit in foveam quam fecit, etc., Impium & impurum demersit Deus in Profundum inferni, quasi plumbam in acquis vehementibus."

34. Comparing the information they provide about afterlife abodes and circumstances with what they convey about the life of the Prophet himself, one is struck by how much seems to have been known about the former and how inaccurate the information often is about the latter.

35. R. Schwoebel, *The Shadow of the Crescent: The Renaissance Image of the Turk (1453–1517)* (Nieuwkoop: B. de Graaf, 1967), p. 213, reflects that the experiences of travelers to the Levant often showed them a people who exhibited more courtesy and charity than Christians showed to one another, and comments that such experiences may well have resulted in a more tolerant attitude on the part of the travelers than might otherwise have been held.

PART TWO

The Contemporary Situation

Regional Studies

15

Sharing Islamically in the Pluralistic Nation-State of India: The Views of Some Contemporary Indian Muslim Leaders and Thinkers

Christian W. Troll

Muslim Minority Status in Historical Perspective: An Unprecedented Challenge

More than three decades ago Wilfred C. Smith, at the beginning of the chapter on India of his seminal work *Islam in Modern History*,[1] made a number of astute observations directly pertinent to our subject. Smith characterized the situation of the Muslims in the Republic of India as unprecedented. Two facts more than anything else, he stressed, combine to create a unique constellation: on the one hand, the Muslims living within the frontiers of the Republic of India inherited an indigenous "thousand-year tradition of imposing dimensions" in all walks of life and, on the other, they share citizenship in the new, secularly constituted republic with an immense number of other people, most of them inheritors of a cultural and religious system that in many ways is different from if not diametrically opposed to that of Islam.

Smith then turned to the specifically religious question: "Here as elsewhere the Muslims are confronted with the general task of reconciling their faith to modernity. In addition, here they have their special minority status. . . . The question of political power and social organization, so central to Islam, has in the past always been considered in yes-or-no terms. Muslims have either had political power or they have not. Never before have they shared it with others."[2] To live with others, "to participate in constructing a life in common," as Smith qualifies in a footnote, presents an unprecedented challenge to them. "It raises the deepest issues both of the meaning of man's being and of social morality. It raises the deepest issues of the significance of revelation, truth, and the relation to other people's faith."[3]

In the final analysis, the problems of Indian Islam do not differ essentially from those facing the whole *umma*—and, in an analogous way, all major religions—namely, how to live as an important religious minority and in shared political responsibility with people of other faiths and ideologies.

Medina: The Foundational Model

The Medinan, or the foundational, model of Islamic political life covered at least the first three decades of the history of Islam. In political terms it represented a city state—more precisely, a religio-political community united by belief in One God who had made known His Will definitively in the Qur'an. All the groups that made up Medinan society, the *bayt al-nabī* (household of the Prophet), the *anṣār* (supporters) and *muhājirūn* (immigrants), the *ahl al-kitāb* (people of the book), were guided by the Prophet whose word and life-example interpreted the will of God and implemented it effectively. After the Prophet's death, the *khalīfa*, the "successor of the Apostle of Allah," had the function of putting into practice the regulations set out in the Qur'anic message. The Qur'anic message was supplemented by the *sunna*, the normative action and teaching of the Prophet.

The ideal of the rule of the Prophet and of the "rightly-guided caliphs" has constituted throughout subsequent Muslim history the "nomocratic ideal for a universal social order." As such it "has never lost its hold upon the imagination of Muslims, although it has never had more than a brushing contact with historical reality."[4]

Historical Mutations

With the establishment and expansion of the Islamic empire and with the spread of the *umma*, Muslim communities came to live in countless new political constellations. Muslims were either rulers or ruled. The division of the world, according to the early developed classical teaching of Islamic law, into *dār al-islām* (abode of Islam) and *dār al-ḥarb* (abode of war) basically guided Muslims in different situations. However, in the spheres of administration and politics, the *sharīʿa*—instead of being an effectively implemented blueprint—began from early on, and increasingly so, to be treated rather as a symbol of the continuous divine guidance and direction of the Muslim community's life. The *ulama*, in the words of Montgomery Watt, "were above all concerned to maintain . . . the charismatic or divinely-instituted nature of the community, and of this they saw the guarantee in its possession—not its carrying out in full—of the divinely-given law, the *sharīʿa*."[5]

Muslim political thought after the watershed of 1258 was characterized by the effort of maintaining the religious and legal rather than the political and constitutional unity of the *umma*. The overriding pattern of post-Mongol-invasion Muslim thought on the temporal order, at least as far as the world of eastern Islam is concerned, has been termed "pious-sultan tradition": "The king must acknowledge the *Sunna* of the Prophet and the *sharīʿa*, as interpreted by the *ulama* (in their role as heirs of the prophets and of Muhammad in particular), as the only way of God; he is allowed, however, to manage the administrative, financial and military affairs of his kingdom according to regulations (*ẓawābiṭ*) of his own devising, and to use extra-*sharīʿa* discretion in the dispension of justice."[6]

New Questioning in Muslim South Asia with the Advent of the British

In the India ruled by sultans, the ulama could live with the sultans' politics of power as long as it was at least the politics of Muslim power. However, the decline of Mughal and Muslim power, the gradually increasing economic and political influence of the East India Company and, later, the establishment of rule by the British crown made the ulama, and many other Muslims for that matter, ask themselves more and more urgently: Can Muslims be the loyal subjects of the British crown?

The main questions asked were these: What is the legal status of the country under the British according to the Islamic laws and to what extent, if any, does the changing political situation affect the religious life of the Muslims? Can a Muslim serve a non-Muslim government? Is it permitted for a Muslim to learn the English language and to dress the English way?[7]

The mainstream body of ulama in nineteenth-century British India did consider the territory under the (Christian) non-Muslims as *dār al-ḥarb*. However, they did not use the term in its technical sense. For them the term *dār al-ḥarb* was not a declaration of war but rather an analysis of the new political situation—in other words, of the overwhelming influence of the East India Company in the Mughal empire, and later, of the rule of the British crown. In the situation thus analyzed they allowed the Muslims actually to cooperate with the British insofar as Islamic values were not violated and as long as their religious and cultural character remained intact.

Many of the ulama, as for instance Shāh ʿAbdul ʿAzīz of Delhi (1746–1824), one of the illustrious sons of Shāh Walīullāh (1703–63), went so far as to declare it lawful to eat with the British, to learn their language, and even to dress like them. The Muslims who asked for legal pronouncements (*istiftā'*) from the *muftīs* were indeed more concerned with the rights which the changing situation could offer them than with their duties as faithful Muslims in a gradually dying *dār al-islām*.[8]

This mainstream attitude toward the British was opposed fiercely by the *mujāhidīn* and their sympathizers who, however, remained clearly a minority if not the exception. Looking at the whole of the nineteenth century with our main question in mind, we would agree with Peter Hardy's assessment: "Throughout the nineteenth century a simulacrum of the medieval relationship between the actual holders of power and the ulama was preserved: the government did not interfere in the ulama's sphere of education in Islam . . . and the ulama did not, with some exceptions, interfere actively in politics."[9]

Arguments in the Wake of Independence

A significant change of outlook occurred only by the end of the first decade of the twentieth century, with the foundation of the All-India Muslim League in 1906 and the winning of separate electorates in 1909, political events which signaled the constitutional recognition in British India of Muslim politics understood as an activity of rallying wills and influencing the decisions of government. With the rise of Indian nationalism and the freedom movement at the turn of the century a new constellation had come about. The vision of an ultimately independent India involved not only collaboration with Hindus and other non-Muslim Indians in the fight for freedom, but also envisaging Indian national values common to all Indians and worth striving for with one's possessions and lives.

Among those preoccupied with effectively projecting the need for unity with the Hindus for independence were Abūl Kalām Azād (1888–1958) in *al-Ḥilal* and *al-Balāgh*; the brothers of the Khilāfat movement, Muḥammad and Shawkat ʿAlī; and the Jamʿiyyat al-ʿUlamā', represented especially by Ḥusayn Aḥmad Madanī (1879–1957). Gradually, with independence becoming a distinct possibility and even an imminent reality, a key question arose: Given the fact that the ulama were by tradition and history familiar with the politics of autocratic polities, how would they adapt their ideas to the politics of constitutional polities conducted, at least in part, according to the liberal Western idiom of representation, public association, and majority voting? And further: To what purpose were Muslims' wills as such to be rallied? Could they be rallied by virtue of their character as Muslims for cooperation with non-Muslims to secure self-government for British India?[10]

The most insightful analysis of the intellectual response given by Azād, the Jamʿiyyat, and Madanī to the questions which the approach first of independence and then of partition inevitably posed would seem to be that of Peter Hardy in *Partners in Freedom—and True Muslims*. One or two points of his analysis need mentioning here.

Azād's chief statement in this matter was his tract of 1920: *Mas'ala-i Khilāfat*. It bears evidence of a significant shift in conceiving of the *sharīʿa*. Whereas the classical scholars of *fiqh* (jurisprudence) saw the sharīʿa as an aggregate of divine commandments already decreed and understood which can be added to by elaboration of detailed applications, Azād sees the sharīʿa as an aggregate of divine commandments, the existing commandments of which can be abrogated by appeal to "the principles" of the "idea" of sharīʿa. The sharīʿa for Azād is "a comprehensive scheme of human welfare"[11] which as such must provide for Muslims' welfare in any situation. If, therefore, the situation requires political cooperation with friendly non-Muslims, it is a reasonable assumption that the sharīʿa does not forbid that cooperation. However, Azād does not outline for an India free from British rule a constitution that would satisfy the requirements of Islam. He does not even outline a constitution for the Indian Muslim community.

This was, however, attempted from the same time onward by the Jamʿiyyat. Here free India essentially was conceived of as a future confederation of two religious and political communities—Muslim and Hindu—which would have cooperated successfully against the British common enemy. Hardy characterizes the kind of relationship between the Muslim community and the Hindu in future India, as envisaged by the ulama of the Jamʿiyyat, to be *imperium in imperio* or political apartheid. The Jamʿiyyat advocated the appointment of an Amīr-i-Hind at the summit of an autonomous Muslim society. Thus the ulama, at least implicitly, rejected the idea of a unitary democratic state in India with authority over all persons and all causes. Instead, they advocated a "functional dualism in the temporal order . . . 'a *sharīʿa* protectorate' wherein the ulama would be free from interference, either by the Hindu majority or by the modern-educated Muslim."[12]

The 1930s saw, on the one hand, the Muslim League holding out a claim for a Muslim state or states on Indian soil and, on the other, Ḥusayn Aḥmad Madanī developing a theory of territorial nationhood or, to translate his own terms, of "united or composite nationalism" (*waṭanī ishtirāk*; *muttaḥida qawmiyyat*). He described it thus: "By the concept of united nationalism we mean the same idea which the Messenger of Allah, prayers and peace be on Him, set down as a principle among the people of Medina. In other words, the inhabitants of India, regardless of their religion, are one Indian nation with one homeland. They will fight against the foreign nation which destroys everything and deprives them of the common national interests in order to achieve their right, to expel the oppressive and merciless force, and shatter the chains of slavery. No one will interfere in the religious affairs of another, and all the peoples who live in India will be free to adhere to their religion and fulfill its commandments."[13]

The position of the Jamᶜiyyat, as stated here by Madanī, is marked by two distinctive features.[14] One concerns the underlying concept of solidarity. Whereas the classical Islamic concept was religious and nomocratic in that according to it Muslims were individually committed to obedience to God, living together because commanded by God, the Jamᶜiyyat's concept of Muslim solidarity was political and nomo-democratic in that Muslims, through persuasion and rallying of wills, are to actively combine to designate authority (e.g., to the Amīr-i-Hind and the *qādī* [judge] courts). According to the classical concept the caliph, divinely instituted by the sharīᶜa, has the duty "to invite to the good and to forbid to the evil." In the Jamᶜiyyat concept the authority of the ulama and of the Amīr-i-Hind rests upon a Muslim public opinion actively and continuously expressed through the organs of the Jamᶜiyyat. The second distinctive feature concerns the kind of nationalism advocated. The free Indian nation will be one of largely self-governing communities. Education is to be kept fully in the hands of the ulama.

Here the question arises: How far will the ulama-educated Muslims be willing and, within Islamic precepts, be able to join their compatriots in shaping and running the fast rising national institutions of a developing and, of necessity, more and more integrated modern state, for example in the field of finance and control of economic development if, culturally, they are to acknowledge themselves as a separate people, in political alliance with Hindus and other non-Muslim compatriots against foreigners?

Muslim Questions for Valid Islamic Response

Thus far we have considered the main features of the background needed for an understanding of the views of a select number of Muslim personalities living in the Republic of India. We now turn to an examination of those views. The overall question put to the respondents interviewed for this study was: "In which ways do select Indian Muslim thinkers conceive of an Islamically valid Muslim participation in the (political) life of the Republic of India (Bharat)?" To this were added five more specific questions:

1. Do you agree that the situation of the Muslim community in India (Bharat) where they participate as a numerical minority in a "sovereign, socialist secular democratic republic," is new in the annals of history? New, in that in this constellation the Muslims as such are neither rulers (*ḥākim*) nor ruled (*maḥkūm*)?

2. If this is so, the need seems to arise for Muslims to develop an Islamic response, or, if you prefer, an Islamically valid rationale and justification for the Muslim community to live in Bharat as co-citizens. Short of such a valid rationale, there would seem to be possible for them only a mere *de facto* acceptance of the new situation, going together with inner discontent arising from an ideological contradiction perceived as irredeemable.
3. In which way will the teaching of Islam be presented and the elaboration and application of the *sharīʿa* be conducted so as to give legitimacy and meaning to the new situation of Muslims in post-partition India?
4. Which particular elements in the foundational sources (Qurʾan and Ḥadīth) and the foundational model (*sīra* of the Prophet) and which, possibly new, ways of understanding them would come into play in such an Islamic response (on the ideological level)?
5. Which modifications in the traditional understanding(s) of the *sharīʿa* and the *uṣūl al-fiqh* would seem to be justified and advisable in the elaboration of an adequate Islamic response to the new Indian Muslim situation?

The study had to be limited to a select, relatively small number of persons, who were asked in writing to respond in person or by letter; from these an even smaller number have been presented here. At the same time an effort was made to cover—however limited and arbitrary the selection had to be for practical reasons—a relatively broad, to some extent representative spectrum of interviewees: ulama, academic teachers and administrators, politicians. The relevant views in print of some personalities who lived and wrote in post-partition India were included in some places.

The views have been presented under five very roughly defined categories in terms of qualifying adjectives which indicate the most conspicuous emphasis of the answers provided: pragmatist; political; modernist; integrist and missionary; and jurisprudentially constructive. Naturally, since most interviewees could be listed under more than one category, the division merely means that the outstanding feature of a particuilar person's response is most adequately, but in no way exhaustively, indicated by the given category.

Pragmatist.—This position denies the newness of the Muslim situation in India and, hence, does not perceive any major problem either on the practical/political or on the theoretical/ideological (e.g., *fiqh*; *kalām*) level.

A typical example is the response given in writing on October 27, 1987 to our question by Capt. N.A. Ameer Ali, the secretary of the Islamic Studies and Cultural Centre in Madras, Tamil Nadu. To the overall question he replies: "I feel that Muslims have been participating in the political life of the Republic of India (*Bharat*). Muslims are in Congress, Janata, Communists (Marxists, Communists [Left]) etc., at the all-India level. They have also enrolled themselves in regional parties. Being Indians, they take part in political activities in a variety of fashions. Such participation, I feel, is valid."

To question 1 he replies: "The assumption that Muslims are neither rulers nor ruled is not correct. They are rulers in the sense that they are members of almost all the ruling parties of the various states as well as the centre. (No single community can be absolute rulers in a multi-racial, secular country like India.) They are ruled in the sense that they obey all the laws of the country except where some special laws are applicable to them."

To question 2 he replies: "Muslims are already living in India as co-citizens and hence 'acceptance of the new situation' does not arise." His comment on question 3 is that it "follows from the assumption that the situation in India after partition is not legitimate. This is absolutely wrong." Questions 4 and 5, Ameer Ali adds, do not need any answer since "there is no question of a new Indian Muslim situation."

Political.—This position considers the situation of the Muslim community in India as new, yet looks at it primarily in political terms and advocates above all a response in terms of change in political outlook and strategy. The views of the former Congress MP, Professor Rasheeduddin Khan of the Jawarharlal Nehru University, expressed orally to me as well as stated in a number of his recent writings, are representative of this position. Professor Khan is a close relative of the late former president of India, Dr. Zakir Husain (d. 1969), and is a renowned political scientist of leftist leanings.

With regard to our question Rasheeduddin Khan writes: "In terms of the contemporary political situation, the basic problem of the Muslims in India is how to reconcile their sense of religious and communal belonging with their political identification with the national process of change in India. . . . This problem is not an isolated problem . . . but part of the larger political challenge facing India and its national policy of secularism and democracy."[15]

Rasheeduddin Khan thinks that a new situation indeed has arisen for the Muslims in India. However, he sees this newness in terms that transcend the confines of the Muslim community since it consists in "a new structuring of power-relationships in India. This has generated a process of secularization and democratic diffusion. All sections of the people, including the Muslims, are caught up, as it were, in a vortex of change. . . . The Muslim response to this is 'limited' by considerations pertaining to them specifically, the first of which is 'their adherence,' as a community, to the traditional view of Muslim polity based on the common law of Islam . . . thereby questioning the total legitimacy of the legislative competence of the democratic law-making processes in India."[16]

Khan sees a solution to the ideological dilemma of Muslims in India in adopting Madanī's theological position, which qualifies the Muslim-Hindu relationship in terms of the concept of *muʿāhada* (treaty) of all those bound together by one national territory and history. Hence, the main overall task, he insists, is "to transcend limitations of community-orientation" by realizing that "As a matter of fact, an Indian Muslim is, precisely in that order, an Indian first and a Muslim next in his sociological, cultural, psychological, and economic and political responses and conditions. Only in terms of faith is he Muslim first and Muslim last, but that is not the concern of the profane problems of politics or secular aspects of social living. The divergence between him and members of another community in his region within India is that of degree but not of kind while the difference between him and his co-religionalists elsewhere in the world—say in Indonesia, Malaysia, Egypt, Nigeria or Albania—is essentially a basic difference in kind. Muslim leadership in India ought to stress this point to undo the effect of tendentious propaganda to the contrary."[17]

In the end, Khan believes, the forces of "faster industrialization, greater diversification of interest, and more democracy will by themselves break relationships based on caste and religious communities."[18]

Syed Shahabuddin, a former career diplomat, MP and member of the Rajya Sabha, and at present the outspoken leader of the recently founded Insaf Party, shares with Rasheeduddin Khan the emphasis on the need for a consistent Muslim Indian political response to the new situation. However, he views "Muslim Indians" as an essentially distinct community, called to organize itself as a whole in distinct political structures, in an India which essentially is "a nation of minorities at all levels." In the face of the fact that, as he sees it, Hindu revivalism increasingly identifies the nation state as the vehicle for the expression of Hindu consciousness, the Indian Muslim response has to be political and institutional. Shahabuddin puts his hope in "a Muslim party with secular, nationalist, democratic credentials . . . [to] 'safeguard the legitimate interests' of the Muslim community."[19] To this effect Shahabuddin founded the Insaf Party which, however, did poorly in the general elections of 1989. Shahabuddin does not seem to see the need for developing, in addition to the political endeavor, an adapted and meaningful Islamic response in terms of *fiqh* and *kalām* restated in the newly arisen predicament of the Muslims in India.

Modernist.—This position emphasizes the need for a radical reinterpretation of Islam on the basis of a modern rereading of the Qurʾan, in the light of the social, ideological, and other changes that have arisen in the modern world. Furthermore, it minimizes the need to adhere to the consensus of the ulama.

A well-known authority on "Muhammadan Law," Professor A.A.A. Fyzee (1899–1981) of Bombay, discussed his views with me on visits to my home in the late seventies. He thought that the basic problem for the Muslims in modern India was that the *sharīʿa* traditionally is conceived of as both law and religion. Whereas law by its very nature is subject to constant change, the heart of religion is unchangeable. Fyzee saw a solution to this clash in a three-part operation: to define religion and law in terms of twentieth-century thought; to distinguish between religion and law in Islam; and to interpret Islam in the light of the science, metaphysics, and theology of the modern world. Fyzee did not believe that God and his will can be truly sovereign, in practice, in a modern state. He advocated the complete separation of religion, whose appeal is "personal, immediate and intuitive," from law, which should be based on the will of the community as expressed in its legislature.[20]

In contrast, the Indian Muslim philosopher and student of comparative religion, Professor Syed Vahiduddin (b. 1909) of Hyderabad and Delhi, stresses the social and universal character of Islam and thus of the *umma*. Yet, not only for practical but also, and above all, for religious reasons he considers it to be necessary to hold apart religious and political concerns. "Muslims should confine the area of immediate cooperation to cultural and religious fields and eschew giving the impression of a political alignment based on religion." An authentic restatement of Islamic religious thought, according to Vahiduddin, is imperative for the Muslims in modern India and in the modern world at large. Such restatement can go far and may provoke controversies but there is no danger of betraying Islam "as long as we remain loyal to [Islam's] metaphysical moorings and remain faithful to the religious spirit." Hence he envisages a reexamination not only of theoretical foundations but also of inbuilt attitudes and perspectives.

For Vahiduddin a key problem and task is the development in Islamic thought and scholarship of an adequate religious hermeneutics. On the basis of an overall understanding of revelation as being multidimensional, it will have to reassess the "semantic equipment of a given time." Such an approach would help to distinguish the moral value content of the Qurʾan from its purely legal aspect. Whereas the moral content has a permanent feature, the legislative infrastructure must not fail to adapt itself to circumstances which are not foreseen. Furthermore, the traditional credal formulations (*ʿaqāʾid*), in contrast to the text of the Qurʾan, cannot claim a final, authoritative character since Islam does not know of clearly stated dogmatic formulations by ecumenical councils binding the whole Church. "Orthodoxy" in Islam cannot be understood in the same way as in Christianity since the Muslim creed has never been officially formulated by any authority comparable to that of a council or synod.

The well-known writer and controversial Bohra reformer Asghar Ali Engineer of Bombay, in a written answer (August 1987) to our question 3 points out that "the teachings of Islam do not conflict with the secular political processes as long as the Muslims are allowed to practice the 'five pillars'." In answer to question 4 he writes: "There is much in the Koran and Hadith which is contextual. . . . The foundational sources do not stand opposed to change provided change does not conflict with the guiding principles laid down in these sources. The foundational model (*sīra*) also bears this out. The Prophet has changed his policies according to the situation. No prophetic vision can be successfully implemented without taking situational constraints into account."

In distinguishing in the foundational sources between the "guiding principles" and the detailed injunctions and in leaving open, at the same time, the question of whose consensus is decisive and how consensus will function validly, Engineer betrays clearly the "modernist" character of this outlook.

Integrist and missionary.—The integrist position considers the Islamic political system to be an essential part of Islam and thinks in terms of the direct rule of God and His Law (theocracy and theo-nomocracy) as an essential condition for a full Islamic life. In India the Jamāʿat-i Īslamī Hind stands most distinctly for this outlook. Syed Shakeel Aḥmad of Hyderabad, a member of the Jamāʿat and declaring himself guided by Mawlānā Ṣadruddīn Iṣlāḥī, the author of the remarkable Qurʾan commentary *Tadabbur-i Qurʾan* and the theorist of the Jamāʿat-i-Islāmī Hind, gave detailed answers in writing (September 15, 1987) to our questions.

In Aḥmad's view the Islamic and the Indian political systems "are at opposite ends to each other and contradict one another ideologically and practically." The "Indian system," as he calls it, is characterized by "popular sovereignty," "democracy" and "secularism" as against "sovereignty of God," "viceregency of man (theo-democracy)" and "laws of the *sharīʿa*" which define the Islamic system. "Hence, a true Muslim should, first, not voluntarily co-operate with the present system but at the same time should not violate civic laws of the country." Second, he "should endeavour to change the present system by peaceful means": "The Islamically valid participation in the political life of the country rallies around these concepts, although a detailed programme has not yet been chalked out in this regard, especially in the area of changing the system through peaceful means."

Aḥmad challenges the idea that Muslims freely participate in a democratic system in India. For him:

> the majority community, i.e. the Hindus, have manipulated the functioning of the political system in such a manner that democracy is resulting in the rule of the majority community only. . . . The Islamic response to the said situation lies in the revival of the missionary spirit in the Muslim community and a full-fledged involvement in the political life of the country.
>
> The ideological concept for the Islamic political system should be propagated from all platforms—social, political, institutional, media and parliamentary forums. . . . This should not be described as participation in the system. It is only a utilization of the available means for propagation of the good cause and proclamation of the truth.

Aḥmad writes that the proper way of Muslim political participation has not yet been elaborated. In any case, "they will have to strive for a new national, secular [*sic*] political party, a true alternative to all other parties. It should stand for India as a federation of communities, the introduction of the proportional representation system, etc. Only when a radical change has been effected in India, will there be provided 'the suitable conditions for the elaboration and explanation of the teachings of Islam and application of *sharīʿa* to the modern problems.' Unless such a practical situation is provided, the reforms needed in its understanding and application can not be dealt with."

Aḥmad's answer to question 4 in a fascinating way expresses the peculiar outlook of the Jamāʿat-i Islāmī Hind. In describing the foundational nature of Islam he links the missionary with the political element: "The Muslim community has been raised as a Missionary community and the foundational sources (Qurʾan and Hadith) and the foundational model (*sira*) are solely manifested by these aspects. The later developments where it acted or appeared as settled community or a nation, can not serve in its present situation. The Muslim community at Mecca or even at Medina initially had been a numerical minority community. At Mecca it was a closely knit (organized and autonomous) group and at Medina it acted as an effective and dynamic partner of the federation of the Medinate communities. Hence, after the revival of its earlier dynamism [here Aḥmad makes it clear that he means politically effective dynamism], the Muslim community may be able to play its historical role in India too."

Jurisprudentially constructive.—This label designates an emphasis placed on "the essentially religious development of Islam" in India. While it rejects an exclusively or preponderantly political approach to solving the problems of the Muslims in India, it stresses the need for applying *ijtihād* as part of a consistent jurisprudential construction in the tradition of classical *fiqh*. Excepting, perhaps, the first of the ulama here presented, whose main emphasis may well be termed religio-moral revivalist, all have begun with modifying traditional *sharʿī* positions in a significant way.

The easily most popular *ʿālim* in contemporary Muslim India, Mawlānā Abūl Ḥasan Ali Nadwī, in a recent speech given at the second World Conference of Religion, Culture and Mission, in Hyderabad/Daccan in March 1987 and published in the original Urdu under the title *The Right Way of Proceeding for the Muslims of India*[21] (in light of their position, the teachings of Islam, historical developments, and their rights) has stated—in a sermon-like exhortation rather than analytical argument—his basic position with regard to our questions, which I also discussed with him.

He considers the situation of the Muslims in contemporary India unique: they neither rule nor are they ruled. Although, technically speaking, they are a minority, it would be wrong to apply this term to them, because they number 130 to 150 million. (Even the official government statistics, Nadwī adds, put them at 100 million.) Considering the role they have played in the history of

India, ruling the country successfully and blamelessly for 800 years, and taking into account the superior religious and moral equipment God has bestowed upon them as the final and best of *umam*, possessing Qur'an, ḥadīth, and *sīra* as well as the fully developed *sharīʿa*, they are bound to be asked by their co-citizens to give decisive leadership. Living in a republican (*jumhūrī*) setup, they hold the balance in lawmaking and other areas of national life. Nadwī appeals to his fellow Muslims to make use of their divinely bestowed gifts and thus to achieve moral excellence and ultimately leadership. Their compatriots inevitably will call upon them to take the lead in service, true guidance, justice, fear of God, and philanthropy (*insān-dosti*).

The way the Qur'anic prophet Yūsuf rose from being a prisoner in a foreign land to be finally entrusted with the financial and economic affairs of Pharaoh's Egypt indicates prophetically what the future has in store for the Muslims in India, if only they sincerely and comprehensively practice Islam. The comparison with the prophet Yūsuf speaks eloquently: as Yūsuf, the son of Ya'qūb, remained a stranger and adhered to the traditions of his people, so the Muslims are called to live in India, to make their unique contribution to their homeland and to succeed in it in every respect—but they must remember that they are strangers, a people (*millat*) set apart through special and divine guidance. Hence Nadwī, in the second part of his speech, stresses the absolute need for them to preserve their national personality (*millī tashakhkhuṣ*) of which their peculiar inherited social and cultural system (*nizam-i muʿashart-o-tahdhib*) and Muslim personal law are an essential and specific part. To ask Muslims to make any concession in this area would amount to demanding of them repudiating (*irtidād*) Islam and, therefore, is inconceivable. It is the civil, republican and religious right (*shahrī, jumhūrī, dīni ḥaqq*) of the Muslims to preserve their *sharīʿa* from any control (*tasalluṭ*) on the part of non-Muslim compatriots or the state.[22]

A question arises similar to the one we posed in to the pre-partition plan of the Jamʿiyyat: How viable is Nadwī's concept of the free Indian nation as one of largely self-governing communities, given the inevitable compulsions to develop, in terms of the modern nation state, pervasive national union in the fields of economic, educational, and even cultural life?

Mawlānā Waḥīduddīn Khān is the leader of the Al-Risāla movement, the editor of a monthly of the same name, and author of numerous books. His response (August 1987) to question 1 immediately marks his position as distinctly different from that of Nadwī: "Islam is not the name of a culture or of a political structure. Islam is the name of a personal action. And the opportunity to practice Islam personally remains the same in all situations, irrespective of whether Islam is politically in power or not."

Question 2 leads him to state that India is neither *dār al-islām* nor *dār al-ḥarb* but rather *dār al-daʿwa'*. "This means that Muslims, while establishing faith on a personal level, should, in equal measure, participate in the worldly matters of the country, just like their fellow-countrymen of other creeds. Furthermore, the presentation of their faith should be carried out peacefully. Permission to do so has been granted to us by the UN Charter of Human Rights as well as by the Indian constitution."

With regard to question 3 he comments: "The fact that the rights of different communities are accepted by the constitution of India is perfectly in consonance with Islam. As far as community matters are concerned, judgments should be based on the law of the country. So far as personal life is concerned, judgments should be based on Muslim personal law."

Replying to question 4 he takes up a sentiment expressed earlier by ulama belonging to or being close to the Jamʿiyyat al-ʿUlamāʾ: "In the present context, I feel that Muslims must look for basic guidance in those teachings of the Qurʾan which were revealed to the Prophet during the thirteen-year period he spent in Mecca—more than half his prophethood. The Prophet immigrated to Medina where he lived for ten years until his death, but it is the Meccan period which has the greater relevance to the prevailing situation in India. That is the period, therefore, which should serve as a model to Indian Muslims."

Regarding tasks of legal construction, Waḥiduddīn remarks that in his view the Salafī school of jurisprudence is, in principle, most relevant to the present-day situation in India since it "enshrines Islamic commands directly taken from the Qurʾan and Hadith whereas Ḥanafī *fiqh* was compiled basically to meet the needs of the ruling period of Islam."

Wahīduddīn's final remark leads to the presentation of the last two ulama of our survey. Here we can only indicate one or two jurisprudentially constructive points of their approach to the complex challenges the new Indian situation presents to the responsible religious scholar in India.

Mawlānā Saʿīd Aḥmad Akbarabādī (1908–85), the former dean of the faculty of Sunni theology at Aligarh Muslim University and for decades the editor of the Urdu monthly *Burhān*, in an essay on "The Predicament of India from the Point of View of the *sharīʿa*," directly deals with the question of the *sharʿī* legitimacy of sharing power with non-Muslims.[23] Basing his argument on the standards of Abū Ḥanīfa's definition—the strictest among the classical schools of law—concerning the conditions that have to be fulfilled to render a given territory *dār al-ḥarb*, he concludes that the Republic of India cannot by any standards be regarded as such, especially since it is not totally dominated (*istīlāʾ*) by the infidels. Such domination would be a fact only if the Muslims were debarred from government and did not enjoy freedom as they do.

Positively then, India, in Akbarabādī's view, is a secular, republican state, the government of which is not in the hands of any single group. Muslims have a share in government.

> Neither India nor any other republican country with a non-Muslim majority can today be considered *dār al-ḥarb*. . . . Akbarabādī reaches the conclusion that the *sharʿī* classification of countries is not applicable to the circumstances which prevail in modern India. . . .
>
> India, therefore, has to be considered by its Muslim inhabitants as their national home. All inhabitants of India, including the Muslims, are one nation, and all are under the obligation to act for the best interests of their country.[24]

Mawlānā Muḥammad Taqī Amīnī (b. 1926), the successor of Mawlānā Saʿīd Akbarabādī as head of the faculty of Sunni theology at Aligarh, in one of his recent writings,[25] deals with the related problem of how Muslims can legitimately (i.e., on *sharʿī* grounds) allow themselves to be voted into parliaments, councils, and local bodies or vote for such in a state which is not organized on theocratic or theo-nomocratic lines but which rather regards itself as the source and highest authority of the law. How can a Muslim believer legitimately bind himself by oath to the organs of a state which expressly does not understand itself as a "divine order?"

By way of preliminary remarks Amīnī stresses the need—in a situation as complex as that of the Muslims in the Republic of India—for adopting a gradual approach and the readiness for compromise, always with the goal in mind to bring about in India ultimately the establishment of religion (*iqāmat-i dīn*). Given the religiously plural character of Indian society and the absence of genuine Islamic life in India today, a secular government like that of the Indian Republic seems to be a boon. It provides the framework for the Muslim *millat* to participate in the politics and lawmaking of the nation, as a first step toward the hoped-for eventual establishment of religion. There is a great difference between accepting secularism as an ideology, by way of belief, and accepting it pragmatically as an inevitable fact, a way of organizing and governing a highly pluralistic state. Not rarely in this world a movement has to adopt such a provisional attitude on the way toward eventually achieving its full objectives and rights.

For Amīnī the Qurʾanic model for this approach and attitude is that of Moses and Aron. God sent them to Pharaoh of Egypt and asked them to "speak gently to him" (S. 20:44), although there was of course available to God the option of providing his servants with the fullness of divine power and assistance. In light of this Qurʾanic model and considering the given circumstances, are we not held to consider participation in the working of parliaments and assemblies in secular India as the legitimate means of representing our Muslim demands and realizing our Muslim rights? Such participation is legitimate and even indicated, if and as long as our objective is thus to service, as far as possible, Islam and humanity, or, at least, "to clear ourselves of blame before your Lord" (S. 7:164). Amīnī quotes this *āya* here as proof. In addition, he refers to some principles (*uṣūl*) as, for example, that of accepting the lesser evil in order to avoid the greater.

Finally, he refers to the model of the pact of Hudaybiyya (628 H.) where the Prophet accepted the shape of pact and oath provisions which in themselves were disagreeable to him and to his companions but which were, in the given situation, a necessary means for "achieving the independent building of the future."[26] Furthermore, an oath of allegiance and a pact practically amount to the same thing. Such pacts or oaths are legitimate on the way toward achieving one's objectives in a given system, under the condition, however, of "keeping one's strength of self" (*khud-mazbuti*). The model here is the Prophet's pact with the Jewish tribes soon after the Hijra and the notion of *umma wāḥida* mentioned in the Constitution of Medina.

In the circumstances of Muslim existence and participation in India there is, above all, a desperate need for bringing about greater unity among different Muslim groups and factions and for consistent and all-round efforts in the fields of religious education and propagation. In the interviews granted to me and in various recent writings Amīnī has outlined in detail how a Muslim consensus (*ijmāʿ*) should be realized and effectively expressed in India. A full presentation of these ideas, however, is the subject of another essay.

Conclusion

This study of Muslim views concerning the question of valid Muslim participation in India was completed in 1988. It has not taken into consideration the two most recent issues that have had a major impact on Hindu-Muslim relations in India. The first centers on the issue raised by Hindu fundamentalists represented by the Vishwa Hindu Parishad (VHT, World Hindu Organization), concerning Muslim demand for retaining the personal status law, which impedes implementation of the directive principle of a common civil code. The handling by the government of the Shah Bano case verdict (April 23, 1985) together with the Muslim Women (Protection of Rights on Divorce) Bill (May 6, 1986), which regulates the maintenance of divorced Muslim women, are perceived by VHT as another instance of appeasement of Muslims by government.

The second issue, which has had even greater impact on the relationship between the Muslim and Hindu communities, is the campaign by the VHT to "liberate" the birthplaces of Shri Rama (Ayodhya) and Shir Krishna (Mathura), as well as the Kashi Vishwanath Temple in Varanasi. Their initial effort to build a temple to Shri Rama at his presupposed birthplace at the site of the Babri Masjid, Babur's mosque in Ayodhya, culminated in the demolition of the Babri Masjid on January 6, 1992 ("Black Sunday"), an event that will have as yet immeasureable consequences for the future of India's Muslims, the Indian Republic, and South Asia as a whole.

The present survey has attempted to show against the background of a historical review both the wide spectrum of relevant Muslim reactions and views and the remarkable flexibility, independence of mind, and creativeness of a few Islamic scholars in contemporary India in the effort to come to terms with a situation that is challenging not only on the practical but also on the ideological level. At the same time, however, this survey highlights the urgent need for further, major advances in Islamic jurisprudential and theological thinking. Such advances remain to be taken on the way to providing eventually a genuinely Islamic rationale and validation for Muslim participation in the life in the democratically and secularly constituted Republic of India.

NOTES

1. Wilfred Cantwell Smith, *Islam in Modern History* (New York: Mentor Books, 1959; 1st ed. 1957), chap. 6.
2. Ibid., p. 287.
3. Ibid., p. 289.
4. Peter Hardy, *Partners in Freedom—and True Muslims* (Lund: Studentlitteratur, 1971), p. 12.
5. William Montgomery Watt, *Islamic Revelation in the Modern World* (London: Oxford University Press, 1968), pp. 102–3.
6. Hardy, *Partners*, p. 17.
7. Mushirul Haq, *Muslim Politics in Modern India* (Meerut: Meenakshi Prakashan, 1970), p. 94.
8. Ibid., pp. 95–97.
9. Hardy, *Partners*, p. 20.
10. Ibid., pp. 20–21.
11. Ibid., p. 30.
12. Ibid., pp. 35, 37.
13. Madani as cited in Yohanan Friedmann, "The Attitudes of the Jamᶜiyyat-i-ᶜUlamaʾ-i Hind to the Indian National Movement and the Establishment of Pakistan," *Asian and African Studies* (Jerusalem) 7 (1971): 190–97. Here quoted from the report in Abubaker A. Bagader, ed., *The Ulama in the Modern Muslim Nation State* (Kuala Lumpur: Muslim Youth Movement of Malaysia, 1983), pp. 55–77.
14. Hardy, *Partners*, passim.
15. Rasheeduddin Khan, "Problems and Prospects of Muslims in India," *Seminar* (New Delhi, June 1968), pp. 25–26.
16. Ibid., pp. 26–27.
17. Ibid., p. 31.
18. Ibid., p. 32.
19. Syed Shahabuddin, "A Muslim-Indian Manifesto," *The Statesman* (New Delhi) 15, no. 8 (1987), Forty Years of Independence Supplement, p. 9.

20. A.A.A. Fyzee, *A Modern Approach to Islam* (New Delhi: Oxford University Press; 1st ed. 1963), pp. 34–113 passim.

21. Abūl Ḥasan Ali Nadwī, *Musalmanan-i Hind ke liye ṣaḥīḥ rāḥ-i ʿamal* (Lucknow: Majlis-i Tahqiqat-o-Nashriyyat-i Islam, 1987).

22. Ibid., p. 25.

23. Saʿīd Aḥmad Akbarabādī, "Hindustan ki Sharʿi Haithiyyat," in *Burhān* (Delhi, July–September, 1966); Friedmann, "Attitudes," passim.

24. Friedman, "Attitudes," pp. 196–97.

25. Muḥammad Taqī Amīnī, *Mursalat, ʾIlmī aur Dīnī*, pt. 1 (Aligarh: Faculty of Diniyyat, 1986).

26. Ibid., p. 218.

16

The Dynamics of Religious Coexistence in Kerala: Muslims, Christians, and Hindus

Roland E. Miller

I would like briefly to examine here the pattern of interreligious relations in the state of Kerala in India. My purpose is to identify what can be learned from that particular history for dealing generally with issues involved in interreligious relations.

Such learning is certainly essential for the people of India beyond the confines of Kerala itself. The matter of interreligious relations continues to be a highly critical one in the life of that nation. Currently there is an almost tangible sense of danger ominously present in Indian society. It is not a feeling that can be well assessed through muted statistical descriptions of interreligious struggles. In the period 1986–88 there were 2,106 officially listed communal incidents in India resulting in casualties and serious unrest.[1] The bare figures, however, cannot express the real psychological impact of these events, especially in certain areas. The minister of state for home affairs, P. Chidambaram, in reviewing the situation, said India had gone through "a three-year period of what I would call competitive religiosity that added an acute dimension to the practice and profession of religion,"[2] and he has also spoken of "the growing sense of alienation and mistrust"[3] among religious communities.

Similarly, the interreligious mood in India cannot fully be grasped by formally analyzing the old/new religious fundamentalisms, on the rise both in the majority segment of the populace and among minorities, and other movements of thought, as though the phenomenon under discussion has to do with purely doctrinal views. Rather, there is an almost visceral level to the emotional reactions, the symbols involved being terms like Ramjanmabhoomi and Babri Masjid; the springs of reaction find their outlets in a variety of social, economic and political streams, and their expression is sometimes unscrupulously channeled by self-interest groups. In short, there is both an affective and an inclusive quality to the instincts and concerns. It is against this background that members of the Rajya Sabha, in their "Appeal for Communal Harmony" (October 12,

1989), noted with grave concern "the machinations of forces of fundamentalism and communalism" and called for all sections of the people "to affirm their faith in the rule of law, preserve and promote amity and harmony, and uphold the secular character and traditions of India."[4]

The general response of contemporary leaders in India to the crisis in inter-religious relations has been not so much to look back into the Indian experience for whatever learning it may provide, but rather to appeal for sanity in the name of the principles of togetherness and secularism. The principle of togetherness was set forth almost poignantly by the vice-chancellors of Indian universities who, in concert, issued the following plea (Srinagar, October 6, 1989):

> We are not a political group but we value—intellectually, culturally and emotionally, the richness that makes India what it is. The identity of India, which is its greatness too, lies in the variety of colors in its religious and cultural tapestry. The dangerous emotions let loose, disregarding this unique feature of our country, must be channelled in a constructive way, lest we should perish.
>
> We appeal therefore to the people of India, particularly all those involved in the crisis, that we should make Ayodhya into a unique cultural and religious center of the whole country—with a mosque, a temple, a church and a gurdwara, and also scholarly institutions to explore, understand and celebrate our great collective heritage.
>
> Let us resolve to convert our current crisis into a movement of universal belonging, a perennial source of togetherness in years to come. Let us stop short of madness and transform our passions into a force for reinforcing the India that is, and that which is seeking expression.[5]

The vice-chancellors, however, do not expound on the nature of the transformational power that will convert crises into positive movements. For Rajiv Gandhi, then prime minister of India, and for similarly minded colleagues, the source of that power is a principle outside of religion itself, namely the principle of secularism in its Indian form. In an address to the Lok Sabha he stated the following:

> A secular India alone is an India that can survive. Secularism is a condition of our existence. It is the essence of our tradition. Secularism and our nationhood are inseparable. We are a multi-lingual society, we are a multi-cultural society, but we are not a multi-national society. The single greatest contribution of India to world civilization is to demonstrate that there is nothing antithetical between diversity. Today's world is in desperate need of learning from India's experience. India's secularism is a global need because global secularism is inseparable from human survival. The never ceasing, running battle with communalism continues, and we must fight it. For India, secularism is not anti-religious or irreligious. The cardinal principle of secularism is equal respect for all religions, Sarva Dharma

> Samabhav. . . . The secular injunction of the Constitution must be carried out in good faith and with deep dedication. Religion must not be mixed with politics.[6]

It is not necessary to assume that in the prime minister's mind was the implication that there are insufficient resources within the religions themselves to deal with the problems created by their own existence, their views, and their expressions, but the logic almost leads to that conclusion. Since the religions which proclaim spiritual powers seem unwilling or unable effectively to draw upon those powers to bring about creatively new and healing situations, society must have recourse to the principle of positive secularism. Some may find such a conclusion understandable but unacceptable. Is it really true that the religions themselves cannot handle the problem of interreligious relations?

Gandhi's words underline the point that the issue of interreligious relations is a global one. It is not merely a Kerala or Indian problem. The loaded Indian term "communalism"—though seldom used in quite the same way and not fully understood outside South Asia—describes a dilemma that is well-nigh universal. It represents, as it were, the underside of the issue, embracing problems that exist both within segments of a single religious community and among discrete religious communities, in many parts of the world. Whatever learning we may have accumulated, therefore, must be shared. It may be suggested that the unique trialogical experience of Kerala state,[7] involving a close living together by Hindus, Muslims, and Christians over a span of thirteen centuries, yields some learning for India as a whole and for the wider human community that is still engaged in its long search for *pas humanitas* within a pluralistic context.

Following a brief introduction to society in Kerala, the interaction among Hindus, Christians, and Muslims in three broad periods will be examined: early Kerala history and its striking interreligious ambience; the incursion of the Portuguese and other Europeans, and its critical impact; and finally the new trends of the modern period of Kerala since 1947, with its suggestive developments. Concluding this overview is a brief reflection on the basic question, namely: In light of this experience, what can be suggested as a sound and enduring basis for viable interreligious living in a pluralistic world?

Kerala

To lead into the discussion, let me provide some general and undoubtedly well-known information. The state of Kerala provides an unusual laboratory for dealing with the question that has just been propounded. A union of former Travancore, Cochin, and Malabar, it is located on the southwest coast of India.

Only about 360 miles long and 50–70 miles wide, a total of 15,002 square miles, within its bounds it contains 25,453,680 people (1981 census; the present estimate is over 28 million).[8] This makes it perhaps the most densely populated geopolitical area in the world (1,697 per square mile in 1981; *ca.* 1,890 today), and much can be said about the implications of the demographic problem. It has a culture and a language called Malayalam, and its citizens are Malayalis.

Kerala's western openness to the sea and the attractiveness of its spices has made it a crossroads of trade from ancient times, opening its people to a host of influences in the past. In modern times, the state has been marked by a combination of progressiveness and turbulence, and has sometimes been viewed as providing a kind of "barometer" for the whole nation. Its people are alert in mind and sensitive in emotion. On the one hand, they are individualistic and divided; on the other hand, they are marked by traditional group loyalties. On the whole well educated, they are nevertheless economically poor and bear in microcosm almost all of the problems of India. In this restless and prophetic milieu, an uncommon religious situation prevails.[9]

Kerala is the only place in the world where Hindus, Muslims, and Christians live together in such numerical equilibrium (although Assam may be compared). Hindus comprise 58.15 percent, Christians 20.57 percent, and Muslims 21.25 percent of the population (1981: Hindus 14,801,347; Christians 5,233,865; Muslims 5,409,687). There is only a tiny sprinkling of other religious adherents, including the remnant of a once flourishing Jewish community. A bare statement of the official membership statistics does not do justice to the inner complexity of the religions; within Christianity, for example, there are more than sixty distinct groups. Furthermore, the erosive effect of secular and materialist philosophies, including that of communism, on traditional religious allegiance blurs the distinctions; modern Kerala has, in fact, freely elected three Marxist governments since 1956. Nevertheless, the reality that three major world religions coexist at such close quarters and in relatively similar proportions creates a unique situation and makes the question of interreligious relations a highly existential one.

Religious Interaction in the Past

The necessity for the different religions to find a viable way of interacting has been a fact of life throughout the history of Kerala. Early Dravidian religion, Aryanizing Brahmanism, Jainism, Buddhism, monism, bhakti, Judaism, Christianity, and Islam each fed the broad stream of Malayali religiosity. Sreedhara Menon summarizes the unique history in these words: "The story of the confluence of religions in Kerala is an exhilarating subject for study. Even in the ancient period Kerala became a meeting ground of all the Indian religions and philosophic systems, as well as the most important world religions."[10]

In the light of this development, the early period of Kerala must be considered as a remarkable one. Perhaps seldom in world history has there been such a successful period of positive interreligious living as seems to have existed in this area from the eighth to the fifteenth centuries. That conclusion may not be unreasonable, even though the evidence is somewhat circumstantial in nature and its interpretation is conditioned by nostalgia. Kerala Hindus, sharers of a faith noted for its tolerance, were at their most hospitable stage. Jews came, possibly after the destruction of Jerusalem, and were given a welcome and special privileges. Christians arrived, perhaps first as west Syrian traders in the fourth century, although Malayali Christians firmly hold that St. Thomas founded the church.[11] They settled in the southern area of the region, were received kindly, intermarried with high caste Hindus, and founded the Syrian church of Kerala. ("Syrian" Christians, interspersed among several denominations, comprise about 65 percent of Christians in Kerala today.)[12]

It is the Syrian Christians who link Kerala Christianity with medieval Christians in the Middle East. During the early period of the church's existence that link was forged not only by the strong St.Thomas tradition itself, or through the retention of Syriac in the liturgy, but also through continued immigration, occasional personal contact, and the provision of episcopal leadership. While in everyday matters Syrian Christians in Kerala absorbed indigenous culture patterns, in ecclesiastical matters they looked to the Middle East, especially for the supply of clergy.[13] At an early stage they established a relationship with the Seleucia-Ctesiphon church of Persia, expressing allegiance to its patriarch and intermittently receiving ordained clergy, especially through the see of Rewardashir. Thus the Nestorian orientation of Syrian Christianity, which lasted for centuries, was established. Later, when the advance of Islam made it more difficult to maintain the Persian connection, Kerala Christians gradually began to turn to west Syria for clerical help, thus bringing the influence of Antioch and the Jacobite tradition into Malayali life. With the coming of the Portuguese, Syrian Christianity in Kerala formally divided into Romo-Syrian and Orthodox Jacobite streams. Despite these affiliations and influences, however, there is no evidence that Malayali Christians themselves became involved in the christological controversies that underlay these divisions; indeed, since the New Testament was not translated into Malayalam until 1830, the basis for such involvement was absent.

It was not only Christians from the Middle East who entered Kerala at an early stage. Arabs also came, both before and after the advent of Islam, in connection with their control of the Indian Ocean trade. They too intermarried and interacted with Hindus, out of which developed the large Mappila Muslim community of Kerala. The word "Mappila," applied to both Muslims and Christians (but now generally limited in use to the Muslims of Malabar), was an honorific term applied to respected and welcome visitors from abroad.[14] Granted that the sources are scanty, through all this we do not discern any sign of the intrusion of religious militance, or even any overt indication of unhappy relationships. As far as can be known, the four communities coexisted in a positive and friendly manner, and even K.M. Panikkar's strong conclusion may be valid: "Malabar was leading a comparatively happy, though politically isolated life. . . . Trade flourished, different communities lived together without friction, and absolute religious toleration existed."[15] We cannot rule out the possible existence of some tensions and, of course, it must be remembered that the number of Jews, Christians, and Muslims at this stage was relatively small.

What was the paste or dynamic that held things together in this "golden age" of toleration? It appears to have been primarily mutual commercial advantage. The Syrian Christians and Arab Muslims were predominantly traders, and they collaborated with the Hindu rajas and merchants to establish a flourishing trade with China, the Middle East, and Europe. The interrelationships in Kerala had started in a friendly way for this reason and it was to the advantage of all concerned that they continue. There are also some indications that the edges of the religions themselves were less hardened than they were to become at a later stage.

From this history arises a question for our day—is mutual commercial advantage a sufficiently enduring basis for interreligious harmony? The question, of course, spills over into a wider frame of reference—is enlightened economic self-interest an adequate basis for forging harmony at international levels between nations, as some evidently have come to believe? The Kerala experience informs us that commercial interaction is indeed an important binding factor in human relations, but subsequent Kerala history also reveals that interrelationships based on economic self-interest alone are built on inadequate foundations. Something more is required. That was to be sadly proved in the next period.

With the coming of the fifteenth century, the age of harmony based on commerce moved to an age of rivalry based on economic and political domination and characterized by a militant religious flavor. The people who ushered in the new age were the Portuguese, heralds of the European period, agents of manifest destiny, and the partly unwitting destroyers of a precious interreligious harmony. They made this impact, largely, by taking over the trade between Kerala and the rest of the world, blocking out the Arabs and the Muslims, and to some extent the Syrian Christians, thus removing the primary basis for the existing relationship. That harmony had not become a deep life principle and so could not resist the new influences. The Portuguese further disturbed matters by making religion itself a part of the fabric of domination, as it were, uniting religion, politics, and economics into one imperialistic whole. Within a century the patterns of interreligious living were radically altered, and up to the twentieth century we have a history of rivalry, deteriorating relations—especially between Hindus and Muslims—and a great deal of tragic violence.

The Impact of Portuguese Christianity

The story of the Portuguese incursion into Kerala and its subsequent impact has yet to be fully told.[16] There is no doubt, however, that the crusading spirit of the Portuguese, born in the medieval matrix of Christian-Muslim encounter, introduced a major new element into the religious scene of southwest India and contributed significantly to a dramatic reversal in relationships.

We will not attempt to trace the history of Portugal's rise in fortune that led to its becoming a dominant maritime power. It is important to recognize in the expressions of that power an extension of the same crusading spirit that drove the Moors from southern Portugal.[17] Prince Henry the Navigator (1394–1460) led the way. This intrepid and brilliant Master of the Order of Christ—which had replaced the Knights Templar in Portugal—probed the western coast of Africa, hopefully seeking a river connection with the believed-in kingdom of Prester John, supposing that this linkage would result in the defeat of Muslims and the regaining of the Holy Land. "It is certain," comments Jayne, "that the master motive which animated the Navigator was neither scientific, commercial nor political. . . . It was essentially religious. Before all else, Prince Henry was a crusader."[18]

It is somewhat difficult, however, to assess the primacy among the various motivations for the Portuguese expansion. Clearly, there were intertwined factors of commerce, imperial power, national energy, and religious zeal. The specific goal of the daring enterprise was the search for a sea route to India. Arabs in conjunction with Egyptians and Venetians controlled the rich India trade, and there was an old and fervent desire to break that stranglehold. As Panikkar suggests: "It was the desire to reach Indian waters and share in the spice trade without going across Egypt that provided motive for the high adventure."[19] What turned this dream into a nightmare for Kerala, however, was its marriage with a militant religious vision and method. Papal bulls (1493 and 1506) had been promulgated, blandly dividing the new world into Portuguese and Spanish hemispheres in the interests of religious conquest, as well as imperial power and commercial advantage. That purpose was clearly evident in the *padroado*, the paper charter granted to the Portuguese.[20] When Vasco da Gama finally landed in Calicut in 1498 in his small but heavily armed vessel, the *San Gabriel*, ushering in the era of European dominance in Asia, this was not only a portent for the future of trade, but it was also a religious sign to the nations. It was not long before the sign was fulfilled. There was a brief, almost humorous moment of rapprochement immediately after the Portuguese landed, when da Gama and his followers prayed in a temple, believing that they were in a Christian church.[21] But when the Hindu king of Calicut (the *zamorin*) hesitated to make a new agreement while his allies, the Muslim merchants, opposed the initiatives of the newcomers, da Gama and the Portuguese struck back with a series of sea attacks, marked by frequent cruelty, that eventuated in the consolidation of Portuguese power in key centers along the Malabar coast.

The religious theory and policy very quickly became quite explicit. When Pedro Cabral followed da Gama in the second voyage to Malabar (1502), King Manuel of Portugal gave the following instructions (as reported by João de Barros): "In order to persuade these people to accept the truths, the priests and friars were to put before them all natural and legal arguments, and employ ceremonies prescribed by Canon Law. And if these people were stubborn in their errors, and would in no wise accept the tenets of the true faith, denying the law of peace which should unite mankind for the preservation of the human race, and raising difficulties and obstacles to the exercise of trade and commerce, the means by which peace and love among men are established and maintained—for trade is the basis of all human policy—they should in this case be taught by fire and sword and all the horrors of war."[22]

In interpreting the pope's rights as reflected in the papal bulls, de Barros further affirms: "The Moors and Gentiles are outside the law of Jesus Christ, which is the true law that everyone has to keep under pain of damnation to eternal fire. If then the soul be so condemned, what right has the body to the privilege of our laws? It is true . . . they are reasoning beings and might if they lived be converted to the true faith, but inasmuch as they have not shown any desire as yet to accept this, we Christians have no duties toward them."[23]

It was the redoubtable Affonso Albuquerque (1453–1515), with his deep hatred for Muslims, who became the living exemplar of that approach. When he captured Goa in 1510, thereby establishing Portuguese power on a strong footing, he sent the following letter to the king of Portugal.

> I burnt the city and put all to the sword. . . . Whenever we could find them no Moor was spared, and they filled the mosques with them and set them on fire. I ordered the farmers and Brahmins to be spared. We counted and found that 6,000 souls of Moorish men and women had been slain. . . . This is the first time that vengeance has been taken in India for the treachery and villainy the Moors have done to your Highness and your people. . . . I am not leaving a single Moorish tomb or building standing, and the men taken alive I have roasted. . . .

> We took here some Moorish women . . . and some poor fellows wished to marry them and remain in the country. . . . I am handing over the property and lands of the Mosque to the Church of St. Catherine, on whose day the Lord gave us the victory on account of her merits, and I am building this Church in the large enclosure of the fortress.[24]

This was the same Albuquerque who conceived a plan to invade Medina, seize the bones of the Prophet, and hold them in ransom in exchange for the Holy Land!

It seemed as though the Crusades were being reborn in southwest India, and the Portuguese did not greatly differentiate in applying their sanctions against those who opposed their will, be they Hindu, Muslim, or indigenous Christian. This became clear at the Synod of Diamper in 1599 when Archbishop Menzies compelled the Syrian Christians to make public profession and written adherence to the Catholic faith. In the process he extirpated their relation with the patriarch of Babylon, burning valuable Syrian manuscripts and books, and placing Malayali Christians under subjection to the Goa Inquisition. It is perhaps too strong to say, as Dorsey does,[25] that "Christian persuasion was quite the exception in the Portuguese system of conversion, and persecution the almost universal rule."[25] There were some thoughtful attempts at communication, and persuasion through the giving of gifts was a normal procedure,[26] but an atmosphere of antagonism prevailed.

The impact of the Portuguese period, followed by the Dutch, British, and French incursions, was far-reaching. Hindu raged against Hindu, the Hindu zamorin of Calicut cooperating with Muslims against the Portuguese, while the Hindu raja of Cochin opposed him, and supported Christians. Christians turned against Christians, as the Syrian and Latin traditions struggled and divided.[27] Indigenous Christians, tending to align with the Christian foreigners, became alienated from those who opposed them. Hindus became suspicious of Christians and the entente between Hindus and Muslims was shattered. Muslims were in a state of distress, as represented by the tragic cries of the famed Zayn al-Dīn in his *Tuḥfat al Mujāhidīn*.[28] There was confusion and trauma, with violence not uncommon. It was only the vital everyday relations of ordinary Hindus, Muslims, and Christians in the towns and villages of Kerala that preserved society from permanent alienation. While not all of the weaknesses in community relations could be traced to Portuguese influence, there can be no doubt of the dramatic and deleterious effects of this period, which continued to modern times.

In the course of time, the Hindus and the foreign Christians achieved a kind of cautious *modus vivendi* and in the end it was the Muslims who felt the deepest sense of alienation. They were oppressed by the formidable Hindu-Christian combination, now apparently turned against them, and were burdened with economic grievances. These emotions were fired by the intrusion of the *jihād* spirit into their active philosophy, partially as the result of a temporary period of Muslim rule from nearby Mysore; this militant spirit from the north, channeled through Tipu Sultan, now penetrated Mappila psychology. Oppressed, aggrieved, and marked by hopelessness, the Mappila Muslims reacted in a way that is common to oppressed and hopeless people anywhere—the reaction was severe and often violent. The flame that was kindled in Portuguese days burned furiously through the British period, and Malabar especially became notorious for its communal unrest. Interreligious living became interreligious struggle, and the golden age of harmony was only a fading memory.

What are the lessons of this period, covering 1500–1921? They are transparent enough, the most obvious one being that violence in religious interrelationships never solves anything for the parties involved, and leaves a heritage of bitterness for generations to come. A second is that interreligious living characterized by the active dominance of one religious group over others is doomed to difficulty. Such a situation inevitably produces reactions, usually resulting in abrasive conflict. A less obvious lesson is that mere coexistence, possibly enforced by some external schoolmaster such as the British came to be in Malabar, is also not a viable pattern for successful interreligious living. In Malabar Hindus and Muslims lived side by side under British control for 150 years (1792–1947), cautiously coexisting to be sure, but not really living together, although many exceptions could be noted. Mere coexistence is essentially a vacuum, which at first opportunity gets filled up with "seven other devils." The final lesson of this period points to the weakness of basing interreligious relationships on common enmity.

Let us consider the latter truth, which is illustrated clearly by a series of startling events that took place in Malabar from 1919 to 1921. In wider India the Hindu-dominated Non-Cooperation Movement, dedicated to liberating the nation from foreign rule, and the Muslim-dominated Khilāfat Movement, dedicated to the defence of the caliphate in Turkey, were drawn together by their opposition to a common enemy, the British. During this period, amazing demonstrations of religious amity took place in Malabar. It was quickly proven, however, that such a marriage of convenience has no enduring strength. A variety of unfortunate circumstances soon led to the notorious Mappila Rebellion of 1921,[29] which not only affected the Hindu-Muslim entente at all-India levels, but which seemed to put the final nail in the coffin of Kerala's interreligious relationships. Mappila Muslims, aroused by the rhetoric of the freedom movement leaders, including Mahatma Gandhi and Shawkat ʾAlī, prematurely rose in a violent protest against British rule. Malabar Hindus, proponents of *ahimsa* and fearful of their safety, pulled back from the conflagration they had helped to kindle. Mappilas, outraged by what they interpreted as betrayal, turned against their compatriots. What had begun in hope ended in disaster. The rebellion wound up with Muslims violently attacking and at times forcibly converting Hindus, and Hindus joining with the hated British Christian imperialists to suppress Muslims. The wheel of relationships had now fully turned.

So Kerala entered the modern period, the heir of both positive and negative experiences in interreligious living. Individually the people of the area were living together in all sorts of ordinary, pragmatic, and healthy day-to-day relationships. Intuitively, they also knew that as religious communities they had to find more positive ways of living together than those of the past four centuries. There was no sustained intellectual and emotional effort, however, to isolate and promote a formal principle of action that could be applied to the task of interreligious living. Is the search for such a formal principle arbitrary, artificial and illusory? Yet, if it is not possible to identify something stronger than is evident in the long history of Kerala relations, are we then doomed to a future of ongoing conflict? Questions such as these faced the Malayalis of Kerala as they began their life in free, post-partition India.

Interreligious Living in Kerala Today

We come to the present. The years since 1947 have introduced new factors into the Kerala interreligious situation including the influence of patriotism, the impact of secularization, and the desire for community self-esteem. Of deeper significance has been the growth of mutual respect. This and other impulses, such as greater mutual awareness, understanding and cooperative action, have worked together to produce what many describe as "Kerala's enviable record in communal harmony." Recent tragic events, however, have also raised the question of whether the need for a fundamental principle of action can be truly and finally met.

Patriotism

On the wider Indian scene the great new event since independence has been nation building, and this has introduced to the people of India a new and conscious policy related to interreligious living. The nation must be unified and developed, and religious interaction must be seen in that light. The freedom movement tended to make things less advantageous for Indian Christians, and the partition movement tended to make things quite disadvantageous for Indian Muslims. The great leaders of India's independence movement, however, stood for religious respect, a special form of secularism that was value-laden, and the affirmation of minorities as key principles for the new nations. Mahatma Gandhi gave his life for those principles, while Pandit Nehru on his part resisted any suggestions that India should revert to a Hindu raj and succeeded in fashioning it as a secular state, marked by respect for religion in general and equality for all religious expressions.[30]

At the same time India embarked on a determined scheme of national integration—the intention of which was to diminish all social, religious, and other differences in the interest of a "larger" principle, namely the good of the nation. Individual religions were not thereby downgraded; in fact, considerable efforts were taken to ensure their legal protection. But hard edges were to be softened, historical differences brought forward from the classical and medieval periods were to be dispelled, and people were to see each other as coworkers in a common cause. Gandhi's philosophy was the model for a basic education scheme that expressed in curricular terms the idea that all children were to experience some form of common prayer and praise as part of their growing up and growing together.

National integration, as a formal principle applied to interreligious living, did not leave Kerala unaffected. The process of integration in the state was further accelerated by the Aikya Kerala movement ("united Malayalis in one state"), which in 1957 resulted in the formation of the present state of Kerala with its linguistic and cultural homogeneity. This had its own effect on interreligious living. The democratic system of government threw together adherents of all religions in a give-and-take legislative process. The state government, the chief Kerala employer, transferred its huge staff every three years, without particular regard for religious affiliations. Development programs of various kinds involved members of one religious persuasion in the service of members of other religious communities. Leaders of all religious communities began throwing their influence into support of the new direction. The revered father of modern Kerala, K.P. Kesava Menon, proposed love of country as the common, binding factor that would overcome communalism. People's religious and cultural differences, he said, would remain, but "the consciousness that they are Indians must grow, and in that they should take pride."[31]

The spirit of love for country, encouraged by pragmatic government pressures toward national integration—is this the looked for, needed, and adequate dynamic for viable interreligious living? Like the economic factor, it is certainly a powerful influence, but it too does not seem strong enough to prevail when the going gets tough. Despite the great emphasis on patriotism, there have been many communal incidents in the nation as a whole, as we have noted, including some in Kerala,[32] indicating that the search for an effective dynamic still must go on.

Secularization

Secularization (sometimes called "secularism") in Kerala has many forms. In general, it is characterized by an emphasis on the practical, tangible, material sides of life in this world, with lesser value placed on spiritual concerns. As traditional religious allegiance correspondingly declines in importance, the very problem of interreligious living is set aside as a nonissue. One form of this approach is communism (a long-time force in the state), which holds that religion is a private matter and not worthy of struggling over as a formal issue. In Kerala, communism seeks to solve the "problem" of religion by privatizing it and by lowering the common estimation of its importance in society, if not denigrating the subject. While this point of view has brought a new perspective on the question of religious interaction and has helped to soften communal emotions, it fails as a principle for interreligious living because it does not take seriously the subject of religion itself.

The impact of the consistent anticommunalism position of Marxist parties in Kerala, however, should not be underestimated. It has helped to modify attitudes and overcome problems. The position is represented by the redoubtable elder statesman of the Communist Party (Marxist), E. M. S. Namboodiripad, who stated: "I declare I am not a Hindu or any other religionist. I am a human being, and I am a Communist."[33] He affirmed that "majority communalism has become the immediate threat to our national unity. . . . It is, however our conviction that effective struggle against majority communalism requires that no quarter is given to minority fundamentalism and communalism."[34]

Self-Esteem

The strong desire for community self-esteem is an aspect of the growing sophistication of the Kerala population. This in part derives from the influence of modernism and education. There is a developing feeling among ordinary people that they do not want to engage any further in the old forms of religious struggle. It is felt that the old style of militancy and contentious relationships reflect invidiously on the image of the particular religion and religious community, and in the interest of community self-respect such reactions are henceforth to be avoided.

This dynamic is felt particularly by the Muslim community in Kerala, a society trying to escape from its inherited reputation for fanaticism, and within the Mappila community it is especially its younger and progressive elements that maintain this view. Christians and Hindus, however, also participate in the thrust for community pride, and community uplift has become a kind of slogan for everyone. The spirit of direct religious rivalry has been absorbed to a degree in a kind of race for educational, economic and social advance, and religious energy has been partially redirected into a competition for community uplift. In the process, community self-esteem has become a driving force. Although the search for community pride has helped and will continue to help create a peaceful context for religious interaction, it is doubtful whether such an *inner-directed* concern can be considered as the effective power for viable interreligious living.

Respect for Others

There is something further in Kerala that seems to come closer to the essence of things. Within the contemporary experience, there is visible an outer-directed attitudinal change that is perhaps best described as mutual respect. The word *respect* may seem prosaic. In the light of Kerala history, however, the term is significant. It represents a powerful force that affects a broad range of relationships. There are many overt signals of this new feeling:

—Muslims picking out universals in the Qur'an and emphasizing them in their literature.
—Muslims speaking with such words as these: "The whole people are subjects of one God. We have, therefore, to live in peace and harmony by honouring all the religious faiths and sentiments. Then only can we build a prosperous India."[35]
—Muslims at the village of Kodur cosponsoring a program of Christian songs, together with Christians and Hindus.
—Christians donating funds for the construction of Muslim mosques and orphanages.
—Christians giving employment to Hindus and Muslims in their charitable institutions.
—Hindus describing Muslims as "serious about their faith," instead of utilizing pejorative phrases familiar in the past.
—Hindus working together in state politics with the Muslim League, considered to be a communal organization.
—A Hindu at Managhat, Palghat District, throwing himself into the flaming hut of his Muslim neighbor and dying to save the lives of two trapped children.

The growing attitude of respect also informs the area of interreligious communication. The sense of mission of the three religions is still vital, and energies and resources continue to be expended on the intentional promotion of the respective faiths. The expressions of that commitment to mission, however, are now generally sensitive rather than aggressive. Change in religious identity, when it occurs, may not be appreciated, but is generally condoned. There is evident a desire for understanding, and mutual respect has significantly increased.

The signals are everywhere and mutual respect is, indeed, a powerful force. The question is, is it strong enough? Is this the principle upon which positive interreligious living can be built? There is a temptation to reply positively. Yet experience indicates that it may not be so. Standing alone, mutual respect may not be able to bear up the structure of religious harmony. It may be argued, however, that by combining mutual respect with three other elements, we can achieve the strength of four pillars. Those elements are mutual knowledge, motivation, and cooperative action.

Mutual Knowledge

We are increasingly alert to the fact that mutual respect must be founded on an educated awareness of other religions. Within Kerala, where Hindus, Muslims, and Christians have lived side by side for so long, there is a considerable quotient of interreligious knowledge in terms of the popular practices of the religious traditions, including festivals, rituals and the like; but there is little mutual knowledge of the intellectual expressions of the respective traditions, and still less of the noble aspects of their artistic and literary heritage. Wherever there have been genuine scholarly efforts to make these known with accuracy, fairness, and common sympathy, the resulting appreciation has been great and there has been a tangible increase in respect and understanding.

Motivation

Second, mutual respect is fundamentally and critically dependent on the element of motivation. During the golden age of Kerala's interreligious harmony, it is clear that Malayalis in some sense wanted to live together and work together in amity. In the end, that motivational element was not strong enough to overcome the tensions that arose. However, the lesson is clear. An "I want to" factor must enter the process of interreligious relations. Despite our historical differences, despite our different approaches and disagreements, and despite the seemingly demonic efforts to destroy human relationships, I want to respect you, and therefore I will. It is within the power of Christian, Hindu, and Muslim religious leaders, according to their respective terms of reference, to plant an "I want to" seed in the heart of that tradition's adherents. That obligation of leadership is thus far only sporadically accepted and lightly proclaimed in Kerala, although there are many remarkable exceptions to that general statement.

Cooperative Action

Third, mutual respect is intimately related to the element of cooperative action on behalf of the general good. The political working together in democratic Kerala for the uplift of society has been so salutary for interreligious relations precisely because of this element. Everywhere where interreligious living is both a necessity and a goal, nothing exceeded the value of joint efforts to help underprivileged and differing people. A notable example of some progress in this area of Kerala's life is its Mahila Samajum, gatherings of women from every segment of society and representing all religions, which are dedicated to practical efforts in life improvement and social development. In many ways, it has been women and youth who have made the signs of hope in the labyrinthine picture of Kerala's social and religious interaction.[36]

The Fifth Pillar

Is mutual respect, founded on objective knowledge, fed by motivational inspiration, and released in cooperative action, the possible principle for positive interreligious living? Events that took place in 1990 were to raise the question of whether something more is needed.

It was the Babri Masjid-Ramjanmabhoomi issue that particularly agitated the nation of India, engulfed it in communal stress, and finally disturbed the communal harmony in Kerala. The site of an existing mosque in Ayodhya (U.P.), founded by the Mughul emperor about 1528, was claimed by some Hindu groups as the birthplace of the deity Ram, as well as the site of an earlier temple. It was argued by the Vishwa Hindu Parishad that the mosque should be moved and a new temple built to replace the one allegedly demolished by the emperor. The subsequent agitations, inflammatory rhetoric, and an ill-fated march (*rathayatra*) culminated in the arrest of the Bharatiya Janata Party leader, an assault on the mosque, the fall of the national government, and a major realignment of parties. In his farewell speech (November 8, 1990), the outgoing prime minister, V. P. Singh, asked the poignant question: "Shall religious polarization divide the country?" He decried the use of religion for purposes of power and to ignite the flames of hatred, declaring: "A resolution that comes out of mutual respect and generosity of spirit will be the strongest foundation of this nation's unity and an abiding testament to religious tolerance."[37]

The impact of these events lapped over into Kerala. Mappila Muslims had already been deeply exercised over the loss of lives and the destruction of homes and mosques experienced by their northern compatriots; however, the geographical distance from the incidents had insulated their reaction. The murder of a madrasa teacher named ʿAlī Musaliar at Kattur, Trichur District, on October 14, 1990, blamed on the Rashtriya Sevak Sangh, not only created deep concern among all Mappilas but also precipitated a series of antisocial events in the following days at Cochin, Quilon, and Tirurangadi. It was to the credit of Malayalis in general, as well as government administrators and the heads of political parties and religious communities, that extreme reactions were largely contained, the difficulties overcome, and peace maintained. Leading the way in the demands for communal harmony, the ruling Communist Party (Marxist) called for a public demonstration of the will of Malayalis to remain calm and to stand together against the communal unrest. On October 30, 1990, it formed a remarkable chain of linked hands, stretching from Manjeshwaram to Parassala, from one end of Kerala to the other, amidst driving rains, thus symbolizing the view of many citizens of the state.

The events of 1990, and the way the events were dealt with in Kerala, revealed two things. The first is that the positive trends in modern Kerala history, noted above, have had cumulative force. All these factors taken together have strengthened the sinews of Malayali interreligious relations materially. The experience indicates that it is possible to alter negative histories and introduce positive change, at least to some degree. The second lesson is that something more is needed to lift the relationships to a level where they cannot be so readily and destructively disturbed.

Is mutual respect, founded on objective knowledge, fed by motivational inspiration, and released in cooperative social action, the possible principle for positive interreligious living? Is this what we have learned from Kerala's long experience? There are those who think that the issue goes deeper, who think that there must be a kind of "fifth pillar" set in the midst of the four.

That pillar is simply described. Some believe that the ultimate resource for positive interreligious living must be a religious one, that it must flow from the spiritual depths of the religions themselves, and that the spiritual ideal to be espoused is the principle of unselfish love. No one has made this point better than Khan Bahadur K. Muhammad in his book *Māppilamār Engottu* ("Whither the Mappilas?").[38] He declares: "When two communities live together, they must forgive much and forget much." He calls on his fellow Mappilas "to improve the condition of their own community and to establish a situation wherein they live in brotherly love on a basis of equality with other communities." They should therefore cast out all religious hostility, cooperate wholeheartedly and trustfully with Hindus, change the attitude of others by their own behavior, and "give honor to all." Although he does not use the precise words, this distinguished Muslim educator is evidently talking about the principle of understanding and forgiving love. This he regards as the force that can really throw bridges across the chasms of misunderstanding and alienation.

Those who share that view will engage in the bridge-building task from the same spiritual center. Without that central pillar the structure of interreligious relations seems impossibly frail, and tends to collapse like a house of cards when even minor stress is put upon it from the social and political realm. In his resignation letter from the central government of India, the minister of state for home affairs, Subodh Kant Sahay, stated (November 4, 1990): "The nation today is confronted with a situation of grave crisis. My experience in the Home Ministry makes me realize that in every State, in every district and almost every village there exist situations of sharp conflicts on caste and communal bases. Never in our past experience in this country, particularly in north India, have we witnessed such widespread violence."[39] This vivid comment comes after forty-five years of intensive national effort to deal with the scourge of communalism. It is not surprising, therefore, that an anguished Kerala voice should inquire: "What then is the reason that makes us humans shed this amalgam of love, understanding and tolerance? What turns us into raving brutes, blind to all reason and understanding? . . . Why is it that compassion loses all its beauty and strength and remains but a quality for the weak?"[40] It is certain that we should join in analyzing basic cause. It is also quite certain that the absence of the strong fifth pillar makes the whole structure weak. Perhaps the voice of the ancient Psalmist needs to be heard: "God is in the midst of her, she shall not be moved."[41] An exegesis appropriate to the field of interreligious relationships might be: "If love is in the midst of her, she shall not be moved."

Yet realism also demands a hearing. It may be suggested by some that although the *ultimate* principle of understanding and forgiving love is the goal toward which we must strive, it is not likely to become the widely accepted and operative principle this side of heaven. Our lot in this world, in a sense, is to be the people of the penultimate. In the interest of moving toward achievable objectives, therefore, is it not perhaps wiser to settle for a *penultimate* principle that is also worthwhile struggling for and that can be practically advanced? Is that principle mutual respect, joined with educated awareness, motivated by genuine desire, and expressed through cooperative action? Will this provide the practical agenda we need? Or is it something else? What arises? What should we do? Employing the words of the vice-chancellors of India's universities, what will "transform our passions" and "convert our current crisis into a movement of universal belonging?" If it is not the above, what then is that sound, sufficiently dynamic and enduring basis for viable interreligious living in trialogical Kerala and in a pluralistic world?

The long search must close in on the answer. It seems appropriate to conclude with a line from Sanjayan (d. 1942), a Malayali poet:

It's getting late,
it's getting late.
Where are you,
My dream?[42]

NOTES

1. Report of the minister of state for home affairs in answer to Rajya Sabha starred question no. 141, of July 27, 1989, cited in *Muslim India* 7, no. 81 (September 1989): 419. A total of 1,024 deaths and 12,352 injured were reported in the official statistics, which some would regard as a low estimate.

2. In a speech to the Lok Sabha, October 12, 1989, quoted ibid. 7, no. 83 (November 1989): 504 ff.

3. In a speech to the Rajya Sabha, May 2, 1989, quoted ibid. 7, no. 78 (June 1989): 264.

4. Ibid. 7, no. 83 (November 1989): 500.

5. Ibid., p. 503.

6. Ibid. 7, no. 78 (June 1989): 246. It is significant that S. Shahabuddin, editor of *Muslim India* and staunch defender of the Indian Muslim community's interests, declares that "at this stage of the political development the priority of a minority group like the Muslim Indian must be to send to the Lok Sabha a group of men of moral integrity and secular commitment . . . call it a secular Lobby, if you like" (7, no. 79 (July 1989): 291). Rafiq Zakaria, *The Struggle within Islam* (New York: Viking Penguin, 1989), gives another view of the ambiguous situation of Indian Muslims caught between the two conflicting forces of secularism and fundamentalism. He states that "no other Muslim in any part of the world is faced with such a dilemma or finds himself so confused and helpless" (pp. 262 f.). For other approaches, cf. Roland E. Miller, "Modern Indian Muslim Responses," in H. G. Coward, ed., *Modern Indian Responses to Religious Pluralism* (Albany: State University of New York Press, 1987), pp. 235–69.

7. An example of the opposite of trialogical awareness is represented by Balraj Madhok, *Indianization* (Delhi: Hind Pocketbook (P) Ltd., 1970), p. 27. A leader of the former Jana Sangh party, he affirmed that "there is no such thing as Muslim culture or Christian culture in India. There is only one culture which is common to all India," and he further commended Indian Muslims who "continued to follow the Hindu way of life" (p. 53).

8. Hindus make up 82.64 percent of the Indian religious tapestry, Muslims 11.43 percent; and Christians 2.43 percent. These and following statistics are taken from the *Census of India*, 1981, especially Paper 4 of 1984: "Household Population by Religion of Household," which corresponds to Series C-VII of 1961 and 1971 Census (Delhi: Registrar General, Government of India, 1984).

9. For the treatment of Kerala, I have made extensive use of Roland E. Miller, *The Mappila Muslims of Kerala—A Study in Islamic Trends* (Madras: Orient Longman, 1976; rev. ed., London: Sangan Books, 1992). This work was originally produced as a doctoral thesis under the warm encouragement and expert guidance of Willem Bijlefeld.

10. Sreedhara Menon, *A Survey of Kerala History* (Kottayam: National Book Stall, 1967), p. 87. See his chapter, "The Confluence of Religions," pp. 87–112.

11. The traditional date cited for the coming of the Jerusalem merchant, Thomas of Cana, is A.D. 345. G. Moraes, *A History of Christianity in India* (Bombay: P. S. Manantala & Sons Pvt. Ltd., 1964), argues strongly in chapter 2 for the St. Thomas tradition and provides a convenient summary of the data. L.W. Brown, *The Indian Christians of St. Thomas* (Cambridge: Cambridge University Press, 1956), holds that the evidence is inconclusive (pp. 43–65). For the Nestorian background to the Syrian church of Kerala, see Eugene Tisserant, *Eastern Christianity in India* (Westminster, Md.: Newman Press, 1957), pp. 181 ff.

12. Manfred Turlach, *Kerala, Politische-Sociale Strukture und Entwicklung eines Indischen Bundeslades* (Weisbaden: Otto Harassowitz, 1970), has an excellent statistical analysis. In 1961, 59.1 percent of the Kerala Christians were Roman Catholic (22.5 percent Latin Catholic, 36.6 percent Syrian Catholic); 20 percent were Orthodox Jacobite Syrian; 7.9 percent were Mar Thoma; 5.5 percent were Church of South India; and 7.5 percent were others.

13. Brown, *The Indian Christians of St. Thomas*, affirms, "They were Christians of Mesopotamia in faith and worship and ethics; they were Indians in all else" (p. 2). Menon, *A Survey of Kerala History*, observes of Syrian Christians today that they "have completely assimilated themselves in the community in which they live by adopting the language, dress and habits of their Hindu brethren. Though Christians in faith, they are Keralites in all other respects" (p. 102).

14. Cf. Miller, *The Mappila Muslims*, pp. 39–51, for the origin of Muslims in Kerala, and pp. 30–32 for the significance of the name *Mappila*.

15. K.M. Panikkar, *Malabar and the Portuguese* (Bombay: D.B. Taraporevala Sons and Co., 1929), p. 24.

16. Edgar Prestage, Affonso de Albuquerque (Watford: no pub., 1929), p. 13; pp. 7–13 provides an excellent evaluation of the extensive Portuguese sources. For the general background to the Portuguese advance, see Charles E. Nowell, *A History of Portugal* (New York: D. Van Nostrandt Co., 1952). Discussions of the Portuguese entry into Kerala include: Alex J.D. Dorsey, *Portuguese Discoveries, Dependencies and Missions in Asia and Africa* (London: Allen & Co., 1893); K.G. Jayne, *Vasco da Gama and His Successors, 1460–1580* (London: Methuen & Co. Ltd., 1910); F.C. Danvers, *The Portuguese in India*, 2 vols (London: W.H. Allen & Company, Ltd., 1894); Panikkar, *Malabar and the Portuguese*; R.S. Whiteway, *The Rise of Portuguese Power in India, 1497–1550* (Westminster: Constable & Co., 1899). For Albuquerque see also vol. 4 of *The Commentaries of the Great Affonso Daboquerque* (by his son), trans. W. de Gray Birch from the Portuguese ed. of 1774, 4 vols. (London: Hakluyt Society, 1884); and H. Morse Stephens, *Albuquerque* (Oxford: Clarendon Press, 1897). Many of the voluminous and often imaginative reports of the Portuguese explorers and administrators are as yet untranslated into English. Note "The Three Voyages of Vasco da Gama," trans. H.E.J. Stanley from Gaspar Correa's *Lendas da India* (London: Hakluyt Society, 1869). Preferred is E.G. Ravenstein's translation of Roteico, the only manuscript by one who actually accompanied the voyage, *A Journal of the First Voyage of Vasco da Gama 1497–1499* (London: Hakluyt Society, 1898). See also Duarte Barbosa, *The Book Duarte Barbosa*, trans. M.W. Dames, 2 vols. (London: Hakluyt Society, 1918). For Portuguese methodology in religious work see Moraes, *A History*,

pp. 121 ff., and for the role of the factory-fortress in extension of commercial, missionary, and political influence, see Marcel Caetano, *Colonizing Traditions, Principles and Methods of the Portuguese* (Lisbon: Agencia Geral do Ultramar, 1951), pp. 20 ff. For the well-documented decline of Portuguese life and influence, see K.P.P. Menon, *A History of Kerala*, 4 vols., ed. T.K. Krishna Menon (Ernakulam: Cochin Government Press, 1934–37), 1: 184 ff. For Muslim feeling and opposition, see Shaykh Zaynu'd-Din, *Tuhfat al-Mujahidin*, trans. S. Muhammad Nainar (Madras: Madras University Press, 1942), and O.K. Nambiar, *The Kunjalis, Admirals of Calicut* (Bombay: Asia Pub. House, 1963). For the Hindu opposition see K.V. Krishna Ayyar, *The Zamorins of Calicut* (Calicut: Norman Publishing Bureau, 1938).

17. Jayne, *Vasco da Gama*, p. 4. Moraes, *A History*, p. 21, affirms that "the Portuguese enterprise was thus a crusade against Islam. It was an act of defence against the Muslim menace"; he makes the astonishing statement that "the Portuguese dealt a staggering blow to aggressive Islam in India and saved South India for the Hindu religion and culture" (p. 119).

18. Jayne, *Vasco da Gama*, p. 11.

19. K.M. Panikkar, *India's Contact with the World in the Pre-British Period* (Nagpur: Nagpur University, 1964), p. 67.

20. Danvers, *The Portuguese in India*, 1: xxxvi. Cf. also pp. 21, 39 f.

21. Roteico was an eyewitness to this peculiar event. King Manuel's triumphant letter to Ferdinand and Isabella of Spain "concerning the Christian people who these explorers reached" is also recorded (app. A, p. 114). He declares that "when they have been fortified in the faith, there will be opportunity for destroying the Moors of those parts."

22. Gaspar Correa in R'emy, *Goa, Rome of the Orient*, trans. L.C. Sheppard (London: Arthur Baker, 1957), p. 34; for another translation, cf. H.E.J. Stanley's version in *Three Voyages* (1869), p. 186, n. 1.

23. Whiteway, *Rise of Portuguese Power*, p. 21.

24. *Cartas*, 1: 26, quoted in Prestage, *Albuquerque*, p. 43.

25. Dorsey, *Portuguese Discoveries*, p. 180.

26. Portuguese records frankly reveal the variety of means employed to carry out the mandate of the *padroado*. Moraes, *A History*, reports that after some time outright grants of money in Goa were discontinued in favor of giving rice at the close of the church service (p. 137). Writing to the king, a Portuguese official suggests (*Documentacão*, 1: 212 f.): "If your Highness desires that many people should turn Christian, order the same gifts to be given to some of the chief men, because when they are converted, the lower people will emulate their example. This can be negotiated with little trouble, as each one has his price."

27. From 1599 the Syrian Christians were loosely united under the Catholic archbishop. In 1653, a section of the Syrian church broke away from Portuguese and papal jurisdiction, resumed its independence, established relations with the patriarch of Antioch, and became the Jacobite church, the forerunner of the Syrian Orthodox Church in Kerala today.

28. "An Offering to Jihad Warriors." Shaykh Zayn al-Dīn (1498–1581) belonged to a noted family of Malabar divines, who wrote chiefly in Arabic.

29. Cf. Miller, *The Mappila Muslims*, pp. 124–53, for an outline of the causes, events, and impact of the rebellion.

30. Prime Minister Rajiv Gandhi, early in his tenure, summarized the Indian view of secularism as a form of coexistence: "How do we define secularism? Do we define it as 'no religion'? We define it as the right of every religion to co-exist with other religions. We acknowledge that right of co-existence by allowing religions to have their own Personal Laws. It does not reduce our secularism. It is, in fact, a strong constituent of our secularism. It is the basic strength of India that every religion has its own freedom of functioning within our framework and we do not try to suppress or change any religion" (speech, Lok Sabha, February 27, 1986, quoted in *Muslim India* 4, no. 39 [March 1986], p. 133). It is the argument of this essay that unless religious coexistence becomes a pro-existence, it becomes some form of no existence.

31. K.P. Kesava Menon, "Communal Sound and Fury in Our Land," in *Mathrubhūmi Annual* (Calicut: Mathrubhūmi Pub. Co., 1973), p. 132.

32. Within Kerala, notably Tellicherry in 1971, Trivandrum in 1982, and Nilakkal in 1983. During the past five years the state has been relatively free of communal incidents. However, in India today discussion of communalism and the analysis of communal incidents is an ongoing preoccupation, and the published literature is extensive. For a convenient survey, see A. Asghar Engineer, ed., *Communal Riots in Post-Independence India* (Bombay: Sangam Books, 1964). There is a current tendency for Christians and Muslims to recognize their mutual interests as minorities. At the same time, the Sikh uprising in the Punjab has significantly affected the picture of interreligious relations, as the national scene becomes increasingly volatile.

33. *Muslim World* 7, no. 83 (November 1989): 488.

34. Ibid. 7, no. 80 (August 1989): 368.

35. Pullangot Mohammed, letter to the editor, *Indian Express*, November 7, 1990, p. 7.

36. An excellent demonstration of the effectiveness of the Mahila Samajum program took place in recent years in Malappuram, headquarters of the administrative district with the highest percentage of Muslim population in India outside of Kashmir (65.5). In an area notorious for religious conflict, Christian, Hindu and Muslim women drew together in a determined and united effort in community uplift that produced remarkable fruits.

37. Speech of November 8, 1990, reported in *Indian Express*, November 9, 1990, p.1. The following month witnessed another surge of communal violence in several urban areas.

38. Khan Bahadur K. Muhammad, *Māppilamār Engottu* (Trichur: Mangalodayam Pvt. Ltd.,1956), pp, 179 f., 188, 200. Malayalam translations mine.

39. Speech of November 4, 1990, reported in *Indian Express*, November 5, 1990, p. 1.

40. F.H. Aderwalla, letter to the editor, *Indian Express*, November 7, 1990, p. 7.

41. Psalm 46, v. 5.

42. K.C. Chaitanya, *A History of Malayam Literature* (New Delhi: Orient Longman Ltd., 1971), pp. 256, 558.

17

Christian-Muslim Encounter in Indonesia

Olaf Schumann

When we think about Islam our thoughts usually are directed toward the Near and Middle East. There Islam originated and there a great deal of the history of interactions between Muslims and Christians has taken place, sometimes in cooperation but most often in competition and warfare. Islam in Southeast Asia[1] has not, until fairly recently, attracted much attention by scholars. This vast area with its various and numerous peoples has not been a topic of major scholarly concern, although it has been of interest to those Christians concerned with the spread of the faith.

In spite of this general scholarly neglect, relations between Christians and Muslims in Southeast Asia have been of decisive importance for many years. With the communist takeover of continental China refugees spread over the area, followed by the missionaries who had been working on the mainland. The majority of the people of the Philippines (with the exception of Mindanao and the Sulu Islands) have been Roman Catholic since the days of the Spanish conquerors in the sixteenth century, and have a long history of interaction with their Muslim neighbors. The former Netherlands Indies, present-day Indonesia, for many years has attracted the interest of Dutch missionaries and even (as an exception to the general lack of scholarly interest in the area) of scholars of Islam.

The Malay world constitutes the largest Muslim community in the world. Indonesia alone, its population of approximately 180 million being 75–80 percent Muslim, contains more Muslims than live in the entire Arab world. But in that country the Christian community, about 4.5 percent of the population, is Roman Catholic, and about 8 percent are Protestants of various denominations. Thus the Christian community in Indonesia is the largest Christian community in Asia. Relations between Christians and Muslims in this area are decisive and determinative for the future of Southeast Asia.

Social, Historical, and Political Background

Christianity and Islam, both of which originated outside Southeast Asia, share much as religions that had to integrate themselves into new surroundings. Both are monotheistic and prophetic, understanding that God as creator has sovereignty over creation—humanity as well as nature—but is not part of that creation. Both are missionary in orientation. As universal religions they are based on the premise that God's commands cannot be restricted to a particular community but must be proclaimed and acknowledged in all areas of the world. Such theological bases have been in tension with the cosmological world view of the inhabitants of Southeast Asia. In their understanding, God, humankind, and nature are but different manifestations of one all-penetrating and all-moving reality or deity. To imagine God as outside or different from the world is a strange notion, and it is neither plausible nor acceptable to consider obedience to demands issuing from a being outside of this divine cosmos. Monotheism itself has been problematic, set over against the notion that the cosmos is filled with "god-like" beings. A primal divine figure is usually considered to have taught the cosmic laws to its descendants, who are understood to be the ancestors of humans. The primal deity or deities are themselves manifestations of an original divine oneness, knowledgeable about and maintaining the rules which created cosmic life. Living according to these rules leads to harmony with all powers acting within the cosmos; obedience to commands coming from outside has no place in this structure.[2]

How were Christianity and Islam to strike roots in this strange world?

Early conversion to Islam.—Up to the twelfth century, while both religions were known in the region, their adherents were foreigners—Muslim Arabs, Persians, Gujaratis, and Bengalis; Nestorian Syrians, Persians, and Mongols.[3] Although these people built churches and mosques, there was no indication of religious propaganda; their relations with the indigenous populations were limited to commercial exchange. In the thirteenth century, however, a Muslim Persian married the daughter of a local ruler in Pasai, North Sumatra, and later converted her family to (Shīᶜite) Islam.[4] Thus the first Muslim dynasty in the region was established.

In the following centuries more of the leading families converted to Islam; if they were rulers their clients usually became Muslim. In this way Islam became influential in the harbor cities and trading centers, although the population of the hinterland was generally untouched. Thus the popular image of Islam spread widely by traders in Southeast Asia is not convincing. And it was generally not until the fifteenth and sixteenth centuries that Islam spread through religious wars.

The most effective agents in the spread of Islam were the teachers, preachers, and holy men (*walīs*, *shekhs*, *mawlās*) who were practicing mystical teachings. Sometimes they founded communities and lived together with their disciples in *tarekats*. They introduced a new lifestyle rooted in Islam and, at least partly, in the sharīᶜa, one to which the common people had access.[5] These walis, who became the backbone of Islamization in Southeast Asia, were in some ways the successors of the former Hindu brahmins and Buddhist *bhiksus* who had followed Indian traders to the area and spread their religion under the protection of the local rulers. Local chronicles contain accounts of the imminent arrival of such teachers and holy men, and how they were accepted by a ruler who, convinced by a dream or other miraculous occurrence, was prepared to adopt a new religion. Rulers were thus often considered to have supernatural powers and to be the representatives of the cosmic order in their realms, their salvatory power over their subjects sanctified by the religious teachers. The walis continued to play this role, supported by the mystically Shīʿite-oriented Islam they proclaimed. Islam thus became legitimate despite its foreign origin. Foreign Muslim merchants also helped in this process. By associating themselves with their indigenous partners, and by intermarrying, they and their religion became integrated into society and the destiny of their new kinship became their own.

The arrival of European Christians.—When the European explorers and traders appeared at the end of the fifteenth century in search of new commercial outlets, they met with local rulers who confessed to be Muslims. The hostile attitudes against the "Saracens" cultivated in Christian Europe carried over to their responses to the Muslims in Southeast Asia, creating from the beginning an atmosphere of suspicion, hostility, and mutual contempt. Exacerbating the situation was the claim of the Europeans to be messengers and agents of a far away king who pretended to have a mandate of rule over all the world (the ideology of the *padroado*). Thus on one side were the Muslim rulers, with Islam by then an "indigenous" religion, and on the other the European foreigners with their strange religion and the competing claims of a king whose throne stood beyond the oceans. The Europeans clearly had no interest in acknowledging, let alone defending, the interests of the local people. Portuguese and Spanish traders and soldiers were accompanied by their priests, many of them preaching the Gospel to people living in or around their fortresses. But those who did become baptized were left alone in their conflict of loyalty. When action was taken against the foreigners, local Christians usually became victims too. Intermarriage, common among the Muslims, was impossible for the Christians. The Portuguese and Spanish Catholic priests were celibate, and British and Dutch Protestants considered intermarriage with indigenous women to be beneath them. Christianity thus could not become legitimate and accepted among the local people as Islam had been. Moreover, foreigners remained the only clerics of Christianity; even in their religious life indigenous Christians were dependent on powers that did not adjust to the local cosmos. No independent indigenous raja became Christian; local interests were left to be defended by the Muslims.

Christians and Muslims in the Movement for Independence

While it is true that rebellions and wars of Muslims against colonialist rulers are of great historical importance, resistance against European colonialism was not promoted only by Muslims. Even in areas with substantial Christian population, resistance arose against the Dutch.[6] Relations between Indonesian Christians and the Dutch were considerably more complicated than was the continuous (although varied) antagonism between the Dutch and the Muslims. Even when they were political opponents the Dutch and the indigenous Christians could not ignore the fact that they shared the same faith. When native Christians were persecuted by Muslim rulers they asked the foreigners for help and protection. On the whole the Dutch preferred the Christians as administrative and military personnel. Improvement of the educational system in the area added to the membership in the indigenous Christian community.

In addition to the Christians and the Muslims a third group played an important historical role in Indonesia—the proponents of pre-Islamic traditional culture based on Adat, represented mainly by feudal rulers and their clients. In frequent warfare between them and the Muslims, the Adat leaders often asked for the help of the Dutch army, widening the gap between the Muslims and the Dutch as well as between themselves and the Muslims. Only in this historical perspective, with the Muslims on one side and the defenders of Adat (who often were nominal Muslims themselves) together with the Christians (and the Dutch) on the other, can many of the current problems in Indonesia be understood.

The rise of the Nationalist Movement at the beginning of the twentieth century opened a new chapter in Christian-Muslim relations. Its aim, supported by most Indonesians, was the termination of Dutch colonial rule. Christians as a confessional group were not represented in two of the oldest nationalist organizations. One of them, Budi Utomo (1908), was promoting ideals of education derived from old Javanese conceptions of humanity and the cosmos.[7] The other, originally a union of Javanese batik traders, in 1912 became Sarekat Islam, a center for nationalist-minded people for whom not only Islam but also other ideologies such as Marxism were interesting as anticolonial ideas.[8]

After World War I a change took place. Christians became active in nationalist (especially youth) groups. Most of these had a regional rather than a religious orientation, like Jong Java, Jong Batak, and Jong Minahasa. In others, however, such as the Jong Islamieten, regional interests were replaced by religious ones. Among the Christian youth a similar role was played by the newly established YMCA/YWCA and, after John R. Mott's visit to Indonesia in 1925,[9] the Student Christian Federation through which Christian youth from different parts of the country met. These youth movements convened a National Youth

Congress in 1928 in which the three pillars of the Indonesian Nationalist Movement were formulated: one country—maintenance of the territorial integrity of the Netherlands' Indies; one people—the unity of all Indonesians in spite of cultural, tribal, and religious variations; one language—Indonesian rooted in Malay, to be used by all Indonesians along with their local and tribal idioms.[10] There was no talk of one religion, as religion was not considered to be a major dividing factor in the common national movement. In a country like Indonesia where bonds of family and tribe and personal contact are more important than formal or official ones, the personal acquaintance of the later national leaders who met at this congress was of utmost significance. They were able to influence the younger members of their organizations in the cause of solidarity that cut across religious lines.

Therefore even during the Japanese occupation (1942–45), Christians participated with so-called secular nationalists in movements preparing for the independence of Indonesia based on a religiously neutral state.[11] For many of them, including Sukarno, the basic idea was an inclusive society based on that of their ancestors before the penetration of foreign religions. This idea of an inclusive society reflected the prevailing ethos of the Adat, the customs and customary law of the different peoples and tribes of the country. This group of secular nationalists was opposed by the Islamieten or Islamists, for whom religion (Islam) is one of the constitutive elements of the state. Their aim was thus to establish an Islamic state based on the sharīʿa.

A compromise was achieved in 1945 when first Muhammad Yamin and after him Sukarno forwarded the Five Principles, later called Pancasila, on which the future state was constitutionally built. That which became the first principle states that the Indonesian state is based on the belief in One Supreme Divinity, in whom every citizen is obliged to believe. It was understood to be the task of the religious communities themselves, however, to define their understanding of that. Religions that fulfill certain criteria inherent in this principle, such as worship of One Supreme Being, following the teachings of a prophet figure and obeying the tenets of their scriptures, are legally recognized. Specifically these are Islam, Protestantism, Roman Catholicism, Hinduism, and Buddhism. Every Indonesian is free to choose or change his or her religion without discrimination.

At one point the Islamieten tried to enlarge the first pillar by adding a special provision that implied the obligation of Muslims to follow the Islamic sharīʿa. In the final form of the Pancasila, however, passed on August 18, 1945, this amendment was not accepted. Had it been, the state would have had a special obligation toward one of the religious communities. Moreover, this would have obliged the state to interfere with the internal affairs of one religion and give it special attention, undermining the neutrality of the state in religious matters.

The compromise of the Pancasila which finally was accepted by both the secular and the Islamic nationalists must be seen against the background of the political developments of the time. Christians and Muslims fought side by side in the period between 1945 and 1949 for Indonesian independence from the Dutch. This was possible for the Christians because of the Pancasila principles. An Islamic state would not have been able to maintain the integrity of the Indonesian territories. On the other hand, the Islamieten never would have accepted a fully secular state. The compromise of the Pancasila, therefore, was the only way to safeguard the goals of the Nationalist Movement and to bind all Indonesians together to defend their independence. Christian participation in the military and political struggle for independence proved their loyalty to the Indonesian state and allowed them to take direct part in the negotiations with the Dutch government. Christians could no longer be mistrusted as agents of a foreign colonial power who were not at home in the Indonesian cosmos.

The possibility of changing Indonesia into an Islamic state was again discussed during the 1950s, but did not win the approval even of the majority of Muslim voters.[12] Still the leaders of the Islamic parties pretended to represent 90 percent of the Indonesian population, and on this unrealistic estimate tried to legitimize their fight for an Islamic state. Finally, in July 1959, Sukarno as president declared the provisional constitution of 1945 final and initiated his "guided democracy." Masjumi, the most outspoken of the Islamic political parties in opposition to Sukarno, was outlawed in 1960 after some of its most prominent leaders became involved in a separatist movement in Western Sumatra.

With the defeat of the radical Islamists, President Sukarno and his Nationalist Party were alone on the political scene along with the communists and the army. The remaining Muslim parties, as well as the Christian, paid him lip service but were not reliable allies. He won the favor of the communists when he proclaimed his concept of "Nasakom" (NASionalisme, Agama [religion], KOMmunisme) as the ideological basis of his "guided democracy." This led to international isolation and economic decay, and Sukarno fell through army intervention in March of 1966. The hopes of Muslims for a revival of Masjumi did not materialize, and Pancasila (despite its misuse during the last years of Sukarno's leadership) remained the dominant ideology of the state.[13]

Christians and Muslims Challenged by the "New Order" after 1966

When finally in January 1968 a new Islamic party was allowed to establish itself as Partai Muslimin Indonesia, provision was made that no former leader of Masjumi might take a position of leadership. Nonetheless, the efforts of Muslims had caused some uneasiness on the part of the Christians. After the prohibition of Masjumi in 1960 all material and ideological resources of the party, with their special concern for Islamic education and welfare, were free to focus on a strategy aimed at strengthening Islamic consciousness among the people. Efforts in Islamic *daʿwa* and *tablīgh*, improved since the early 1960s, resulted in growing tensions between Muslims and Christians.

And like the Muslim community, Christian churches began to wake up to a growing awareness of their social responsibilities. The Second Vatican Council and the World Council of Churches' Conference on Church and Society (Geneva, 1966) both had an impact on Indonesian Christian efforts at improved social programs. Already the Fifth General Assembly of the Council of Churches in Indonesia in 1964 had gathered to discuss the "renewal of society through revolution," a slogan much in use at that time of Sukarno's revolution. Christians combined this theme with the social role of the church under the leadership of Christ. Christian mission and Islamic daʿwa both were interpreted with a strong social and ethical accent, leading to growing competition between the two. Each community accused the other of using social programs as a pretext for proselytizing.

In this context the new and still provisional head of state, Suharto, convened a conference of Christian and Muslim leaders in 1967. They were not able to produce a common statement about their future relations because Christians opposed a provision which would have stopped Christian mission and especially diaconia "among people who adhere already to a religion."[14] They justified their position both theologically and by pointing to the Islamic daʿwa which was carried out systematically in predominantly Christian areas. Despite this failure, the meeting did prompt some willingness on both sides to work together. The first common programs of community development started in the late 1960s.

The rationale for these programs was participation in national development characterized by the "New Order" government of Suharto.[15] But these programs of cooperation and dialogue soon led to a deadlock caused by growing interference of government functionaries who tried to propagate the government's emphasis on economic and physical development. The motivations and aims of the religiously inspired social programs, which tended to free themselves from administrative interference, were met with increasing suspicion by the government. In addition to disregarding spiritual values, the government was seen as increasingly corrupt and subject to manipulation by the wealthy. As open opposition by the country's religious leaders—interpreted as criticism of Pancasila and thus subversive of national stability—was impossible, they silently withdrew their support. Pancasila, misused as a shield to defend current development, lost its reputation in the eyes of many Indonesians.

In the meantime, talking about the old aim of establishing an Islamic state had given way to an effort to shape new laws introduced by the government in such a way that they would comply with Islamic legal conceptions. There was heated controversy in 1973 when the government tried to introduce a bill to make marriage a civil act. After considerable protest from the Muslim community, the government agreed that marriage should be legalized by a representative of the respective religious community, authorized by the government. Muslims were allowed to bring legal disputes related to marriage to the Islamic courts, although their decisions had to be confirmed by state courts. This concession by the government was seen by non-Muslim Indonesians as a sign of weakness. They feared that such capitulation might lead to Islamization through the back door. On the other side, the original secular bill was interpreted by some Islamists as a covert attempt at Christianization of Indonesian society.

Relations between the religious communities were not helped when a 1976 World Council of Churches meeting of the Commission on World Mission and Evangelization, attended by a Christian and a Muslim participant from Indonesia, issued a statement strongly urging Christian churches and religious organizations "to suspend their misused diaconia activities in the world of Islam." The conference further urged that all material assistance donated by outside churches and religious organizations "henceforth be distributed wherever possible through or in cooperation with the governments."[16] Despite the opening statement that mission and daʿwa are recognized religious duties of their respective communities, the impression was that diaconia was always "misused."

At the Indonesian Council of Churches meeting in Central Java, held right after the World Council session, President Suharto indirectly referred to the commission's statement as being in accord with the policy of his government, and urged the churches to channel all foreign aid through the Department of Religious Affairs. Two years later, this intention was legally enforced when the then newly appointed minister for religious affairs, General Alamshah Ratu Prawiranegara, included it in two letters of instruction he issued. Members of the Christian community refused to accept a politically motivated restriction of their religious self-understanding and activity, pointing again to the fact that since Islamic daʿwa among Christians was not affected by these instructions, the letters could only be understood as a move against Christians. They agreed, however, to discuss with Muslims an "ethical code" according to which mission and daʿwa should be conducted. These matters thus clearly remained as topics of continuing dispute between Christians and Muslims in Indonesia.[17]

Toward Cooperation for a New Society

In the meantime, a discussion had been initiated in the late 1960s among young Muslim intellectuals about the vision of the Islamic student organizations for future Islamic society. They were concerned to develop practical and acceptable alternatives to the old concept of an Islamic state. One of the main concerns was the role of the *sharīʿa*. The earlier Jakarta Charter had urged that Muslims be obliged by the state to follow the sharīʿa, but the elections of 1955 had proven that no majority could be obtained for this aim. In 1969 some of the prominent Muslim student leaders took up the Qurʾanic insistence that humans are God's vice-regents on the earth, and claimed that such a task could not be fulfilled if Muslims had to obey laws set at an earlier time in history, and that they had to be free to adjust the rules to current needs. One of the results of the ensuing heated debates was a greater awareness on the part of some Muslim leaders of the pluralistic character of Indonesian society. Pointing to the fourth pillar of the Pancasila, many agreed that mutual deliberation and consensus should include, on equal terms, representatives from other religious groups in helping define the future ideological and moral orientation of Indonesians. In the task of nation building every group should participate and no one, these Muslims included, could force others to accept concepts against their will.[18]

In 1980 a forum was established through the Department for Religious Affairs where religious questions and matters of interreligious relations could be discussed. Members of the forum were to be the leaders of the different religious communities. The forum is charged with considering the relationship of the first pillar of the Pancasila, the belief in one supreme divinity, to the other pillars of inclusive humanity, nationalism, consensus, and social justice. One of the important questions is whether the first pillar stands in the center and the others derive their meaning from it (a position held by many Muslims) or whether all five pillars are equally interrelated. In the context of this forum, leaders of the religious communities have the chance to meet and to try to resolve issues that otherwise would be discussed within their individual communities.

Because of their comparatively better education, Christians in the past in Indonesia have tended to dominate cultural, economic, and political life. Their solidarity with the underprivileged often was hidden in the struggle for prestige. The efforts of Muslims in the 1960s to improve their educational system as well as to send students to Western countries to study has resulted in a new generation of Muslim intellectuals able to compete with Christians for leading positions. As a result there is a much better chance that the conversations among members of the two communities can be conducted on a more equal footing. An important variable in the present scene is Islamic "fundamentalism." This movement inevitably will grow if questions of social justice and legal security are not taken seriously by those in power, and if Christian intellectuals refuse to accept Muslim counterparts as equals. The opportunity to cooperate with Muslims in the social field, as well as in the field of developing moral and ethical standards, is an important way for Christians to express their solidarity with and responsibility for the whole Indonesian people and not just for their own community.

Theological Implications

The obligation to cooperate has been stressed by a number of actions undertaken by the Indonesian government since 1978 to strengthen the role of Pancasila in political, social, and religious life. A law was passed in 1985 that obligates all social organizations to include an article in their constitutions accepting Pancasila as the sole basis of their social and national life and activities. I would like to conclude here by reflecting briefly on the theological implications for the religious communities in Indonesia of the implementation of this 1985 law.

It is easy to say that religious institutions have complied with the law because they had no other choice. In fact, however, it has presented these communities with another opportunity to offer their own vision of how society should develop. Putting this vision into the framework of Pancasila can mean that it is not just the government that defines what Pancasila means. Considering the pluralistic character of Indonesian society with its five acknowledged religious communities, it is clear that such a contribution from each would work toward complementarity and cooperation rather than support the domination of any one. It gives the opportunity to the Islamic and Christian groups finally to develop a vision of society that is really inclusive, taking into account the rights and tasks of other communities as well as their own. The impetus for cooperation necessitates the identification of a theological rationale and justification that acknowledges the existence of adherents of other religions and faiths.

Not many religious thinkers in Indonesia have yet accepted this challenge as a specifically theological one. But those who do are coming up with some quite remarkable ideas concerning the future role of religions in Indonesia. This concern is obvious in the titles of some of the books and articles that have appeared in the last few years from younger, primarily Muslim, thinkers: "New Directions of Islam: The Voice of the Younger Generation"; "Opening a New Way for Islam"; "Indonesian Islam: Planning the Future"; "Aspirations of the Islamic Umma in Indonesia"; "One Islam: A Dilemma"; "To Enter the Common Future: Task and Responsibility of the Religions of Indonesia" (compiled by a Christian with Muslim, Hindu, and Buddhist contributors).[19]

Several thinkers are worth noting in some detail as significant contributors to this new form of conversation. One is Nurcholis Madjid, known for his earlier attack against the "Islamic state" concept heralded by the older generation.[20] In a recent article entitled "The Actualization of the Teachings of Ahlussunnah Wal Jamaʾa"[21] he develops the theme that the understanding of an exclusive Islamic society is unacceptable in Indonesian society. He cites historical precedent for an antisectarian perspective, arguing that Muslims should accept other interpretations of truth provided they are consonant with belief in one God. Thus, he says, the exclusive claim to truth and knowledge goes against the Word of God and its spirit. What is demanded from believers is mutual respect and understanding.

Madjid makes use of two arguments that occur frequently in the writings of some of the members of the traditionalist Sunni organization Nahdlatul Ulama, and especially its chairman Abdurrahman Wahid. One of these is the point that *islām* in the Qurʾan does not point to a distinctive group of the followers of Muhammad, but refers to the attitude of people who surrender themselves to God. Another refers to the Qurʾanic anthropology which concedes that the *fiṭra*, or human nature, preserves the recognition of God's oneness in every person. "Islam is the religion of humanity (*fiṭra*) which makes its ideals to run parallel to the universal ideals of humankind." These ideals have continually to be developed, and in the process of that development non-Muslim Indonesians also must contribute. A political system in Indonesia should therefore work in a way that benefits all Indonesians together.[22]

Another protagonist of cooperation between Muslims and non-Muslims in Indonesia is Abdurrahman Wahid, elected general chairman of the Nahdlatul Ulama in 1984. Generally considered a traditionalist, he is nonetheless not a proponent of a kind of frozen *taqlīd*. In an article entitled "Indigenization of Islam"[23] he urges a reshaping of traditional religious laws and legal prescriptions according to local needs and with a contextual understanding of justice and righteousness. He refers to a principle of Shāfiʾite law according to which customs and habits become arbiters. He understands blind execution of verbal formulations of a text actually to be un-Islamic. The agenda of Islamic thought, he says, should be determined by the needs of society rather than Islamic theories dictating society's agenda.

The actual problems of Indonesian society, he says, center on the implementation of social justice, democracy, and equality before the law. These are the priorities on the agenda of Muslims as they themselves decide if Islam is to be a practical and dynamic world view rather than a nebulous ideology which hides its ineffectiveness behind slogans and external, formalistic attitudes. Having thus determined the agenda of priorities for Islamic reflection and action, Abdurrahman Wahid reflects about the framework in which Muslims can work for the implementation of justice, democracy, and equality. Muslims and their non-Muslim neighbors must struggle for the goals of Pancasila together. Like Nurcholis Madjid he justifies this by pointing to the fiṭra of humankind. But his anthropology is broadened somewhat by the inclusion of Sufi conceptions about the nature of the human being. Iḥsān, the highest stage of human progress toward God, is defined as love toward one's neighbor whomever he might be, which stands together with the love of God.[24] Thus according to Wahid both Islamic dogmatics and Islamic mysticism urge Indonesian Muslims into a close and cooperative relationship with non-Muslims.

On the Christian side, since the proclamation of independence Pancasila has been regarded as the safeguard of their religious freedom and the basis for their participation in national developments. But Christians must bear responsibility for the fact that in many aspects the Pancasila has not yet been implemented in a satisfactory way. Therefore many Christians also feel that the time has come to reflect in more theological terms about this situation. Together with their co-citizens they feel the urgent need to develop standards of moral and ethical behavior relevant to their developing society. According to the original understanding of Pancasila, such standards should grow out of the religious communities themselves and are then to be worked on intercommunally. Christians, like Muslims, have to come to some insight into the theological meaning of such interdependence with adherents of other faiths in the context of their nation. Both groups are realizing that such reflection can be conducted internally but also dialogically. The latter way has been chosen by the research department of the Communion of Churches in Indonesia. By offering an annual seminar in which representatives of the different religious communities are invited to share their insights on the challenges before them, it tries to contribute to the kinds of common efforts that are being envisaged and proposed by Muslim thinkers such as Nurcholis Madjid and Abdurrahman Wahid.[25]

Good conditions exist today both for the growth of mutual trust and respect between Christians and Muslims and for theological reflection in both communities about their relationship with their co-citizens in a common community.[26] This is in fact what Pancasila, agreed upon by national consensus at the very beginning of the independence of the Indonesian nation, requires of them. But they also must search for justification in their own religious self-understanding. And essential to the process is the resolve of the Indonesian government and other constitutional forces serving as protectors of the liberty offered by Pancasila to maintain strict neutrality and evenhandedness in dealing with the different religious communities that make up this multicultural and multireligious nation.

NOTES

1. Southeast Asia in this article refers to the region where peoples speak Malay or Malaic languages and adhere to the general patterns of Malay culture.

2. A recent important study on the Javanese world view has been presented by Franz Magnis Suseno, *Javanische Weisheit und Ethik: Studien zu einer ostlichen Moral* (Munich–

Vienna: Oldenbourg, 1981) esp. chap. 4; cf. Clifford Geertz, *The Religion of Java* (Glencoe: Free Press, 1960), and Niels Mulder, *Mysticism and Every Day Life in Contemporary Java* (Singapore: University Press, 1978). For further basic studies on traditional religions and their world views see Hans Scharer, *Ngaju Religion* (The Hague: M. Nijhoff, 1963); Philip L. Tobin, *The Structure of the Toba-Batak Belief in the High God* (Amsterdam: J. Van Campen, 1956); Peter Suzuki, *The Religious System and Culture of Nias, Indonesia* (The Hague: Excelsior, 1959); W. Stohr, "Die Religionen der Altvolker Indonesiens und der Philippines" in W. Stohr and Piet Zoetmulder, eds., *Die Religionen Indonesiens* (Stuttgart: n. p., 1965).

3. There are references in Arabic lists on Asian episcopies to the presence of Nestorians in "Fansur" near Baros on the west coast of Sumatra. These are discussed in the history of the Catholic Church in Indonesia. That these Christians are declared to have been Catholics by the compiler seems to be somewhat anachronistic. See *Sejarah Gereja Katolik Indonesia*, 5 vols. (Ende-Flores: Arnoldus, 1974), 1: 27 ff.

4. D.G.E. Hall, *A History of Southeast Asia* (London: Macmillan, 1961), p. 205; P.M. Holt et al., eds., *The Cambridge History of Islam* (Cambridge: Cambridge University Press, 1970), 2: 124 ff.

5. S.Q. Fatimi, *Islam Comes to Malaysia* (Singapore: Malaysian Sociological Research Institute, 1963).

6. T.B. Simatupang, "Kurzer Ruckblick auf die Geschichte der christlichen Kirche in Indonesia," in Rolf Italiaander, ed., *Indonesiens verantwortliche Gesellschaft* (Enlargen: Verlag der Evang. Lutheran Mission, 1976), pp. 37–85, esp. p. 44; see further remarks on Patimura's rebellion in I.H. Enklaar, *Josef Kam, Apostel der Molukken* (The Hague: Boekencentrium, 1963), pp. 28 ff., and M. Sapija, *Sejarah Perjuangan Pattimura* (Jakarta: Djambatan, 1957). An extensive survey on the participation of Christians in the National Movement was compiled by T.B. Simatupang et al. "Partisipasi Kristen dalam Revolusi Bidang Politik," in W.B. Sidjabat, ed., *Partisipasi Kristen dalam Nation Building di Indonesia* (Jakarta: BPK, 1968), pp. 3–35.

7. M.C. Ricklefs, *A History of Modern Indonesia* (Bloomington: Indiana University Press, 1981), pp. 156 ff.

8. Special mention is given to the rebellion of Thomas Matulesia, known as Pattimura, who fought the Dutch when they returned to the Moluccas in 1817 after the British interregnum. Like all other rebellions, it was unsuccessful. But it shows that even in the Moluccas, where most of the indigenous soldiers of the Dutch colonial army were recruited, solidarity with the foreigners was limited. Christian teaching stimulated a feeling for justice and human dignity. It was not without meaning that at the time when the Dutch soldiers entered the church of Saparua during Pattimura's rebellion, they found a Bible on the altar, open to Psalm 17. See Deliar Noer, *The Modernist Muslim Movement in Indonesia 1900–1942* (Singapore–Kuala Lumpur–New York: Oxford University Press, 1973), pp. 101 ff.

9. C.H. Hopkins, *John R. Mott 1865–1955: A Biography* (Geneva and Grand Rapids: Eerdmans, 1979), pp. 650 ff.

10. John Ingleson, *Road to Exile: The Indonesian Nationalist Movement 1927–1934* (Singapore: Heinemann Educational Books, 1979), pp. 65 ff.; A.K. Pringgodigdo, *Sejarah Pergerakan Rakyat Indonesia* (Jakarta: Pen. Dian Rakyat, 1978), pp. 100 ff.; *Bunga Rampai*

Sumpah Pemuda: Dihimpun Yayasan Gedung-gedung Bersejarah Jakarta (Jakarta: Balai Pustaka, 1978).

11. A great deal has been written about this period of decisive struggle for the future of the constitution and the final compromise in support of the concept of Pancasila. Controversies about its "correct" interpretation have not yet come to an end. Only a few books are cited in order to help provide a better understanding of the different positions: Harry J. Benda, *The Crescent and the Rising Sun* (Bandung and The Hague: W. van Hoeve, 1958), esp. pp. 169 ff.; B.J. Boland, *The Struggle of Islam in Modern Indonesia* (The Hague: M. Nijhoff, 1971) VKI, p. 59; Wendelin Wawar, *Muslime und Christen in der Republik Indonesia* (Wiesbaden: F. Steiner, 1974), esp. pp. 38 ff.; Notonagoro, *Pancasila Dasar Falsafah Nagara* (Jakarta, n.d.); H.E. Saifuddin Anshari, *Piagam Jakarta 22 Juni 1945* (Bandung: Pustaka, 1981), esp. pp. 212 ff.; Marcel Bonnef et al., *Pantjasile—trente annes de débats politiques en Indonesie* (Paris: Éd. de la Maison des Sciences de l'homme, 1980), Études insulindiennes archipel. No. 2.

12. During the elections for the parliament and those for the Konstituante (a body elected to draft the final Indonesian Constitution) in 1955, all Islamic parties together achieved not more than 43.5 percent of the vote. This means that half of the Muslim community disagreed with the constitutional and legal aims of the Islamic parties, and parted with the Muslim and non-Muslim supporters of Pancasila as it was formulated on August 18, 1945.

13. C. van Dijk, *Rebellion Under the Banner of Islam* (The Hague: M. Nijhoff, 1981), VKI, p. 94; Holk H. Dengel, *Darul-Islam. Kartosuwirjos Kampf um einen islamischen Staat Indonesien*, Beitrage zur Sudasienforschung (Stuttgart: Steiner Verlag Wiesbadn, 1986), p. 106; Bernhard Dahm, *Sukarnos Kampf um Indonesiens Unabhangigkeit* (Frankfurt and Berlin, 1966; Ithaca: Cornell University Press, 1969), pp. 249 ff.; H. Feith, *The Decline of Constitutional Democracy in Indonesia* (Ithaca, N.Y.: Cornell University Press, 1962).

14. Mohammad Natsir, *Islam dan Kristen di Indonesia* (Bandung: Pelajar–Bulan Sabit, 1961), esp. pp. 188 ff., 219ff.; see also Frank L. Cooley, *The Growing Seed: The Christian Church in Indonesia* (Jakarta: BPK Gunung Mulia, 1981), esp. pp. 212 ff.

15. A. Mukti Ali, appointed minister for religious affairs in 1971, had participated in the International Dialogue held at Ajlatoun, Lebanon in 1970. He favored this cooperation between the adherents of different religious groups. According to him such working together was more effective among the common people to overcome mistrust and suspicion based on religious diversity than theological discussions which were important mainly to religious leaders. See his contribution in Stanley J. Samartha, ed., *Dialogue Between Men of Living Faiths* (Geneva: World Council of Churches, 1971).

16. "Christian Mission and Islamic Daʿwa," *International Review of Missions* (Geneva: World Council of Churches), 65: 260 (October 1976). The statement of consultation is on pp. 457 ff.

17. Olaf Schumann, "Herausforderung der Kirchen durch den Islam: Beispiel Indonesien," *Okumenische Rundschau* 30 (1981): 55–70, esp. p. 61. The secretariats of the Council of Churches in Indonesia and the Catholic Bishops Conference in Indonesia published together a statement in which they protested against these instructions: *Tinjauan mengenai Keputusan Menteri Agama No. 70 dan 77 Tahun 1978*. As an answer, the

government issued another letter of instruction signed by both the minister for home affairs and the minister for religious affairs. This confused matters more and was consequently neglected. Muslims continued to point to the two letters.

18. B.J. Boland, "Discussion on Islam in Indonesia Today," in *Studies on Islam*, ed. Konnklijke Nederlandse Akademie van Wetenschappen (Amsterdam and London: North Holland Publishing Company, 1974), pp. 37–50; for a different emphasis, see Harun Nasution and Hadji Abdul Malik Karim Amrullah in R. Italiaander, ed., *Indonesiens* (Erlangen: Verlag der Evang, 1976), pp. 107–21, 122–46.

19. *Arab Baru Islam: Suara Angkatan Muda*, a special issue of *Prisma*, 1984; Fakhry Ali and Bahtiar Effendy, eds., *Merabah Jalan Baru Islam* (Bandung: Mizan, 1986); M. Dawam Rahardjo, ed., *Islam Indonesia: Menatap masa depan Islam* (Jakarta: P3M, 1989); Bosco Carvallo and Dasrizal, eds., *Aspirasi Umat islam Indonesia* (Jakarta: Leppenas, 1988); Haidar Bagir, ed., *Satu Islam: sebuah dilemma* (Bandung: Mizan, 1986); J. Garang, ed., *Memasuki Masa Depan Bersama: Tugas dan Tanggungjawab agama-agama di Indonesia* (Jakarta: Litbang PGI, 1989).

20. Nurcholis Madjid et al., *Pembaharuan Pemikiran Islam* (Jakarta: Bulan Bintag, 1972); E. Saifuddin Anshari, *Kritik atas faham dan gerakan "Pembaharuan" Drs. Nurcholis Madjid* (Bandung: Bula Sabit, 1973); Nurcholis Madjid, *Islam: Kemodernan dan keindonesieniaan* (Bandung: Mizan, 1987).

21. "Aktualisasi Ajran Ahlussunah wal Jamaʿa," in M. Dawam Rahardjo, ed., *Islam Indonesia*, pp. 61–80.

22. "Cita-cita politik kita," in Carvallo and Dasrizal, eds., *Aspirasi*, pp. 1–36.

23. "Primbumisasi," in Carvello and Dasrizal, eds., *Aspirasi*, pp. 81–96.

24. In this context, he points to the roofs of the traditional mosques in Java as represented by the mosque of Demak with its three layers symbolizing the three "i"s. This form of their roofs was derived from the old Meru or pagoda style of Hindu buildings which can still be seen in Bali. For his understanding of *dār al-ṣulḥ*," see his foreword in Einar H. Stompul, *NU dan Pancasila* (Jakarta: Sinar Harapan, 1989).

25. A collection of such presentations was published by J. Garang (see note 19, above). Cf. T.B. Simatupang, "Agama-agama dalam pembangunan Negara Pancasila: Dialog, kerjasama dan pemberitaan," in his *Dari Revolusi ke Pembangunan* (Jakarta: BPK Gunung Mulia, 1987), pp. 145–59.

26. For further details and discussion of most recent events, see Olaf Schumann, "Staat und Gesellschaft in heutigen Indonesia," in *Die Welt des Islam* 33 (1993).

18

The Direction of Christian-Muslim Relations in Sub-Saharan Africa

Johann Haafkens

Of an estimated population of over 500 million in sub-Saharan Africa, nearly 30 percent are believed to be Muslim[1] and about 53 percent Christian.[2] Naturally the percentages of Muslims and Christians vary widely in the different subregions of Africa. In West Africa, for example, an area with over 150 million inhabitants in 1981, Muslims constituted some 47 percent of the population and Christians 37 percent. For northeastern Africa these percentages were, respectively, 53.7 and 35, for East Africa 13.4 and 62.6, for Central Africa 8.4 and 44.2, for areas near the Indian Ocean 5.6 and 50.8, and for southern Africa 1 and 77.6.[3]

These figures naturally are tentative, with Muslim sources generally providing much higher estimates of the percentage of Muslims. In statistics published by the Islamic Foundation, for example, the percentage of Muslims in sub-Saharan Africa is given at around fifty.[4] However, there is general agreement that in this area with a rapidly growing population, there are hundreds of millions of persons for whom relations between Christians and Muslims are of at least potential interest and concern. Polarization along religious lines could seriously jeopardize the future of this part of the world; the maintenance of good neighborly relations between Christians and Muslims therefore is a matter of considerable importance.

Christian-Muslim Relations before 1800

Three Christian kingdoms were established in the Nile valley in present-day Sudan somewhere around A.D. 580. From north to south these were Nobatia or al-Maris, Makuria or al-Muqarra, and Alodia or Alwa. The first two kingdoms were united and became known as Nubia with the capital Dongola.[5] For six centuries, the relationship of Nubia with Muslim Egypt was governed by a treaty and can be characterized as generally peaceful. Within the kingdoms, Christian-Muslim relations were harmonious. However, the Turkish Mamluk soldier kings of Egypt overthrew Nobatia in the thirteenth century. Makuria fell somewhat later and Alwa came under Muslim rule in 1504. The disappearance of Christianity in Nubia is seen by several scholars to be a consequence of the continuous Arab migration into the area, the urban character of the Christian civilization, and the geographical isolation of the Christian kingdoms.[6]

Christian Ethiopia has had a long history of interaction with Muslims. Around the year 615, when the Muslims suffered severe persecutions in Mecca, a number of them found refuge with the negus in Axum. These included ʿUthmān, a close companion of the Prophet and his third successor, and the Prophet's daughter Ruqayyā, ʿUthmān's wife. The Christian ruler refused to honor the request of a delegation sent from Mecca to extradite the Muslims. This decision in favor of the Muslims seems to have been influenced by an awareness on the side of the negus of an affinity between Christianity and the faith of Islam.[7]

Nonetheless, Ethiopia through its long history has seen a good many armed struggles between Christians, concentrated in the highlands, and Muslims in the lower areas. This was particularly the case from the late thirteenth to the sixteenth century. In the well-known war of Ahmad Gran against the Christian empire in the sixteenth century both sides received outside support, the Christians from the Portuguese and the Muslims from the Turkish pasha of Zabid in Yemen.[8] After this war the condition of the Christian empire was stabilized and a sort of *modus vivendi* between Christians and Muslims was reached. The status of the Muslim minority in the Christian heartland of Ethopia was comparable to the status provided for "protected people" (Jews, Christians) in Islamic countries. On the whole, in spite of the above mentioned wars, an atmosphere of religious tolerance has generally prevailed in Ethiopia.[9]

Turning to the East African coast we find that when the Portuguese arrived at the end of the fifteenth century, they discovered there the flourishing cities of the Muslim Swahili, a people of Afro-Asian (Arab, Persian) origin.[10] Almost immediately an armed conflict broke out which lasted until the first part of the eighteenth century. The hostility of the relations between Christians and Muslims in the area is clearly reflected in an important Swahili literary document of the time, the epos entitled "Heraklios."[11] This epos is an evocation of a war between the Prophet Muhammad and Heraklios, the Christian emperor of Byzantium. It was composed in 1728, a year before the Swahili people in alliance with Arabs from Oman drove the Portuguese out of the city of Mombasa.

Even such a brief review of these early centuries illustrates the checkered nature of Christian-Muslim relations in sub-Saharan Africa. There have been moments and periods when interaction has been harmonious, as with the first Christian-Muslim encounter in Ethiopia around 615. One can cite positive relationships for a number of centuries between Christian Nubia and Muslim Egypt, as well as periods in the later history of Ethiopia when religious tolerance prevailed. Of course there also have been times of confrontation and war. It is noteworthy, though, that several such conflicts were directly related to the tensions in the Christian-Muslim relationship in the Mediterranean and actually involved people from outside Africa. And where relationships were harmonious this may have been due, in a large measure, to resources and circumstances within the sub-Saharan African community itself which seem to make it possible for people to live together peacefully in culturally and religiously plural societies.

The Period of European Dominance, 1800–1960

When the era of European dominance began around the turn of the nineteenth century, Islam had been present for many centuries in several parts of Africa south of the Sahara. This was particularly the case in the Sahel area, from the Atlantic Ocean to the Nile. Islam had made a great impact on society and culture especially in West and northeastern Africa. The Muslim presence in East Africa was established in the coastal areas rather than inland, and extended as far south as Mozambique and Madagascar.

There were long periods in the history of Islam in Africa when Muslims lived peacefully together with adherents of African traditional religions. To a great extent that seems to be due to the fact that Islam was seen through the lens of traditional African views of life. Rulers were able to become Muslims without abandoning a number of pre-Islamic customs and religious practices, which was especially convenient when many of their subjects did not become Muslims. Sufi orders often played a major role in making Islam accessible for African people.

A very different tone was set when the spread of Islam came about through the Islamic reform movements. Reformers advocated a purification of Islam on the basis of its Arabic sources: the Qurʾan, the Traditions (*ḥadīth*), and the *sharīʿa*. In West Africa, for example, between 1700 and 1900, revolutionary revival movements led to the establishment of a number of Islamic states. In these cases toleration in the context of a symbiotic relationship between Islam and African traditional religion clearly was not the expectation. Rulers accused of being halfhearted Muslims, of disobeying the sharīʿa, and of concluding alliances with non-Muslims were overthrown. Armed force was used to establish, maintain, and extend these states.

Into these differing kinds of situations came the European colonial powers. As they moved to take over parts of Africa they not surprisingly met with firm resistance from Muslims as well as other groups. Once they had established their authority, however, the Europeans generally adopted a pragmatic approach to Islam. Where there were influential Muslim rulers or leaders, their authority was often recognized on condition that they cooperate with the administration. The British developed a system of indirect rule, for example, which was applied in such places as northern Nigeria and Sudan. In some cases this system actually strengthened the authority of Muslim rulers in areas where traditional religion was predominant.[12] As part of an effort to avoid tensions, colonial authorities even imposed restrictions on Christian missions in strongly Muslim areas.[13] In places where Muslims were less influential, the colonial administration actively supported the educational work of Christian missions. Here the authorities not only did nothing to encourage or favor Islam but sometimes, as in Zaire, actively tried to contain its influence and spread. The general policy was actually one of freedom of religion, but there was a tendency to limit the contacts of African Muslims with Muslims elsewhere for fear of the spread of anticolonial ideas.[14]

The changes that occurred in African society during the colonial period contributed to a considerable growth in the Muslim community in many countries. As increased security provided new opportunities for Muslim traders, Islamic commercial communities grew and spread to new areas. Moreover, Islam became an option for an increasing number of people who were not satisfied, under the new conditions, with the traditional African way of life. This phenomenon extended even to the upper strata of African society; several traditional rulers became Muslim in this period, as for example the king of the Bamoun in Foumban, Cameroon (around 1917).[15]

For the missionaries, who came mainly from Europe, influenced by centuries of rivalry between Christianity and Islam in the Mediterranean area, Islam in Africa was clearly seen as a danger and a force to be combatted. Missionary strategists worked out plans to set up a string of mission stations designed to act as a barrier to stop the spread of Islam to the south. At a synod meeting in 1908 of the Anglican Diocese of Western Equatorial Africa, for example, special attention was given to the fact that Islam was rapidly gaining ground in Yoruba country in Nigeria. As one of the speakers commented: "The Church must face this fact as a country faces an enemy, and determine upon a definite plan of campaign."[16] The Christian missionary response to the development of Islam in a number of areas of sub-Saharan Africa was characterized by ignorance, distrust, alarm, and a spirit of competitiveness (see, e.g., Bone, 1984 and 1987 for a discussion of the reaction of missionaries to the spread of Islam in Malawi).[17] In some cases Western missionary writings about Islam brought about Muslim responses in other parts of the world which then found their way back to Africa. Around 1880, for example, Muslims in Sierra Leone were reading *The*

Revelation of Truth, a book written in Arabic by an Indian Muslim, Rahmatullah al-Hindi, in response to a well-known missionary publication on Islam entitled *The Balance of Truth*.[18]

Although Christian missionaries obviously were concerned about the influence of Islam in Africa, they concentrated their efforts mainly on areas where Islam had little or no impact. Much of this, of course, was due to the practical realities of what was possible to accomplish. The Church Missionary Society, for example, according to Crampton, "never [had] the human and financial resources for extensive work in the Northern Emirates" of Nigeria, where Islamic influence was strong.[19] Much of what characterized the Christian-Muslim encounter in this colonial period, then, was actually the absence of encounter. As Christians consciously avoided contact with Islamic communities, so Muslims too tended to withdraw from engagement with Christians. The tendency in many areas seems to have been for each community to live its own life without acknowledging the existence of the other any more than was necessary.[20]

Such an approach of exclusivism and mutual avoidance, however, did not always prevail and clearly did not characterize traditional society in Africa. In 1969, for example, a king of Sierra Leone sent one son to England to learn about Christianity, and another to Futa Jallon in Guinea to study Islam.[21] The traditional oracle of the Yoruba in Nigeria could declare, on the one hand, that certain children were destined to become Muslims, and on the other that Christian missionaries should be allowed to settle in Ibadan in spite of the objections of local Muslims.[22] This inclusive approach is related to the African understanding of human life in community.[23]

It is this sense of community, no doubt, which enabled Anglican clergymen in Lagos, in the last decade of the nineteenth century, to study not only Arabic but the religion of Islam itself under the direction of local bilingual Muslim teachers.[24] Living in close contact with Muslims, Christian leaders in Nigeria expressed appreciation for the African character of Islam, its spirit of self-reliance, and the absence of racialism and clericalism among Yoruba Muslims. These characteristics of Islam often were cited as exemplary for Christians.[25] Courtesy and a sense of moderation, reflecting Yoruba cultural values, generally prevailed in relationships between Christians and Muslims. It should be noted, however, that this courtesy did not affect the deep commitment of such Christians to evangelism, while the Muslims also remained adamant and assertive about their religion and faith.[26] In western Nigeria, Muslims initially watched the advent of Christianity with concern and mounted a sort of passive resistance. Later they became increasingly responsive to Christian presence, ready to engage in generally good-natured public discussions, and less suspicious of modern education.[27]

To a very real extent, nationalism, often drawn upon as a common goal in the development of a strong educational program in Africa, served to bring together Christians and Muslims in a kind of reinforcement of the traditional African sense of community. Dr. Edward Blyden, a nineteenth-century educator who served for some time as a minister in the Presbyterian Church in Monrovia, and as a church missionary agent in Sierra Leone, is well-known for his efforts to create modern educational institutions for the advancement of the people of Africa. As a nationalist, he felt that both the Christian and the Muslim academic traditions should be harnessed for this purpose. He even launched the idea of the establishment of an institute of higher Islamic learning. His efforts on this score, however, received considerably more sympathy from the colonial governors than from the leadership of the mission organizations.[28]

It seems to be the case, then, that missionaries responded for the most part to the Muslim presence in Africa in a spirit of conflict and rivalry rather than of cooperation. This of course had significant impact on the newly founded Christian communities. It must be said, however, that the real encounters between members of the two faiths were determined by more than the formal or historical relationships between Christianity and Islam. Sharing life in community as sons and daughters of Africa, and living in a similar colonial situation, Christians and Muslims often maintained personal relations much more respectful and cordial than one might expect from official pronouncements.

Postindependence Developments, 1960–1975

By 1960, many countries in sub-Saharan Africa had attained, or were in the process of attaining, their political independence. It was the beginning of a new era in the history of this part of the world, a time of renewal and of hope for a better future. Leaders everywhere emphasized the need for national unity—people from different linguistic, cultural, and religious backgrounds were challenged to work hand in hand to build the new Africa.

Within the Christian community much thought was given at this time to the future role of the church in Africa. An All-Africa Church Conference was held in Ibadan, Nigeria in 1958, for example, with the title: "The Church in Changing Africa." In 1960 the Christian Council of Nigeria commissioned a study resulting in a lengthy report on Christian responsibility in an independent Nigeria. Among the issues addressed in both of these examples was the relationship of Christians and Muslims. A Protestant process of consultation on this particular matter led in 1959 to what was called the Islam in Africa Project.[29] (The name of the organization was changed in 1987 to Project for Christian-Muslim Relations in Africa.) Following wide-ranging discussions which extended over a good many years, the purpose of the project finally was formulated as follows:

"To keep before the Churches in Africa their responsibility for understanding Islam and the Muslims of their region in view of the Churches' task of interpreting faithfully in the Muslim world the Gospel of Jesus Christ."[30]

Under the responsibility of the Islam in Africa Project (IAP), area committees were established in Sierra Leone, Ghana, Benin, Nigeria, Cameroon, Ethiopia, Kenya, and Malawi and training programs were organized which were well received in the local churches. In a number of countries Muslims agreed to come to IAP seminars to help participants gain a better understanding of Islam. Several small books were published by IAP advisors, such as *Islam and Christianity, 90 Questions and Answers*,[31] and *Christian Witness among Muslims*. The type of relationship with Muslims that the project advocated is reflected in the words of an Anglican clergyman, the Rev. F.O. Segun (later bishop of Lagos), quoted in the 1962 report "Christian Responsibility in an Independent Nigeria": "The approach . . . should always be by love, by readiness for a deeper understanding of each other's point of view, and above all, by living what we profess and leaving the issues in God's hands."[32] The project can be described on the one hand as an effort to find a genuine Christian way of practicing the traditional African values of life in community. From another angle, it can be understood as an effort of the Christian community, in its relationship to Muslims, to witness to Christ in a spirit of evangelical love, respecting others in their religious commitments.

It is important to note that the IAP program was not just the concern of a few interested persons. It was developed in Africa through an extensive process of consultation and found ready welcome and support within Protestant churches on the continent. This, of course, did not mean that old attitudes of suspicion, confrontation, or withdrawal suddenly disappeared. It did mean, however, that a reorientation was taking place within the churches. Thinking about the relationship between Christians and Muslims took a new direction, changing its primary focus from rivalry and conflict to an emphasis on life-in-community. The positive experiences that members of the two faiths had in encountering each other (experiences that occurred but were not often cited in earlier days) were more and more taken into account as Christians reconsidered their relationship with Muslims.

This reorientation happened not only in Protestant communities. In Francophone West Africa, where most Christians belong to the Roman Catholic Church, the Regional Episcopal Conference established a "Commission on (other) Religions" while the Second Vatican Council (1962–65) was still in session. The dogmatic Constitution on the Church of 1964 and the 1965 Declaration on the Relations of the Church with the Non-Christian Religions were major incentives leading to the establishment of this commission. The Constitution mentions Muslims as people "who profess to hold the faith of Abraham, and worship with us the One, Merciful God, who will judge mankind on the last day." The Declaration explicitly states that "the Church has also a high regard for the Muslims." In a statement on Christian-Muslim relations, it says: "Over the centuries many quarrels and dissensions have arisen between Christians and Muslims. The Sacred Council now pleads with all to forget the past, and urges that a sincere effort be made to achieve mutual understanding, for the benefit of all men, let them together preserve and promote peace, liberty, social justice and moral values."

These statements were warmly welcomed by many Catholic missionaries in West Africa, who found there a reflection of their own experiences of encounter with Muslims.[33] As P.B. Clarke rightly observes, the Declaration was in some measure a vindication of the efforts of both Christians and Muslims in Senegal and elsewhere in West Africa to encourage dialogue between their respective faiths.[34] In 1969 the Episcopal Conference appointed a special commission to deal with Christian-Muslim relations. This commission developed training programs, in many ways similar to those organized by the IAP. Among other things, the commission prepared a clear and simple presentation of Islam for African Christians under the French title: "Connais-tu ton Frère?" (Do you know your brother?), translated into English as "Let us understand each other."

In Nigeria, Father Victor Chukwulozie has been involved in the organization of Christian-Muslim encounters since 1962. At his initiative, a meeting of Catholic and Muslim leaders took place in Ibadan in 1974.[35] The Catholic Church in West Africa clearly took steps to move from confrontation to dialogue, although Francophone West Africa was the only region in the continent where the Catholics formally developed a program on Christian-Muslim relations. As is true for Protestants, this did not mean that the problems of the past were somehow eliminated, but rather that efforts were made to see these relations in a new light.[36]

For a better understanding of what happened to Christian-Muslim relationships in this period, it is useful to consider specific developments inside the respective communities. Within the churches, serious efforts were put forth to make Christianity more relevant to African realities. Traditional African culture and religion as well as national life were taken into consideration. The title of a series of radio lectures by the Reverend Professor E. Bolaji Idowu of the University of Ibadan, *Towards an Indigenous Church*, is very significant in this regard.[37] The awareness that the church had something important to learn from the traditional African understanding of life certainly contributed to the new approach to Christian-Muslim relations in Christian circles.

Within the Muslim community, developments in this period were largely a continuation of what had been initiated during the colonial period—the further development of structures and institutions to enhance the life of the community in the new society. There was a strong emphasis on the provision of modern education in a specifically Islamic environment. In Nigeria, Muslim societies like the Ansar-ud-Deen founded in 1923, the Nawair-ud-Deen founded in the 1930s, and the Jamaʿatu Nasril Islam were particularly active in this respect. A Muslim women's society founded in 1958, called Isabatudeen, established a Muslim girls' grammar school in 1964 in Ibadan.[38] Islamic literature in English and French was being published, and Qurʾan translations were widely distributed. Organizations of Muslim women, youth, and students became very active. Missionary work was undertaken, efforts were made to establish national Muslim organizations, and international relations were strengthened.[39] Even the traditional Muslim understanding of the relationship between God and human beings was changing, with the emphasis more on human responsibility than on God's omnipotence.[40] Such changes made Islam appear more similar to Christianity than in the past and did not really jeopardize the hope for increasingly harmonious Christian-Muslim relations.

During this period, however, there were some clear concerns among Christians about the growing strength of the Muslim community. The above-mentioned 1962 report to the Christian Council of Nigeria, "Christian Responsibility in an Independent Nigeria," expressed the hope that there could be real political freedom and economic progress there, but at the same time noted that "as independence approached there were deep-seated fears on the part of the Christian population regarding their future in the 'Muslim' North."[41] In fact, Christian worries in relation to Islam were being allayed by a number of factors. While around 1960 the feeling was widespread among Christians that the growth in the number of Muslims in Africa was far outstripping the numerical growth in Christianity, there was much more of a balance than was feared.[42] In the political field, the Nigerian civil war (1967–70) did not lead to a general polarization between Christians and Muslims, and after the war a considerable effort was made toward national reconciliation. In 1972 a peace accord concluded in Sudan raised hopes for a peaceful coexistence of Christians and Muslims in a country that had been ravaged by civil war. Senegal, with a large Muslim majority, remained peaceful under a Christian president, Leopold Sedar Sengor, as did Cameroon, a country where Christians constitute a majority, under Muslim president Ahmadu Ahidjo.

In 1974, Dr. Musa Abdul of the Department of Arabic and Islamic Studies at the University of Ibadan cochaired a dialogue meeting at the University of Legon in Ghana organized by the World Council of Churches. In his paper, entitled "A Community of Religions," he expressed the spirit of tolerance and cooperation that characterized the 1960s as a time of optimism and hope for better relations between the communities: "I regard every Christian as brother/sister and fellow seeker in an identical quest and a comrade against materialism and its concomitant evils."[43] Indeed here there were signs of hope.

Recent Trends Toward Polarization

The reality is that many of the hopes of the sixties have not materialized. In certain Muslim circles the Western democratic principles on which the new African nations were based have come under serious criticism. A. R. I. Doi wrote in 1975 that Nigerian Muslim scholars who went to Europe or America for higher education more often than not returned with a much greater degree of modern Islam consciousness. In spite of their apparent acceptance of Western values, they have engaged in a subsequent apologetic attack on Western culture and Western secularism. This phenomenon has continued among Muslim intellectuals who emphasize that Islam is the only way and the law of Islam the only viable basis for a modern state. In this process they reject not only Western democracy and Marxism, but also traditional African concepts of community life.[44] These voices are heard not only in Nigeria[45] and in the Sudan, where the National Islamic Front is an articulate protagonist of sharīʿa law, but also in Senegal and elsewhere.

Revivalist Muslim authors such as the Egyptian Sayyid Quṭb, and Mawlana Mawdūdī from Pakistan, are widely read among Muslims in Africa. In a Kenyan textbook on Islam for secondary school and teacher training colleges, for example, Quṭb's Muslim Brotherhood in Egypt and Mawdūdī's Jamāʿat-i-Islāmī are presented as exemplary movements.[46] The Islamic revolution in Iran has given a new impetus to advocates of the sharīʿa as the basis of national life. Christians, who have adopted the principle of a state which is neutral in religious matters, generally reject these ideas, which they fear will lead to inequality before the law for citizens of different religious persuasions. There is a sense in which the matter of the sharīʿa took many Christians by surprise as they began to discover that there are significant groups of Muslims who do not accept the consensus on statehood which was reached at the time of independence.

This issue is not merely a theoretical matter. Considerable tension arose in Nigeria around 1978, when the place of the sharīʿa in the national constitution was discussed. Since then friction between Christians and Muslims has been on the increase, and there are signs of a real polarization along religious lines. The debate on Nigeria's membership in the Organization of the Islamic Conference plays an important role. Outbursts of violence involving the loss of human life and the destruction of property (including church buildings) have taken place in Kano (1982) as well as in Kaduna state (1987). In Sudan the 1972 peace accord collapsed when civil war broke out. The introduction of sharīʿa laws in 1983 was pivotal in the conflict. The sharīʿa was seen by its opponents as an instrument of Islamization and Arabization. Tension has not run as high in Senegal, but reports that revivalist Muslim preachers warn Muslims in villages to guard their own identity and not to befriend Christians are a matter of real concern. Such a development clearly calls into question previously existing harmonious relationships.

The rising tide of Muslim radicalism in Africa, receiving significant support from outside the continent, does have an impact on the way Christians view their relationship with Muslims. Those who hoped that rivalry and conflict would gradually decrease are deeply concerned that the movement seems to be leading in the opposite direction. Many factors serve to complicate relations. In addition to the radicalism, there are socioeconomic and political differences between Christians and Muslims which reveal a religious dimension. Moreover, Islam and Christianity are both missionary religions. Within the two communities in Africa, and strongly supported from sources outside the continent, plans continue to be developed for the Christianization or the Islamization of all of Africa. Mutual awareness of such plans, inevitable in today's world of ready communication, raises suspicion and increases tension. This is especially true when, often erroneously, local communities are identified with such plans.

Conclusion

After independence there was a widespread feeling in Africa that Christian-Muslim relations were moving in a new direction, that there was a turn for the better. Resources within the society and within the two religious communities were identified in the hope of enhancing such a development. Now it has become evident that a considerable effort will be needed to maintain the momentum toward a more harmonious relationship.

Meanwhile, Christian-Muslim dialogue continues and the resources are still available. In 1989 at a Christian-Muslim colloquium in Arusha, Tanzania, organized by the World Council of Churches, there were moments of great tension. However, under the wise leadership of an Anglican bishop from Sierra Leone, the Right Reverend Dr. Michael Keili, and of a Muslim who is Uganda's ambassador in Saudi Arabia, His Excellency Badru Kateregga, there was no break in relations. Thus it was possible for the final report on the meeting to conclude that the colloquium did in fact maintain a spirit of cordiality throughout, and that there was clear evidence of a willingness to accommodate each other's views.[47]

The Right Reverend John Onaiyekan, one of the leading Nigerian Catholic theologians, concludes his article about the sharīʿa in Nigeria as follows: "God did not make a mistake when He put us all together here in one geographical zone. Since we all invoke Him, albeit under various Names, we must meet the challenge we have assumed to live in unity and harmony as one indissoluble Sovereign Nation under God [a reference to the Nigerian constitution]. This is a duty we owe to ourselves, to the coming generations, to mankind, and to God Himself."[48] Whenever and wherever, by Muslims and Christians, the matter of Christian-Muslim relations in Africa is approached in this spirit, there is hope for the future.

NOTES

1. R. Delval, *A Map of the Muslims in the World* (Leiden: E.J. Brill, 1984).

2. David Barrett, *World Christian Encyclopedia* (Nairobi: Oxford University Press, 1982).

3. Barrett, *World*; Delval, *A Map*; Johannes Haafkens, "Statistics of Religious Adherence in Africa: Muslims and Christians," in J.P. Rajeshekar, ed., *Christian-Muslim Relations in Eastern Africa* (Geneva: Lutheran World Federation, 1988), pp. 124–29.

4. M.M. Ahsan, *Islam, Faith and Practice* (Nairobi: Islamic Foundation, 1985); Haafkens, "Statistics."

5. Basil Davidson, *Africa: History of a Continent* (New York: Spring Books [Hamlyn], 1972), p. 132; Yusuf Fadl Hasan, "The Penetration of Islam in Eastern Sudan," in I.M. Lewis, ed., *Islam in Tropical Africa* (London: Oxford University Press, 1966), p. 144.

6. Hasan, "The Penetration," pp. 146–54; Davidson, *Africa*, p. 137.

7. Alfred Guillaume, *The Life of Muhammad: A Translation of Ishaq's Sirat Rasul Allah*, 2d imp. (Lahore, Karachi, Dakka: Oxford University Press, Pakistan Branch, 1968), pp. 146–53.

8. E.J. Van Donzel and Anqasa Amin, *La Porte de la Foi* (Leiden: E.J. Brill, 1969), p. 11.

9. E. Ullendorff, "Habash, I. Historical Background," in *Encyclopedia of Islam*, new ed. (Leiden: E.J. Brill, London: Luzac & Co., 1971), 3: 4–5. For a different view of the Christian-Muslim relationship in Ethiopia see A.R. Moten, "Islam in Ethiopia," in *Africa Events* (Alperton, U.K.) 6, no. 5 (May 1990): 32–35.

10. Davidson, *Africa*, pp. 203–7; A.I. Salim, "Kenya," in *Encyclopedia of Islam*, new ed., 4: 885–91.

11. Jan Knappert, *Het Epos van Heraklios* (Amsterdam: Meulenhoff, 1977).

12. E.P.T. Crampton, "Christianity in Northern Nigeria," in O. Kalu, ed., *Christianity in West Africa: The Nigeria Story* (Ibadan: Daystar Press, 1978), pp. 56 ff.

13. Ibid., pp. 48–53.

14. J. Spencer Trimingham, *Islam in West Africa* (London: Oxford University Press, 1959), p. 218.

15. The growth of the Muslim community is highlighted by figures given by David Barrett in the *World Christian Encyclopedia* (1982). He mentions an increase in the percentage of Muslims in Nigeria from 25.9 percent to 43.4 percent between 1900 and 1963, and an increase in Tanzania from 7 percent to 33.2 percent betwen 1900 and 1957. The estimated increase between 1900 and 1970 for Mali is from 30 percent to 78 percent, for Burkina Faso from 10 percent to 35 percent, and for Sierra Leone from 10 percent to 38 percent.

16. T.G.O. Gbadamosi, *The Growth of Islam among the Yoruba, 1841–1908* (London: Longman, 1978), p. 230.

17. D. Bone, "The Christian Missionary Response to the Development of Islam in Malawi: 1875–1940," *Bulletin of Islam and Christian-Muslim Relations in Africa* (Birmingham) 2, no. 3 (1984), 1–23; D. Bone, "The Development of Islam in Malawi and the Response of the Christian Churches: 1940–1986," ibid. 5, no 4 (1987), 7–24

18. Edward W. Blyden, *Christianity, Islam and the Negro Race* (Edinburgh: Edinburgh University Press, 1967; first published 1887), p. 3.

19. Crampton, "Christianity," p. 71.

20. Lamin O. Sanneh, "Christian Experience of Islamic Daʿwa, with Particular Reference to Africa," *International Review of Missions* (Geneva) 65 (1976): 417–21; Bone, "Islam in Malawi," pp. 18–19.

21. Lamin O. Sanneh, *West African Christianity: The Religious Impact* (London: C. Hurst & Co., 1983), p. 130.

22. Gbadamosi, *Growth*, pp. 126–27.

23. M.A. Oduyoye, "The Value of African Religious Beliefs and Practices for Christian Theology," in K. Appiahkubi and S. Torres, eds., *African Theology en Route* (New York: Orbis Books, 1979), pp. 110–11.

24. Gbadamosi, *Growth*, p. 129.

25. Ibid., pp. 143–44.

26. Ibid. pp. 146–47.

27. Sanneh, *West African Christianity*, pp. 217–19.

28. Ibid., pp. 214–20; Blyden, *Christianity*, pp. 82–107.

29. John Crossley, "The Islam in Africa Project," *International Review of Missions* 61 (1972): 150–60; Johannes Haafkens, "Naar gemeenschappelijke verantwoordelijkheid als belangrijk moment in de relaties tussen Christenen en Moslims in Afrika," *Wereld en Zending* (Amsterdam) 10, no. 1 (1981): 54–61.

30. A significant role in these discussions was played by Willem A. Bijlefeld, who lived in Nigeria from 1959 to 1966, serving the project in a central coordinating capacity as leader of its team of advisers and, after 1965, as director of its study center in Ibadan.

31. Abd-ul-Massih, *Au Seuil de l'Islam* (Yaounde: Ēditions Clé, 1965); Abd-ul-Massih, *Islam and Christianity, 90 Questions and Answers* (Ibadan, Daystar Press, 1967).

32. "Christian Responsibility in an Independent Nigeria," a report prepared for the Christian Council of Nigeria, p. 97.

33. J. Stamer, "Report of the Episcopal Commission for Relations between Christians and Muslims in West Africa," *Bulletin on Islam and Christian-Muslim Relations in Africa* (Birmingham) 5, no. 3 (1987): 18–20.

34. P.B. Clarke, "Christian Approaches to Islam in Francophone West Africa in the Post-Independence Era (c. 1960–1983): From Confrontation to Dialogue," *Bulletin on Islam and Christian-Muslim Relations in Africa* (Birmingham) 1, no. 2 (1983): 3.

35. Victor Chukwulozie, *Muslim-Christian Dialogue in Nigeria* (Ibadan: Daystar Press, 1986), pp. 70 ff.

36. Stamer, "Report," pp. 21–22.

37. E. Bolaji Idowu, *Towards an Indigenous Church* (London: Oxford University Press, 1965).

38. A.R.I. Doi, "Islam in Nigeria: Changes Since Independence," in E. Fashole-Luke,

et al., eds., *Christianity in Independent Africa* (Ibadan: Ibadan University Press, 1978), p. 336; E.O. Oyelade, "Islamic Movements in Yorubaland: Challenges and Responses in Christian-Muslim Relations," paper presented at the November 1984 Consultation of the Christian Councils in West Africa on Christian-Muslim Relations.

39. Doi, "Islam," pp. 338–39, 346–50.

40. Ibid., pp. 343–44.

41. "Christian Responsibility," p. 89.

42. Dean S. Gilliland, *African Religion Meets Islam, Religious Change in Northern Nigeria* (Lanham, New York, London: University Press of America, 1986), pp. 169–72.

43. S. Babs Mala, "Attitudes of Nigerian Muslim Intellectuals towards Christian-Muslim Relations," *Bulletin on Islam and Christian-Muslim Relations in Africa* (Birmingham) 1, no. 4 (1984): 14.

44. It is interesting to note the significant parallels between these ideas and the principles applied by the revolutionary founders of Islamic states in West Africa in the eighteenth and nineteenth centuries.

45. Joseph Kenny, "Sharīʿa in Nigeria—A Historical Survey," *Bulletin on Islam and Christian-Muslim Relations in Africa* (Birmingham) 4, no. 1 (1986): 1–21; J. Onaiyekan, "The Sharīʿa in Nigeria: A Christian View," ibid. 5, no. 3 (1987): 1–17.

46. M.A. Quraishy, *Textbook on Islam*, Book 2 (Nairobi: Islamic Foundation, 1987), pp. 301–12.

47. "A Christian-Muslim Colloquium in Tanzania," *Current Dialogue* (Geneva: World Council of Churches) 17 (1989): 17.

48. Onaiyekan, "The Sharīʿa," p. 15.

19

Muslims in Europe in the Late Twentieth Century

Jorgen S. Nielsen

There has been a continuous Muslim presence in Europe virtually since the beginning of Muslim history. For the most part it has consisted of small communities and individuals. But at times the presence has encompassed historically significant communities such as that in Spain and, in continuity with the present, the Tartars, Bosnians, Albanians, and other Muslim peoples of eastern Europe.

This essay is concerned primarily with the present Muslim communities of western Europe, communities which are overwhelmingly the consequence of the imperial and postimperial history of modern Europe. Such communities started at a low level in the German states during the eighteenth century with renegade soldiers and prisoners from the Ottoman and later also the Russian armies supplemented by merchants and diplomats. The Ottoman dimension was strengthened during the late nineteenth century as the unified German state rapidly built up Turkish interests after the dismissal of Bismarck.[1]

British and French history shows the imperial link most clearly. The British East India Company started recruiting Indians almost from the beginning of its presence in India. To this was added significant Yemeni recruitment through Aden after the Suez Canal was opened in 1869.[2] Two world wars brought soldiers and sailors in growing numbers. Much of this early immigration to Britain of people of various religious backgrounds, including Muslim, was related directly to employment in the imperial communications and military machine. In France, on the other hand, there is a continuity of immigration for employment in mines and industry, probably related to France's chronic underpopulation during the nineteenth and early twentieth centuries. During both world wars a significant proportion of indentured labor from North Africa was forced into the defense industries or, in the Second World War, to build military installations for the German occupying power.[3]

After 1945, having absorbed demobilized military personnel, European industry soon began to extend its efforts to find labor to satisfy the fast growing economies. In Britain the search began in the Caribbean, spread to India during the 1950s, and toward the end of the decade into Pakistan, mainly West but also soon East, the later Bangladesh. In addition, people came for work from other parts of the empire, having left situations of conflict such as that in Cyprus in the 1950s, in East Africa because of nationalization policies, and later in various parts of the Middle East because of regional conflicts.[4]

France also began importing labor from North Africa, a process which after a pause during the Algerian war of independence picked up again during the 1960s.[5] West Germany came into the field slightly later because it first had to absorb the many Germans leaving eastern Europe. But then it turned to southern Europe and, finally, in 1961 signed the first labor supply treaty with Turkey. This model was followed with other supply countries in the succeeding years, while countries such as the Netherlands, Belgium, Denmark, Sweden, and Switzerland followed suit.[6]

Throughout this period we are talking of "primary" immigration, people coming to seek work usually for a limited period of a few years. From the Muslim areas of recruitment the movement was overwhelmingly of young men. This situation changed with far-reaching consequences in 1962 in Britain, when the first Commonwealth immigration act came into effect, and in 1973–74 in mainland Europe when governments closed the doors to primary immigration because of a sudden economic retrenchment. The pattern became one of family reunion, as wives and children also migrated.

By the end of the 1970s, communities of Muslim background in western Europe were beginning to approach a demographic balance between men and women, settled in families with children. But it was obviously a very young community, with few older members and the great majority of adults in the age of parenthood.[7] So the ground was laid for a continuing expansion in numbers even as governments during the 1980s laid down ever stricter limitations on immigration. By 1985 these restrictions were so tight that immigration virtually had ceased. But it was replaced by a growth in the numbers of people seeking political asylum. Any continuing Muslim arrival into Europe in the late 1980s must be seen as part of the refugee question, although clandestine immigration through Spain and Italy continues.

By the end of the 1980s the total Muslims in western Europe was probably in the region of 7 million, an increase of 1.5 million over the decade. Any attempt to produce figures is fraught with error, because official government population statistics and censuses usually do not include information on religion. So data have to be deduced from other figures, such as numbers of foreign citizens, making the assumption that Algerians, Tunisians, Moroccans, Turks, and Pakistanis are of Muslim background. Only unreliable corrections can be made for the minorities of those nationalities that are not Muslim, such as Syrian or Armenian Christians. The question becomes yet more difficult when considering people from countries with several large religious communities, such as India, Lebanon, Egypt, Yugoslavia, and countries of sub-Saharan Africa. But with these provisos in mind, one can "guesstimate" 2.5 million in France, 1.7 million in West Germany, 1 million in Britain, about 300,000 each in Belgium and the Netherlands, about 200,000 in Italy, 100,000 each in Austria and Switzerland, and smaller numbers although still in the tens of thousands in the Scandinavian countries, Spain, and Portugal.[8]

Immigration and Settlement

The circumstances under which Muslim communities have arrived and are settling have contributed to their perceptions of their surroundings and of the space they have made and can make for themselves in the matrix of European society. Particularly in the British case, the ease of entry during the early years contrasts starkly with the difficulties experienced now after almost thirty years of relentless tightening of the entry rules. The obstacles are both legal and administrative, to the point that only a few thousand people a year now succeed in gaining entry clearance to join spouses, parents, or children already there. Recent research in Britain suggests that perhaps as many as 80 percent of children denied entry by officials, because of doubt raised about the authenticity of the claimed relationship, can be shown by genetic "fingerprinting" to be genuine offspring. It is not much easier in France or Germany, with the result that there are growing numbers of people working without legal status—and therefore exposed to exploitation by unscrupulous employers. Another consequence is that spouses legally married in the country of origin are being prevented from joining their partners in Europe. In Germany a marriage has to last one year before a wife can join her husband; in Britain a spouse has to show that the primary purpose of entry is marriage and not employment. A side effect of these stringent regulations is the difficulty experienced by relatives wanting to visit for such reasons as family celebrations or funerals, and often finding they have to wait many months for visas.

Once they have succeeded in entering, the next major hurdle for immigrants has been finding employment. The labor treaties adopted by West Germany have meant that a laborer hired in the country of origin by a specific employer entered with a permit to work only for that employer. In the Netherlands similar arrangements often have applied. Work permits are required throughout Europe for foreigners, and the restrictions on changing employment or type of employment are relaxed only gradually with the length of stay. With a full work permit, attained usually after ten years of residence (although the period differs somewhat among countries), the holder is still vulnerable if unemployed or somehow in conflict with the law. Spouses'—usually wives'—right of residence is almost totally dependent on that of their partners. If one is divorced or widowed a deportation order is a not unusual result.

In Britain the situation on the surface is different, in that most Muslims have become British citizens. On entry as Commonwealth citizens, therefore, they have had the right to full participation in the economic and political life of the country. In reality this has been restricted by racial discrimination which means that they often have been employed below their training and have suffered consistently higher rates of unemployment.[9]

We have already pointed to the major shift in the nature of immigration toward family reunion, which took place after 1962 in Britain and a decade later elsewhere. This shift has been crucial in bringing out the religious dimension in immigrant and ethnic minority communities.[10] So long as single men were the chief category of people involved, their religious life—if they wished to pursue it—could be limited to regular prayer and care with food. As already stated, some employers did feel able to make minimal attempts at recommendations, but it was often many years before any kind of policy was achieved regarding the wider recognition of religious sensitivities in employment.

When there is a change from living singly to living with wife and children, immediately a great many new practical issues arise. Family realities underscore tensions between European health and social welfare policies and traditional Islamic cultural practices. Often the health services have been the slowest part of the public sector to adapt to cultural and religious minorities. As a result "traditional" medicine continues to be actively practiced among Muslim communities. Perhaps more serious, it is becoming clear that psychologists and psychiatrists are only just beginning to realize that they have difficulty functioning across religious and cultural boundaries.[11]

Education in a new environment raises challenges across the board. In many ways the school has become the focus of the tension between diversity and integration. This has been aided by a tendency in recent decades in Europe to see the school as one of the main arenas in which to change attitudes and social structures—often called "social engineering." The school is thus the place to which European educationists look for the shaping of a future society, whether it be multicultural, pluralistic, nationalistic, or whatever, depending on one's political point of view. Muslim parents are ambivalent about this. On the one hand, they see successful participation in the education system and subsequent professional achievements of the children as guaranteeing the prosperity of the family. On the other hand, they fear that the school is subverting central components of the traditional way of life: gender roles, parental authority, and ultimately cultural and religious authority.

Muslim Institutions

It is quite clear that only with the growth of Muslim family life in Europe has there been any soil in which Muslim institutions could grow. The change from individual to family life has been a major determining factor in the spread of mosques. There has been a significant rise in the opening of new mosques in Britain from 1964 on, and a similar rise in other European countries began a decade later. Although statistics are not reliable, by the end of the 1980s the number in France was probably well over one thousand, in Britain about five hundred, and in West Germany somewhere between those two estimates.[12]

Given the very different context of the operation of mosques in Europe as compared to the countries of origin, it is to be expected that changes are taking place. These changes come about because the needs of the community itself are changing, as well as because of the very different institutional and legal context in which they have to operate. The concept of an "Islamic cultural center," a widespread term for larger mosques with their associated bookshops, teaching, and publicity, is strange in the Muslim tradition. It is becoming more common to have weddings solemnized in community mosques where this was seldom done before. The larger newly built mosques are having morgues designed into them for ease of Muslim burial. Mosque committees, themselves a new phenomenon, are having to find ways of responding to Muslim needs which were never previously addressed to the mosque—except perhaps in the pristine days of the Prophet and the early caliphs.

The management of mosques, usually taken care of by the state in the country of origin, has had to be taken up by the communities themselves. It is therefore an element of the whole process of the formation of Muslim organizations in the various countries of Europe. It is difficult to describe beyond vague generality the ways in which Muslims in Europe have organized themselves. The process and format of organization is closely dependent on the circumstances in each individual country, and the nature of the organization has so far been closely dependent on the heritage of the country of origin.

Most organizations in Europe have sprung out of the continuing history of Muslim movements in the countries of origin. Even where many mosques have been founded and run by small groups arising locally, Muslims have felt it useful or necessary to link in to the wider networks. Among the Muslim Turks in Germany, for example, the Sulaymanli movement played a dominant role up to the end of the 1970s and continues to be important. Beside it are the smaller Nursi and Milli Gorus groups among the Sunnis. The Alevis have their own less formal network.[13] But this latter also has to be more circumspect, since the German and Turkish governments retain quite close cooperation, a cooperation based on the former's refusal to recognize that Germany is a country of immigration, and on the latter's need to keep some degree of control over its expatriate population. After the military coup of September 1980, the Turkish government expanded the role in Germany of the Department of Religious Affairs (Diyanet) of the Prime Minister's Office. As a result, during the 1980s the Diyanet's German branch based in Cologne has been spreading its control over Turkish mosques to the extent that it has taken away the lead position from the Sulaymanlis.

This change in influence has been assisted not only by German officialdom, but also by the facilities available to organizations in German law. Virtually all the mosques were originally founded as voluntary associations (*eingetragenes Verein*, or *e.v.*), their direction in the hands of a committee elected by the members, at least legally. As Diyanet supporters have succeeded in getting themselves elected onto these committees, they have had the associations' status changed to that of foundation (*Stiftung*), where control is in the hands of nominated trustees.

While the situation in Germany is dominated by Turkish perspectives, there are also significant Muslim communities of other ethnic and cultural origins, forming possibly the most influential network of converts in western Europe. This raises questions related particularly to religious education, such as who should design the curriculum and whether it should be given in Turkish or German, questions still far from being solved.[14]

All governments of the countries of origin, not only the Turkish, are concerned to preserve as much influence as possible over their expatriate communities. Some of them know from bitter experience that the communities in Europe are a base which exiled or opposition politicians and movements can use to great effect. France experienced this during the Algerian war of independence and interned thousands of Algerians in France in an effort to cut off sources of support to the Front de Libération Nationale (FLN).[15] The underground movements in Turkey during the years leading up to the 1980 coup, movements ranging across the political spectrum, found support, a propaganda base, and a safe haven among the Turkish communities in Germany. Benazir Bhutto's return to power in Pakistan in 1988 used supporters in Britain as a springboard, as did her opponents in turn.

It is probably in France and Britain that Muslim organizations are most splintered. In France, Algerians can relate to the pro-FLN Amicales, a movement which seems to be weakening in the face of groups in opposition. The

Moroccan government is probably the most successful in keeping a tight hold over its expatriates through its own Amicales as well as through extensive informal networks. At present, all of these various organizations and movements are under pressure from the fast-growing influence of the Jamāʾat al-Tablīgh movement, appearing in French under the banner of "Foi et proutique." At the same time the growth in the Turkish and sub-Saharan (particularly Senegalese) presence has brought in new variations and traditions in the last decade or so.

It is to avoid too much of such foreign influence that some European legal systems insist on having their own nationals on the boards and committees of registered associations. In Belgium this does not appear to have prevented particular groups from gaining control behind an official "front" of Belgian committee members. One study has suggested that the Tablīgh movement is the real influence behind the official leadership of the Brussels Central Mosque, in this case Muslim ambassadors.[16] Such a restriction, however, was a major limitation on the development of Muslim institutional life in France, until the limitations on foreign associations were canceled in 1981. Since then the number of registered associations has risen drastically, with an accompanying growth in variety.[17]

In Britain the variety can be attributed to the range of ethnic origins as well as to a customary ease of access to association. There is no requirement to register associations, as in most of the rest of Europe, unless one wants tax exemption as a charity, which is not too difficult to achieve. One attempt a few years ago by a Muslim foundation to list Muslim youth associations identified about fifteen hundred, of which over one thousand only existed as a letterhead![18] Apart from the various associations linked with the many smaller ethnic groups, or the minority Shīʿite communities, the organizational scene is dominated by the movements of Muslim India. Chief among these are the Deobandis and their rival, the much splintered Barelwis. Smaller but with a very high public profile have been organizations sponsored by the Jamāʿat-i-Islāmī. Here there is also the Tablīgh movement in its original Indian form related to Deobandi mosques and institutions including two "colleges."[19]

Again, however, it is important to note that the situation in the host country can also encourage such splintering. In Denmark, any group of parents over a certain number has an automatic right to government funding for a private school, and several have been established since the mid-1970s. But as such schools have grown in size, factions within the parent body have sometimes increased to the point where a subgroup is able to start a viable school of its own, thus splintering the original one.[20] Similarly in Sweden, where government funding is available to religious congregations over a certain size (to give them some degree of equality with the state Lutheran church), several Muslim "congregations" have split when they have become large enough to become two viable ones.[21]

Given these circumstances, it is not surprising that there has been little success anywhere in Europe at forming effective and stable federations of Muslim organizations in any one country. The evidence so far is that single-issue federations have been more successful. In Germany persons of various theological and ethnic backgrounds have formed a group in opposition to a proposed curriculum for Islamic religious instruction, introduced on a trial basis by the government of North-Rhein-Westphalia in cooperation with the German branch of the Diyanet.[22] In Birmingham, England, sixty local Muslim organizations have held together for nearly a decade to pressure the local education authority to take Muslim educational concerns seriously.[23] The campaigns against Salman Rushdie's *The Satanic Verses* have provided cohesion for a variety of organizations in Britain. But even in this instance there are at least two national action committees, as there are two councils of mosques, with little coincidence between the two sets. In Belgium there is particular pressure from the government to find a representative body that can speak for all the Muslims. Attempts by the Central Mosque in Brussels to form such a body, however, repeatedly run up against the opposition of one or another group.

There arguably has been more success at creating networks across national boundaries, but in many ways such networks are based on traditional foundations rather than representing an adaptation into new circumstances within a given country. Among the Turks, the Sulaymanli, Nursi, Milli Gorus, and Diyanet networks across Germany, the Netherlands, Belgium, and France are each stronger than any links among them in Germany. The same can be said of similar movements among North Africans or Pakistanis across European boundaries. In addition, some of the networks of traditional Sufi orders are finding a new role in linking together their various branches which, having come from mutually distant parts of the Muslim world, now find themselves in close proximity within Europe. Various groups with Naqshabandī or Alawi links are particularly active. The Tablīgh movement too, having had unusual success in crossing ethnic and state boundaries in the Muslim world, is repeating its success in Europe.[24] Finally, some ties are being established across boundaries both of European states and traditional movements, such as the cooperation involving a Naqshabandī group in Birmingham, a Milli Gorus mosque in Hamburg, and the large Shīʿite mosque also in Hamburg.

In some countries Islam has a legal status which is commonly described by the term "recognition." This is far from being the case in every country; despite repeated demands by some Muslims in Britain for recognition by the government, the legal status does not exist and it is unclear how the government is supposed to respond. The comparison is made with Austria and Belgium, where Islam has been "recognized."[25] In Austria this took place in 1979, when the government decided that a law of 1912 was applicable to Muslims in Austria today. In 1974, Belgium had added Islam to the list of religions recognized. In both cases recognition is linked to the existence of an organization representing Islam. Austrian Muslims have had to create a federal council to be able to take advantage of the benefits flowing from recognition: access to religious broadcasting on radio and television and Islamic instruction for Muslim children in school. In Belgium, the government nominated the Brussels Central Mosque as the organization responsible for implementing Islamic religious instruction by Muslim teachers paid for by the provincial governments.[26] Particularly in the Belgian case, it took many years before implementation could be achieved and the situation remains unsatisfactory, partly because the mainly Moroccan and Turkish Muslims feel no identity with or loyalty toward the Brussels mosque.[27]

West German state and federal authorities continue to resist demands for recognition. In German law it is not a question of recognizing Islam as a religion but of recognizing a Muslim organization as a "public law body" (*Korperschaft offentlichen Rechts*). The only advantage to the state that might flow from such recognition would be that it could collect a "church tax" from Muslims who are members of that organization. Access to religious instruction and most other facilities does not require recognition.

While the arguments and demands continue, it must be said that the question of recognition itself is clearly of far greater concern than the specific practical advantages that might accrue. The issue is one of recognition in the wider sense, acknowledgment that Muslims are now a legitimate part of European societies. Muslims are conscious of being a "new religion" in Europe, from the start having cultural, legal, and material disadvantages in relation to the long-established churches. But being part of one of the great world religions, part of a worldwide Muslim community with a rich heritage and current significance, also makes them feel that they should be both recognized and treated as equals of members of the churches. This is illustrated perhaps most clearly in the Danish case. The constitution guarantees religious freedom, confirms the establishment of the Lutheran state church, and creates the category of "recognized faith communities," a category which provides no legal or other advantages not otherwise available. As a result of Muslim demands for recognition as such a faith community, the government has declared that the category is "defunct," a response which does not deter the Muslims from seeking the recognition nonetheless.

Muslim and European

The settlement of Muslim communities of significant size has inevitably raised challenges to traditions, both Muslim and European. Given sheer power relationships—political, economic, cultural, demographic—it is to be expected that it is the Muslim minorities who have had to carry the weight of adapting. Traditional institutions such as the mosque, as well as those of more recent origin such as particular movements and organizations, have changed and are continuing to change in order to respond to circumstances and needs different from those of the past.

The character of this adaptation is strongly influenced by two particular overlapping factors. On the one hand is the ethnic and cultural variety among the Muslims in Europe. They have come from many different parts of the Muslim world and are mixing in European cities. With this immigrant generation has arrived the variety of cultural baggage from different countries, regions, even villages. In the alien context each often has been forced to defend a particular tradition as being Islamic while finding that a neighbor was defending a different tradition in the same terms. It has been necessary to abandon exclusive claims to Islamic legitimacy without abandoning Islamic legitimacy as such, as well as to identify those aspects of the way of life that are culturally relative and to categorize them apart from the central and absolute Islamic core.

The second factor that must be taken into consideration is the generation of young Muslims born or raised in Europe. Much has been written about a lost generation "between two cultures," marginalized youth, and the like. But it is also these young people, in Britain and France now establishing families of their own, who have been through a European system of education and have experienced the wider society positively as well as negatively, who are consciously undertaking the analysis of Islam and its cultural expression necessary for Islam to remain meaningful to them and their children. They meet in numerous informal groups to study the Qurʾan and ḥadīth as texts relevant to their own life situation. They are not bound either by the social pressures of traditional village society or by the fourteen hundred years of Islamic scholarly tradition. Here is where the bases are being laid for European expression of Islam. Whether those expressions will be ones that favor the full participation of Muslims in European society, or whether they will be highly critical and even antagonistic toward their host culture, is a matter still to be settled.

Regardless of that determination, the European context clearly will be the major influence on how Muslims perceive their place and contribution, as was shown in the various technical issues discussed earlier. But it goes much deeper, as indicated in the events of the last two years. For in the last analysis, the question must be how far European society itself is prepared to adapt. It is an adaptation that is extremely difficult to contemplate, as European cultures seem to have entrenched themselves to a degree unusual in history. Monocultural and monolingual nation states, often legitimating one religion and one legal system, grew up in the eighteenth and nineteenth centuries. Their identity, self-confidence, often very *raison d'être*, was founded on superiority over others internally and externally.[28] Dutch, British, and French imperialism was an extension of the internal imperialism of industrial capitalism which subjugated regional and working-class cultures and interests, turning them into the tools of the ruling establishment if they could not be crushed.

What we have inherited in the late twentieth century is a complex of apparently inflexible structures which can only consider the integration of alien minorities if those minorities agree to complete assimilation. We have religious freedom—on condition that it is our definition of religion that is applied. So family law is outside the scope of religion, and other practices, such as dietary requirements, the cycles of worship and festivals, and the like can be given credence only as "exceptions." The explicit and implicit assumptions of our universal education deny all absolutes that are not secular. Religious organization can only take the form of a recognizably "ecclesiastical" structure with, for example, a "cathedral"-like building like Brussels Central Mosque. Political participation depends on citizenship, which requires loyalty to a nation state whose history and culture is both alien to and unaccepting of minorities.

The events of 1989 in western Europe have brought these tensions starkly into the open. In Britain, with echoes in other western European countries, the affair of Salman Rushdie's *The Satanic Verses* has shown how little importance many Muslim leaders attach to the structures of the wider society, as they have formulated many of their declarations and pronouncements in tones designed to reinforce their support rather than influence their ostensible targets. The episode has also confirmed how little significance the wider society attaches to the ethnic and religious minorities. The cultural establishment, the "glitterati," have betrayed a double standard, some have said hypocrisy, in their own favor. Only parts of the church have seen fit to try to understand Muslims' sense of outrage in the matter. Again it has become clear that groups who have been marginalized in economy, culture, and social structures cannot rely on the patronage of those in power to improve their position but have to take their fates into their own hands.

In Belgium, the issue of education came to the fore when the Brussels Central Mosque proceeded to establish a Muslim nursery school after repeated failed attempts to obtain government permission. Some of the protest from the Belgian side concentrated on the lack of legal form, but the majority of the public outcry was over the question of Islamic education and its compatibility—or more often its alleged lack thereof—with Belgian education.

In France, the ideological *laicistes* had insisted in the spring that laicism was the only reliable guarantor of religious freedom in the context of the Rushdie affair. Six months later, they campaigned against the wearing of headscarves by Muslim girls in school on the grounds that it constituted a threat to the open, secular principles of the French state.

These "crises" have been a culmination of developments and should not have come as a surprise. Over the years, the reaction of German constitutional lawyers to the Muslim demand for "recognition" has been that the Muslims are not a permanently settled population, and that they are arguably in breach of the Basic Law in having loyalties outside of it and in being against equality of the sexes. The same lawyers do not appear to perceive similar problems, for example, in relation to either the Roman Catholic Church or the Jewish community, both "recognized." In Britain, the issue of education increasingly has become the key indicator of a similar double standard. Legal access to publicly funded church schools continues while Muslims and others are prevented from obtaining similar privileges by administrative and political maneuvers. The 1988 Education Reform Act, both in its provisions regarding religious education and school worship ("mainly Christian") and in the political pronouncements about parts of the new National Curriculum (although the details are often much better than such pronouncements would suggest), has given the clear message to all ethnic and religious minorities that their interests and perceptions are marginal. They may be considered as exceptions but are not part of the mainstream.

As young people grow up through the European educational system, they are acquiring the skills, attitudes, and expectations associated with being European—despite all the obstacles placed in their way deliberately or otherwise. They have ideals that are both Islamic and European, and they test reality against these ideals. When the test fails, there is the potential for conflict. Perhaps it is not coincidence that this conflict has been concentrated in Britain and France where immigration and settlement were earliest. The last decade of this century will see the tensions spread to the rest of Europe. The test for Europe is to learn the lessons now, so as to be able to turn these tensions toward constructive rather than destructive ends.

NOTES

1. M.S. Abdullah, *Geschichte des Islam in Deutschland* (Graz: Styria, 1981), pp. 13–36; Abdel-Raouf Sinno, *Deutsche Interessen in Palastine 1841–1989* (Berlin: Baalbek Verlag, 1982), pp. 255 f.

2. M.M. Ally, "History of Muslims in Britain, 1850–1980" (Master's thesis, University of Birmingham, 1981), pp. 13–36; R.B. Serjeant, "Yemeni Muslims in Britain, *The Geographical Magazine* 17, no. 4 (1944): 143–47.

3. Alain Gillette and Abdelmakeu Sayad, *L'immigration algérienne en France*, 2d ed. (Paris: Éditions Entente, 1984), pp. 40–60; C.R. Ageron, "L'immigration maghrebine en France: un survol historique," in M. Morsy, ed., *L'Islam en Europe a l'époque moderne* (Paris: Sindbad, 1985), pp. 201–22.

4. E.J.B. Rose, *Colour and Citizenship: A Report on British Race Relations* (London: Oxford University Press, 1969), pp. 65–90, remains a good account of the main phase of immigration into Britain.

5. Ageron, "L'Immigration," and J. F. Legrain, "Aspects de la présence musulmane en France," *Dossiers du SRI* 2 (September 1986).

6. N. Abadan-Unat, "Turkish migrants to Europe (1960–1975)," in Abadan-Unat, *Turkish Workers in Europe 1960–1975* (Leiden: E.J. Brill, 1976), pp. 6 f.

7. For Britain see Office of Population Censuses and Surveys, *Census 1981: Country of Birth, Great Britain* (London: OPCS, 1983), pp. 114 f., and *Labor Force Survey 1979* (London: OPCS, 1982), p. 35; see also annual issues from 1985. For France, see J. Wisniewski, *Étrangers en France: Des chiffres et des hommes* (Paris: Hommes et migrations, 1986).

8. For a small attempt at a reasoned estimation, see Jorgen S. Nielsen, "Muslims in Europe: An Overview," *Research Papers: Muslims in Europe* 12 (December 1981), updated in a forthcoming article, "Migrant Muslims in Europe," *Encyclopedia of Islam*, 2d ed. (Leiden: E.J. Brill).

9. Donald E. Smith, *The Facts of Racial Disadvantage: A National Survey* (London: PEP, 1976), pp. 68, 214 f.

10. See S. Baron, "The Bengali Muslims of Bradford," *Research Papers: Muslims in Europe* 13 (March 1982), pp. 12 f.

11. See, for example, articles by B. Ineichen and R. Cope in *New Community* 15, no. 3 (April 1989): 335–56, which, although they deal with Afro-Caribbean experiences, well illustrate the point being made.

12. For Britain, see J. S. Nielsen, "Muslims in Europe," *Renaissance and Modern Studies* 31 (1987): 67, and the annual OPCS, *Marriage and Divorce Statistics* (London: OPCS), which records the number of registered mosques. For France see Legrain, "Aspects," pp. 20 f. Much of the following information is based on the unpublished documentation submitted by national delegates to the annual *Journées d'Arras*.

13. K. Kreiser, "Islam in Germany and the German Muslims," *Research Papers: Muslims in Europe* 28 (December 1985): 9–29; J. Blaaschke, "Islam und Politik unter turkischen Arbeitsmigranten," in J. Blaschke and M. van Bruinessen, eds., *Jahrbuch zur Geschichte und Gesellschaft des Vorderen und Mittleren Orients 1984* (Berlin: Express Edition, 1985), pp. 295–366.

14. See several of the papers collected in J. Lahnemann, ed., *Erziehung zur Kulturbegegnung* (Hamburg: EBV-Rissen, 1986).

15. Gillette and Sayad, *L'Immigration*, pp. 64–68.

16. F. Dassetto, "The Tabligh Organizations in Belgium," in T. Gerholm and Y. G. Lithman, eds., *The New Islamic Presence in Western Europe* (London: Mansell, 1988), pp. 159–73.

17. Cf. Legrain, "Aspects."

18. This was told to me by the researcher who was trying to compile the list.

19. F. Robinson, *Varieties of South Asian Islam* (Warwick, U.K.: University of Warwick, Centre for Research in Ethnic Relations, 1988).

20. A. Olesen, *Islam oq undervisning i Denmark* (Aarhus: Aarhus Universitetsforlag, 1987).

21. *Muslim i Sverige* (Norrkoping: Statens Invandrarverk, 1981).

22. *Religiose Unterweisung fur muslimische Kinder, Curruculumentwurf Stufe 1–4* (Soest, 1989).

23. One achievement of this Muslim Liaison Committee was the production in 1986 by the Birmingham Education Committee of *Guidelines on Meeting the Religious and Cultural Needs of Muslim Pupils*; cf. D. Joly, "Ethnic minorities and education in Britain," *Research Papers: Muslims in Europe* 41 (March 1989).

24. See Dassetto, "The Tabligh Organizations."

25. See J. S. Nielsen, "Forms and Problems of Legal Recognition for Muslims in Europe," *Research Papers: Muslims in Europe* 2 (June 1979).

26. F. Dassetto and A. Bastenier, *L'Islam transplante* (Antwerp: Editions EPO, 1984), pp. 174–77.

27. Ibid., pp. 180 ff.

28. I have argued this case more extensively in "Zusammenleben verschiedener Kulturen-Erfahrungen in Europa," in Lahnemann, *Erziehung zur Kulturbegegnung*, pp. 135–47.

20

Challenges Facing Christian-Muslim Dialogue in the United States

Sulayman S. Nyang

My purpose here is to introduce briefly the history and the present composition of the Muslim community in the United States of America and to identify the areas that deserve special attention in the dialogue between Muslims and Christians in this country. For the purpose of this study dialogue is defined as a process by which members of the two religious communities try to build bridges between their respective groups as they jointly and separately grapple with the basic issues of life, individually and collectively, in the United States and seek to bring about greater understanding between the two communities not only in terms of their different definitions of self and community, but also in terms of their different attitudes toward each other's beliefs, rituals, festivals, and behavioral patterns. What needs to be emphasized in this context is the absolute necessity to respect each community's unqualified right to self-definition. There is no dialogue when one group defines the other's identity and expects its members to accept this—and this holds true for both Muslims and Christians.

Because of the still widespread unfamiliarity with the Muslim community in the United States, a short introduction to its history will precede a discussion of the realities and the potentials of Muslim-Christian dialogue in this country.

A Brief History of Islam in the United States

It is self-evident that any discussion of Islam in the United States needs to deal both with the communities of Muslims who came from elsewhere and with the Afro-American presence in this country. The history of the coming of Muslims from overseas prior to World War II can be divided into three main periods.

The first period is the pre-Columbian phase, a timespan about which controversy continues because of the scarcity—according to some, the total absence—of reliable historical data. Leo Wiener, the Harvard scholar who wrote *Africa and the Discovery of America*,[1] maintained that the Indians living in modern Mexico were in contact with the people of northwest Africa, more specifically, with Mali. The author supported his controversial thesis by citing ethnographic, archaeological, and linguistic data. Wiener's claim was indirectly supported by the British historian Basil Davidson through his publications on the history of the western Sudanic kingdoms of Ghana, Mali, and Songhai.[2]

He reported that Mansa Abubaker of Mali embarked on an ambitious expedition across the Atlantic Ocean. Without any familiarity with Wiener's study, Davidson reached the conclusion that the Malian king and his entourage probably landed successfully somewhere in the New World.[3] The author relied primarily on the writings of an Arab historian, al-Omari, who first referred to this African adventure across the Atlantic.[4] Among other authors who wrote along the same lines is Guyanese scholar Ivan Van Sertima, who in his *They Came Before Columbus* also argued that Africans from the western part of that continent came to the New World before the arrival of the man from Genoa; and several of these Africans, Van Sertima holds, were Muslims.[5]

Unless further evidence is found to substantiate this thesis of a pre-Columbian Muslim presence in America, it will remain in the eyes of many a far too tentative and speculative idea—although some others will undoubtedly continue to consider it a most meaningful starting point for the history of Islam on this continent.

The second period coincides with the slave trade which brought many Muslim men and women to this country. Allan Austin has collected all the material he could find related to the history of Muslim slaves in the United States[6] and his study provides ample evidence of the presence of several Muslims who were actively practicing the faith of Islam and were well versed in its teachings. One of these figures was Ayub Ibn Sulayman Diallo (known to American historians as Job Ben Solomon Jallo). This African prince from Bondu was apprehended and sold into slavery. He spent many years in Annapolis, Maryland, where his fantastic memorization of the Qur'an distinguished him from most other slaves. In his *The Fortunate Slave* Douglas Grant recapitulated the story of Diallo, who escaped the terror of slavery because he was ransomed by a British official who heard of his plight and was familiar with his royal origins in Africa. Grant tells us that the British official secured Diallo's freedom and then took him to England where he met British royalty on his way back to Bondu.[7]

Another Muslim who spent several decades in America serving as a slave on a Mississippi plantation was Abdur Rahman (erroneously called Abdurahahman). This African prince was not able to secure his freedom until he wrote a letter in Arabic to the sultan of Morocco asking for intercession on his behalf. The sultan called on the U.S. president and the latter obliged. This presidential intervention led to the release of Abdur Rahman and his wife, but not to that of his children. Abdur Rahman left under the auspices of the American Colonization Society and went to his country in West Africa by way of Liberia, but he died on the way—a broken man.[8]

Yorro Mahmud (erroneously Anglicized as Yarro Mamout), another Muslim slave, arrived in this country as a teenager and lived to be 134 years of age. The American artist Charles Willson Peale immortalized Yorro in a diary sketch of him.[9] Yorro used to walk around Georgetown in Washington, D.C., doing the *dhikr* ("remembrance, mention," a ritual of invocation and praise of God) and insisted on a strict adherence to the Muslim prohibition of pork and to other Muslim laws and regulations.

Omar Ibn Sayyid was a slave whose claim to fame was his escape to Fayetteville, North Carolina, where he entered a church and began to write on its walls verses from the Qu'ran. This act of desperation later led to his acquisition by one of the planters of his day. It is reported that he converted to Christianity and died as an old man in that part of the South. His memory has recently been resurrected by the community of African-American Muslims in Fayetteville, followers of Imam Warith Deen Muhammad,[10] who personally took the initiative for the establishment of the Omar Ibn Sayyid Foundation. At the time of the inauguration of the foundation a symposium of Muslim scholars converged at the city to discuss the Islamic experience in America.

There is no consensus as to the precise number of Muslim slaves during this period of American history. Allan Austin estimated that perhaps 10 percent of all African slaves were Muslims.[11] This figure seems reasonable but it cannot be taken as definitive. The pattern of distribution of Muslims in West Africa varies throughout the period of slavery. Whatever their exact number, Muslim slaves were invariably the victims of religious warfare between their small communities and the neighboring *jāhiliyya* groups, the dominant non-Muslim majority. One of the many obstacles they had to face was the practice of southern Protestant slave masters to deny slaves any opportunity to pass their religion on to their descendants, a situation that was not different from, for example, that in Brazil.

The third phase is the time after the opening of the Suez Canal. This period brought hundreds and thousands of Muslims from the Middle East, South Asia, Central Asia, Southern Europe, North Africa, and Southeast Asia. The first group to arrive in the United States in the last two decades of the nineteenth century consisted of Arab Muslims from the Ottoman Empire. Following in the footsteps of their Christian Arab neighbors who had been coming to the United States for a decade or two earlier, these Muslim immigrants did not intend, initially, to settle permanently in this country but rather to make a fortune as quickly as possible and then to return home. But despite their original plan, many of them decided to stay for good and the majority of these immigrants found their homes along the eastern seaboard and in the Midwest. On the eastern seaboard some made their living as either peddlers or factory workers. Those in the Midwest found their fortune on farms or made their way into the factories emerging in those areas, many of them specifically attracted to this region because of the job opportunities provided by the automobile industry in Detroit. The large numbers of people from the Arab world who settled in this Michigan city and its environs have made Dearborn (a suburb of Detroit) the cultural Mecca of the American Arab.

The Arab Muslim immigration to the United States occurred almost simultaneously with that of South Asian Muslims, mainly from the Punjab. Following in the footsteps of their Sikh brethren, these Muslims went to the western part of the United States by way of Philippines. Many of them were recruited into farm labor and their coexistence with Hispanic Americans led to some conjugal bonds with that segment of the American population. Willows, California was the first major settlement for these South Asians. Their numbers were small in the early part of this century, but the size of their community increased when students from South Asia came to the United States, especially between the world wars.

Another Muslim community that developed in the United States during this period was that of southern European Muslims. Scattered between the eastern seaboard and the Midwest, these Muslims were mainly Bosnians and Albanians, with a relatively small group of Croatians. They had followed the example of their Christian compatriots who had emigrated to this part of the world well before them. As some Arab Muslims who found themselves in an unfamiliar cultural environment occasionally looked for their orientation toward Christian fellow Arabs who had preceded them and who already had found their place in this new world, so many of the Muslim southern Europeans have over the last century found succor and emotional support from their Christian countrymen at critical times in their sojourn in these lands, as evidenced in stories about mutually beneficial cooperation between Muslim and Christian Albanians as well as between Yugoslavians of the two faiths.

Then there were those who came from the Soviet-occupied parts of Central Asia. Unwilling to accept the Soviet agenda for their countries, determined to establish a new life for themselves elsewhere, and encouraged by U.S. authorities to emigrate, many came, mostly via Turkey.

There is some evidence that Muslims from North and sub-Saharan Africa also came to the United States during this third period. FBI material obtained under the Freedom of Information Act by Robert Hill[12] refers to a small but active Muslim community in Pittsburgh, Pennsylvania, which had an Islamically oriented organization known as the African Muslim Welfare Society of North America (AMWSNA). It drew its members from both the immigrant and the native-born population. From 1927 to 1928 the community had an imam from the Sudan.

During this period a number of Muslims from Somalia and other points along the Suez Canal landed in New York and at other American ports, either as stowaways or as sailors who decided to jump ship because of their attraction to life in this country. Many of these Muslims seem to have congregated around the Afro-Arab West Indian musician who had converted to Islam in the 1920s, Shaykh Dawud Faisal. Together with his wife, Sister Khadija, another Afro-Caribbean, he established the Islamic Mission to the United States of America, based in Brooklyn, New York, following in the footsteps of Muhammad Webb, to be mentioned below.

The aforegoing background brings us to a discussion of the role and place of native-born American Muslims. The earliest indigenous Muslim organization in the United States was established in the last decade of the nineteenth century by Muhammad Alexander Russell Webb, an American diplomat who was actively involved in the American theosophical movement. Committed to that movement's objective of studying the great religions of the world, Webb came across Islam in his research, felt deeply attracted to it, and decided to devote the rest of his life to its propagation in the United States. His conversion dates from the period that he served as U.S. consul in Manila, the Philippines. His discovery of the truth of Islam opened new doors of opportunity for him in the Muslim world. He traveled to the Indian subcontinent and befriended several important Muslims who would later give him significant moral and financial support. He established a *daʿwa* movement in Manhattan, New York, and founded a journal called *The Moslem World.*[13] Through this journal, through his *Islam in America*[14] and in various lectures, Webb sought to make a case for Islam, especially before fellow Westerners, and to remove some of the most serious distortions of Islam prevalent in the West. On that last point he concluded in 1893, in one of his lectures at the World's Parliament of Religions held in Chicago, that "there is no system that has been so wilfully and persistently misrepresented as Islam, both by writers of so-called history and by the newspaper press. There is no character in the whole range of history so little, so imperfectly, understood as Mohammed."[15]

Of the other American Muslim movements the most important historically is the Nation of Islam, founded by Farad Muhammad, the elusive immigrant who is variously described as a Hijazi, a Palestinian, a Syrian, and a Middle Easterner. Whatever his real origins, Farad Muhammad has entered history as the source of the teachings, now identified with the Nation of Islam, which came to the public view in the late 1950s and early sixties, largely because of the activities of Malcolm X, the national spokesman for the movement's long-term leader, Elijah Muhammad. Malcolm X became a celebrity in black radical circles in the United States because of his flamboyant rhetoric and his severe social critique of American society. Bold, courageous, and defiant, he catapulted the Nation of Islam (NOI) to national visibility and very soon brought himself face to face with Christian leaders in both the white and black communities.

The Nation of Islam underwent a major transformation in 1975 following the death of Elijah Muhammad. Inherited by Elijah's son, Imam Warith Deen Muhammad, this powerful movement was gradually transformed (with several name changes—the Bilalians, the World Community of Islam in the West, and the American Muslim Mission) into a veritable Sunni Muslim organization. It is now the largest single Muslim organization among the indigenous and immigrant Muslims. Its message is circulated around the United States through its weekly publication, *The Muslim Journal*. With branches scattered all over the country, this movement, which has been decentralized since the late 1980s, has Imam Muhammad as its spiritual head and none of the infrastructure established by Elijah Muhammad.[16]

However the transformation of the old organization was not universally accepted. Several splinter groups have surfaced since 1975. There are the followers of the eloquent minister Louis Farrakhan, who still advocates the old teachings in his *Final Call*. The second splinter group is that founded by Silas Muhammad, who started out in California in the late 1970s before moving to Atlanta, Georgia. The third group is that which was founded by John Muhammad, an old NOI follower who teaches that he is indeed the only true successor to his late brother, Elijah Muhammad. The fourth group was founded by one self-styled caliph Emmanuel Muhammad; he too claimed to be the only true successor to the late Elijah Muhammad and operated in the mid-seventies out of Baltimore. Another group are the Five Percenters. Founded by Clarence Thomas X, this group came into being in the late sixties. All of these splinter groups have minuscule support in the U.S. Muslim communities except for the reconstituted Nation of Islam of Louis Farrakhan.[17]

Besides the Nation of Islam, an organization whose pre-1975 history was dismissed in Sunni Muslim circles as heretical, there were several Sunni Muslim groupings within the African-American communities. They were the Islamic Party of North America, the Darul Islam movement, the Islamic Brotherhood, Inc., and the Ḥanafī movement. All these organizations came into being as a result of their founders' exposure to some form of Sunni teachings in the United States. The Islamic Party of North America was created—according to its historian, Abdul Fattah Griggs of the Institute of Islamic Involvement in Winston-Salem, North Carolina—to correct the wrong ideas about Islam propagated by the old Nation of Islam. This attempt at correcting the NOI message within the black community embittered the NOI leadership and many battles ensued in the 1970s. But the preaching of true Islam by the Islamic Party leadership brought this group of African-Americans closer to the immigrant Muslims and simultaneously exposed them to the possibility of dialogue with "the white Christian devil."

The Darul Islam movement, which also came into being in the early 1970s, was a loose federation of *masajid* (mosques) along the eastern seaboard. Committed to *da'wa* and to a *jihād* at the spiritual level, it earned a reputation for toughness and serious adherence to Islamic values. As a result of their fierce advocacy of orthodox Islam, the leaders of the Darul Islam movement soon found themselves locked in combat with the leaders of the old Nation of Islam. Another organization that operated out of New York and had some impact in the eastern seaboard area was the Islamic Brotherhood, Inc. Founded and led for many years by Brother Tawfiq, it served a limited constituency through its *masjid* (mosque) and its publication, *The Western Sunrise.*

The Ḥanafī movement was founded by Abdul Haalis, a former member of the Nation of Islam who defected in the early 1970s because of serious disagreement with Elijah Muhammad. Committed to the teachings of true Islam and unwilling to accept anything from his old teacher and master, Abdul Haalis established a center for his group at a Sixteenth Street Northwest address in Washington, D.C. It has been alleged in the media that this place was bought for the group by the famous basketball star Kareem Abdul Jabbar. Again the rivalry between this group and the old Nation of Islam led to violence within the black community. The outside world came to know about this power struggle when the media in Washington, D.C. reported that some members of the Nation of Islam based in Philadelphia struck against the family and followers of Abdul Haalis staying at the Sixteenth Street residence of the Hanafis. Dissatisfied with the judgment of the courts regarding the crime perpetrated against his group by the Nation of Islam, including the violent murder of several people, Abdul Haalis decided to take the law into his own hands by seizing illegally the Islamic Center of Washington, D.C., the B'nai B'rith, and the Municipal Building. This act of defiance led to the jailing of Abdul Haalis and many of his disciples. Today, the Hanafi movement seems to be in a state of total disintegration.[18]

Even a very incomplete historical survey as presented above gives an idea of the tremendous variety within Islam in the United States, a diversity one clearly needs to take into account when considering the prospects of Muslim-Christian dialogue in this country. But before proceeding with that topic, I would like to mention briefly some recent efforts to bring about a greater degree of cooperation between individual Muslims and among the various Muslim organizations on this continent. While the Federation of Islamic Associations (FIA) functions primarily as an umbrella organization for Arab Muslims,[19] other organizations seek to bring together much more ethnically diverse groups of Muslims for common action and mutual strengthening, especially the Islamic Society of

North America (ISNA), the Islamic Circle of North America (ICNA) and the Tablīgh movement.[20] The answer to the question whether these organizations are prepared to function also as centralized points of contact for Muslim-Christian dialogue on this continent will determine to a large degree the possibilities of dialogue at a wider than local level.

Major Issues for Muslim-Christian Dialogue in America

It is an understatement to say the diversity within the Muslim community in the United States is matched by that within the Christian community in this country, and every generalized assertion about Muslim-Christian dialogue in America is, therefore, a questionable abstraction. What can be done within the confines of this article is to suggest for this dialogue a number of agenda items that deserve consideration, leaving it to the participants in every concrete dialogue event to decide what the priorities are for their particular exchange and what in their situation are the specific implications of the general topics here proposed. In this part of the world, as anywhere else, some of the issues are more directly related to the local, regional, or national state of affairs than other topics which seem to arise in Muslim-Christian conversations almost everywhere and at all times. But even in the case of the latter, the exact progress of the discussion and its ultimate outcome will be determined by the distinct points of view and the concrete circumstances of each group of participants. In what follows I shall indicate briefly some of the widely recognized challenges to common action and three potentially divisive areas, and then conclude with a few observations on the phenomena of secularization and secularism as important aspects of the situation in which we find ourselves in this country as well as in some other parts of the world.

Some Widely Recognized Challenges to Common Action

Dialogue in action means collaboration of people from two or more faith communities in areas of concern to both or all. In order to prepare for these cooperative efforts and in order to deepen them, many feel the need also for another type of dialogue, a mutual exploration of each other's perspectives on these issues. With regard to both—the concrete common action and the agenda for the discursive dialogue—it is often difficult if not impossible to distinguish between religious and nonreligious aspects of the problems we are facing, and between theological and ideological perspectives. With due recognition of the significance of all nonreligious factors, I shall focus in this short essay on religious and theological issues. The first area for common action is the whole complex field of human rights. For Muslims "the essence of all human rights is the equality of the entire human race, which the Qur'an assumed, affirmed and confirmed. It obliterated all distinctions among men except goodness and virtue (*taqwā*)," Fazlur Rahman once wrote.[21] Several points of convergence between Muslims and Christians are discernible here; the belief in God who created all of us in God's image; the recognition of our common human predicament, created as equals, with the implied protest against any form of racial superiority; and the emphasis on human accountability, very pronounced in the Qur'an where human beings are seen as God's vice-gerents on earth, stressing their moral responsibility. Muslim and Christian perspectives on human rights have already been discussed elaborately and in depth on many occasions,[22] not infrequently with a Muslim caveat against excessive "Western" permissiveness when dealing with the question of the freedom of the individual. Muslims often stress that the well-being of society has priority over individual claims to freedom and that, in Fazlur Rahman's words, "'obligations and rights' are the obverse and converse of the same coin; the one obviously cannot subsist for any length of time without the other."[23]

To Muslims, as well as to many Christians in Latin America and elsewhere, human rights, peace, and social justice are closely interrelated issues. For any society peace depends not only on the international balance of military forces but also on the extent to which social justice is practiced within the country. Peace is inextricably linked with the question of justice for the poor and the powerless. Peace without justice is fragile; and justice without peace is discomforting. For Muslims, the life of the Prophet serves as an inspiring example in the field of social service to others. Though the Prophet was not a rich man, he demonstrated human kindness in his dealings with his companions, his wives, his friends, and most importantly, in his attitudes toward the poor, the weak, the sick, and the helpless—the *miskīn*. We need to recognize that the fundamental teachings of both our religious traditions are not always affected in the everyday realities of so-called Muslim or Christian societies. As far as the essence of Islam and human rights is concerned, it is certainly true that in many Muslim lands dictators are in power and that there is no sign that their grip over these lands is weakening. Because of this reality it becomes necessary for Muslims interested in the upholding of human rights in Muslim lands to develop not only theological arguments for their cause but the necessary support systems around the world, and we as Muslims living in the West must work together with our non-Muslim neighbors to create the vehicle for change in the political fortunes of our fellow human beings around the world. In the modern world where democracy has established itself as the most open and accommodating system for people of divergent belief systems, it is to be expected that Muslims living under democratic systems of government would seek to promote worldwide their view that social tranquility is inextricably bound up with social justice and a full and honest recognition of human rights.

Three Potentially Divisive Areas

Doctrinal disputes have marred Muslim-Christian relations through the centuries and continue to constitute a potential source of tension, especially in situations where leaders of both communities of faith allow their zealots unrestricted freedom to criticize and deeply offend the others. Admittedly, there is the authority of civil society and its political power to curb and control the excesses of religious fanatics. But even short of the manifestations of excessive intolerance, there are numerous instances of common distortions of the faith and the convictions of people of a particular religious community. Not unlike some other sections of the population, Muslim Americans or Muslims in the United States have to face up to the challenges of negative press within the American cultural universe. This litany of negativism can only be tackled effectively and successfully when the average Muslims know that their Christian neighbors share many things in common with them and begin through the dialogical process to educate their neighbors about Islam. This is not an easy task, for religion and politics are two dangerous topics which are often conveniently excluded from the subjects of neighborly conversations. In all of this, Muslims in the United States and Canada need to accept fully the reality of their minority status and should appreciate the religious diversity within this continent rather than seeing it as a threat. As Muslims have the task and responsibility to inform and educate the general public and especially the Christian communities and their leadership in this country about Islam, so Christians need to educate Muslims about the Christian faith as Christians themselves define and articulate it in the universe of American religious discourse. It is indeed dangerous and unwise for Muslims to assume that their view of the Christian faith is shared by Christians. The dialogical process at its best allows people to state their beliefs without others second-guessing them on the accuracy of their account of their own beliefs.

The second potentially divisive issue is the "missionary" or "daʿwa-istic" character of both Islam and Christianity. An international dialogue conference on "Christian Mission and Islamic Daʿwa" held in the 1970s[24] has shown once again that it is almost impossible to avoid serious tensions around this subject even when people come together in a spirit of dialogue. One of the urgent tasks is the clarification of the language we use. As many Muslims have emphasized that daʿwa is not proselytization, so many Christians draw a sharp distinction between mission and proselytization—all of them, Muslims and Christians, expressing their strong opposition to any form of coercion.

At the level of official contacts between the two communities of faith it may be possible, difficult as it is, to discuss the issue of conversion in a somewhat detached manner. Where the greatest tension, pain, and agony are experienced is often at the level of personal decisions and family life. Since this is a society where the rights of the individual are respected by the political order, it is naive and unrealistic not to expect that occasionally members of one community will cross the boundary line between their parental faith community and a newly adopted one. Jews, Catholics, and Protestants have faced similar predicaments and their experiences may be of some help in a number of cases. But even when a *modus vivendi* can be worked out that allows for an intimate relationship and for close cooperation *without* conversion of any person involved, the situation still deserves careful and patient attention and constant counsel.

The third and last issue to be mentioned here relates to one specific aspect of the minority status of U.S. Muslims, namely the rather widespread feeling of being marginalized in American society also, and especially, politically. The burden of being constantly confronted with caricatures of one's religious tradition should not be underestimated. But no matter how understandable the apprehensions are, Muslims should remember that for many decades in American society, religious minorities such as the Catholics and Mormons also found the majority faith community hostile. This hostility was largely due to fears and suspicions. It took many years of education and information to turn things around. Muslims are now faced with similar challenges. They need to realize that their identity in the American context is not negatively defined by U.S. law, and that the Christian community is not *ipso facto* anti-Muslim. The Muslims can depoliticize conflicts with members of other religious groups only when they are integrated within the American political system and are in close contact with leaders of the various religious groupings in the country. Since the politicization of religion often begins in the religious establishment, it makes good political sense for Muslims to build bridges of communication and dialogue with leaders of all major religious communities.

Secularization, Secularism, and the Muslim-Christian Dialogue

Even if one is inclined to question the usefulness of this particular terminology, which is difficult if not impossible to translate in many Asian and African languages, one still needs to admit that the distinction between secularization and secularism—a distinction used frequently by Christians in the West and found relatively rarely in Muslim literature—points to a very important issue. What is meant in this context by "secularization" is a process of historization, of desacralization, or, as I would like to call it, of detraditionalization of human life. Secularization implies the recognition of the existence of "secular" dimensions of life and an acceptance of the value and validity of "secular" knowledge. Dialogue itself can therefore be seen as, at least to some extent, one of the results of the process of secularization. Instead of trying to interpret and direct all of life from within one's own religious tradition, one now acknowledges that we need to explore jointly the questions that relate to all those dimensions of life which we share with all other people. As far as openness to new knowledge is concerned, from whichever source it comes, Muslims often remind each other of the Prophetic challenge "to seek knowledge even if it is in China" and of the attitude of the early Muslims who, coming out of Arabia, benefited immeasurably from the wealth of knowledge found in the areas and cultures with which they came into contact. Believers who are not prisoners to tradition do not need to shy away from new insights and new knowledge, from wherever it comes.

Secularization, then, does not mean in any way a curtailment of the freedom to worship God. It is the term "secularism," and not the word "secularization," that derides an ideological position which denies or at least ignores the transcendent dimension of life or, as in Muslim language, of the reality of *al-ghayb* (the unseen) and *al-ākhira* (the hereafter). Deeply concerned about this phenomenon, many religious figures continue to plead for a joint effort of all believers in God to counteract the trend toward godlessness in some parts of the world and, equally important and related to it, the trend toward crass materialization and as such vulgarization of human life. These appeals are meaningful as long as they do not obscure the reality of an even wider community than that of all believers in God, namely the one inherent in the very fact of our common humanness.

Fortunately, serious reflection has begun on what it means to carry out the Muslim-Christian dialogue in a secularized environment and an at least partly secularist society, in Europe[25] as well as in the United States. These explorations will need to be taken up by much larger numbers of Muslims and Christians than those presently involved in these discussions. The realization of what secularization and secularism mean may well turn out to be a blessing if it leads Muslims and Christians to realize that Muslim-Christian dialogue should not be an exclusive concern with each other and a withdrawal of these two communities of faith from the world and from other believers and "nonbelievers," but that we meet, as Muslims and Christians, not just to understand each other more fully and to strengthen our relationship, but ultimately in order to be jointly of greater service to this world and to all those in need.

NOTES

1. Leo Wiener, *Africa and the Discovery of America* (Chicago: Innes & Sons, 1922).

2. Basil Davidson, *Lost Cities of Africa* (Boston: Little, Brown, 1959), pp. 74–75. This story of an African visit to the New World in pre-Columbian times is based on chapter

ten of Ibn Faḍl Allah al-Omari's *Masālik al-Abṣār fī Mamālik Amṣār* (Cairo, c. 1342 A.H.) The Arabic original was translated and published in Paris by Gaudefroy-Demombynes in 1927.

3. Ibid.

4. Al-Omari's chapter 10 addresses those issues.

5. Ivan Van Sertima, *They Came before Columbus* (New York: Random House, 1976).

6. Allan D. Austin, *African Muslims in Antebellum America* (New York: Garland, 1984).

7. Douglas Grant, *The Fortunate Slave* (London: Oxford University Press, 1968).

8. Terry Alford, *Prince among Slaves: The Story of an African Prince Sold in the American South* (New York: Oxford University Press, 1977).

9. For details on Yorro, see "Yorro Mamout: Maryland Muslim," in Sidney Kaplan, *The Black Presence in the Era of the American Revolution* (New York: Graphic Society Ltd., 1973), pp. 218–19; Sulayman S. Nyang, "Islam in North America," in Stewart Sutherland et al., *The World's Religions* (London: Routledge, 1988), pp 521–22.

10. Imam Warith Deen Muhammad supported the effort by agreeing to deliver the keynote address launching the Omar Ibn Said Foundation in Fayetteville, North Carolina.

11. Austin, *African Muslims*, chap. 1.

12. Robert Hill, who edited the Marcus Garvey Papers, shared with me some of his research findings on the Islamic groups which were directly or indirectly related to the Garvey movement. These documents were obtained from the U.S. government under the Freedom of Information Act.

13. For details on Muhammad Alexander Russell Webb, see Emory H. Tunison, "Mohammed Webb: First American Muslim," in *The Arab World* 1, no. 3 (1945): 13–18. See also his "Philosophical Islam," a lecture delivered in the Public Garden, Hyderabad Deccan, India (November 25, 1892).

14. Webb's *Islam in America* (1893) was divided into eight short chapters.

15. Quoted in Tunison, *Mohammed Webb*, p. 15.

16. For a recent assessment of the old Nation of Islam and its two major successor organizations, see Steven Barboza, "A Divided Legacy," *Emerge* (April 1992): 26–32.

17. The followers of the late Honorable Elijah Muhammad are now divided into six groups: the followers of Imam Warith Deen Muhammad (the largest group); the followers of Minister Louis Farrakhan under the reconstituted Nation of Islam; the followers of Silas Muhammad of Atlanta, Georgia; the followers of John Muhammad; the followers of self-styled Caliph Emmanuel Muhammad; and the followers of the group called the Five Percenters. This last group is influential among some of the rap groups in the United States.

18. The Hanafis have been out of the limelight since their daring seizure of the Islamic Center of Washington, the Municipal Building of the District of Columbia and the B'nai B'rith office in Washington, D.C.

19. See Abdo el-Kholy, *The Arab Moslems in the United States of America* (New Haven, Conn.: Yale University Press, 1966).

20. Information about these national Muslim organizations can be gleaned from the *Islamic Horizon*, *The Minaret*, *The Muslim Journal*, and *Message International*.

21. Fazlur Rahman, *Major Themes of the Qur'an* (Minneapolis-Chicago: Bibliotheca Islamica, 1980), p. 45.

22. See, e.g., the various articles on "Les droits de l'homme en Islam et en Christianisme," in *Islamochristiana* 9 (1983): 1–248.

23. Rahman, *Major Themes*, p. 46.

24. *Christian Mission and Islamic Dawah: Proceedings of the Chambesy Dialogue Consultation* (Leicester: The Islamic Foundation, 1982); originally published in *International Review of Missions*, 65, no. 260 (1976): 365–460.

25. See, e.g., the Christian-Muslim reflections in *Witness to God in a Secular Europe*, ed. Jan Slomp (Geneva: Conference of European Churches, 1985).

21

The *Umma* in North America: Muslim "Melting Pot" or Ethnic "Mosaic"?

Frederick Mathewson Denny

The concept of *umma*, "religious community," is one of the central coordinates of the Islamic worldview.[1] The early generations of the Muslim umma tried to maintain unity and concord—as the Qur'an commands—and they succeeded to a considerable extent, especially in the acceptance of the Qur'an as common scripture and the example (Sunna) of the Prophet Muhammad as the perfect model for following the "Straight Path." Furthermore, the Islamic worship practices of obligatory prayers, almsgiving, fasting in the month of Ramadan, and pilgrimage to Mecca have always been remarkably uniform worldwide, regardless of sectarian, ethnic, national, or other differences. It is at this ritual-liturgical level, unregulated by any clerical class, that Muslims demonstrate their ideal of unity most forcefully, and where they take strength for their somewhat less successful but nevertheless persistent efforts to apply the *sharī'a* to all aspects of their common life.

It may be that the Qur'anic concept of a unified and balanced community, the "best umma drawn from humankind" (S. 3:110), is more idealistic than the actual world can sustain. Nevertheless the Islamic umma ideal continues to inspire reformers, who often remember an umma of the olden times that embraced the diverse nations, cultures, and races of Muslims in a harmonious whole within a material as well as spiritual civilizational matrix.

It is surprising that the Muslim communities of North America should now become the testing ground for a microcosm of the global umma as it seeks authentic expression and embodiment in a new age.[2] The Muslim communities of North America—there is no single one—may well develop an organic as well as spiritual unity in the decades to come. Whatever happens, the Muslims' experiences in North America (and Europe) will doubtless have important consequences for world Islam.

Muslims in North America

It has become trite, although it remains true, to say that Islam is a "complete way of life," ideally. As Muslims migrate to Western countries, they go through various levels of culture shock learning to live in societies that are, to them, very alien and, in some respects, repugnant. The reasons for migration vary from desiring better economic conditions and occupational opportunities, to wanting freedom from persecution by totalitarian governments, to getting a better education and other things.

During the past 20–30 years the Muslim population of North America has grown to perhaps as many as 3 million in the United States and 200,000 in Canada. Muslims in North America may be classified under three main categories. The largest, in both the United States and Canada, is the immigrants. The next largest is the African-American Muslim population, while the smallest is the category of indigenous converts, mostly white.[3]

The major immigrant ethnic groups in North America are Arabs, Indo-Pakistanis, and Iranians, although other ethnicities are also present (such as Bangladeshis, Africans, Turks, Bosnians, and small numbers of Malaysians and Indonesians). Members of these groups are by no means all Muslims, although many are at least nominally. Among the Iranians, for example, are Jews, Bahais, and Zoroastrians, as well as secularized persons who emigrated because of the Iranian Islamic revolution of 1978–79. The Muslims among the Iranians are almost all of the Shīᶜite branch of Islam and thus, when religious, tend to associate with other Shīᶜites, at least for worship and religious education. Probably most but certainly not all Shīᶜites in North America are Iranian. Many come from East Africa (of Indian heritage) and others come from Iraq, Lebanon, and Yemen, as well as Pakistan. In the case of Shīᶜites, as also with Sunnis, there is sometimes a fit between ethnic and/or national origins and sectarian adherence. A large Twelver Shīᶜite Islamic center in Toronto attracts participants of Iranian, Arab, and South Asian background, including some Sunnis.[4]

The various Arab communities—such as the old and sizable one in the Detroit/Dearborn, Michigan area—are the longest-standing immigrant Muslim populations in North America. They started arriving toward the end of the nineteenth century and swelled in numbers after World War II. Many came to North America to work in the automobile plants of the Midwest or the mills and factories of New England.[5] Arab-American Muslims include some of the most assimilated Muslim immigrants. The long-established Islamic Center of Greater Toledo, for example, is perhaps the most Americanized Muslim congregation. While its roots were planted and nourished by Syrians and Lebanese, its numbers now include some 30 different national and ethnic backgrounds in a membership of more than 600 families. Some nearby old Arab-American mosques of Dearborn and Detroit also became quite Americanized, but in recent years the trend has been for new immigrants of Islamist (cf. "fundamentalist") convictions to "take over" the old assimilated mosques and turn them toward normative Islam as their deliverers conceive it.[6]

More recently, Pakistani immigrants have come to North America in great numbers. They are both visible and active in Islamic affairs, whether in mixed ethnic Muslim contexts or their own ethnic circles.[7] In the above-mentioned Toledo mosque, the Pakistani-American members have come to exert great influence, partly because of their vigor and Islamic dedication, but also because of their command of English, their generally high economic, social, educational, and occupational status, and their savoir faire. There are more than fifty physicians, for example, belonging to the Toledo center, many of whom are from South Asia. Other frequently noted occupations include scientific research fields, engineering, computer science, finance, and academia, both administration and the professoriate. Toledo is not unique, either in its diversity or in the high status of many of its members. Similar congregations can be found in large Islamic centers, for example, in Los Angeles and Orange County, California; Houston, Texas; central New Jersey; and London and Toronto, Ontario.

Pakistani-American influence has become so great in North American Islamic affairs that anxieties are being raised among other immigrant Muslims. One informant, for example, told me that her father, a Palestinian-American pillar of long standing of a major urban mosque founded by Arab-Americans, worries now that the Pakistanis are going to "take over" their establishment. This Muslim of Arab ethnicity considers Pakistani and all other Muslims, regardless of their ethnic or national origins, to be brothers; this, however, does not dispel the strong sense of ethnic difference and accompanying cultural competitiveness and rivalry. Pakistani-American, Indian, and other immigrant Muslim populations may also have strong loyalties to Islamic missionary and ideological movements based in their regions of origin, such as the Jamaʾat i-Islami and the Jamāʾat al-Tablīgh of South Asia, both of which have major international followings.[8]

In Canada, which is officially multicultural, the mosque represents the universality of Muslims. But there, as in the United States, mosques and Islamic centers are increasingly sorting out their constituents along ethnic lines. Pakistanis, for example, like to sustain all-night vigils in the mosques during the sacred fasting month of Ramadan. A well-established mosque in Toronto serves also as a Turkish cultural center, with business meetings conducted in Turkish. Arab and Pakistani Muslims in North America have no hesitation about conducting worship together and attending conferences and supporting Islamic activities where they interact effectively. But, as a Pakistani-Canadian Muslim leader told Yvonne Haddad, "We worship together but then the Pakistanis go back to their curries and the Arabs to their kebabs."[9] My field research a dozen years after Haddad published hers finds the same thing in a variety of regions both in Canada and the United States. If anything, the separate community consciousness of ethnic diversity among Muslims may be greater than before, perhaps because of larger numbers and sectarian and/or ideological differences, even among Sunnis.

Immigrant Muslims and their children and grandchildren tend to be middle and upper middle class in status. That is not generally true, however, of the second largest category of Muslims in the United States, the African-Americans, most of whom are indigenous. Many African-American Muslims trace their roots back to the Nation of Islam movement founded in the 1930s by Elijah Muhammad as a radically separatist venture focused on rejection of white values and connections and the pursuit of black religious, social, and economic goals.

It is not possible to rehearse this important and absorbing story here, but it should be known—although generally is not—that the vast majority of African-American Muslims are now mainline Muslims and not part of the old "Black Muslim" movement.[10] The older movement underwent a revolutionary change after the leader died in 1975 and his son—the designated successor Warith Deen Muhammad (earlier Wallace D.)—fundamentally altered the course of the movement, finally declaring that it would henceforth be mainstream Sunni Muslim. The original movement has continued as the Nation of Islam under the leadership of Minister Louis Farrakhan.[11] It is not considered to be an authentic Islamic movement by mainstream Muslims, especially those with strong normative convictions—and this would include most immigrants from Islamic countries—who are offended by its claims.[12]

Muslim African Americans recognize various leaders and movements as providing special and valuable messages more or less in conformity with Islam. The differences between them, viewed from within the African-American community, appear rather less definitive than when viewed from outside, because of racial and class solidarity, or at least sympathy, that seeks to avoid conflict. One context where Muslim African Americans come together in their divisions is in correctional institutions, where so many young African-American males, especially, discover and embrace Islam. There are serious disagreements between African-American Muslim groups, but the trend continues to be toward the practice of universal Islam as guided by Qur'an and Sunna, as has happened with the great majority of Muslim African Americans who follow the leadership of Imam Warith Deen Muhammad.

Muslim African Americans are a crucial bridge between Muslim immigrant communities and the generality of Americans. (I refer, here, to the United States, not Canada, which is a different case.) On the one hand, Muslim African Americans are in an excellent position to serve as cultural and spiritual translators to the newcomers, with whom they have trusting relationships as fellow Muslims. On the other hand, non-Muslim Americans—especially Jews and Christians—can be greatly helped in understanding and appreciating Islam and Muslims and their potentialities in America by the example, activities, and interpretations of Muslim African-Americans. When one listens to the speeches and sermons of people like Imam Siraj Wahhaj of Masjid Taqwā in Brooklyn, Dr. Ihsan Bagby of the Islamic Resources Institute in California, or Imam Warithu Deen Umar, president of the National Association of Muslim [prison] Chaplains, one is aware of hearing American voices with Islamic convictions. The African-American sociologist and student of the religion of African Americans, C. Eric Lincoln, wrote almost a decade ago of the successor of Elijah Muhammad, his son Warith Deen, that his

> struggle for orthodoxy is, first of all, a struggle to break through the double isolation involved in being black in white America and Muslim in the citadel of Western Christianity. Both Warith and his predecessor were aware from the beginning that there is a world beyond the West, but while Elijah's claims to affiliation and affinity with the world of Islam were both tentative and pro forma, Warith Muhammad fully intends to enlist that world by enlisting in it. If he is successful, the isolation of Black Muslims qua Muslims will of course be transcended in the international fellowship of the Islamic faith. . . . At the present rate of growth, the Muslims will soon be our third largest religious presence following the Protestants and Catholics. How this will affect a religious climate which has always considered Blacks a class apart awaits the determination of history, but there is a convention that every new religious option makes the neglected soul more dear. In that case, Islam may well play a vital part, direct and indirect, in the reconstruction of our traditional attitudes about race and religion.[13]

There is a wide gap between the economic, educational, and occupational levels of African-American Muslims and those from the immigrant and other indigenous categories introduced earlier. This poses the greatest imaginable challenge to Muslims here in realizing the goal of a united and harmonious umma. A transcribed forum of four leading African-American Muslim leaders was published in 1989 in *Islamic Horizons*,[14] the magazine of the Islamic Society of North America (ISNA), the largest Muslim organization and, in my opinion, a potential denominationalizing instrument.[15] The forum was wide-ranging, covering issues of group identity, African Americans' role in developing the umma in the West, racism, civil rights, the nomenclature of ethnicity (e.g., "Black"/"Afro-" vs. "African-American"/"Negro"), criteria for Islamic leadership, social consciousness and community building, political involvement of Muslims in North America, and conflicts between the Muslim immigrant community and Muslim African Americans.

After acknowledging major problems between African Americans and immigrants, one of the panelists declared:

> *Al-Ḥamdulillāh* [Thank God!], I think it is getting better. We still have some obstacles to overcome. A lot of prejudices from different people. From both sides really. There's an attitude among African-Americans, 'I ain't gonna take nothing from no *foreigner*.' We *have* experienced that with brothers coming from overseas to disrupt our communities. And there are some brothers who are very bitter. On the other hand, we've had situations where brothers have come with a more humble approach and wanted to listen to what you say. And I think that is important. But overall the relationship is getting *much* better. We are able to operate on a level that we have today with the brothers. And that's a lot of progress. . . . We can sit down with the immigrant brothers. I don't even like to use the term. (28; editor's emphasis)

The speaker, Al-Amin Abdul Latif, is imam of a masjid in Brooklyn. His term "brothers" has a double meaning: fellow African Americans and immigrant Muslims, who are part of the larger, more inclusive umma. Dr. Ihsan Bagby, another panelist who was at the time of the meeting a high official in ISNA's educational programs, immediately added "Actually, all of these terms—immigrant, African-American—kind of throw you off the whole perspective. I mean, we're African-Americans, but we are Muslims first. And anything we talk about is defined by that" (28).

The panel continued in this vein, agreeing that only the Qur'an can define the boundaries and mutual responsibilities of the umma. As Jamil Al-Amin (the former H. Rap Brown) observed:

> Again, Allah has given definition in the Qur'an and it is the only way we can have any sense of character, how Allah has defined the believer, the pious person, the hypocrite, those who are in the state of rebellion, and the unbelievers. This has to be the criteria. It is as Allah defines and as the Prophet has elaborated upon. We're safe when we do that. When we go outside this context, we prejudice Islam. We have to be particular about this. The word *Muslim* stands alone throughout the Qur'an. And we are making terms, *immigrant Muslims* and *indigenous Muslims*. We keep that old conversation going and what it does is reinforce the barriers that we talk about breaking down. (29, editor's emphasis)

At a more practical level, the panelists discussed ways to increase Muslim unity in North America. One panelist said that there is no way except in worship, which is Allah's main command of His obedient servants. If worship is carried out faithfully, then Allah will provide the unity. Another panelist thought that rational planning was also required, but the two disagreed. While acknowledging the social and cultural distance between immigrants and African-Americans, one panelist recalled the early umma's resolution of such distance by deliberate and wide-scale intermarriage between those who made the Hijra from

Mecca and the host Medinans, and afterward between migrating Muslims and indigenous peoples in much more distant locales. Panelist Ishaq Abdul-Hafiz, a Muslim chaplain in California federal prisons, observed:

> Many of the immigrants who come here—we do have to look at this aspect—have been persecuted. Many never practiced Islam until they came here and saw there was another flow of the spirit of Islam. So now, *inshā'Allāh*, to blend this, we have to implement the Qur'an and *ḥadīth*. . . .
>
> Intermarriages, what role did that play when Islam spread to new lands? What was the effect of the immigrant Muslims marrying the indigenous? We have to start marrying each other's children. (28)

At this point Dr. Bagby said: "Uh oh! Guess who's coming to dinner?" (28)

The Umma: "Melting Pot" or "Ethnic Mosaic"?

I have not heard the term "melting pot" used by Muslims,[16] although Ishaq Abdul-Hafiz's suggestion of "blending" comes close, especially when he specifies intermarriage as a main solution to ethnic divisions among Muslims. Canadians do not approve of the melting pot metaphor, but prefer to characterize their multiculturalism as a "mosaic" of peoples contributing their special qualities to Canadian life while retaining their distinctiveness.[17]

It may be that both metaphors—melting pot and mosaic—could be positively applied to the umma ideal. For example, at the annual Hajj (pilgrimage to Mecca), the white *ihram* garment worn by males may be understood to symbolize the common faith and order of Muslims worldwide, as well as the fact of each person's death as a great leveling experience (there is an *ars moriendi* aspect to the shroud-like *ihram*). Islam also has a strong egalitarianism and a tradition of relative freedom from racism and ethnicism. But the dress of female pilgrims is not the required white uniform of the males; rather, women are free to wear their national and ethnic dress, which displays and celebrates the creative diversity of the umma. The fact that male and female pilgrims wear different types of garments also illustrates the diversity of roles performed by men and women: the former are public agents in the global cause of Islam whereas the latter maintain the domestic, one could say cultural and customary spheres. The two—the public and the domestic—reinforce the traditional regulation of Muslim society while exhibiting both melting pot and mosaic characteristics. Thus Muslims can be somewhat comfortable with the dominant American and Canadian social myths as they apply to their own condition within the process of building the umma in North America.

At the 1991 annual meeting of ISNA in Dayton, Ohio the official theme was

"Developing an Islamic Environment in North America." One of the most frequently raised issues was that of ethnic divisions and their threat to Muslim unity and therefore to the mission of spreading Islam in North America. But an even greater fear is of assimilation into a non-Muslim melting pot and a consequent loss of identity and values. Muslims are asking how they are going to be able to retain their valued ethnic and cultural heritage as Pakistanis, Indians, Arabs, Turks, Bangladeshis, and so forth while developing a strong common Muslim environment that will protect them from the perceived destructive and immoral aspects of the dominant secular culture of North American life. Added to these concerns is the worry that if they do not get politically involved in the dominant ethos, they will suffer from protracted marginalization.

ISNA itself is a large-scale effort to unite Sunnis by serving as an umbrella organization for a variety of more specialized organizations.[18] In ISNA-related discourse there is a great deal of talk about "establishing the umma" in North America. Both ethnic exclusiveness and anything resembling sectarianism or denominationalism are anathema to most Muslims and considered sinful. But, they ask, how are we Muslims specifically going to arrange our affairs and establish concrete institutions for our community in pluralistic, secular, industrialized societies except by proximate measures? One possibility is that some kind of associational approach, structurally and functionally resembling denominationalism of the most ecumenical variety, will provide a type of provisional structure for these ends in North America, where no official religious—let alone Islamic—establishment can look after the affairs of its adherents. Whether such organizations will be divided along lines of Sunnism and Shīᶜism remains to be seen.[19]

The classic sociological theory of the "church" type of religious community held that members were born into it and that it encompassed and impinged upon them—sometimes in determinative ways—whether or not they were individually observant.[20] By this definition, many if not most immigrant Muslims belonged to something like "churches" in their native countries. This is especially true if they hailed from Saudi Arabia, Pakistan, or postrevolutionary Iran, where "church" and state are coterminous. The openness of the denominational model would appear to be appropriate to a mixed Sunni organization like ISNA. ISNA's aim is to be the means whereby the umma is established in North America and as such it has the long-term intention of being a kind of church, at least for the Sunni majority here. ISNA seeks to be as complete a representation and embodiment of the universal umma as may be possible in North America, including an ordering system of Sharīᶜa law that many Muslims want to see operating alongside U.S. and Canadian law, particularly in personal status matters such as marriage, divorce, custody, and inheritance.[21] If Islamic personal status laws were to be permitted to operate in Canada and the

United States, the further consolidation of ummatic concerns might be enhanced and ethnic distinctions and divisions among Muslims weakened as an Islamic legal community gained ground.[22]

Muslims in North America, whether immigrant, African American or other, must make a special effort to sustain their Muslim identity as a minority faith in a sea of secularism, irreligion, and different forms of religion. In the short term, ethnicity provides a strong factor of identity preservation. But ethnicities may experience a steady decrease in their strength over generations unless strong institutions, such as special separationist practices and communities, are established.[23] Most African Americans are not Muslims and a sizable proportion of immigrants from the Middle East and South Asia are either non-Muslim or nonobservant people of Islamic heritage. Arab-American organizations include both Muslims and Christians, as well as nonreligious members. (A high proportion of Arab Americans are in fact Christians, reflecting heavy recent as well as former emigration from Lebanon, Jordan, the West Bank, Egypt, and Syria, countries that are losing their Christian populations.) Many Iranian organizations in North America are based on shared cultural rather than religious concerns. Pakistani organizations tend to be more Islamically oriented, whether or not religion is the purpose of their association. Yet, in the last case, ethnicity is very strong. Further, Pakistani immigrants tend to be group endogamous,[24] whereas Arabs and Iranians frequently marry outside their ethnic boundaries. African Americans marry mostly within their ethnic and racial groups, partly from preference but also because of racism. Imam Ishaq Abdul-Hafiz's call for intermarriage among Muslim groups, quoted above, expresses an openness to interracial and interethnic marriage between African-American and other Muslims that I have witnessed in other places, as well.[25]

There is a clear tug-of-war between what some Muslims like to call "ummatic" concerns and imperatives and what actually divides Muslims from each other, whether political disagreement, Sunni-Shīʿite sectarian division, or ethnicity, class differences, and race.[26] Muslims have always held up a unified umma as their ideal. But this is easier to do when individual Muslim societies stay put in their national and ethnic regions. When significant populations are set in motion, as is happening with large-scale migration, Muslims come face to face with their actual differences beneath the transcending levels of creed, cultus, and romantic myth.

In the past, Muslims have often had a successful history of interaction and blending, including large-scale intermarriage following trade, migration, and invasion. (An example of the first is Indonesia, of the second North Africa, and of the third India, although none of these is purely one or the other.) It is too early to predict whether and to what extent the umma ideal will succeed in bringing Muslims in North America to melting point.[27] Based on consideration of past cases, however, it is safe to assume that Muslims will strengthen their ummatic ties here in both traditional and adaptive ways. They will do this through intermarriage and concerted ventures while continuing to display rich ethnic diversity in a general spirit of mutual respect and concord based both on their Islamic convictions and their minority consciousness.[28]

Author's note

The author gratefully acknowledges the Council on Research and Creative Work and the Graduate Council on the Arts and Humanities of the Graduate School of the University of Colorado–Boulder for several grants-in-aid and a CRCW Faculty Fellowship that have made the field research for this paper possible. He also gratefully acknowledges the extensive hospitality and help that many Muslim spokespersons and agencies, as well as other colleagues and institutions, have provided in his field travels in Canada and the United States.

NOTES

1. For a detailed discussion of the concept of umma in Islam see Frederick M. Denny, "The Meaning of *Ummah* in the Qur'an," *History of Religions* 15, no. 1 (August 1975): 34–70.

2. An absorbing analysis of Islamic revivalism and the challenge of restoring the umma as a dynamic and creative reality in these times is Ziauddin Sardar's *The Future of Muslim Civilization* (Petaling Jaya, Malaysia: Pelanduk Publications, 1988).

3. See the recent review "How to Count Muslims," a sidebar to the article "The Rise of Islam in America: How Will this Change Jewish Self-Identification?" by Jonathan D. Sarna, in *Moment: The Magazine of Jewish Culture and Opinion* 16, no. 2 (June 1991/Sivan 5751): 38. Recent attempts at estimating the Muslim American population are reviewed, including that of Barry A. Kosmin and Jeffrey Scheckner, "Estimating the Muslim Population of the United States in 1990" (City University of New York, April 1991), which placed the number at only 1.5 million. For the Muslim population of Canada, I rely on the recent book by Zohra Husaini, *Muslims in the Canadian Mosaic: Socio-Cultural and Economic Links with their Countries of Origin* (Edmonton, Alberta: Muslim Research Foundation, 1990), pp. 20–27. Husaini relies partly on Canadian census records, which put the Muslim population at 100,000 in 1981, the first year in which Muslims were counted. Muslim leaders in Canada think that is a serious undercounting. Adding that probability to high immigration and birthrates since yields a current conservative estimate of 200,000.

4. A useful overview of the Iranian community is Maboud Ansari, "Iranians in America: Continuity and Change," in Vincent N. Parillo, ed., *Rethinking Today's Minorities*, Contributions in Sociology, no. 93 (New York: Greenwood Press, 1991), pp. 119–42.

5. The literature on Arabs in North America, particularly in the United States, is increasing. See, for example, the pioneering study of Abdo el-Kholy, *The Arab Moslems in*

the United States: Religion and Assimilation (New Haven, Conn.: Yale University Press, 1966); *Arabs in the New World: Studies on Arab-American Communities*, edited by Sameer Y. Abraham and Nabeel Abraham (Detroit: Wayne State University Center for Urban Studies, 1983), especially the chapters by Yvonne Haddad, "Arab Muslims and Islamic Institutions in America: Adaptation and Reform," pp. 64–81, and Sameer Y. Abraham, Nabeel Abraham, and Barbara Aswad, "The Southend: An Arab Muslim Working-Class Community," pp. 163–84; see also Baha Abu-Laban, *An Olive Branch on the Family Tree: The Arabs in Canada* (Toronto: McClelland and Stewart, 1980).

6. See Haddad, "Arab Muslims and Islamic Institutions in America," pp. 74–76. The Toledo mosque seems to be better able to defend itself against takeover by outside Islamist interlopers through its diplomatic finesse and strong and astute governing board, which enjoys final authority and fully understands its corporate rights under U.S. and Ohio law. The imam told me that when a visitation of critical outsiders appears, he refers them to his superiors because he cannot himself change the situation, being merely an employee. The "employers," namely the governing board, receive such visitors graciously and generally succeed in guiding the encounter to an amicable conclusion without giving up the mosque's relatively liberal and mildly assimilationist profile as an "American" Muslim congregation. I have treated the Toledo case at greater length in my *Islam and the Muslim Community* (San Francisco: HarperSanFrancisco, 1987), chap. 5.

7. See Regula B. Qureshi and Saleem M.M. Qureshi, "Pakistani Canadians: The Making of A Muslim Community," in Earle H. Waugh, Baha Abu-Laban, and Regula B. Qureshi, eds., *The Muslim Community in North America* (Edmonton: University of Alberta Press, 1983), pp. 127–48.

8. See Mumtaz Ahmad, "Islamic Fundamentalism in South Asia: The Jamaat-i-Islami and the Tablighi Jamaat of South Asia," in Martin E. Marty and R. Scott Appleby, eds., *Fundamentalisms Observed*, The Fundamentalism Project (Chicago and London: University of Chicago Press, 1991), pp. 457–530.

9. Yvonne Yazbeck Haddad, "Muslims in Canada: A Preliminary Study," in Harold Coward and Leslie Kawamura, eds., *Religion and Ethnicity* (Waterloo, Ont.: Wilfrid Laurier University Press, 1978), p. 80.

10. For the evolution of the Nation of Islam, see Clifton E. Marsh, *From Black Muslims to Muslims: The Transition from Separatism to Islam, 1930–1980* (Metuchen, N.J.: Scarecrow Press, 1984), and Martha F. Lee, *The Nation of Islam: An American Millenarian Movement*, Studies in Religion and Society, vol. 21 (Lampeter, Wales: The Edwin M. Mellen Press, 1988).

11. See Lawrence H. Mamiya, "Minister Louis Farrakhan and the Final Call: Schism in the Muslim Movement," in Waugh, Abu-Laban, and Qureshi, eds., *The Muslim Community in North America*, pp. 234–55. The author reflects that "with its move to Sunni orthodoxy, the American Muslim Mission [a transitional name for the former "Black Muslims" who followed Warith Deen Muhammad into the new dispensation of mainline Sunnism] will be less subject to the conflicts between charismatic personalities. A more routinized, institutionalized charisma, the 'charisma of office' to use Weber's term, will help thwart some of the conflicts that have plagued Muslims [i.e., Black Muslims] in the past. As Ms. Akbar [Evelyn Akbar, secretary of the Oakland, California mosque]

said, 'Consistently as a community we have been followers of personality rather than knowledge. Now we have knowledge'" (p. 252).

12. A pamphlet widely circulated among American and Canadian Muslims at the 1991 annual meeting of the Islamic Society of North America (Labor Day weekend, Dayton, Ohio) and the joint 1991 annual meetings of the ISNA-affiliated Association of Muslim Social Scientists and the American Association of Scientists and Engineers (Romulus, Michigan, October 25–27) condemns what its author calls "Farrakhanism." See M. Amir Ali, *Islam or Farrakhanism?* (Chicago: The Institute of Islamic Information and Education, 1991).

13. C. Eric Lincoln, *Race, Religion, and the Continuing American Dilemma* (New York: Hill and Wang, 1984), pp. 168–69.

14. "Muslim Americans," *Islamic Horizons* (Special Convention Issue) 18, nos. 7–8 (July–August 1989): 24–30.

15. I have speculated on the possible development of denomination-like Islamic movements in "Church/Sect Theory and Emerging North American Muslim Communities: Issues and Trends," a paper delivered at the annual meeting of the Society for the Scientific Study of Religion, Virginia Beach, Va., November 1990. I do not foresee Muslim denominations organized around differences in doctrines and practices—as in Protestantism—but it may be that a quasi-denominational model will prove useful in developing an organized and operational North American Islamic community and not just the ummatic ideal that most talk about now. In mid-April 1992 there was a gathering of Muslims from all over North America in Indianapolis, Indiana (near ISNA's Plainfield headquarters) for a first-ever "Islamic Coordinating Conference" to discuss ways and means of Muslim unity in North America. ISNA represents a powerful centering impulse, but is sometimes criticized for being bureaucratic and out of touch with local concerns, whereas powerful regional centers are increasingly reaching out—with programs, publications, and services—to provide widely visible leadership. Examples of the latter are the Islamic Society of Orange County, in Garden Grove, California; the Islamic Center of Southern California, in Los Angeles; The Islamic Society of Central Jersey, between New Brunswick and Princeton; and the Islamic Center of Greater Toledo, Ohio. In Canada there is, for example, the influential Islamic Centre of Toronto and Jami Mosque, on Boustead Avenue. I see the Islamic centers and mosques here as similar to American congregationalist-type societies: locally autonomous, democratic, and independent but with a desire for some kinds of larger associations for joint purposes and economies of scale (as in supporting publications, media outreach, school development, and humanitarian causes).

16. For a brief, mordant estimate of the "melting pot" theme in American social history, see Nathan Glazer and Daniel Patrick Moynihan, *Beyond the Melting Pot: The Negroes, Puerto Ricans, Jews, Italians and Irish of New York City*, 2d ed. (Cambridge, Mass.: MIT Press, 1970), pp. 288–92.

17. The title of John Porter's classic sociological study of Canadian ethnic groups, *The Vertical Mosaic* (Toronto: University of Toronto Press, 1965), contains the clear sense of Canada's highly stratified society. The mosaic metaphor suggests an artwork with the richer, warmer skin colors clustered toward the bottom and the cooler whites, grays and

blues toward the top, where the so-called charter groups, with roots in Britain and France, continue to dominate the federation. See also Husaini, *Muslims in the Canadian Mosaic.*

18. A comprehensive study of ISNA is Herman Meredith Bowers, "A Phenomenological Study of the Islamic Society of North America," Ph.D. diss., Southern Baptist Theological Seminary, 1989.

19. When I mention the Sunni-Shīʿite division in Muslim company, I am sometimes provided with a patient lecture about there being no fundamental division like that in Islam, at least in any sense beyond politics. However, when I listen to participants in ISNA and ICNA (Islamic Circle of North America), for example, I often hear that those organizations are regulated according to Sunni principles. We may have here a matter that is acceptable to raise intramurally but unwelcome when heard from the lips of outsiders.

20. For literature and general discussion of this point, see Denny, "Church/Sect Theory and Emerging North American Muslim Communities." Persons are also born into their ethnicities. For an incisive analysis of the concept of ethnicity—including its relationship to religion—see Wsevolod W. Isajiw, "Definitions of Ethnicity," *Ethnicity* 1, no. 1 (1974), reprinted in *Ethnicity and Ethnic Relations in Canada: A Book of Readings*, 2d ed., ed. Rita M. Bienvenue and Jay E. Goldstein (Toronto: Butterworth, 1985), pp. 5–17.

21. See *Oh! Canada! Whose Land, Whose Dream? Sovereignty, Social Contracts and Participatory Democracy: An Exploration into Constitutional Arrangements*, compiled and written by Syed Mumtaz Ali and Anab Whitehouse for the Canadian Society of Muslims, Toronto, 1991 (161 pp.). The authors place Muslim personal status concerns within the ongoing and fateful national debate about what Canada is to be. The Canadian Society of Muslims is a small but confident as well as intellectually and legally sophisticated Sufi-oriented organization based in Toronto. There is a broadly Sunni-based Fiqh Council of North America, which seeks sharīʿa-grounded understandings and solutions for situations that arise because of the North American context of Muslim life.

22. At ISNA meetings a marriage bureau conducts a brisk business. The back section of *Islamic Horizons* carries several pages of "Matrimonials," advertisements by Muslim men and women seeking partners. The ads often include ethnic information, but they also often exhibit openness to any Muslim of good faith. Examples of each kind: "American (Italian) Muslima [i.e., female Muslim], 39, never married, no children, educated, attractive and cultured seeks educated, professional Muslim for loving marriage filled with laughter and devotion." "Arab Muslim, living in B.C., Canada, educated, professional, speaks three languages, looking for Arabic Muslima, 20–28, well-educated, moderate, open-minded, well-dressed & pretty. Pref. Canadian or USA. Letter/phone." Some of the ads for husbands are placed by parents, which in part shows the more conservative tradition of the immigrant who wants to maintain propriety by suggesting an arranged marriage, in which families and not merely individuals are fully involved and in which female and family honor are guarded. An example: "Pakistani family seeks correspondence for their two daughters (graduating from a prestigious U.S. univ) from Pakis-

tani bachelors, Muslim, non-smoking, Dr., Eng., or Ph.D. pref. Phone/photo/details appreciated." All from *Islamic Horizons* 18, nos. 7–8 (July–August 1989): 60–62.

23. At the 1991 ISNA convention meeting I heard the Amish model mentioned a number of times in connection with establishing a pure Islamic environment. Most commentators clearly rejected such a solution as both unrealistic and un-Islamic. But one of the articles in the "ISNA Companion," the official program of the twenty-eighth annual convention, held over Labor Day weekend in September 1991 called for, as the title has it, "Developing an Islamic Environment through a Peace Village." The author, Atouf Yassine, writes that a separate, experimental Islamic village, to be built on "a huge piece of land" to be acquired somewhere in the American or Canadian countryside, "will provide a total *living experience* in which Islamic values are to be observed and applied. An Islamic court should play a positive role by making significant decisions on all village affairs. The village has to protect, support, maintain, teach, prepare, stimulate, motivate, encourage, change and strengthen the residents. It has to be like a safe house, protecting the inhabitants from further deadly, infectious effects of the non-Muslim environment" (p. 31, author's emphasis).

24. This is true of most peoples of the South Asian subcontinent. See Regula B. Qureshi, "Marriage Strategies among Muslims from South Asia," in Earle H. Waugh, Sharon McIrvin Abu-Laban, and Regula Burckhardt Qureshi, eds., *Muslim Families in North America*" (Edmonton: University of Alberta Press, 1991), p. 187.

25. For a pessimistic appraisal of race relations in America, see Andrew Hacker, *Two Nations: Black and White, Separate, Hostile, Unequal* (New York: Scribner's, 1992).

26. Race is understandably a highly sensitive issue among Muslims in North America. While most Muslims acknowledge the racism of the dominant white societies toward themselves and other minorities, it is more painful when racism is discovered in intra-Muslim relations, as sometimes happens. For a recent examination of majority (i.e., European white) racism against the Muslim minority, see Zuhair Kashmeri's penetrating analysis of immigrant Muslim experiences in *The Gulf Within: Canadian Arabs, Racism and the Gulf War* (Toronto: James Lorimer & Co., Publishers, 1991).

27. For an empirical study of American Muslims' attitudes towards marriage, intermarriage (whether with Muslims of differing ethnic/national/racial backgrounds or with non-Muslims), divorce, custody, and related matters, see Yvonne Yazbeck Haddad and Adair T. Lummis's ground-breaking *Islamic Values in the United States: A Comparative Study* (New York: Oxford University Press, 1987), pp. 144–54. This book also contains much valuable material on ethnicity and assimilation. Also highly recommended are several articles in the important collective work, cited above, *Muslim Families in North America*, edited by Waugh, Abu-Laban, and Qureshi, such as Abu-Laban's typological study of "Family and Religion among Muslim Immigrants and their Descendants," pp. 6–31, Nimat Hafez Barazangi's "Parents and Youth: Perceiving and Practicing Islam in North America," pp. 132–53, and Qureshi's "Marriage Strategies among Muslims from South Asia," pp. 185–212.

28. Although this essay has included all of North America in its purview, it is not to be imagined that Canada and the United States, however similar in many ways, are to be

equated with each other with respect to what ethnicity, multiculturalism, civil rights, and other things may mean in the two countries. For a brief overview of the differences, including penetrating observations on "manifest destiny," national identity, and civil religion, see Earle H. Waugh, "North America and the Adaptation of the Muslim Tradition: Religion, Ethnicity and the Family," in Waugh, Abu-Laban and Qureshi, eds., *Muslim Families in North America*, pp. 80–87.

Ideological and Theological Reflections

22

Some North African Intellectuals' Presentations of Islam

Jacques Waardenburg

In this essay I aim to investigate ways in which some leading Algerian, Moroccan, and Tunisian scholars have articulated their thinking on Islam in French publications and how they have initiated an intellectual discourse about Islam with French readers. Under the influence of French language, culture, and intellectual thought they treated their problems through logical argumentation and used data resulting from scholarly research to answer more general questions, putting the facts within a more theoretical framework.

Insofar as members of older generation of the North African intelligentsia have been educated according to the French system, they have been imbued by French culture and intellectual thought, besides the properly Arabic and Islamic education they received. They also have taken up current French ideas about *l'intellectuel*, the thinking man. He has qualities beyond those of a pragmatic scientist or a man of accumulated erudition, qualities which distinguish him also from those who proclaim convictions or preach a faith. Such an intellectual indeed distances himself from current opinions and judgments, established institutions and loyalties. He is basically a free man. He develops his own ideas and positions in relation to what he sees as major problems and assumes his responsibility with regard to the society in which he lives and works. And then, typically, he writes. The same holds true for the six intellectuals I am dealing with here.

Not only French intellectual thinking, therefore, but also the type of the French intellectual has had an impact on the members of a certain French-educated North African elite. This was also the case when they developed their ideas in opposition to ideas of French nationalism and to French depreciatory views of Islam. Whether Islam was approached as a subject of literary and historical inquiry in France itself, of empirical investigations in the field in North Africa, or as part of the globe's many cultures and religions, the general and current view in France has been until recently to consider Islam as medieval, an old-fashioned religious tradition left behind by the march of history and civilization. As far as I have been able to see, there was scarcely a discourse between French and North African intellectuals on an equal footing until after World War II and particularly the fifties. Similar ethnocentric views of Islam have been current, however, in other Western countries as well.

It is in North African French language publications that the impact of intellectual thought of French origin is clearest, particularly in the way in which authors reflect on Islam as part of their cultural heritage and their vision of the future. Such publications can shed light on other questions as well. How do the authors explain, interpret, and articulate Islam to a French public which professes various faiths and ideologies including that of *laicité* (secular society), but shares a cultural framework of which Islam until now cannot be said to have been part. To what extent did these authors, once independence had been achieved, feel the need to identify themselves, their society and culture, constructively and to accentuate precisely those norms and values, symbolized by Islam, that distinguished them from French culture? They may have taken such Islamic norms and values as subjects of detached study, last remnants from a lost past, but they also recognized in them elements of an Islamic ideal structure which still has a normative quality. In any case, by consciously integrating Islam in their newly assumed identity and by speaking about it, North African intellectuals started a new type of discourse with French society and culture. The very fact that their books and articles have been brought out by French publishers and by journals in France shows that there has been an interest in them in France, at least among a more educated public. One may also assume that these authors, by choosing to write in French, have engaged in a discourse not only with French readers but also with their compatriots and others for whom the French language is the privileged vehicle of intellectual discourse.

I am leaving aside here historical and sociological studies about North African society and culture, French literature by authors from the region, and publications by North African authors in Arabic as well as in European languages other than French. Also excluded are texts read in French by North African participants in international meetings like the seminars on Islam in Algiers, the Muslim-Christian dialogues organized in Tunis, and the many other meetings of Euro-Arab and Muslim-Christian dialogue in which North African speakers have been involved. What follows is not a study of Islam in North Africa nor a study of North African contributions to various dialogue efforts, although some publications on these subjects with contributions by North African authors are mentioned in the notes.

Hence I am restricting this account to six prominent North African intellectuals in the French tradition, nearly all of whom have written a substantial *thèse d'État* (dissertation for a state doctorate). Scholarly research by these authors, however, is treated here only insofar as it reveals a particular interpretation of Islam. Since these writings are few, and in any case unique, it will be difficult to draw any general conclusion here about North African writings on Islam. The main French language publications of these authors are mentioned in the notes at the end of this paper.

Some Common Features

The publications of the authors chosen are distinguished by certain common features. First of all, they do not preach Islam, warn of French culture, or announce a last judgment to Western civilization. Second, the authors are very much aware of a common history between Islam and Europe, the southern and the northern shores of the Mediterranean, North Africa and France. By concentrating on France, however, they tend to neglect the equally common history of North Africa with Italy, Spain, and Portugal on the one hand and the Ottoman Empire on the other. The relations between North Africa and more distant European countries (Great Britain, the Netherlands, and Germany) as well as the common history of the Balkans and Russia with the Ottoman Empire also fall outside their sights. They hardly mention the Palestine-Israel conflict or the earlier history of the Jews in Europe. A third characteristic is that these authors envisage a common future with France, Europe, and the world at large, and that they are committed to this future. A fourth common feature is the extent to which these publications comply with the more formal demands of French culture: written in excellent French and mostly provided with copious notes and references, they witness to erudition and *esprit*.

The influence of French intellectual thought on these authors reveals itself particularly in their predominantly rational interpretation of Islam. Transrational views of Islam, as were propounded at the time by Louis Massignon and Henry Corbin in Paris, seem not to have found much of an echo among them. The cooler critical reflection, on the contrary, of scholars like Robert Brunschvig and Régis Blachère, Claude Cahen, and Maxime Rodinson has certainly had an impact. The work of Louis Gardet, promoting understanding by the use of reason, sympathetic study, and personal dialogue has also borne fruit. We have difficulty in discovering clear traces of French doctrinal positivism, or even the work of Durkheim, in the work of our six authors. But they seem to have been exposed to Marxian analysis and certain hermeneutical problems when they studied at French universities in the fifties and sixties.

The Straightforward Presentation of Islam: Malek Bennabi

Following an earlier work in French on *Le phénomène coranique*,[1] Malek Bennabi (born 1905, Algerian engineer) published in 1954 his *Vocation de l'Islam*,[2] a straightforward presentation of Islam as a driving force in Algerian society. Written shortly after the Arab-Israeli war of 1948, the book was published in 1954 in the series *Frontières ouvertes* through which Seuil publishing house in Paris at the time drew attention to a number of Third World countries in a wider perspective than that of French politics. In the foreword Bennabi significantly defines his stand towards H. A. R. Gibb's *Modern Trends in Islam*,[3] a French translation of which had appeared in 1949. He thoroughly rejects Gibb's idea that the Arab mind is atomistic and incapable of discerning laws, and that the humanism of modern reform movements in Islam is due to the influence of European culture rather than to specific Qur'anic orientations. Bennabi mocks European "humanism" which went out to subdue and colonize the rest of the world. He takes seriously, however, Gibb's description of what Bennabi calls the "quasi infantile pathology" of the Muslim world and he stresses that many Muslims can profit and learn from Gibb's diagnosis. Bennabi is willing to listen to orientalists.

Even after forty years Bennabi's remains a prophetic book, foreshadowing the terrible Algerian war which would follow. Describing what he calls "post-Almohad" society and its decline compared to the standard of classical Muslim civilization, Bennabi argues that this "post-Almohad" society made man "colonizable," prone to be colonized, not only because of aggression from outside but particularly because of its inner weakness and pretense to self-sufficiency. The author welcomes the reformist and modernist movements in the second half of the nineteenth and the early twentieth centuries, seeing in them a Renaissance expressed in Islamic terms. When describing post–World War I history and the colonial impact of France on North Africa and of the West on the Muslim world at large, Bennabi analyzes critically the internal and external factors of what he calls chaos. Not only the modern Muslim world but also the modern Western world which enjoys the semblance of power finds itself in a moral chaos, for colonialism "kills the colonized materially and the colonizer morally."[4]

Bennabi calls for a new phase in the Muslim renaissance, in which the complex of *colonisabilité* will be overcome, the social values of Islam observed, and a religious reform starting from the Qur'an carried out as a prerequisite for social reforms. Perceptively, he observes that the center of the Muslim world is moving eastward in the direction of Pakistan, India, and even Indonesia.

Bennabi's presentation in French already contains the main elements of a prolific *daʿwa* literature which was to appear in nearly all Islamic languages during the four following decades, calling for Muslim societies to renew themselves by returning to the sources of Islam and castigating the moral failure of the West. Looking back, one cannot but be astonished that a book like this has not been read more widely in the West, since in its critical analysis it exemplified a lucid Muslim reading of the signs of the times, while showing intellectual and moral self-restraint.

Description of Arab-Islamic and European Civilization Side by Side: Hichem Djait

The Tunisian historian Hichem Djait (born in 1935) has published in French scholarly works on the early history of the town Kufa (1986)[5] and also on the intricate relationships between religion and politics during the first decades of Islam after Muhammad's death (1989).[6] Of special interest in our context, however, are his work on the Arab-Islamic personality (1974)[7] and his book on Europe and Islam (1978).[8]

His first book, *La personnalité et le devenir arabo-islamique* (1974), stands in what we may call the more personalist tradition of North African thinkers. In 1964, for instance, the Moroccan author Mohamed Aziz Lahbabi, influenced by French personalist philosophy, published a booklet on Muslim personalism in which he develops the basic notions on the human person to be found in Qurʾan and Sunna. Ten years later Djait tries to describe in his book the profile of the Muslim person as it emerged historically within the Arab setting, in both the Mashriq and the Maghrib. The term "Arab-Islamic (or Arab-Muslim) personality" has become current particularly in North African (Tunisian) thinking. It has served to identify the (North African) Arab Muslim, in particular over against Europe, stressing his particular history and destiny. This special concern for the human person is continued by authors committed to interreligious dialogue, such as Mohamed Talbi, and by Mohammed Arkoun in his more critical philosophical thinking. Compared to Arab thinkers of the Middle East, North African authors generally distinguish themselves by a certain realism, critical rationalism, and a "personalizing" perception of human relationships and reality. Besides discussing the Arab-Muslim person, Djait also deals with Arab unity, the organization of society and the state, and, in a separate chapter, "Reform and renewal in religion." Here Djait calls for a renewed vision of faith, both intellectually and in the heart, and refers to both Muslim and European philosophers (for example, Iqbal and Hegel).

Djait's book *L'Europe et l'Islam* (1978), as the title indicates, treats Euro-Arab relationships throughout history. The first part deals with the way in which Islam has been viewed by Europeans. After a description of the general medieval and more modern Europocentric vision of Islam, Djait concentrates on three special topics: French intellectuals and Islam (Enlightenment thinkers, travelers, present-day intellectuals); European scholarship and Islam (Renan's ideological bias, Islamicist orientalists' achievements, and Europocentric or Christianocentric biases including modern anthropology, where he discusses in particular Lévi-Strauss' views on Islam and Muslim societies); and finally the relationship between German thought (which most Muslim authors admire) and Islam (focusing in particular on the ideas of Hegel and Spengler). Throughout this part of his book Djait shows perspicacity and lucidity in the way in which he describes particular European views. He is not uncritical of France; he complains about the provincial and closed character of French as compared with American universities[9] and he correctly observes that whereas France has always attracted "liberal" Europeanized intellectuals from Arab and other Muslim countries, it has hardly welcomed Muslim thinkers representing what Djait calls an "Islamic authenticity."[10] This is true indeed. Louis Massignon's sympathies for the Arabs and Islam, and the settling of more traditional Muslim thinkers like Muhammad Hamidullah in Paris, were exceptional; in general both laicist and Catholic France have not been much interested in taking the religious faith, substance, contents, or message of Islam seriously as an alternative. Throughout the nineteenth and the twentieth centuries until now Islam has been perceived in France simply according to the parameters of the political, laicist, and ecclesiastic Catholic positions in the country.

The second part of Djait's book deals more explicitly with Islam and Europe as two historical structures. He describes Europe's historical dynamism and Islam's insistence on universal values, and stresses the need to reread and rewrite world history in a less Europocentric and more universal perspective. He presents the properties of Islam as a civilization, a culture, and a body politic: characteristic features in history, evident breaks in historical continuity with the arrival of the Europeans, and problems of alienation and historical backwardness in a more universal perspective. Interestingly enough, the book closes with a chapter on the specific features not of Islam but of Europe. There is a little menu of everything, seen through thick French pebble glasses; Djait presents his somewhat gloomy reflections on the future of European culture very much as French journalists at the time wrote about other civilizations. Compared to others, however, Djait's is a more liberal, universalist spirit.

Reaching for Dialogue: Ali Merad and Mohamed Talbi

The Algerian historian Ali Merad (born 1929) is known for his scholarly work on the reformist movement in Algeria between the two world wars[11] (1967) and the religious thought of Ibn Badis (1889–1940), who during those years wrote a commentary of the Qur'an along reformist principles (1971).[12] His little booklet on contemporary Islam (1984)[13] is a rather unproblematic factual presentation, in which the period after 1960 is hardly treated except for some very general data and a brief description of the ways in which Islam is expanding.

As a professor at the University of Lyon III, and more recently, Paris IV, Merad has been involved in dialogue efforts between Muslim and (mainly Catholic) Christians in France. He also looks for dialogue on a practical level to improve the often miserable condition of so many North Africans in France in the present time of unemployment, political pressures, and general uncertainty about the future. In 1978 he made available to the French public a modest anthology of religious Islamic texts. His *Charles de Foucauld au regard de l'Islam* (1975)[14] describes with appreciation a Christian hermit (d. 1917) who tried to provide a link between France and Christianity on the one hand, and North Africa and Islam on the other.

The Tunisian scholar Mohamed Talbi (born 1920), now a retired professor of history at the University of Tunis, is also committed to promoting dialogue between Muslims and Christians, perhaps more in ethical and religious terms than the others. His scholarly work led to his extensive *thèse d'État* on the Tunisian dynasty of the Aghlabids (800–909)[15] preceding the Shīʿī dynasty of the Fāṭimids who took power in Tunisia in 909 and conquered Egypt in 969.

During the last twenty years Talbi has participated in a number of official and personal dialogues with Christians in both North Africa and Europe. In an article on Islam and the West, published in 1987, he complains about the current poverty of Muslim initiatives or even responses in the matter of Euro-Arab or Islamo-Christian dialogue. In a brochure on the subject, published some ten years ago, he explicitly declared Islam to be open to dialogue with other faiths and cultures. In 1989 he and the French Orthodox Christian Olivier Clément published together a large book called *Un respect têtu*,[16] "A Dogged Respect," in which both authors testify to the search for common truth. For Talbi the Muslim-Christian dialogue is not just a social event but a significant religious matter, and he has done whatever has been possible to promote such a dialogue in Tunisia and elsewhere. His *Mémoires*, published in Arabic in 1992, deal in part with problems of dialogue.

Comparative Historical Analysis: Abdallah Laroui

The Moroccan historian Abdallah Laroui (born 1933), professor at the University of Rabat, has published in French two scholarly historical studies. The first is on the history of the Maghrib (1970),[17] and the second, his *thèse d'État*, on the origins of Moroccan nationalism (1977).[18] He has also brought out three volumes of essays which have made him widely known outside the circle of specialists: on contemporary Arab ideology (1967),[19] on the crisis of Arab intellectuals (1974),[20] and on Islam and modernity (1987)[21]; the first two of these have been translated into English.

As a historian inspired by Marxian principles, Laroui normally carries out his analysis of Arab Muslim societies, their history, and their ideologies without speaking much about Islam as a religion. One interesting exception is his fierce rebuttal of Gustav E. von Grunebaum's theory and practice of cultural analysis.[22] Laroui establishes the primacy of what he calls "real" history over "cultural" history as von Grunebaum understood it; he also shows that von Grunebaum's assumptions and presuppositions made him describe and evaluate Islam as a medieval and premodern culture, inherently different from, if not opposed to, the modern West. Subsequently Laroui tries to put von Grunebaum's model and his many scholarly findings within a broader framework of historical study. At the end of his criticism, however, Laroui proposes four domains in the study of Islam which ought to be approached successively: Islam as history, including power with all its local and temporal specificities; Islam as culture (with a process of continuous traditionalization); Islam as morality, with a basic "Muslim personality" and a characteristic lifestyle and behavior; and Islam as a faith. In Laroui's view the domain of faith has hardly been elucidated in Islamic studies until now and does not simply coincide with the study of *fiqh*, *kalām* and *akhlāq* (ethics). Faith has to be studied as the fourth and highest level of society, determined by the three underlying levels of history, behavior, and culture. Laroui apparently thinks, for instance, of an inquiry into the logical foundations of the Sunna, a present-day reinterpretation of the various cathechisms (*ʿaqīdas*) written in Islamic history, and a study in depth of the concept of Islamic faith with its characteristic resistance to all that is not Islamic. In Laroui's scheme the level of faith cannot influence the first level, that of power; it is rather the infrastructural situation which precedes faith and conditions any realization and historical articulation of it. For Laroui, Islam evidently is not a static entity; the word *islām* indicates each time a new reality.

As he argues in *Islam et modernité* (1987), the issue is not so much a "return" of Islam since the middle of the nineteenth century (or earlier or later, depending on the region), but rather what he calls a "neo-Islam" with an ideological structure quite different from that of "classical" Islam. Its strengthening since the 1970s is largely due to political forces, in particular new kinds of relationships between Arab countries. Whereas formerly such countries as Egypt, Syria, and Iraq had been centers of Arab culture, during the last decades countries like Saudi Arabia, the Gulf states, and Libya have become rich and have furthered this "neo-Islam" in order to legitimate their new role of ideological domination, as Laroui interprets it. The masses are sensitive to any appeal to Islam; everywhere in the world there is a resurgence of tradition and this holds equally true for the Muslim countries. "Neo-Islam," which represents a resurgence of Islamic tradition, poses sociopolitical rather than religious problems, the latter belonging to the domain of religious feeling.[23]

His volume on Islam and modernity contains two essays (chapters 5 and 6) illustrating the kind of comparative historical analysis Laroui wants to make of analogous developments in the history of Europe and Islam. One example is his comparison between Ibn Khaldūn (1332–1406) and Machiavelli (1468-1527)—two thinkers who both discovered, the latter apparently independently of the former, a new field of investigation and knowledge which until then had been largely unexplored: man as a political being. Laroui contends that they used the same method because they had the same epistemological postulates. He subsequently analyzes some striking differences between the two thinkers, explaining particular features of Ibn Khaldūn's work compared to that of Machiavelli by means of the Islamic elements of the world view in which Ibn Khaldūn worked. Both thinkers, however, refused utopian solutions, employed formal logic in analyzing political life, and sought to offer conclusive proofs for their arguments. Both accepted a permanent dualism between consciousness (*conscience*) and instinct and both envisaged man as a sociopolitical animal.

The second example of comparative historical analysis which Laroui offers concerns the rationalism of the European (especially French) Enlightenment and that of the Salafiyya reformists. According to Laroui, Voltaire's interpretation of religion on the one hand and Jamāl al-Dīn al-Afghānī's reinterpretation of Islam on the other both refer to a kind of natural, rational religion without need of mediation and accessible to every human being. Again, having given this similarity between the two schools of thought, Laroui analyzes some striking differences between them, such as the acceptance or negation of evil as a metaphysical problem. The author proceeds in this line of thought, and posits Islam as a "naturalism for human usage."[24]

Subsequently, Laroui proposes other comparisons: between the "marginal" thinkers of Islam and the eighteenth-century Enlightenment philosophers, between gnostic currents in both contexts, especially in regions bordering each other, and between various attitudes to life to be found in both cultures. The interest of such comparisons for Laroui is in the first place methodological. He sees that they can also function, however, to facilitate a better understanding between the two civilizations, which since the beginning have been characterized by a nearly perennial structural opposition to each other.

The Effort to Raise Thought on Commonly Recognized Problems: Mohammed Arkoun

The last of our six North African intellectuals is Mohammed Arkoun, an Algerian of Berber origin (born in 1928). He studied in Paris and since 1961 has been a professor of the history of Islamic thought at the University of Paris III. Arkoun has done a special study of the tenth-century Muslim intellectual Miskawayh (936–1030), whom he characterizes as a true humanist (1961, 1969, 1970).[25] A number of Arkoun's scholarly essays were collected in volumes on Islamic thought (1977),[26] readings of the Qur'an (1982),[27] and a critique of Islamic reason (1984).[28] Smaller books deal with Arab thought (1975),[29] and with ethics and politics in Islam (1986).[30] Arkoun is committed to interreligious dialogue, especially with Christians, and published several books on this subject together with Christian authors [with Louis Gardet (1978),[31] with Arosio and Borrmans (1982),[32] and with the Islamic-Christian research group on Scriptures (1987)[33]]. His basic approaches and findings were synthesized in a smaller book, *Ouvertures sur l'Islam*, "Overtures to Islam" (1989),[34] which will be our point of departure here.

If, with the exception of Malik Bennabi, the preceding authors can be qualified as historians, sometimes using a sociological approach as in the case of Laroui, Arkoun seems to be a born philosopher and subsequently an erudite (*adīb*), familiar with the arts in general, the humanities and social sciences in particular, and semiology (semiotics) specifically. In his writings and at conferences he addresses himself to a Western public, the French in particular, as well as to a younger Muslim student generation, and if I see it correctly, to the critically thinking faithful of religious traditions in general and in particular of the monotheistic faiths.

To start with the last concern: Arkoun observes and criticizes the existence of a kind of complicity among the faithful of the three monotheistic religions in order to preserve their respective dogmatic definitions, using them to establish themselves and their community continuously as an "orthodoxy" instead of striving for a new space of intelligibility (*OI*, p. 9). For instance, Islam like Christianity has entertained a medieval vision, of a theological nature, of other religions and communities. Both in Christianity and in Islam particular theological systems have had an enormous impact on all the ways in which people have understood themselves and the world. This framework of perception has continued to exist until the present day. Even though scholarly research has brought about the secularization of the conditions of intelligibility and understanding in large measure, people continue to have a perception of each other biased by the divisions which originally were established by the religions (OI, pp. 22–23).

As far as Islam is concerned, until recently it has been characterized by a religious discourse which Arkoun terms "mythical," that is, constantly drawing on the Qur'an. However, with a growing openness to Europe in the course of the nineteenth and twentieth centuries, a new "liberal" trend arose among Muslim intellectuals, favorable to imitation of the Western cultural model. This meant the rise of a discourse alternative to the traditional religious one: a Western discourse in which Western values dominated.

From the beginning of the twentieth century on, sometimes earlier and sometimes later, there arose a new, secular nationalist trend which was furthered by a reformist Islamic trend. Both opposed the liberal trend which had been open to the West. From this time on Islam ceased to be used as a *religious* discourse of a mythical nature drawing on the Qur'an. Rather it has become a mobilizing *ideological* discourse manipulating popular and traditional beliefs in order to recommend and impose purely political projects such as those of the Arab nation, the Arab socialist revolution, or the Islamic state. Here directed ideology has taken the place of myth (*OI*, pp. 25–26).

Arkoun lays his finger on similar politically directed attempts to ideologize the religious-mythical contents of the Jewish and Christian traditions at the present time, as a consequence of which each religion defends its own starting points, postulates, and dogmas ever more ideologically.

This degeneration of the faiths, however, in fact began much earlier, and in this connection it is relevant to see how Arkoun presents the beginning of Islam. As he sees it, Muhammad basically introduced a new political system in the Arabia of his day, a system which was articulated with the help of a new religious symbolism and made particular use of the symbolism of the alliance between God and mankind. A new semiological system replaced what came to be called the *Jāhiliyya*, and a new state surpassing tribal solidarities arose to apply and impose the new political order. But in Islam, as earlier in Judaism, the original creative religious symbolism degenerated into juridical codes, automatic rituals, scholastic doctrines and—last but not least—ideologies of domination (*OI*, pp. 36–38).

Indeed, this development was closely linked to the process of empire building which led to a government control (*étatisation*, *Verstaatlichung*) of Islam. With the growth and subsequent centralization of the caliphal empire not only did a judiciary emerge which needed a common juridical code, but also a subordination of the religious to the political took place (*OI*, p. 39). Whereas during Muhammad's lifetime there had been a double—symbolic as well as political—expression of leadership (as Arkoun puts it, the Qur'an is the best witness to Muhammad's creativity in the realm of "symbolic realism"), this ended abruptly once the empire had been established. Not only was this sort of creativity at an end but, on the contrary, the symbolic capital which was conveyed by the Qur'an was now used to construct an Islam which was both "official" (with government blessing) and "orthodox" (eliminating rival interpretations from power). And whereas in the Qur'an the sacred was purified and concentrated in the person of God, in the Muslim societies of subsequent periods the sacred on an empirical level was again dispersed in a number of objects, as had been the case before

Islam, and a sacralization of Qur'an and Sunna took place so that they were defended in apologetic literature at all costs (*OI*, pp. 40–41).

Thus according to Arkoun, Islam arose as a political system with a religious symbolism of its own; during the imperial period this religious symbolism was systematized rationally in the religious sciences which represented official orthodox Islam supported by the state. In the twentieth century a new politicization of Islam took place, in the course of which the religious discourse, with its symbolic and mythical elements, made room for an ideological discourse which used those elements for political purposes. Especially since the sixties an ideological "Islamic" model has evolved which armors itself against scholarly inquiry; it contains a universe of the collective imagination, ideologically depicted as "Islamic" (*OI*, p. 27). And what has happened to Islam has also happened to Judaism and Christianity with their particular official and orthodox versions of religion, their ideologizations in the course of the twentieth century, and their growing degradation into politics.

Arkoun then discusses a subject hardly envisaged by other Muslim scholars until now: the essentially critical role of *science of religion* in the study of the three great monotheistic religions and their mutual relations. He observes a continuous—historical and contemporary—rivalry among the three communities of Judaism, Christianity, and Islam. All want to monopolize the management of what Arkoun calls the "symbolic capital," this monopolization being linked to what is called "Revelation" by these three religious traditions. Arkoun adds that the theologians of each community are responsible for the management of the symbolic capital which represents the community's "goods of salvation," and for legitimizing in this way each community's natural will to dominate. The construction of a "Judeo-Christian" vision of the history of salvation, which includes Judaism and Christianity but excludes Islam, is a recent product of such activity (*OI*, pp. 16–17). In this way the most sacred values of these traditions have been changed into communal "property," a "symbolic capital" which is managed by theologians and through which each community constitutes and legitimates its own separate identity over against the others.

It is to the science of religion that Arkoun assigns the task of a thorough criticism of theological reasoning (*OI*, p. 17). In fact, the sciences of man and society, that is to say the humanities and social sciences, should take charge of all those matters in dispute which have been bequeathed by the theological constructions of former times. Historical research, for instance, can show how different groups have drawn from a common stock of signs and symbols to produce their respective exclusive systems of belief and nonbelief (*OI*, p. 20). Science of religion must also analyze the dimension of the imaginative (*l'imaginaire*) as it arose in the three religions and the many societies constituting them. It should make a special effort to reach the radical dimension which these three traditions have in common, as a counterweight to the many efforts made to show their distinctiveness. At the end, Arkoun is deeply concerned with the nature of the data claimed to be Revelation by the three religious traditions. He pleads for a modern kind of theology able to discuss the phenomenon of Revelation as a special issue in itself, in a perspective of "comparative theology" which will go beyond the polemics and beyond what Arkoun calls "exchanges of false tolerance" (*OI*, p. 45) between the three religious traditions. We shall come back to these broad tasks assigned by Arkoun to the scholarly study of religion in general, and the three monotheistic traditions in particular, but let us first stress another ongoing concern of his.

Arkoun is very much concerned about the kind of knowledge which not only the Islamic theological disciplines but also the West has acquired of Islam. He questions the objective nature and the validity of the latter (*OI*, p. 13). Is much of this knowledge not a construct of the Western collective imagination, especially in the way in which Islam is presented by the media and at schools in the West? In particular during the last twenty years, the Western media have transposed a present-day hard-line construct of Islam by Muslim "Islamists" to the West, where it simply has become part of the Western collective imagination connected with Khomeini and political extremism. At the present time, instead of a better mutual knowledge and understanding between the two religious traditions, there is rather a confrontation of two different realms of collective imagination, the Muslim and the Western one. So where then does real knowledge start? Islamic studies worthy of the name should abandon thinking about Islam as something existing in itself and instead examine and interrogate Islam in the light of the modern sciences of man and society (*OI*, p. 11).

Significance for Islamic Studies and Other Religious Studies

I would like to assess the work of the various authors discussed, who have expressed themselves within the framework of French intellectual thought, in terms of Islamic Studies. Indeed, any Christian-Muslim encounter on an intellectual level demands not only a common effort to understand the Christian faith, but also a like effort to understand the Islamic faith. An encounter between people who do not seriously investigate their own and the other's religion may result in a dialogue but not one in intellectual terms.

It appears to me that descriptive studies of twentieth-century intellectual movements in Islam and the Muslim commonwealth, such as have been carried out by an author like Ali Merad, are indispensable, if only for the degree of information they offer: scholars coming from the tradition studied are often better placed than outsiders to describe such movements accurately, providing they do not bow to current fashions and ideologies. In Ali Merad's particular case, he also pays attention to the description of meetings between Muslims and Christians at the present time, both in Muslim countries and in Europe.

Such descriptive studies of twentieth-century developments can be usefully supplemented on the one hand by studies of the cultural history of Islam in earlier times and its impact on the identity of present-day Muslims and, on the other hand, by studies of the relations between the Muslim and European worlds which have also left their mark on present-day Muslim identity and contemporary relations between Muslims and Europeans. The work of an author like Hichem Djait offers this kind of cultural history, covering what is common to Europe and Islam and what is specific to the Arab-Muslim world. Whereas nearly all European historians have described Arab and Islamic history as a different, even separate history from that of Europe, the awareness of a common, not only Mediterranean but even Euro-Arab history is now gaining ground.

History, however, is much more than cultural, and certainly religious, history. Solid studies of the economic, demographic, ethnic, and political determinants of the history of Arab-Muslim regions and their relations with Europe are still very much lacking, if certain descriptions of North African history from the biased point of view of French colonial history are discounted. The work of an author like Abdallah Laroui is important in various respects. He not only describes North African history and its determinant factors as a development originating in the region itself, and twentieth-century Arab ideological movements in terms of similar infrastructural determinants, but also presents an analysis in depth of the way in which analogous ideas and trends of thought developed in Europe and in the Arab world. Here again there is the awareness of a cultural history held in common notwithstanding the particular traits of Muslim and European thought, traits which in times of political and ideological struggle were quickly absolutized. More than is the case with the authors mentioned before, Laroui's work has for such a study its own coherent epistemology, critical of ideology, inspired but not slavishly determined by Marxian principles of historical research.

None of these scholars just mentioned, however, has focused principally on Islam as a religion. This is the contribution of Malek Bennabi, whose work is unique in the sense that forty years ago already it presented the Qur'an and Islam to French readers as a religious and ideological recourse for Muslim societies. It is an honest intellectual search for independence and dignity, on a religious as well as political level, but it now has a documentary rather than a scholarly importance in terms of Islamic studies and the study of religion generally.

The only North African scholar writing in French who has made a concerted original effort in the field of Islamic Studies in our time is Mohammed Arkoun, and I would like to summarize the respects in which his work represents a precious contribution to Islamic Studies, the study of religion generally, and Christian-Muslim encounter on an intellectual level which is both critical and self-critical. More than any other Muslim scholar of Islam I know, Arkoun raises questions inescapable for the Islamic, Christian, and also Jewish traditions, and it would indicate a decline of intellectual capacities if the questions raised by Arkoun, difficult as they may be, were not appropriately discussed, if not answered, by intellectual minds of younger generations, Muslims and non-Muslims alike.

Arkoun, first of all, wants critical scholarship, real science of religion, to be applied to Islam. Specifically he calls for the application of historical, sociological, and anthropological methods to the study of Muslim societies and Islamic history in general, and semiotic and linguistic methods to the study of Islamic texts. This includes a consistent effort to reveal the political interests and implications of expressions which most scholars of Islam until now have tended to study for their cultural and religious significance.

A good example is his treatment of what happened to Muhammad's original symbolic word expressions contained in the Qurʾan (*OI*, pp. 35, 38, 46). After the creative moment of an open religious discourse as offered in the Qurʾan, the "symbolic capital" contained in Qurʾan and Ḥadīths was fought over by different factions in the community who wanted to control its "symbolic charge," which they needed to legitimate their thirst for political power. In a next phase this symbolic charge was tamed and rationalized in various disciplines of a theological nature, such as *tafsīr* and *ʿilm al-ḥadīths*, *fiqh* and *kalām*, and as the price of this rationalization the texts in question gradually lost much of their symbolic power. Much later, with the growth of European influence and the rise of secular thinking, the symbols which had functioned in a religious discourse started to operate as simple signals in an ideological discourse in which religious aims and purposes had largely been lost. And whereas formerly such signals used to indicate whether one belonged to the "traditional" or the "modern" wing of society, in the last twenty years the trend of meaning has been inverted, with the accent being put on the affirmation of an Islamic identity. The veil, for instance, has changed from a "traditional" into a self-assertive symbol, like the short beard and other signals which mean nowadays "properly Islamic," whereas thirty years ago they indicated a traditionalism of bygone times.

In his study of Islam within the parameters of the modern sciences of man and society Arkoun opens up completely new subjects of research that can and should be studied in other traditions as well. What, for instance, are the conditions in which particular politicoreligious "imaginatives" (*imaginaires*) arise, such as what Arkoun calls the "Medinan experience" under the Prophet and afterwards under the Rashidun caliphs? What have been the social and cultural conditions of the evolution of both the rational and the imaginative aspects of Islamic life and thought in particular times and places? How should the rational and the imaginative perception of the past by Muslim authors and historians be distinguished and evaluated historically?

Second, Arkoun represents rational enlightenment in his thinking about both his own religion and religion in general. I contend that he stands in the line of Western critical thought when he applies modern historical and social scientific criticism to what he calls "Islamic reason/rationality" (*la raison islamique*), that is to say, classical Islamic thought patterns and their ideological effects, which he judges critically. I call him an Enlightenment thinker in so far as he has faith in reason and knowledge and sees dogmatism, sacralization, and ideologization as major barriers to thought. This attitude also shows up in his high regard for modern reason, to which he assigns—after it has destroyed false kinds of knowledge—an essentially constructive function. Modern reason strives for a kind of knowledge that integrates both the rational and the imaginative, and seeks what Arkoun calls a "comprehensive intelligibility" (*intelligibilité compréhensive*). A good example is his call for a philosophical criticism of the notions of Truth as held in the monotheistic religions (*OI*, p. 89). The way in which truth has been conceived in them has led to mutual exclusiveness; for any serious communication and dialogue (*réciprocité des consciences*), this concept of truth has simply to be abandoned, which means a serious epistemological rupture. Another example is his consistent criticism of Islamic reason/rationality (*OI*, pp. 71, 105) understood as a theological construct, by which he wants to introduce what he calls "modern reason" (scientific and philosophical) and to put an end to intellectual stagnancy. It is time to unmask the harmful ideological effects (*OI*, p. 79) of a situation which has been sacralized for more than ten centuries (*OI*, p. 77).

As part of his search for rational enlightenment Arkoun has virtually opened up new domains of research in Islamic Studies, even though he may have derived the approaches from elsewhere. First he uses the notion of discourse, and that of religious discourse in particular, as a broad guiding concept, for instance in Qur'anic studies, even broaching a theory of religious discourse (*OI*, p. 69). Another area he opened up is the application of semiotic theory and techniques as a key to the search for meaning, speaking for instance of Muhammad's *islām* as a new semiological system opposed to the old *jāhiliyya* system. Arkoun has a keen nose for problems of meaning. He opposes Marcel Gauchet's idea of "the debt of significance" (*la dette de sens*) as a heuristic key to having access to latent meanings (*OI*, pp. 33–34), drawing attention to present-day ideological trends where meaning is simply imposed on the subject under study. He contends that we have to do with an impoverishment of meaning and a degeneration of symbolic universes nowadays (*OI*, pp. 35, 47–48, 137) and affirms, for instance about the present-day Muslim context, that "one observes a degeneration of myth to mythologies, a dilapidation of the symbolic capital left by Islam, a reduction of the sign to a signal" (*OI*, p. 121). He has developed and applied a theory of "reading" a text (*OI*, p. 71) in broader philosophical terms and with greater objectivity than is usual in current hermeneutical theory and practice. Finally I want to stress that it is Arkoun who has opened up the field of the imaginative (*l'imaginaire*) and its relation to historical and social reality in Islamic Studies which, in good empirical tradition, has been rather hesitant toward the study of imaginative expressions. In this respect too, Arkoun must be recognized as a pioneer.

Third, Arkoun urges closer cooperation between scholars on the subject of the three monotheistic religions, Judaism, Christianity, and Islam, and their relations. Common research should center on what is called in all three religions "Revelation" (*OI*, pp. 53–61). Science of religion should study the orthodox and other teachings of the three religions on the subject of their historical and theological origin, the ideological and psychological functions of such teachings, and their semantic and anthropological limits and even inadequacies. The fact that a text is held to be revelation should be seen primarily as a linguistic and cultural datum to be studied. Theological discourses on Revelation, including the ways in which they have reified "revelations," should be subjected to scientific inquiry. In all three cases it was the oral discourse that was the primary vehicle of revelation and in all three cases there is an analogous relationship between the "spoken words" and the "heavenly Word."

In particular the textual fixation of the religious discourse had far-reaching consequences. It made "Revelation" accessible only from within an official closed corpus of fixed texts, which put man in a hermeneutical situation. It enabled various groups of people to sacralize, transcendentalize, and absolutize their own behavior and words by appealing to chosen texts of scripture; this has created unbearable situations, for instance, in the Muslim discourse of today. Arkoun wants to consider Revelation again as an event of meaning and a source of living tradition, something which opens to the future and is definitively opposed to repetitive behavior and the formation of rigid and closed systems of thought. Revelation properly understood provides human beings with mental space and creates a spiritual ethos; in practice, however, in all three religions it has served to legitimate domination, which is contrary to its primary function (*OI*, p. 72).

Fourth, the work of Arkoun destroys the idea still current in the West that a critical study of Muhammad (*OI*, chap. 9) and the Qur'an (*OI*, chaps. 6–8) by Muslims is not possible; he breaks a taboo. He explicitly pleads for a comparative historical study of the three "Book religions" (*OI*, p. 120). He has an enlightened critical and self-critical attitude to all received ideas about anything Islamic, whether held by Muslims or Western scholars. In this vein he compares, for instance, the relations between religion and state in Islam and Christianity, offering new insight (*OI*, chap. 3). Refreshingly, he shows no tendency to glorify, magnify, or estheticize Islam, and certainly no inclination to enter into polemics or apologetic reasoning.

One senses how much Arkoun is concerned with the current ideologizations of Islam: "the triumph of an area of society's imagination which is qualified as 'Islamic'" (*le triomphe d'un imaginaire social qualifié d'islamique*). He offers a proper definition of ideologization: "There is an ideological derivation in Islamic thinking whenever an author . . . establishes as a closed cognitive system a Qur'anic discourse which initially was open" (*il y a dérive idéologique dans le cadre de la pensée islamique chaque fois qu'un auteur—lui-même écho plus ou moins fidèle d'une école, d'une communauté, d'une tradition—érige en système cognitif clos un discours coranique initialement ouvert* (*OI*, p. 158). He also gives an acceptable explanation of such an ideologization of Islam as of any religion: when there are attacks from the outside, the Muslim world assembles around an Islam made ideologically efficient (*il a fallu se rassembler autour d'un Islam orthodoxe, dogmatique, rigide, mais idéologiquement efficace*) (*OI*, p. 131). In recent times, for instance, the Salafiyya and subsequent movements have developed a "mythological" vision of original Islam and classical Islam, as something ideologically useful which is rooted in a society's imaginative universe (*imaginaire social*) (*OI*, pp. 27, 131).

Over against the perennial tendency to ideologization, not only in religion but also in scholarship, Arkoun proclaims a plural methodology, open problematics, and a philosophical attitude, "in order to go beyond the ravaging ideologies" (*OI*, p. 127). No wonder that Arkoun, as a committed thinker and scholar, wants to make a sharp distinction between the theoretical Islamology of Western universities, of philological inspiration, and an applied Islamology which intends to read and study Islam's past and present on the basis of the present-day expressions and questions of Muslim societies. Applied Islamology should address itself to the largest possible public but without incurring the condemnation, haughty rejection, or even indifference of erudite scholars (*OI*, p. 8).

Applied Islamology

The expression "applied Islamology"[35] was coined by M. Arkoun probably in analogy to the expression "applied anthropology," which the French anthropologist Roger Bastide introduced.[36] In a way, all Islamology which is not purely academic—that is to say, an exclusively scholarly pursuit—constitutes some kind of "applied" scholarship, and even pure scholarship plays a role in society and in relations between people from different societies. In the case of the six authors under consideration, the social relevance of their research is striking.

Of the four historians Laroui concentrates on Moroccan history and the rise of the national movement, Merad explores the role of reformist Islam in the national movement of Algeria, Talbi works on Tunisian history in earlier times, and Djait devotes himself to the study of Arab history in the first century and a half with particular attention to the role of Islam. Furthermore, Laroui has paid attention to the Arab intelligentsia facing present-day problems of the Arab world and Talbi has cherished the cause of dialogue on a personalist basis, beyond the frontiers of confessional systems and communal structures, stimulating Muslims to take part in it. Merad, too, has been open to dialogue, also in a practical sense with a view to improving the situation of North Africans living in France. Djait has a vivid sense of the rise and decline of cultures and civilizations and has been concerned about inter-Arab and Arab-European relations.

Of the two authors concentrating on Islam, Bennabi has been concerned with Islam as a resource for the moral and ideological reconstruction of Algeria and Arkoun's basic concern has been the study of the humanist tradition in Islamic intellectual history and the role of the human person. Whereas Bennabi has made a concerted effort to mobilize his people in the framework of an Islamic movement, Arkoun has been sensitive to the manipulation of religion by manifold interests which has taken place throughout the history of Islamic and other religious traditions. When he subjects the forms of established religion to a critical analysis, he is inspired not only by rational enlightenment, which employs the human and social sciences, but also by the Qur᾽an with its religious symbolism. He has developed his ideas both in publications and in many lectures given in Muslim and Western countries.

As a consequence, all six authors are profoundly aware of the relevance of their work for the future of their societies, their own countries, the Arab world, and the wider Muslim world. It would have been strange if this had not been the case, and this distinguishes them quite naturally from Western scholars scarcely ever concerned with the future of Muslim societies for their own sake. So all six authors are also involved in the practical effects of their studies on Muslim societies beyond the academic sphere and have their place in "applied" Islamology.

For Arkoun, however, applied Islamology has a special meaning; it serves what I would like to call an intellectual renewal of Islam and potentially all monotheistic religions. Knowing classical Islamology well and recognizing what it has achieved in terms of textual studies, he sees its limitations as being a purely Western discourse and defining Islam by means of classical texts alone. In his view this Western Islamology should be subject to epistemological self-criticism, assimilate the many new developments in the human and social sciences, and develop an awareness of the problems with which Muslim societies are confronted today.

Over against classical Islamology, applied Islamology as conceived by Arkoun leads to a different orientation in research. It is meant to overcome a certain distrust which Muslims feel toward orientalism by promoting active cooperation between Muslim and non-Muslim scholars. Applied Islamology must ultimately create conditions under which freedom of thinking can be restored and developed. Muslim thought needs to be liberated from old taboos, obsolete mythologies, and the weight of current political forces and ideologies. More than before Muslim thought should take part actively in the intellectual ventures in which Western thought has been involved for centuries, and this again in all freedom. Applied Islamology should take seriously, and respond to, the vital concerns of Muslim thought at the present time. Accordingly, the Islamologist "applying" his or her knowledge should be not only a scholar but also a promoter of all reflection which aims at renewal and emancipation. When studying Islam, applied Islamology introduces comparative research and questions Islamic materials in the same way as the modern human and social sciences investigate materials of other religions. Fifth, applied Islamology should subject the Islamic theological system to critical inquiry just like that which needs to be directed at theological systems in other religions. For at least the three monotheistic religions, theologies have functioned largely as "cultural systems of mutual exclusion" which legitimate opposing interests and stand in the way of true communication and dialogue.

Conclusion

The task set out at the beginning of this essay was to analyze the ways in which six North African intellectuals have presented Islam in French during recent decades. The first conclusion must be that none of the authors confines himself to simple presentation; each communicates results of scholarly research and search for scholarly cooperation. Moreover, some of them formulate broader questions which apply not only to Islam but to Christianity as well, which is an invitation to dialogue on an intellectual level.

A second conclusion is that it is no longer French scholars who study and teach Islamic history, thought, and institutions in France as was the case in the days when our six authors were students. Many scholars from North African countries are now carrying out research in this field and a scholarly debate has started on the ways in which Islamic Studies are to be pursued. Differences in approach depend not only on different theoretical frameworks and methodologies but also on the different causes to which scholars are dedicated, those from Muslim societies naturally being aware of the relevance and application of their work for the future of their societies.

Thirdly, I would say that Arkoun's appeal to broaden Islamic Studies beyond the study of texts deserves our sympathy and participation, even though many Western researchers are basically specialists in textual work and not always able to situate such texts and their various interpretations and applications in their intellectual and religious, historical, and social context as ideally should be done. Moreover, the lack of concern, or even interest, of many Western researchers in the present-day problems of Muslim societies, which irritates Arkoun and many other Muslim scholars, must be deplored. However, within the context of academic freedom it falls to the responsibility of individual researchers to remedy this; measures cannot be dictated from above though pedagogy can be improved. But for research to be carried out by scholars of different backgrounds, including those coming from the Muslim societies studied, cooperation appears to be a sound demand and a scholarly necessity.

Finally I would suggest the necessity for similar inquiries into the ways in which Islam in recent times has been presented by scholars from Egypt and other countries of the Arab East, from Turkey and Iran, from the former USSR and China, from Pakistan and India, from Indonesia and Malaysia, and from West and East Africa, not to speak of turning our attention to the ways in which Muslims in North America and Europe present Islam nowadays.

NOTES

1. Malek Bennabi, *Le phénomène coranique: Essai d'une théorie sur le Coran* (Alger: Sharikat al-Nahḍa li ʾl-ṭibaʿa wa ʾl-Nashr, 1946), English translation *The Qurʾanic Phenomena* (Chicago: Kazi Publications, 1988).

2. Malek Bennabi, *Vocation de l'Islam* (Paris: Seuil, 1954), English Translation *Islam in History and Society* (Chicago: Kazi Publications, 1988). See also the first part of the autobiography of the author, *Mémoires d'un témoin du siècle* (Alger: Entreprise Nationale du Livre, 1965, 1990).

3. H.A.R. Gibb, *Modern Trends in Islam* (Chicago: University of Chicago Press, 1947), French translation by Bernard Vernier, *Les tendances modernes de l'Islam* (Paris: G.P. Maisonneuve, 1949).

4. Bennabi, *Vocation*, p. 111.

5. Hichem Djait, *Al-Kufa: Naissance de la ville islamique* (Paris: Maisonneuve et Larose, 1986).

6. Hichem Djait, *La grande discorde. Religion et politique dans l' Islam des origines* (Paris: Gallimard, 1989).

7. Hichem Djait, *La personnalité et le devenir arabo-islamique* (Paris: Seuil, 1974).

8. Hichem Djait, *L'Europe et l'Islam* (Paris: Seuil, 1978), English translation *Europe and Islam* (Berkeley: University of California Press, 1985).

9. Djait, *L'Europe et l'Islam*, p. 47.

10. Ibid., p. 86.

11. Ali Merad, *Le réformisme musulman en Algérie de 1925 à 1940. Essai d'histoire religieuse et sociale* (Paris & The Hague: Mouton, 1967).

12. Ali Merad, *Ibn Badis, commentateur du Coran* (Paris: Geuthner, 1971).

13. Ali Merad, *L'Islam contemporain* (Paris: Presses Universitaires de France, 1984, 1987).

14. Ali Merad, *Charles de Foucauld au regard de l'Islam* (Paris: Chalet, 1975). For Ali Merad's contributions to Muslim-Christian dialogue see for instance his contributions in Armand Abecassis, Ali Merad, and Daniel Pézeril, *N'avons-nous pas le même Père?* (Paris: Chalet, 1972) and in Jean Paul Gabus, Ali Merad, and Youakim Moubarac, *Islam et christianisme en dialogue* (Paris: Cerf, 1982).

15. Mohamed Talbi, *L'émirat aghlabide 184–296/800–909. Histoire politique* (Paris: A. Maisonneuve, 1966). He also published *Ibn Khaldūn et l'histoire. Réflexions sur un thème d'actualité* (Tunis: Maison tunisienne de l'édition, 1973).

16. Mohamed Talbi and Oliver Clément, *Un respect têtu* (Paris: Nouvelle Cité, 1989). Compare Mohamed Talbi, *Islam et dialogue. Réflexions sur un thème d'actualité* (Tunis: Maison tunisienne de l'édition, 1972, 1979). See also Mohamed Talbi, "Islam et Occident. Les possibilités et les conditions d'une meilleure compréhension," *Les Cahiers de Tunisie* 33 (1987): 5–46.

17. Abdallah Laroui, *L'histoire du Maghreb. Essai de synthèse* (Paris: Maspero, 1970), English translation *The History of the Maghrib: An Interpretive Essay* (Princeton: Princeton University Press, 1977).

18. Abdallah Laroui, *Les origines sociales et culturelles du nationalisme marocain, 1830–1912* (Paris: Maspero, 1977).

19. Abdallah Laroui, *L'idéologie arabe contemporaine: Essai critique* (Paris: Maspero, 1967, 1977).

20. Abdallah Laroui, *La crise des intellectuels arabes: Traditionalisme ou historicisme?* (Paris: Maspero, 1974), English translation *The Crisis of the Arab Intellectual: Traditionalism or Historicism?* (Berkeley: University of California Press, 1977).

21. Abdallah Laroui, *Islam et modernité* (Paris: La Découverte, 1987). See also his *L'Algérie et le Sahara marocain* (Casablanca: Serar, 1976).

22. Chap. 3 of *La crise des intellectuels arabes* (1974), "Les Arabes et l'anthropologie culturelle: Remarques sur la méthode de Gustave von Grunebaum" (pp. 59–102 of the French edition).

23. Laroui, *Islam et modernité*, pp. 94–95.

24. Ibid., p. 145.

25. Mohammed Arkoun, *Deux Epîtres de Miskawayh. Edition critique* (Damascus: Institut Français d'Études Arabes, 1961); *Traité d'éthique. Trad. française annotée du Tahdhīb al-akhlāq de Miskawayh* (Damascus: Institut Français d'Études Arabes, 1969, 1988); *L'humanisme arabe au IVe/Xe siècle. Miskaway philosophe et historien* (Paris: Vrin, 1970, 1982).

26. Mohammed Arkoun, *Essais sur la pensée islamique* (Paris: Maisonneuve et Larose, 1977, 1984).

27. Mohammed Arkoun, *Lectures du Coran* (Paris: Maisonneuve et Larose, 1982, 1989).

28. Mohammed Arkoun, *Pour une critique de la raison islamique* (Paris: Maisonneuve et Larose, 1984).

29. Mohammed Arkoun, *La pensée arabe* (Paris: Presses Universitaires de France, 1975, 1985).

30. Mohammed Arkoun, *L'Islam, morale et politique* (Paris: Unesco & Desclée de Brouwer, 1986).

31. Mohammed Arkoun and Louis Gardet, *L'Islam, hier, demain* (Paris: Buchet-Chastel, 1978, 1982).

32. Mohammed Arkoun, M. Arosio, and M. Borrmans, *L'Islam, religion et société* (Paris: Cerf, 1982).

33. Groupe de Recherches Islamo-Chrétien (G.R.I.C.), *Ces Écritures qui nous questionnent. La Bible et le Coran* (Paris: Centurion, 1987).

34. Mohammed Arkoun, *Ouvertures sur l'Islam* (Paris: Grancher, 1989). Hereafter cited in text as *OI* with page numbers.

35. Mohammed Arkoun, "Pour une islamologie appliquée," first published in 1976 and reproduced in his *Pour une critique de la raison islamique* (1984), chap. 1 (pp. 43–63).

36. Roger Bastide, *Anthropologie appliquée* (Paris: Payot, 1971).

23

Christians in a Muslim State: The Recent Egyptian Debate

Yvonne Yazbeck Haddad

The contentious nature of the debate on the status and role of non-Muslims in an Islamic state has persisted for several decades in Egypt. Much literature has been produced, with a great deal clearly at stake in whether a given author belongs to the minority (in this case mainly Coptic Christian) or the majority Muslim community. At times, the debate has appeared as a free-for-all engaged in, among others, by religious and secular activists (both Christian and Muslim), parliamentarians, commentators, and religious leaders as well as scholars.

It is clear that while the focus is Egypt, the nature of the modern world is such that those engaged are not only responding to internal policy issues on the Egyptian scene, but are also attuned to Western opinion expressed on the matter. In some cases, they actually choose to address and refute what they consider to be erroneous or inflamatory commentary published by Western scholars.[1] The context, therefore, is global in perspective and not limited to internal considerations. The debate proceeds from a feeling of disempowerment and defeat that has enveloped the Muslim world and a perception that it is virtually encircled by hostile powers not only bent on the destruction of the community's strength but also on keeping it underdeveloped and dependent.

At the same time, within the Egyptian context itself, discussions of minority rights along with issues of human rights and democratization are seen as potentially threatening to those in power who do not want to see changes in the status quo. Under the slogan of national unity and national security, political leaders have tended to discourage such discussion for fear of discord.[2] Regardless of such efforts and of government control of the press, however, the issue of religious minorities has been highly visible in recent public discourse. It has also been claimed to be of paramount importance by those who seek to gain control of the political process in Egypt with the goal of bringing about an Islamic state with the institution of the sharīʿa as its constitution.

The discussion on Christian minorities within the context of an Islamic state as it has been engaged by contemporary Muslim commentators appears to have centered on three general rubrics. The subject is ostensibly the same—that is, majority-minority relations—but there are subtle differences in the tone in which that subject is addressed as well as in the direction of the discussion.

The first rubric relates to the classical Islamic term *dhimmī*, traditionally applied to protected (or covenanted) non-Muslim people who chose to continue to live within the context of the abode of Islam and consequently agreed to special rights and duties. The *dhimmī* status was abrogated as a result of European pressure on the Ottoman sultan to revoke Islamic laws governing such a status. Two royal prescripts, the Hatti Humayun (1840) and the Hatti Sherif (1860) thus attempted to alter the role of religious minorities in the empire, giving Christian and Jewish subjects rights equal to those of Muslims. (They were relieved of paying the *jizya* tax in 1855 in the Ottoman Empire and 1856 in Egypt.) It was not until the formation of the modern nation states that the constitutional rights of religious minorities as equal citizens were affirmed.

The content of the second rubric is the more modern discussion of Islamic principles as measured against those of the Euro-American model of the nation state with reference to majority-minority relations. On the one hand, it involves the awareness that "the term minorities did not appear in the nineteenth century in European political discourse, or as a particular category in international law except when great powers interfered in the affairs of the Ottoman Empire under the pretext of protecting the Christian subjects."[3] On the other hand, there is the recognition that the conversation is taking place today in a set of circumstances radically different from those that obtained at the beginning of Islam when the "rules" were first set up. At the time of the Rightly Guided Caliphs, the Christians were the majority in lands conquered by Muslims. It was thus a case of the minority ruling the majority. Today Christians in Egypt, where the issue is being engaged, are the minority within an essentially Islamic state. There is a qualitative as well as a quantitative difference in this existential reality which raises serious questions. Can *dhimmī* status be applicable today given the fact that it was created to deal with different circumstances? And if it is in some way applicable, can it provide adequately for the rights of the minority population?

The growth of Muslim migration to Europe and North America during the last four decades has tempted some to raise issues of parity of treatment of religious minorities in "Christian" and "Muslim" countries. These are depicted in different ways reflecting the point the author is trying to make. Some Muslim authors, for example, have pointed to European democracies where the constitutional guarantees have not provided minorities with equal access to economic and political power or educational and employment opportunities as justification for similar treatment of Copts by Muslims.[4] Others such as Ṣāliḥ Jawdih, editor of *Al-Muṣawwar*, have advocated the adoption of the goal of Islamic unity to replace Arab unity as a means of putting an end to "Pharaonic extremism," an obvious reference to the Copts. Sensitivity to Coptic sentiment, he said, is unnecessary since Muslims are able to live comfortably in France, Italy, and Germany. "So what trouble does a Christian face if he lives in the context of an Islamic country?" One Coptic respondent to Jawdih argued that the two situations are not parallel since European countries are not established on a religious basis. The author also reminded Jawdih that the Muslims in Europe are foreigners, living on a temporary basis as students, diplomats, and other kinds of visitors, whereas the Copts have lived in Egypt for over fifty centuries and have no intention of becoming foreign nationals in their own country.[5]

The third rubric under which discussion of majority-minority concerns is taking place grows out of ideas initiated in the Indian subcontinent by the Jamaᶜat-i-Islami. It has as its content the issue of government control by committed Muslims, with the corollary of second class status for those who have a different religious affiliation or a different interpretation of Islam. In its Egyptian form it appears to have been developed as a kind of parallel to the concept of the Marxist ideological state insofar as it allows for no toleration of those with different perceptions. From this perspective, Islam is a system or ideology, not a set of doctrines, beliefs, and practices. There is a divine mandate to implement this system in the world, and to eradicate all other systems which by definition must be considered ungodly. This perspective is stated with particular cogency, for example, by Amir Hasan Siddiqi of the University of Karachi:

> Since the Islamic state is basically an ideological state, only those persons are to be primarily entrusted with its administration who believe in its ideology, are conversant with its spirit, and have dedicated themselves to the promotion of the objectives of the state. And since Islam is the basic ideology of the state, it is Muslims alone who can be genuinely expected to dedicate themselves fully to running such a state and undergoing all sacrifices that might come in the way of keeping that state a going concern. This does not mean that the Islamic State taboos the utilization of non-Muslims in the service of the state. This only means that while availing of the services of non-Muslims, due care should be taken that the Islamic character of the state is not compromised and the ideological demands are not sacrificed at the altar of so called "tolerance." This is possible only if the basic policy-making positions are held by those who are deeply and wholeheartedly committed to Islam. In this respect the Islamic state may be regarded as having something in common with the communist state, but the cruel treatment meted out by the Communist Party to non-Communists is conspicuous only for its absence in Islamic societies.[6]

From this Islamic perspective, the world is divided into believers and nonbelievers. The nonbelievers are followers of what Siddiqi calls a "godless cult," and as long as they survive "Islam cannot flourish and will not be able to achieve its ideal." Thus this cult "must be rooted out of the universe so that the religion of God may flourish."[7]

While it is true that the Muslim Brotherhood in Egypt has demanded the establishment of an Islamic state since Ḥasan al-Bannā, who advocated tolerating *dhimmīs* as a separate community,[8] the definition of this state appears to have become much sharper, with unequivocal demands, as a consequence of the repression of the Muslim Brotherhood under the Nasser regime and the encounter of its leaders with the teachings of Abū al-Aʿlā al-Mawdūdī. As the idea of such a state was developed by such Egyptian thinkers as Sayyid Quṭb[9] and ʿAbd al-Qādir ʿAwda,[10] it became radicalized. Mawdūdī had called for a complete separation between Muslims and non-Muslims based on his interpretation of the Qurʾan and the practice of the Prophet, insisting that religious minorities deserve to suffer the consequences of belonging to a minority faith.[11] He wrote that since there is no precedent of non-Muslim advisors in the Medinan state, none can be associated with the running of an Islamic state. Mawdūdī's ideas have been refuted by writers in both India[12] and Egypt[13] who insist that these beliefs are neither Qurʾanic nor from the Sunna. His countryman Rafiq Zakaria went as far as to imply that they might be a fabrication. "Mawdūdī's contention that as there were no non-Muslim advisers in the Medinan state, no non-Muslim can be associated with the running of an Islamic state, is a travesty of history."[14]

Events in Egypt as well as other Muslim countries have influenced the context of the debate. Two major occurrences in the seventies have been of special significance: the Islamic Revolution in Iran and the Lebanese Civil War. The success of the revolution was perceived by advocates of the implementation of the sharīʿa as a vindication of the Qurʾanic understanding that when a people are totally devoted to God, obedient in fulfilling all his commandments and willing to strive in his way, they can bring down a mighty tyrant regardless of his accumulated power. It spawned a variety of texts dealing with the subject of Islam and politics, some of which addressed the issue of the role of religious minorities in an Islamic state.

The Lebanese fratricide cast doubt on the faithfulness of Christian citizens in a Muslim state. The fact that the Phalangists colluded with Israel against the Palestinians and against Arab interests raised grave questions as to whether the Muslim majority population can trust the Christian citizens of the state. Israel's ability to recruit a predominantly Christian militia to implement its policies in South Lebanon, dismembering the state and uprooting its Muslim population, along with the collusion of the militia with the Israelis in perpetrating the massacres of unarmed Palestinian children, women, and old men in Khyam in 1978 and in the refugee camps of Sabra and Shatila in 1982, raise continuing questions about Christian loyalty. Have Christians always been colluding with

Western interests, for example in becoming champions of nationalism at the turn of the century, and will they continue to work for the interest of a "Judeo-Christian conspiracy" (American-Israeli coalition) against Arab interests?

In looking at the various Muslim writings of the last two decades that address the issue of religious pluralism in an Islamic state, one can see a spectrum of approaches. At one end are the teachings of the Islamic groups who insist that the state is an all-encompassing system, regulating every minute aspect of life and producing uniform Muslim individuals who can be identified not only by the clothes they wear, the culture they maintain, the demeanor they assume, and the expressions they use, but also in their relations to other people. At the other end are the writings of those who, while operating within the framework of an Islamic culture and life style, seek new interpretations of Islamic principles that not only are relevant for modern life but also are in accord with the accepted universal norms of the modern world.[15]

Falling between the two polarities, a number of concerned Egyptian intellectuals within the Islamic movement have been engaged in reflection on questions of authenticity in the modern world, the prospects and future of an Islamic state, and the role of religious minorities within this state. They range from mainline authors of the Muslim Brotherhood such as Yūsuf al-Qaraḍāwī[16] to moderate voices from within the Islamic movement such as Aḥmad Kamāl Abū al-Magd,[17] Fatḥī ʿUthmān,[18] ʿAbd al-ʿAzīz Kāmil,[19] and Muḥammad Salīm al-ʿAwwā.[20] The authors see themselves as attempting to provide new interpretations that in the words of al-ʿAwwā portray Islam as a system that "summons to faith in God and the call for the love and respect of humanity, a call for good works." Another group of writers who have addressed the topic are from what is called the "Islamic Left," including such people as Ḥasan al-Ḥanafī, Muḥammad Aḥmad Khalafallāh, Muḥammad ʿAmāra, and Ṭāriq al-Bishrī.

Yūsuf al-Qaraḍāwī, a Muslim Brotherhood member whose writings have been very influential in the Egyptian context, wrote a book in 1983 that addressed the issue of non-Muslims in a Muslim state. The book was published at the time when relations between Copts and Islamic revivalist groups were very tense because Coptic property was being destroyed by angry mobs—episodes that appeared after the Iranian revolution, which inspired growing demands for the institution of the sharīʿa as the constitution of Egypt. While the book is apologetic in tone, affirming the tolerance evident in the history of Islam, it does outline some areas of liberty currently enjoyed by Copts that would be restricted in an Islamic system. Such restrictions as he suggests, however, are in no way comparable either to the demands of the conservative Islamic groups or to the fears that Copts have about such demands. Thus while al-Qaraḍāwī's work outlines the classical model as defined within the Islamic heritage, he presented it in such a light that other authors have been able to use his definition and broaden its scope to provide a more progressive Islamic interpretation as defined in the Qur'an and the sunna of the Prophet.

For al-Qaraḍāwī, the word *dhimma* means *ʿahd*, a covenant, a pledge to provide security for the People of the Book. It is the covenant of God, of the Prophet, and of the Muslims. He draws parallels between this concept and the concept of citizenship in the modern state. Thus People of the Book, in contemporary terms, carry an Islamic citizenship. This covenant is eternal in nature, affirming the non-Muslims in their religion while they abide under Islamic law except in matters pertaining to their faith.[21]

The rights of the non-Muslims as *dhimmīs* include protection from external aggression[22] and internal oppression, a guarantee of their peace and security. They are not to be touched "by hand or tongue," says al-Qaraḍāwī, and their property and honor are to be safeguarded. This extends even to property deemed unacceptable in Islam such as wine and pork. He insists that any Muslim who destroys such property has to compensate the owner. He also reports that although there is controversy among the classical jurists as to whether the killing of a *dhimmī* by a Muslim is punishable by death or whether the hand of the thief who steals from a non-Muslim should be amputated, such acts are considered major crimes.

Al-Qaraḍāwī was writing at a time when kiosks and sidewalk stalls were selling an increasing number of books that attacked Christian doctrines, Western persecution of Muslims, and what was and continues to be seen as the heritage of Western crusader-colonialist-Zionist mentality. Nonetheless he argued that in the Islamic system non-Muslims are guaranteed freedom of religion since Islam does not insist on their conversion.[23] The basis for their treatment is revealed in S. 60:8–9 of the Qur'an which does not advocate their eradication but rather affirms that the essential principles of their treatment are toleration, justice, and mercy.[24] People of the Book have a special relationship to Muslims regardless of the fact that they have corrupted their scripture.[25] Since the covenant is undergirded by a belief system that prescribes all relationships, the following Islamic principles obtain: (1) all human beings have dignity regardless of race or color (S. 17:70); (2) religious difference is valid as an expression of divine will since He gave His creation the freedom of choice in action and belief (S. 18:29; 11:118); (3) Muslims are not enjoined to judge nonbelievers for their unbelief, nor to punish them for their waywardness (10:99; 22:68–69; 42:15); (4) God has decreed justice, despises oppression and punishes the oppressors (S.5:8).[26]

In the Islamic state, the covenanted relationship between Muslims and the People of the Book is one of reciprocity. While their rights are guaranteed by divine prescript, so are their duties outlined. The first duty expected from non-Muslims according to al-Qaraḍāwī involves the sensitive issue of the *jizya*, which some Islamic groups have insisted is a humiliation tax levied on the People of the Book because of their refusal to convert to Islam. They argue that while the sharīʿa enjoins the toleration of scriptural unbelievers, it insists on their inferiority. This interpretation they base on a S. 9:29 of the Qurʾan: "Fight against those given the scripture but do not believe in God or the Last Day, nor forbid that which God has forbidden through His Messenger, and follow not the religion of truth until they pay the tribute readily, being brought low." Al-Qaraḍāwī insists that the jizya is a tax collected from able-bodied men of the People of the Book who are not drafted into the army, and is not collected from women, children, old men, monks, the blind, the insane, or anyone unable to carry arms. In fact, the Islamic system guarantees that religious minorities are provided with social security benefits for old age or in cases of poverty. The jizya is collected from non-Muslims as a substitute for two religious obligations prescribed on Muslims: *jihād* and *zakāt* (tithing). Al-Qaraḍāwī accuses the orientalists and the missionaries of demonizing this issue by depicting it as a tax to humiliate and punish non-Muslims for their refusal to convert.[27]

The second duty al-Qaraḍāwī lists as expected from non-Muslims is to abide by the rules of the sharīʿa. They are allowed to work and make a living but not to take interest. They are banned from selling wine and pork in Muslim lands, opening bars for drinking, or importing liquor into Muslim countries even if it is for their own consumption. This restriction is to stop the spread of evil.[28] Non-Muslims can be employed by the government except in positions that are religious in nature such as imam, head of state, judge among Muslims, supervisor of charitable donations, or leader of the armed services. "Leadership of the armed services is not a secular position but is an act of worship in Islam, for jihād is the acme of Islamic acts of worship."[29]

A third duty of the covenanted people, he says, is to respect the feelings of the Muslims by not flaunting their religious symbols which are offensive to Muslims. This was at a time when the Egyptian government, in order to placate demands by Islamic groups, had instituted what Copts saw as a moratorium on granting permits for church construction, even halting the completion of the new Cathedral of St. Mark in Cairo. Al-Qaraḍāwī notes that Muslims are particularly sensitive to such things as visible artifacts and institutions associated with Christianity and its religious celebrations (as well as Christian missionary activity, which is seen as defaming Islam).

> They should not display their symbols and crosses in Muslim territory and should not establish a church in a Muslim city where none existed before. This is an order since such a display is considered an affront to Islamic sentiment which may precipitate discord and disturbances.[30] . . . They are not allowed to curse Islam, its Prophet and its Book publicly, nor to propagate doctrines or ideas that

> contradict the doctrines of the state and its religion, unless it is part of their doctrine such as the Trinity and the crucifixion. Nor are they permitted to publicly consume wine or eat pork or other commodities that Islam forbids. It is also forbidden for them to sell such to Muslims since that would lead to the corruption of Islamic society. They must not eat or drink publicly during Ramadan out of respect for the feelings of Muslims.[31]

Al-Qaraḍāwī addresses the Coptic apprehension that under a state based on the sharīʿa they would be asked to wear clothing that would identify them according to their religious affiliation.[32] As for the distinctive dress that People of the Book have been forced to wear at different times in history in order not to offend Muslim sensibility, says al-Qaraḍāwī, this issue has been exaggerated by the orientalists. There are no specific religious restrictions that must be replicated in each time and place, as some jurists have understood; it is merely a case of some rulers giving orders that they felt pertained to the public good at a specific time. Given other circumstances such orders should be either reformed or canceled.[33]

While Christians living in an Islamic state are expected to respect Muslim sensitivities, Muslims do not need to reciprocate. Al-Qaraḍāwī argues that tolerance does not demand a Muslim to "freeze" the commandments of his God and his religion, or to suspend the punishments to be meted out to sinners in order to please the non-Muslim minorities, or to avoid hurting their sensibilities. "I do not know what bothers the Christian or the Jew about the cutting of the hand, whether Muslim or non-Muslim, the lashing of the adulterer or the drunkard, or other commandments or punishments."[34] His book even concludes with the affirmation that "it is not tolerance to dissolve the essential differences among religions, to equate *tawḥīd* [oneness of God] with the Trinity, the abrogating and the abrogated. These ideas lead to contradictions. They separate rather than bring together; they destroy and do not build."[35]

Another Muslim writer who has devoted considerable attention to relations between Muslims and Copts in Egypt, maintaining an ongoing dialogue with the Coptic community, is Ṭāriq al-Bishrī. In his introduction to a biography of Makram ʿUbayd, the Egyptian nationalist who struggled against British colonialism to bring about an independent Egypt in the early part of the century, he identifies what he sees to be the real concern facing Egyptian Muslims today.[36]

> It appears from this study that secularism is the necessary vehicle to realize equality between Muslims and Copts in citizenship. . . . [However] there is another matter that I hope we will not neglect, and that is that this experience was useful in isolating the Islamic political tide which sees secularism as antithetical to its principles and doctrines. This view places the movement in a dilemma between the desired goal of affirming the equality of all citizens regardless of religion and

> its political Islam . . . and secularism which is projected as a means of bringing Muslims and Copts together, [at the same time] rupturing another unity between the nationalistic trend and the Islamic trend.[37]

For Ṭāriq al-Bishrī, this potential rift between the two forces within the Islamic community necessitates new efforts at Islamic jurisprudence that can foster closer relations and cooperation between Muslims and Copts and ensure the full equality and participation of Copts in a clearer and more comprehensive way while being inclusive of the concerns of members of the Islamic groups. The experience of the first half of this century, he says, has led Coptic politicians to believe that secularism is a necessary means of maintaining the current relationship between the two communities in Egypt.[38] He addresses the issue of Coptic concern that in an Islamic state they would not only be underrepresented but that their opportunities for employment would be drastically reduced. Islam has no qualms about Muslims working for non-Muslims or vice versa, he says, and is open to the employment of Jews and Christians in high positions in an Islamic state. For validation he quotes Muslim Brotherhood leader Muḥammad al-Ghazālī: "In reality, Islam looks at the covenanted Jews and Christians as having become politically Muslim in terms of their rights and duties, while on the personal level they maintain their doctrines, worship, and matters pertaining to personal status. [Islam] establishes its social structure based on interaction and cooperation."[39]

The idea that Egypt is basically made up of two peoples, Muslims and Copts, which has been espoused by some commentators, in some ways actually has served to disadvantage the Copts. It has made them a target of resentment on the part of Islamic revivalists who have identified them as an impediment to the implementation of the sharīʿa because of the claim that their rights would be curtailed. Some Muslim writers, such as Muḥammad Salīm al-ʿAwwā, reject this "two peoples" concept entirely. Al-ʿAwwā says that such an affirmation not only plays into the hands of those who seek to stoke the fires of division, but is essentially untrue since Egyptians are in reality one race which has seen continuous intermarriage between the original inhabitants (Copts) and those who came to the valley (Muslims). It is also incorrect in that it gives the erroneous impression that there is a basic separation in sentiment, or in cultural or social customs. He cites Dr. Abd al-Razzāq al-Ṣanhūrī, who was instrumental in modernizing law in Egypt at the turn of the century. "When we speak of the Islamic *umma*, I do not mean to refer exclusively to the society of Muslims. Rather I refer to a distinctive society which is a historical product of the cooperative efforts of all the religious groups that have lived and worked together under the banner of Islam and have presented us with a corporate heritage for all the inhabitants of the Islamic East."[40]

For al-ʿAwwā, Muslims and Copts share a common heritage which is the sharīʿa. This has provided the foundation for a particular Arab or Eastern civilization with a distinctive personality whether it be Muslim, Christian, or Jewish. The notion that Christians actually share the sharīʿa serves to make them insiders rather than outsiders, an integral part of a more inclusive Islamic society. According to al-ʿAwwā it is the duty of all concerned to uphold this common heritage, the principles of which he sees as the only guarantee of independent thought and legislation and of the persistence of a distinctive civilization.[41] He says that Muslims and Christians are partners in the homeland which was divided by the imperialists. The institution of the sharīʿa promises to bring Islamic unity based on Islamic principles, and to render the nation independent of those who would subsume it under their own power. "Non-Muslims have been partners with Muslims in the fatherland since the beginning of the Islamic state."[42]

Recognizing the issues that have led to conflict in the past, al-ʿAwwā says that those conflicts have been based on a misunderstanding of the essence of the relationship among the communities. For him, besides the divine injunction (S. 60:8–9) concerning the relationship with People of the Book, other Qurʾanic verses serve to enhance the quality of the relationship as one of basic trust. They allow Muslims to eat the food of the People of the Book and to marry their women, thus entrusting to them with raising the children of the Muslims.[43] Furthermore, the teachings of the Prophet advocate caring for non-Muslims. The Prophet said, "Whoever harms a *dhimmī*, I am his enemy and he who is my enemy will be my enemy on the Day of Judgment." He also said, "He who harms a *dhimmī* has harmed me. And he who harms me, harms God."[44] The Medinan constitution signed by the Prophet assured the People of the Book the right to full citizenship and freedom of worship, based on the Qurʾanic affirmation that "There is no compulsion in religion" (S. 2:256).

Al-ʿAwwā goes on to say that the Islamic state that was established by the Prophet and the caliphs came to an end by the elimination of the office of the caliphate, the subsequent hegemony of Western imperialism, and the suspension of the rule of the sharīʿa. The current Muslim states exhibit a new kind of Islamic sovereignty based not on conquest but on the existence of an Islamic majority. They have come into existence as a consequence of resistance to foreign oppression by Muslims and non-Muslims together. The non-Muslim minority has participated in establishing the state, a fact that calls for new jurisprudence. This could not have been addressed by former jurists because these conditions did not obtain at their time.[45] "The tree of its independence has been watered by the blood of all its children. The campaign for its freedom was a [consequence] of the actions of the intellectuals and politicians from both groups. What should its children do? Should they fight that the nation should be for some and the *dhimma* for the others?"[46]

While affirming that the primary bond in Islam is one that is based on religious affiliation, al-ʿAwwā insists that difference in religion should not imply enmity. The People of the Book are neighbors, friends, and partners in the administration of the state.[47] The Christian and Muslim community are one people, although they may disagree as to the details that should govern their lives. When there is disagreement the majority should choose in the spirit of brotherhood and sincere nationalism what is in the interest of maintaining a structure of independence and cohesion as necessitated by modern developments.[48] "If the choice, without hesitation, is national strength in place of weakness, unity instead of discord, power in place of humilation, we invite the Copts to join us in re-creating the glories of the east, its strength and its unity."[49]

Fahmī Huwaidī, another Muslim writer addressing the issue of non-Muslim minorities in an Islamic state, notes that the relations of Christians and Muslims have been formed by both communities and not by Islam alone. He sees a crucial need to distinguish between the Qurʾanic text and the context in which it was revealed, and to rely solely on *ḥadīth* narratives that have been determined to be accurate. Huwaidī faults those in the Muslim community who believe that recognition of the legitimacy of the "others" means a recognition of the truth and validity of their beliefs. He cites the Qurʾan as proof. Islam from its beginning has recognized the existence of the "other," whether as individuals or as nations:

> Those who believe, and those who are Jews, Sabaeans, and Christians, whoever believes in God and the Last Day and do acts of righteousness, no one needs fear for them, nor do they grieve. (S. 5:69)
>
> You have your religion and I have mine. (S. 109:6)
>
> For each We have appointed a divine law and a path. Had God willed, He would have made you one community. (S. 5:48)
>
> Had God willed, He would have united them in Guidance. Do not be among those who are ignorant. (S. 6:35)
>
> Had your Lord willed, all those on earth would have believed, would you coerce people until they become believers. (S. 10:99)

From these verses Huwaidī develops an Islamic typology of brotherhood defining Muslim relations with others. The first is "the brotherhood of religion in which all Muslims unite." The second is the brotherhood of the worship of God in which the Muslims meet people who belong to divine religions. The third is the brotherhood of humanity where the Muslims meet with all human beings regardless of whether their religions are of divine or human origin.[50]

God's creation is to be respected because of the human role of *khalīfa*, vice-regent of God on earth. This Huwaidī says is assigned to all human beings, Muslim and non-Muslim, since all are creatures of God. It both guarantees that minorities have full rights in a truly Islamic state and recognizes "the legitimacy of the others" based on the value of the person and the brotherhood of all human beings. This legitimacy is not contingent on the validity or falsehood of their doctrines; rather, "it is based on the truths Islam affirmed from the beginning: their humanity, their right to security, dignity and protection."[51]

Huwaidī recognizes that a great deal of the bitterness that is expressed in the public discourse on the subject by the *duʿāt* (missionaries) has been oppressive for both Muslims and non-Muslims, yet it is understandable if seen in the context of centuries of victimization.

> We must register that there are wounds in the Muslim memory that are difficult to ignore, that the Muslims have suffered and continue to suffer a great deal from non-Muslims. It is possible to say without exaggeration that the Muslims are victims in this situation. It is not easy to eradicate from that memory the agonies and horrors of the Crusades. It is not easy for the Muslims to forget the suffering of their brethren in Spain and Sicily. It is difficult for contemporary Muslims to forget their own suffering under the hegemony of British imperialism in the east and French imperialism in North Africa and to ignore the sorrow of Muslim minorities in various Asian and African nations and the oppression and suffering inflicted on them by non-Muslims.[52]

The victimizing of Muslims at the hand of Christians is a theme that is increasingly cited by a variety of authors as a response to Western accusations that Islam discriminates against religious minorities. A few authors recognize that Muslims have no monopoly on the painful memory of suffering and persecution in the past, and that Copts have a legitimate cause for apprehension, having suffered under different Islamic governments. Huwaidī's perspective on this is shared by Fatḥī ʿUthmān, who writes: "[Copts] may have bad memories of oppressive rule administered in the name of Islam or an unkind discussion by a Muslim. It is the right of the non-Muslim citizens to have assurances about their legal status, their rights and future, and to have the Islamic perception regarding their treatment and to clarify to them the difference between eternal established principles and juridical efforts and explanations which have been influenced by historical change that produced selected rulings."[53]

If either community comprising the Egyptian nation, Muslim or Coptic, sees itself as a victim, this produces a tension in the relationship. Selective historical memory and consciousness raising can lead to fear, apprehension, and division. For Huwaidī the historical record by itself is not sufficient to establish a proper and friendly relationship between Muslims and non-Muslims. Yet, it does show that such a relationship is possible if it is grounded in the effort to establish a just society predicated on human dignity, actively seeking to fulfill the role of agent of God in building the universe. This goal cannot be achieved until there is a clarification of the issues that act as an impediment to the proper treatment of minorities.[54]

In the final analysis, for Huwaidī, "*Dhimma* is a contract, not a condition,"[55] to be maintained in perpetuity. Such an interpretation opens up the possibility for new jurisprudence which is necessary in order to engage the Copts in the process of the Islamic reforms desired. According to this view, periods of mutual respect and cooperation must be highlighted by contemporary researchers in order to raise the proper consciousness as well as recover the history of the community. This is the only way to liberate the community from the legacy colonialism left in its wake, a legacy that some Muslims believe "robbed" them of their history and distorted their principles and achievements in order to sow discord and create antagonisms.[56]

In a later publication, Huwaidī reacts against opinions expressed by ʿAbd al-Jawād Yāsīn in his *Muqadimma fī Fiqh al-Jāhiliya al-Muʿāsira*. Yāsīn argues that in an Islamic state there must automatically be a division between Muslims and non-Muslims with the former having authority over the people of the dhimma. If they do not accept that status they are people of war and enmity. He opposes nationalism as what he calls an alternative to religion, the obvious choice of religious minorities in Egypt because it gives them equality with Muslims without having to pay the jizya. As members of the Islamic state, he says, "they would be in a perpetual condition that makes them aware of the power, greatness, eminence, goodness, generosity and tolerance of Islam."[57]

Commenting on this perspective Huwaidī says that such language naturally causes apprehension among Copts. He makes seven points in refuting Yāsīn's ideas. (1) These divisions of humanity are not legal divisions in perpetuity but are interpretations made by jurists at different times contingent on particular circumstances. (2) Muslim pride in their religion is one thing, but being arrogant toward others and projecting Muslims as "God's chosen people" is quite another. God has created all people from one soul, and is the lord of all. (3) Different religions exist because of God's will, as stated in S. 18:29, "Whoever wills let him believe, and whoever wills let him be a kafir," thus it is not understandable that some people should seek vengeance on those who do not belong to Islam. (4) Since the principle in jurisprudence says: "They have what we have and are responsible for what we are responsible for," implying equality in duties and rights, it is not clear why Yāsīn rejects the equality between the Muslim and the non-Muslim. (5) Yāsīn's assessment that *dhimmī* status inevitably means paying the jizya and not participating in government, and that Muslims cannot rely on Christians in time of war, shows that he is ignorant of other Muslim authors. (6) The division of people into religions does not have a strong background in Islamic thought; the first treaty of the Prophet with the Jews indicates that he considered them "one nation with the Muslims." (7) Finally, it seems that Yāsīn is ignorant of changes in history and geography. He talks about *dār al-islām* as though it still exists in its former greatness as at the time of the Umayyads. *Dār al-islām* today is forty-five weak and scattered nations, and "the abode of war, which he rejects, is what the Muslims of our day depend on for their food, clothing, war and peace."[58]

Thus the questions that have been debated have ranged over issues of jurisprudence—whether the sharīʿa is a fixed divine mandate not open to reinterpretation for modern life; of divine election—whether the Muslim community has been mandated by God to govern the world by the prescripts of the sharīʿa; of loyalty—whether Muslims can trust non-Muslims in positions of authority to be faithful to the interests of the nation; of equity—whether the Copts are getting their fair share or, as some Islamic groups have contended, are receiving more than is their due; of freedom of religion—whether this freedom should allow Copts to build new churches in urban areas where their congregations have now established residence, or to propagate their beliefs as their Christian faith calls them to do; of appropriate behavior—whether Copts are offending their Muslim neighbors by observing practices represensible to Muslims or are not themselves being permitted to enjoy the freedom of religion promised under Islamic law.

It is clear that there is some consensus in the literature of the contemporary Egyptian debate written by those addressing the issue from within the Islamist perspective. They all affirm the validity of the teachings of the Qurʾan and the Prophet Muḥammad as well as historical precedent as the basic foundation on which the role of the non-Muslims has to be defined. While some members of Islamic groups have highlighted and sought to implement details from the classical writings that focus on restrictions on non-Muslims, others have championed a more open process in which there is a reassessment of these teachings in their historical context and in terms of their validity as eternal truths.

There is a recognition among Muslim scholars that the divergence in the interpretation of what constitutes valid precedent is a major challenge to contemporary Muslim society. On the one hand are scriptural verses, prophetic pronouncements, political treaties between Islamic governments and their Christian subjects, and juridical pronouncements that affirm tolerance and the duty of Muslims to provide security and freedom of worship. On the other hand, a second set of documents (scripture, ḥadīth, treaties, and juridical opinion) relegate the dhimmīs to second class status and impose a variety of restrictions on their social, economic, political, cultural, and religious activities.[59] While some authors have raised questions about the authenticity of some of the documents, there continues to be a major question about who decides which set of documents is valid, and what guarantees minorities have that more liberal interpretations will apply should the sharīʿa be instituted as the constitution of Egypt. Will the majority continue to engage the Copts in the redefinition of the future of the nation as well as provide human and civil rights as redefined by the international order?

Even the most liberal among the Islamists affirm that Islam as a total way of life defines the whole culture. Christian minorities are allowed to operate freely only as long as they define themselves within the parameters of the law of the majority. While these more liberal authors have attempted to open the issue for reinterpretation by new jurisprudence more attuned to the times, they continue to affirm the validity of the past. This naturally causes apprehension among the Copts as they seek to hold the Muslims to teachings of tolerance that are espoused as the foundation of Islam.

The Coptic minority hears both groups: those seeking additional restrictions on minorities in order to humiliate them because of their errant ways, and those who advocate cooperation and a new jurisprudence. Copts seek the right to propagate their religious beliefs publicly, celebrate their faith, and share it with others as commanded by Christ. They wonder whether a redefinition of Muslim sensibilities, if one were to take place, would provide for the possibility of a vibrant Coptic community. And aware that in the history of their relations with Muslims there have been interludes of tolerance as well as of tension, they continue to wonder whether such pluralism as Islam can tolerate within its parameters in the modern context leaves room for the minority religious community to survive, to redefine its cultural identity as differing from that of the majority if they so choose, and to participate with full membership in the Egyptian state.

NOTES

1. See, for example, Fahmī Huwaidī, *Muwāṭinūn lā Dhumiyyūn: Mawqiʿ Ghayr al-Muslimīn fī Mujtamaʿ al-Muslimīn* (Beirut: Dār al-Shūrūq, 1985), p. 118, where he attacks Bernard Lewis for accusing Islam of essentially affirming the ideal of "war against the Christian world" (p. 217); Majid Khaduri's treatment of the topic in his *War and Peace in the Law of Islam* (p. 237) stating that *dhimmīs* cannot be full citizens in an Islamic state; and Hisham Sharabi's assertion in his *Arab Intellectuals and the West* (p. 23) where he reports that while the Muslim feels at ease in his homeland, the indigenous Christians feel in constant jeopardy because they feel like strangers. Both authors are accused of basing their treatment on Shafīʿi law and ignoring other opinions from within Islam.

2. Samīra Baḥr, *Al-Aqbāt fī al-Ḥayāt al-Siyāsiyya al-Miṣriyya* (Cairo: Maktabat al-Anglo al-Miṣriyya, 1979), p. 6; cf. his *Al-Madkhal li Dirāsat al-Aqalliyat* (Cairo: Maktabat al-Anglo al-Miṣriyya, 1982).

3. Huwaidī, *Muwāṭinūn*, p. 42.

4. "The children of Muslims under Communist or Crusader governments are forced to study atheism and Communism and are restricted from fulfilling their religious duties. They are often forbidden to practice the tenets of their religion concerning marriage as well as other matters that conflict with the prevailing system": Farghalī Shuqayrī, *Fī Wajh al-Muʾāmara ʿalā Taṭbīq al-Sharīʿa* (al-Manṣūra: Dār al-Wafāʾ, 1986), p. 89.

5. Samīra Baḥr, *al-Aqbāt*, p. 146.

6. Amir Hassan Siddiqi, *Non-Muslims under Muslim Rule and Muslims under Non-Muslim Rule* (Karachi: Jamʿiyatul Falah Publications, n.d.), p. 2.

7. Siddiqi, *Non-Muslims*, p. 3.

8. Ḥassan al-Bannā, *Majmūʿat Rasāʾil al-Imām al-Shahīd Ḥasan al-Bannā* (Beirut: Al-Muʾssasa al-Islāmiyya li ʾl-Ṭibāʿa Waʾl-Nashir, 1980). For additional material on the Muslim Brotherhood see below.

9. Sayyid Quṭb, *Maʿālim fī al-Ṭarīq* (Cairo: Maktabat Wahba, 1964); cf. his *Naḥwa Mujtamaʿ Islāmī* (Amman: Maktabat al-Aqṣā, 1969).

10. ʿAbd al-Qādir ʿAwda, *Al-Islām wa Awḍāʿunā al-Siyāsiyya* (Beirut: Muʾassat al-Risāla, 1980).

11. Muhammad Munir, *From Jinnah to Zia* (Lahore: Vanguard Books, 1980), p. 65.

12. Rafiq Zakaria, *The Struggle within Islam* (London: Penguin, 1989) p. 292. He also cites other Indian authors affirming his ideas. See Sayyid Abdul Latif, *Bases of Islamic Culture* (Hyderabad: Institute of Indo-Middle East Studies, 1959), pp. 13–23, 179–85; K. G. Saiyidain, *Islam the Religion of Peace* (New Delhi, 1976), pp. 21–71.

13. Muḥammad Saʿīd al-ʿAshmāwī, *Al-Islām al-Siyāsī* (Cairo: Sīnā li-al-Nashr, 1987), p. 24. ʿAshmāwī attributes Mawdūdī's interpretation to a feeling of an inferiority complex combined with persecution, minority status, hatred of colonialism, and ignorance about Islam.

14. Zakariya, *The Struggle*, p. 292.

15. See, for example, the work of Abdullahi A. An-Naʿim of the Sudan: "Religious Minorities under Islamic Law and the Limits of Cultural Relativism," *Human Rights Quarterly* 9 (1987): 10, and *The Second Message of Islam* (Syracuse: Syracuse University Press, 1987).

16. Yūsuf al-Qaraḍāwī, *Al-Ḥall al-Islāmī: Fariḍatun wa Ḍarūra* (Cairo: Maktabat Wahba, 1977).

17. See Aḥmad Kamāl Abū al-Magd's "Bal al-Islām wa-al-ʿUrūba maʿan," *Majallat al-ʿArabī* 264 (October 1980); "Naḥwa Ṣīghatin Jadīda li-al-ʿAlāqa Bayn al-Qawmiyya al-ʿArabiyya wa-al-Islām," *Kitāb al-Qawmiyya al-ʿArabiyya wa-al-Islām* (Beirut: Markaz Dirāsāt al-Waḥda al-ʿArabiyya, 1980); *Ḥiwār la Muwājaha* (Cairo: Dār al-Shurūq, 1988).

18. Fathī ʿUthmān, "Iqtirān al-Qawmiyya bi-al-ʿAlmāniyya Maṣdar Shukūk al-Islāmiyyin," *Majallat al-ʿArabī* 266 (January 1981); see also his *Dawlat al-Fikr* (Kuwait: al-Dār al-Kuwaitiyya, 1968).

19. ʿAbd al-ʿAzīz Kāmil, "Al-Islām wa-Dawruhu fī Bināʾ al-Insān al-Muʿāsir," paper

delivered at the conference on Confluence of Islamic Conscience and Christian Conscience in Confronting the Challenges of Development, Tunis, November 1974; cf. his *Al-Islām wa-al-Mustaqbal* (Cairo: Dār al-Maʿārif, 1975); *Maʿ al-Rasūl wa-al-Mujtamaʿ fī Istiqbāl al-Qarn al-Hijrī al-Khāmis ʿAshar* (Kuwait: Muʾassasat al-Ṣabāh li-al-Nashr wa-al-Tawzīʿ, 1980).

20. Muḥammad Salīm al-ʿAwwā, *Fī al-Niẓām al-Siyāsī li al-Dawla al-Islāmiyya* (Cairo: Dār al-Shurūq, 1989).

21. He based this on the works of Sarakhsī, *Sharḥ al-Siyar al-Kabīr*, 1: 140, Kāsānī's *Badāʾiʿ*, 5: 281, and Ibn Qudāma's *Mughnī*, 5: 516. For details see Yūsuf al-Qaraḍāwī, *Ghayr al-Muslimīn fī al-Mujtamaʿ al-Islāmī* (Beirut: Muʾassasat al-Risālah, 1983), p. 7.

22. According to Ḥanbalī jurisprudence in *Maṭālib Ulī al-Nahī*, 2: 602–3, and al-Qarāfī's *Al-Furūq*, 3: 14–15, it is the duty of Muslims to fight to protect the people of the *dhimma* (al-Qaraḍāwī, *Ghayr al-Muslīmīn*, pp. 9–10).

23. al-Qaraḍāwī, *Ghayr al-Muslīmīn*, pp. 12 ff.

24. "God does not forbid you those who did not fight against you on account of religion and did not drive you out of your homes, that you should show them kindness and deal justly with them. Lo, God loves the just. God forbids you to befriend only those who fought against you on account of religion and have driven you out of your homes and helped to expel you. Those who befriend them are wrongdoers" (S. 60:8–9).

25. al-Qaraḍāwī, *Ghayr al-Muslīmīn*, p. 6.

26. Ibid., p. 49.

27. Ibid., pp. 33, 55.

28. Ibid., p. 21.

29. Ibid., p. 23.

30. Ibid., p. 20.

31. Ibid., p. 41. He goes on to say that even though the New Testament allowed the drinking of wine, it is not a Christian prescription for them to drink it (p. 44).

32. In earlier times, for example, Christian women had to wear blue rather than white or green headcoverings.

33. al-Qaraḍāwī, *Ghayr al-Muslīmīn*, p.60.

34. Ibid., p. 80.

35. Ibid., p. 81.

36. Ṭāriq al-Bishrī, "Introduction," in Muṣṭafā al-Fīqī, *Al-Aqbāṭ fī al-Siyāsa al-Miṣriyya: Makram ʿUbayd wa-Dawruhū fī al-Ḥaraka al-Waṭaniyya* (Cairo: Dār al-Shurūq, 1985). He notes that Makram's "Copticness" was not an issue in his striving for Egypt, so much so that the reader of the biography may even forget the fact that he was a Copt.

37. Ibid., p. 8.

38. Ibid., p. 9.

39. Muḥammad al-Ghazālī, *al-Taʿaṣṣub bayn al-Masīhiyya wa-al-Islām*, p. 55, as quoted in Ṭāriq al-Bishrī, *al-Muslimūn wa al-Aqbāṭ fī Iṭār al-Jamāʿa al-Waṭaniyya* (Cairo: Al-Hayʾa al-Miṣriyya al-ʿĀmma li al-Kitāb, 1980), p. 706.

40. al-ʿAwwā, *Fī al-Niẓām*, p. 12.

41. Ibid., p. 18

42. Ibid., p. 27.

43. Ibid., p. 32.
44. Ibid., p. 37.
45. Ibid., pp. 38–41.
46. Ibid., p. 41.
47. Ibid., pp. 33–34.
48. Ibid., p. 18.
49. Ibid., p. 21.
50. Huwaidī, *Muwaṭinūn*, p. 225.
51. al-ʿAwwā, *Fī al-Niẓām*, pp. 81, 91.
52. Huwaidī, *Muwāṭinūn*, p. 7.
53. Muḥammad Fatḥī ʿUthmān, "Qabl Taqnīn Aḥkām al-Sharīʿa ka-Asās li-Taṭbīqiha," *Majallat al-Muslim al-Muʿāṣir* 11 (July–September 1977): 87.
54. Huwaidī, *Muwāṭinūn*, pp. 72–73.
55. al-ʾAwwā, *Fī al-Niẓām*, p. 37.
56. Huwaidī, *Muwāṭinūn*, p. 72.
57. Fahmī Huwaidī, *al-Tadayyun al-Manqūṣ* (Cairc. Al-Ahram, 1988), p. 243, citing Yāsīn, p. 59.
58. Huwaidī, *al-Tadayyun*, p. 24.
59. Hamān ʿAbd al-Rahīm Saʿīd, "al-Waḍʿ al-Qanūnī li-Ahl at-Dhimma fī al-Mujtamaʿ al-Islāmī Mustamadan min al-Qurʾān al-Karīm wa-al-Sunna al-Sharīfa wa-al-Wathāʾiq al-Siyāsiyya fī ʿAhd al-Nabī Ṣalla Allāhu ʿAlayhi wa-Sallam wa-Khulafaʾuhu al-Rashidīn," *Dirāsāt* 9, no. 1 (June 1982): 156–57.

24

Ismāʿīl al-Fārūqī in the Field of Dialogue

Kenneth Cragg

"Right you are if you think you are," wrote the Italian novelist Luigi Pirandello. The remark captures the paradox of all "dialogue." The criteria we bring to it are predetermined—since there is no such thing as "a vacant mind," nor any worthwhile faith that is uncommitted. Nor, if it were otherwise, would it be "us" coming to it. Even the necessary capacity to question or suspend our criteria turns on the temper they generate and the instincts they have instilled. Furthermore, a possessiveness—us of them in the mind and they of us in the psyche—makes problematic any independence of them which would not be a forfeiture of ourselves. An actual pluralism of mind and soul seems not only daunting but spiritually impossible. Is not that conclusion proved by the consensus among many practitioners of "dialogue" to persist somehow with an "identity" of faith and allegiance while, nevertheless, readily assenting to the legitimacy of others doing the same while the issues between them remain radically unresolved and even quite contradictory? Has "dialogue" virtually stopped short because—on any other terms—reality allows us only impasse? If so, is there not a sense in which impasse is really all there is? Courtesy proves to be all that truth expects of us.

Perhaps it is well, after several decades of contemporary involvement with each other in the saga of *daʿwa*, mission, and *ḥiwār*, dialogue, to take stock of what the experience teaches us. How intellectually genuine, how spiritually authentic, is our will to mutuality? How adequately "plural" can our intentions be? There is no writer within Islam more apt to confront us with that question than Ismāʿīl al-Fārūqī (1921–86). Robust, even magisterial, his positions always were and there were times when his assessments of Judaism and Christianity left the reader wondering whether he had ever really taken their point. Yet any such impression, by Jew or Christian, was simply the other side of a contrast cherishing the meaning he had failed to register. Or, as Hamlet might have put the situation, "by the image of my cause I see/The portraiture of his." It was precisely in being provocative that Ismāʿīl al-Fārūqī sharpened the issues in exciting the emotions. Such was the zest—if also (in the exact sense) the prejudice—of his scholarship.

To attempt a comprehensive study of his lifework brings a lively and loving sense of irony, in two main directions. There was, as we must explore, a sustained repudiation (as far as Islamic theology was concerned) of the dimension of the tragic, a rejection of the centrality—indeed the very presence—of that dimension in the being of God as Christianly understood. Yet his own experience of life was shot through with personal tragedy. His family roots in the Ramleh area of what became Israel in 1948 and his share in the ongoing tragedy of Palestinian displacement immersed him, and his thinking, in the mystery of pain, resentment, privation, and distress. That prevailing circumstance of his mind and story shadowed all his work. His energies in debate were the measure of his struggle with adversity. It is true that his entrepreneurial competence and his vigor in its pursuit in the setting of the United States enabled him to ensure the economics of a life henceforward devoted to study and letters. Yet anguish awaited him in a final outrage when he and his wife were struck down in their home on the very eve of the publication of their joint masterpiece, *The Cultural Atlas of Islam*. Vulnerability is a common human condition, but some know it more desperately and bitterly than others. In a retrospect like that of the Fārūqīs it would be false to truth and to them if any study were to be merely academic or should fail to penetrate beyond "dialogue" to the sacrament of the mystery in suffering. For me it will always be important to seek the text of the life as well as the text of the writing.

In this light, the other irony of Ismāʿīl al-Fārūqī's scholarship, alongside its being ill at ease with tragedy in theology, was its rejection of paradox. Arabic itself, of course, is hard put to express "paradox." It resorts to phrases like "a saying with apparent contradiction," which do not quite possess the feel of "the eloquence of silence," or "strength in weakness." For al-Fārūqī, paradox was evasion, the sign of an untidy mind or a perverse will. It offended against the sure principle of rationality which Islam, as he saw it, possessed and enshrined. He insisted that "the test of internal coherence precludes the recourse to paradox as theological principle."[1] There was, he thought, something he called metareligion which "approved" faith as based on certainty of evidence assured on the ground that "whatever is repugnant to reason is repugnant to Allah."[2] Such conformity of the true faith (Islam) to internal coherence as constituting the validity of "revelation" was not to be seen as an imposition upon God, but was a necessity for man, since God "did not operate in a vacuum."[3]

This confidence had large implications for al-Fārūqī's understanding of scriptures, of ethics, and of politics. It did not stay, however, to wonder whether the "nonvacuum" of divine ways—that is, their enmeshment with humanity—might not bring back paradoxicality precisely because the divine will had opted to hinge, for human purposes of law and grace, on the interengaging will of the human, a situation implicit no less in the prophethood of Muhammad than in the (Christianly alleged) incarnation of "the Word made flesh." Revelation would then turn, not only on the unity of its divine source, but also on the susceptibility of the human to contain and recognize it. When that human condition of all theism is understood, the certainty—and, indeed, the excitement—of paradox returns into partnership with all our believing.

What can be attempted here must be more an essay than a full analysis. It will relate broadly to five fields of al-Fārūqī's dialogue scholarship, namely his monumental volume coauthored with Lois Lamyāʾ al-Fārūqī, *The Cultural Atlas of Islam* (New York: Macmillan Publishing Co., 1986); *Christian Ethics: A Historical and Systematic Analysis of Its Dominant Ideas* (Montreal: McGill University Press, 1967); *ʿUrūbah and Religion: A Study of the Fundamental Ideas of Arabism and of Islam at Its Highest Moment of Consciousness* (Amsterdam: Djambatan, 1962); a short but significant manual in the Major World Religions Series, *Islam* (Niles, Illinois, 1979); and his concern to develop a purely Islamic sociology in *Islamization of Knowledge: General Principles and Workplan* (Herndon, Va.: International Institute of Islamic Thought, 1982).

But reflection on these sources of his mind may well be prefaced by a little exercise in provocation—an instinct of which al-Fārūqī would have approved. It has to do with our supposed consensus about Abraham as somehow embracing and uniting us all. I wonder, teasingly, whether this plea of Abraham is not a way of eluding—or eliding—problems and ask, further, whether we would not be wiser to begin and end with God? Is not Abraham too historicomythical a figure truly to serve our relationships? I am familiar enough with the arguments and with the role of ancient genealogy in the definition of identity. But do we not each make of Abraham whom we will? He is, for Judaism, the fount of the right "seed," the progenitor of the faithful by his free exile but only, also, by the proper lineage after him. For Islam he is the great iconoclast, the breaker of false gods and, only via Ishmael, the founder of the *Kaʿba* and the great *Ḥanīf*, who was "neither Jew nor Christian." The New Testament possesses him as having exemplified a "faith-relationship" with God which antedated the Mosaic covenant and so could be a precedent for the grace that obviated Law. So Paul.

If we have these diverse "interests" in Abraham does he really make us "a family" seeing that so much significant and deliberate differentiation is located in his name and legend? Further, is there not something a little lofty in "Semitic cousinry," when we become aware of Asia, of Hindus and the Buddha? Is there any authentic coziness in Abraham? And does "history" matter? Who knows what tribal enmities lie (in both senses) within the narratives of the patriarchs, coming—we may presume—in their present written form from times when those enmities were current history? Why do we always overlook Keturah (Gen. 25:1–4) with Abraham's other progeny beyond the contenders, Isaac and Ishmael? If Abraham was a powerful tribal force in southern Palestine in what (?) century, will his aura suffice to bridge our disparities in more than tokens in potential tension? Had not our search for the mutual better begin and end in God? Theology would be a surer rendezvous than putative fatherhood and archaeology.

There are many points at which this crucial question of history and belief arises and, with it, the issue of what al-Fārūqī himself has called "the human necessity" conditioning "revelation" (as distinct from a divine untrammeledness). It attaches, for example, to the identity in the Qur'an of the patriarchal and the prophetic. Al-Fārūqī insists, in line with sūra 3:84 and elsewhere, that Abraham and Jeremiah brought the same message. Does the *Sitz im Leben* of what that message could have been not matter? In the pain and trauma of tragic exile Jeremiah is "a breaker of idols" only in the sense of decrying and defining, through personal anguish, corporate infidelity to a covenant Jews should never have understood in the "separatist" sense with which, for al-Fārūqī, they distorted and suborned the significance of Abraham.[4] Will it be loyal to history to identify "Judaism" and "the religion of Abraham?" Symbolic figures, to be sure, are not and need not be tied to historians' research, nor hobbled by their findings. There will always be legitimate enigmas around the historization of myth and the mythicization of history, since what faith possesses is not chronicles but meanings.

Nevertheless, meanings become inauthentic if, once alerted to its claims, they dispense with honesty.[5] This is particularly so when we are occupied not with interior possession of our faiths, but with the venture of their mediation in dialogue. For it is then that we are taken (or are we?) out of our privacies of concept and criterion into those that obtain for others. We need them to conspire together to join them rather than conspire separately to exclude them. To a certain degree, all our dogmas are a form of self-consciousness and it is when we truly bring our "selves" to meeting that the proposition/affirmation/negation part of "us" as dogmatists finds the open modesty it needs. Can we look back over the field of dialogue and think that this has happened?

Ismā'īl al-Fārūqī's "advocacy" of the Abrahamic faiths was—on strictly Islamic terms—also the prosecution of two of them. The thesis of his two earlier works (*'Urūbah* and *Christian Ethics*) is direct and simple, taking in its confident stride those issues of "history" which might have given it pause. Briefly, the Jews and Judaism turned the whole Abrahamic meaning into crippling and confining separatism, making "the God of all," into "the God of Abraham, Isaac and Jacob." The covenant, which—within nature—really means "the virtue of happiness and the happiness of virtue," available to all and sanctioned by axiology and history as "the will of God," was misread into a Jewish perquisite: There followed a whole misconstruing symbolized in the banishment of Hagar. Instead of sharing in the spiritual genius of "Arabness" with which it properly belonged, Jewry developed the circumcising peculiars of "land-right" in "covenant," and, with them, all the entail of exceptionality of which Zionism is the present shape. The call of Abraham, for which no scriptural "reason" is ever given save that of sheer obedience, was never meant for this conclusion. By perversity "Hebrews as a whole were never converted to the Judaic faith"[6]—the faith of Abraham, whose original "monotheism" was annexed to become the Mosaic version. In this way monotheism itself was, as it were, purloined—and with it the range of "the Semitic"—into being an exclusively Jewish possession.

As for "Christianity"—it has to be sharply distinguished from the "Christianism" which al-Fārūqī defines as the faith of the Christian centuries. While Jesus, to be sure, was "not a Christian," the term "Christianity," duly adjusted, is used to denote what the faith so named should have been, had sorry misguidance not overtaken it. The authentic Gospel of Jesus had as its central feature a direct and costly correction of Jewish particularism and privilege. This, for al-Fārūqī, was the main thrust of Jesus' mission, the burden of his heavenly mandate as "messenger." But, while blessedly calling "Judaism" back to its true identity within the obedience of Arabness and axiology, the significance of Jesus was perverted into trinitarian theology and the Hellenized christology of the Church. This left to the Qur'an and Islam the necessity of "re-Semiticizing" Jesus, liberating him from the *ḍalāl*, the misguidedness and calumny, of Christianism.

Summary does not do justice to the *ipse dixit* in these theses, nor to the enormous issues they leave unnoticed or unresolved—for example, how Judaism, properly understood, originated after the fall of Jerusalem and the loss of the Temple in A.D. 70 or how one could account for the very existence, as literature, let alone as faith, of the New Testament documentation. The emergence of the Church via conviction of Resurrection is read as "the bright idea" of Peter that all had been somehow foretold and was not, therefore, occasion for shame or guilt on the part of the disciples.[7] Some of the keen anticipation attending the publication of *Christian Ethics* had to do with the fact that here was a young and lively Muslim scholar who had taken pains to acquire needful disciplines of Greek and textual New Testament study and could, therefore, bring to discussion the requisite expertise. Sadly that promise was only technically, not radically, fulfilled. The scholar remained immersed in the a priori which he brought to the techniques, so that their application missed the dimensions—as the first Christians knew them—of what was going on in the New Testament. Nowhere are the crux of christology, the impetus to it, its consistency with the theology of divine unity, and its relevance to the whole perspective of Prophethood, ever seriously probed. Messianism, "saviorism," incarnation, and redemption simply became an a priori anathema to al-Fārūqī's scholarship as being *ab initio* excluded by the prejudgments he was minded to bring. These, sadly, took no account of the logic, discernible in Islam itself (the prophetic as biographic, the sacrament of the *āyāt*, and the implications for law of human *jāhiliyya*), which might have entailed a longer patience with the evidence—not to say with the sanctities of cherished conviction. Are we not all too roughshod over the field of dialogue?[8] Do we well only to subject the other to verdicts that preempt the hearing we should give them?

If so, one of the necessities is to suspect in ourselves the "separatism" of which we accuse others. All religious identities, precisely because they concern ultimates and think themselves in trust with things nonnegotiable, are tenacious of their own and retentive of adherence. Much of our dialogue lives uneasily here and may even be subtly recruited to our defense. It may be useful, in this context, to turn to al-Fārūqī's indictment of things Judaic.

There is valid point in his strictures on Jewish separatism, his censure of an Abraham callous to the claims of Hagar, his charge against the likes of Nehemiah and the divorce of "foreign wives." The conviction of exceptionality has, indeed, been the cross of Jewry down the centuries. Scholarship may not be unanimous. But there is strong ground for al-Fārūqī's belief that his "re-Semiticized Jesus" indeed strove against Jewish separatism. Luke would certainly agree with him. But reproach of Jewry, on this ground, needs perceptive reticence. Jewry is perhaps only the extreme form of a defensive solidarity. All, to some degree, partake in it. It is true that the ethnic factor, the cult of "birth" and "seed," is the most recalcitrant and obdurate—though Jewry has long ago been ethnically various. Yet what if other identities substitute a doctrinal factor, a cultural shape, for the ethnic and make baptism or the *shahāda* witness a Christian, and Islamic, "circumcision," not of the flesh but of the soul? Will not separatism persist? Is there not a point in the Jewish charge that those "universal Semites," Christians and Muslims, have only a phony "universalism" in that exclusivism characterizes their attitudes? They patently exceptionalize themselves. Al-Fārūqī's "Arabness," as somehow metaphysical as well as demographic, seems to prove the point.

It is right, furthermore, to note how boundaries are needed to ensure that the vehicles of truth or salvation or orthodoxy are kept safe from dilution by insulation, from atrophy by assertion. To that extent Judaic exceptionality is not exceptional. All religions know the paradox of particularizing the universal, in sacred text, sacred time, sacred space, and sacred office. Affirmation and contrast underline each other. The mark of the "sect" is an intensified seclusion from contagion. But even would-be "churches," though they may strive for "comprehension," cannot avoid sectarian temptation. All structures of faith must in some way transact "apartness." That it is so creates both the vocation and the tribulation of dialogue. It is not unfair to underline it as emerging forcefully in the work of al-Fārūqī. Sincerity always wants to cordon itself, in some measure, if it is to approve itself.[9]

We may reflect that Islam has its own forms of this dilemma. One belongs with the strictly Arabic ambit and orbit of final divine revelation, as contrasted with the potentially multilingual translatability of revelation elsewhere. The Arabicity of the holy Qurʾan has always been seen as inseparable from its authority. Arabism and Islam, as al-Fārūqī insists, are not to be thought identical. But where "the Word is not made flesh," but is made text, it is vested inalienably in its chosen language, the custody and pride of which will always wait upon it, to the disadvantage of all other tongues.

A further factor in Islamic "privacy" has to do with parenthood as the due instrument of its security. There is the tradition that all are born "Muslim": it is parents who divert the young from Islam by non-Muslim nurture. Yet sexuality, procreation, and parenthood are among "the signs of God," and, given the doctrine of creation which Islam shares, must be seen as diversely God-given. Was the Creator at fault in diversifying the racial, parental factor in our *maṣīr*, our becoming? How adamant Islam is that parenthood should allow no neutrality in education that might endanger faith even while making it potentially more free and more responsible to reasons rather than submission and conformity. Perhaps, then, there should be some guardedness about undue reproach of the Nehemiahs, the Gentile-avoiders, of Jewry. At least the issue is a taxing remit from *ʿUrūbah and Religion*.[10] Dialogue has surely to engage with the will to exclusivism not least when it claims the intention to be universal.

This thought brings us back to al-Fārūqī's quite resolute disavowal, as only "pseudo-Christian," of those very dimensions which historic Christianity has received and affirmed as its lifeblood, namely "God in Christ," Jesus-Messiah, the Cross and Resurrection, the Holy Spirit in the Church, the New Testament writings, the Eucharist, and the apostolate of all believers. He sees its mission as "subversion," its redemption as evasion of law, and its sacraments as misconstrued. The charges are many and categorical and often formulated in terms that provoke despair about genuine encounter rather than inform a will to it. Perhaps, at an earlier juncture from where we now need to be, that was the merit in him. At least response could understand that it must learn to keep despair at bay and take due measure of what it was about. If so, the belligerence was salutary. Yet, too often, even so, it obscures the point by its impatience.

A now familiar example occurred in the conference at Chambesy, Switzerland in 1976 on "Christian Mission and Islamic *Daʿwah*." When discussion turned to the theme of Incarnation, "God in Christ," a distinction was made between claiming the *fact* of it and allowing the *possibility*. That it *might* be congruent with the very sovereignty of God—indeed, essential to it—derived conceptually from metaphors like "shepherd," or "father," where status was not in immunity but obligation. To think a shepherd inherently debarred from shepherding would be quite nugatory of shepherdhood. Could not it be so, likewise, with "God?" One should not deny to the divine what might be perceptibly within divineness in respect of human need, if "God," like "friend" was a relational word. Veto on the possibility of "incarnation"—given suitably divine reasons for that initiative (lesser initiatives being already in hand in "messengers" and "prophets")—would be denying divine sovereignty by limiting its prerogatives and doubting its freedoms. But, al-Fārūqī retorted: "By that argument, God might become a brick." The retort, as sheer bathos, ignored the whole careful consideration as to the *congenially* divine.[11] Mutual reflection as to what might, or might not, be "proper to God" was foreclosed by hasty ridicule. The episode, trivial in its way, seems a warning against bland dismissiveness. Nor may it be rightly read as scotching a conspiracy to "read things Christian into things Islamic," or to infer what Islam ought to be in regret that it is not.[12] For divine relationality to man, to history, and to time is explicit and integral to Islam itself. The question is not whether but how far? Or that "non-vacuum" of divine action, in prophet-sending and the entrusted creaturehood of man—what is it that duly occupies it, engages with it, initiates for it and through it in the divine intention? Or what, in New Testament vocabulary, is the *pleroma* of *kenosis* which tenants it like drama in a theater? The questions are inseparable from the very meaning of Islam and the appeal of the Qur'an.

The very wealth of meaning here—even if we feel that "in beckoning, it baffles"[13]—requires that we try to assess it, if here from one angle only. One focus among many would be to ask whether or not theology needs theodicy. The particle *ʿalā* is used in the Qur'an of *Allāh* with the implication of "obligation."[14] Is there any "ought" attached *to* the being of God? There are many *from* God, attaching to the being of man. For, as Fazlur Rahman as well as al-Fārūqī have emphasized, Islam is insistently the religion of divine command. "Let all men agree to establish the divine will first."[15] If no theodicy, no "justification" of God is rightly to be sought or feasibly to be had, we are left with enormous burdens liable to sink theism itself. We are left with a vacuum for "heaven." Do not creation, the mandate to man, nature amenable to human dominion, prophethood, law, guidance, and *dhikr*, in the setting of the sacrament of all experience, spell reciprocity between God and man of a kind to make the wrongness of history and the enigma of human evil a proper area of the divine compassion? Thus far, surely, we agree. But how far may the compassion *will* to go as the self-consistency of God, how far *need* to go in meeting the predicament of man? Surely here is the crux of the dialogue that necessarily binds Muslim to Christian and Christian to Muslim if either is to be authentic. It is here, rather than in sharing Abraham, that our business lies. Dialogue must mean a refusal to evade it.

The theodicy question, with its mutual implications, obviously spills into the interpretation of man and history in respect of *ẓulm* (wrongdoing), *fitna* (temptation), *istighnāʾ* (self-sufficiency), *ḍalāl* (going astray), *ithm* (iniquity), and *dhanb* (sin), by which the Qurʾan describes the rebelliousness of mankind. Here the pressure of the reality of waywardness is eased by a Muslim confidence in the efficacy of revelation *ipso facto*, of communal solidarity in the true *umma*, of due habituation in the *arkān al-dīn*, and of the writ of the Islamic state. Here, where current dialogue has so much to undertake, al-Fārūqī held a robust assurance and could be round with Christian misgiving about those prescripts. His handling of the equation he makes between apostasy and treason in *Islam*, published as textbook in 1979, makes this crystal clear. He writes that leaving the umma of Islam means "repudiation of the Islamic state," and continues, "That is why Islamic law has treated people who have converted out of Islam as political traitors. No state can look upon political treason directed to it with indifference. It must deal with the traitors, when convicted after due process of law, either with banishment, life imprisonment or capital punishment. . . . But Islamic political theory does allow converts to emigrate from the Islamic state provided they do so before proclaiming their conversion. . . . But once their conversion is proclaimed, they must be dealt with as traitors to the state."[16]

What this implies for the climate of dialogue is not hard to guess. The identity of creed and polity, of the Muslim worshiper with the Muslim subject, could hardly be more total. Faith can scarcely be religious if "treason" is its antithesis. Exile becomes the condition of feasible doubt and, in effect, the non-Muslim world its only haven. The sanctions of belief must surely be other than political, and so dire, if genuine dialogue is not to be per se subversive. Happily practice is often better than theory in this matter within the umma. Where the non-umma obtains, the politicization of Islam is inoperative. But otherwise it is clear that dialogue needs to take legal stock of its own legitimacy and paradox is with us again. For the non-Muslim within Islamic *dawla* (state), according to theory of *ahl al-dhimma*, has liberty of belief and religious law but not of faith articulation vis-à-vis Muslims in their umma. Dialogue de facto needs undergirding as dialogue de jure. Evil must be truly discerned.

These points lead into concerns which became paramount in al-Fārūqī's activity in the last decade of his life and may be seen to underlie the impulse to the superb task which *The Cultural Atlas* fulfilled. He set himself to develop what he saw as an exclusively Islamic sociology. One may wonder whether any "-ology" can be unilaterally possessed or posited by any one religion, given the sharedness of the factors—secularity, technology, modernity—which engage all sociologists. One might even suspect that to be unilateral here implied the irrelevance of dialogue itself or its consignment to more indulgence by scholars and ʿ*ulama*ʾ in abstractions. If theism is, indeed, embattled by what is modern or postmodern, does it not need all the allies it can get?

To be sure, societies do vary endlessly with the variety of the cultures and races which faiths inform. In that sense, sociology might well require Islamic treatment, though there can be no Islamic aeronautics, just as there is no Christian biology. However, both those faithful fly planes and are alive. Does not something of the present global, plural situation make social, moral, and personal issues common in all societies? Certainly it was such circumstantial interpenetration that inspired al-Fārūqī's quest for an Islamic sociology. Outside the umma of Islam, he saw Muslims imperiled in their Islam by the insistent contagion of habits, notions, norms he read as non-Islamic. Within the umma, commerce, development, technology, Hollywood, and much else brought those same inimical influences to bear on Muslim life and worship. Higher education, in particular, was the crucial sphere of this assimilation to the un-Islamic. Was it not sociology that alleged or implied the nonfinality of religious belief, the psychic nature of religious rites? Did it not unloose piety from its moorings, filch the faithful from their truths, by making all things relative to social forces, leaving nothing in command? Effete Christianity might tolerate this erosion of itself and Judaism find rebuttal in militant Zionism. But Islam was the religion of divine command. As in the stoning of *al-Shayṭān* (Satan) in the *ḥajj*, it must "give the lie to the liar,"[17] and by repudiation of *al-Rajīm*, "let God be God."

To develop, teach, propagate, and actualize an Islamic sociology he saw as the necessary answer to the umma's dangers, not obscurantist and blind, but by an intellectual construct which knew its own mind and worked for its application within the structure of contemporary science, education, and techniques. But only Islam held the clues, the perspectives, the incentives by which its self-defense and its mission to the world could coincide in action. He called for an outright "Islamization of modern knowledge." "All our previous reformers have thought of was to acquire the knowledge and power of the West. They were not even aware of the conflict of Western knowledge with the vision of Islam. It is our present generation which first discovered the conflict as we lived it in our own intellectual lives. But the spiritual torture the conflict had inflicted upon us caused us to wake up in panic, fully aware of the rape of the Islamic soul taking place before our very eyes in the Muslim universities."[18] In that urge to "recast the whole legacy of human knowledge from the standpoint of Islam," he laid down the first principles of an Islamic epistemology, derived from the unity of God, understood as the harmony of truth and knowledge. Modern disciplines had to be mastered along with the legacy of Islam, in order to "launch Islamic thought on the trajectory which leads it to the fulfillment of the divine pattern of *Allah*." His "workplan" in this aim was developed into the International Institute of Islamic Thought.

As a vibrant implied protest against Eurocentrism or Westernism in current history, al-Fārūqī's thought must be saluted and understood. But can there really be an Islamic psychology, an Islamic mechanics of politics, an Islamic science of society? There can, surely, only be a will—in his own words—"to establish the specific relevance of Islam to each area of modern knowledge." That specific relevance is, indeed, enormous and has been gratefully saluted, not to say expounded, by Christians and others from outside Islam. It has to do with the sole sovereignty of God, the creaturehood of man, the *khilāfa* within nature, the sacramental character of sensory and sexual experience, the liability of man to judgment, the reality of al-ghayb, and the ever urgent plea: *Rabbī, zidnī ʿilman* (Lord increase my knowledge).[19]

But the Qurʾanic source and ground of these bearings of an "islamicized knowledge of ourselves," of time and space and God, is not well erected into a sole *fons et origo*—not if we are to believe in the common word of all "the prophets." And are there not conditions of their writ and mandate over us, and their implementation in us, which turn on the patience, the long-suffering, the grace within the tragedy, which classical Islam, for its own reasons, has willed, for the most part, to exclude from the kind of reckoning these receive in the Christian and also in the Jewish idiom? If that is so, then we need each other, and the dialogue adequate to give us to each other is reinstated. If "panic"—the word in the quotation—is appropriate, then it describes us all. If, in the light of divine Lordship, it is not the word, then the ressurance about God and truth can hardly be unilateral.

These paragraphs do not pretend to suffice in tribute, criticism, and exposition concerning the work of a formidable, lively, resourceful, belligerent, and tenacious practitioner of dialogue; we mourn his passing and esteem his legacy. It may be fitting to recall the words of the German poet Rainer Maria Rilke, who said in another context (that of personal grief, rather than intellectual exchange): "Be gentle with yourself, and try to love the questions." And always, when dealing with questions about and between ourselves, we mean that we are more than questions.

NOTES

1. Ismāʿīl R. al-Fārūqī, *Christian Ethics: A Historical and Systematic Analysis of the Dominant Ideas* (Montreal: McGill University Press, 1967), p. 11.
2. Ibid., p. 33.
3. Ibid., p. 14.
4. Ismāʿīl R. al-Fārūqī, *ʿUrūbah and Religion* (Amsterdam: Djambatan, 1962), p. 9.
5. One might compare the wry notice in a pharmacy: "We dispense with accuracy."

6. al-Fārūqī, *ʿUrūbah*, p. 16.

7. al-Fārūqī, *Christian Ethics*, p. 6.

8. One way to avoid being so would be to see in "religion" "a humane science" (as suggested by Wilfred Cantwell Smith) where diversity of form expresses identity of meaning in the ultimate. But that "solution" has issues of its own.

9. Though "sincerity," sociologists warn us, is simply the state of being deceived by our own propaganda.

10. There have been tragic recent cases of parental conflict over children in mixed and sundered marriage and of the harsh intransigence of Muslim fathers.

11. See *International Review of Missions* (Geneva) 65, no. 260 (October, 1976): 400–9.

12. As has been alleged at times against the present writer.

13. Recalling the lines of the Amherst poetess, Emily Dickinson: "This world is not conclusion, A sequel stands beyond. . . . /It beckons and it baffles: Philosophies don't know,/And through a riddle at the last, Sagacity must go." (*Collected Poems* [New York: Chatham River Press, 1982], p. 183).

14. E.g., S. 6:12, *kataba ʿalā nafsihi al-raḥma*; cf. S. 6:54.

15. *Christian Ethics*, p. 33. It seems odd (a) how it is "divine" if it needs our "establishing," and (b) how we could do so in the context of agnosticism about the divine nature: "Let God be whom He may."

16. Ismāʿīl R. al-Fārūqī, *Islam* (Niles, Ill.: Argus Communication, 1979), p. 68.

17. Is not this the inner significance of "the stoning" *rajm* at Jamrat al-ʿAqaba? In the heavenly conclave (S. 2:30 f.) where God announced the bestowal of the *khilāfa* on man, Satan repudiates the whole idea as a fond and foolish policy. This is the implication of his refusal to "worship" Adam. It is in decrying the dignity of man that he is defiant of God. It then becomes *his* policy so to tempt and ensnare man that God may be made to realize His own folly over man. It therefore becomes, in turn, the calling of man to disprove the disprover, to repudiate the repudiator, and—so doing—to vindicate God. This, then, becomes the motif, the hidden drama of history, the drama to which prophethood, guidance, and *Islam* relate. Psalm 8.2 ("Out of the mouth of babes . . . silence the accuser") sees in ongoing human procreation the unfailing loyalty of God to His design and the continuing hope, via the generations, of human meaning achieved and Satan routed.

18. Ismāʿīl R. al-Fārūqī, *Islamization of Knowledge* (Herndon, Va.: International Institute of Islamic Thought, 1982), p. 14.

19. S. 20:114. See a critical Muslim discussion of al-Fārūqī's "workplan" in Ziauddin Sardar, *Islamic Futures: The Shape of Ideas to Come* (London: Mansell, 1985), pp. 85–106.

25

Religious Pluralism in the Thought of Muḥammad Kāmil Ḥussein

Harold S. Vogelaar

Those who knew Muḥammad Kāmil Ḥussein well would agree, I think, that his interpretation of Islam was very personal and did not follow traditional paths. He sometimes referred to his own ideas as "aberrations," which Webster defines as having a slight variance from the normal and typical. One might even argue that his variance from traditional Islam was more than slight.

But if religion is defined as a tradition of human response to the call of one who is beyond all religion, and emphasis placed on the word response (in its contemporary form) rather than on tradition, then the "aberrational" thinking of Ḥussein reaches deep into the religious spirit and has much to offer contemporary search for faith. In his own quiet way Ḥussein suggested that if it is to remain credible in today's world, traditional religion, and the moral strength it generates, need to be informed by the response of both modern science and the scientific community. This may mean altering or setting aside some ancient forms and formulations of faith; so be it. The alternative is spiritual atrophy. In some cases, he said, those who insist on traditional patterns of speech resemble a blind man talking to a deaf man, a phrase borrowed and relished by Ḥussein. To insist, for example, that a religion is complete and must be taken in its entirety with no latitude for growth through individual discretion, reasonable debate, and honest doubt is an outmoded idea. Such an "all or nothing" attitude, he felt, is tantamount to speaking of great things and making them small and is designed to bring reproach and scorn upon a dimension of the human spirit meant to be ennobling and uplifting.

Ḥussein was no theologian but a highly respected "lay" professional, a physician who used his love for medicine to evolve a therapeutic synthesis between religion and science. He saw it as the only sensible path to world community. That, plus the fact that he lived and wrote during a time of great intellectual ferment in Egypt (post–World War II), makes it understandable why

Egyptian scholars and scientists alike still refer to him affectionately as "our teacher."

Muḥammad Kāmil Ḥussein was born in 1901 in Sabq, a village in the Nile Delta, the son of a teacher and small farmer. His early training was conservative and pious. His father died when he was three and subsequently the family moved to Cairo where he came under the influence and tutelage of an uncle who was an ardent student of Muḥammad ʿAbduh, the Grand Mufti. Ḥussein was an apt pupil whose ability led him as a young adult to medical school and study in England and France. There he was introduced to the rationalism of Auguste Comte, which impressed him greatly; he was particularly intrigued with Comte's scientific positivism. With his Islamic upbringing Ḥussein developed a theory that religion and science could and would ultimately be blended into a rational whole. Ḥussein was saddened by the political turmoil of his own country and appalled at the mindless futility of the war in Europe (i.e., World War II). These factors urged him on to find a way to bring science and religion together to produce a peaceful and just society in which people could live in mutual respect. Over the years, Ḥussein held a variety of positions: he was a physician and orthopedic surgeon, professor of orthopedic surgery at Cairo University, rector of Ain Shams University, prime motivator for the Isʿāf Emergency Hospital in Cairo, and a private practitioner. Moreover, his medical career was enriched by his avid involvement with literature, archeology, ancient Egyptian medicine, and social reform. He is the only Egyptian to have been awarded state prizes in both literature and science.

Since some of Ḥussein's writings pertaining to interfaith relations have already found their way into English,[1] I will here attempt to examine his thoughts on religion under three interrelated headings: first, that Ḥussein's works represent a layperson's attempt to shift the focus of theology from transcendence to immanence; second, that this focus on the immanence of God constitutes, for Ḥussein, a restructuring of religion; and third, that though his thoughts may be radical they are, within Islam, both time-honored and timely.

Ḥussein Shifts Theological Thinking

In his well-known book *Modern Trends in Islam*, H. A. R. Gibb makes reference to a radical shift in Christian thinking that occurred during the nineteenth century. He refers to the fact that prior to this time all Christians accepted the proposition that "the God whose existence could be demonstrated by rational proofs was a transcendent Being quite distinct from the world which he had created."[2] During the nineteenth century this old rational theology, which had been destroyed by Kant, was replaced by a new defense of religion which relied upon the "consciousness of the divine to be found in the souls of men; and this tendency to emphasize an immanent rather than a transcendent God was strengthened by the prevailing concept of development or evolution."[3]

One can see in Ḥussein a similar shift in the understanding of God, which can be explained in large part by two factors. First one must recognize his growing fascination and then complete commitment to the scientific method as a way of approaching reality. As a young man he pondered why there should be such a large gap between the ideal and the real and whether what is called the ideal has any basis in reality or is simply an arbitrary construct. For example, he asked, why should ascetics make such a point of fasting when they are hungry and of suppressing all their natural desires? Isn't this a distortion of what is natural and good? Doesn't this represent the utilization of enormous energy and willpower "on the part of these people to do one better than God?"[4] Eventually he felt it did. He argued that to be physically ordinary or what medical people call "normal" is a rare but excellent state in which to be and that mentally one should also strive to be normal or strong-minded. He defined such a person as "one who has a keen sense of realities and facts; who reacts naturally and strongly to surroundings; who has a definite aim and clear realistic imagination and keen desire to develop all his power."[5] He concluded that anything, even religious law, that contradicts or obstructs the development of this natural person, or, in the language of philosophy, the "ideal man," must be considered a distortion and therefore wrong. For Ḥussein two faculties, the natural and the strong—which he "happily found in the art of Michaelangelo"[6]—with their emphasis on individualism and human aspirations were the philosophical basis for his growing faith in science and its ability to unveil reality.

Ḥussein came to believe that the analytical method of science, as defined by Descartes and others, is not simply the correct method but the only means available for arriving at the truth in the investigation of any problem. "We believe that all of nature from the atom to the stars and all the laws about living organisms up to the physiology of the most complicated organ in man are within the sphere of investigation by the analytical and experimental methods of our modern sciences."[7] For Ḥussein the true miracle of science is "not breaking the sound barrier or reaching the moon but rather participation in things formerly forbidden such as the human psyche, morals and conscience."[8] He believed that eventually all other disciplines would bow to the reign of science. "It has already remarkably expanded on a horizontal plane. My contention is that it has developed sufficient vigor, confidence and width of outlook to make it capable of expanding upwards into the realm of morality and religion."[9]

Muḥammad ʿAbduh, whom Ḥussein learned to admire through his uncle, had associated the sphere of reason with the natural and social sciences, thus hoping to avoid a conflict with the metaphysics of religion. For him science and philosophy had no place in the metaphysical sphere. What ʿAbduh failed to realize is that science will not be content to leave any area of life outside its purview, including metaphysics. Ḥussein knew this full well but was quite certain, as ʿAbduh was not, that a whole new concept for the metaphysics of religion was essential and that the one science could encourage would not conflict with but rather confirm and stabilize the role of religion rightly understood.[10]

A second factor impelling Ḥussein toward a radical shift in theological thinking was the Second World War. For him it signaled a tremendous moral watershed in the history of civilizations. Like many compatriots, he came to admire the West, and following his study in Europe made bold to tell the Academy of Arabic Language that sooner or later all developing countries would follow the Western pattern. But his admiration was primarily for its scientific achievements and the commitment of its intellectual community to the pursuit of science. His diaries amply confirm this.[11]

He was less admiring of the philosophical and metaphysical underpinning of Western civilization which, the war convinced him, was enormously "out of synch" with its scientific advancements. He called the West an imposing and magnificent civilization but one that was tottering and coming apart at the seams. It was like a huge monster with body and muscles of steel but a heart shriveled and full of corruption. World War II exposed it for what it was: "This great stupid war . . . has laid naked all the ugliness of Europe, an ugliness which would have been more revolting if it were not so nauseating. By Europe I mean a stage in the development of human thought and not [a] geographical area. . . . Such a colossal structure of violence, hatred, vengeance, cruelty, deceit and lies could not have been created in a decade or two. It is the culmination of processes in European history of thought which are centuries old."[12]

It is clear from the tone of Ḥussein's reflections that he believed there was a dreadful sickness at the core of a civilization which had reached its creative peak. This does not mean, however, that he held, as some two-thirds' of world thinkers now do,[13] that the brutal war (along with colonialism and Marxism) constituted a summing up of Western thought and tradition, as though the light of its ideal had gone out or its sickness was ineradicable. Rather, for Ḥussein, the transition evidenced by the war was part of a great natural evolution marking an end to the era of "Christianism," by which he meant the whole "philosophical system underlying Christianity and the allied religions," and the beginning of the scientific age, an age that was here to stay.

"Christianism," or the age of religion, Ḥussein argued, had failed completely to prevent the Second World War, and in many ways had actually precipitated it.[14] His book, *City of Wrong*, which grew out of reflections on WW II, is an emotional, literary reaction to that catastrophic event and movingly depicts the utter failure of traditional religion to prevent it. In that book, he develops the theme that minds steeped in religion and law at their creative peak, epitomized by Jew and Roman, could not and did not prevent the crucifixion of Christ, "the supreme tragedy of humanity," but actually aided and abetted it. In the brutalities of the West through colonialism, world wars (and Marxism?), "Christianity and the allied religions" had shown themselves to be of one mind with the ancient Jews and Romans, as those who participate in extinguishing the light of conscience, who continue to crucify innocence. The atomic bomb, after all, did not fling itself upon humanity. It was released by human beings very much shaped by the legacy of "Christianism." To borrow a line from *City of Wrong*, these contemporary people too were "caught . . . in a vortex of seducing factors and taken unawares amid them they faltered. Lacking sound and valid criteria of action, they foundered utterly, as if they had been a people with neither reason nor religion."[15]

But if *City of Wrong* was an emotional reaction to the war and its moral decadence, his *Unity of Knowledge* was a reasoned, scientific response to it. In the isolation of his study, removed from the market place of life, Ḥussein attempted to map out the structure of human nature, individually and collectively. He saw it as an edifice nobly embedded in the laws of nature, an image so ideal, so real and certain and scientifically verifiable that once described in lay language, it could not fail to attract and inspire all people even as it fascinated and inspired Ḥussein. In *City of Wrong* the Wiseman assured the Greek philosopher that the time would come when men would rationally understand the relationship between things intangible and things material.[16] In *Unity of Knowledge* Ḥussein attempted to explore this understanding and, in a therapeutic way, to point to a physiological basis for morality and a psychological basis for religion.

With Freud and many others, Ḥussein held to the idea that truth, scientifically expressed, is an agreement between the mind and reality, a conformity of the intellect with what exists outside and independently of the mind. It was this concept of truth, quite apart from its effect on behavior, and his conviction that the known laws of nature can be extrapolated to apply, *mutatis mutandis*, to the unknown,[17] that enabled him to say that human ideals have a natural and therefore a physiological foundation. Even conscience, the highest of these human laws, functioning as a type of moral imperative, has such a basis.

Ḥussein admitted that most people attribute conscience to some remote force, but argued that this is unnecessary since science provides a natural explanation. Conscience is really the law of inhibition, a law the action of which can be clearly seen in the function of the nervous system that regulates the body's organic activities. The heart, for example, has two sets of nerves, one increasing and the other diminishing its stimulation. This arrangement assures that it will confront all conditions with minimum exposure to danger. People's actions, concludes Ḥussein, are just like the heartbeat, representing a tension between active desire and inhibition.[18]

This law of inhibition, when it relates to immaterial values located in the brain, becomes the law of conscience. It makes decisions not just of feasibility but of desirability, not just of what is dangerous but of what is good for one's mental health. It does this through a combination of electrically charged brain waves which may or may not be chemically induced. The criteria for determining the soundness of judgments thus made, for example being honest and courageous, is that they be "orderly in their origin . . . [and] follow agreeable channels" in the brain. Such sound judgments make a person feel relaxed while wrong conduct does not. Implicit in such thinking is that if the interrelatedness of all things could be perceived correctly, such knowledge would be conducive to orderly and decent behavior.[19] This does not mean that what ought to be is different from what actually is, but that there is no way of knowing what ought to be apart from seeing things the way they really are. In this way "oughtness" springs not from some unknown, untried, hoped-for future but from an increasingly known and knowable past. It is enough to discover and describe what is because somehow the truth of that will set people free to be what they truly are.

Could this mean that in the final analysis conscience for Ḥussein turns out to be simply another word for Islam? The thought is intriguing. Muḥammad ʿAbduh had already conceived of Islam as a principle of restraint to enable Muslims to distinguish what is good and acceptable among the many winds of change. He too had felt obliged to rescue true Islam from the bonds of blind tradition and to study the implications for modern society. Can we see Ḥussein doing essentially the same thing, except that by substituting conscience for Islam he avoids the laborious task of sorting through a whole history of traditional thought while at the same time preserving the moral force behind it? Perhaps. It is certainly true that he spends little time trying to unravel a tangled Islamic past, much of which he considers irrelevant to modern society.

His view, however, is more radical. It is more accurate to say that he equates God and conscience. In this we see a distinct movement away from a transcendent to an immanent concept of God. In traditional Islam the voice of God, who is transcendent and quite distinct from the world He created, becomes public through Qurʾanic revelation. In *City of Wrong* that same voice speaks most surely to the individual heart through the universal language of conscience. In *Unity of Knowledge* conscience (God?) is equated with the natural law of inhibition.

Ḥussein realized that such an approach to religion, which begins from man and not God, from science and not revelation, could be disturbing to many. People would think that any theory suggesting a natural source for religious ideas denies their intrinsic value and thereby endangers the human social order. He argued, however, that a natural explanation for transcendent values need not lessen mankind's position in the universe. "What is greater than that man should feel that the pulse of his heart, the heat of his blood, his feelings and arts are nothing but part of the great forces, the simplest of which move the heavens and earth, the stars and planets."[20]

Thus one can see, I think, how Ḥussein's commitment to science and the evolutionary process of history required for him a radical or, as he called it, a "Copernican shift" in the focus of theology. It was a shift that would demand the restructuring of religion as traditionally understood.

Immanence Means Restructuring Religion

Although Ḥussein's faith in science as a way forward through the morass of human evil was unshakable, it did not mean he advocated the abandonment of all forms of traditional religion. What it meant was that religion and religious language would have to be reformulated and restructured to accommodate two views of reality: one for those minds shaped by the age of religion, in which revelation is seen to come from above, descending from heaven through prophets, and inscribed in holy books which may or may not be extant; and the other shaped by science, where revelation proceeds through knowledge which is derived from the scientific method and experimentation. For people sharing the latter perspective there is no need for a recognized authoritative religious text or tradition, only a sound and proven way of approaching reality. Such a reformulation could take place, Ḥussein believed, if religion would return to its original and natural function, that of giving outward expression to an inner experience, namely the innate experience of faith, "in a true and pure manner," following the example of the great prophets. Such a transformation would constitute a return to the natural course of events. It is understandable from this perspective why religion gradually overstepped its role of expressing pure faith, since prior to the development of modern science people had no alternative but to apply religious answers to scientific questions. The human mind, after all, abhors a vacuum. That, however, has now changed and religion ought willingly to relinquish much of its secular power and return to its original and natural function.

To define the nature of religion's original and therefore "natural" function and to explore its implications for society was to become a life-long study for Ḥussein. He was fairly certain from his reading of history that he knew what that function was. Increasingly he came to see faith as one of the most intense peculiarities of human life, as essential to being human as air is to being alive.

It is, he said, an innate characteristic as real as love and beauty and, like them, has no appreciable historical evolution but remains a constant in the human self. But it needs to express itself in people's external life in a form acceptable to the self just as the innate characteristic of beauty needs art to find its suitable external expression. Faith does this, declared Ḥussein, in an orderly fashion through religion. Religion then is to faith what art is to beauty. Thus faith is innate, beyond reason, changeless—while religion is external, reasoned, and subject to change.

The expression of faith "in a true and pure manner" did not mean for Ḥussein a particular religious system. It meant rather an expression that would be true and natural for any given individual depending on his peculiar temperament and psychological makeup. It follows that people may still prefer to be Jews, Christians, Muslims, even Buddhists and Hindus, but there is now no theological reason for them to do so. The only critical matter is to find a religious expression which is true and natural for any given individual. He expressed this in different ways. Some people, he said, are motivated by a fear of God, others by a love for God, and still others by a hope in God. It is true that Ḥussein felt that these expressions correspond respectively to Judaism, Christianity, and Islam, but one senses that his concern is not so much to characterize each religion as to insist that people must have the freedom to choose that religious expression which suits them best. Only when this is allowed can true purity of the heart be achieved. And only then will the great outward diversity of religions disclose a deep complementary and unitive character within them, namely the universal character of faith, which, when free to express itself diversely, will demonstrate its ability to create human unity.

It is important to point out here that for Ḥussein, purity of heart does not necessarily come through belief in God, or at least in the traditional concept of God. God, like lofty precepts, need not be conceived as transcendent and external, wholly other. God's existence "is all that is certain, or that can be established scientifically. Anything other than that, about the attributes of God, is purely anthropomorphic. . . . When we believe in God we are convinced of his existence."[21] For some God may be the transcendent Deity of tradition; for others, God may be likened to an inner "pole" of attraction which, like the magnetic pole, draws the compass of the soul to itself. Purity, then, is the movement of the soul toward this force which acts on the nature of man.[22]

It is clear from the above that Ḥussein could be accused of what Gibb calls dualism or double-mindedness, where science and religion simply function on parallel lines. Ḥussein was, after all, no theologian, nor was he interested in "the theology of the theologians."[23] It would be a mistake, however, to think that he would have been content with such parallelism. Clearly he believed religion should be seen as a part of the phenomena of life, as the natural way to express faith, but not as a movement which demands absolute loyalty to the point of dividing and destroying human community.

> He who bears arms or harms people in the name of the defence of religion sets religion above God, who has ordained love, not murder.[24]
>
> God never commands evil, but always goodness, peace and love. Everything that persuades you otherwise is polytheism though you think it is done in obedience to God's command. Those who injure people in pursuit of sound creeds, who burn heretics alive, who are extremely harsh on those who differ with them credally, all suppose they are pleasing God by this evil they commit, but God is never pleased by evil. They are in error no matter how good they are or how worthy their aims. The dividing line between guidance and error is that your actions do no one any harm.[25]

Religion should return to its original and natural function in society, that of giving expression to the inner core of faith found in all people. Once this happens, religion and science can cooperate in uniting a world fragmented by war and injustice. Unlike nationalism or any other "-ism" that can misuse science for destructive and demonic self-serving purposes, there is something so powerful and universal about faith, expressed in diverse religions, that it has the capacity and capability of maximizing the benefits of science for all. The age of science, therefore, is intended not to replace religion, but to restructure it. In providing a modern scientific foundation for the ideals and morals traditionally taught by religion, science and religion may be able to provide that sound and valid criterion of action so utterly lacking in events leading up to World War II. It may also provide common people, even atheists, with an understanding of faith and religion that does not disgust them or turn them into bigots. It may even bring them into the "hallowed valley."[26]

Ḥussein's Reception Within Islam

As extreme or aberrational as Ḥussein's thoughts on religion can sometimes be, they are not without precedent in the history of Islam, albeit generally within the philosophical and sufi traditions. There is, for example, the whole Muʿtazilite tradition with its commitment to reason and its teaching that morality is an inherent quality within human nature. There was also the classic attempt by Ibn Rushd[27] to harmonize religion and philosophy and Ibn Ṭufayl's famous *Ḥayy ʾIbn Yaqẓān*[28] where one discovers the perfect religion (Islam) through a study of nature alone. In the thirteenth century the sufi Muḥyīddīn Ibn al-ʿArabī in his book *The Bezels of Wisdom* (Fuṣūṣ al-Ḥikam) spoke powerfully of the immanence of God. He argued that "he who asserts that God is [purely] transcendent is either a fool or a rogue, even if he be a professed believer."[29] Ibn al-

ʿArabī's argument, of course, is that God must be conceived as both transcendent and immanent if justice is to be done to the concept of *tawḥīd*, the oneness of being. Nevertheless his work met with strong opposition from the orthodox and in recent time was banned from being republished in Egypt.

Another writer of extraordinary stature to touch on the subject of God's immanence was the Persian poet Jalāl al-Dīn al-Rūmī. These haunting words from his *Mathnavī* may depict a spirit shared by Ḥussein. God is speaking:

> Was it not I that summoned thee to service?
> Did I not make thee busy with my name?
> Thy call 'Allah!' was my 'Here am I,'
> Of all those tears and cries and supplications
> I was the magnet, and I gave them wings.[30]

To one degree or another all of these men and movements were trying to harmonize Islam to a world view different from its own; all met with some degree of resistance. Standing in that tradition, Ḥussein felt impelled to defend the intellectual prestige of religion even as he explored the moral responsibility of science. He saw the problem not simply as a debate between faith in reason and faith in God or between faith in the Greek heritage and in the Judeo-Christian-Islamic heritage, but rather that both these traditions are in serious trouble and both are inadequate to meet the needs of modern society. For this reason it is not realistic or even feasible to speak of a retrieval or revival of either system. One must think rather in terms of a reformulation of both under the guidance and tutelage of science. He argued not that religion and philosophy have no essential place in a modern world, but that the forces that will shape and determine their place are not ancient texts and traditions, however hallowed, but the requirements of an ever expanding scientific world view.

Ḥussein did not articulate the problem as certain scientists have done, namely that "the type of religion which looks to a realm other than the world about us for criteria of the good life is not a religion in man's interest."[31] He said instead, though perhaps with the same intent, that such religion risks losing the interest of modern folks unless it is reformed and then bolstered in its task of delineating the straight path by sound scientific methods. Ḥussein, as we have seen, tried to do this primarily by ascribing scientific bases to the moral nature of man, not as something mystical outside the self, but rather as a fixed and permanent entity, part of the very structure of the self.

He also saw science as tremendously significant in the struggle for freedom, progress, and peace. His love for it kept him from becoming a narrow nationalist. He was patriotic but the source of his loyalty was not Arab history or Islamic thought but a vision of humanity that extended far beyond the borders of any particular country or culture. He had a progressive view of man similar in many ways to Jacques Maritain's concept of "humanisme integral"[32] helping people to become more truly human by emphasizing their original grandeur and encouraging them to participate in all that can enrich them in nature and history. He was willing to champion national causes but only to the extent that this would help rather than hinder people in developing their faculty of reason and using the forces of the physical world to secure and maintain personal liberty.

It was inevitable that Ḥussein's commitment to science would eventually bring him into conflict with traditional religion. That it did so is fortunate since the challenge motivated his most significant literary contributions.

In the area of interfaith dialogue his pursuit and practice of personal freedom allowed him to range far afield and, perhaps more than any other Muslim, to penetrate deeply and thoughtfully into the mysteries of other faiths, in particular that of Christianity. In *City of Wrong*, for example, he broke fresh ground in showing that the two religions need confront each other no longer as rivals and bitter opponents, but at least potentially as friends and allies based on a sincere desire for mutual understanding, although this was not his explicit purpose in writing the book.[33] For many his willingness to probe patiently into the mysteries of the Christian faith and to be sensitive to what they mean to believers, an attitude so evident in *City of Wrong*, constitutes his greatest contribution to interfaith dialogue. Louis Gardet called this attitude an "example of that which can be a common spiritual search."[34]

Unlike al-Afghānī and many others, Ḥussein never espoused the belief that of the three monotheistic religions only Islam is capable of finding a perfect *modus vivendi* with science since it alone can accommodate itself to rational thought.[35] He knew that the misfortunes of Judaism and Christianity can equally befall Islam when confronted with the same challenges. Islam has no unique characteristic either to protect it from the eroding power of secular thought or to make it more hospitable to scientific inquiry. Like all religions it will suffer the fate of becoming anachronistic if its leaders refuse to make concessions to modern thought. It is religion as a phenomenon and not a single expression of it that stands in imminent danger of becoming unintelligible.

This is not to imply that Ḥussein wanted to discredit traditional arguments for morality. As we have seen, he did not. To do so would entail a "very great loss and deprive multitudes of a faith that purifies."[36] Nor did he argue that traditional expressions of faith have already become completely obsolete and incapable of satisfying the human spirit. He admitted that even primitive expressions of faith are essential for people who find them satisfying and cleansing. But such people should be aware that the relentless discoveries of science are eroding the foundations of their religious edifices and may eventually make them crumble, not because they are wrong but because they were fashioned for another day and age. Might it not be better, he asked, and in the long run more fruitful for the human spirit to allow the firm findings of science to shape the present and future form of religion defined as a response of faith? Ḥussein felt that he was arguing not through the influence of materialism[37] but simply out of realism. Such reliance on science he saw to be the surest way to enhance the greatness and dignity of humans. "When something is placed in its rightful position in the general order, then great things become truly great."[38]

Perhaps, being a doctor and not a theologian, his solutions are too decisive, too clinical. Certainly he glossed over a great deal of history in a way that few theologians would feel comfortable doing. Commenting on this Suhayr al-Qalamāwī writes: "In all the books and articles of Doctor Kamil Ḥussein, the individual and group problems of suffering and pleasure, of misery and oppression, of fear and of the end, recur continuously. In all his books and writings he approaches these questions with the scalpel of the doctor, who studies, compares, draws conclusions. . . . In all his writing there dominates this decisive tone which we call the opinions and prescriptions of the doctor, who has finished the examination, [and] plumbed the depths of the illness."[39]

Whether Ḥussein has actually "plumbed the depths" will be a question for future readers to ponder. What is certain is that he was not afraid to be venturesome and to take risks in trying to find a correlation between the things he believed and the things he knew. In doing so he employed the language of both theology and science, trying earnestly to avoid the dogmatism so often found in the one and the secular spirit so common to the other. It was his way of offering what he believed to be healing counsel. Mohamed Talbi wrote:

> Neither Islam nor any other faith in God has another choice today than to accept adventure. Science, in pushing back further each day the frontiers of mystery and the universe, poses questions for us before which neither philosophers nor theologians can abdicate without denying that which is fundamentally and radically man. It requires from everyone increased reflection, and on the part of believers, spurred on by the new problem, a rereading of the Revelation. Ought one to emphasize that the response cannot be a simple and vague concordance as was often the case with Islam since the Renaissance? . . .
>
> A new exegesis, not denying the riches and positive acquisitions of the past, is necessary and needs a climate of adventure, of exchange and of tension for being up to date and responsive to every disquiet. . . .
>
> This exegesis ought to integrate with neither complexity nor timidity, all that exists. Certainly the risks of crisis, deviation and aberration are real, and their consequences ought not to be minimized. But is it not the natural vocation of a religion to be perpetually in crisis, that is to say, in tension and flux?[40]

Such was the work and thought of Dr. Kāmil Ḥussein—to undertake the "risks of crisis, deviation and aberration." He quietly and courageously accepted both the challenge and the risk of this momentous task because through it and beyond it he saw the genuine possibility of contributing something toward solving some of the riddles of life he had pondered as a youth; of liberating the human spirit from those irrational and devastating passions which until now have kept mankind from realizing its highest ideals; of providing a way for all to find their own "hallowed valley."

NOTES

1. Notably Muḥammad Kāmil Ḥussein, *City of Wrong: A Friday in Jerusalem* (New York: Seabury Press, 1966), and *Hallowed Valley* (Cairo: American University Press, 1977), both translated by Kenneth Cragg. See also Cragg's *The Pen and The Faith: Eight Modern Muslim Writers and the Qur'an* (London: George Allen & Unwin, 1985), pp. 126–44, for an excellent summary of Ḥussein's thoughts.

2. H. A. R. Gibb, *Modern Trends in Islam* (Beirut: Librairie du Liban, 1975), p. 45.

3. Ibid.

4. The author's doctoral thesis at Columbia University (1976) completed under the title "The Religious and Philosophical Thought of M. Kāmil Ḥussein, an Egyptian Humanist," p. 49, hereafter referred to as Dissertation.

5. Muḥammad Kāmil Ḥussein, Diary of 1928, p. 7 (in Arabic; in possession of author).

6. At one point he described this "natural" person as "a creature capable of rising by his own intrinsic powers of good to the divine state" (Diary of 1941, pp. 9–10).

7. Ḥussein, Diary of 1928, p. 51.

8. Ibid., p. 53.

9. Ḥussein, "Science of the Transcendental" (lecture before a meeting of The Temple of Understanding, Princeton, N.J., October 1971), p. 1.

10. Dissertation, p. 56. For a discussion on ʿAbduh's view of religion and science see Charles C. Adams, *Islam and Modernism in Egypt*, (London: Oxford University Press, 1933), pp. 134–35. Cf. views of Muḥammad Ḥusayn Haykal who, like ʿAbduh, was keen on keeping dogma and science effectively apart: Haykal, *Fī Manzil al-Waḥī* (al-Qāhira: Dār al-Kutub, 1938), p. 634. One can see in Ḥussein's strong attachment to science an attempt, perhaps, to create space for intellectual freedom in his part of the world otherwise hedged and restricted by rigid forms of traditional and religious belief. Science could become that neutral ground on which all passions, other than the passion to pursue truth in a scientific way, could be set aside, calmed, or tempered, and then reclaimed for constructive activity. This becomes quite clear, for example, as we begin to look at his reconstruction of religious thought. During the seventies he would lament that much of the intellectual high ground gained during the thirties, forties, and fifties in Egypt was being lost to neoconservative movements.

11. Ḥussein, Diary of 1941, pp. 5–6.

12. Ḥussein, Diary of 1948, p. 35.

13. Girilal Jain, former editor of the *Times of India*, proposes that "'1989 could well mark the end of the period that began in 1789 with the French Revolution and the start of a radically new one.' He has a hard time seeing the Holocaust and the Gulags 'as ab-

errations in an otherwise humane and beneficent Christian West. I have come to believe that these developments speak of ineradicable sickness at the core of that civilization.' . . . 'I find it extraordinary,' writes Jain, 'that anyone should regard Marxism as a deviation from Western philosophy. It is in reality a summing up of Western thought and tradition'" (*Context* 22, no. 9 [1990]: 2).

14. Ḥussein, Diary of 1941, p. 21. The use of the term "Christianism" allows Ḥussein to criticize Islam without actually naming it.

15. Ḥussein, *City of Wrong*, p. 3.

16. Ibid., p. 189.

17. Muḥammad Kāmil Ḥussein, *Unity of Knowledge* (Cairo: Maktab at al-Nahḍa al-Miṣriyya, 1974), p. 88.

18. Ibid., p. 149

19. Dissertation, p. 175. One is reminded here of the novel by Brian Bates, *The Way of Wyrd, Tales of an Anglo-Saxon Sorcerer* (Century Publishing, 1983), p. 74, in which he attempts to reconstruct the training and initiation of an Anglo-Saxon sorcerer. Wat Brand, the Christian scribe who sets out to uncover the pagan mysteries, ends up by becoming the apprentice of the sorcerer himself, a Mr. Wulf, who at one point upbraids Wat for his atomized view of life: "You are labelling pieces of the world with words, then confusing your word-hoard for the totality of life. You see life as if you were viewing a room by the light of a single moving candle; then you make the error of assuming that the small areas you are seeing one at a time are separate and cannot be seen as one. Since the small areas of your life are thus seen as separate, you have to invent ways of connecting them. This is the fallacy of the ordinary person's view of life, for everything is already connected." In Bates's book it is the sorcerer, of course, who sees it as one. For Ḥussein, it was never sorcery but religion that claimed to see the connectedness of all things, and indeed had to because there were no other plausible explanations. Today, however, the only plausible and trustworthy explanations are those coming through science and the scientific method.

20. Ḥussein, *Unity of Knowledge*, pp. 171 ff.

21. Ibid., p. 162.

22. Ḥussein, *Hallowed Valley*, pp. 27 ff.

23. Dissertation, p. 179.

24. Ḥussein, *City of Wrong*, p. 195;

25. Muḥammad Kāmil Ḥussein, *adh-Dhikr al-Ḥakīm* (Cairo: Maktabat an-Nahḍa al-Miṣriyya, 1972), p. 16. Ḥussein's views here show marked similarity to those of an-Naẓẓām and al-Baṣrī. For them as for Ḥussein it was thought impossible that God would do anything but good for his creatures, in fact, that God did not have the power to do evil.

26. "The hallowed valley is the place on earth, the point in time, the state of mind, where you reach upward beyond the form of external things, beyond your own nature and the necessities of life, and even beyond the bounds of intellect. . . . It is where your hopes are altogether good and your dreams worthy, having no springs of evil willed by you or willed against you. . . . In the hallowed valley you hear the voice of conscience, clear and plain, enjoining upon you unconfusedly the obligations of the good,

and leading you undeviatingly towards the truth—conscience as the very voice of God" (*The Hallowed Valley*, p. 12).

27. See G.G. Hourani, *On the Harmony of Religion and Philosophy*, a translation, with introduction and notes, of Ibn Rushd's *Kitāb faṣl al-Maqāl*, with its appendix (Ḍamīma) and an extract from *Kitāb al-kashf ʾan manāhij al-adilla* (E.J.W. Gibb Memorial Series [London: Luzac, 1961]).

28. Ibn Ṭufayl, *The History of Ḥayy ʾIbn Yaqẓān*, trans. from Arabic by A.S. Fulton, (London: Chapman and Hall, 1929).

29. Ibn al ʾArabī, *The Bezels of Wisdom*, trans. R.W.J. Austin (New York: Paulist Press, 1980), p. 73.

30. *The Mathnawī*, quoted by R.A. Nicholson in *The Mystics of Islam* (first published 1914) (London: Routledge and Kegan Paul, 1975), p. 113.

31. Max Otto, *Science and the Moral Life* (New York: A Mentor Book, New American Library, 1949), p. 147.

32. Aziz Ahmad, *Islamic Modernism in India and Pakistan 1857–1964* (Oxford: Oxford University Press, 1967), p. 272.

33. Dissertation, p. 10.

34. L. Gardet, Review of *La cité inique*, in *Arabica* 22, 2 (1975): 217.

35. Albert Hourani, *Arabic Thought in the Liberal Age, 1798–1939* (London: Oxford University Press, 1967), p. 123

36. Ḥussein, lecture on "The Science of the Transcendental," at the Temple of Understanding, Princeton, N.J., October 1971, p. 2.

37. Ḥussein, *Unity of Knowledge*, p. 142.

38. Ibid.

39. Suyahr al-Qalamāwī, "Taʾmmulāt ḥawl al-Wādī al-Muqaddas" (Meditations about the Hallowed Valley).

40. Mohamed Talbi, *Islam et Dialogue* (Paris: Maison de l'Édition, 1972), pp. 44–46, as quoted by Marc Chartier in "Penseur's musulmans contemporains," *IBLA* 133 (1974), 18.

26

"He Walked in the Path of the Prophets": Toward Christian Theological Recognition of the Prophethood of Muhammad

David A. Kerr

"What say ye of Muhammad?" The archaism is intended, a reminder that this is perhaps the oldest question Muslims ask of Christians, Jews, and people of other religions with which Islam has engaged through history. In view of the Qurʾanic charge of *takdhīb*—"crying lies"—against the Children of Israel who denied Muhammad,[1] it was at least prudent of the eighth- and ninth-century Assyrian patriarch Timothy (d. 823) to answer the question, as put to him by the ʿAbbāsid caliph al-Mahdī with the opinion that "he [Muhammad] walked in the path of the prophets."[2] Ambiguity may have been part of the patriarch's intention.[3] In any event this oldest recorded Christian answer has left itself open to as much, or as little, as later generations have chosen to read into it. For the most part it has been ignored, as Christian polemics followed the more accusatory precedent of ninth-century al-Kindī (fl. 813–833) who influenced both oriental and occidental Christianity in their traditional assault upon the integrity of the Prophet of Islam.[4]

Due to the obvious theological problems which, from a Christian point of view at least, lurk within the question, it has arguably been more by prudence than neglect that the modern search for irenic dialogue between Christianity and Islam respectfully has chosen to circumvent the issue. The Second Vatican Council broke new dogmatic ground in 1964 when its constitution on the Church, Lumen Gentium, acknowledged the place of Muslims in "the plan of salvation" based on their faith in and adoration of "the one merciful God." Within the plan of history, however, the council preferred to acknowledge Muslims' "profession to hold the faith of Abraham" than to mention their more characteristic adherence to the faith of Muhammad.[5] Muhammad's ministry and message were again passed over in silence when the council elaborated its esteem for Muslims in the 1965 Nostra Aetate declaration.[6]

Subsequent Catholic elaborations of guidelines for Christian-Muslim dialogue,[7] based on the teaching of the Vatican Council, deal cautiously with the question, recognizing that "one of the most clear-cut differences between Christians and Muslims appears to be that concerning Prophets."[8] At most they try to clarify the problem: "For secular history the prophet marks a stage on the way of moral and religious progress; within the framework of salvation history his importance depends on the measure in which he announces God, our Judge and Savior."[9]

In his magisterial research on modern developments of Christian thought on Islam, the Lebanese Catholic scholar Youakim Moubarac criticized what he terms this "definition au rabais" (cut-price definition),[10] insisting that Christians need to decide definitely whether or not Islam is truly a religion based in prophecy. The same point was made, more diplomatically, by the cardinal archbishop of Madrid at the opening of the 1977 international Muslim-Christian Congress of Cordoba: "How is it possible to appreciate Islam and Muslims without showing appreciation for the Prophet of Islam and the values he has promoted? Not to do this would not only be a lack of respect, to which the (Vatican) Council exhorts Christians, but also neglect of a religious factor of which account must be taken in theological reflection and religious awareness."[11] Yet the controversy which occurred in this very congress—the only international occasion of Christian-Muslim dialogue on the theme "Positive Esteem for Muhammad and Jesus in Christianity and Islam"[12]—evidences the difficulty which belies the best-intended effort to come to theological terms with our question.

The most recent version of the Roman Catholic *Guidelines for Dialogue between Christians and Muslims*, prepared by Father Maurice Borrmans, urges deeper and more objective study of the problem within the "differing definitions of prophethood" which distinguish Muslim and Christian religious thought; "Christians," Borrmans concludes, are inclined to perceive that Muhammad was a great literary, political and religious genius, and that he possessed particular qualities which enabled him to lead multitudes to the worship of the true God. But, at the same time, they find in him evidence of mistakes and important misapprehensions. They also discern in him marks of prophethood."[13]

The principal ecumenical Protestant/Orthodox publication on Christian-Muslim dialogue in Europe, *Christians and Muslims Talking Together*,[14] acknowledged in 1982 that "up to now Christians in Europe have not paid sufficient attention to the teaching and mission of Muhammad." It continues: "With the new Muslim presence in Europe we have the opportunity to come to new assessments in co-operation with Muslims themselves."[15] At an important Christian-Muslim consultation two years later in Salzburg, convened by the Conference of European Churches, one of the items commended for further reflection and action was stated as follows: "Christians respect the prophetic tradition of the Old Testament. It calls people to repentance in the service of the One God. It is unjust to dismiss Muhammad out of hand as a false prophet. Christians may recognize Muhammad as part of the same prophetic tradition, and in the past some have done so. We must nevertheless ensure that our Muslim friends understand the subtle differences between the two perspectives, for Christians confess that the Word became flesh and dwelt among us (Jn. 1:14)."[16]

While this statement has the merit of placing the issue of Muhammad's prophecy on the agenda of Christian-Muslim meetings in Europe today, its incondite composition betrays such confusion of thought as would surely provoke Moubarac's most caustic criticism—a case of "cut-price definition" in which allusions to Muhammad's comparability with Hebrew prophets and justice are couched in ambiguous reference to "the subtle differences" between Christian and Islamic views of prophethood. It is difficult to discern where this statement contributes to an understanding of how "Christians may recognize Muhammad as part of the same prophetic tradition," except in its sense of the injustice of declaring him false.

The purpose of this article is not to resolve the problems inherent in well-intended but confused Christian confessional and ecumenical statements about the theological importance of our question. Nor does it essay a theological answer, for this would be to ignore foolishly the methodological lessons Willem Bijlefeld has tried to teach those who study Christian-Muslim relations since the 1959 publication of his *De Islam als Na-Christelijke Religie*, ("Islam as a Post-Christian Religion: An Inquiry into the Theological Evaluation of Islam, Mainly in the Twentieth Century").[17] We shall try, rather, to chart some individual Christian thinkers, from the mid-twentieth century, who have attempted to create theological space for Muhammad as a "post-Christian" prophet within their respective theological understandings of the Christian tradition. We use the term "post-Christian" in the manner of Bijlefeld, in preference to "anti-Christian" or "semi-(potentially) Christian," which arise from what he identifies as "false anticipations" based in surmise more than the thorough theological inquiry without which dialogue dissolves into platitude.[18] Clarification of the views of seven chosen Christian scholars from the Catholic, Orthodox, and Anglican traditions will, it is hoped, evidence new possibilities in "inclusive" Christian thought about Muhammad in answer to an age-old Muslim question.

Louis Massignon

In an important interview entitled "Le Signe Marial," given to a Catholic missionary journal in 1948,[19] the great French Catholic scholar of Islam, Louis

Massignon, offered his most succinct theological account of Muhammad's prophethood. The original French is terse almost to the point of defying translation. "To be 'false' it is necessary to prophesy falsely. 'Positive prophecy' is generally shocking for those who hear, preaching as it does a reversal of human values. But Muhammad, who believed in such total reversal in a terrifying manner, could not have been but a 'negative prophet,' quite authentically. He never pretended to be an intercessor or saint . . . but affirmed that he was a witness, the Voice which cries in the desert the final separation of the good from the evil, the witness of separation."

Massignon's primary point was to defend Muhammad from the charge of being a false prophet. In definition of Muhammad's authentic prophethood, however, he introduced a distinction between "positive" and "negative" prophecy which can easily mislead. Far from contrasting true and false prophecy, he used "positive" and "negative" to distinguish two attributes of authentic prophecy. Positive prophecy challenges and reverses human values which are prone to weakness and sin. While this accounts for much of Muhammad's ministry as social reformer, Massignon wanted to say more: that Muhammad was also a negative prophet in the sense of bearing witness to "the final separation of the good from the evil." Negative prophecy is therefore an eschatological category in Massignon's thought, the ultimate concern of a negative prophet being to bear witness of the Last Day when God would disclose "the transcendant secret of the glory of the just God."[20]

In Massignon's reading of Muhammad's history, this was the prophet's superior role in Medina. In marked contrast to frequent Christian disapproval of Muhammad's Medinan period, Massignon judged that "his entire politics succinctly reflected his contrasting the concrete problem to be resolved with that which his faith dictated to his heart."[21] This faith was most clearly expressed, according to Massignon, when Muhammad proclaimed to the Medinan Jews "the virginal secret of the perfect transcendence of the glory of God."[22] For this Massignon coined the phrase "the Marian sign,"[23] meaning that Muhammad's prophethood in Medina consisted ultimately of his witnessing the secret of the virginity of Mary, mother of Jesus the Messiah—an eschatological truth for all of humankind that Jesus' Second Coming will reveal the perfect freedom of God's glory in salvation, and in judgement of those who may have sought to "domesticate" the Messiah with a physical genealogy, or to have "carnalized" the Incarnation.[24]

The Marian-Christic focus of Massignon's idea is one that recurs in many of his writings. He sensed an equivalence between Mary and Muhammad: as Mary bore the Messiah in Bethlehem, so it was Muhammad's "Marian sign" in Medina that witnessed the Messiah's Second Coming. It is this that, according to Massignon, qualified Muhammad eschatologically as a "negative prophet."

Without addressing the issue of his finality in explicit terms, the equivalence he drew between Mary and Muhammad implies that the latter represents a point of culmination: as Mary was unique in her immaculacy, Muhammad was definitive in the negative, eschatological character of his prophecy; neither is to be repeated. By further implication, Massignon gave positive significance to Muhammad's "post-Christian" chronology: if his prophethood occurred after Jesus' first coming, it is his very anticipation of the Second Coming that commends him for Christian acceptance as an authentically eschatological prophet.

Charles Ledit

Contemporary and friend of Louis Massignon, Canon Charles Ledit published, in 1956, a study under the title *Mahomet, Israel et le Christ.*[25] Clearly influenced by Massignon's vision of an Abrahamic community embracing Jews, Christians, and Muslims,[26] Ledit turned to Thomas Aquinas for Thomist theological categories of prophethood in his assessment of Muhammad. Written in the intention of inviting "Jews, Muslims and Christians to become conscious of the community of their destinies" (*MIC* 10), his discussion of Islam in its history and "in the heart of the Prophet" (*MIC* 70–119)[27] culminated in an attempt to include the three religious traditions within the Abrahamic blessing which he believed them to share. Hence his vision of "a community of destinies": Jesus, the Incarnate Word of God's promise to Abraham, inaugurated the Kingdom of God in foretaste of its eschatological fulfillment in his Second Coming; Israel, called to anticipate this eschatological fulfillment, sacrificially prepared God's Kingdom as a temporal and spiritual reality in the political order of human society; Ishmael's vocation, through the civilizational achievement of the Arabs, was to achieve that which, by infidelity, Israel refused—God thus showing "the fullness of the help upon which Israel could have counted had it served [God] with a pure heart" (*MIC* 144–74).

Ledit's historical symbolization of Massignon's vision of the Abrahamic blessing raises critical questions which need not detain us here.[28] More relevant to our discussion is his attempt to fit Muhammad, the principal subject of the book, into a framework of Thomistic understanding of prophethood. Adopting Aquinas' definition of prophecy as a charism—"that is, a free gift communicated by God to certain men to elucidate the faith of others" (*MIC* 160)—Ledit identified two types of prophetic office from the several classifications in the six articles which Thomas devoted to the topic in his *Summa Theologica.*[29]

The major prophetic office is that which receives and communicates "faith in Christ's Incarnation"[30]; this Ledit called "theological prophecy" (*MIC* 162),[31] which serves to lead "humanity to sacramental participation in the mystery of the Holy Trinity by redemption" (*MIC* 162). Though this type of prophecy ended with Jesus Christ, Aquinas recognized another kind of prophecy under "the guidance of human acts" by which "at all times men were divinely instructed about what they were to do, according as it was expedient for the spiritual welfare of the elect."[32] Ledit called this "directive prophecy" which functions as "a divine guarantee in human affairs" for the direction of human communities (*MIC* 163). Following Aquinas' view that "at all times there have not been lacking persons having this spirit of prophecy," Ledit called upon the biblical evidence of prophets outside Israel—Adam, Noah, Melchizedek, Job, Ahikar, Daniel—as grounds for accepting Muhammad as a directive prophet (*MIC* 174).

Reverting then to his framework of an Abrahamic symbolization of history, Ledit proposed that Muhammad should be recognized as the culminating point of "extra-biblical" prophecy "since grace is addressed this time to a son of Abraham, precisely to hasten Israel's return before the grand apocalyptic wrath" (*MIC 174*).

The Thomist concept of prophecy for the guidance of human acts—Ledit's "directive prophecy"—does not presuppose intellectual or moral perfection on the part of the prophet. Ledit therefore did not attribute sinlessness to Muhammad and made no concession to the Islamic doctrine of prophetic infallibility (*ʿiṣma*). He assessed Muhammad's moral example in more culturally relative terms and in his desire to demonstrate consistency between the Meccan and Medinan periods of Muhammad's teaching, he chose to deal firstly with the latter, in light of which he reviewed the Meccan period as laying the foundations for the Medinan achievement.

The publication of Ledit's work provoked theological controversy, particularly among Thomist scholars of Islam who mostly rejected his views.[33] Massignon was more favorable, at least to Ledit's intention, which he saw as a loyal attempt at reconciliation between Jews, Christians, and Muslims "divided from one another by the profanity of their temporal administrations."[34]

Michel Hayek

Massignon's vision of "Abrahamic community" raises the question of the place of Ishmael in Christian reflection on Islam. Allusions to Ishmael abound in his thought and that of his disciples, including Charles Ledit as already instanced in passing. The most elaborate treatment of this subject within the Massignonian school belongs to Father Michel Hayek—a Maronite scholar-priest and contemporary of Youakim Moubarac—who published *Le Mystère d'Ismael* in 1964.[35]

In concept and content Hayek's book marks a distinctly different approach than can be found in earlier Protestant attempts to equate Muhammad and Ishmael, the classic if idiosyncratic example being the biblical-literalist theory of Charles Forster's *Mahometanism Unveiled.*[36] Hayek, by contrast, places scarcely any theological reliance on the genealogical connection between Ishmael and Muhammad, though he refers to the traditions that identify Muhammad's people as descendants of the Ishmaelite tribes. Ishmael's "mystery" is considered, rather, in terms of a typological development of the New Testament antithesis between flesh and spirit, rejection and election, slavery and liberty. Hayek construes Ishmael as "the child of flesh, the slave and the excluded," emphasizing that he yet remains the child of Abram/Abraham, for which reason he cannot be deemed theologically extraneous to the purpose of God in "the Abrahamic cycle" of faith.

In what sense, then, does Hayek's theological vision include Ishmael? "He constitutes the first, natural stage in the realization of the plan of God . . . an Old Testament in the Old Testament," symbolizing natural human adoration of the *mysterium tremendum* of the one God in obedience to the divine will (*LMI* 224). Abraham's prayer in Genesis 17:18 ("O that Ishmael might live before Thee") is interpreted as his confirmation of this fact, at the very moment when, in his own faith journey, Abraham is stretched beyond the limits of natural religion into a deeper or higher experience of faith which Hayek sees to be symbolized in the typology of Isaac, "the child of miracle and the testimony of the capability of divine omnipotence beyond natural limits." In this typology of faith Abraham experiences "another means of salvation, that of grace" (*LMI* 225).

If Ishmael "excluded" himself from this stage by succumbing, in Hayek's view, to the temptation of remaining within the certain but limited realm of natural or human faith, he thereby was to remain effectively the "preparation of the revelation of the supernatural promises" of God, by "reconciling the nations with a natural revelation limited to faith in God, unique, creator and judge" (*LMI* 241). This is analogous to Hayek's estimation of Islam's role in history: positive in the sense of bringing vast domains of humanity into true faith in the one God, expressed in a profoundly ethical civilizational enterprise; yet problematic—in Hayek's understanding of Christian faith—in that Islam and Islamic civilization have evidently refused God's gift of supernatural faith which is "the substance of things hoped for, the evidence of things not seen" (*LMI* 241).[37]

Hayek does not regard Ishmael's "exclusion" in terms of permanent rejection or condemnation. God cares for and listens to Ishmael, whose Hebrew name denotes that "God has heard." By analogy the same can be said of Islam which shares Ishmael's *baraka* (blessing; *LMI* 232). To this truth Muhammad himself bore witness, proclaiming "no other message than that of an invitation to humankind to adore God, their Lord," whose compassion knows no limits as God extends a divine love inclusively to all who believe (*LMI* 235). "No other religion more than Islam," in Hayek's estimation, "could have confirmed this biblical truth in so impressive, massive and continuous manner" (*LMI* 241). He thus concludes that "the grace of prophethood on the life of Muhammad" is clearly discernible, "an exceptional grace" which converted so many outside Israel from potential to "actual, real faith" (*LMI* 241).

Hayek remains somewhat ambiguous as to whether this actual faith is really sufficient for Muslims to find salvation apart from the Gospel. His poetic imagination is perhaps impatient with the systematic distinctions that mark Ledit's work, though it evokes contemporary Catholic ideas of "ordinary" and "extraordinary" modes of salvation. With greater clarity, however, Hayek emphasizes Islam as a challenge to Christians to live faithfully to the exceptional promises of God in the Gospel. Following Massignon he rests his case in eschatological perspective: it is the prophetic role of Muhammad, the prophet of the "excluded" faithful, to witness the truth of Christ's Second Coming which alone can bring into being the "universal Messianic reconciliation" (*LMI* 254) of Jews, Christians, and Muslims.

George Khodr

Attention to the views of Bishop George Khodr moves us away from the Massignonian realm of French Catholic reflection on Islam to the Eastern Orthodox tradition of the Middle East, and specifically to the Byzantine Church of Antioch, one of the member churches of the ecumenical movement of the World Council of Churches. It was to this body's Central Committee that Bishop Khodr lectured in 1970 on "Christianity in a Pluralist World: The Economy of the Holy Spirit,"[38] on the occasion of the WCC's establishing a formal program unit on "Dialogue with People of Living Faiths and Ideologies."

In his lecture Khodr challenged Western Protestants to understand the mission of the church as being "to nurture the spiritual tradition of religions it encountered by 'improving' them from within . . . while not 'alienating' them" (*MT* 42). Relating this to the New Testament assurance that God "did not leave himself without witness" (Acts 14:17), he exemplified his point in the history of the Eastern church by citing the precedent of the Assyrian (Nestorian) Church's approach to Islam: "God can, if He pleases, send witnesses to those who have neither been able to see the uplifting manifestations of Christ in the face which we (Christians) have made bloody by our sins, or in the seamless robe which we have torn by our divisions. . . . The prophetic character of Muhammad is defined in Nestorian texts on the basis of a specific analysis of the Muhammadan message. But there is no blurring of the centrality and ontological uniqueness of Jesus Christ" (*MT* 42).

Khodr does not specify which of the Assyrian texts he has in mind, but it may be assumed that they would include the one referred to at the beginning of this article, Patriarch Timothy's dialogue with Caliph al-Mahdī. This text states that "Muhammad walked in the path of the prophets" on the following reasoning: "Muhammad is 'worthy of all praise' and 'walked in the path of the prophets' because he taught the unity of God; he taught the way of good works; he opposed idolatry and polytheism; he taught about God, his word and his spirit; he showed zeal by fighting against idolatry with the sword; like Abraham he left his kinsfolk rather than worship idols."[39]

If Khodr alluded to this text, the fact that he did not cite it must temper any speculation as to how he would weigh it theologically. But in another article, written about the same time as the one already mentioned, Khodr offered a fascinating cultural-religious understanding of the Prophet Muhammad. Dealing in Christian perspective with the general theme of "Arabism,"[40] he esteemed Muhammad for embodying and giving religious expression to "the dynamic of the Arab people in search of unity on the eve of the Hijra."[41] If the "nationalistic" concept of Muhammad as the ethnic prophet for the Arabs comes to mind,[42] it must be emphasized that Khodr's concept of Arabism is catholic in its composition and universalist in its implication. In his own words: "Unity born of monotheism, continuity born of the Arab tradition, universality born of humanism expressed first in literature, later scientifically—these are the components of Arabism from its genesis. . . . Islam in its origins expressed the dynamic of the Arab people in search of unity on the eve of the Hijra. Muhammad expressed and incarnated this unity, giving it religious content."[43]

Arabism, for Khodr, is "a vocation of inclusion" to which "the structure of dialogue" is elemental.[44] Muhammad shaped the catholic nature of Arabism in a creatively synthetic way by combining Jewish, Christian, and pre-Islamic Arab traditions into "the muhammadan revelation" . . . or as Moubarac would say, "under the tent of Abraham."[45] Far from arguing a theory of historical derivation, Khodr interprets Muhammad's achievement in terms of his reaffirmation of the universality of Arabism against tendencies which, untrue to the Arab character, presumed "a monopoly of truth in the Judeo-Christian tradition." Muhammad's lasting significance, in Khodr's estimation, lies in his (Khodr's) perception that "Arabism, at the religious level, is the bearer of biblical catholicity," evident in fact that "the Qur'an vibrates with a powerful nostalgia of Christ."[46]

The key to Khodr's theological approach to Muhammad is found less in christology than in the doctrine of the Holy Spirit, pneumatology. Proceeding from a trinitarian doctrine of God, to which Khodr is Orthodoxly loyal, he envisions the whole cosmos as bearing "the mark of God" (*MT* 43), nature and human history therefore being sacred. As Christ is "the true covenant between God and the cosmos" which makes creation capable of receiving the Spirit, the

Spirit "is present everywhere and fills everything by virtue of an economy distinct from that of the Son" (*MT* 46). Between the Spirit and the Son there is "a reciprocity and mutual service," and it is this that creates, in Khodr's theology, the "hidden bond" between Christ and Muhammad, the mystery of which will only be revealed with Christ's Second Advent (*MT* 46).

Kenneth Cragg

The most thorough essay in Christian accounting of Muhammad to have been attempted in recent years is the work of the Anglican bishop and scholar of Islam, Kenneth Cragg. *Muhammad and the Christian: A Question of Response*[47] was inspired, as the rest of his voluminous work, by his search for "a community in truth" (*MT* 141) which would retrieve past failures of historic relationship between Christianity and Islam. To this goal he has sought to tread a path that avoids two obnoxious dangers: negative Christian judgments of Muhammad which "admit no extenuation" (*MT* 160)[48]; and "the refusal to allow that the autonomies of religions have other than one humanity" (*MT* 123)—the latter by way of response to scholars, especially in North America, who have charged him with "Christianizing" Islam.[49]

Yet it is most definitely by "Christ-criteria" (*MC* 145) that Cragg construes "Christian relation to Islamic theism, and so to all the issues about Muhammad" (*MC* 148), but in the conviction that "loyalty to Islamic essentials beings us more vitally into Christian fields of meaning than anything else could—and more hopefully" (*MC* 124).

Insisting that a Christian acknowledgment of Muhammad must rest on authentically biblical grounds, he assesses Muhammad's preaching as follows: "In the broadest terms it means the rule of God, the reality of divine power, wisdom, mercy and justice. It means the strong permeation of the human scene with a consciousness of God, his claim, his creating, his sustaining, his ordaining. That awareness by which Islam lives is sure enough to contain all those issues which the Christian must be minded to join when he studies the predicates of his New Testament theology" (*MC* 145).

In this perspective Cragg discerns the foundation of "a recognizably shared theism warranting community across disparity" (*MC* 145). But it is in the realm of shared human experience and deepest human need that Cragg questions the sufficiency of Muhammad's prescriptions. The Qur'anic command (*amr*) and its directive pedagogy find their corollary, he judges, in the didactic and hortatory style of Muhammad's ministry. This leads him to ask one of his recurrent questions of Islam: what happens when human minds remain unreceptive, obstinate, obstructive, recalcitrant? His answer is also characteristic of his oft-rehearsed assessment of Islam: "The whole logic of the Prophet's career is that the verbal deliverance of prophetic truth fails of satisfaction and must therefore pass to the post-Hijrah invocation of power . . . in the effective surmounting of the long-term obdurate" (*MC* 155).

Cragg's "disquiet about the Islamic power-assurance" (*MC* 150) leads to his sense of antithesis between the ministries of Muhammad and Jesus, which is the more problematic because of the essential unity of their conviction about the rule of God. Muhammad's *hijra* (migration from Mecca to Medina) evokes for Cragg a paradigm of "the kingdoms of this world . . . nationalist, competitive, exclusivist, political and coercive" (*MC* 130); Jesus' passion offers the opposite paradigm. "The Messianic task and the political arm are not compatible,"[50] Cragg concludes, and in these terms he defines the difference between Messiahship and Prophethood.[51]

In no sense does this diminish Cragg's recognition of Muhammad as prophet. Rather it is to argue, by "Christ-criteria," that the human condition needs more than prophethood to meet its deepest needs. It is in suffering messiahship that Cragg identifies the love of God which "does indeed meet our deepest human yearning but, in so doing, most surely vindicates the divine supremacy."[52] He insists that it is to this same truth that the inner logic of the Qur'an itself points, which enables him to conclude: "If we question or regret the Caesar in Muhammad, it will only be for the sake, in their Qur'anic form, of those same 'things of God' which move us to acknowledge him."[53]

Cragg would seem, then, to be drawing a distinction between the content of Muhammad's "prophecy" and the method of his "prophethood," affirming the former while criticizing the latter. Problematic as this may appear, it illustrates the dilemma that another Anglican bishop and scholar of Islam, the late David Brown, thought to be inescapable in Christian dialogue with Islam: "the Christian finds himself in an ambiguous position with respect to Islam, saying both 'yes' and 'no' at the same time."[54] Alan Race, another British Anglican scholar, conceptualizes this position as "inclusivist" in the sense that it accepts the spiritual power and depth of another religion, while yet judging such power as insufficient for salvation apart from Christ. "To be inclusivist" he defines as "to believe that all non-Christian religious truth belongs ultimately to Christ and the way of discipleship which springs from him. Inclusivism therefore involves its adherents in the task of delineating lines between the Christian faith and the inner dynamism of other faiths."[55]

Hans Küng

Cragg's publication of *Muhammad and the Christian* was shortly followed by Hans Küng's *Christentum und Weltreligionen* (1985), which quickly appeared in

English translation as *Christianity and the World Religions.*[56] His discussion of Islam focused significantly on Muhammad, whom he recognized as bearing many personal, social, ethical, and spiritual resemblances to the Hebrew prophets. In summary: Muhammad's prophethood was initiated not at the invitation of his community but by a personal vocation, the effect of which penetrated his entire mission, leading him to confront the sociopolitical malaise of his day with a message of warning which originated not in his own mind but in divine revelation coming from God, the unique, kind and merciful creator who, as the sole legitimate object of human gratitude, is intolerant of idolatry and demands social justice of all who submit in obedience to the divine will (*CWR* 25–26). Küng therefore asks whether it is not the same God who speaks to both the Hebrew prophets and Muhammad. "Does not the 'Thus says the Lord' of the Old Testament correspond to the 'Speak' of the Qur'an, and the Old Testament's 'Go and proclaim' to the Qur'an's 'Stand up and warn'?" (*CWR* 26).

Answering these questions in the affirmative, Küng was no less sensitive than Cragg to the tension between similarity and difference. He expressed it as "a continuum in discontinuity," for which he offers no resolution in mundane history. It is a matter rather of an historical dialectic which must continue until "no religion will be left standing, but the one Inexpressible to whom all religions are orientated."[57]

Discontinuity is essential to Küng's appreciation of Muhammad's originality. According to this view, "Muhammad is discontinuity in person, an ultimately irreducible figure, who cannot simply be derived from what preceded him, but stands radically apart from it as he, with the Qur'an, establishes permanent new standards. In that respect Muhammad and the Qur'an represent a decisive break, a departure from the past, a shift toward a new future (*CWR* 25).

For Küng's elaboration of these "permanent new standards" we must turn to another of his works, *Theology for the Third Millenium: an Ecumenical View.* Here he suggests two principal criteria for discerning what is "true and good" in religions: their ability to enhance the human condition "against the background of the Absolute"; and their capacity for self-renewal and reformation.[58] Muhammad is vindicated, Küng argues, on both these criteria. The Qur'an is as convincing as the Decalogue, the Sermon on the Mount, the Bhagavad-Gita, or the sermons of the Buddha in confronting humanity with the divine imperative as the source of human enhancement. With equal conviction Küng recognizes that "Muhammad has functioned as a religious archetype for a large part of the human race; down through the ages people have repeatedly, consciously fallen back on him, on the earliest Muslim community, on the Qur'an" (*CWR* 25).

Accepting that Muhammad functions authentically as a prophet for Muslims, Küng reflects on what this should mean for the Christians as part of a single humanity and world history. He points out that although the office of prophet has been inert in Christian history since the Montanist crisis of the late second century,[59] it continues to have New Testament authority. New Testament scripture, therefore, carries the expectation of prophets after Jesus, and does not reject them if their teaching is in basic agreement with his. Assessing this to be the case with Muhammad, Küng calls for an extension of the Vatican II references to Muslims: "The same church must, in my opinion, also respect that the one whose name is absent from the same declaration out of embarrassment, although he and he alone led Muslims to pray to this one God, so that once again through him, Muhammad, the Prophet, this God 'has spoken to mankind'" (*CWR* 27).

The church's obligation to acknowledge Muhammad's prophethood, according to Küng, is required subjectively in terms of its inner needs as much as objectively in recognition of what Muhammad has been and continues to be for Muslims. "[Christianity] also needed, even after Christ, the prophetic corrective, the prophets of the church and—we see this today even more clearly—the prophets and the enlightened ones outside the church as well, among whom the prophet Muhammad and the Buddha should no doubt be included par excellence."[60]

It is in respect of historical Christianity's need of prophetic corrective that Küng posits a dialectical relationship between Islam and Christianity. By way of cultural analogy more than historical identification, he suggests that Islam is to Hellenistic Christianity as was Jewish Christianity to the early development of the Christian tradition itself. While in no sense disavowing the cultural legitimacy of Gentile Christianity's adaptation to Hellenism, Küng insists on the dialectical value of its seeking to retrieve "that original and thus thoroughly legitimate Christological option which, pushed aside and concealed, originated in the oldest Judeo-Christian church community." He admits to being strongly influenced, if not fully persuaded, by the argument that this early form of Jewish Christianity was "for centuries . . . handed down by the scattered Jewish Christian communities living east of the Jordan, who probably spread it all the way into Arabia, where Muhammad finally encountered it" (*CWR* 127). If Muhammad, as the Qur'an insists, recapitulated an original understanding of Jesus' message, the church—Küng argues—needs to embrace Muhammad's insights in order to retrieve that which was obscured in its own Hellenistic development. Interestingly Küng presses this point not so much as a matter of history as within the context of christological discussion which he envisions as including Christians, Jews, and Muslims in "the very necessary trilateral dialogue" (*CWR* 126).

It should be noted, however, that whether he is speaking of Jesus or Muhammad, Küng rejects the category of "finality" as a way of understanding either religion or prophethood. Axiomatic to his thought is that history is always penultimate in relation to its future eschatological fulfilment. It is in the penultimacy of history, therefore, that Küng recognizes Muhammad to be normative for Muslims, as is Jesus for Christians. Moreoever, the nature of history is always relative, and religions, as historical contructs, interact relatively with one another. In the dialectic of history Küng acknowledges the many differences between Christianity and Islam, but searches for what, in dialectical terms, he sees as the "synthesis of Jesus and Muhammad" (*CWR* 126). In history's eschatological fulfillment, however, he believes that "there will no longer be standing between religions a figure that separates them, no more prophet or enlightened one, not Muhammad and not the Buddha. Indeed even Jesus Christ . . . will no longer stand as a figure of separation."[61]

Montgomery Watt

William Montgomery Watt is known firstly as an historian of Islamic religion, and particularly of Muhammad's life and ministry.[62] At several points throughout his Islamic writing, however, he has expressed his own philosophical and theological ideas on interreligious relations, reflecting the fact that he was originally schooled in philosophy and theology. It is no surprise, therefore, that his published thought in later years has focused substantially on Christian-Muslim relations.[63]

In the opening paragraphs of a recent (1988) review of Muhammad's early preaching, he is forthright in his estimation of his subject: "I consider Muhammad was truly a prophet, and I think that we Christians should admit this on the basis of the Christian principle that 'by their fruits you will know them,' since through the centuries Islam has produced many upright and saintly people."[64]

He elaborates this judgment in his latest book, *Muslim-Christian Encounter: Perceptions and Misperceptions*, where he argues that "such a view does not contradict any central Christian belief," though he adds, "It has, however, to be made clear to Muslims that Christians do not believe that all Muhammad's revelations from God were infallible, even though they allow that much of divine truth was revealed to him."[65]

Twenty-five years earlier, Watt explored the nature of a prophet as "a religious leader who brings religious truth in a form suited to the needs of his society and age" (*TR* 149). Distinguishing the prophet from both the poet and the mystic, he defined the prophet's teaching as "an ideational synthesis, including dynamic ideas in projection, [which] express some essential features of the world in which the prophet and his contemporaries have to live" (*TR* 149). The prophet presents a vision which requires action, in contrast the quiescence of the mystic, and in distinction from the poet, the prophet's vision exhibits sufficient coherence for his ideas to become "the basis of a systematic world-view, that is, a dogmatic system" (*TR* 150). For this to be possible, Watt argues, the prophet's ideas must come from a source much greater than personal unconsciousness, as evidenced by the prophets' sense of an invasive "revelation" coming from a source outside themselves. Following Carl Jüng, however, Watt interprets this as the prophet being in intuitive touch with "the collective unconscious or the movement of Life" (*TR* 151). It is this that elevates the ideational synthesis of a prophet beyond the needs of a particular society, enabling it to function as "the core of the religious ideation of vast civilizations" (*TR* 151).[66]

Examples of such transformative prophetic ideational synthesis Watt finds in Jesus and Muhammad. While recognizing the difficulties involved in extending a prophet's teaching and vision from one culture to another, he suggests that the problems are only resolvable through a combination of intellectual, ethical, and spiritual travail. It is in these terms that Watt asks the simple question of religions in history: do they work for the general moral well-being of their adherents?

In *Islam and Christianity Today: A Contribution to Dialogue*, Watt gives primacy of place to ethical criteria, on the principle that reality is to be construed in terms of action: *ago ergo sum*.[67] It is by the ethics of what it does that a religion may be judged "true" as a means of providing a satisfactory quality of life for individuals and communities. He makes the same point succinctly in his latest book: "If the quality of life [which he equates with the 'fruits' of religion] is in general good, then it can be said that the system of belief is more or less true."[68] In contrast to Cragg's focus upon *jihād* as the hallmark of Islam, Watt discerns the fruits of Islam in the Qur'anic value of *ṣabr*—"patience" which comes from obedience to God's command with the reward of "the great success" (*al-fawz al-mubīn*) on the Last Day. In this he sees the characteristic mark of Muhammad's prophetic message, and applied to Muslim experience in history he equates it with "the attainment of a supremely meaningful life."[69]

He thus concludes: "On [this] basis . . . a religious community developed, claiming to serve God, numbering some thousands in Muhammad's lifetime, and now having several hundreds of million members. The quality of life in this community has been on the whole satisfactory for the members. Many men and women in the community have attained to saintliness of life, and countless ordinary people have been enabled to live decent and moderately happy lives in difficult circumstances. These points lead to the conclusion that the view of reality presented in the Qur'an is true and from God, and that therefore Muhammad is a genuine prophet."[70]

Conclusion

It has become almost de rigueur that surveys of Christian attitudes toward other religions are expressed in terms of typologies of exclusivism, inclusivism, and pluralism.[71] In these terms our seven examples of modern Christian thinkers about the question of Muhammad's prophethood range between the inclusivist and pluralist paradigms—the exclusivist position being excluded by the terms of reference with which the paper began.

By various Christian theological criteria all seven have attempted to "include" Muhammad by affirming his prophetic stature. The "inclusivist" position, propounded by Alan Race, relates the truth of other faiths to an inclusive understanding of God's salvific work in Christ. Within this typology of Christian affirmation of Muhammad's prophethood we may discern at least three variants: an eschatological focus which treats Muhammad as the extra-Christian witness to Christ's Second Coming as Messiah—a theory for which Massignon finds corroboration in the Qur'an, Ledit in an interpretation of Thomist categories of prophethood, and Hayek in an analogical reflection on Ishmael; a messianic focus which, as Cragg exemplifies, addresses the human condition in the order of mundane history and assesses Muhammad's prophethood to have been genuine but rather less than the "more than a prophet" New Testament witness of Jesus; and a pneumatological focus which relates Muhammad to "the economy of the Holy Spirit" in Khodr's interpretation of the "catholicity" of Arab culture.

The views of Küng and Watt conform more clearly to the pluralist paradigm which is theistic, not christic in focus, and which posits many authentic paths to God. Their estimation of Muhammad's prophethood depends on ethically pragmatic criteria, tested in the Qur'an and in the history of Islam as an historical religion. Their understanding of Christian-Muslim relationship is based not in a "history of salvation" but in "history as dialectic."

Prompted by the demands of Christian-Muslim dialogue as each scholar seems to have been, their discussions must be read as essentially intra-Christian in nature. Their Christian theological criteria largely fail to address Islamic understandings of prophecy and prophethood. Moreover, while they deal with the Muhammad of history, much less account is given to the Muhammad of Islamic doctrine, piety, prayer, and politics.

This begs a deeper question: are Christian and Muslim theologies of prophethood compatible?[72] Cragg, who wrestles with this question most deeply, seems to incline to a negative answer, though his analysis of prophethood and messiahship ignores the "political" focus of much contemporary liberation theology. It is perhaps from this quarter that new Christian perspectives on Muhammad could eventually emerge.

Understandings of prophethood themselves turn on theologies of revelation, a central issue which occurs only obliquely in the foregoing assessments of Muhammad. Montgomery Watt rightly emphasizes this in drawing attention to new lines of inquiry opened by Fazlur Rahman.[73] It is in this area of theological inquiry that Christians and Muslims should search for "a new statement of the nature of revelation" without which it will be difficult to move to fuller mutual acceptance of their normative human personifications of faith.

NOTES

1. The Qur'an sees the sin of *takdhīb* as universal in human history—the mark of unbelief (*kufr*) which causes people to "cry lies" against God's signs (S. 2:39) and God's prophets (S. 23:44). This universal human tendancy to declare false the truth of divine revelation the Qur'an sees exemplified in the history of the Children of Israel who rejected and persecuted their prophets (S. 5:73), and in similar spirit denied Muhammad (S. 6:147); in different words but with similar sense the Qur'an lays this allegation upon both Jews (*yāhūd*) and Christians (*naṣāra*) who will never "be satisfied with thee [Muhammad] unless thou follow their form of religion" (S. 2:120).

2. R. Caspar, "Les versions arabes du dialogue entre le Catholicos Timothee 1 et le Caliphe Al-Mahdi," *Islamochristiana* 3 (1977): 107–75; Jean-Marie Gaudeul, *Encounters and Clashes: Islam and Christianity in History* (Rome: Pontificio Istituto di Studi Arabi & Islamici, 1984), 1: 34–36.

3. Gaudeul (*Encounters*, p. 36) acknowledges the "openness" of the patriarch's answer but suggests that "there may be a certain amount of prudence in it as well: speaking ill of Muhammad entailed the death penalty" for Christians living under Islamic rule.

4. G. Anawati, "Polémique, apologie et dialogue islamo-chrétiens: positions classiques et positions contemporaines," *Euntes Docete* (Urbaniana, Rome) 22 (1969): 375–452; Gaudeul, *Encounters*, pp. 51–54. For the full text of this work, see W. Muir, trans., *The Apology of al-Kindy* (London: Smith and Elder, 1882); cf. T. Arnold, *Preaching of Islam: a History of the Propagation of the Muslim Faith* (London: Constable, 1935), pp. 121–30.

5. W.M. Abbott, *The Documents of Vatican II* (New York: Guild Press), p. 35.

6. Ibid., p. 663.

7. L. Gardet and J. Cuoq, *Guidelines for Dialogue between Christians and Muslims* (Rome: Ancona, 1969); M. Borrmans, *Orientations pour un Dialogue entre Chrétiens et Musulmans* (Paris: Cerf, 1981), trans. R.M. Speight, *Guidelines for Dialogue between Christians and Muslims* (New York: Paulist Press, 1990).

8. Gardet and Cuoq, *Guidelines for Dialogue*, p. 131.

9. Ibid., p. 132.

10. Y. Moubarac, *Pentalogie Islamo-Chrétienne* vol. 3, *L'Islam et le Dialogue Islamo-Chrétien* (Beirut: Éditions du Cenacle Libanais, 1972–73), p. 188.

11. Emilio G. Aguilar, "The Second International Muslim-Christian Congress of Cordoba (March 21–27, 1977)," in Richard W. Rousseau, ed., *Christianity and Islam: The Struggling Dialogue* (Scranton, Penn.: Ridge Row Press, University of Scranton, 1985), p. 165.

12. Ibid., p. 163. The record of the proceedings of this congress was first published in *Islamochristiana* (Rome: Pontificio Istituto di Studi Arabi & Islamici) 3 (1977), 207–28. The report is reprinted in Rousseau, ed., *Christianity and Islam*, pp. 161–83.

13. Gardet and Cuoq, *Guidelines for Dialogue*, pp. 57–58.

14. First published in German under the title *Christen und Muslime im Gesprach*

(Frankfurt am Main: Verlag Otto Lambeck, 1982). The result of an international European working party convened by the church's Committee for Migrant Workers, it was subsequently translated into Swedish, Dutch, and French and was published in English in 1984 (trans. K. Cracknell, British Council of Churches, London).

15. Cracknell, *Christen und Muslime im Gesprach*, p. 36.

16. Conference of Éuropean Churches, *Witness to God in a Secular Europe* (Geneva, 1984), p. 56.

17. W. Bijlefeld, *De Islam als Na-Christelijke Religie* (The Hague: Van Keulen, 1959).

18. Ibid., p. 324.

19. Louis Massignon interview, *Rhythmes du Monde* (Paris) 3 (1948): 7–16, esp. p. 8.

20. Moubarac offers his own interpretation of Massignon's *pròphete negatif* as follows: "défenseur farouche de l'unicité divine contre toutes les idolatries et du mystère de Dieu contre toute formulation susceptible d'évacuer le *ghayb* ou mystère divin" (Y. Moubarac, ed., *Les Musulmans: Consultation Islamo-Chrétienne* [Paris: Beauchesne, 1971], p. 16). An eschatological element may be implied by this definition but is not explicit.

21. Quoted from J. Waardenburg, *L'Islam dans le Miroir de l'Occident* (Paris: Mouton, 1962), pp. 147–48.

22. Massignon interview, p. 9.

23. Massignon's term arises from the Qur'anic statement "And We made the son of Mary and his mother as a sign" (S. 22:50). An alternative term used by Massignon for the same idea, drawn from the same Qur'anic text, is "the sign of the two."

24. Massignon interview, pp. 8–9.

25. Charles Ledit, *Mahomet, Israel et le Christ* (Paris: La Colombe, 1956), hereafter cited in text as *MIC*, with page numbers.

26. For Massignon's concept of "le cycle abrahamique," see Guy Harpingy, *Islam et le Christianisme selon Louis Massignon* (Louvain-la-Neuve: Centre de l'histoire des religion, 1981), pp. 79–106.

27. Ledit uses this term to embrace Muhammad's ministry in Mecca and Medina, which he discusses in terms of his understanding of the prophet's inspiration and intentions.

28. Suffice it to say that Ledit's treatment of Israel suggests a variation on the traditional Christian theme of Israel's displacement from providential history, the falsity of which has emerged in recent Christian-Jewish dialogue.

29. St. Thomas Aquinas, *Summa Theologica: Complete English Edition in 5 Volumes*, trans. Fathers of the English Dominican Province (Westminster, Md.: Christian Classics, 4: 1883–1905.

30. Ibid., article 6.

31. The French original is "la prophétie théologale," meaning prophecy empowered by the divine word, or *logos*, which, citing Colossians 1:26, Ledit defined as "the revelation of the mystery hidden in the Christ since the beginning of the world."

32. St. Thomas Aquinas, p. 1906, where he elaborates upon Proverbs 29:18.

33. Moubarac, *Les Musulmans*, pp. 350, 356.

34. Ibid., p. 357, n. 19.

35. Michel Hayek, *Le Mystère d'Ismael* (Paris: Maison Mame, 1964). Hayek dedicated

his book "to the living memory of Louis Massignon" in fulfilment of their dialogue on the subject of Abraham. Hereafter cited in text as *MDI* with page numbers.

36. Charles Forster, *Mahometanism Unveiled* (London: J. Duncan, 1829), 2 vols. The most recent discussion of this work is to be found in the article by C. Bennett, "Is Isaac without Ishmael Complete? A Nineteenth-Century Debate Re-visited," in *Islam and Christian-Muslim Relations*, ed. C. Troll (Birmingham: Centre for the Study of Islam and Christian-Muslim Relations [CSIC], Selly Oak Colleges), pp. 42–55; also "Victorian Images of Islam," *International Bulletin of Missionary Research*, ed. G. Anderson (New Haven, Conn.) 15, no. 3 (July 1991): 116–17.

37. Hayek's quotation is from Hebrews 11:1, not Romans 4:16 as his citation suggests. It is clear, however, that his whole argument is of the nature of an exegesis of the relationship of law and grace in Romans 4.

38. George Khodr, "Christianity in a Pluralist World: The Economy of the Holy Spirit," first published in English translation in *Ecumenical Review* (World Council of Churches, Geneva) (April 1971), pp. 118–28; it has been republished several times, most accessibly in *Mission Trends No. 5: Faith Meets Faith*, ed. G. Anderson and T. Stransky (New York: Paulist Press, 1981), pp. 36–49. Khodr's lecture is hereafter cited in text as *MT*, with page numbers.

39. William Young, *Patriarch, Shah, and Caliph* (Rawalpindi, Pakistan: Christian Study Centre, 1974), pp. 202–3.

40. Moubarac, *Pentalogie*, 5: 185–99.

41. Ibid., p. 189.

42. The view, for example, of twelfth-century Paul of Antioch (d. 1180), who deemed that "Muhammad was sent only to those of the Arabs who were in ignorance" (P. Khoury, ed./trans., *Paul d'Antioche, Évêque Melkite de Sidon* [Beirut: Imprimerie Catholique, 1965], pp. 170–71), a view strongly contested by several Muslim theologians (Thomas F. Michel, *A Muslim Theologian's Response to Christianity: Ibn Taymiyya's al-Jawāb al-Saḥīḥ* [Delmar, N.Y.: Caravan Books, 1984], pp. 87 f.).

43. Quoted in Moubarac, *Pentologie*, 5: 189.

44. Ibid., p. 191.

45. Moubarac uses this phrase as the title of the final section of the fifth volume of his *Pentalogie Islamo-Chrétien*, in which Khodr's article on "Arabite" has pride of place.

46. Ibid., p. 191.

47. Kenneth Cragg, *Muhammad and the Christian: A Question of Response* (London: Darton, Longman and Todd, and Maryknoll, N.Y.: Orbis Books, 1984).

48. Cragg applies his criticism to the work of Sir William Muir and David Margoliouth.

49. Cragg (*Muhammad and the Christian*) presses his point in rejoinder to the criticisms of Charles Adams and Marshall Hodgson. For a full discussion of the methodological issues involved, see W.A. Bijlefeld, "The Danger of 'Christianizing' Our Partners in Dialogue," *The Muslim World* 57 (1967), 171–77. References to Cragg in text are given as *MC*, with page numbers.

50. Kenneth Cragg, *Jesus and the Muslim: An Exploration* (London: George Allen and Unwin, 1985), p. 154.

51. Cragg's analysis reiterates an antithesis between Muhammad and Jesus, featured in his first book, *The Call of the Minaret*, originally published in 1956 (Oxford University Press; 2d ed., Orbis Books [Maryknoll, N.Y.] and Daystar Press [Ibadan, Nigeria], 1985). "What is the final relationship of the messenger of God to those to whom he is sent when they refuse to hear? The Muhammadan decision here is formative of all else in Islam. It was the decision for community, for resistance, for external victory, for pacification and rule. The decision for the Cross—no less conscious, no less formative, no less inclusive—was the contrary decision" (2d. ed., pp. 84–85). While Cragg's development of this polarity becomes a distinctive feature of his work, its origins may lie in Pascal's *Pensées*: "Mahomet a pris la voie de réussir humainement, Jesus Christ celle de périr humainement" (quoted by Hendrik Kraemer in *The Christian Message in a Non-Christian World* [New York: Harper and Bros., 1938], p. 223 in support of his similar criticism of Islam).

52. Cragg, *Muhammad and the Christian*, p. 159.

53. Ibid.

54. David A. Brown, *A New Threshold: Guidelines for the Churches in Their Relations with Muslim Communities* (London British Coucil of Churches and the Conference of Missionary Societies of Great Britain and Ireland, 1976), p. 17.

55. A. Race, *Christians and Religious Pluralism: Patterns in the Christian Theology of Religions* (Maryknoll, N.Y.: Orbis Books, 1982), p. 38.

56. H. Küng, J. van Ess, Heinrich von Stietencron, and Heinz Bechert, *Christianity and the World Religions: Paths of Dialogue with Islam, Hinduism, and Buddhism*, trans. Peter Heinhegg (London: Collins and Garden City, N.Y.: Doubleday, 1986), hereafter cited in text as *CWR*, with page numbers.

57. H. Küng, *Theology for the Third Millenium* (New York: Doubleday, 1988), p. 255.

58. Küng, *Theology*, pp. 240–45.

59. See "Montanism" in M. Eliade, ed., *The Encyclopedia of Religion*, 10: 81–82. The article by F. Massigberd, "Was Montanism a Jewish-Christian Heresy?" (*Journal of Ecumenical Theology* 17 [1966]: 145–58), provokes interesting ideas which point in the direction of Küng's analysis of the Jewish-Christian character of original Islam. Is it possible to interpret Qur'an 61:6 in terms of a recurrence of "Montanism" in Arabia in the person of Muhammad?.

60. Küng, *Theology*, p. 251.

61. Küng, *Theology*, p. 255.

62. William Montgomery Watt, *Muhammad at Mecca* (Oxford: Clarendon Press, 1953), and *Muhammad at Medina* (Oxford: Clarendon Press, 1956).

63. Watt's earliest essay into the nature of religion and of interreligious relationships, especially between Christianity and Islam, appeared in 1963: *Truth in the Religions: A Sociological and Pyschological Approach* (Edinburgh: University Press), hereafter cited in text as *TR*, with page numbers. Later works include "Thoughts on Muslim-Christian Dialogue," *Hamdard Islamicus* (Hamdard National Foundation, Pakistan) 1, no. 1 (Summer 1978): 1–52; *Islam and Christianity Today: A Contribution to Dialogue* (London: Routledge and Kegan Paul, 1983); and *Christian-Muslim Encounter: Perceptions and Misperceptions* (London: Routledge and Kegan Paul, 1991).

64. W.M. Watt, *Muhammad's Mecca: History in the Qur'an* (Edinburgh: University Press, 1988), p. 1.

65. Watt, *Christian-Muslim Encounter*, p. 148.

66. Watt, *Truth in the Religions*. He reiterates this perception of prophethood in *Muhammad at Mecca* (p. 67) and *Christian-Muslim Encounters* (p. 28).

67. Watt, *Islam and Christianity Today*, p. 12.

68. Watt, *Christian-Muslim Encounter*, p. 133.

69. Watt, *Islam and Christianity Today*, p. 21.

70. Ibid., p. 135.

71. See Race, *Christians and Religious Pluralism*, Gavin D'Costa, *Theology and Religious Pluralism: the Challenge of Other Religions* (New York: Blackwell, 1986).

72. See, further, J. Jomier, "The Idea of the Prophet in Islam," *Bulletin: Secretariatus pro non-Christianis* (Vatican) 6/3, no. 18 (1971), 149–63, where he argues their incompatibility, and expresses grave caution against the Christian theological enterprise reviewed in this paper.

73. Watt, "Thoughts on Muslim-Christian Dialogue," p. 38, quoting F. Rahman, *Islam* (New York: Doubleday Anchor, 1968), p. 272.

27

Suspending or Postponing Theological Judgment? A Second Look at W. A. Bijlefeld's *De Islam als Na-Christelijke Religie*

John B. Carman

It is now more than thirty years since the publication in Dutch of W. A. Bijlefeld's dissertation, *Islam as a Post-Christian Religion (De Islam als Na-Christelijke Religie)*.[1] In the hope of acquainting the English-reading public with its contents, I wrote a long review that appeared in the 1960 spring and summer issues of the *Henry Martyn Institute Bulletin in India*.[2]

I want first to relate some points from that review and then to share some reflections on the major issues Bijlefeld has raised, especially on an unresolved problem for myself: in what ways and for how long should the Christian student of another religion try to suspend theological evaluation? I shall leave it to Bijlefeld himself and others to update the book's involvement in detailed issues of Islamic and Christian theology.

Summarizing Bijlefeld's Conclusions

Christian interpreters through the centuries, Bijlefeld maintained, have generally agreed in giving Islam a special status as a "post-Christian" religion, since it acknowledges Jesus as a prophet and Christians as "People of the Book," but these interpreters can be divided between those who gave a negative and those who gave a partially positive evaluation of Islam. In his dissertation Bijlefeld rejected both types of interpretation. Islam is not "anti-Christian" in the sense of deliberately rejecting the Christian Gospel, for it is impossible to decide to what extent Jews and Christians failed to communicate or even actually corrupted the biblical message and to what extent the Qur'an rejects what should be seen as the core of the biblical message. On the other hand, Bijlefeld also rejected the characterization of Islam as "semi-Christian," or a "Christian sect." Many of the same terms have different meanings in the Bible and the Qur'an; similarities in language may hide the real differences in content. For example, the notion of God's omnipotence, according to many Christians, cannot be understood without reference to the cross.

If for Christians the identity of God is expressed in the language of Father, Son, and Holy Spirit, can we simply refer to the First Person of the Trinity as "God"? What did the author propose? To suspend or postpone judgment about Islam's claim to Divine revelation. This means, on the one hand, to reject the notion of "Satanic influences" on Islam but, on the other hand, to refrain from listing common elements in the two religions or speaking about a common worship of God transcending differing theological conceptions. Positively, this position accepts that parts of the biblical revelation are in full accord with Islam and takes seriously the Muslim conviction that the other Books of Revelation convey the same message as the Qur'an.

The most important positive implication of this position is the appeal to the Christian community to try to bring about a real meeting between Muslims and Christians that will help effect what has not yet happened, a decisive encounter of Islam with the Christian Gospel.

The author's refusal thirty years ago to accept the notion of common belief "in the one God beyond our knowledge of Him" was based on his conviction that "we only know God in the relation in which He has made himself known to us," and "we can only try to understand when and to what extent the Qur'an's testimony to God agrees or differs with Christian knowledge of God through the biblical revelation." However, he considered there to be a common basis for discussion, which also includes Judaism, of the three religions as "theocentric and historical religions of revelation." Within this triadic relationship there are also distinct bilateral relations. The author affirmed both the Church's special relation to Israel and the unique relationship between the Church and Islam.[3]

Initial Reactions to the Book

When I first read the dissertation I was full of admiration for the way Bijlefeld had organized such an extensive literature into two opposing positions illustrated with many apt quotations. I was also struck with his comments on what he called the "impression of chaos." He noted that these Christian theological interpreters were generally blind to their inadequate understanding of Islam. I suggested in my review, however, that each group of interpreters might have been seeing a different side of what is really there, that testimony from God and human opposition to God could be expected to occur together. This theological insight I owed to Bijlefeld's former teacher in Groningen, Gerardus van der Leeuw, and not surprisingly therefore, I shared with Bijlefeld van der Leeuw's view that "Christian theology should respect the Science of Religion as an independent discipline seeking to understand and interpret but not to evaluate religions." Such evaluation "in the light of God's revelation in Israel and in Jesus Christ" is the specific task of Christian theology. I noted in my review the importance of Bijlefeld's reiterating these views of van der Leeuw "at the present time when two other approaches are widely followed." One is an objective approach following the method of the natural sciences. The second and seemingly opposite view, "now very popular among Christian students of other religions," "denies that any scientific objectivity is possible in studying religions."[4]

In the first chapter of his book Bijlefeld treated *suspension of evaluation* as appropriate to history and phenomenology of religion but *evaluation* as the very heart of the theological approach to religion. In the rest of the book, however, he maintained that "with respect to Islam this *epochē* or suspension of judgment is necessary even in the area of specific theological appraisal, at least with respect to a final evaluation of Islam's claim to Divine revelation." To this conclusion I raised a number of objections and stated my alternative theses.

1. It is doubtful whether we can avoid theological judgments or whether we ought to in matters affecting Christian relations to their Muslim neighbors.
2. A total judgment is illegitimate, not because Muslims have not yet been adequately confronted with the biblical message but because Islam as a total system or an entire community cannot give an unqualified "Yes" or "No" to the Gospel. Any alternative religious path is in some sense a "No," but within that alternative many positive affirmations of the Gospel are possible.
3. In our lives as Christians, ostensibly a "Yes" to God in Christ, there are often serious rejections of the Gospel, and "another religion's attitude to Christianity can make us more aware of the ways in which we ourselves say 'No' to Christ."
4. The light of God's revelation should not be limited to cases where a religion acknowledges God's revelation to or through the patriarchs and prophets of Israel and Jesus of Nazareth. All religions, including Islam and Christianity, are in a double relation to God that is "both negative and positive, in which there is opposition to God's will, but also positive relation to the Creative Word by whom all things are made and to the Redeeming Word in whom all things will be summed up and created anew."
5. "The God who speaks in the Gospel is the same God who has spoken to men of primitive cultures and of great civilizations, to simple men and to sophisticated philosophers. He has been speaking thus, and men have been

responding with both acceptance and rejection of God's call, often mixed in the same religious act or the same religious consciousness. Thus we should expect to find that there is a mixture of the 'Yes' and the 'No' in Muhammad's response, not only to the Christian Kerygma, but also to God's revelation of Himself through His creation (as apprehended by the religions of the Arabs and by Greek philosophy) and to the special promptings of God which Muhammad received as an individual."[5]

Thirty Years Later on Another Continent

When I wrote that review, Bijlefeld was in Africa and I was in India. A few years later both of us came to the United States, and we have spent most of our time since working in theological education related to an expanding though still modest part of North American academic life: the study of religion. The change of location as well as the passage of time give a new perspective on the subject matter of this book.

We are still, however, in a postcolonial era, living at a time in which Western orientalists and Western Christian missionaries are subject to a great deal of criticism, not only about their own blind spots and prejudices, but about the West's continuing exploitation of the resources of the rest of the world population and Westerners' continuing confidence that they know what is best for the rest of the world, as regards both political freedom and economic development. We who are trained in the art of sympathetic listening or empathetic understanding may try to make up for the continuing insensitivity of our Western culture to the grievances of Asia and Africa and Latin America by taking all these criticisms very seriously indeed. Those criticisms include an attack on what are seen as the outrageous claims of Christians concerning their community, their path to salvation, and the triumph of their God. Christian scholars are easily reduced to an awkward silence or an embarrassed *mea culpa*.

The secularism of thirty years ago is still strong, with a rationalistic approach that dismisses religion as outmoded superstition, condemns it as instrument of oppression, or, at its most generous, seeks to find psychological insights or social values in what are regarded as the crumbling belief systems of traditional religions. At the same time, many students and teachers accept a cultural relativism that assumes that all religions are no more than expressions of their respective cultures, cultures that cannot be measured by any values but their own.

Any assertion of a traditional religious claim seems shockingly out of place in academic and enlightened circles, though in the world outside the academy "fundamentalism" may still be a powerful threat. It is hardly surprising that in this environment one must be courageous or foolhardy to propose a Christian theological statement with any traces of so-called "triumphalism." During the last thirty years, opportunities for interreligious dialogue have expanded, and many Christian scholars have proposed liberal revisions of Christian theology as their contribution to such dialogue. Such contributions have often been greeted with enthusiasm, but sometimes also—behind the scenes—with more than a little skepticism. Do such liberal theologians really speak for the Christian community, or only for themselves? On the other hand, Western scholars who scrupulously refrain from expressing theological judgments have often evoked severe misgivings. "What are they hiding," our partners in dialogue sometimes ask themselves, "if they will not be straightforward about what they really believe?"

What Bijlefeld eloquently proposed was neither a liberal revision of Christian theology nor evasion concerning the Christian Gospel, but a frank admission that Christians have no way of giving a simple answer to what may be a Muslim's initial question, before the dialogue can even begin: Do you accept Muhammad as a prophet of God?

There is an even more fundamental matter that most Muslims simply assume: that we all believe in God. This assumption certainly underlies insistence by many Muslims, as the basis for dialogue, that "we both believe in the one God." Even though Bijlefeld recognized that practical circumstances may compel Christians to affirm this wording—for example, in Indonesia with the acceptance of the five common principles (*Pancasila*)—he could not then accept the theological argumentation often used as the basis of this affirmation.

Before returning to this central and continuingly relevant question of which questions the religious scholar should attempt to answer, it may be useful to place the concept of "post-Christian religion" in a broader context. There are some who would place many new religions during the last two thousand years in this category, but I think more especially of religious movements during the last two hundred years that are similar to Islam in being self-consciously related to the Christian tradition and yet in some fashion independent of the official church, claiming a distinct or inspired interpretation. Clearly the Mormons and the Christian Scientists represent such movements that now often claim status as Christian denominations. The status of the much more recently founded Unification Church is more controversial.

When the Brahmo Samaj was started in the nineteenth century it was closer to Unitarian Christianity than to any Hindu group; it has moved away from Christianity during most of its subsequent history, though for a brief period under the leadership of Keshub Chunder Sen, it moved toward a merger of Christian, Hindu, and Muslim devotionalism. Many of the African Independent Churches exhibit comparable semi-independence from Christian churches with ties to the West, but nevertheless often consider themselves as a revival or reform of pure Christianity. All of these movements are of fairly recent origin; thus far none has had such spectacular growth as early Islam, and none has become such an effective military and political force. None has yet become such a threat to the continuing existence of organized Christian churches and therefore none has generated the amount of virulent Christian polemic as did early Islam, though the attitude of many Korean Christians toward the Unification Church is sharply and vigorously negative and certainly the Church of the Latter Day Saints suffered repeated persecution at the hands of Christians during its early history.

In the case of most of the "post-Christian" movements there has been discussion among Christians as to whether the movement should be considered anti-Christian, semi-Christian or authentically Christian—or none of the above. If we ask whether an indefinite postponement of Christian evaluation would be an appropriate approach to these movements, we see how much not only the nature of a particular movement but the history of its relationship to the Christian community affects our answer. In many cases the specific issue has been whether some kind of mutual recognition is possible, and to postpone a decision is in effect to confirm the connection or separation that prevailed when the issue arose.

Related to the issue of community connection is obviously the attitude toward individual or group conversion from one group to another. More specifically, should the group organize efforts ("missions") to secure such conversion? Bijlefeld's suspension of theological judgment does not preclude an active proclamation of the Gospel. Indeed, such proclamation is essential. Yet if there is the possibility of a future collective reform of Islam, it is unclear whether proclamation should be accompanied by active encouragement to Muslims to shift their socioreligious allegiance. That same ambiguity obtains if Muslims are collectively placed in a semi-Christian category, just as it does in the ambivalent Muslim attitude toward conversion of Jews and Christians. On the one side is the Christian view that regards Islam as one of many non-Christian religions. On the other side is the view held explicitly by a small number of liberal Christians that conversion of Muslims to Christianity should be discouraged. This view coincides with the practical experience of many Christian neighbors of Muslims in many parts of the world, that efforts to convert Muslims are unsuccessful and only provoke Muslim animosity toward Christians. Similar issues continue to arise with respect to Christian missionary efforts toward other and more recent "post-Christian religions." Sometimes the practical problem is reversed (as has been the case with Islam): Christians are invited to convert to the new religion.

The other general question about the issues Bijlefeld raised is this: should the indefinite suspension of theological evaluation apply only in the case of "post-Christian religions"? Most of the older missionary theology assumed a negative evaluation of all "pagan" religions: they are not interpreted as responses to Divine revelation. By the time this book was written, the views of Karl Rahner were already affecting Roman Catholic thinking on this issue; since then that influence has increased and spread to Protestant circles as well. I am now struck by an interesting parallel between the way Karl Rahner dealt with pre-Christian religions (by which he seemed to mean, in principle, all religions "outside the Church") and the way Bijlefeld treated Islam as a "post-Christian religion." While Father Rahner ascribed a potentially salvific value to other religions as cultic systems, Bijlefeld thirty years ago wanted to leave open a decision on the revelatory status of Islam. For both interpreters, however, the crucial point of decision lies in the future, the future when a significant encounter will actually take place. The temporary efficacy of these religions, according to Rahner, will cease at the point that incorporation into the Church becomes a realistic possibility for them. Despite Bijlefeld's emphasis on Islam's post-Christian character, placing the crucial theological decision in the future puts Islam in a theologically pre-Christian position! If even with respect to Islam, which has so evidently been in a continuing relation with the Christian tradition, the Christian theologian must remain silent because the encounter is still incomplete, how much more should the theologian suspend judgment with respect to all religions without any traceable Christian influence, where the encounter has hardly begun?

Bijlefeld's book is an appeal for dialogue, for much more effective meeting between Muslims and Christians, and for much more dialogical scholarship in Islamic Studies. Much has been said and been written about dialogue in the past thirty years. Sometimes the rhetoric seems to go far beyond our achievements in actual dialogue, but certainly considerable progress has been made. Enthusiastic reports about the fruits of dialogue, at least with respect to Christian-Hindu dialogue, are sometimes put in terms of requirements for dialogue. If openness is interpreted as "mutual conversion," most conservative religious people on both sides may withdraw. Even informal conversation, moreover, has a certain representative character. One is not just speaking for oneself; one is representing a position about which there is some community consensus and usually some historical stability. I should add that one is also listening, not only for one's own edification, but in order to report back to one's own community. Thus stability of convictions is as important to dialogue as is willingness to listen, and openness to change of mind about misconceptions should not mean a *requirement* to alter one's convictions. The widening of horizons and deepening of faith that sometimes happens as a result of dialogue is a gift of the Spirit that should not be confused with the human arrangements we make for dialogue.

My own view of dialogue is that we should avoid any requirements other than mutual goodwill and a felt need to rectify serious ignorance and misunderstanding. Nevertheless, a Christian wishing to engage in dialogue must realistically expect that those belonging to other religious communities are likely to present some minimal lists of their theological, philosophical, or ethical concerns as their prerequisites for dialogue. In some cases the requirement may be shaped by a current issue, witness frequent Jewish insistence on Christians' recognizing the legitimacy of the state of Israel, or Sri Lankan Buddhists wanting a mutual covenant to refrain from making converts. In these and many other such cases, the so-called prerequisite, or "nonnegotiable demand," is precisely what should come up for serious discussion. Nevertheless, we still are challenged case by case to decide now on some tentative position that will enable dialogue to proceed. I should like to ask Bijlefeld, after his extensive experience in dialogue during the last forty years, whether he would still object to the argumentation used to substantiate the affirmation that "we both believe in the one God."

It seems to me that Christians can affirm the unity of the three Persons of the Trinity without identifying Muslim belief in God with a truncated Christian notion of the Creator. There are certainly plenty of differences concerning the doctrine of God, but different Christian traditions all point in the direction of a substantial assent with Islamic understandings of God: the more fluid theology of the New Testament Christianity, the Greek Orthodox notion of the Father as originating principle of the Trinity, and the general Christian affirmation (over against Marcion) of God in covenant with Israel, an affirmation so strongly reaffirmed in the Reformed Churches as sometimes to lead to unitarianism! To this we could add the medieval theistic doctrine shared by some Jewish, Muslim, and Christian thinkers, the willingness of Arab-speaking Christians in a largely Islamic environment to continue to use the name Allah for God, and finally, the personal experience of many Muslim converts to Christianity, that even before encountering the God proclaimed in the Christian Gospel, they knew God.

The question of the extent of agreement in our faith in God is put to the test when the question arises of including worship in our dialogue. For me the question is difficult to answer in Hindu-Christian dialogue, despite all the similarities between some Hindu and some Christian doctrines of God about which I have written. I do not see such difficulty in Muslims and Christians joining together in worship.

On the matter of the status of Muhammad as Prophet and Apostle of God, on the other hand, I agree with Bijlefeld's position of thirty years ago but I would put the matter the other way round. It is because Christianity is "pre-Islamic" that Christians have rather shaky warrants for affirming any later claim to postbiblical prophecy. It has been difficult for Christian communities to decide on the claim for prophecy or other gifts of the Spirit in their own midst; it is still more difficult to achieve the necessary *consensus in the community* for theological judgments about those who claim to be prophets at the edge of the Christian community. Here suspension of judgment seems to me appropriate, but there is no getting away from the fact that such a position will seem grudging and even insulting to Muslims. Such awkwardness comes with dialogue and it is well for Christians to remember this if they are offended by a Jewish refusal, justifiable on Jewish grounds, to recognize Christian claims about Jesus of Nazareth.

Postponement of Evaluation in Theory and Practice: A Confession and a New Resolve

My own position on these issues and therefore the basis for my critique of Bijlefeld's book was developed during a series of monthly meetings held in the Bijlefelds' home in Leiden several years before the completion of his dissertation. The strongest influence on my thinking came from Bijlefeld's former teacher at the University of Gröningen, Gerardus van der Leeuw. The Bijlefelds' encouragement and advice during my stay in Leiden also helped me to develop a conviction that hospitality is itself an important ingredient in the scholarly process, and certainly in situations of dialogue. My theoretical position thirty years ago included:

1. distinguishing but not separating phenomenological understanding and theological evaluation,
2. postponing evaluation until one has gained sufficient understanding,
3. avoiding sweeping evaluations, either negative or positive, and
4. seeking guidance from the lives and thought of converts to Christianity when trying to determine the elements in other religions that could be considered "preparation for the Gospel."

My "theology of religion" of thirty years ago still seems to me right *in theory* but when I look at what I have so far accomplished, I seem *in practice* to have been following the indefinite postponement of specific theological evaluations of religion that Bijlefeld then advocated with respect to Islam. I have hardly begun to work out a Christian theological assessment of specific aspects of Hindu life and thought. I have made considerable use of Christian concepts as I try to understand Hindu thought, and I am beginning to use Hindu concepts in a comparative look at Hindu and Christian theology. This comparison, however, I consider part of my effort at understanding, not a theological evaluation.

The object of understanding seems to recede as I advance, so that on many subjects I do not yet understand enough to undertake responsible evaluation. Perhaps, however, this is just an excuse, because it is easier to remain silent in a theological environment where my "Christian inclusivism" may be considered outdated in an age of "religious pluralism." If I had continued to live in India as part of the Indian Christian community I should certainly have been virtually forced to undertake some assessments. Whether my caution is growing wisdom or intellectual cowardice I do not know. I believe that there are many truths that remain in God's hidden counsels and not at our academic disposal, and that there are others that may be disclosed in good time, if not to the individual scholar, then to the prayerfully searching community. In the meantime, dialogue remains an imperative for Christians, not as a substitute for evangelism or for traditional scholarship, but as, in this closing decade of the twentieth century, their necessary accompaniment. The decisive point in the future, after all, is not the point of sufficient understanding for me or for my partner in dialogue, but the point beyond our grasp where the One beyond our grasp grasps us all in His judgment and mercy.

NOTES

1. Willem Abraham Bijlefeld, *De Islam als Na-Christelijke Religie: een Onderzoek naar de Theologische Beoordeling van de Islam, in het Bijzonder in de Twintigste Eeuw* (Islam as a Post-Christian Religion: An Inquiry into the Theological Evaluation of Islam, Mainly in the Twentieth Century, with a summary in English.) Dissertation for obtaining the degree of doctor of theology at the State University of Utrecht (the Netherlands), defended on 18 June, 1959 (The Hague: Van Keulen, 1959).

2. John B. Carman, "A New Assessment of the Christian Encounter with Islam," *Bulletin of the Henry Martyn Institute of Islamic Studies* (Hyderabhad, India) (spring 1960): 38–51; (summer 1960): 13–32.

3. Ibid. (spring), pp. 39–43.

4. Ibid. (summer), pp. 23–27.

5. Ibid., pp. 27–31.

28

Comments on a Few Theological Issues in the Islamic-Christian Dialogue

Seyyed Hossein Nasr

The crucial questions and difficulties that confront serious ecumenism are above all of a metaphysical and theological order and must be confronted in a sincere and serious manner if a profound understanding is to be created between the two sides. It is too late for diplomatic platitudes and the kind of relativization which in the name of ecumenical understanding belittles issues of major theological concern, creating so-called human accord at the expense of truncating, reducing, or distorting the Divine Message.

I believe that seven outstanding theological and metaphysical issues can be identified between Islam and Christianity which need to be studied, elaborated, and better understood in order that a more profound harmony and comprehension between Christians and Muslims can be fostered. Specific cases of interaction between Christian and Muslim communities and groups, of course, raise other issues as the attention shifts to human and social considerations. From the theological perspective, however, these seven points remain crucial and need much further reflection by those theologians and religious scholars on both sides who are concerned with a deeper understanding between Christianity and Islam.

I

The first and most complex question is not so much that of the nature of God but rather of the way in which God manifests Himself. The nature of God is of course itself the basic reality of both religions and has been dealt with by numerous generations of Christian and Muslim theologians, philosophers, and gnostics (in the sense of *ʿurafāʾ* in Islam rather than the sectarian gnostics of the early Christian centuries). Despite the difference of emphasis in the two religions, namely the insistence of Christians upon trinity and of Muslims upon unity, it is not difficult to reach an accord on the ultimate nature of God, the One Reality. The works of such persons as al-Ghazzālī, Rūmī, and Ibn ʿArabī on the Islamic side and Erigena and Nicolas of Cusa on the Christian side provide the necessary metaphysical and theological doctrines on the basis of which one can formulate a doctrine of the nature of God which would be acceptable to either religion. What is needed is a further effort on the part of both Christians and Muslims to provide formulations of traditional and orthodox doctrines in a contemporary context along the lines found in the works of F. Schuon[1] and also in the writings of such Christian theologian-scholars as Louis Massignon, Louis Gardet, Wilfred Smith, and Willem Bijlefeld.[2]

What is much more difficult to understand in its full theological significance across the Christian-Islamic religious frontiers is the way in which the Divine Reality manifests Itself. Here one comes to the question of theophany (*tajallī*) and incarnation (*ḥulūl*) and the relation between the Divine (*lāhūt*) and the human (*nāsūt*). Both religions, of course, accept the primacy of the Divine and the blinding reality of God. But they differ as to whether that Transcendent and Divine Reality can become manifested in the world of becoming and if so, what constitutes the meaning of manifestation. Islam rejects the incarnation, fixing its gaze upon the Absolute as such, which cannot become incarnated without entering into the domain of relativity. Christianity places its emphasis not on the Absolute as such but on the manifestation of the Absolute as the son or the Truth incarnate.

Debates within Christianity concerning the Divine and human natures of Christ actually have been and are of great significance for the debates between Christianity and Islam over this issue. Were Islam to carry out a dialogue with some of the Eastern Christian churches, there would be quite a different theological climate of discourse precisely because of other christologies which were cultivated by some of the early Eastern churches. Does *lāhūt* enter in *nāsūt*, or is it simply reflected in it? Can the two become united in a single reality or do they remain apart? Many of these issues were discussed by early Muslim scholars in works on "schools and sects" (*al-milal waʾl-niḥal*) in the context of early Islamic-Christian debates. But they have not been discussed sufficiently in the contemporary context by theologians and religious thinkers who would take their own tradition seriously. There is no denying the fact that serious Muslim thinkers cannot accept the penetration of *lāhūt* into *nāsūt* or the incarnation of God in any form unless incarnation be understood in a metaphysical and symbolic sense. In any case it is important to realize the central significance of this issue in any Christian-Islamic dialogue that seeks to go beyond simple formalities and human niceties.

II

The second question of great theological significance is that of finality. Islam claims finality for itself in the present period of human history and asserts that there will be no major religious message, including the revelation of a new *sharīʿa* and Sacred Book, until the second coming of Christ and the ending of human history. The history of the past fourteen centuries has in fact vindicated the Islamic view insofar as no major religion comparable to Buddhism, Christianity, or Islam has appeared since the descent of the Qurʾan. The Islamic attitude toward religious movements that have appeared more recently, such as Bahāʾism and the Aḥmadiyya in the nineteenth century, is well-known precisely because they negate the basic Islamic doctrine concerning the Prophet Muhammad as the Seal of Prophets, *Khatam al-anbiyāʾ*. Although the particulars of these two religious movements are not the same, in both cases the question of finality of prophethood has been at the center of this confrontation with Islam.

As for Christianity, its founder never claimed to be the "Seal of Prophets." Yet he spoke on the one hand of false prophets who would arise after him and on the other of the rule of the Paraclete, which Muslims identify with the coming of Islam, equating the name of the Prophet as Ahmad with the Paraclete.[3] If the identification of the rule of the Paraclete with the coming of Islam is rejected and Islam is simply identified with the false prophets mentioned by Christ, then there is of course no possibility of a serious religious dialogue and one is back to the position taken by the majority of Christian theologians since the advent of Islam. But as far as Christianity is concerned, the very existence of Islam poses a greater challenge than its finality. In any case it remains for Christian theologians to delve more deeply into the doctrine of the Paraclete in its relation with the Islamic revelation.

The problem of finality is more acute as far as Muslims are concerned because Christianity in its own way also claims finality for itself. Nor in fact could the "sense of the Absolute" in every religion not bring with it a sense of finality of the message of that religion for those who have accepted it. But it is finality in a historic sense that is particularly problematic in the Islamic understanding of Christianity, for the vast majority of Christians have interpreted the saying of Christ, "I am the way, the Life and the Truth," to mean "I am the only Way" and also the final way. Such a view obviously makes any discourse with a religion which comes after rather than precedes Christianity historically impossible. This issue certainly plays a role in the contrast between current Christian theological studies of Judaism and of Islam. In any case the question of finality as understood in the two religions must be thoroughly studied and elaborated, both as this question relates to the sense of the Absolute in each religion and as it relates to their particular views concerning historical finality.

Furthermore, this question, which is obviously related to the issue of "final things" or eschatology in each religion, cannot be discussed without considering those secular philosophies of time and of history for which historical finality in the religious sense is meaningless, philosophies which were born in the Renaissance and the seventeenth century and reached their peak of influence in the nineteenth century. These philosophies have influenced Christian thought much more than they have Islamic thought, where the traditional doctrine of the terminal nature of history of humanity is widely held. An in-depth examination of the question of finality in the context of Christian-Islamic dialogue requires taking into consideration the view of an indefinite linear history in which there can never be any finality except through some unforeseen natural cataclysm and not because of a divine intervention in human history. In earlier centuries, both Christian and Islamic thought had to confront other views of time, including that of cyclic time as expounded by later schools of Greek philosophy, distinct from the traditional view of cosmic cycles found to this day in Hindu doctrines. The modern philosophical challenge is, however, of a different nature and needs to be considered fully in any Christian-Islamic dialogue, especially since so much of Christian thought has been influenced by these modern philosophical ideas during the past two centuries.[4]

III

The next question of considerable theological import in the Christian-Islamic dialogue is that of the meaning and status of sacred scripture in the two respective traditions. A great deal of discussion concerning this issue has already taken place in both camps but much of it has been in the form of soliloquies which fail to address the main issues involved. On the Christian side the status of the Qur'an has been taken to be the same for Muslims as the Bible is for Christianity. Even the meaning of the Qur'anic revelation has been evaluated in the context of Christian theological understanding of revelation as this understanding has been modified and even distorted as a result of the epistemological premises of modern philosophical schools of thought based on rationalism and empiricism. There have been a few Western Christian theologians such as Wilfred C. Smith who have taken the Islamic meaning of sacred scripture as it pertains to the Qur'an seriously, but such figures have been rare. Most Western scholars of Islam have sought to criticize the Islamic understanding of scripture, and many have even gone so far as to claim that for fourteen centuries Muslims have failed to understand how simplistic and naive their understanding of revelation and sacred scripture really is.[5]

Western Christianity's understanding of sacred scripture has itself changed to a large extent during the past two centuries, at least in many of the churches. The application of rationalistic and empirical methods of research and so-called higher criticism have removed the sense of the sacred from the Bible even for many who are still believers, reducing Christian and Jewish sacred scripture also for them—as for the nonbelievers in the West—to either literature or history. These developments are taken by many Christians to be universal and global, like so many other intellectual trends and philosophies that have emanated from the West during the past two centuries and for which their proponents have claimed and still claim universal validity and applicability. Christian students of Islam have then proceeded to apply their own findings, experiences, and methods to Islam, all defined by a particular cultural context, and to teach Muslims what their own sacred scripture really means and what the status and reality of the Qur'an are.

On the Islamic side, Jewish and Christian scriptures have rarely been studied seriously and have been dealt with by many contemporary Muslim thinkers under the category of abrogated texts, *mansūkh*, with which one does not have to bother. Some have in fact dealt with the Bible in a manner that is in sharp contrast to the dignified language of the Qur'an where all sacred scriptures are mentioned with great respect. The long tradition of exegesis and discussion of the meaning of *naskh* or abrogation have rarely been seriously pursued and applied by present-day Muslim scholars dealing with Christian-Islamic dialogue. While many Christian students of the Qur'an seek to impugn the sacrosanct character of the text in Muslim eyes—by comparing the text to that of the Bible, which has been reduced for many in the West to a historical document of human inspiration or of partly divine inspiration interpreted in human terms—most Muslims are happy to discuss the Christian scriptures as simply abrogated or as humanly altered, as is also claimed by so many modernized Christians themselves.

Such attitudes and approaches leave out of consideration the most crucial and essential issues which must be resolved if there is to be better mutual understanding. What is the sense of the sacred as it applies to scripture in the Christian case and in the Muslim perspective? Wherein do they differ? How does the role of the Bible in the Christian perspective resemble and differ from the role of the Qur'an in Islam? These and many other questions need to be addressed more profoundly from both sides. Christians cannot create better understanding of Islam by destroying the sacrosanct nature of the Qur'an through the application of Western methods irrelevant to Islam any more than Muslims can gain a better understanding of Christianity by simply dismissing the Bible as abrogated or distorted by human interventions. Muslims in fact need to know that there are people in the West, both Jewish and Christian, who hold views concerning sacred scripture which are close to those of Muslims. Regrettably, until recently such groups have in general not been among those interested in Christian-Islamic dialogue.

IV

The fourth question concerns sacred language. The lack of understanding by most Christians of the significance of Arabic as the sacred language of Islam is related directly to the fact that Christianity has no sacred language of its own. Rather, it has several liturgical languages ranging from the Aramaic spoken by Christ and still used in the Christian mass among the Assyrians of Iraq and western Iran to Greek, Latin, Slavic, and even Arabic itself as used by Arab Christians. Not enough theological attention has been paid in Christian circles to the difference between sacred, liturgical, and vernacular languages and their role in the economy of different religious worlds. This has been due partly to the lack of appreciation by followers of one religion of where the sacred is to be found in the other religion, and partly to the difference in the structure and form of the Christian and Islamic revelations.

There is also a lack of parallelism in relation to this issue between Islam and Christianity as a result of the fact that in the present-day context Islam is not strong enough politically, economically and militarily to interfere in the life of the West, Christian or otherwise, while the reverse is obviously not true. Muslims had no influence whatsoever in the decision of the Catholic Church to discontinue the Latin mass, but Christian as well as so-called humanistic and secular missionaries functioning in the Islamic world have played a considerable role over the past century and a half in seeking to limit the spread of Qur'anic Arabic through a thousand and one programs both outside and within the Arab world. These attempts have not gone unnoticed by Muslims and constitute a major stumbling block in Christian-Islamic understanding. Christians who are earnest in their attempt to create better Christian-Islamic relations should put aside political machinations and study the meaning of sacred language as understood not only by Muslims but also by orthodox Jews. It is also important for Muslims to comprehend the role of liturgical languages in Christianity in contrast to the use of Arabic as the sacred language of Islam.

V

Another important question, which is related to how the sacred is situated differently within the structure of the two religions, is that of sacred law in general and in particular sexuality as governed by sacred law. It is now fairly well known that the very concept of law in Islam differs from what is prevalent in the West and that sacred law in Christianity refers to the spiritual and moral principles enunciated by Christ, whereas the sacred law, *sharīʾa* in Islam involves not only principles but also their application to daily life in the form of legal codifications. It is now necessary to bring out further the human, social, and political implications of this theological difference in the understanding of law so as to permit a better mutual understanding between the two communities. Only then can there be a change in the current situation in which many in the West criticize Islam for holding on to rigid laws while times change, as if time rather than God's Will were the ultimate determining factor of human life,[6] while Muslims continue to criticize Christians because they seem to have no immutable laws at all.

No issue in this domain is as controversial as sexuality, considered sacred in Islam and a consequence of original sin by the mainstream of Western Christian theology. For over a millennium Christians have viewed Muslims as hedonists and Muslims have loathed the Christian attitude toward sexuality as unnatural and against God's plan for His creation. Each religion emphasizes one aspect of the complex reality of sexuality, and there seems to be no way of reconciliation save by pointing to the fact that sexuality is a reality with different and contrasting aspects. It can lead the soul to God as well as to dispersion and perdition. Each religion appears to have chosen one aspect of this reality and made it central without neglecting the other aspect completely.[7]

Mutual misunderstanding on this point is further aggravated by the collapse of traditional Christian sexual ethics in the West with all its latent consequences for the whole social fabric. For centuries Christian missionaries compared and contrasted the chaste, monogamous Christian marriage with the "immoral" polygamy of Muslims and depicted the Islamic East in terms of harems and concubines. Today, however, there are some practices in the West, even among still nominal Christians, in comparison to which the wildest depictions of the harem of some pasha in "orientalist" literature appear as tame as the description of monastic scenes. All of this has added further confusion to a major issue which needs to be studied not only sociologically and anthropologically, as has been the case for the most part until now, but also theologically in a dialogical context.

VI

The sixth point of great importance in the Christian-Islamic dialogue that needs to be mentioned here is the life of Christ as seen in the two religions. Paradoxically, theological christology is not as acute a problem as his historical life. Islamic christology actually resembles certain forms of early Christian christology, such as the Ebionite, which were discussed and rejected by the magesterium and which can now be discussed anew in an intra- as well as interreligious context. The much more difficult problem, if the two religions are taken seriously, is the historical life of Christ.

If one rejects the life of Jesus as recorded in the gospels and accepted in Christian tradition for nearly two thousand years, then there is of course no problem to discuss. Nor would there be an obstacle to Islamic-Christian understanding if the Qur'anic account of the life of Jesus the Son of Mary were to be brushed aside as simply a distorted version which reached Arabia and was then incorporated into the Qur'an. If, however, one takes the claims of the two sides seriously, accepting both the traditional Christian account and the Qur'anic account as true, then there is an obvious problem especially as far as the end of that life is concerned (setting aside for the moment the question of filial relationship and the incarnation). Was Christ crucified or was he taken alive to Heaven and not crucified as asserted by Islam? Here one faces what seems to be an insurmountable obstacle. While this problem may have been placed there providentially to preserve both Christianity and Islam as distinct religions, it is nevertheless an issue which must be confronted squarely and discussed seriously.

Modern epistemologies, based upon empiricism and a one-to-one correspondence between the knowing subject and the known object, would be at a loss to find a way out of this impasse. Traditional epistemologies which take into account both levels of reality of consciousness—that is, the knowing subject and the known object—however, could provide a solution were they to be taken seriously. One could say that such a major cosmic event as the end of the earthly life of Christ could in fact be "seen" and "known" in more than one way, and that it is God's will that Christianity should be given to "see" that end in one way and Islam in another. Be that as it may, it is essential to consider this question theologically and metaphysically in any serious Christian-Islamic dialogue even if the solution proposed cannot be accepted easily by those who find themselves bound to the epistemological premises of rationalism and empiricism.

VII

The seventh and final point to be mentioned here is perhaps the most subtle and elusive one. It concerns that silent and often unnoticed partner in Christian-Islamic dialogue, namely, modernism and, in increasingly important ways, postmodernism, phenomena which have influenced and continue to influence Christianity much more than Islam. When various religious questions are discussed in a dialogical situation, it is often forgotten that the Christian position is not one of a St. Augustine or St. Bernard or even Martin Luther or John Wesley. Many ideas and practices which are now defended as Christian are the result of antireligious and secularist forces of modernism before which certain Christian thinkers have retreated or which they have joined during the past few centuries. There is in fact no serious dialogue possible without taking this fact into account, especially since for several centuries most Christians have identified themselves completely with modern Western civilization and many continue to do so today.

Muslims are fully aware that Christian missionaries often have tried to defend the superiority of Christianity in many parts of the world with the help of modern medicine and technology, as if the superiority of the message of Christ were proven by the fact that vaccines were developed in France in the nineteenth century. It is only recently with the collapse of the modern world view and the catastrophes brought upon the whole ecosystem of the planet by modern technology that many Christians gradually are beginning to distance themselves from a civilization which was once Christian but can no longer lay claim to such a status. Still it is essential to be aware of the fact that the silent partner, modernism, continues to be present in Christian-Islamic dialogues, whether they be theological or political.

Such awareness is difficult to attain because almost unconsciously many Christians, including a large number of theologians, identify the historical processes which Western civilization has experienced as the inevitable historical process which is to be experienced sooner or later by every other society on the surface of the earth. From this perspective there must be a period of rationalism and humanism, leading to the separation of religion from many domains of life and of various branches of knowledge from theology. In most cases where dialogue is carried out, Western Christian partners tend to reify their own experience and judge Islam accordingly. This attitude creates a particularly difficult barrier to overcome at a time when the Islamic world, representing a civilization as well as a religion, is seeking to assert its own identity. It thereby wants to follow a path different from that followed by the West from its Christian medieval phase to Renaissance humanism, to the scientific revolution, through the secularization of knowledge with the rise of rationalism and empiricism, the Age of Enlightenment, Romanticism, the Age of Ideology, and up to the present century. The very assertion of an Islamic identity by Muslims today thus poses a challenge to Christian-Islamic dialogue based on earlier assumptions of the identification of Christianity with Western civilization including its modern developments and the belief that there is but one historical process to be followed by all civilizations and human collectivities if they are to survive historically. It is a challenge by no means insurmountable but which must be understood in all its profound dimensions including the acceptance of the presence of this third partner in Christian-Islamic dialogues, a partner which is outwardly silent but which influences deeply the ongoing religious and theological dialogue.

Concluding Remarks

It might appear strange that such basic questions as the nature of God, the soul, eschatology, the status and meaning of creation and the natural order, and many other issues have not been mentioned here. The reason is that although these are basic issues, and in the case of "the theology of nature" a most timely one, they have either been discussed in various sources already or can be resolved fairly easily by turning to the rich theological traditions of the two religions wherein they have been discussed extensively. If these discussions were fully understood, such issues would not pose obstacles to mutual Christian-Islamic understanding.

The seven points mentioned above explicitly, however, are more divisive and require greater theological attention at the present moment in the history of Christian-Islamic dialogue. In drawing the attention of those seriously involved in religious dialogue to these issues, it is my hope that they can be more satisfactorily addressed and treated. Such a treatment would in turn be of great assistance to mutual understanding if one were to respect both the Christian and Islamic positions in the spirit of authentic ecumenism to which Willem Bijlefeld has devoted so much of his scholarly life.

NOTES

1. F. Schuon has dealt with this subject and also the more general questions of the relation between Christianity and Islam in many of his works such as *Christianity/Islam—Essays on Esoteric Ecumenism*, trans. G. Polit (Bloomington, Ind.: World Wisdom Books, 1985); *In the Face of the Absolute* (Bloomington, Ind.: World Wisdom Books, 1989); and his earliest and most significant book in the field of comparative religions, *The Transcendent Unity of Religions* (Wheaton, Ill.: The Theosophical Publishing House, 1984). He has also dealt with the Islamic attitude to Christian doctrine of the nature of the Divinity and vice versa in his *Understanding Islam*, trans. D.M. Matheson (London: Allen & Unwin, 1975). See also "Form and Substance in Religions," in his *Islam and the Perennial Philosophy*, trans. P. Hobson (London: Festival of the World of Islam, 1976), esp. pp. 17 ff., where specific comparisons of the profoundest nature are made between Christian and Islamic doctrines.

See also S.H. Nasr, "The Islamic View of Christianity," in *Christianity Among World Religious*, ed. Hans Küng and Jurgen Moltmann, *Concilium* (1986): 3–12; "The *Philosophia perennis* and the Study of Religion" in his *Need for a Sacred Science* (forthcoming); and *Religion and Religions: The Challenge of Living in a Multi-religious World*, The Loy H. Witherspoon Lecture in Religious Studies (Charlotte: University of North Carolina, 1985).

2. Many Western Islamicists have discussed the Islamic doctrine of the Divine Nature in comparison with Christian teachings without being themselves theologians, while more recently certain Christian theologians such as H. Küng have dealt with the same subject without being Islamicists. But Christian theologian scholars who have been serious Christian thinkers as well as being well versed in Islamic thought have been relatively rare. That is why the work of scholars such as those cited here stands out in any discussion of the theological dimension of the Christian-Islamic dialogue.

3. In the Qur'an (S. 61:6) Jesus says, "O children of Israel! Lo! I am the messenger of Allah unto you, confirming that which was (revealed) before me, in the Torah, and bringing good tidings of a messenger who cometh after me, whose name is the Praised One (Aḥmad)" (Pickthall translation). Aḥmad, the praised one, is *periklytos* in Greek and Muslim commentators through the centuries have believed that the term *paracletos* in the gospels is an alternation of *periklytos* and that Christ referred directly to the Prophet of Islam when he spoke of the coming of the Paraclete. This has been dealt with extensively by H. Corbin in many of his works, especially *En Islam iranien* (Paris: Gallimard, 1970–71), 1: 171, 4: 280. See also M. Lings, *Symbol and Archetype* (Cambridge, U.K.: Quinta Essentia, 1991), pp. 39–40.

4. This is not the place to deal with this complicated issue, which involves the view of history of the Abrahamic religions, possessing certain significant differences among themselves; the traditional doctrine of cycles as found in Hinduism; the ancient doctrine of cosmic cycles as they were separated from their metaphysical basis in antiquity and presented as the simple repetition of cosmic events; and the modern idea of a secularized historical time marching forward either indefinitely or toward some secularized form of religious eschatology as one finds in Marxism. See S.H. Nasr, *Knowledge and the Sacred* (Albany: State University of New York Press, 1981) chap. 7, addressing the metaphysical foundation of the rapport between eternity and time and the question of cyclic versus linear conceptions of history and providing in the notes many references to works on this complicated and at the same time crucial subject.

5. Such views have been espoused even by those like Kenneth Cragg who have claimed and in fact shown some sympathy for Islam and Muslims.

6. On this complex and at the same time crucial question see "The *Sharīʿa* and Changing Historical Conditions," in S.H. Nasr, *Islamic Life and Thought* (Albany: State University of New York Press, 1981), pp. 24–30.

7. This question has been examined in depth by F. Schuon in his discussion on "The Problem of Modern Divergencies," in his *Christianity/Islam*, pp. 109–17.

CONTRIBUTORS

+ ☽

Mahmud Mustafa Ayoub, professor of Islamic studies, Temple University, served from 1978 to 1987 as a research associate at the Centre for Religious Studies, University of Toronto. He has published extensively on Islam. His books include: *Redemptive Suffering in Islam: A Study of the Devotional Aspects of 'Ashūrā' in Twelver Shī'ism*; *The Qur'an and Its Interpreters*, vol. 1; and *The Great Tiding, An Annotated Translation of the Thirtieth Part of the Qur'an*.

Willem A. Bijlefeld, distinguished senior professor at Hartford Seminary, edited *The Muslim World* from 1967 to 1992. His extensive publications on Islam include *Islam as a Post-Christian Religion: An Inquiry into the Theological Evaluation of Islam, Mainly in the Twentieth Century* and the forthcoming *Winding Quest for a "Christian Theology of Islam."*

Issa J. Boullata, professor of Arabic language and literature, Institute of Islamic Studies, McGill University, served as editor of *The Muslim World*, *Al-ʿArabiyya*, and *Mundus Arabicus*. His translations include *Wallace Stevens* (into Arabic); *Flight Against Time* (from Arabic); *Ahmad Amin: My Life* (from Arabic with an introduction). His books include *Modern Arab Poets, 1950–1975*; *Critical Perspectives on Modern Arabic Literature* (ed.); and *Al-Rumānṭīqiyya wa Maʿālimuhā fī al-Shiʿr al-ʿArabī al-Ḥadīth* (Outlines of Romanticism in Modern Arabic Poetry).

John B. Carman, Parkman Professor of divinity and professor of comparative religion, Harvard Divinity School, Harvard University, is the author of several books and numerous articles in such areas as the comparative study of religion and Christian theological interpretation of religion. Among his books are *The Theology of Ramanuja: An Essay in Interreligious Understanding*; *Village Christians and Hindu Culture: Study of a Rural Church in Andhra Pradesh, South India* (with P. Y. Luke); and *Majesty and Mercy in Comparative Religion: Polar Opposites in the Concept of God* (forthcoming).

Kenneth Cragg, former professor of Arabic and Islamics at Hartford Seminary and editor of *The Muslim World*, was Warden of St. Augustine's College in Canterbury, England and Bye-Fellow of Caius College, Cambridge. He has published translations from Taha Husain, Kamil Husain, and Muḥammad ʿAbduh and is author of numerous works on Islamic and Christian themes, including

The Theology of Unity, a translation of Muḥammad ʿAbduh's theological work *Kitāb al-Tawḥīd* with an Introduction (coauthored); *The Event of the Qur'an*; *The Mind of the Qur'an*; *The Call of the Minaret*; *Jesus and the Muslim*; *The House of Islam*; *Muhammad and the Christian*; and *The Pen and the Faith*.

Frederick Mathewson Denny, professor of religious studies at the University of Colorado, Boulder, has published *Islamic Ritual Practices: A Slide Set and Teacher's Guide* (with Abdulaziz A. Sachedina); *An Introduction to Islam*; and *Islam and the Muslim Community*.

Johann Haafkens, secretary and general adviser to the Project for Christian-Muslim Relations in Africa (formerly the Islam in Africa Project), has published *Chants Musulmans en Peul: Textes de l'héritage religieux de la communauté Musulmane de Maroua, Cameroun, publiés avec introduction et traduction*.

Wadi Z. Haddad, professor of Islamic studies, Hartford Seminary, has been an editor of *The Muslim World* since 1980. His publications include *Kitāb al-Muʿtamad fī uṣūl al-dīn of Abū Yaʿlā ibn al-Farrāʾ* and *The Roots of Islamic Law*, a translation of Muhammad Saʿid al-Ashmawi's *Uṣūl al-Sharīʿa* with an introduction (forthcoming).

Yvonne Yazbeck Haddad, professor of Islamic history, University of Massachusetts, Amherst, edited *The Muslim World* from 1980 to 1988. Her publications include *Islamic Values in the United States: A Comparative Study* (coauthored); *Women, Religion, and Social Change* (coedited); *Contemporary Islam and the Challenge of History*; *The Islamic Understanding of Death and Resurrection*; *The Islamic Impact* (coedited); and *Mission to America: Five Islamic Sectarian Communities in North America* (coauthored).

David A. Kerr, director of the D.B. Macdonald Center and professor of Islamic studies at Hartford Seminary, has published *Jews, Christians and Muslims* (ed.) and *The Life of Muhammad* (forthcoming).

Donald P. Little, professor and director of the Institute of Islamic Studies, McGill University, has published *An Introduction to Mamluk Historiography*; *A Catalogue of the Islamic Documents from Ḥaram al-Sharīf in Jerusalem*; *History and Historiography of the Mamluks*; and *Essays on Islamic Civilization* (ed.).

Roland E. Miller, professor of religious studies, Luther Northwestern Theological Seminary, has published *The Mappila Muslims of Kerala: A Study in Islamic Trends* and *The Sending of God*.

Seyyed Hossein Nasr, university professor of Islamic studies, George Washington University, is president of the Foundation for Traditional Studies. His publications include *Ideals and Realities of Islam*; *Islamic Art and Spirituality*; *Islam* *and the Plight of Modern Man*; *Traditional Islam in the Modern World*; *Sufi Essays*; *Islamic Life and Thought*; and *Introduction to Islamic Cosmological Doctrines*.

Jorgen S. Nielsen, director, Centre for the Study of Christian-Muslim Relations, Selly Oak Colleges, Birmingham, U.K., has published *Secular Justice in an Islamic State: Mazalim under the Bahri Mamluks, 662/1264–789/1387*; *Muslims in Britain: An Annotated Bibliography* (with Daniele Joly); and *Islamic law and Its Significance for the Situation of Muslim Minorities in Europe*.

Sulayman S. Nyang, professor and director of the Department of African Studies, Howard University, has published *Islam, Christianity and African Identity* and *Reflections on the Human Condition*. He is former editor of the *American Journal of Islamic Studies*.

James E. Royster, associate professor of religious studies at Cleveland State University, has published "Muhammad as Teacher and Exemplar," *The Muslim World* (1978); "Sufi Shaykh as Psychotherapist," *Psychologiqia* (1979); and "Bondage and Freedom," *Darshana International* (1980).

Daniel J. Sahas, associate professor, University of Waterloo, has published *Icon and Logos: Sources in Eighth-Century Iconoclasm*; *John of Damascus on Islam, the "Heresy of the Ishmaelites*; and *Katechesis: He horimansis tou somatos*.

Annemarie Schimmel, professor of Indo-Muslim culture at Harvard University and professor of Islamic studies at the University of Bonn, has published *Das Mysterium der Zahl: Numerology and Customs Connected with Numbers*; *Islam in the Indian Subcontinent*; *Pearls from the Indus: Studies in Sindhi Culture*; *Stern und Blume: Symbolism in Persian Mystical Poetry*; and *Pakistan, ein Schloss mit tausend Toren*.

Olaf Schumann, dean of the Faculty of Theology, University of Hamburg, has published *Der Christus der Muslime: Christologische Aspekte in der arabisch-islamischen Literatur*.

Hadia Dajani-Shakeel, associate professor of Middle East and Islamic studies, University of Toronto, has published "Jerusalem in the Consciousness of the Counter-Crusade," in *The Meeting of Two Worlds: Cultural Exchange Between East and West during the Period of the Crusades*; "Peace in the Qur'an and Prophetic Tradition," in *Exploring Justice and Peace: Religious Perspectives*; "Images of the Franks in Medieval Arabic Writings," *Hamdard Islamicus* (1985).

Jan Slomp, moderator of the Islam in Europe Committee of the Conference of European Churches and the Council of Roman Catholic Episcopal Conferences in Europe, is also moderator of the Islam Committee of the Netherlands Council of Churches. He served as editor of the missiological journal *Wereld en Zend-*

ing (1977–88) and has published numerous articles in English, German, French, Dutch, Spanish, and Indonesian on Christian-Muslim relations, Islam in the Netherlands, and Islam in Europe.

Jane I. Smith, vice president and dean of academic affairs, Iliff School of Theology, has published *The Islamic Understanding of Death and Resurrection* (coauthored); *Women in Contemporary Muslim Society* (ed.); *The Precious Pearl* (translation with notes of Abū Ḥamīd al-Ghazālī's *al-Durra al Fākhira*); *The Concept of 'Islam' in the History of Qur'anic Exegesis*; and *Mission to America: Five Islamic Sectarian Communities in North America* (coauthored).

R. Marston Speight, director of the Office on Christian-Muslim Relations of the National Council of the Churches of Christ in the U.S.A. and adjunct professor of Islamic studies, Hartford Seminary, is coauthor (with Kenneth Cragg) of *Islam from Within*, and author of *Christian-Muslim Relations: An Introduction for Christians in the United States of America*; and *God is One: The Way of Islam*.

Mark N. Swanson, currently teaching at the Evangelical Theological Seminary in Cairo, has published "A Study of Twentieth-Century Commentary on Sūrat al-Nūr (24): 27–33," in *The Muslim World* (1984).

Christian W. Troll, currently teaches at the Centre for the Study of Islam and Christian-Muslim Relations, Selly Oak Colleges, Birmingham, U.K.

Harold S. Vogelaar, professor at Lutheran Seminary, Chicago, has published "Middle East Mosaic: An Egyptian Pope" and "Dr. M. Kamil Husayn: Reflections on Science and Religion."

Jacques Waardenburg, professor of science of religion at the University of Lausanne (Switzerland), is author of *L'Islam dans le miroir de l'Occident*; *Les Universités dans le Monde arabe actuel*; *Classical Approaches to the Study of Religion: Aims, Methods, and Theories of Research*; *Zien met anderman's ogen*; *Reflections on the Study of Religion, Including an Essay on the Work of Gerardus van der Leeuw*; and *Islam: Norm, ideaal en werkelijkheid*.

Antonie Wessels, professor and dean of the Faculty of Theology at the Free University, is author of *A Modern Biography of Muhammad: A Critical Study of Muhammad Husayn Haykal's Hayat Muhammad*; *De nieuwe arabische mens: Moslims en christenen in het Arabische Oosten*; *De moslimse naaste: op weg naar een theologie van de islam*; and *Twee watermeloenen in een hand: de acteurs in het libanese drama*.

SELECT BIBLIOGRAPHY

+ ☽

Abadan-Unat, N. "Turkish Migrants to Europe (1960–1975)." In Abadan-Unat, *Turkish Workers in Europe 1960–1975*. Leiden: E.J. Brill, 1976.

Abdel-Wahab, H.H. "Coup d'oeil général sur les apports ethniques étrangers en Tunisie." *Cahiers de Tunisie* 18, nos. 69–70 (1970): 151–69.

Abdullah, M.S. *Geschichte des Islam in Deutschland*. Graz: Styria, 1981.

Abdul Latif, Sayyid. *Bases of Islamic Culture*. Hyderabad: Institute of Indo-Middle East Culture, 1959.

Abd-ul-Massih. *Au Seuil de l'Islam*. Yaounde: Éditions Clé, 1965.

———. *Islam and Christianity: 90 Questions and Answers*. Ibadan: Daystar Press, 1967.

Abraham, Sameer Y., and Nabeel Abraham, eds. *Arabs in the New World: Studies on Arab-American Communities*. Detroit: Wayne State University Center for Urban Studies, 1983.

Abū al-Magd, Aḥmad Kamāl. "Bal al-Islām wa-al-ʿUrūba maʿan" (Rather Islam and Arabism together). *Majallat al-ʿArabī* 264 (October 1980).

Abū-Laban, Baha. *An Olive Branch on the Family Tree: The Arabs in Canada*. Toronto: McClelland and Stewart, 1980.

Abū-Manneh, Butrus. "The Georgians in Jerusalem in the Mamluk Period." In Amnon Cohen and Gabriel Baer, eds., *Egypt and Palestine: A Millennium of Association (868–1948)*. New York: St. Martin's Press, 1984.

Abū Qurra, Theodore. "Letter to David the Jacobite." In Qusṭanṭīn Bāshā, *Mayāmir Thawudūrus Abī Qurra usquf Ḥarrān* (The epistles of Theodore Abū Qurra the Bishop of Harran). Tripoli, Lebanon: n.p., 1904.

Abū Shama, ʻAbd al-Raḥmān al-Makdisī. *Kitāb al-Rawḍatayn fī Akhbār al-Dawlatayn al-Nūriyya wa ʾl-Ṣalāḥiyya*. Cairo: Al-Muʾassasa al-Miṣriyya al-ʿĀmma li ʾl-Taʾlīf wa ʾl-Tarjama wa ʾl-Nashr, 1962.

Adams, Charles J. "The History of Religions and the Study of Islam." In Joseph M. Kitagawa, ed., *The History of Religions: Essays on the Problem of Understanding*. Chicago: University of Chicago Press, 1967.

———. "Islamic Religious Tradition." In L. Binder, ed., *The Study of the Middle East*. New York-London: John Wiley and Sons, 1976.

———. "Islam and Christianity: The Opposition of Similarities." In Roger M. Savory and Dionisius Agius, eds., *Logos Islamikos*. Toronto: Pontifical Institute of Mediaeval Studies, 1984.

Affifi, A.E. *The Mystical Philosophy of Muhyid Din-Ibnul ʿArabi*. London: Cambridge University Press, 1939.

Ageron, C.R. "L'immigration maghrebine en France: un survol historique." In M. Morsy, ed., *L'Islam en Europe à l'époque moderne*. Paris: Sindbad, 1985.

Aguilar, Emilio G. "The Second International Muslim-Christian Congress of Cordoba (March 21–27, 1977)." In Richard W. Rousseau, ed., *Christianity and Islam: the Struggling Dialogue*. Scranton: Ridge Row Press, University of Scranton, 1985.

Ahmad, Mumtaz. "Islamic Fundamentalism in South Asia: The Jamaat-i-Islami and the Tablighi Jamaat of South Asia." In Martin E. Marty and R. Scott Appleby, eds. *Fundamentalism Observed*. Chicago and London: University of Chicago Press, 1991.

Ahsan, M. M. *Islam, Faith and Practice*. Nairobi: Islamic Foundation, 1985.

Ahwānī, Aḥmad Fu'ād al-. *Al-Taʿlīm fī Ra'y al-Qābīsī min ʿulamā' al-Qarn al-Rābiʿ* (Teaching, according to al-Qābīsī, a fourth-century scholar). Cairo: Maṭbaʿat Lajnat al-Ta'līf wa-al-Tarjama wa-al-Nashr, 1364/1945.

______. *Al-Taʿlīm fī Ra'y al-Qābīsī min al-Alūsī, Abū al-Faḍl Shihāb al-Dīn Maḥmūdī, Rūḥ al-Maʿānī fī Tafsīr al-Qur'ān al-ʿAẓīm wa 'l-Sabʿ al-Mathānī* (Teaching according to al-Qābīsī in Abū al-Faḍl Shihāb al-Dīn Maḥmūdī al-Alūsī's 'the essential meaning in the interpretation of the Gracious Qur'an and the seven couplets'). 30 vols. Beirut: Dār al-Fikr, 1398/1979, vol. 10.

Akbarabādī, Saʿīd Aḥmad. "Hindustān ki Sharʿī Ḥaithiyyāt" (The status of India in Islamic Law). *Burhān* (Delhi) (July–September 1966): 190–97.

Alford, Terry. *Prince Among Slaves: The Story of an African Prince Sold in the American South*. New York: Oxford University Press, 1977.

Ali, Amir. *Islam or Farrakhanism?*. Chicago: The Institute of Islamic Information, 1991.

Ali, Fachry, and Bahtiar Effendi, eds. *Merambah Jalan Bar Islam* (Clearing the path for Islam). Bandung: n.p., 1986.

Ally, M. M. "History of Muslims in Britain, 1850–1980." Master's thesis, University of Birmingham, 1981.

Amīnī, Muḥammad Taqī. *Murasalāt, ʿIlmī aur Dīnī* (Correspondence: scientific and religious). Pt. 1. Aligarh: Aligarh University Faculty of Religion, 1986.

Anawati, Georges C. "An Assessment of the Christian-Islamic Dialogue." In Kail C. Ellis, ed., *The Vatican, Islam, and the Middle East*. Syracuse, N.Y.: Syracuse University Press, 1987.

______. "Polémique, apologie et dialogue islamo-chrétiens: positions classiques et positions contemporaines." *Euntes Docete* (Urbaniana, Rome) 22 (1969): 375–451.

______. "L'Islam à l'heure du Concile: Prolégomènes à un dialogue islamo-chrétien." *Angelicum* 41 (1914): 145–68.

Andrae, S. Tor. *In the Garden of Myrtles*. Trans. Birgitta Sharpe. Albany: State University of New York Press, 1988.

Ansari, Maboud, "Iranians in America: Continuity and Change." In Vincent N. Parillo, ed., *Rethinking Today's Minorities*. Contributions in Sociology, no. 93. New York: Greenwood Press, 1991.

Anshari, H. E. Saifuddin. *Kritik atas faham dan gerakan "Pembaharuan" Drs. Nurcholis Madjid* (A critique of the concepts and movement of "Renewal" of Drs. Nurcholis Madjid). Bandung: Bula Sabit, 1973.

______. *Piagam Jakarta 22 Juni 1945*. Bandung: Pustaka, 1981.

Antes, Peter. "Dialog oder doppelter Monolog?" In Udo Tworuschka, ed., *Gottes ist der Orient, Gottes is der Okzident*. Cologne-Vienna: Bohlau, 1991.

______. "Theologie als Dialoghindernis?" In Ludwig Hagemann and Ernst Pulsfort, eds., *Festschrift fur A. Th. Khoury zum 60 Geburtstag*. Altenberge: Telos, 1990.

Aquinas, St. Thomas. *Summa Theologica: Complete English Edition in Five Volumes*. Maryland: Fathers of the English Dominican Province, 1981, vol. 4.

Arkoun, Mohammed. "Émergences et problèms dans le monde musulman contemporain (1960–1985)." *Islamochristiana* 12 (1986): 135–61.

Arnaldez, Roger. *Jésus fils de Marie, prophète de l'Islam*. Paris: Desclée, 1980.

Arnold, T.W. *Preaching of Islam: A History of the Propagation of the Muslim Faith*. London: Constable, 1935.

Asad, Muhammad, trans. *The Message of the Qur'an*. Gibraltar: Dar al-Andalus, 1980.

ʿAshmawī, Muḥammad Saʿīd al-. *Al-Islām al-Siyāsī* (Political Islam). Cairo: Sīna li-al-Nashr, 1987.

Aṣlaḥ, Muḥammad. *Tadhkirat-i Shuʿara-i Kashmīr* (Anthology of the poets of Kashmir). Ed. Sayyid Husamuddin Rashdi. 5 vols. Karachi: Iqbal Academy, 1969–70, vol. 2.

ʿAttār, Fariduddīn, *Musibatnāmā* (Chronicle of crises). Ed. N. Wisal. Tehran: Zawwar, 1338sh/1959, chap. 36.

Austin, Allan D. *African Muslims in Ante Bellum America*. New York: Garland, 1984.

ʿAwda, ʿAbd al-Qādir. *Al-Islām wa Awḍāʿunā al-Siyāsiyya* (Islam and our political condition). Cairo: Maktabat Wahba, 1978; Beirut: Mu'assasat al-Risāla, 1980.

ʿAwwā, Muḥammad Salīm al-. *Fī al-Niẓām al-Siyāsī li al-Dawla al-Islāmiyya* (The political system in the Islamic State). Cairo: Dār al-Shurūq, 1989.

Ayoub, Mahmoud Mustafa. "The Death of Jesus, Reality or Delusion? A Study of the Death of Jesus in Tafsir Literature." *The Muslim World* 70 (1980): 91–121.

———. "The Word of God in Islam." In N.M. Vapori, ed. *Orthodox Christians and Muslims*. Brookline, Mass: Holy Cross Orthodox Press, 1986.

Baar, Marius. *Das Abendland am Scheideweg*. Asslar: Schulte and Gerth, 1979. English trans. *The Unholy War*. Trans. Victor Carpenter. Nashville, Tenn.: T. Nelson, 1980.

Bagir, Haidar, ed. *Satu Islam: sebuah dilemma* (Unified Islam: A dilemma). Bandung: Mizan, 1986.

Bahr, Samira. *Al-Aqbat fī al-Hayat al-Siyāsiyya al-Misriyya* (The Copts in Egyptian political life). Cairo: Maktabat al-Anglo al-Misriyya, 1979.

———. *Al-Madkhal li Dirāsat alʿAqliyyāt* (An introduction to philosophical studies). Cairo: Maktabat al-Anglo al-Misriyya, 1982.

Bakri, Abu ʿUbayd al-. "Kitab al-Masalik wa-l-Mamalik (The book of systems and kingdoms)." In *Description de l'Afrique Septentrionale par Abou-Obeid-el-Bekri*. Algiers: Imprimerie du Gouvernement, 1957.

Balic, Smail. "The Image of Jesus in Contemporary Islamic Theology." In Annemarie Schimmel and Abdaljavad Falaturi, eds., *We Believe in One God*. New York: Seabury Press, 1979.

Bannā, Ḥassan al-. *Majmūʿat Rasā'il al-Imām al-Shahīd Ḥasan al-Bannā* (A collection of the treatises of the Martyred Imam Ḥasan al-Bannā). Beirut: Al-Mu'assa al-Islāmiyya li'l-Tibaʿa wa'l-Ṣiḥahāfa wa'l-Nashr, 1980.

Baqillānī, Abū Bakr Muḥammad Ibn al-Ṭayyib al-. *al-Inṣāf* (The just treatment [of theology]). Ed. Muhammad Zahid ibn al-Hasan al-Kawthari. Cairo: Maktab Nashr al-Thaqafa al-Islamiyya, 1950.

———. *Iʿjaz al-Qur'an* (The inimitability of the Qur'an). Ed. Amad Saqr. Cairo: Dar al-Maʿarif bi-Masr, 1954.

———. *Kitab al-Tamhid*. Ed. Richard J. McCarthy, S.J. Beirut: Librairie Orientale, 1957.

Barbosa, Duarte. *The Book Duarte Barbosa*. Trans. M.W. Dames. 2 vols. London: Hakluyt Society, 1918.

Barrett, David. *World Christian Encyclopedia*. Nairobi: Oxford University Press, 1982.

Barth, Karl. *Kirchiche Dogmatik*. Vol. 1, pt. 1. Munich: Kaiser Verlag, 1935. Vol. 1, pt. 2. Zurich: Evang. Verlag, 1948. English edition *Church Dogmatics*. Vol. 1, pt. 1. Trans. G.T. Thomson. Edinburgh: T. & T. Clark, 1936. Vol. 1, pt. 2. Intro. Helmut Gollwitzer; ed. and trans. G.W. Bromiley. New York: Harper & Row, 1962.

Bayḍāwī, Abū Saʿīd (Abd Allāh Nāṣir al-Dīn al-. *Anwār al-Tanzīl* (The lights of revelation). Cairo: Dar al-Kutub al-ʿArabiyya al-Kubra, n.d.

Becker, Carl H. "Christliche Polemik und Islamische Dogmenbildung." *Zeitschrifte for Assyrioloie* 26 (1912): 175–95.

Benda, Harry J. *The Crescent and the Rising Sun*. Bandung and The Hague: W. van Hoeve, 1958.

Bennabi, Malek. *Islam in History and Society*. Chicago: Kazi Publications, 1988.

______. *Le phénomène coranique: Essai d'une théorie sur le Coran*. Alger: Sharikat al-Nahḍa li ʾl-Ṭibāʿa wa ʾl-Nashr, 1964.

______ *The Qurʾanic Phenomenon*. Chicago: Kazi Publications, 1988.

Benton, John. *Self and Society in Medieval France. The Memoires of Guibert of Nogent*. New York: Harper, 1970.

Berchem, Max van. *Matériaux pour un corpus inscriptionum arabicarum*. Cairo: L'Institut Français d'Archéologie Orientale, 1922.

Bijlefeld, Willem Abraham. *De Islam als Na-Christelijke Religie: een Onderzoek naar de Theologische Beoordeling van de Islam, in het bijzonder in de Twintigste Eeuw* (Islam as a Post-Christian Religion: An Inquiry into the Theological Evaluation of Islam, Mainly in the Twentieth Century), with a summary in English. The Hague: van Keulen, 1959.

Bilz, Jacob. *Die Trinitätslehre des heiligen Johannes von Damaskus*. Forschungen zur christlichen Literatur- und Dogmengeschichte IX, 3. Paderborn: Ferdinand Schöningh, 1909.

Binder, Leonard, ed. *The Study of the Middle East*. New York-London: John Wiley and Sons, 1976.

Bishop, Eric F.F. "The Jerusalem that Now Is." *International Review of Missions* 37 (1948): 427–36.

Bishrī, Ṭāriq al-. *Al-Muslimūn waʾl-Aqbāṭ fī iṭār al-Jamāʿ al-Waṭaniyya* (Muslims and Copts in the context of the national community). Cairo: Al-Hayʾa al-Miṣriyya al-ʿĀmma li ʾl-Kitāb, 1980.

______. "Introduction." In Muṣṭafā al-Fīqī, *Al-Aqbāt fī al-Siyāsa al-Miṣriyya: Makram ʿUbayd wa-Dawruhu fī al-Ḥaraka al-Waṭaniyya* (Copts in Egyptian politics: Makram ʿUbayd and his role in the national movement). Cairo: Dār al-Shurūq, 1985.

Blaaschke, J. "Islam und Politik unter turkischen Arbeitsmigranten." In J. Blaschke and M. van Bruinessen, eds., *Jahrbuch zur Geschichte und Gesellschaft des Vorderen und Mittleren Orients 1984*. Berlin: Express Edition, 1985.

Blackney, Raymond B. *Meister Eckhart: A Modern Translation*. New York: Harper and Row, 1941.

Blyden, Edward W. *Christianity, Islam and the Negro Race*. 1887; reprint, Edinburgh: University Press, 1967.

Boland, B.J. "Discussion on Islam in Indonesia Today." In *Studies on Islam*. Konnklijke Nederlandse Akademie van Wetenschappen. Amsterdam: North Holland Publishing Company, 1974.

______. *The Struggle of Islam in Modern Indonesia*. The Hague: M. Nijhoff, 1971.

Bonis, K.G. *Euthymiou tou Malake, metropolitou Neon Patron (Hypate) (deuteron hemisy xii hekatont.), Ta sozomena. Teuchos Bʾ. Dyo Engomiastikoi Logoi, nyn to proton ekdidomenoi, Eis ton autocratora Manuel I ton Comnenon (1143–80)* (Euthimious of Malake, Metropolitan of Neon Patron [Hypate], [the second half of the twelfth century]; Facsimile B; Two eulogies from the speeches of of Manuel I of Comnenon (1143–

80). Athens: n.p., 1949.

Bonnef, Marcel, et al. *Pantjasile—trente annes de débats politiques en Indonesie*. Paris: Ėd. de la Maison des Sciences de l'homme, 1980.

Borrmans, M. *Orientations pour un Dialogue entre Chrétiens et Musulmans*. Paris: Cerf, 1981. English translation by R. M. Speight, *Guidelines for Dialogue between Christians and Muslims*. New York: Paulist Press, 1990.

Bowers, Herman Meredith. "A Phenomenological Study of the Islamic Society of North America." Ph.D. dissertation, Southern Baptist Theological Seminary, 1989.

———. *Études sur Saʿid ibn Batriq et ses sources*. Louvain: E. Peeters, 1983.

Brenner, H. "Protestantische Orthodoxie und Islam. Die Herausforderung der turkischen Religion in Spiegel evangelischer Theologen des ausgehenden. 16. und 17. Jahrhunderts." Theological dissertation, Heidelberg University, 1986.

Breydy, Michael, ed. and trans. *Das Annalenwerk des Eutychios von Alexandrien: Ausgewählte Geschichten und Legenden kompiliert von Saʿid ibn Batriq um 935 A.D.* Louvain: E. Peeters, 1985.

Brinkmann. *Die Theosophie des Aristokritos*. Rhein, Germany: Mus. LI, 1896.

Brown, David A. *A New Threshold: Guidelines for the Churches in Their Relations with Muslim Communities*. London: British Council of Churches and the Conference of Missionary Societies of Great Britain and Ireland, 1976.

Brown, Leslie W. *The Indian Christians of St. Thomas*. Cambridge: Cambridge University Press, 1956.

Brown, Stuart E. *The Challenge of the Scriptures: The Bible and the Qurʾan*. Maryknoll, N.Y.: Orbis Books, 1989.

———. "A First Step in a Dialogue on Spirituality: Impressions of a Conference." *Islamochristiana* 12 (1987): 169–76.

Brundage, James. *The Crusades: A Documentary Survey*. Milwaukee, Wis.: Marquette University Press, 1962.

Burkle, Horst. *Missionstheologie*. Stuttgart: Kahlhammer, 1979.

Cachia, Pierre, ed., and W. Montgomery Watt, trans. *Eutychius of Alexandria: The Book of the Demonstration (Kitab al-Burhan)*. Louvain: Secrétariat du Corpus SCO, 1960–61.

Caputo, John D. *The Mystical Element in Heidegger's Thought*. Athens: Ohio University Press, 1978.

Carman, John B. "A New Assessment of the Christian Encounter with Islam." Pts. 1 and 2. *Bulletin of the Henry Martyn Institute of Islamic Studies* (Hyderabad, India; Spring 1960): 38–51 (Summer 1960): 13–32.

Carré, Olivier. *Mystique et Politique: Lecture révolutionnaire du Coran par Sayyid Qutb, Frère musulman radical*. Paris: Cerf/Presses de la Fondation Nationale des Sciences Politiques, 1984.

Carvallo, Bosco, and Dasrizal, eds. *Aspirasi Umat islam Indonesia*. Jakarta: Leppenas, 1988.

Caspar, Robert. "Pour une vision chrétienne du Coran." *Islamochristiana* 8 (1982): 25–55.

———. "Les versions arabes du dialogue entre le Catholicos Timothée 1 et le Caliphe Al-Mahdi." *Islamochristiana* 3 (1977).

Chaitanya, K. C. *A History of Malayan Literature*. New Delhi: Orient Longman Ltd., 1971.

Chalandon, Ferdinand. *Les Comnène. Études sur l'Empire byzantine au XIe et au XIIe siècles*. Vol. II (2) *Jean II Comnène (1118–1143) et Manuel I Comnène (1143–1180)*. New York: Burt Franklin, 1912.

Chase, Frank H., Jr., trans. *Saint John of Damascus: Writings*, vol. 37. The Fathers of the

Church: A New Translation. Washington, D.C.: Catholic University of America Press, 1958.

Cheikho, Louis. *Eutychii Patriarchae Alexandrini Annales*. Beirut: E. Typografico Catholico, 1906–9.

Chittick, William C. "Belief and Transformation: The Sufi Teachings of Ibn al-ʿArabi." *The American Theosophist* 74 (1986).

———. *The Sufi Path of Knowledge: Ibn al-ʿArabī's Metaphysic of Imagination*. Albany: State University of New York Press, 1989.

Chukwulozie, Victor. *Muslim-Christian Dialogue in Nigeria*. Ibadan: Daystar Press, 1986.

Clark, James M. *The Great German Mystics: Eckhart, Tauler and Suso*. Oxford: Basil Blackwell, 1949.

———. *Meister Eckhart: An Introduction to the Study of His Works With an Anthology of His Sermons*. London: Thomas Nelson and Sons, 1957.

Clark, James M., and John V. Skinner. *Meister Eckhart: Selected Treatises and Sermons Translated from Latin and German with an Introduction and Notes*. London: Faber and Faber, 1958.

Clarke, P. B. "Christian Approaches to Islam in Francophone West Africa in the Post-Independence Era (c. 1960–1983): From Confrontation to Dialogue." *Bulletin on Islam and Christian-Muslim Relations in Africa* (Birmingham) 1, no. 2 (1983).

Colledge, Edmund, and Bernard McGinn, trans. and intro. *Meister Eckhart: The Essential Sermons, Commentaries, Treatises, and Defense*. Classics of Western Spirituality. New York: Paulist Press, 1981.

Colpe, Carsten. "Historische und theologische Grunde fur die abendlandische Angst vor dem Islam." In Carsten Colpe, ed., *Problem Islam*. Frankfurt am Main: Athenaum, 1989.

Cooley, Frank L. *The Growing Seed: The Christian Church in Indonesia*. Jakarta: BPK Gunung Mulia, 1981.

Corbin, Henry. *Creative Imagination in the Sufism of Ibn ʿArabi*. Trans. Ralph Manheim. Bollingen Series 91. Princeton: Princeton University Press, 1969.

———. *En Islam iranien*. Vols. 1, 4. Paris: Gallimard, 1970–71.

Cracknell, Kenneth. *Towards a New Relationship: Christians and People of Other Faith*. London: Epworth, 1986.

Cragg, Kenneth, *The Call of the Minaret*. 1st ed. Oxford University Press, 1956; 2d ed., Maryknoll, N.Y.: Orbis Books, and Ibadan, Nigeria: Daystar Press, 1985.

———. *The Christian and Other Religions*. Oxford: Mowbrays, 1977.

———. "God and Salvation (An Islamic Study)." *Studia Missionalia* 29 (1980): 155–66.

———. *Jesus and the Muslim: An Exploration*. London: George Allen and Unwin, 1985.

———. "Persons, Situations, Books." *The Muslim World* 43 (1953): 197–207

———, comp. *Alive to God. Muslim and Christian Prayer*. London: Oxford University Press, 1970

Crampton, E. P. T. "Christianity in Northern Nigeria." In O. Kalu, ed., *Christianity in West Africa: The Nigeria Story*. Ibadan: Daystar Press, 1978.

Crollius, Ary A. Roest. "Salvation in the Qurʾan." *Studia Missionalia* 29 (1980): 125–40.

Cumont, Franz. "La conversion des Juifs byzantins au IXe siècle." *Revue de l'instruction publique en Belgique* 46 (1903): 8–15.

———. "Une formule grecque de renonciation au Judaism." *Bormannheft der Wiener Studien* 24, no. 2: 233–34.

———. "L'origine de la formule grecque d'abjuration imposée aux musulmans." *Revue de l'Histoire des Religions* 64 (1911): 143–50.

Cuoq, Joseph. *L'Église d'Afrique du Nord du IIe au XIIe siècle*. Paris: Éditions du Centurion, 1984.

Dachroui, F. "Contribution à l'histoire de Fatimides en Ifriqiyya." *Arabica* 8 (1961): 189–203.

———. "Les commencements de la prédication isma'ilienne en Ifriqiyya." *Studia Islamica* 20 (1964): 89–102.

Dahm, Bernhard. *Sukarnos Kampf um Indonesiens Unabhangigkeit*. Ithaca, N.Y.: Cornell University Press, 1969.

Daniel, Norman. *The Arabs and Mediaeval Europe*. London and New York: Longman, 1975; 2d ed. 1979.

———. *Heroes and Saracens. An Interpretation of the Chansons de Geste*. Edinburgh: University Press, 1984.

———. *Islam and the West. The Making of an Image*. Edinburgh: University Press, 1960.

———. *Islam, Europe and Empire*. Edinburgh: University Press, 1966.

———. "Sarrasins, Chevaliers et maines dans les Chansons de geiste." *MIDEO* 17 (1986): 115–24.

Danvers, Fredrick Charles. *The Portuguese in India*. 2 vols. London: W.H. Allen & Company, Ltd., 1894.

Darraj, Ahmad. *al-Mamālīk wa ʾl-Firanj fī al-Qarn al-Tāsiʿ al-Hijrī—al-Khāmis ʿAshar al-Milādī* (The Mamlūks and the French in the ninth century Hijrī/fifteenth century A.D.). Cairo: Dār al-Fikr alʿArabī, 1961.

———. *Wathaʾiq Dayr Sahyun bil-Quds al-Sharif* (Documents of the Monastery of Sahyun in Jerusalem). Cairo: Maktabat al-Anglu al-Misriyya, 1968.

Dassetto, F. "The Tabligh Organizations in Belgium." In Tomas Gerholm and Yngre Lithman, eds., *The New Islamic Presence in Western Europe*. London: Mansell, 1988.

Dassetto, F., and A. Bastenier. *L'Islam transplante*. Antwerp: Editions EPO, 1984.

Davidson, Basil. *Africa, History of a Continent*. New York: Spring Books [Hamlyn], 1972.

———. *Lost Cities of Africa*. Boston: Little, Brown, 1959.

D'Costa, Gavin. *Theology and Religious Pluralism: The Challenge of Other Religions*. New York: Blackwell, 1986.

Delval, R. *A Map of the Muslims in the World*. Leiden: E.J. Brill, 1984.

Dengel, Holk H. *Darul-Islam. Kartosuwirjos Kampf um einen islamischen Staat Indonesien*. Beitrage zur Sudasienforschurg. Stuttgart: Steiner Verlag Wiesbaden, 1986.

DeValve, Robert Henry. "The Apologetic Writings of Yahya b. ʿAdi." Ph.D. thesis, Hartford Seminary, 1973.

Di Matteo, Ignazio. *Ibn Taymiyya, o Riassunto del suo opera al-Jawab al-Sahih li-man baddala din al-Masih*. Palermo: 1912.

Djait, Hichem. *Al-Kūfa: Naissance de la ville islamique* (Paris: Maisonneuve et Larose, 1986.

———. *Europe and Islam*. Berkeley: University of California Press, 1985.

———. *La grande discorde: Religion et politique dans l'Islam des origines*. Paris: Gallimard, 1989.

Dodge, Bayard. *The Fihrist of al-Nadim, a Tenth-Century Survey of Muslim Culture*. 2 vols. New York and London: Columbia University Press, 1970.

Doi, A.R.I. "Islam in Nigeria: Changes Since Independence." In E. Fashole-Luke et al. *Christianity in Independent Africa*. Ibadan: Ibadan University Press, 1978.

Dölger, Franz. *Corpus des griechischen Urkunden der Mittelalters und der neuern Zeit*. Vol. 2: *Regesten von 1025–1204*. München-Berlin: R. Oldenbourg, 1925.

———. *Regesten der Kaiserurkunden des ostromichen Reiches von 565–1453*. Vol. 2. *Regesten von 1025–1204*. Berlin: Munich University; Druck University, Verlag von R. Oldenbourg, 1925.

Dorman, Harry Gaylord, Jr. *Toward Understanding Islam: Contemporary Apologetic of Islam and Missionary Policy*. New York: Teachers College, Columbia University, 1948.

Dorsey, Alex J.D. *Portuguese Discoveries, Dependencies and Missions in Asia and Africa*. London: Allen & Co., 1893.

Dretke, James P. *A Christian Approach to Muslims:* Reflections from West Africa. Pasadena: William Carey Library, 1979.

Eckhart, Meister. *Parisian Questions and Prologues*. Trans. Armand Maurer. Toronto: Pontifical Institute of Mediaeval Studies, 1974.

Engineer, A. Asghar, ed. *Communal Riots in Post-Independence India*. Bombay: Sangam Books, 1964.

Enklaar, I.H. *Josef Kam, Apostel der Molukken*. The Hague: Boekencentrium, 1963.

Evers, Georg. "Christen und Muslime im Gesprach." In *Evangelische Mission* 18 (1986): 86–87.

Fakhry, Majid. *A History of Islamic Philosophy*. New York and London: Columbia University Press, 1970.

Falaturi, Abdaljavad. "The Experience of Time and History in Islam." In Annemarie Schimmel and A. Falaturi, eds., *We Believe in One God*. New York: Seabury Press, 1979.

Faruqi, Ismail R. al-. "History of Religions: Its Nature and Significance for Christian Education and the Muslim-Christian Dialogue." *Numen* 12 (1965): 35–65, 81–86.

———. *Islam. Niles, Ill.: Argus Communication, 1979.*

———. *Islamization of Knowledge*. Herndon, Va.: International Institute of Islamic Thought, 1982.

Faruqi, Ziya-ul-Hasan. *The Deoband School and the Demand for Pakistan*. Bombay: Asia Publishing House, 1963.

Fatimi, S.Q. *Islam Comes to Malaysia*. Singapore: Malaysian Sociological Research Institute, 1963.

Fattal, Antoine. *Le statut légal des non-Musulmans en pays d'Islam*. Beirut: Imprimerie Catholique, 1958.

Feith, H. *The Decline of Constitutional Democracy in Indonesia*. Ithaca, N.Y.: Cornell University Press, 1962.

Feki, Habib. *Les idées religieuses et philosophiques de l'ismaelisme fatimide (organization et doctrine)*. Faculté des Lettres et Sciences Humaines de Tunis. 6e Serie: Philosophie-Littérature. Vol. 13. Tunis: Publications de l'Université de Tunis, 1978.

Fox, Matthew, intro. and comm. *Breakthrough: Meister Eckhart's Creation Spirituality in New Translation*. Garden City, N.Y.: Image Books, 1980.

Fraigneau-Julien, B. "Un traité anonyme de la Sainte Trinité attribué à Saint Cyrille d'Alexandrie." *Recherches de Science Religieuse* 49 (1961): 188–211.

Franck, Frederick, trans. *The Book of Angelus Silesius*. Santa Fe, N.M.: Bear and Company, 1985.

Friedmann, Yohanan. "The Attitudes of the *Jamᶜiyyat-i-ᶜUlamaʾ-i Hind* to the Indian National Movement and the Establishment of Pakistan." *Asian and African Studies* (Jerusalem) 7 (1971): 157–80.

Fritsch, Erdmann. *Islam und Christentum im Mittelalter: Beiträge zur Geschichte der muslimischen Polemik gegen das Christentum in arabischer Sprache*. Breslauer Studien zur historischen Theologie, vol. 17. Breslau: Müller & Seiffert, 1930.

Fyzee, A.A.A. *A Modern Approach to Islam*. 1st ed. New Delhi: Oxford University Press, 1963.

Gabus, Jean-Paul. "Approches Protestantes de l'Islam." In Jean-Paul Gabus, Ali Merad, and Youakim Moubarac, *Islam et Christianisme en dialogue*. Paris: Cerf, 1982.

Garang, J., ed. *Memasuki Masa Depan Bersama: Tugas dan Tanggungjawab agama-agama di Indonesia* (Moving toward the future together: The task and responsibility of religions in Indonesia). Jakarta: Litbang PGI, 1989.

Gardet, Louis, and M.M. Anawati. *Introduction à la théologie musulmane: Essai de théologie comparée*. Paris: J. Vrin, 1948.

Gaudeul, Jean-Marie. *Encounters and Clashes. Islam and Christianity in History*. 2 vols. Rome: Pontificio Istituto di Studi Arabi & Islamici, 1984.

Gbadamosi, T.G.O. *The Growth of Islam among the Yoruba, 1841–1908*. London: Longman, 1978.

Geertz, Clifford. *The Religion of Java*. Glencoe: Free Press, 1960.

Geffre, Claude. "Le Coran, une Parole de Dieu différente?" *Lumière et Vie* 163 (July–August 1983): 21–32.

Gennep, F.O. van. *De terugkeer van de verloren vader* (The return of the lost father). Baarn: Ten Have, 1989.

Gervers, Michael, and Ramzi Jibran Bikhazi, eds. *Conversion and Continuity*. Toronto: Pontifical Institute of Mediaeval Studies, 1990.

Ghazali, Abu Hamid al-. *Al-Durra al-Fakhirah: The Precious Pearl*, Jane I. Smith, trans. Missoula, Mont.: Scholars Press, 1979.

Gibson, Margaret Dunlop. *An Arabic Version of the Acts of the Apostles and the Seven Catholic Epistles, from an Eighth or Ninth Century MS in the Convent of St. Catherine on Mount Sinai, with a Treatise 'On the Triune Nature of God.' Studia Sinaitica*, no. 7. London: C.J. Clay & Sons, 1899.

Gillette, Alain, and Abdelmalek Sayad. *L'immigration algérienne en France*. 2d ed. Paris: Éditions Entente, 1984.

Gilliland, Dean S. *African Religion Meets Islam: Religious Change in Northern Nigeria*. Lanham, New York, London: University Press of America, 1986.

Gort, J.D., H.M. Vroom, R. Fernhout, and A. Wessels, eds. *Dialogue and Syncretism: An Interdisciplinary Approach*. Grand Rapids: W.B. Eerdmans; Amsterdam: Editions Rodpi, 1989.

Graf, Georg. *Die Philosophie und Gotteslehre des Jahjâ ibn ʿAdî und späterer Autoren: Skizzen nach meist ungedruckten Quellen*. Münster: Aschendorffsche Buchhandlung, 1910.

———. "Ein bisher unbekanntes Werk des Patriarchen Eutychius von Alexandrien." *Oriens christianus* n.s. 1 (1911): 227–44.

———. "Zu dem bisher unbekannten Werk des Patriarchem Eutychios von Alexandrien." *Oriens Christianus* 2 (1912): 136–37.

Grant, Douglas. *The Fortunate Slave*. London: Oxford University Press, 1968.

Griffith, Paul J. *Christianity through Non-Christian Eyes*. Maryknoll, N.Y.: Orbis, 1990.

Griffith, Sidney H. "The Controversial Theology of Theodore Abû Qurrah (c.750–c.820 A.D.), a Methodological Comparative Study in Christian Arabic Literature." Ph.D. diss., Catholic University of America, Washington, D.C., 1978.

———. "The Monks of Palestine and the Growth of Christian Literature in Arabic." *The Muslim World* 78 (1988): 1–28.

———. "'*The Monks of Palestine*,' or '*Greek into Arabic: Life and Letters in the Monasteries of Palestine in the Ninth Century*'; The Example of the *Summa Theologiae Arabica*." *Byzantion* 56 (1986): 117–38.

Guillaume, Alfred. *The Life of Muhammad: A Translation of Ishaq's Sirat Rasul Allah*. 2d. impr. Lahore, Karachi, Dakka: Oxford University Press, Pakistan Branch, 1968.
Haafkens, Johannes. "Statistics of Religious Adherence in Africa: Muslims and Christians." In J.P. Rajeshekar, ed., *Christian-Muslim Relations in Eastern Africa*. Geneva: Lutheran World Federation, 1988.
Hacker, Andrew. *Two Nations: Black and White, Separate, Hostile, Unequal*. New York: Scribner's, 1992.
Haddad, Rachid. *Le trinité divine chez les théologiens arabes (750–1050)*. Beauchesne Religions 15. Paris: Beauchesne, 1985.
Haddad, Robert M. "Iconoclasts and *Muʾtazila*: The Politics of Anthropomorphism." *The Greek Orthodox Theological Review* 27 (1982): 287–324.
Haddad, Yvonne Y. *Contemporary Islam and the Challenge of History*. Albany: SUNY Press, 1981.
______. "Muslims in Canada: A Preliminary Study." In Harold Coward and Leslie Kawamura, eds., *Religion and Ethnicity*. Waterloo, Ont.: Wilfrid Laurier University Press, 1978.
Haddad, Yvonne Yazbeck, and Adair T. Lummis. *Islamic Values in the United States: A Comparative Study*. New York: Oxford University Press, 1987.
Haenchen, Ernst. *Die Apostelgeschichte*. Gottingen: Vandenhoeck & Ruprecht, 1965- 1966.
Hagemann, Ludwig. *Der Kurʾan in Verstandnis und Kritik bei Nikolaus von Kues Ein Beitrag zur Erhellung islamich-Christlicher Geschichte*. Frankfurt am Main: Josef Knecht, 1976.
Haik, Michel. *Al-Masīḥ fī al-Islām* [Christ in Islam]. Beirut: Catholic Press, 1961.
Hall, D.G.E. *A History of Southeast Asia*. London: Macmillan, 1961.
Hamidullah, Muhammad. *Muslim Conduct of State*. Hyderabad: Government Press, 1942.
Hamza, Si Boubakeur. *Le Coran: Traduction nouvelle et commentaires*. 2 vols. Paris: Fayard/Denoel, 1972.
Haq, Mushirul. *Muslim Politics in Modern India*. Meerut: Meenakshi Prakashan, 1970.
Ḥaqqī, Ismāʿīl. *Rūḥ al-Bayān* (The essence of explication). 10 vols. Beirut: Dār al-Fikr, n.d.
Hardy, Peter. *Partners in Freedom—and True Muslims*. Lund: Studentlitteratur, 1971.
Harnack, Adolf von. *Reden und Aufsatze*. Vol. 2. Giessen: J. Ricker, 1904.
Harpigny, Guy. *Islam et Christianisme selon Louis Massignon*. Louvain-la-Neuve: Centre de l'histoire des religion, l'Université Catholique, 1981.
Hasan, Yusuf Fadl. "The Penetration of Islam in Eastern Sudan." In I.M. Lewis, ed., *Islam in Tropical Africa*. London: Oxford University Press, 1966.
Haydar, Ahmad. "Mittelalterliche Vorstellungen von dem Propheten der Sarazenen, mit besonderen Berucksichtigung der Reisebeschreibung des Bernhard von Breidenback 1483." Ph.D. diss., Freie Universitat, Berlin, 1971.
Hayek, Michel. *Le Christ de l'Islam*. Paris: Seuil, 1959.
Ḥijāzī, Muḥammad Maḥmūd. *Al-Tafsīr al-Wāḍiḥ* (The clear interpretation). 30 vols., 6th ed. Cairo: Matbaʿat al-Istiqlāl al-Kubrā, 1389/1969.
Hock, Klaus. "Christliche Mission und islamische Daʿwa: 'Sendung' und 'Ruf' in geschichtlichen Wandel." *CIBEDO Beitrage* 3, no. l (1989): 11–26.
______. *Der Islam in Spiegel westlicher Theologie*. Cologna-Vienna: Bohlau, 1986.
Holoch, George, trans. *The Raft of Mohammad: Social and Human Consequences of the Return to Traditional Religion in the Arab World*. New York: Paragon House Publishers, 1988.
Holt, P.M., et al., eds. *The Cambridge History of Islam*. Vol. 2.Cambridge: Cambridge Uni-

versity Press, 1970.

Hopkins, C.H. *John R. Mott 1865–1955: A Biography*. Geneva and Grand Rapids: Eerdmans, 1979.

Horst, L., trans. *Das Metropoliten Elias von Nisibis Buch vom Beweis der Wahrheit des Glaubens*. Colmar: E. Barth, 1886.

Husaini, Zohra. *Muslims in the Canadian Mosaic: Socio-Cultural and Economic Links with Their Countries of Origin*. Edmonton, Alberta: Muslim Research Foundation, 1990.

Hussey, J.M. *The Byzantine World*. New York: Harper Torchbooks, 1961.

Huwaidī, Fahmī al-. *al-Tadayyun al-Manqūṣ* (The deficient religiosity). Cairo: al-Ahrām, 1988.

———. *Muwāṭinūn lā Dhumiyyūn: Mawqiᶜ Ghayr al-Muslimīn fī Mujtamaᶜ al-Muslimīn* (Citizens, not protected people: the status of non-Muslims in Muslim society). Beirut: Dār al-Shurūq, 1985.

Ibn Abī Zayd al-Qayrawānī, ᶜAbd Allāh ibn ᶜAbd al-Raḥmān (d. 386/996). *Kitāb al-Jāmiᶜ: Al-Sunan wa-al-Adāb wa-al-maghāzī wa-al-tārīkh* (The comprehensive book on tradition, manners, raids, and history). Beirut: Muʾassasat al-Risala, and Tunis: Al-Maktaba al-ᶜAtiqa, 1982.

Ibn ᶜArabi, Muhyiddin. *The Bezels of Wisdom*. Trans. R.W.J. Austin. New York: Paulist Press, 1980.

———. *Journey to the Lord of Power*. Trans. Rabia Terry Harris. London: East West Publications, 1981.

Ibn al-Athīr, ᶜIzz al-Dīn. *Al-Kāmil fī al-Tārīkh* (A comprehensive history). Vol. 10. Beirut: Dār al-Kutub al-ᶜIlmiyya, 1987.

———. *Al-Tārīkh al-Bāhir fī ʾl-Dawla al-Atbakiyya* (The dazzling history of the Atabak state). Baghdad: Al-Muthannā, 1963.

Ibn Hammad. *Histoire des Rois Obaidides (Les Califes Fatimides)*. Trans. and ed. M. Vondeheyden. Paris: Paul Geuthner, and Algiers: Jules Carbonel, 1927.

Ibn ᶜIdhārī, Abū alᶜAbbās al-Marrākushī. *Histoire de l'Afrique et de l'Espagne intitulée Al-bayanoʾl-Moqrib*. 2 vols. Trans. and annot. E. Fagnan. Algiers: Imprimerie Orientale P. Fontana, 1901–4.

Ibn Jubayr, Muḥammad. *Riḥlat Ibn Jubayr* (The journey of Ibn Jubayr). Beirut: Dār al-Hilāl, 1981.

Ibn Kathīr, ᶜImād al-Dīn Abī al-Fidāʾ. *Tafsīr al-Qurʾān al-ᶜAẓīm* (The interpretation of the Glorious Qurʾan). 2d ed. 7 vols. Beirut: Dār al-Fikr, 1389/1970.

Ibn Munqidh, Usāmā. *Kitāb al-Iᶜtibār* (The book of reflection or "a Syrian gentleman"). Princeton: Princeton University Press, 1930.

Ibn al-Qalānisī, Ḥamza. *Dhayl Tārīkh Dimashq* (Supplement to the history of Damascus). Beirut: Maṭbaᶜat al-Ābāʾ al-Yasūᶜiyyīn, 1908.

Ibn Sahddād, Bahāʾ al-Dīn. *Al-Nawādir al-Sulṭāniyya wa-Maḥāsin al-Yūsufiyya* (Anecdotes of the sultanate and the good qualities of the Yusifiyya). Cairo: Al-Dār al-Miṣriyya li ʾl-Taʾlīf wa ʾl-Tarjama, 1964.

Ibn Taymiyya, Taqī al-Dīn Ahmad. *Al-Jawāb al-Saḥīḥ li-man Baddala Dīn al-Maṣīh* (The correct reply to those who have changed the religion of Christ). 4 vols. in 2. Cairo: Maṭbaᶜat al-Madanī, n.d.

Idowu, E. Bolaji. *Towards an Indigenous Church*. Ibadan: Oxford University Press, 1965.

Idris, H.R. *La Berberie Orientale sous les Zirides Xe-XIIe siècles*. Paris: Adrien-Maisonneuve, 1962.

———. "Fêtes chrétiennes célébrées en Ifriqiya à l'époque ziride." *Revue Africaine* 98

(1954): 261–76.

______. ed. and trans. *Manāqib d'Abū Isḥāq al-Jabanyānī par Abū 'l-Qāsim al-Lābidī et Manāqib de Muḥriz b. Ḫalaf par Abū 'l-Ṭāhir al-Fārisī*. Publication de la Faculté des Lettres d'Alger, 31. Paris: Presses Universitaires de France, 1959.

Ineichen, B., and R. Cope. *New Community* 15, no. 3 (April 1989): 335–56.

Ingleson, John. *Road to Exile: The Indonesian Nationalist Movement 1927–1934*. Singapore: Heinemann Educational Books, 1979.

Isfahani, Muhyi al-Din al-. *Epître sur l'Unité et la Trinité, Traité sur l'Intellect, Fragment sur l'âme*. Text arabe edité et annoté par M. Allard et G. Troupeau. Beirut: Imprimerie Catholique, 1962.

ʿIyād, Al-Qāḍī. *Tartīb al-Madārik wa-Taqrīb al-Masālik li-Maʿrifat Aʿlām Madhhab Mālik* (A systematic and lucid presentation toward the knowledge of the luminaries of the Maliki school of law). 8 vols. Rabat: Wizārat al-Awqāf wa-al-Shu'ūn al-Islāmiyya, 1965–83.

Izutsu, Toshihiko. *Sufism and Taoism: A Comparative Study of Key Philosophical Concepts*. Berkeley: University of California Press, 1983.

Jalil, Abd-el. *Marie et l'Islam*. Paris: Beauchesne, 1950.

Jami, ʿAbdurrahman. *Divan-i Kamil* (Collection of Kamil's poetry). Tehran: Payruz, 134sh/1962.

Jayne, Kingsley Garland. *Vasco da Gama and His Successors, 1460–1580*. London: Methuen, 1910.

Jeffery, Arthur. "Ibn al-ʿArabi's Shajarat al-Kawm" (Ibn al-ʿArabi's "Tree of Being"). *Studia Islamica* 10 (1959): 43–77; 11 (1959): 113–60.

______, ed. *A Reader on Islam*. The Hague: Mouton, 1962.

Joly, Daniele. "Ethnic minorities and education in Britain." *Research Papers: Muslims in Europe* 41 (March 1989): 1–28.

Jomier, Jacques. "Eine neue Form des christlich-islamischen Dialogs." *CIBEDO Beitrage* 2, no. 2 (1988): 38–44.

______. "Review." *Revue Thomiste* 87 (1987): 690–97.

______. "Prophetisme biblique et prophetisme Coranique." *Revue Thomiste* 77 (1977): 600–9.

______. "Le salut selon l'Islam." *Studia Missionalia* 29 (1980): 141–54.

Kāmil, ʿAbd al-ʿAzīz. *Al-Islām wa-al-Mustaqbal* (Islam and the future). Cairo: Dār al-Maʿārif, 1975.

______. *Maʿ al-Rasūl wa-al-Mujtamaʿ fī Istiqbāl al-Qarn al-Hijrī al-Khāmis ʿAshar* (With the Messenger [Muhammad] and society in meeting the Islamic fifteenth century). Kuwait: Mu'assasat al-Ṣabāḥ li-al-Nashr wa-al-Tawzīʿ, 1980.

Kashmeri, Zuhair. *The Gulf Within: Canadian Arabs, Racism and the Gulf War*. Toronto: James Lorimer & Co., Publishers, 1991.

Katz, Stephen T., ed. *Mysticism and Philosophical Analysis*. New York: Oxford University Press, 1978.

______, ed. *Mysticism and Religious Traditions*. New York: Oxford University Press, 1983.

Kaufhold, Herbert. *Die Rechtssamlung des Gabriel von Basra und ihr Verhaltnis zu den anderen juristischen Sammelwerken der Nestprianer*. Berlin: J. Schweitzer, 1976.

______. *Syrische Texte zum Islamischen Recht*. Munich: Verlag der Bayerischen Akademie der Wissenschaften, 1971.

Kelley, Carl Franklin. *Meister Eckhart on Divine Knowledge*. New Haven, Conn.: Yale University Press, 1977.

Kenny, Joseph. "Shariʿa in Nigeria—A Historical Survey." *Bulletin on Islam and Christian-Muslim Relations in Africa.* (Birmingham) 4, no. 1 (1986): 1–21.

Khaduri, Majid. *War and Peace in the Law of Islam.* New York: AMS Press, 1979.

Khalīl, Samīr. "Thiyūdūrus Abū Qurra" (Theodore Abū Qurra). *Majallat al-Majmaʿ al-ʿIlmī al-ʿArabī, al-Qism al-Suryānī* (The Arab Science Academy Journal, the Syriac section) (Baghdad) 7 (1984): 138–60.

———. "Une théologie arabe pour l'Islam." *Tantur Yearbook 1979–80*, 57–84

Khan, Rasheeduddin. "Problems and Prospects of Muslims in India." *Seminar*, New Delhi, June, 1968.

Khāzin, ʿAlāʾ al-Dīn ʿAlī Ibn Muḥammad Ibn Ibrāhīm al-. *Lubāb al-Taʾwīl fī Maʿānī al-tanzīl* (The essence of allegorical interpretation of the meaning of revelation). 4 vols. Beirut: Dār al-Maʿrifa, n.d.

Kholy, Abdo el-. *The Arab Moslems in the United States of America.* New Haven, Conn.: Yale University Press, 1966.

Khoury, Adel-Théodore. "Apologetique byzantine contre l'Islam (VIIIe-XIIIe s.)." *Proche Orient Chrétien* 29 (1979): 242–300; 30 (1980): 132–74; 32 (1982): 14–49.

———. *Polémique byzantine contre l'Islam (VIIIe -XIIIe s.).* Leiden: E.J. Brill, 1972.

———. Les th*éologiens byzantines et l'Islam, I: Textes et auteurs (VIIIe-XIIIe s.).* Louvain: Éditions Nauwelaerts, 1969.

Khoury, Paul, trans. and ed. *Paul d'Antioche: Évêque Melkite de Sidon (XIIe s.).* Recherches publiées sous la direction de l'Institut de Lettres Orientales 24. Beirut: Imprimerie Catholique, 1965.

Kinānī, Muṣṭafā al-. *Al-ʿAlāqāt bayn Ganawā wa ʾl-Fāṭimiyyīn fī ʾl-Sharq al-Awsaṭ, 1095–1171 A.D.* (The relationship between Genoa and the Fatimids in the Middle East, A.D. 1095–71). Alexandria: Al-Hayʾa al-Miṣriyya al-ʿĀmma li ʾl-Kitāb, 1981.

Kittel, Gerhard F. *Theologisches Worterbuch zum Neuen Testament.* Vol. 6. Stuttgart: W. Kahlhammer, 1959.

Knappert, Jan. *Het Epos van Heraklios* (The epic of Heraclius). Amsterdam: Meulenhoff, 1977.

Knitter, Paul. *No Other Name? A Critical Survey of Christian Attitudes Toward the World Religions.* Maryknoll, N.Y.: Orbis Books, 1985.

Kohlbrugge, D.J. and J. van der Werf. *De Ware Jozef* (The true Joseph). Nijkerk: G.F. Callenbach, 1973.

Kotter, Bonifatius, ed. *Die Schriften des Johannes von Damaskos herausgegeben vom Byzantinischen Institut der Abtei Scheyern: II. Ekdosis akribēs tēs orthodoxou pisteō, Esposito Fidei.* Patristische Texte und Studien, vol. 12. Berlin and New York: Walter de Gruyter, 1973.

———. *Die Schriften des Johannes von Damaskos.* Vol. 4. *Liber de haeresibus: Opera Polemica.* Berlin: Walter de Gruyter, 1981.

Kraemer, Hendrik. *The Christian Message in a Non-Christian World.* New York: Harper & Bros., 1938.

Kreiser, K. "Islam in Germany and the German Muslims." *Research Papers: Muslims in Europe* 28 (December 1985): 9–29.

Küng, Hans, Josef van Ess, Heinrich von Stietencron, and Heinz Bechert. *Christianity and the World Religions: Paths of Dialogue with Islam, Hinduism, and Buddhism.* Trans. Peter Heinegg. Garden City, N.Y.: Doubleday, 1986.

———. "Christianity and World Religions: The Dialogue with Islam as One Model." *The Muslim World* 77 (1987): 80–95.

______. *Theology for the Third Millenium*. New York: Doubleday, 1988.
Lahnemann, J., ed. *Erziehung zur Kulturbegegnung*. Hamburg: EBV-Rissen, 1986.
Lampros, S. P. *Michael Acominatou tou Choniatou. Ta Sozomena*. Vol. 2. Groningen: Verlag Bouma's Boekhuis, 1968.
Landron, Bénédicte. "Apologétique, polémique et attitudes nestoriennes vis-à-vis de l'Islam entre le VIIIe et le debut du XIVe siècle." Thèse de doctorat, Université au Paris, Sorbonne, 1978.
Lee, Martha F. *The Nation of Islam: An American Millenarian Movement*, Studies in Religion and Society, vol. 21. Lampeter, Wales: The Edwin M. Mellen Press, 1988.
Lelong, Michel. *Deux Fidélités une espérance*. Paris: Cerf, 1979.
______. "Mohammed, prophète de l'Islam." *Studia Missionalia* 33 (1984): 251–75.
______. *Si Dieu l'avait voulu*. Paris: Éd. Tougui, 1986.
Lewicki, Tadeusz. *Études maghrebines et soudanaises*. Vol. 1. Varsovie: Éditions scientifiques de Pologne, 1976.
Lezine, A. "Mahdiya, quelques précisions sur la 'ville' des premiers Fatimides." *Revue des Études Islamiques*, 1967.
Lings, M. *Symbol and Archetype*. Cambridge: Quinta Essentia, 1991.
Little, Donald P. "Three Arab Critiques of Orientalism." *The Muslim World* 69 (1979): 110–31.
______. "Haram Documents Related to the Jews of Late Fourteenth Century Jerusalem." *Journal of Semitic Studies* 30 (1985): 227–64, 368–70.
Macdonald, D. B. "Allah." In *Shorter Encyclopedia of Islam*. Ithaca, N.Y.: Cornell University Press, 1965.
Madhok, Balraj. *Indianization*. Delhi: Hind Pocketbook (P) Ltd., 1970.
Madjid, Nurcholis, et al. *Pembaharuan Pemikiran Islam* (Modernizing Islamic mentality). Jakarta: Bulan Bintag, 1972.
______. *Islam: Kemodernan dan keindonesieniaan* (Islam: Modernization and Indonesian contextualization). Bandung: Mizan, 1987.
Magoulias, Harry J., trans. *O City of Byzantium: Annals of Niketas Choniates*. Detroit: Wayne State University Press, 1984.
Makdisi, George. "The Tanbīh of Ibn Taimīya on Dialectic: The Pseudo-ʿAqilan Kitāb al-Farq." In Sami A. Hanna, ed., *Medieval and Middle Eastern Studies in Honor of Aziz Suryal Atiya*. Leiden: E.J. Brill, 1972.
Makhlouf, Avril Mary. "The Trinitarian Doctrine of Eutychius of Alexandria (877–940 A.D.)." *Parole de l'Orient* 5 (1974): 5–20.
Mala, S. Babas. "Attitudes of Nigerian Muslim Intellectuals towards Muslim-Christian Relations." *Bulletin on Islam and Christian-Muslim Relations in Africa* (Birmingham) 1, no. 4 (1984): 11–20.
Maqrīzī, al-. *Ittiʿāẓ al-Ḥunafāʾ bi akhbār al-Aʾimma al-Fāṭimīyyin al-Khulafāʾ* (The Hanafites' learning a lesson from the chronicles of the Fāṭimid Imamate-Caliphate). Vol. 2. Cairo: Al-Maʿhad al-ʿIlmī al-Faransī, 1964.
Marrakushi, Ibn Idhari al-. *Histoire de l'Afrique et de l'Espagne intitulée Al-bayanoʾl-Moqrib*. 2 vols. Trans. E. Fagnan. Algiers: Imprimerie Orientale P. Fontana, 1901–4.
Marsh, Clifton E. *From Black Muslims to Muslims: The Transition from Separatism to Islam, 1930–1980*. Metuchen, N.J.: Scarecrow Press, 1984.
Martin, Richard C., ed. *Approaches to Islam in Religious Studies*. Tucson: University of Arizona Press, 1985.
Massigberd, F. "Was Montanism a Jewish-Christian Heresy?" *Journal of Ecumenical The-*

ology 17 (1966).

Masʿudi, Masdar F., ed. *Islam Indonesia: Menatap Masa Depan* (Indonesian Islam: A look at the future). Jakarta: P3M, 1989.

Māturīdī, Abū Manṣūr al-. *Kitāb al-Tawḥīd* (The theology of unity). Ed. Fathalla Kholeif. Beirut: Dar el-Machreq Éditeurs, 1970.

Mayer, Hans Eberhand. *The Crusades*. Oxford: Oxford University Press, 1981.

McCarthy, Richard J. *The Theology of Al-Ashʿarī*. Beirut: Imprimerie Catholique, 1953.

McGinn, Bernard, ed. *Meister Eckhart: Teacher and Preacher*. Classics of Western Spirituality. New York: Paulist Press, 1986.

Memon, Muhammad Umar. *Ibn Taimīya's Struggle Against Popular Religion*. Religion and Society 1. The Hague and Paris: Mouton, 1976.

Merad, Ali. *Ibn Badis, commentateur du Coran*. Paris: Geuthner, 1971.

———. *L'Islam contemporain*. Paris: Presses Universitaires de France, 1984, 1987.

Mérigoux, Jean-Marie. "Lettres du Fr. Riccoldo adressees a l'Église du Ciel." *Sources* (Fribourg, Switzerland) 12 (Sept.–Oct. 1986): 204–12.

———. "L'ouvrage d'un frère Précheur florentin en Orient à la fin du xiiie siècle, le 'Contra legem Sarracenorum' de Riccoldo da Monte di Croce." *Memorie Domenicane* 17 (986): 1–144

———. "Un precurseur du dialogue islamo-chrétien, frère Ricolodo." *Revue Thomiste* 3 (1973): 609–21.

Meyendorff, John. *Christ in Eastern Christian Thought*. Crestwood, N.Y.: St. Vladimir's Seminary Press, 1975.

Michel, Thomas F. *A Muslim Theologian's Response to Christianity: Ibn Taymiyya's al-Jawab al-Sahih*. Delmar, N.Y.: Caravan Books, 1984.

Miller, Roland E. *The Mappila Muslims of Kerala: A Study in Islamic Trends*. Madras: Orient Longman, 1976.

———. "Modern Indian Muslim Responses." In H.G. Coward, ed. *Modern Indian Responses to Religious Pluralism*. Albany: State University of New York Press, 1987.

———. *A Survey of Kerala History*. Kottayam: National Book Stall, 1967.

Miskotte, K.H. *Als de goden zwijgen: over de zin van het oude testament*. Amsterdam: 1956. Trans. by John W. Doberstein, *When the Gods Are Silent*. New York: Harper and Row, 1967.

Mitchell, R.J. *The Spring Voyage: The Jerusalem Pilgrimage in 1458*. London: John Murray, 1964.

Moore, Johannes C. de. *Uw God is mijn God; over de oorsprong van het geloof in de ene God* (Your God is my God: On the origin of belief in one God). Kampen: Kok, 1988.

Moraes, G. *A History of Christianity in India*. Bombay: P.S. Manantala & Sons Pvt. Ltd., 1964.

Moubarac, Youakim. *Pentalogie Islamo-Chretienne*. Vol. 3: *L'Islam et le Dialogue Islamo-Chrétien*. Beirut: Éditions du Cenacle Libanais, 1972–73.

———. *Recherches sur la pensée chrétienne et l'Islam dans les temps modernes et a l'époque contemporaine*. Beirut: Publ. de l'Université Libanaise, 1977.

———, ed. *Les Musulmans: Consultation Islamo-Chrétienne entre Muhammad Arkoun et Youakim Moubarac*. Paris: Beauchesne, 1971.

Moubarac, Youakim, and Guy Harpigny. "L'Islam dans la reflexion théologique du christianisme contemporain." *Concilium* 116 (1976): 28–38.

Muir, W., trans. *The Apology of al-Kindy*. London: Smith and Elder, 1882.

Mulder, Niels. *Mysticism and Every Day Life in Contemporary Java*. Singapore: University Press, 1978.

Muldoon, James. *Popes, Lawyers and Infidels*. Philadelphia: University of Pennsylvania Press, 1979.

Munir, Muhammad. *From Jinnah to Zia*. Lahore: Vanguard Books, 1980.

Nadwi, Abul Hasan Ali. *Musalmanan-i Hind ke liye sahih rah-i ʿamal* (The Muslims of India and the right course for action). Lucknow: Majis-i Tahqiqat-o-Nashriyyat-i Islam, 1987.

Naʾim, Abdullahi A. an-. "Religious Minorities under Islamic Law and the Limits of Cultural Relativism." *Human Rights Quarterly* 9 (1987).

______. *The Second Message of Islam*. Syracuse: Syracuse University Press, 1987.

Nasr, Seyyed Hossein. *Islamic Life and Thought*. Albany: State University of New York Press, 1981.

______. "The Islamic View of Christianity." In *Christianity Among World Religions*. Eds. Hans Küng and Jurgen Moltmann. *Concilium* 183 (1986): 3–12.

______. *Knowledge and the Sacred*. Albany: State University of New York Press, 1981.

______. *Religion and Religions: The Challenge of Living in a Multi-Religious World*. The Loy H. Witherspoon Lecture in Religious Studies. Charlotte: University of North Carolina, 1985.

______. *Three Muslim Sages: Avicenna-Suhrawardi-Ibn ʿArabī*. Cambridge, Mass.: Harvard University Press, 1964.

______, ed. *The Essential Writings of Frithjob Schuon*. Amity, N.Y.: Amity House, 1986.

Natsir, Mohammad. *Islam dan Kristen di Indonesia* (Islam and Christianity in Indonesia). Bandung: Pelajar–Bulan Sabit, 1961.

Nau, F. "Un Colloque du Patriarche Jean avec L'Émir des Agareens." *Journal Asiatique*. 11 ser. 5 (1915): 225–79.

Newbigen, Lesslie. *The Gospel in a Pluralistic Society*. Grand Rapids, Mich.: Eerdmans; Geneva: World Council of Churches Publications, 1989.

Nicholson, Reynold A. *Studies in Islamic Mysticism*. Cambridge: Cambridge University Press, 1921.

Nicolay, Nicolas de, and Dauphin of Arfeuile. *Les Navigations, Peregrinations et Voyages faicts en la Turquie*. Antwerp: G. Silvius, 1576.

Nielsen, Jorgen. "Forms and Problems of Legal Recognition for Muslims in Europe." *Research Papers: Muslims in Europe* 2 (June 1979): 1–19.

______. "Muslims in Europe: An Overview." *Research Papers: Muslims in Europe* 12 (December 1981): 1–31.

Nisābūrī, Niẓām al-Dīn al-Ḥasan ibn Muḥammad ibn al-Ḥusayn al-Qummī al-. *Gharāʾib al-Qurʾān wa-Raghāʾib al-Furqān* (The marvels and desideratum of the Qurʾan). Ed. Ibrāhīm ʿAtwah ʿAwaḍ. 30 vols., 1st. ed. Cairo: al-Bābī al-Ḥalabī, 1384/1964.

Noer, Deliar. *The Modernist Muslim Movement in Indonesia 1900–1942*. Singapore–Kuala Lumpur, New York: Oxford University Press, 1973.

Nowell, Charles E. *A History of Portugal*. New York: D. Van Nostrandt Co., 1952.

Nuʿmān, al-Qādi Ibn Muḥammad al-. *Kitāb al-Majālis wa-l-Musāyārāt* (The book concerning meetings and the disposition to be accommodating). Tunis: Al-Matbaʿa al-Rasmiyya liʾl-Jumhūriyya al-Tūnisiyya, 1978.

Oduyoye, M.A. "The Value of African Religious Beliefs and Practices for Christian Theology." In K. Appiahkubi and S. Torres, eds., *African Theology en Route*. New York: Orbis Books, 1979.

Olesen, A. *Islam oq undervisning i Denmark* (Islam and education in Denmark). Aarhus: Aarhus Universitetsforlag, 1987.

Omant, H. "Journal d'un Pélerin Français en Terre-Sainte (1383)." *Revue de l'Orient Latin* 3 (1895).

Onaiyekan, J. "The Shariᶜa in Nigeria: A Christian View." *Bulletin on Islam and Christian-Muslim Relations in Africa* (Birmingham) 5, no. 3 (1987): 1–17.

Oosten, Jarich. "Cultural Anthropological Approaches." In Frank Whaling, ed., *Contemporary Approaches to the Study of Religion*. Vol. 2. Berlin–New York–Amsterdam: Mouton, 1985.

O'Shaughnessy, Thomas J. "Sin as Alienation in Christianity and Islam." *Boletín de la Asociación Espanola de Orientalistas* 14 (1978): 127–35.

———. *Word of God in the Qur'an*. 2d rev. ed. Rome: Biblical Institute Press, 1984.

Palacios, Asin. "Logia et agrapha Domini Jesu." *Patrologia Orientalis* 13 (1919): 335–431; 19 (1926): 532–624.

Perier, Augustine. *Petits Traités Apologètiques de Yahya Ben ᶜAdi*. Paris: J. Gabalda and Paul Geuthner, 1920.

Peters, F. E. *Jerusalem: The Holy City in the Eyes of Chronicles, Visitors, Pilgrims and Prophets from the Days of Abraham to the Beginnings of Modern Times*. Princeton: Princeton University Press, 1985.

Pieris, Aloysius. *Love Meets Wisdom: A Christian Experience of Buddhism*. Maryknoll, N.Y.: Orbis, 1988.

Pirone, Bartolomeo. *Eutichio, Patriarca di Alessandria (877–940): Gli Annali*. Studia Orientalia Monographiae, no. 1. Cairo: Franciscan Centre of Christian Oriental Studies, 1987.

Pitra, Jean Baptiste. *Hymnographie de l'Église Grecque*. Rome: Impr. de la civita cattolica, 1867.

Pocock, Edward. *Contextio Gemmarum, sive, Eutychii Patriarchae Alexandrini Annales*. 2 vols. Oxford: H. Robinson, 1658–59.

Prescott, H. F. M. *Jerusalem Journey: Pilgrimage to the Holy Land in the Fifteenth Century*. London: Eyre and Spottiswoode, 1954.

———, trans. *The Wanderings of Felix Fabri*. Palestine Pilgrims' Text Society. Reprinted in 2 vols. from the 1889–97 ed. New York: AMS Press, 1971.

Prestage, Edgar. *Affonso de Albuquerque*. Watford: n.p., 1929.

Pringgodigdo, A. K. *Sejarah Pergerakan Rakyat Indonesia* (A history of movements among the people of Indonesia). Jakarta: Pen. Dian Rakyat, 1978.

Pruett, Gordon E. "Duncan Black Macdonald: Christian Islamicist." In Asaf Hussain, Robert Olson, and Jamil Qureshi, eds., *Orientalism, Islam, and Islamists*. Brattleboro, Vt.: Amana Books 1984.

Qalqashandī, Aḥmad Ibn ᶜAlī al-. *Ṣubḥ al-Aᶜsha fī Ṣināᶜat al-Inshā* (Subḥ al-Aᶜshā and the art of writing composition). 14 vols. Cairo: Al-Mu'assasa al-Miṣriyya li'l Ta'līf wa'l Tarjama wa'l-Nashr, n.d., vol. 13.

Qaraḍāwī, Yūsuf al-. *Ghayr al-Muslimīn fī al-Mujtamaᶜ al-Islāmī* (Non-Muslims in Islamic society). Beirut: Mu'assasat al-Risāla, 1983.

———. *al-Ḥall al-Islāmī: Farīḍatun wa-Ḍarūra* (The Islamic solution: A religious duty and a necessity). Cairo: Maktabat Wahbah, 1977.

Quraishy, M. A. *Textbook on Islam*. Book 2. Nairobi: Islamic Foundation, 1987.

Qurṭubī, Abū ᶜAbd Allāh Muḥammad Ibn Aḥmad al-Anṣārī al-. *Al-Jāmīᶜ li-Aḥkām al-Qur'ān* (The comprehensive compilation of the statutes of the Qur'an). Ed. Aḥmad ᶜAbd al-ᶜAlīm al-Burdūnī. 20 vols., 2d ed. Cairo: Dār al-Kātib al-ᶜArabī, 1387/1967.

Quṭb, Sayyid. *Maʿālim fī al-Ṭarīq* (Milestones on the road). Cairo: Maktabat Wahbah, 1964.

______. *Naḥwa Mujtamaʿ Islāmī* (Toward an Islamic society). Amman: Maktabat al-Aqṣā, 1969.

______. *Fī Ẓilāl al-Qurʾān* (In the shade of the Qurʾan). 1st printing, Cairo: Dār Iḥyāʾ al-Kutub al-ʿArabiyya, 1953. 4th printing, Beirut: Al-Dār al-ʿArabiyya liʾl-Ṭibāʿa waʾl-Nashr waʾl-Tawziʿ, n.d. 7th ed., 8 vols. Beirut: Dār Iḥyāʾ al-Turāth al-ʿArabī, 1391/1971.

Race, A. *Christians and Religious Pluralism: Patterns in the Christian Theology of Religions.* Maryknoll, N.Y.: Orbis Books, 1982.

Rahman, Falzur. *Major Themes of the Qurʾan.* Minneapolis-Chicago: Bibliotheca Islamica, 1980.

Raillon, François. "Christiens et musulmans en Indonesie: les voies de la tolérance." *Islamochristiana* 15 (1989): 135–67.

Ravenstein, Ernest G., ed. and trans. *A Journal of the First Voyage of Vasco da Gama, 1497–1499.* London: Hakluyt Society, 1898.

Rāzī, Fakhr al-Dīn al-. *Al-Tafsīr al-Kabīr* (The comprehensive interpretation [of the Qurʾan]). 30 vols. 1st ed. Cairo: al-Maṭbaʿa al-Bahiyya Miṣriyya, 1357/1938, vol. 16.

Regel, W. [Vasilii Eduardovich]. *Fontes rerum byzantinarum.* Petropoli: S. Eggers & S. and I. Glasunof. Leipzig: Voss' Sortiment (G. Haessel), 1892–1917, vol. 1.

Richard, Jean. *The Latin Kingdom of Jerusalem.* Trans. J. Shirly. Amsterdam: North Holland Publishing Co., 1979.

Ricklefs, M.C. *A History of Modern Indonesia.* Bloomington: Indiana University Press, 1981.

Riḍā, Muḥammad Rashīd, *Tafsīr al-Manār* (Al-Manār's interpretation [of the Qurʾan]). 2d ed., 10 vols. Beirut: Dār al-Maʿrifa, n.d.

______. *Tafsīr al-Qurʾān al-Ḥakīm* (The interpretation of the Gracious Qurʾan). 4th printing. Cairo: Dār al-Manār, 1954.

Riedel, Siegfried. *Sunde und Versohnung in Koran und Bibel.* Erlangen: Verlag der Ev. Luth. Mission, 1987.

[Risciani, Noberto.] *Documenti e Firmani.* Jerusalem: Tipografia dei PP. Francescani, 1936.

Ritter, Hellmut. *Das Meer der Seele.* Leiden: E.J. Brill, 1957.

Robinson, F. *Varieties of South Asian Islam.* University of Warwick, Centre for Research in Ethnic Relations, 1988.

Robson, James. "Stories of Jesus and Mary." *The Muslim World.* 40 (1950): 236–43.

Rose, Eliot Joseph Benn. *Colour and Citizenship: A Report on British Race Relations.* London: Oxford University Press, 1969.

Rose, Richard B. "Islam and the Development of Personal Status Laws among Christian Dhimmis: Motives, Sources, Consequences." *The Muslim World* 72 (1982): 159–79.

Roteico. *A Journal of the First Voyage of Vasco da Gama.* Trans. E.G. Ravenstein. London: Hakluyt Society, 1898.

Roux, Jean-Paul. *Les Explorateurs au Moyen Age.* Paris: Fayard, 1981.

Runciman, Steven. *A History of the Crusades.* Vol. 2. New York: Cambridge University Press, 1988.

Sahas, Daniel J. "The Formation of Later Islamic Doctrines as a Response to Byzantine Polemics: The Miracles of Muhammad." *The Greek Orthodox Theological Review* 27 (1982): 307–24.

______. *John of Damascus on Islam: The "Heresy of the Ishmaelites".* Leiden: E.J. Brill, 1972.

Said, Edward W. *Orientalism*. New York: Pantheon Books, 1978.

Saiyidain, K.G. *Islam the Religion of Peace*. New Delhi: Islam and the Middle Age Society, 1976.

Ṣāliḥī, Muḥammad Ibn Ṭūlūn al-. *Al-Qalāʾid al-Jawhariyya fī Tārīkh al-Ṣāliḥiyya* (The exquisite essentials in the history of al-Ṣāliḥiyya). Vol. 1. Damascus: Maktab al-Dirāsāt al-Islāmiyya, 1949.

Samartha, Stanley J., ed. *Dialogue Between Men of Living Faiths*. Geneva: World Council of Churches, 1971.

Sanneh, Lamin O. "Christian Experience of Islamic Daʿwa, with Particular Reference to Africa." *International Review of Missions* (Geneva) 65 (1976).

———. *West African Christianity: The Religious Impact*. London: C. Hurst & Co., 1983.

Sapija, M. *Sejarah Perjuangan Pattimura* (A history of the Pattimura independence movement). Jakarta: Djambatan, 1957.

Sardar, Ziauddin. *Islamic Futures: The Shape of Ideas to Come*. London: Mansell, 1985.

Sarrāj, Abū Naṣr as-. *Kitāb al-Lumaʿ fīʾl-Taṣawwuf* (The book of radiance in Sufism). Ed. Reynold Alleyne Nicholson. London, Leiden: Luzac and Brill, 1914.

Scharer, Hans. *Ngaju Religion*. The Hague: M. Nijhoff, 1963.

Schimmel, Annemarie. "Islam." In C. Jouco Bleeker and Geo Widengren, eds. *Historia Religionum, Handbook for the History of Religions*. Vol. 2. Leiden: E.J. Brill, 1971.

———. *Mystical Dimensions of Islam*. Chapel Hill: University of North Carolina Press, 1975.

Schlink, M. Basilea. *Wo liegt die Wahrheit? Ist Mohammeds Allah der Gott der Bibel?* Darmstadt-Eberstadt: Verl. Evang. Marienschwesternschaft, 1982.

Schlumberger, Gustave. *Un Empereur Byzantin au Dixième Siècle: Nicephore Phocas*. Paris: Librairie de Firmin-Didat et Cie., 1890.

Schumann, Olaf. *Der Christus der Muslime*. Gutersloh: Gerd Mohn, 1975; 2nd ed. Cologne: Bohlau, 1988.

———. "Herausforderung der Kirchen durch den Islam: Beispiel Indonesien." *Okumenische Rundschau* 30 (1981): 55–70.

———. "Herausgefordert durch die Pancasila: Die Religionen in Indonnesien." In Udo Tworuschka, ed. *Gottes ist der Orient, Gottes ist der Okzident*. Cologne: Bohlau, 1991.

———. "Staat und Gesellschaft im heutiger Indonesien." *Die Welt des Islam* 33 (1993).

Schurmann, Reiner. "The Loss of the Origin in Soto Zen and in Meister Eckhart." *The Thomist* 42 (April 1978).

———. *Meister Eckhart: Mystic and Philosopher*. Bloomington: Indiana University Press, 1978.

Schwoebel, R. *The Shadow of the Crescent: The Renaissance Image of the Turk (1453–1517)*. Nieuwkoop: B. de Graaf, 1967.

Seale, Morris S. *Muslim Theology: A Study of Origins with Reference to the Church Fathers*. London: Luzac & Co., 1964.

Secretaritus pro non-Christians. *Guidelines for a Dialogue Between Muslims and Christians*. Rome: Ancora, 1969.

Segesvary, Victor. *L'Islam et la Réforme: étude sur l'attitude des réformateurs zurichois envers l'Islam (1510–1550)*. Lausanne: Éd. L'Age d'homme, 1978.

Senac, Philippe. *L'Image de l'Autre*. Paris: Flammarion, 1983.

Sepmeijer, Floris. *Een Weerlegging van het Christendom uit de 10e Eeuw: De brief van al-Hasan b. Ayyub aan zijn broer ʿAli* (A tenth-century refutation of Christianity: The letter of al-Hasan b. Ayyub to his brother ʿAli). Kampen: W. van den Berg, 1985.

Serjeant, R.B. "Yemeni Muslims in Britain." *The Geographical Magazine* 17, no. 4 (1944): 143–47.

Shahabuddin, Syed. "A Muslim Indian Manifesto." *The Statesman* (New Delhi) 15, no. 8 (1987).

Shākir, Maḥmūd Muḥammad, ed. *Tafsīr al-Ṭabarī* (Al-Ṭabarī's interpretation [of the Qur'an]). Cairo: Dār al-Maʿārif bi-Miṣr, n.d.

Sharfī, ʿAbd al-Majīd al-. *al-Fikr al-Islāmī fī al-Radd ʿalā al-Naṣārā ilā Nihāyat al-Qarn al-Rābiʿ/al-ʿĀshir* (Islamic thought concerning the refutation of Christians to the end of the fourth century hijrī/tenth century A.D.). Tūnis: al-Dār al-Tūnisiyya liʾl-Nashr and Algiers: al-Muʾassasa al-Waṭaniyya liʾl-Kitāb, 1986.

Shawkīnī, Muḥammad Ibn ʿAlī B. Muḥammad al-. *Fatḥ al-Qadīr al-Jāmiʿ bayn fannay al-Riwāya wa ʾl-Dirāya min ʿilm al-Tafsīr* (The revelation of the Powerful [God] combining the two arts of narration and experience in the science of interpretation). 3d. ed. 5 vols. Beirut: Dār al-Fikr, 1393/1973, vol. 2.

Shirvani, Khaqani. *Divan* (A collection of poems). Ed. Ziaʾuddin Sajjadi. Tehran: Zawwar, 1338sh/1959.

Shorter, Hylward. *Toward a Theology of Inculturation*. Maryknoll, N.Y.: Orbis, 1988.

Shrady, Maria, trans. and foreword, and Josef Schmidt, intro. and notes. *Angelus Silesius: The Cherubinic Wanderer*, Classics of Western Spirituality. New York: Paulist Press, 1986.

Shuqayrī, Farghalī. *Fī Wajh al-Muʾāmara ʿalā Taṭbīq al-Sharīʿa* (Confronting the conspiracy against the application of Islamic law). Al-Manṣūra: Dār al-Wafāʾ, 1986.

Siddiqi, Amir Hassan. *Non-Muslims under Muslim Rule and Muslims under Non-Muslim Rule*. Karachi: Jamʿiyatul Falah Publications, n.d.

Siddiqi, Muzammil Husain. "The Doctrine of Redemption: A Critical Study." In Khurshi Ahmad and Zafar Ishaq Ansari, eds., *Islamic Perspectives*. Leicester, U.K.: The Islamic Foundation, 1979.

______. "Muslim and Byzantine Christian Relations: Letter of Paul of Antioch and Ibn Taymiya's Response." In N.M. Vaporis, ed., *Orthodox Christians and Muslims*. Brookline, Mass.: Holy Cross Orthodox Press, 1986.

Simatupang, T.B. "Agama-agama dalam pembangunan Negara Pancasila: Dialog, kerjasama dan pemberitaan" (The role of religions in the formation of the nation based on the five foundational principles: dialogue, cooperation, and dissemination). In Simatupang, T.B., ed., *Dari Revolusi ke Pembangunan* (From revolution to national development). Jakarta: BPK Gunung Mulia, 1987.

______. "Kurzer Ruckblick auf die Geschichte der christlichen Kirche in Indonesia." In Rolf Italiaander, ed., *Indonesiens verantwortliche Gesellschaft*. Enlargen: Verlag der Evang. Lutheran Mission, 1976.

Simatupang, T.B., et al. "Partisipasi Kristen dalam Revolusi Bidang Politik" (Christian participation in the political arena of revolution). In W.B. Sidjabat, ed., *Partisipasi Kristen dalam Nation Building di Indonesia* (Christian participation in nation building in Indonesia). Jakarta: BPK, 1968.

Sinno, Abdel-Raouf. *Deutsche Interessen in Palastine 1841–1989*. Berlin: Baalbek Verlag, 1982.

Slomp, Jan. "Can Christians Recognize Muhammad as a Prophet?" In Jan Slomp, ed., *Witness to God in a Secular Europe*. Geneva: Conference of European Churches, 1985.

Smith, Donald E. *India as a Secular State*. Princeton: Princeton University Press, 1963.

———. *The Facts of Racial Disadvantage: A National Survey.* London: PEP, 1976.

Smith, Margaret. *The Way of the Mystics: The Early Christian Mystics and the Rise of the Sufis.* New York: Oxford University Press, 1978.

Smith, Wilfred Cantwell. *Islam in Modern History.* New York: Mentor Books, 1959.

———. "Is the Qur'an the Word of God?" In Smith, *Questions of Religious Truth.* New York: Charles Scribner's Sons, 1967.

Speight, R. Marston. "Attitudes toward Christians as Revealed in the *Musnad* of al-Tayalisi." *The Muslim World* 63 (1973): 249–68.

———. "The *Musnad* of al-Tayalisi: A Study of Islamic Hadith as Oral Literature." Ph.D. diss., Hartford Seminary, 1970.

———. "The Place of the Christians in Ninth Century North Africa, According to Muslim Sources." *Islamochristiana* 68 (1978): 47–65.

———. "Temoignage des sources musulmanes sur la présence chrétienne au Maghreb de 26/647 à 184/800." *Revue de l'Institut des Belles Lettres Arabes* (Tunis) 129 (1972): 73–96.

Srawley, James Hebert, ed. *The Catechetical Oration of Gregory of Nyssa.* Cambridge: Cambridge University Press, 1956.

Staehlin, G. *Die Apostelgeschichte.* Gottingen: Vandenhoeck & Ruprecht, 1968.

Stamer, J. "Report of the Episcopal Commission for Relations between Christians and Muslims in West Africa." *Bulletin on Islam and Christian-Muslim Relations in Africa* (Birmingham) 5, no. 3 (1987).

Stanley, H. E.J., trans. "The Three Voyages of Vasco da Gama." In Gasper Correa, *Lendas da India.* London: Hakluyt Society, 1869.

Starkey, Peggy. "Agape: A Christian Criterion for Truth in the Other World religions." *International Review of Missions* 74, no. 296 (1985): 425–63.

Stefanides, Vasileios K. *Ekklesiaspike Historia.* Athens: Asper, 1959.

Stephens, H. Morse. *Albuquerque.* Oxford: Clarendon Press, 1897.

Stern, S.M. "An Embassy of the Byzantine Emperor to the Fatimid Caliph al-Muʿizz." *Byzantion* 20 (1950): 239–58.

Stohr, W. "Die Religionen der Altvolker Indonesiens und der Philippines." In W. Stohr and Piet Zoetmulder, eds., *Die Religionen Indonesiens.* Stuttgart: n.p., 1965.

Stompul, Einar H. *NU dan Pancasila* (Nahdatuk Ulama Muslim Party and its relation to the Indonesian philosophy of Pancasila or "the five foundational principles"). Jakarta: Sinar Harapan, 1989.

Sturzl, Erwin A. *Elizabethan and Renaissance Studies.* Salzburg, Austria: Institut fur Anglistik und Amerikanistik, Universitat Salzburg, 1986.

Suermann, Harald. Ein Disput des Johannan von Litharb." *CIBEDO Beitrage zum Gesprach zwischen Christen und Muslimen* 3, no. 5-6 (1989): 182–90.

———. *Die geschichtstheologische Reaktion auf die einfallenden Muslime in der Edessenischen Apokalyptik des 7. Jahrhunderts.* Frankfurt/M: P. Lang, 1985.

———. "Orientalische Christen und der Islam." *Zeitschrift fur Missionswissenschaft und Religionswissenschaft* 67 (1983): 120–36.

Sumption, Jonathan. *Pilgrimage: An Image of Medieval Religion.* Totowa, N.J.: Rowman and Littlefield, 1975.

Sundermeier, Theo. "Die religiose und politische Herausforderung des Islam." In *Evangelische Mission.* 15 (1983): 37–49.

Suseno, Franz-Mgnis. *Javanische Weisheit und Ethik: Studien zu einer ostlichen Moral.* Munich–Vienna: Oldenbourg, 1981.

Suyūṭī, Jalāl al-Dīn al-, and Jalāl al-Dīn Al-Maḥallī. *Tafsīr al-Jalālayn* (The [Qur'an] interpretation of the two Jalāls). Beirut: Dār al-Kitāb al-Lubnānī, n.d.

Suzuki, Peter. *The Religious System and Culture of Nias, Indonesia.*The Hague: Excelsior, 1959.

Sweetman, J. Windrow. *Islam and Christian Theology*. Vols. 1, 2. London: Lutterworth Press, 1945–55.

Ṭabarī, Muḥammad Ibn Jarīr al-. *Jāmiᶜ al-Bayān ᶜan Āy al-Qur'ān*. (The lucid and comprehensive interpretation of the verses of the Qur'an). 30 vols. Vol. 28. Beirut: Dār al-Fikr, 1398/1978.

______. *Tafsīr al-Ṭabarī* (Al-Tabari's interpretation [of the Qur'an]). Ed. Mahmud Muhammad Shakir. Cairo: Dār al-Maᶜārif bi-Miṣr, n.d.

Ṭabarsī, Abū ᶜAlī al-Faḍl Ibn al-Hasan al-. *Majmaᶜ al-Bayān fī Tafsīr al-Qur'ān*. (The lucid and comprehensive interpretation of the Qur'an). 30 vols. Beirut: Dār Maktabat al-Ḥayāt, 1380/1961, vol. 28.

Ṭabāṭabā'ī, Muḥammad Ḥusayn al-. *al-Mīzān fī Tafsīr al-Qur'ān* (The balanced interpretation of the Qur'an). 2d. ed., 20 vols. Beirut: al-Aᶜlami, 1394/1974, vol. 19.

Tisserant, Eugene. *Eastern Christianity in India*. Westminster, Md.: Newman Press, 1957.

Tobin, Frank. *Meister Eckhart: Thought and Language*. Philadelphia: University of Pennsylvania Press, 1986.

Tobin, Philip L. *The Structure of the Toba-Batak Belief in the High God*. Amsterdam: J. Van Campen, 1956.

Tour, Augustin Dupré La. "A New Departure in Islamo-Christian Studies." *Theological Review* 3, no. 2 (1980): 5–9.

Trempelas, P. *Ekloge Hellenikes Orthodoxou Hymnologias* (Selections of Greek Orthodox hymns). Athens, n.p., 1949.

Trimingham, J. Spencer. *Islam in West Africa*. London: Oxford University Press, 1959.

Troupeau, Gérard. "Ibn Taymiyya et sa réfutation d'Eutychès." *Bulletin d'Études Orientales* 30 (1978): 209–20.

Turlach, Manfred. *Kerala, Politische-Sociale Strukture und Entwicklung eines Indischen Bundeslades*. Wiesbaden: Otto Harassowitz, 1970.

Ṭūsī, Abū Jaᶜfar Muḥammad ibn al-Ḥasan ibn ᶜAlī ibn al-Ḥasan al-. *Al-Tibyān fī Tafsīr al-Qur'ān* (Exposition in the interpretation of the Qur'an). Ed. Aḥmad Qāṣir al-ᶜĀmilī. 10 vols. Beirut: al-Aᶜlami, n.d., vol. 10.

ᶜUlaymī, Mujīr al-Dīn al-. *Al-Uns al-Jalīl fī Tārīkh al-Quds wa 'l-Khalīl* (Splendid Familiarity with the History of Jerusalem and Hebron). 2 vols. Amman: Maktabat al-Muḥtasib, 1973.

Ullendorff, E. "Habash, I. Historical Background." *Encyclopedia of Islam*. New ed. Leiden: E.J. Brill, and London: Luzac & Co., 1971.

ᶜUthmān, Fatḥī. *Dawlat al-Fikr* (The power of thought). Kuwait: al-Dār al-Kuwaitiyya, 1968.

______. "Iqtirān al-Qawmiyya bi 'l-ᶜAlmāniyya Maṣdar Shukūk al-Islāmiyyīn" (The combination of nationalism and secularism as a source of the Islamists' suspicion). *Majallat al-ᶜArabī* (Kuwait) 266 (January 1981).

Vander Werff, Lyle L. *Christian Mission to Muslims, the Record: Anglican and Reformed Approaches in India and the Near East, 1800–1938*. South Pasadena, Calif.: William Carey Library, 1977.

Van Dieten, Ioannes Aloysius, ed. *Nicetae Choniatae: Historia*. Corpus Fontium Historiae Byzantinae, vol. 11, part 1. Trans. Harry J. Magoulias. Berlin: Walter de Gruyter,

1975.
Van Dijk, C. *Rebellion Under the Banner of Islam*. The Hague: M. Nijhoff, 1981.
Van Donzel, E.J., and Anqasa Amin. *La Porte de la Foi*. Leiden: E.J. Brill, 1969.
Van Ess, Josef. *Die Erkentnisslehre des ʿAdudaddin al-Ici: Übersetzung und Kommentar des Ersten Buches seines Mawaqif*. Akademie der Wissenschaften und der Literatur: Veröffentlichungen der orientalischen Kommission, vol. 22. Wiesbaden: Franz Steiner, 1966.
———. "The Logical Structure of Islamic Theology." In G.E. von Grunebaum, ed., *Logic in Classical Islamic Culture: First Giorgio Levi Della Vida Biennial Conference*. Wiesbaden: Otto Harrassowitz, 1970.
Van Sertima, Ivan. *They Came before Columbus*. New York: Random House, 1976.
Vasiliev, A.A. *History of the Byzantine Empire 324–1453*. Madison: University of Wisconsin Press, 1961.
Veinstein, Gilles, ed. *Mehmed Effendi, Le paradis des infidèles*. Paris: Librarie François Maspero, 1981.
Visser t'Hooft, Willem Adolph. *No Other Name: The Choice Between Syncretism and Christian Universalism*. Philadelphia: Westminster Press, 1963.
Vitry, Jacque de. *The History of Jerusalem*. Trans. A. Steward. London: The Palestine Pilgrims Text Society, 1896.
Volney, C.F. de Chasseboeu f. comte de. *Travels through Stria and Egypt, in the years 1783, 1784, and 1785*. 2 vols. Trans. from the French. London: G. Robinson, 1805.
Waardenburg, J. Jacques. *L'Islam dans le Miroir de l'Occident*. Paris: Mouton, 1962.
———. *Religionen und Religion. Systematische Einfuhrung in die Religionswissenschaft*. Berlin–New York: Walter de Gruyter, 1986.
Waldburger, Andreas. *Missionare und Moslems: Die Basler Mission in Persien 1833–1837*. Basel: Basileia Verlag, 1985.
Waldman, Marilyn Robinson. "New Approaches to 'Biblical' Material in the Qurʾan." *The Muslim World* 75 (1985): 1–16.
Walshe, Maurice O'Connell, trans. and ed. *Meister Eckhart: Sermons and Treatises*. 3 vols. Dorset, England: Element Books, 1987.
Wāqidī, Abū Muḥammad ʿAbd Allāh ibn ʿUmar ibn Wāqid. *Futūḥ Ifrīqiyya* (The conquest of Africa). 2 vols. Tunis: al-Maṭbaʿa al-ʿUmūmiyya, 1315/1897.
Watt, William Montgomery. *Christian-Muslim Encounter: Perceptions and Misperceptions*. London: Routledge and Kegan Paul, 1991.
———. *The Formative Period of Islamic Thought*. Edinburgh: University Press, 1973.
———. *Islam and Christianity Today: A Contribution to Dialogue*. London–New York: Routledge and Kegan Paul, 1983.
———. *Islamic Revelation in the Modern World*. London: Oxford University Press, 1968.
———. *Muhammad at Mecca*. Oxford: Clarendon Press, 1953.
———. *Muhammad at Medina*. Oxford: Clarendon Press, 1956.
———. "The Study of Islam by Orientalists." *Islamochristiana* 14 (1988): 201–10.
———. "Thoughts on Muslim-Christian dialogue." *Hamdard Islamicus* (Hamdard National Foundation, Pakistan) 1, no. 1 (Summer 1978): 1–52.
———. *Truth in the Religions: A Sociological and Pyschological Approach*. Edinburgh: University Press, 1963.
Watwat, Rashiduddin. *Divan* (A collection of poems). Ed. Saʿid Nafisi. Tehran: Barani, 1339sh/1960.

Waugh, Earle H., Baha Abu-Laban, and Regula B. Qureshi, eds. *The Muslim Community in North America*. Edmonton: University of Alberta Press, 1983.

Wawer, Wendelin. *Muslime und Christen in der Republik Indonesia*: Wiesbaden: F. Steiner, 1974.

Welch, Claude. *Graduate Education in Religion: A Critical Approach*. Missoula: University of Montana Press, 1971.

Wensinck, A.J. *The Muslim Creed: Its Genesis and Historical Development*. Cambridge: University Press, 1932, and London: Frank Cass & Co., 1965.

Wessels, Antonie. "Biblical Presuppositions for or against Syncretism." In J. D. Gort, H. M. Vroom, R. Fernhout, and A. Wessels, eds., *Dialogue and Syncretism: An Interdisciplinary Approach*. Grand Rapids: Eerdmans; Amsterdam: Ed. Rodopi, 1989.

Whiteway, R. S. *The Rise of Portuguese Power in India, 1497–1550*. Westminster: Constable & Co., 1899.

Wickham, Lionel R. "Soul and Body: Christ's Omnipresence." In Andreas Spira and Christoph Klock, eds., *The Easter Sermons of Gregory of Nyssa: Translation and Commentary*. Patristic Monograph Series, no. 9. Philadelphia: Philadelphia Patristic Foundation, Ltd., 1981.

Wiebe, Donald. *Religion and Truth: Towards an Alternative Paradigm for the Study of Religion*. The Hague: Mouton, 1981.

Wielandt, Rotraud. *Offenbarung und Geschichte im Denken moderner Muslime*. Wiesbaden: Franz Steiner, 1971.

Wiener, Leo. *Africa and the Discovery of America*. Chicago: Innes & Sons, 1922.

Wijoyo, Alex Soesito. "The Christians as Religious Community According to the Hadith." *Islamochristiana* 8 (1982): 83–105.

William of Tyre. *A History of the Crusades*. Vol. 2. New York: Cambridge University Press, 1988.

Wilms, Franz-Elmar. *Al-Ghazālī's Schrift wider die Gottheit Jesu*. Leiden: E.J. Brill, 1966.

Wisniewski, J. *Étrangers en France: Des chiffres et des hommes*. Paris: Hommes et migrations, 1986.

Wisniewski, Roswitha. "Christliche Antworten auf den Islam in fruhmittelalterlicher deutscher Dichtung." In Albert Zimmermann and Ingrid Craemer-Ruegenberg, eds., *Orientalische Kultur und Europaisches Mittelalter*. Berlin–New York: Walter de Gruyter, 1985.

Woods, Richard. *Eckhart's Way*. Wilmington, Del.: Michael Glazier, 1986.

Wysham, William N. "Jesus in the Poetry of Iran." *The Muslim World* 42 (1952): 104–11.

Yalaoui, Mohammed. *Un poète chiite d'Occident au IVeme/Xeme siècle: Ibn Hani al-Andalusi*. Tunis: Publications de l'Université de Tunis, 1976.

Ye'or, Bat. *The Dhimmī, Jews and Christians under Islam*. Rutherford-Madison-Teaneck: Fairleigh Dickinson University Press, 1985.

Zakaria, Rafiq. *The Struggle within Islam*. New York: Viking Penguin, 1989.

Zamakhsharī, Abū al-Qāsim Jār Allāh Maḥmud ibn ʿUmar al-. *Al-Kashshāf ʿan Ḥaqāʾiq al-Tanzīl wa-ʿUyūn al-Aqāwīl fī Wujūh al-Taʾwīl* (Unveiling the truth of the revelation and the notable sayings concerning the various aspects of allegorical interpretation). 4 vols. Beirut: Dār al-Kitāb al-ʿArabī, n.d.

Zirker, Hans. *Christentum and Islam. Theologische Verwandschaft und Konkurrenz*. Dusseldorf: Patmos, 1989.

INDEX

+ ☽

Abandāa (festival), 185–86
Abdia ben Belon, 226
ʿAbduh, Muḥammad (d. 1905), 48, 49, 412, 413–14, 416
Abdul, Musa, 308
ʿAbdul ʿAzīz (Indian shah), 247
Abdul-Hafiz, Imam Ishaq, 348, 350
Abraham (Abram): al-Faruqi's advocacy of, 11, 401–4; Manuel I Comnenos compared to, 118; as a *muslim*, 51; as a Muslim prophet, 226, 426; Muslims as descendants of, 119, 131, 132, 432–33; and religious pluralism, 56–57, 61, 62–63, 401–2, 430; unity with the Word of God, 91
Abram. *See* Abraham (Abram)
Abubaker, Mansa, 329
Abū Bakr, 167, 183
Abū Ḥanīfa, 258
Abū Qurra, Theodore, 69–70, 96, 100, 111
Abū Shāma, 203
Academy of Arabic Language, 414
Adam: compared to God, 69–70; compared to Jesus, 65, 69, 78; conception of, 68; as a Muslim prophet, 226
Adams, Charles J., 24, 25, 26
Adat, 288, 289
ʿĀḍid, al-, 205
ʿādil, al-Malik al-, 200
Afghānī, Jamāl al-Dīn al-, 366, 421
Africa. *See* Maghrib; North Africa; sub-Saharan Africa; *names of specific countries*
Africa and the Discovery of America (Wiener), 328–29
African-American Muslims, 9, 328–35, 343, 345–48
African Independent Churches, 451–52
African Muslim Welfare Society of North America (AMWSNA), 331–32
Afrusha, 216
Ahidjo, Ahmadu, 308
ahl al-kitāb (people of the book), 210, 246, 386
ahl al-kufr (people of unbelief), 185
ahl al-sunna, 85
Aḥmad, Syed Shakeel, 255–56
Ahmad Gran, war of, 301
Aḥmadiyya movement, 459
Aikya Kerala movement, 274
Akbarabādī, Saʿīd Aḥmad (mawlānā), 258–59
ākhira, al- (the hereafter), 339
Alawi movement, 321
Albuquerque, Affonso, 270–71
Alevi movement, 319
Alexandrian church fathers, 159
Alexius I Comnenos (Byzantine emperor), 114, 117
ʿAlī, Muḥammad, 248
ʿAlī, Shaukat, 248, 272
Alice (daughter of Baldwin III), 204
All-Africa Church Conference, 305
Allat, 73
All-India Muslim League, 248, 249, 276
Alūsī, Abū al-Faḍl Shihāb al-Dīn Maḥmūd al-, 72, 73, 76
Amalric I (king of Jerusalem), 196, 202–3, 205
amān (safe conducts), 194, 198, 214
ʿAmāra, Muḥammad, 385
Ameer Ali, Capt. N.A., 251–52
American Colonization Society, 330
American Muslim Mission, 333
Amicales movement, 319–20
Amin, Jamil Al- (H. Rap Brown), 347
Amīnī, Muḥammad Taqī (mawlānā), 259–60
Amīr-i-Hind, 249–50
Anawati, Georges C., 18, 21, 26, 27
Andalusī, Ibn Hānī al-, 187, 188–89
Anglican Diocese of Western Equitorial Africa, 303
Annals (Eutychius), 95
anṣār (supporters), 246
Ansar-ud-Deen, 308
Anvarī, Awḥad ad-Dīn ʿAli, 148
Apocrypha, 143
apologetic literature, 18–19, 84, 87, 95–107
apotaxis (statement of renunciation), 109
applied Islamology, 375–77
Apuleius, Lucius, 151
Arabs and Mediaeval Europe, The (Daniel), 16
Aristotelian logic, 84, 88
Aristotle, 88, 233
Arkoun, Mohammed, 10, 362, 366–70, 371–75, 376–78
Armenian Christians, 316
Aron, 259
Arosio, M., 367
Arvieux, Laurent d' (chevalier), 232, 237
Asad al-Dīn Shirkūh, 196, 197, 205
Ashʿarite school, 85, 86
Assam, state of (India), 266